American History I

American History I

(HIS105) OS Collection

Lumen Learning

American History I by Lumen Learning *is licensed under a* Creative Commons Attribution-ShareAlike 4.0 International License, *except where otherwise noted.*

Cover Image: "Declaration of Independence – National Archives – Washington, DC" by Josh Hallett from https://flic.kr/p/6shrhc licensed under a Creative Commons Attribution-ShareAlike License.

Published by SUNY OER Services
Milne Library
State University of New York at Geneseo
Geneseo, NY 14454

Distributed by State University of New York Press

Except where expressly noted otherwise, the contents of this course are based on materials originally published by Lumen Learning CC-BY-SA Creative Commons Attribution-ShareAlike License. The original version of the materials as published as Survey of American History I may be access for free at https://courses.lumenlearning.com/suny-fmcc-ushistory1os2xmaster/.

ISBN: 978-1-64176-020-1

This book was produced using Pressbooks.com, and PDF rendering was done by PrinceXML.

Contents

About This Book   9

1. The Americas Before 1492

Introduction   3
The Americas   5
Primary Source Reading: A Slave Revolt   17
Primary Source Reading: The Life of Gustavus Vassa   20

2. Early Globalization: The Atlantic World, 1492-1650

Introduction   27
Portuguese Exploration and Spanish Conquest   29
New Worlds in the Americas: Labor, Commerce, and the Columbian Exchange   39
Challenges to Spain's Supremacy   47
Colonial Rivalries: Dutch and French Colonial Ambitions   55
Primary Source Reading: Aztec Accounts of the Conquest   61
Primary Source Reading: Vasco De Gama   64

3. English Settlements in America

Introduction   69
English Settlements in America   70
The Impact of Colonization   86
Primary Source Reading: Jamestown Charter   93
Primary Source Reading: Bradford, History of Plymouth Plantation   100

4. Rule Britannia! The English Empire, 1660-1763

Introduction   107
Charles II and the Restoration Colonies   108
The Glorious Revolution and the English Empire   118

An Empire of Slavery and the Consumer Revolution	123
Great Awakening and Enlightenment	129
Wars for Empire	136
Primary Source Reading: The Social Contract	142
Primary Source Reading: A Treatise on Tolerance	144

5. Imperial Reforms and Colonial Protests, 1763-1774

Introduction	147
Confronting the National Debt: The Aftermath of the French and Indian War	148
The Stamp Act and the Sons and Daughters of Liberty	156
The Townshend Acts and Colonial Protest	164
The Destruction of the Tea and the Coercive Acts	173
Disaffection: The First Continental Congress and American Identity	179
Primary Source Reading: Common Sense	184
Primary Source Reading: "Give Me Liberty or Give Me Death!"	188
Primary Source Reading: The Declaration of Independence	191

6. America's War for Independence, 1775-1783

Introduction	197
Britain's Law-and-Order Strategy and Its Consequences	199
The Early Years of the Revolution	210
War in the South	218
Identity during the American Revolution	224

7. Creating Republican Governments, 1776-1783

Introduction	233
Common Sense: From Monarchy to an American Republic	234
How Much Revolutionary Change?	240
Debating Democracy	250
The Constitutional Convention and Federal Constitution	258
Primary Source Reading: The U.S. Constitution	267

8. Growing Pains: The New Republic, 1790-1820

Introduction	279
Competing Visions: Federalists and Democratic-Republicans	281
The New American Republic	290
Partisan Politics	298
The United States Goes Back to War	307
Primary Source Reading: The Alien and Sedition Acts	313

Primary Source Reading: The Star-Spangled Banner	316

9. Industrial Transformation in the North: 1800-1850

Introduction	323
Early Industrialization in the Northeast	324
A Vibrant Capitalist Republic	335
On the Move: The Transportation Revolution	343
A New Social Order: Class Divisions	348

10. Jacksonian Democracy, 1820-1840

Introduction	357
A New Political Style: From John Quincy Adams to Andrew Jackson	358
The Rise of American Democracy	367
The Nullification Crisis and the Bank War	372
Indian Removal	378
The Tyranny and Triumph of the Majority	386
Primary Source Reading: "An Address to the Whites"	392
Primary Source Reading: Speech to Congress on India Removal	393
Primary Source Reading: Jackson and the Bank of the U.S.	395

11. A Nation on the Move: Westward Expansion, 1800-1860

Introduction	401
Lewis and Clark	402
The Missouri Crisis	410
Independence for Texas	414
The Mexican-American War, 1846–1848	421
Free Soil or Slave? The Dilemma of the West	430
Primary Source Reading: The Great Nation of Futurity	436

12. Cotton is King: The Antebellum South, 1800-1860

Introduction	443
The Economics of Cotton	444
African Americans in the Antebellum United States	451
Primary Source Reading: Twelve Years a Slave	460
Primary Source Reading: John Calhoun on Slavery	467
Primary Source Reading: Fredrick Douglass	471
Primary Source Reading: The Life of Plantation Field Hands	478

13. Troubled Times: The Tumultuous 1850s

Introduction	483
The Compromise of 1850	484
The Kansas-Nebraska Act and the Republican Party	496
John Brown and the Election of 1860	505
The Dred Scott Decision and Sectional Strife	511

14. The Civil War, 1860-1865

Introduction	519
The Origins and Outbreak of the Civil War	521
Early Mobilization and War	529
1863: The Changing Nature of the War	536
The Union Triumphant	548
Primary Source Reading: The Emancipation Proclamation	555
Primary Source Reading: Lincoln's 2nd Inaugural Address	558
Primary Source Reading: Stephens' Cornerstone Address	560

Appendices

The Declaration of Independence	567
The Constitution of the United States	572
Presidents of the United States of America	591
U.S. Political Map	594
U.S. Topographical Map	595
United States Population Chart	596
Further Reading	598

About This Book

Your Survey of American History I textbook is a compilation of articles written by instructors for universities
around the country. The entire compilation is provided free of charge online through a Creative Commons license. You can access or even copy all the material here, for your own reference, even after the semester ends.

Different Versions

An electronic version is made available via your course at https://courses.lumenlearning.com/suny-fmcc-ushistory1os2xmaster/.
You may also purchase a physical copy at the College Bookstore. The electronic version has
access to multimedia content including video, slideshows, and interactive activities. The print version will have all the same reading material, but not include the multimedia content.

About the Author

There are many different authors; look to the "Licenses and Attributions" section at the end of each chapter to identify contributors. This compilation was edited by Anna Biel at Fulton-Montgomery Community College.

1. The Americas Before 1492

Introduction

Globalization, the ever-increasing interconnectedness of the world, is not a new phenomenon, but it accelerated when western Europeans discovered the riches of the East. During the Crusades (1095–1291), Europeans developed an appetite for spices, silk, porcelain, sugar, and other luxury items from the East, for which they traded fur, timber, and Slavic people they captured and sold (hence the word *slave*). But when the Silk Road, the long overland trading route from China to the Mediterranean, became costlier and more dangerous to travel, Europeans searched for a more efficient and inexpensive trade route over water, initiating the development of what we now call the Atlantic World.

In pursuit of commerce in Asia, fifteenth-century traders unexpectedly encountered a "New World" populated by millions and home to sophisticated and numerous peoples. Mistakenly believing they had reached the East Indies, these early explorers called its inhabitants Indians. West Africa, a diverse and culturally rich area, soon entered the stage as other nations exploited its slave trade and brought its peoples to the New World in chains. Although Europeans would come to dominate the New World, they could not have done so without Africans and native peoples.

In Europe supported by Africa and America (1796), artist William Blake, who was an abolitionist, depicts the interdependence of the three continents in the Atlantic World; however, he places gold armbands on the Indian and African women, symbolizing their subjugation. The strand binding the three women may represent tobacco.

Attributions

CC licensed content, Shared previously

- US History. **Authored by**: P. Scott Corbett, Volker Janssen, John M. Lund, Todd Pfannestiel, Paul Vickery, and Sylvie Waskiewicz. **Provided by**: OpenStax College. **Located at**: http://openstaxcollege.org/textbooks/us-history. **License**: CC BY: Attribution. **License Terms**: Download for free at http://cnx.org/content/col11740/latest/

Public domain content

- William Blake-Europe Supported By Africa and America 1796. **Authored by**: William Blake. **Located at**: http://commons.wikimedia.org/wiki/File:William_Blake-Europe_Supported_By_Africa_and_America_1796.png. **License**: *Public Domain: No Known Copyright*

The Americas

Learning Objectives

By the end of this section, you will be able to:

- Locate on a map the major American civilizations before the arrival of the Spanish
- Discuss the cultural achievements of these civilizations
- Discuss the differences and similarities between lifestyles, religious practices, and customs among the native peoples

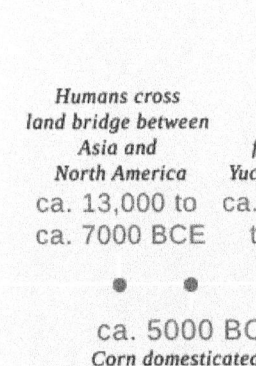

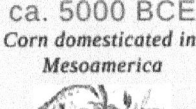

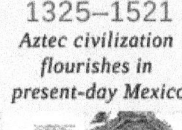
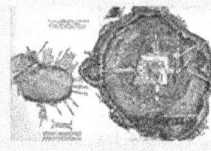

Humans cross land bridge between Asia and North America ca. 13,000 to ca. 7000 BCE

Mayan civilization flourishes in Yucatán Peninsula ca. 2000 BCE to 900 CE

Leif Ericson arrives in present-day Canada ca. 1000

Black Death decimates Europe 1346

Columbus arrives in Bahamas 1492

ca. 5000 BCE Corn domesticated in Mesoamerica

622 Muhammad receives vision for Islam

ca. 1100 Cahokia at its peak near modern St. Louis

1325–1521 Aztec civilization flourishes in present-day Mexico

1400–1532 Inca Empire thrives in South America

(credit: modification of work by Architect of the Capitol)

Between nine and fifteen thousand years ago, some scholars believe that a land bridge existed between Asia and North America that we now call **Beringia**. The first inhabitants of what would be named the Americas migrated across this bridge in search of food. When the glaciers melted, water engulfed Beringia, and the Bering Strait was formed. Later settlers came by boat across the narrow strait. (The fact that Asians and American Indians share genetic markers on a Y chromosome lends credibility to this migration theory.) Continually moving southward, the settlers eventually populated both North and South America, creating unique cultures that ranged from the highly complex and urban Aztec civilization in what is now Mexico City to the woodland tribes of eastern North America. Recent research along the west coast of South America suggests that migrant populations may have traveled down this coast by water as well as by land.

Researchers believe that about ten thousand years ago, humans also began the domestication of plants and animals, adding agriculture as a means of sustenance to hunting and gathering techniques. With this agricultural revolution, and the more abundant and reliable food supplies it brought, populations grew and people were able to develop a more settled way of life, building permanent settlements. Nowhere in the Americas was this more obvious than in Mesoamerica.

THE FIRST AMERICANS: THE OLMEC

Mesoamerica is the geographic area stretching from north of Panama up to the desert of central Mexico. Although marked by great topographic, linguistic, and cultural diversity, this region cradled a number of civilizations with similar characteristics. Mesoamericans were **polytheistic**; their gods possessed both male and female traits and demanded blood sacrifices of enemies taken in battle or ritual bloodletting. Corn, or maize, domesticated by 5000 BCE, formed the basis of their diet. They developed a mathematical system, built huge edifices, and devised a calendar that accurately predicted eclipses and solstices and that priest-astronomers used to direct the planting and harvesting of crops. Most important for our knowledge of these peoples, they created the only known written language in the Western Hemisphere; researchers have made much progress in interpreting the inscriptions on their temples and pyramids. Though the area had no overarching political structure, trade over long distances helped diffuse culture. Weapons made of obsidian, jewelry crafted from jade, feathers woven into clothing and ornaments, and cacao beans that were whipped into a chocolate drink formed the basis of commerce. The mother of Mesoamerican cultures was the Olmec civilization.

This map shows the extent of the major civilizations of the Western Hemisphere. In South America, early civilizations developed along the coast because the high Andes and the inhospitable Amazon Basin made the interior of the continent less favorable for settlement.

Flourishing along the hot Gulf Coast of Mexico from about 1200 to about 400 BCE, the Olmec produced a number of major works of art, architecture, pottery, and sculpture. Most recognizable are their giant head sculptures and the pyramid in La Venta. The Olmec built aqueducts to transport water into their cities and irrigate their fields. They grew maize, squash, beans, and tomatoes. They also bred small domesticated dogs which, along with fish, provided their protein. Although no one knows what happened to the Olmec after about 400 BCE, in part because the jungle reclaimed many of their cities, their culture was the base upon which the Maya and the Aztec built. It was the Olmec who worshipped a rain god, a maize god, and the feathered serpent so important in the future pantheons of the Aztecs (who called him Quetzalcoatl) and the Maya (to whom he was Kukulkan). The Olmec also developed a system of trade throughout Mesoamerica, giving rise to an elite class.

THE MAYA

After the decline of the Olmec, a city rose in the fertile central highlands of Mesoamerica. One of the largest population centers in pre-Columbian America and home to more than 100,000 people at its height in about 500 CE, Teotihuacan was located about thirty miles northeast of modern Mexico City. The ethnicity of this settlement's inhabitants is debated; some scholars believe it was a multiethnic city. Large-scale agriculture and the resultant abundance of food allowed time for people to develop special trades and skills other than farming. Builders constructed over twenty-two hundred apartment compounds for multiple families, as well as more than a hundred temples. Among these were the Pyramid of the Sun (which is two hundred feet high) and the Pyramid of the Moon (one hundred and fifty feet high). Near the Temple of the Feathered Serpent, graves have been uncovered that suggest humans were sacrificed for religious purposes. The city was also the center for trade, which extended to settlements on Mesoamerica's Gulf Coast.

The Olmec carved heads from giant boulders that ranged from four to eleven feet in height and could weigh up to fifty tons. All these figures have flat noses, slightly crossed eyes, and large lips. These physical features can be seen today in some of the peoples indigenous to the area.

The Maya were one Mesoamerican culture that had strong ties to Teotihuacan. The Maya's architectural and mathematical contributions were significant. Flourishing from roughly 2000 BCE to 900 CE in what is now Mexico, Belize, Honduras, and Guatemala, the Maya perfected the calendar and written language the Olmec had begun. They devised a written mathematical system to record crop yields and the size of the population, and to assist in trade. Surrounded by farms relying on primitive agriculture, they built the city-states of Copan, Tikal, and Chichen Itza along their major trade routes, as well as temples, statues of gods, pyramids, and astronomical observatories. However, because of poor soil and a drought that lasted nearly two centuries, their civilization declined by about 900 CE and they abandoned their large population centers.

The Spanish found little organized resistance among the weakened Maya upon their arrival in the 1520s. However, they did find Mayan history, in the form of glyphs, or pictures representing words, recorded in folding books called codices (the singular is *codex*). In 1562, Bishop Diego de Landa, who feared the converted natives had reverted to their traditional religious practices, collected and burned every codex he could find. Today only a few survive.

El Castillo, located at Chichen Itza in the eastern Yucatán peninsula, served as a temple for the god Kukulkan. Each side contains ninety-one steps to the top. When counting the top platform, the total number of stairs is three hundred and sixty-five, the number of days in a year. (credit: Ken Thomas)

> **Visit the** University of Arizona Library Special Collections **to view facsimiles and descriptions of two of the four surviving Mayan codices.**

THE AZTEC

When the Spaniard Hernán Cortés arrived on the coast of Mexico in the sixteenth century, at the site of present-day Veracruz, he soon heard of a great city ruled by an emperor named Moctezuma. This city was tremendously wealthy—filled with gold—and took in tribute from surrounding tribes. The riches and complexity Cortés found when he arrived at that city, known as Tenochtitlán, were far beyond anything he or his men had ever seen.

According to legend, a warlike people called the Aztec (also known as the Mexica) had left a city called Aztlán and traveled south to the site of present-day Mexico City. In 1325, they began construction of Tenochtitlán on an island in Lake Texcoco. By 1519, when Cortés arrived, this settlement contained upwards of 200,000 inhabitants and was certainly the largest city in the Western Hemisphere at that time and probably larger than any European city. One of Cortés's soldiers, Bernal Díaz del Castillo, recorded his impressions upon first seeing it: "When we saw so many cities and villages built in the water and other great towns on dry land we were amazed and said it was like the enchantments . . . on account of the great towers and cues and buildings rising from the water, and all built of masonry. And some of our soldiers even asked whether the things that we saw were not a dream? . . . I do not know how to describe it, seeing things as we did that had never been heard of or seen before, not even dreamed about."

Unlike the dirty, fetid cities of Europe at the time, Tenochtitlán was well planned, clean, and orderly. The city had neighborhoods for specific occupations, a trash collection system, markets, two aqueducts bringing in fresh water, and public buildings and temples. Unlike the Spanish, Aztecs bathed daily, and wealthy homes might even contain a steam bath. A labor force of slaves from subjugated neighboring tribes had built the fabulous city and the three causeways that connected it to the mainland. To farm, the Aztec constructed barges made of reeds and filled them with fertile soil. Lake water constantly irrigated these **chinampas**, or "floating gardens," which are still in use and can be seen today in Xochimilco, a district of Mexico City.

In this illustration, an Aztec priest cuts out the beating heart of a sacrificial victim before throwing the body down from the temple. Aztec belief centered on supplying the gods with human blood—the ultimate sacrifice—to keep them strong and well.

Each god in the Aztec pantheon represented and ruled an aspect of the natural world, such as the heavens, farming, rain, fertility, sacrifice, and combat. A ruling class of warrior nobles and priests performed ritual human sacrifice daily to sustain the sun on its long journey across the sky, to appease or feed the gods, and to stimulate agricultural production. The sacrificial ceremony included cutting open the chest of a criminal or captured warrior with an obsidian knife and removing the still-beating heart.

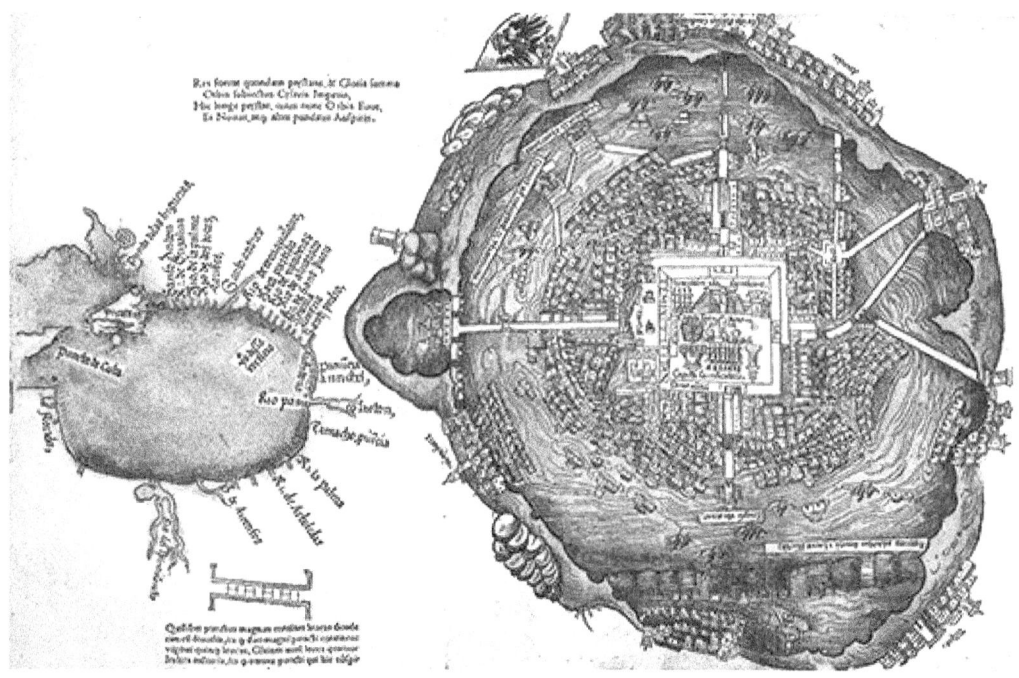

This rendering of the Aztec island city of Tenochtitlán depicts the causeways that connected the central city to the surrounding land. Envoys from surrounding tribes brought tribute to the Emperor.

Explore Aztec-History.com to learn more about the Aztec creation story.

The Aztec Predict the Coming of the Spanish

The following is an excerpt from the sixteenth-century Florentine Codex of the writings of Fray Bernardino de Sahagun, a priest and early chronicler of Aztec history. When an old man from Xochimilco first saw the Spanish in Veracruz, he recounted an earlier dream to Moctezuma, the ruler of the Aztecs.

> Said Quzatli to the sovereign, "Oh mighty lord, if because I tell you the truth I am to die, nevertheless I am here in your presence and you may do what you wish to me!" He narrated that mounted men would come to this land in a great wooden house [ships] this structure was to lodge many men, serving them as a home; within they would eat and sleep. On the surface of this house they would cook their food, walk and play as if they were on firm land. They were to be white, bearded men, dressed in different colors and on their heads they would wear round coverings.

Ten years before the arrival of the Spanish, Moctezuma received several omens which at the time he could not interpret. A fiery object appeared in the night sky, a spontaneous fire broke out in a religious temple and could not be extinguished with water, a water spout appeared in Lake Texcoco, and a woman could be heard wailing, "O my children we are about to go forever." Moctezuma also had dreams and premonitions of impending disaster. These foretellings were recorded after the Aztecs' destruction. They do, however, give us insight into the importance placed upon signs and omens in the pre-Columbian world.

THE INCA

In South America, the most highly developed and complex society was that of the Inca, whose name means "lord" or "ruler" in the Andean language called Quechua. At its height in the fifteenth and sixteenth centuries, the Inca Empire, located on the Pacific coast and straddling the Andes Mountains, extended some twenty-five hundred miles. It stretched from modern-day Colombia in the north to Chile in the south and included cities built at an altitude of 14,000 feet above sea level. Its road system, kept free of debris and repaired by workers stationed at varying intervals, rivaled that of the Romans and efficiently connected the sprawling empire. The Inca, like all other pre-Columbian societies, did not use axle-mounted wheels for transportation. They built stepped roads to ascend and descend the steep slopes of the Andes; these would have been impractical for wheeled vehicles but worked well for pedestrians. These roads enabled the rapid movement of the highly trained Incan army. Also like the Romans, the Inca were effective administrators. Runners called **chasquis** traversed the roads in a continuous relay system, ensuring quick communication over long distances. The Inca had no system of writing, however. They communicated and kept records using a system of colored strings and knots called the **quipu**.

The Inca people worshipped their lord who, as a member of an elite ruling class, had absolute authority over every aspect of life. Much like feudal lords in Europe at the time, the ruling class lived off the labor of the peasants, collecting vast wealth that accompanied them as they went, mummified, into the next life. The Inca farmed corn, beans, squash, quinoa (a grain cultivated for its seeds), and the indigenous potato on terraced land they hacked from the steep mountains. Peasants received only one-third of their crops for themselves. The Inca ruler required a third, and a third was set aside in a kind of welfare system for those unable to work. Huge storehouses were filled with food for times of need. Each peasant also worked for the Inca ruler a number of days per month on public works projects, a requirement known as the **mita**. For example, peasants constructed rope bridges made of grass to span the mountains above fast-flowing icy rivers. In return, the lord provided laws, protection, and relief in times of famine.

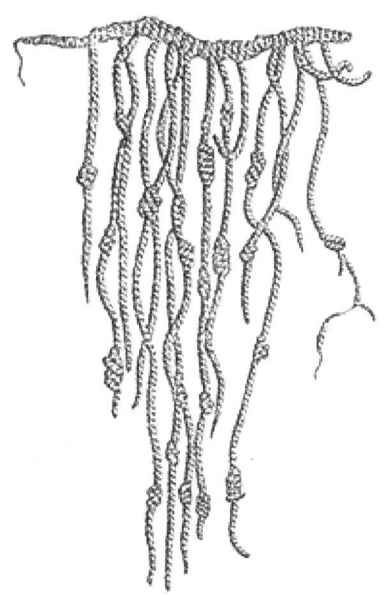

The Inca had no written language. Instead, they communicated and kept records by means of a system of knots and colored strings called the quipu. Each of these knots and strings possessed a distinct meaning intelligible to those educated in their significance.

The Inca worshipped the sun god Inti and called gold the "sweat" of the sun. Unlike the Maya and the Aztecs, they rarely practiced human sacrifice and usually offered the gods food, clothing, and coca leaves. In times of dire emergency, however, such as in the aftermath of earthquakes, volcanoes, or crop failure, they resorted to sacrificing prisoners. The ultimate sacrifice was children, who were specially selected and well fed. The Inca believed these children would immediately go to a much better afterlife.

In 1911, the American historian Hiram Bingham uncovered the lost Incan city of Machu Picchu. Located about fifty miles northwest of Cusco, Peru, at an altitude of about 8,000 feet, the city had been built in 1450 and inexplicably abandoned roughly a hundred years later. Scholars believe the city was used for religious ceremonial purposes and housed the priesthood. The architectural beauty of this city is unrivaled. Using only the strength of human labor and no machines, the Inca constructed walls and buildings of polished stones, some weighing over fifty tons, that were fitted together perfectly without the use of mortar. In 1983, UNESCO designated the ruined city a World Heritage Site.

Located in today's Peru at an altitude of nearly 8,000 feet, Machu Picchu was a ceremonial Incan city built about 1450 CE.

> Browse the British Museum's World Cultures collection to see more examples and descriptions of Incan (as well as Aztec, Mayan, and North American Indian) art.

NORTH AMERICAN INDIANS

With few exceptions, the North American native cultures were much more widely dispersed than the Mayan, Aztec, and Incan societies, and did not have their population size or organized social structures. Although the cultivation of corn had made its way north, many Indians still practiced hunting and gathering. Horses, first introduced by the Spanish, allowed the Plains Indians to more easily follow and hunt the huge herds of bison. A few societies had evolved into relatively complex forms, but they were already in decline at the time of Christopher Columbus's arrival.

In the southwestern part of today's United States dwelled several groups we collectively call the Pueblo. The Spanish first gave them this name, which means "town" or "village," because they lived in towns or villages of permanent stone-and-mud buildings with thatched roofs. Like present-day apartment houses, these buildings had multiple stories, each with multiple rooms. The three main groups of the Pueblo people were the Mogollon, Hohokam, and Anasazi.

The Mogollon thrived in the Mimbres Valley (New Mexico) from about 150 BCE to 1450 CE. They developed a distinctive artistic style for painting bowls with finely drawn geometric figures and wildlife, especially birds, in black on a white background. Beginning about 600 CE, the Hohokam built an extensive irrigation system of canals to irrigate the desert and grow fields of corn, beans, and squash. By 1300, their crop yields were supporting the most highly populated settlements in the southwest. The Hohokam decorated pottery with a red-on-buff design and made jewelry of turquoise. In the high desert of New Mexico, the Anasazi, whose name means "ancient enemy" or "ancient ones," carved homes from steep cliffs accessed by ladders or ropes that could be pulled in at night or in case of enemy attack.

To access their homes, the cliff-dwelling Anasazi used ropes or ladders that could be pulled in at night for safety. These pueblos may be viewed today in Canyon de Chelly National Monument (above) in Arizona and Mesa Verde National Park in Colorado.

Roads extending some 180 miles connected the Pueblos' smaller urban centers to each other and to Chaco Canyon, which by 1050 CE had become the administrative, religious, and cultural center of their civilization. A century later, however, probably because of drought, the Pueblo peoples abandoned their cities. Their present-day descendants include the Hopi and Zuni tribes.

The Indian groups who lived in the present-day Ohio River Valley and achieved their cultural apex from the first century CE to 400 CE are collectively known as the Hopewell culture. Their settlements, unlike those of the southwest, were small hamlets. They lived in wattle-and-daub houses (made from woven lattice branches "daubed" with wet mud, clay, or sand and straw) and practiced agriculture, which they supplemented by hunting and fishing. Utilizing waterways, they developed trade routes stretching from Canada to Louisiana, where they exchanged goods with other tribes and negotiated in many different languages. From the coast they received shells; from Canada, copper; and from the Rocky Mountains, obsidian. With these materials they created necklaces, woven mats, and exquisite carvings. What remains of their culture today are huge burial mounds and earthworks. Many of the mounds that were opened by archaeologists contained artworks and other goods that indicate their society was socially stratified.

Perhaps the largest indigenous cultural and population center in North America was located along the Mississippi River near present-day St. Louis. At its height in about 1100 CE, this five-square-mile city, now called Cahokia, was home to more than ten thousand residents; tens of thousands more lived on farms surrounding the urban center. The city also contained one hundred and twenty earthen mounds or pyramids, each dominating a particular neighborhood and on each of which lived a leader who exercised authority over the surrounding area. The largest mound covered fifteen acres. Cahokia was the hub of political and trading activities along the Mississippi River. After 1300 CE, however, this civilization declined—possibly because the area became unable to support the large population.

INDIANS OF THE EASTERN WOODLAND

Encouraged by the wealth found by the Spanish in the settled civilizations to the south, fifteenth- and sixteenth-century English, Dutch, and French explorers expected to discover the same in North America. What they found instead were small, disparate communities, many already ravaged by European diseases brought by the Spanish and transmitted among the natives. Rather than gold and silver, there was an abundance of land, and the timber and fur that land could produce.

The Indians living east of the Mississippi did not construct the large and complex societies of those to the west. Because they lived in small autonomous clans or tribal units, each group adapted to the specific environment in which it lived. These groups were by no means unified, and warfare among tribes was common as they sought to increase their hunting and fishing areas. Still, these tribes shared some common traits. A chief or group of tribal elders made decisions, and although the chief was male, usually the women selected and counseled him. Gender roles were not as fixed as they were in the patriarchal societies of Europe, Mesoamerica, and South America.

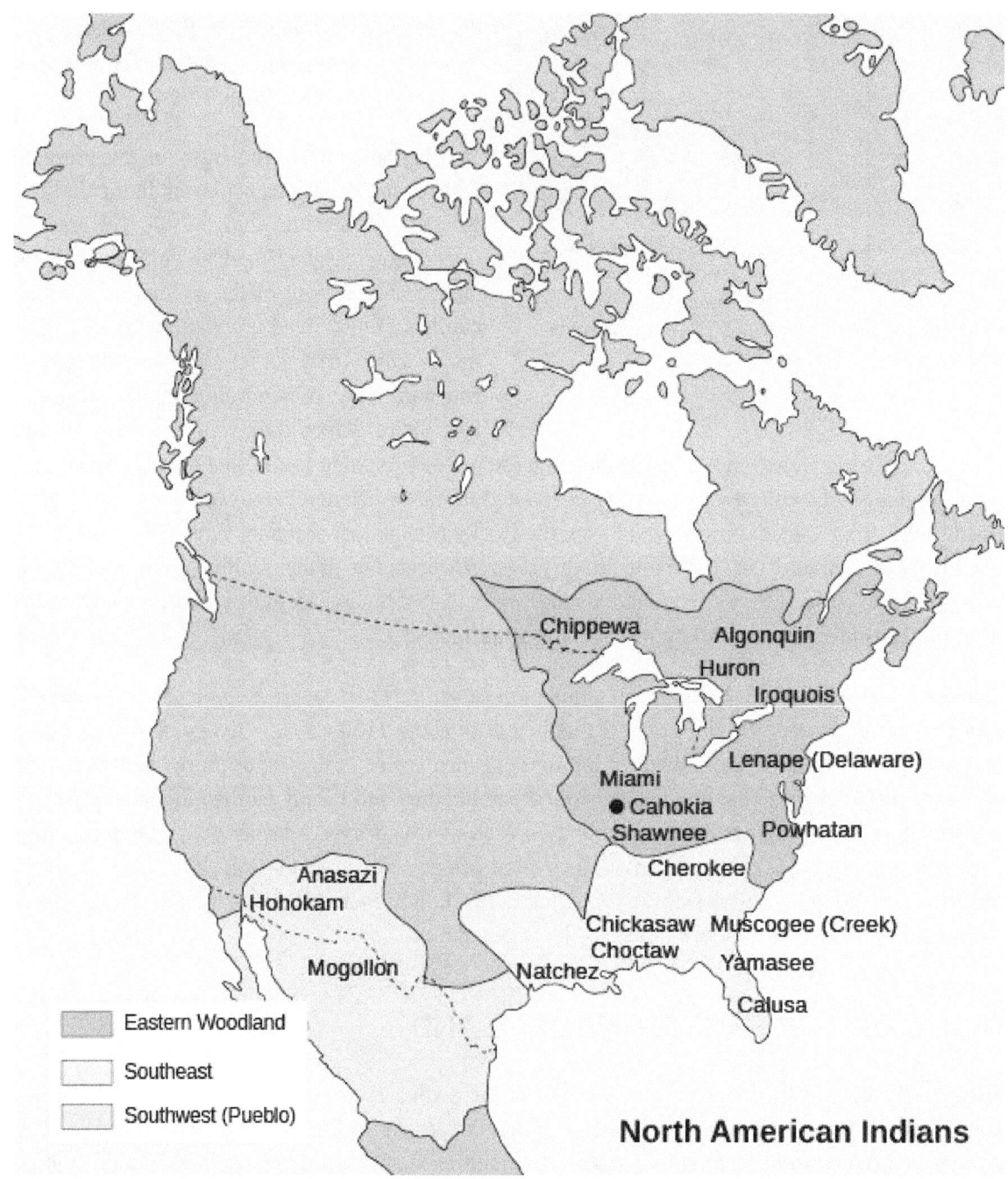

This map indicates the locations of the three Pueblo cultures the major Eastern Woodland Indian tribes, and the tribes of the Southeast, as well as the location of the ancient city of Cahokia.

Women typically cultivated corn, beans, and squash and harvested nuts and berries, while men hunted, fished, and provided protection. But both took responsibility for raising children, and most major Indian societies in the east were matriarchal. In tribes such as the Iroquois, Lenape, Muscogee, and Cherokee, women had both power and influence. They counseled the chief and passed on the traditions of the tribe. This **matriarchy** changed dramatically with the coming of the Europeans, who introduced, sometimes forcibly, their own customs and traditions to the natives.

Clashing beliefs about land ownership and use of the environment would be the greatest area of conflict with Europeans. Although tribes often claimed the right to certain hunting grounds—usually identified by some geographical landmark—Indians did not practice, or in general even have the concept of, private ownership of land. There were tribal hunting grounds, usually identified by some geographical landmark, but there was no private ownership of land. A person's possessions included only what he or she had made, such as tools or weapons. The European Christian worldview, on the other hand, viewed land as the source of wealth. According to the Christian Bible, God created humanity in his own image with the command to use and subdue the rest of creation, which included not only land, but also all animal life. Upon their arrival in North America, Europeans found no fences, no signs designating ownership. Land, and the game that populated it, they believed, were there for the taking.

Section Summary

Great civilizations had risen and fallen in the Americas before the arrival of the Europeans. In North America, the complex Pueblo societies including the Mogollon, Hohokam, and Anasazi as well as the city at Cahokia had peaked and were largely memories. The Eastern Woodland peoples were thriving, but they were soon overwhelmed as the number of English, French, and Dutch settlers increased.

Mesoamerica and South America had also witnessed the rise and fall of cultures. The once-mighty Mayan population centers were largely empty. In 1492, however, the Aztecs in Mexico City were at their peak. Subjugating surrounding tribes and requiring tribute of both humans for sacrifice and goods for consumption, the island city of Tenochtitlán was the hub of an ever-widening commercial center and the equal of any large European city until Cortés destroyed it. Further south in Peru, the Inca linked one of the largest empires in history through the use of roads and disciplined armies. Without the use of the wheel, they cut and fashioned stone to build Machu Picchu high in the Andes before abandoning the city for unknown reasons. Thus, depending on what part of the New World they explored, the Europeans encountered peoples that diverged widely in their cultures, traditions, and numbers.

- https://www.openassessments.org/assessments/1090

Review Question

1. What were the major differences between the societies of the Aztec, Inca, and Maya and the Indians of North America?

Answer to Review Question

1. North American Indians were fewer in number, more widely dispersed, and did not have the population size or organized social structures of the Maya, Aztec, or Inca societies. The Eastern Woodland peoples, in particular, lived in small clan groups and adapted to their singular environments. Some North American Indians lived by hunting and gathering rather than cultivating crops.

Glossary

Beringia an ancient land bridge linking Asia and North America

chasquis Incan relay runners used to send messages over great distances

chinampas floating Aztec gardens consisting of a large barge woven from reeds, filled with dirt and floating on the water, allowing for irrigation

matriarchy a society in which women have political power

mita the Incan labor tax, with each family donating time and work to communal projects

quipu an ancient Incan device for recording information, consisting of variously colored threads knotted in different ways

activation energy the amount of initial energy necessary for reactions to occur

matriarchy a society in which women have political power

chinampas floating Aztec gardens consisting of a large barge woven from reeds, filled with dirt and floating on the water, allowing for irrigation

matriarchy a society in which women have political power

Attributions

CC licensed content, Shared previously

- US History. **Authored by**: P. Scott Corbett, Volker Janssen, John M. Lund, Todd Pfannestiel, Paul Vickery, and Sylvie Waskiewicz. **Provided by**: OpenStax College. **Located at**: http://openstaxcollege.org/textbooks/us-history. **License**: *CC BY: Attribution*. **License Terms**: Download for free at http://cnx.org/content/col11740/latest/

Primary Source Reading: A Slave Revolt

PREMEDITATED A REVOLT

James Barbot, Jr., a sailor aboard the English slaver Don Carlos, describes a slave uprising that took place aboard the vessel.

About one in the afternoon, after dinner, we, according to custom caused them, one by one, to go down between decks, to have each his pint of water; most of them were yet above deck, many of them provided with knives, which we had indiscreetly given them two or three days before, as not suspecting the least attempt of this nature from them; others had pieces of iron they had torn off our forecastle door, as having premeditated a revolt, and seeing all the ship's company, at best but weak and many quite sick, they had also broken off the shackles from several of their companions feet, which served them, as well as billets they had provided themselves with, and all other things they could lay hands on, which they imagin'd might be of use for this enterprize. Thus arm'd, they fell in crouds and parcels on our men, upon the deck unawares, and stabb'd one of the stoutest of us all, who receiv'd fourteen or fifteen wounds of their knives, and so expir'd. Next they assaulted our boatswain, and cut one of his legs so round the bone, that he could not move, the nerves being cut through; others cut our cook's throat to the pipe, and others wounded three of the sailors, and threw one of them over-board in that condition, from the fore-castle into the sea; who, however, by good providence, got hold of the bowline of the fore-sail, and sav'd himself…we stood in arms, firing on the revolted slaves, of whom we kill'd some, and wounded many: which so terrif'd the rest, that they gave way, dispersing themselves some one way and some another between decks, and under the fore-castle; and many of the most mutinous, leapt over board, and drown'd themselves in the ocean with much resolution, shewing no manner of concern for life. Thus we lost twenty seven or twenty eight slaves, either kill'd by us, or drown'd; and having master'd them, caused all to go betwixt decks, giving them good words. The next day we had them all again upon deck, where they unanimously declar'd, the Menbombe slaves had been the contrivers of the mutiny, and for an example we caused about thirty of the ringleaders to be very severely whipt by all our men that were capable of doing that office….

I have observ'd, that the great mortality, which so often happens in slave-ships, proceeds as well from taking in too many, as from want of knowing how to manage them aboard….

As to the management of our slaves aboard, we lodge the two sexes apart, by means of a strong partition at the main mast; the forepart is for men, the other behind the mast for the women. If it be in large ships carrying five or six hundred slaves, the deck in such ships ought to be at least five and a half or six foot high, which is very requisite for driving a continual trade of slaves: for the greater height it has, the more airy and convenient it is for such a considerable number of human creatures; and consequently far the more healthy for them, and fitter to look after them. We build a sort of half-decks along the sides with deals and spars provided for that purpose in Europe, that half-deck extending no father than the sides of our scuttles and so the slaves lie in two rows, one above the other, and as close together as they can be crouded....

The planks, or deals, contract some dampness more or less, either from the deck being so often wash'd to keep it clean and sweet, or from the rain that gets in now and then through the scuttles or other openings, and even from the very sweat of the slaves; which being so crouded in a low place, is perpetual, and occasions many distempers, or at best great inconveniences dangerous to their health....

It has been observ'd before, that some slaves fancy they are carry'd to be eaten, which make them desperate; and others are so on account of their captivity: so that if care be not taken, they will mutiny and destroy the ship's crue in hopes to get away.

To prevent such misfortunes, we use to visit them daily, narrowly searching every corner between decks, to see whether they have not found means, to gather any pieces of iron, or wood, or knives, about the ship, notwithstanding the great care we take not to leave any tools or nails, or other things in the way: which, however, cannot be always so exactly observ'd, where so many people are in the narrow compass of a ship.

We cause as many of our men as is convenient to lie in the quarter-deck and gun-room, and our principal officers in the great cabin, where we keep all our small arms in a readiness, with sentinels constantly at the doors and avenues to it; being thus ready to disappoint any attempts our slave might make on a sudden.

These precautions contribute very much to keep them in awe; and if all those who carry slaves duly observ'd them, we should not hear of so many revolts as have happen'd. Where I was concern'd, we always kept our slaves in such order, that we did not perceive the least inclination in any of them to revolt, or mutiny, and lost very few of our number in the voyage.

It is true, we allow'd them much more liberty, and us'd them with more tenderness than most other Europeans would think prudent to do; as, to have them all upon deck every day in good weather; to take their meals twice a-day, at fix'd hours, that is, at ten in the morning, and at five at night; which being ended, we made the men go down again between the decks; for the women were almost entirely at their own discretion, to be upon deck as long as they pleas'd, nay even many of the males had the same liberty by turns, successively; few or none being fetter'd or kept in shackles, and that only on account of some disturbances, or injuries, offer'd to their fellow captives, as will unavoidably happen among a numerous croud of such savage people. Besides, we allow'd each of them betwixt their meals a handful of Indian wheat and Mandioca, and now and then short pipes and tobacco to smoak upon deck by turns, and some coconuts; and to the women a piece of coarse cloth to cover them, and the same to many of the men, which we took care they did wash from time to time, to prevent vermin, which they are very subject to; and because it look'd sweeter and more agreeable. Toward the evening they diverted themselves on the deck, as they thought fit, some conversing together, others dancing, singing, and sporting after their manner, which pleased them highly, and often made us pastime; especially the female sex, who being apart from the males, on the quarterdeck, and many of them young sprightly maidens, full of jollity and good-humour, afforded us abundance of recreation; as did several little fine boys, which we mostly kept to attend on us about the ship.

We mess'd the slaves twice a day, as I have observed; the first meal was of our large beans boil'd, with a certain quantity of Muscovy lard….The other meal was of pease, or of Indian wheat, and sometimes meal of Mandioca…boiled with either lard, or suet, or grease by turns: and sometimes with palm- oil and malaguette or Guinea pepper I found they had much better stomachs for beans, and it is a proper fattening food for captives….

At each meal we allow'd every slave a full coconut shell of water, and from time to time a dram of brandy, to strengthen their stomachs….

Much more might be said relating to the preservation and maintenance of slaves in such voyages, which I leave to the prudence of the officers that govern aboard, if they value their own reputation and their owners advantage; and shall only add these few particulars, that tho' we ought to be circumspect in watching the slaves narrowly, to prevent or disappoint their ill designs for our own conservation, yet must we not be too severe and haughty with them, but on the contrary, caress and humor them in every reasonable thing. Some commanders, of a morose peevish temper are perpetually beating and curbing them, even without the least offence, and will not suffer any upon deck but when unavoidable to ease themselves does require; under pretence it hinders the work of the ship and sailors and that they are troublesome by their nasty nauseous stench, or their noise; which makes those poor wretches desperate, and besides their falling into distempers thro' melancholy, often is the occasion of their destroying themselves.

Such officers should consider, those unfortunate creatures are men as well as themselves, tho' of a different colour, and pagans; and that they ought to do to others as they would be done by in like circumstances….

Source: James Barbot, Jr., "A Supplement to the Description of the Coasts of North and South Guinea," in Awnsham and John Churchill, Collection of Voyages and Travels (London, 1732).

Attributions

Public domain content

- A Supplement to the Description of the Coasts of North and South Guinea. **Authored by**: James Barbot, Jr.. **Located at**: http://www.vgskole.net/prosjekt/slavrute/5.htm. **Project**: Collection of Voyages and Travels. **License**: *Public Domain: No Known Copyright*

Primary Source Reading: The Life of Gustavus Vassa

The Life of Gustavus Vassa, by Olaudah Equiano was the first first-ever slave autobiography, using his slave name, written after he was freed and living living in England. The autobiography covers all of Equiano's life – his boyhood in the Gold Coast, his capture and transportation to the West Indies, and his success in business – a success which enabled him to buy his freedom. Chapter Two, given here, relates his capture and transportation in Africa. Chapter 5 relates the abuse of slaves in the West Indies.

The autobiography was a success. It helped open us the opposition to slavery which began to gather force towards the later 18th century.

The Life of Gustavus Vassa

Chapter 2

The Atlantic Voyage

The first object which saluted my eyes when I arrived on the coast, was the sea, and a slave ship, which was then riding at anchor, and waiting for its cargo. These filled me with astonishment, which was soon converted into terror, when I was carried on board. I was immediately handled, and tossed up to see if I were sound, by some of the crew; and I was now persuaded that I had gotten into a world of bad spirits, and that they were going to kill me. Their complexions, too, differing so much from ours, their long hair, and the language they spoke, (which was very different from any I had ever heard) united to confirm me in this belief. Indeed, such were the horrors of my views and fears at the moment, that, if ten thousand worlds had been my own, I would have freely parted with them all to have exchanged my condition with that of the meanest slave in my own country. When I looked round the ship too, and saw a large furnace of copper boiling, and a multitude of black people of every description chained together, every one of their countenances expressing dejection and sorrow, I no longer doubted of my fate; and, quite overpowered with horror and anguish, I fell motionless on the deck and fainted. When I recovered a little, I found some black people about me, who I believed were some of those who had brought me on board, and had been receiving their pay; they talked to me in order to cheer me, but all in vain. I asked them if we were not to be eaten by those white men with horrible looks, red faces, and long hair. They told me I was not: and one of the crew brought me a small portion of spirituous liquor in a wine glass, but, being afraid of him, I would not take it out of his hand. One of the blacks, therefore, took it from him and gave it to me, and I took a little down my palate, which, instead of reviving me, as they thought it would, throw me into the greatest consternation at the strange feeling it produced, having never tasted any such liquor before. Soon after this, the blacks who brought me on board went off, and left me abandoned to despair.

I now saw myself deprived of all chance of returning to my native country, or even the least glimpse of hope of gaining the shore, which I now considered as friendly; and I even wished for my former slavery in preference to my present situation, which was filled with horrors of every kind, still heightened by my ignorance of what I was to undergo. I was not long suffered to indulge my grief; I was soon put down under the decks, and there I received such a salutation in my nostrils as I had never experienced in my life: so that, with the loathsomeness of the stench, and crying together, I became so sick and low that I was not able to eat, nor had I the least desire to taste any thing. I now wished for the last friend, death, to relieve me; but soon, to my grief, two of the white men offered me eatables; and, on my refusing to eat, one of them held me fast by the hands, and laid me across, I think the windlass, and tied my feet, while the other flogged me severely. I had never experienced any thing of this kind before, and although not being used to the water, I naturally feared that element the first time I saw it, yet, nevertheless, could I have got over the nettings, I would have jumped over the side, but I could not; and besides, the crew used to watch us very closely who were not chained down to the decks, lest we should leap into the water; and I have seen some of these poor African prisoners most severely cut, for attempting to do so, and hourly whipped for not eating. This indeed was often the case with myself. In a little time after, amongst the poor chained men, I found some of my own nation, which in a small degree gave ease to my mind. I inquired of these what was to be done with us? they gave me to understand, we were to be carried to these white people's country to work for them. I then was a little revived, and thought, if it were no worse than working, my situation was not so desperate; but still I feared I should be put to death, the white people looked and acted, as I thought, in so savage a manner; for I had never seen among any people such instances of brutal cruelty; and this not only shown towards us blacks, but also to some of the whites themselves. One white man in particular I saw, when we were permitted to be on deck, flogged so unmercifully with a large rope near the foremast, that he died in consequence of it; and they tossed him over the side as they would have done a brute. This made me fear these people the more; and I expected nothing less than to be treated in the same manner. I could not help expressing my fears and apprehensions to some of my countrymen; I asked them if these people had no country, but lived in this hollow place? (the ship) they told me they did not, but came from a distant one. 'Then," said I, "how comes it in all our country we never heard of them?" They told me because they lived so very far off. I then asked where were their women? had they any like themselves? I was told they had. "And why," said I, "do we not see them?" They answered, because they were left behind. I asked how the vessel could go? they told me they could not tell; but that there was cloth put upon the masts by the help of the ropes I saw, and then the vessel went on; and the white men had some spell or magic they put in the water when they liked, in order to stop the vessel. I was exceedingly amazed at this account, and really thought they were spirits. I therefore wished much to be from amongst them, for I expected they would sacrifice me; but my wishes were vainÑ-for we were so quartered that it was impossible for any of us to make our escape.

While we stayed on the coast I was mostly on deck; and one day, to my great astonishment, I saw one of these vessels coming in with the sails up. As soon as the whites saw it, they gave a great shout, at which we were amazed; and the more so, as the vessel appeared larger by approaching nearer. At last, she came to an anchor in my sight, and when the anchor was let go, I and my countrymen who saw it, were lost in astonishment to observe the vessel stop and were now convinced it was done by magic. Soon after this the other ship got her boats out, and they came on board of us, and the people of both ships seemed very glad to see each other. Several of the strangers also shook hands with us black people, and made motions with their hands, signifying I suppose, we were to go to their country, but we did not understand them.

At last, when the ship we were in had got in all her cargo, they made ready with many fearful noises, and we were all put under deck, so that we could not see how they managed the vessel. But this disappointment was the least of my sorrow. The stench of the hold while we were on the coast was so intolerably loathsome, that it was dangerous to remain there for any time, and some of us had been permitted to stay on the deck for the fresh air; but now that the whole ship's cargo were confined together, it became absolutely pestilential. The closeness of the place, and the heat of the climate, added to the number in the ship, which was so crowded that each had scarcely room to turn himself, almost suffocated us. This produced copious perspirations, so that the air soon became unfit for respiration, from a variety of loathsome smells, and brought on a sickness among the slaves, of which many diedÑ-thus falling victims to the improvident avarice, as I may call it, of their purchasers. This wretched situation was again aggravated by the galling of the chains, now became insupportable; and the filth of the necessary tubs, into which the children often fell, and were almost suffocated. The shrieks of the women, and the groans of the dying, rendered the whole a scene of borror almost inconceivable. Happily perhaps, for myself, I was soon reduced so low here that it was thought necessary to keep me almost always on deck; and from my extreme youth I was not put in fetters. In this situation I expected every hour to share the fate of my companions, some of whom were almost daily brought upon deck at the point of death, which I began to hope would soon put an end to my miseries. Often did I think many of the inhabitants of the deep much more happy than myself. I envied them the freedom they enjoyed, and as often wished I could change my condition for theirs. Every circumstance I met with, served only to render my state more painful, and heightened my apprehensions, and my opinion of the cruelty of the whites.

One day they had taken a number of fishes; and when they had killed and satisfied themselves with as many as they thought fit, to our astonishment who were on deck, rather than give any of them to us to eat, as we expected, they tossed the remaining fish into the sea again, although we begged and prayed for some as well as we could, but in vain; and some of my countrymen, being pressed by hunger, took an opportunity, when they thought no one saw.them, of trying to get a little privately; but they were discovered, and the attempt procured them some very severe floggings. One day, when we had a smooth sea and moderate wind, two of my wearied countrymen who were chained together, (I was near them at the time,) preferring death to such a life of misery, somehow made through the nettings and jumped into the sea: immediately, another quite dejected fellow, who, on account of his illness, was suffered to be out of irons, also followed their example; and I believe many more would very soon have done the same, if they had not been prevented by the ship's crew, who were instantly alarmed. Those of us that were the most active, were in a moment put down under the deck, and there was such a noise and confusion amongst the people of the ship as I never heard before, to stop her, and get the boat out to go after the slaves. However, two of the wretches were drowned, but they got the other, and afterwards flogged him unmercifully, for thus attempting to prefer death to slavery. In this manner we continued to undergo more hardships than I can now relate, hardships which are inseparable from this accursed trade. Many a time we were near suffocation from the want of fresh air, which we were often without for whole days together. This, and the stench of the necessary tubs, carried off many.

During our passage, I first saw flying fishes, which surprised me very much; they used frequently to fly across the ship, and many of them fell on the deck. I also now first saw the use of the quadrant; I had often with astonishment seen the mariners make observations with it, and I could not think what it meant. They at last took notice of my surprise; and one of them, willing to increase it, as well as to gratify my curiosity, made me one day look through it. The clouds appeared to me to be land, which disappeared as they passed along. This heightened my wonder; and I was now more persuaded than ever, that I was in another world, and that every thing about me was magic. At last, we came in sight of the island of Barbadoes, at which the whites on board gave a great shout, and made many signs of joy to us. We did not know what to think of this; but as the vessel drew nearer, we plainly saw the harbor, and other ships of different kinds and sizes, and we soon anchored amongst them, off Bridgetown. Many merchants and planters now came on board, though it was in the evening. They put us in separate parcels, and examined us attentively. They also made us jump, and pointed to the land, signifying we were to go there. We thought by this, we should be eaten by these ugly men, as they appeared to us; and, when soon after we were all put down under the deck again, there was much dread and trembling among us, and nothing but bitter cries to be heard all the night from these apprehensions, insomuch, that at last the white people got some old slaves from the land to pacify us. They told us we were not to be eaten, but to work, and were soon to go on land, where we should see many of our country people. This report eased us much. And sure enough, soon after we were landed, there came to us Africans of all languages.

We were conducted immediately to the merchant's yard, where we were all pent up together, like so many sheep in a fold, without regard to sex or age. As every object was new to me, every thing I saw filled me with surprise. What struck me first, was, that the houses were built with bricks and stories, and in every other respect different from those I had seen in Africa; but I was still more astonished on seeing people on horseback. I did not know what this could mean; and, indeed, I thought these people were full of nothing but magical arts. While I was in this astonishment, one of my fellow-prisoners spoke to a countryman of his, about the horses, who said they were the same kind they had in their country. I understood them, though they were from a distant part of Africa; and I thought it odd I had not seen any horses there; but afterwards, when I came to converse with different Africans, I found they had many horses amongst them, and much larger than those I then saw.

We were not many days in the merchant's custody, before we were sold after their usual manner, which is this: On a signal given, (as the beat of a drum) the buyers rush at once into the yard where the slaves are confined, and make choice of that parcel they like best. The noise and clamor with which this is attended, and the eagerness visible in the countenances of the buyers, serve not a little to increase the apprehension of terrified Africans, who may well be supposed to consider them as the ministers of that destruction to which they think themselves devoted. In this manner, without scruple, are relations and friends separated, most of them never to see each other again. I remember, in the vessel in which I was brought over, in the men's apartment, there were several brothers, who, in the sale, were sold in different lots; and it was very moving on this occasion, to see and hear their cries at parting. O, ye nominal Christians! might not an African ask youÑ-Learned you this from your God, who says unto you, Do unto all men .as you would men should do unto you? Is it not enough that we are torn from our country and friends, to toil for your luxury and lust of gain? Must every tender feeling be likewise sacrificed to your avarice7 Are the dearest friends and relations, now rendered more dear by their separation from their kindred, still to be parted from each other, and thus prevented from cheering the gloom of slavery, with the small comfort of being together; and mingling their sufferings and sorrows? Why are parents to lose their children, brothers their sisters, husbands their wives? Surely, this is a new refinement in cruelty, which, while it has no advantage to atone for it, thus aggravates distress; and adds fresh horrors even to the wretchedness of slavery.

Attributions

Public domain content

- Life of Gustavus Vassa. **Authored by**: Olaudah Equiano. **Located at**: http://legacy.fordham.edu/halsall/mod/Vassa.asp. **Project**: Internet Modern History Sourcebook. **License**: *Public Domain: No Known Copyright*

2. Early Globalization: The Atlantic World, 1492-1650

Introduction

The story of the Atlantic World is the story of global migration, a migration driven in large part by the actions and aspirations of the ruling heads of Europe. Columbus is hardly visible in this illustration of his ships making landfall on the Caribbean island of Hispaniola. Instead, Ferdinand II of Spain (in the foreground) sits on his throne and points toward Columbus's landing. As the ships arrive, the Arawak people tower over the Spanish, suggesting the native population density of the islands.

This historic moment in 1492 sparked new rivalries among European powers as they scrambled to create New World colonies, fueled by the quest for wealth and power as well as by religious passions. Almost continuous war resulted. Spain achieved early preeminence, creating a far-flung empire and growing rich with treasures from the Americas. Native Americans who confronted the newcomers from Europe suffered unprecedented losses of life, however, as previously unknown diseases sliced through their populations. They also were victims of the arrogance of the Europeans, who viewed themselves as uncontested masters of the New World, sent by God to bring Christianity to the "Indians." The Spanish enslaved Native Americans, forcing them to bring whatever gold could be found to fill Spanish coffers.

After Christopher Columbus "discovered" the New World, he sent letters home to Spain describing the wonders he beheld. These letters were quickly circulated throughout Europe and translated into Italian, German, and Latin. This woodcut is from the first Italian verse translation of the letter Columbus sent to the Spanish court after his first voyage, Lettera delle isole novamente trovata by Giuliano Dati.

Attributions

CC licensed content, Shared previously

- US History. **Authored by**: P. Scott Corbett, Volker Janssen, John M. Lund, Todd Pfannestiel, Paul Vickery, and Sylvie Waskiewicz. **Provided by**: OpenStax College. **Located at**: http://openstaxcollege.org/textbooks/us-history. **License**: *CC BY: Attribution*. **License Terms**: Download for free at http://cnx.org/content/col11740/latest/

Portuguese Exploration and Spanish Conquest

Learning Objectives

By the end of this section, you will be able to:

- Describe Portuguese exploration of the Atlantic and Spanish exploration of the Americas, and the importance of these voyages to the developing Atlantic World
- Explain the importance of Spanish exploration of the Americas in the expansion of Spain's empire and the development of Spanish Renaissance culture

---

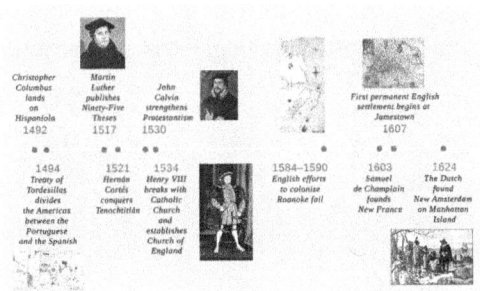

Portuguese colonization of Atlantic islands in the 1400s inaugurated an era of aggressive European expansion across the Atlantic. In the 1500s, Spain surpassed Portugal as the dominant European power. This age of exploration and the subsequent creation of an Atlantic World marked the earliest phase of **globalization**, in which previously isolated groups—Africans, Native Americans, and Europeans—first came into contact with each other, sometimes with disastrous results.

PORTUGUESE EXPLORATION

Portugal's Prince Henry the Navigator spearheaded his country's exploration of Africa and the Atlantic in the 1400s. With his support, Portuguese mariners successfully navigated an eastward route to Africa, establishing a foothold there that became a foundation of their nation's trade empire in the fifteenth and sixteenth centuries.

Portuguese mariners built an Atlantic empire by colonizing the Canary, Cape Verde, and Azores Islands, as well as the island of Madeira. Merchants then used these Atlantic outposts as debarkation points for subsequent journeys. From these strategic points, Portugal spread its empire down the western coast of Africa to the Congo, along the western coast of India, and eventually to Brazil on the eastern coast of South America. It also established trading posts in China and Japan. While the Portuguese didn't rule over an immense landmass, their strategic holdings of islands and coastal ports gave them almost unrivaled control of nautical trade routes and a global empire of trading posts during the 1400s.

The travels of Portuguese traders to western Africa introduced them to the African slave trade, already brisk among African states. Seeing the value of this source of labor in growing the profitable crop of sugar on their Atlantic islands, the Portuguese soon began exporting African slaves along with African ivory and gold. Sugar fueled the Atlantic slave trade, and the Portuguese islands quickly became home to sugar plantations. The Portuguese also traded these slaves, introducing much-needed human capital to other European nations. In the following years, as European exploration spread, slavery spread as well. In time, much of the Atlantic World would become a gargantuan sugar-plantation complex in which Africans labored to produce the highly profitable commodity for European consumers.

Elmina Castle

In 1482, Portuguese traders built Elmina Castle (also called São Jorge da Mina, or Saint George's of the Mine) in present-day Ghana, on the west coast of Africa. A fortified trading post, it had mounted cannons facing out to sea, not inland toward continental Africa; the Portuguese had greater fear of a naval attack from other Europeans than of a land attack from Africans. Portuguese traders soon began to settle around the fort and established the town of Elmina.

Although the Portuguese originally used the fort primarily for trading gold, by the sixteenth century they had shifted their focus. The dungeon of the fort now served as a holding pen for African slaves from the interior of the continent, while on the upper floors Portuguese traders ate, slept, and prayed in a chapel. Slaves lived in the dungeon for weeks or months until ships arrived to transport them to Europe or the Americas. For them, the dungeon of Elmina was their last sight of their home country.

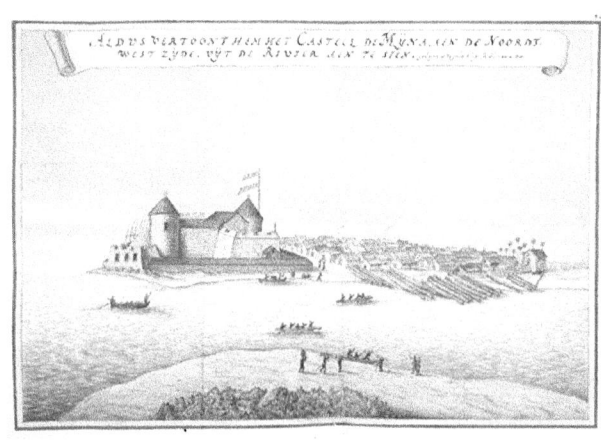

Elmina Castle on the west coast of Ghana was used as a holding pen for slaves before they were brought across the Atlantic and sold. Originally built by the Portuguese in the fifteenth century, it appears in this image as it was in the 1660s, after being seized by Dutch slave traders in 1637.

SPANISH EXPLORATION AND CONQUEST

The Spanish established the first European settlements in the Americas, beginning in the Caribbean and, by 1600, extending throughout Central and South America. Thousands of Spaniards flocked to the Americas seeking wealth and status. The most famous of these Spanish adventurers are Christopher Columbus (who, though Italian himself, explored on behalf of the Spanish monarchs), Hernán Cortés, and Francisco Pizarro.

The history of Spanish exploration begins with the history of Spain itself. During the fifteenth century, Spain hoped to gain advantage over its rival, Portugal. The marriage of Ferdinand of Aragon and Isabella of Castile in 1469 unified Catholic Spain and began the process of building a nation that could compete for worldwide power. Since the 700s, much of Spain had been under Islamic rule, and King Ferdinand II and Queen Isabella I, arch-defenders of the Catholic Church against Islam, were determined to defeat the Muslims in Granada, the last Islamic stronghold in Spain. In 1492, they completed the Reconquista: the centuries-long Christian conquest of the Iberian Peninsula. The Reconquista marked another step forward in the process of making Spain an imperial power, and Ferdinand and Isabella were now ready to look further afield.

Their goals were to expand Catholicism and to gain a commercial advantage over Portugal. To those ends, Ferdinand and Isabella sponsored extensive Atlantic exploration. Spain's most famous explorer, Christopher Columbus, was actually from Genoa, Italy. He believed that, using calculations based on other mariners' journeys, he could chart a westward route to India, which could be used to expand European trade and spread Christianity. Starting in 1485, he approached Genoese, Venetian, Portuguese, English, and Spanish monarchs, asking for ships and funding to explore this westward route. All those he petitioned—including Ferdinand and Isabella at first—rebuffed him; their nautical experts all concurred that Columbus's estimates of the width of the Atlantic Ocean were far too low. However, after three years of entreaties, and, more important, the completion of the Reconquista, Ferdinand and Isabella agreed to finance Columbus's expedition in 1492, supplying him with three ships: the *Nina*, the *Pinta*, and the *Santa Maria*. The Spanish monarchs knew that Portuguese mariners had reached the southern tip of Africa and sailed the Indian Ocean. They understood that the Portuguese would soon reach Asia and, in this competitive race to reach the Far East, the Spanish rulers decided to act.

This sixteenth-century map shows the island of Hispaniola (present-day Haiti and Dominican Republic). Note the various fanciful elements, such as the large-scale ships and sea creatures, and consider what the creator of this map hoped to convey. In addition to navigation, what purpose would such a map have served?

Columbus held erroneous views that shaped his thinking about what he would encounter as he sailed west. He believed the earth to be much smaller than its actual size and, since he did not know of the existence of the Americas, he fully expected to land in Asia. On October 12, 1492, however, he made landfall on an island in the Bahamas. He then sailed to an island he named **Hispaniola** (present-day Dominican Republic and Haiti). Believing he had landed in the East Indies, Columbus called the native Taínos he found there "Indios," giving rise to the term "Indian" for any native people of the New World. Upon Columbus's return to Spain, the Spanish crown bestowed on him the title of Admiral of the Ocean Sea and named him governor and viceroy of the lands he had discovered. As a devoted Catholic, Columbus had agreed with Ferdinand and Isabella prior to sailing west that part of the expected wealth from his voyage would be used to continue the fight against Islam.

Columbus's 1493 letter—or ***probanza de mérito*** (proof of merit)—describing his "discovery" of a New World did much to inspire excitement in Europe. *Probanzas de méritos* were reports and letters written by Spaniards in the New World to the Spanish crown, designed to win royal patronage. Today they highlight the difficult task of historical work; while the letters are primary sources, historians need to understand the context and the culture in which the conquistadors, as the Spanish adventurers came to be called, wrote them and distinguish their bias and subjective nature. While they are filled with distortions and fabrications, *probanzas de méritos* are still useful in illustrating the expectation of wealth among the explorers as well as their view that native peoples would not pose a serious obstacle to colonization.

In 1493, Columbus sent two copies of a *probanza de mérito* to the Spanish king and queen and their minister of finance, Luis de Santángel. Santángel had supported Columbus's voyage, helping him to obtain funding from Ferdinand and Isabella. Copies of the letter were soon circulating all over Europe, spreading news of the wondrous new land that Columbus had "discovered." Columbus would make three more voyages over the next decade, establishing Spain's first settlement in the New World on the island of Hispaniola. Many other Europeans followed in Columbus's footsteps, drawn by dreams of winning wealth by sailing west. Another Italian, Amerigo Vespucci, sailing for the Portuguese crown, explored the South American coastline between 1499 and 1502. Unlike Columbus, he realized that the Americas were not part of Asia but lands unknown to Europeans. Vespucci's widely published accounts of his voyages fueled speculation and intense interest in the New World among Europeans. Among those who read Vespucci's reports was the German mapmaker Martin Waldseemuller. Using the explorer's first name as a label for the new landmass, Waldseemuller attached "America" to his map of the New World in 1507, and the name stuck.

Columbus's *Probanza de mérito* of 1493

The exploits of the most famous Spanish explorers have provided Western civilization with a narrative of European supremacy and Indian savagery. However, these stories are based on the self-aggrandizing efforts of conquistadors to secure royal favor through the writing of *probanzas de méritos* (proofs of merit). Below are excerpts from Columbus's 1493 letter to Luis de Santángel, which illustrates how fantastic reports from European explorers gave rise to many myths surrounding the Spanish conquest and the New World.

> This island, like all the others, is most extensive. It has many ports along the sea-coast excelling any in Christendom—and many fine, large, flowing rivers. The land there is elevated, with many mountains and peaks incomparably higher than in the centre isle. They are most beautiful, of a thousand varied forms, accessible, and full of trees of endless varieties, so high that they seem to touch the sky, and I have been told that they never lose their foliage. . . . There is honey, and there are many kinds of birds, and a great variety of fruits. Inland there are numerous mines of metals and innumerable people. Hispaniola is a marvel. Its hills and mountains, fine plains and open country, are rich and fertile for planting and for pasturage, and for building towns and villages. The seaports there are incredibly fine, as also the magnificent rivers, most of which bear gold. The trees, fruits and grasses differ widely from those in Juana. There are many spices and vast mines of gold and other metals in this island. They have no iron, nor steel, nor weapons, nor are they fit for them, because although they are well-made men of commanding stature, they appear extraordinarily timid. The only arms they have are sticks of cane, cut when in seed, with a sharpened stick at the end, and they are afraid to use these. Often I have sent two or three men ashore to some town to converse with them, and the natives came out in great numbers, and as soon as they saw our men arrive, fled without a moment's delay although I protected them from all injury.

What does this letter show us about Spanish objectives in the New World? How do you think it might have influenced Europeans reading about the New World for the first time?

The 1492 Columbus landfall accelerated the rivalry between Spain and Portugal, and the two powers vied for domination through the acquisition of new lands. In the 1480s, Pope Sixtus IV had granted Portugal the right to all land south of the Cape Verde islands, leading the Portuguese king to claim that the lands discovered by Columbus belonged to Portugal, not Spain. Seeking to ensure that Columbus's finds would remain Spanish, Spain's monarchs turned to the Spanish-born Pope Alexander VI, who issued two papal decrees in 1493 that gave legitimacy to Spain's Atlantic claims at the expense of Portugal. Hoping to salvage Portugal's Atlantic holdings, King João II began negotiations with Spain. The resulting Treaty of Tordesillas in 1494 drew a north-to-south line through South America; Spain gained territory west of the line, while Portugal retained the lands east of the line, including the east coast of Brazil.

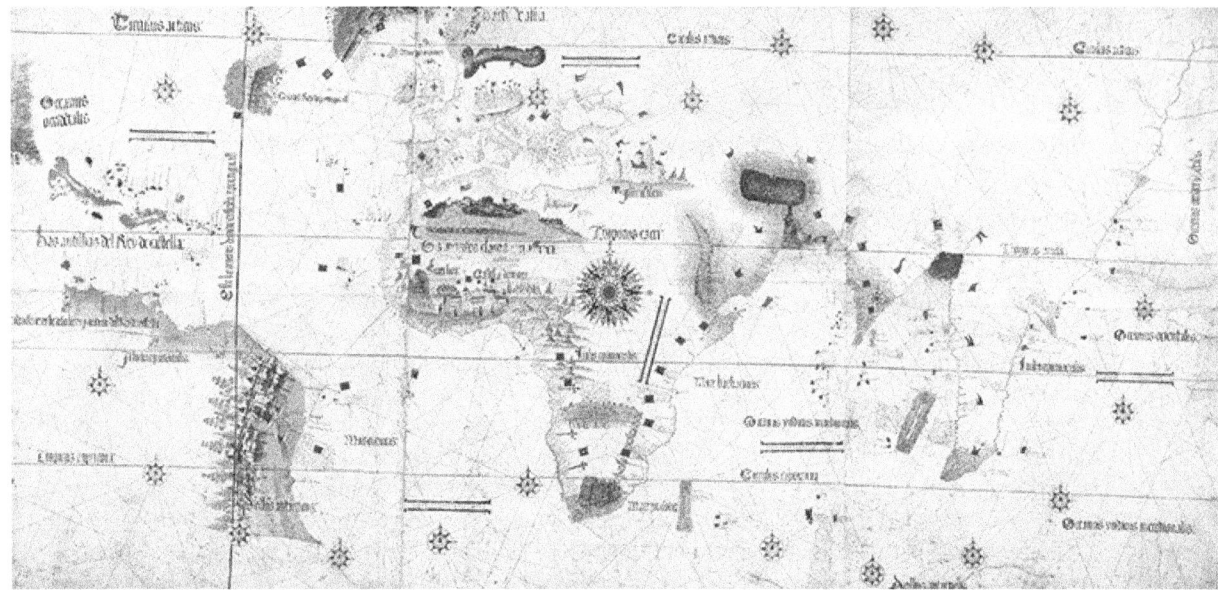

This 1502 map, known as the Cantino World Map, depicts the cartographer's interpretation of the world in light of recent discoveries. The map shows areas of Portuguese and Spanish exploration, the two nations' claims under the Treaty of Tordesillas, and a variety of flora, fauna, figures, and structures. What does it reveal about the state of geographical knowledge, as well as European perceptions of the New World, at the beginning of the sixteenth century?

Columbus's discovery opened a floodgate of Spanish exploration. Inspired by tales of rivers of gold and timid, malleable natives, later Spanish explorers were relentless in their quest for land and gold. Hernán Cortés hoped to gain hereditary privilege for his family, tribute payments and labor from natives, and an annual pension for his service to the crown. Cortés arrived on Hispaniola in 1504 and took part in the conquest of that island. In anticipation of winning his own honor and riches, Cortés later explored the Yucatán Peninsula. In 1519, he entered Tenochtitlán, the capital of the Aztec (Mexica) Empire. He and his men were astonished by the incredibly sophisticated causeways, gardens, and temples in the city, but they were horrified by the practice of human sacrifice that was part of the Aztec religion. Above all else, the Aztec wealth in gold fascinated the Spanish adventurers.

Hoping to gain power over the city, Cortés took Moctezuma, the Aztec ruler, hostage. The Spanish then murdered hundreds of high-ranking Mexica during a festival to celebrate Huitzilopochtli, the god of war. This angered the people of Tenochtitlán, who rose up against the interlopers in their city. Cortés and his people fled for their lives, running down one of Tenochtitlán's causeways to safety on the shore. Smarting from their defeat at the hands of the Aztec, Cortés slowly created alliances with native peoples who resented Aztec rule. It took nearly a year for the Spanish and the tens of thousands of native allies who joined them to defeat the Mexica in Tenochtitlán, which they did by laying siege to the city. Only by playing upon the disunity among the diverse groups in the Aztec Empire were the Spanish able to capture the grand city of Tenochtitlán. In August 1521, having successfully fomented civil war as well as fended off rival Spanish explorers, Cortés claimed Tenochtitlán for Spain and renamed it Mexico City.

The traditional European narrative of exploration presents the victory of the Spanish over the Aztec as an example of the superiority of the Europeans over the savage Indians. However, the reality is far more complex. When Cortés explored central Mexico, he encountered a region simmering with native conflict. Far from being unified and content under Aztec rule, many peoples in Mexico resented it and were ready to rebel. One group in particular, the Tlaxcalan, threw their lot in with the Spanish, providing as many as

200,000 fighters in the siege of Tenochtitlán. The Spanish also brought smallpox into the valley of Mexico. The disease took a heavy toll on the people in Tenochtitlán, playing a much greater role in the city's demise than did Spanish force of arms.

Cortés was also aided by a Nahua woman called Malintzin (also known as La Malinche or Doña Marina, her Spanish name), whom the natives of Tabasco gave him as tribute. Malintzin translated for Cortés in his dealings with Moctezuma and, whether willingly or under pressure, entered into a physical relationship with him. Their son, Martín, may have been the first mestizo (person of mixed indigenous American and European descent). Malintzin remains a controversial figure in the history of the Atlantic World; some people view her as a traitor because she helped Cortés conquer the Aztecs, while others see her as a victim of European expansion. In either case, she demonstrates one way in which native peoples responded to the arrival of the Spanish. Without her, Cortés would not have been able to communicate, and without the language bridge, he surely would have been less successful in destabilizing the Aztec Empire. By this and other means, native people helped shape the conquest of the Americas.

Spain's acquisitiveness seemingly knew no bounds as groups of its explorers searched for the next trove of instant riches. One such explorer, Francisco Pizarro, made his way to the Spanish Caribbean in 1509, drawn by the promise of wealth and titles. He participated in successful expeditions in Panama before following rumors of Inca wealth to the south. Although his first efforts against the Inca Empire in the 1520s failed, Pizarro captured the Inca emperor Atahualpa in 1532 and executed him one year later. In 1533, Pizarro founded Lima, Peru. Like Cortés, Pizarro had to combat not only the natives of the new worlds he was conquering, but also competitors from his own country; a Spanish rival assassinated him in 1541.

Spain's drive to enlarge its empire led other hopeful conquistadors to push further into the Americas, hoping to replicate the success of Cortés and Pizarro. Hernando de Soto had participated in Pizarro's conquest of the Inca, and from 1539 to 1542 he led expeditions to what is today the southeastern United States, looking for gold. He and his followers explored what is now Florida, Georgia, the Carolinas, Tennessee, Alabama, Mississippi, Arkansas, Oklahoma, Louisiana, and Texas. Everywhere they traveled, they brought European diseases, which claimed thousands of native lives as well as the lives of the explorers. In 1542, de Soto himself died during the expedition. The surviving Spaniards, numbering a little over three hundred, returned to Mexico City without finding the much-anticipated mountains of gold and silver.

Francisco Vásquez de Coronado was born into a noble family and went to Mexico, then called New Spain, in 1535. He presided as governor over the province of Nueva Galicia, where he heard rumors of wealth to the north: a golden city called Quivira. Between 1540 and 1542, Coronado led a large expedition of Spaniards and native allies to the lands north of Mexico City, and for the next several years, they explored the area that is now the southwestern United States. During the winter of 1540–41, the explorers waged war against the Tiwa in present-day New Mexico. Rather than leading to the discovery of gold and silver, however, the expedition simply left Coronado bankrupt.

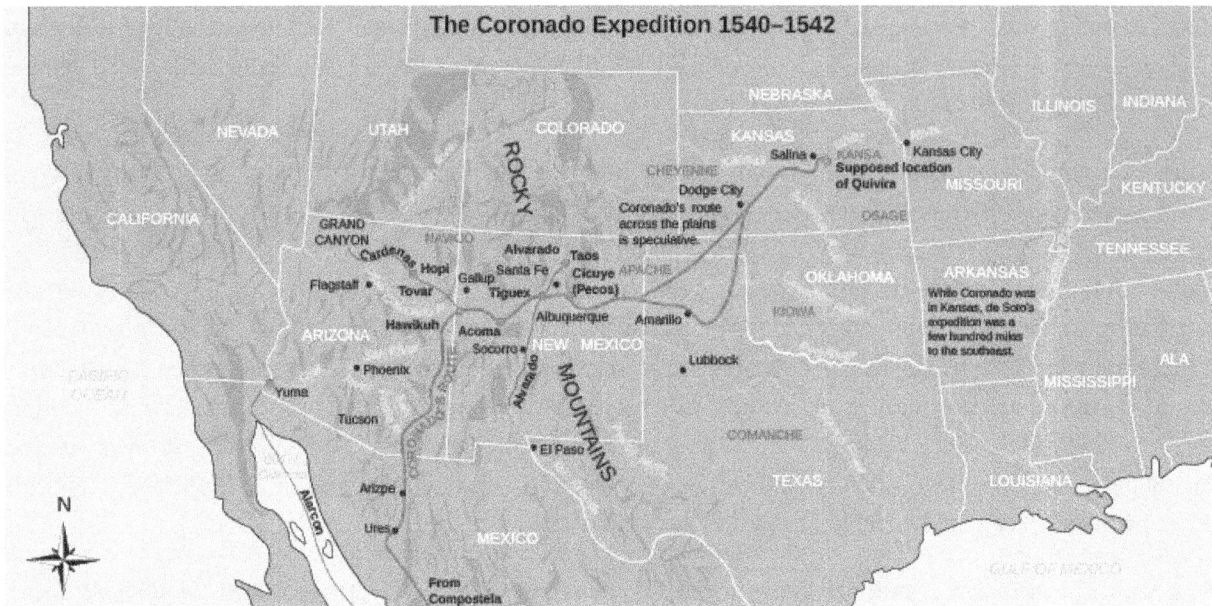

This map traces Coronado's path through the American Southwest and the Great Plains. The regions through which he traveled were not empty areas waiting to be "discovered": rather, they were populated and controlled by the groups of native peoples indicated. (credit: modification of work by National Park Service)

THE SPANISH GOLDEN AGE

> Explore the collection at The Cervantes Project for images, complete texts, and other resources relating to Cervantes's works.

Spain attracted innovative foreign painters such as El Greco, a Greek who had studied with Italian Renaissance masters like Titian and Michelangelo before moving to Toledo. Native Spaniards created equally enduring works. *Las Meninas (The Maids of Honor)*, painted by Diego Velázquez in 1656, is one of the best-known paintings in history. Velázquez painted himself into this imposingly large royal portrait (he's shown holding his brush and easel on the left) and boldly placed the viewer where the king and queen would stand in the scene.

The exploits of European explorers had a profound impact both in the Americas and back in Europe. An exchange of ideas, fueled and financed in part by New World commodities, began to connect European nations and, in turn, to touch the parts of the world that Europeans conquered. In Spain, gold and silver from the Americas helped to fuel a golden age, the Siglo de Oro, when Spanish art and literature flourished. Riches poured in from the colonies, and new ideas poured in from other countries and new lands. The Hapsburg dynasty, which ruled a collection of territories including Austria, the Netherlands, Naples, Sicily, and Spain, encouraged and financed the work of painters, sculptors, musicians, architects, and writers, resulting in a blooming of Spanish Renaissance culture. One of this period's most famous works is the novel *The Ingenious Gentleman Don Quixote of La Mancha*, by Miguel de Cervantes. This two-volume book (1605 and 1618) told a colorful tale of an *hidalgo* (gentleman) who reads so many tales of chivalry and knighthood that he becomes unable to tell reality from fiction. With his faithful sidekick Sancho Panza, Don Quixote leaves reality behind and sets out to revive chivalry by doing battle with what he perceives as the enemies of Spain.

Las Meninas (The Maids of Honor), painted by Diego Velázquez in 1656, is unique for its time because it places the viewer in the place of King Philip IV and his wife, Queen Mariana.

Section Summary

Although Portugal opened the door to exploration of the Atlantic World, Spanish explorers quickly made inroads into the Americas. Spurred by Christopher Columbus's glowing reports of the riches to be found in the New World, throngs of Spanish conquistadors set off to find and conquer new lands. They accomplished this through a combination of military strength and strategic alliances with native peoples. Spanish rulers Ferdinand and Isabella promoted the acquisition of these new lands in order to strengthen and glorify their own empire. As Spain's empire expanded and riches flowed in from the Americas, the Spanish experienced a golden age of art and literature.

https://www.openassessments.org/assessments/1092

Critical Thinking Questions

1. Why did the authors of *probanzas de méritos* choose to write in the way that they did? What should we consider when we interpret these documents today?

Answers to Critical Thinking Questions

1. *Probanzas de méritos* featured glowing descriptions of lands of plenty. The Spanish explorers hoped to find cities of gold, so they made their discoveries sound as wonderful as possible in these letters to convince the Spanish crown to fund more voyages. When we read them now, we need to take the descriptions with a grain of salt. But we can also fact-check these descriptions, whereas the Spanish court could only take them at face value.

Glossary

Hispaniola the island in the Caribbean, present-day Haiti and Dominican Republic, where Columbus first landed and established a Spanish colony

probanza de mérito proof of merit: a letter written by a Spanish explorer to the crown to gain royal patronage

Attributions

CC licensed content, Shared previously

- US History. **Authored by**: P. Scott Corbett, Volker Janssen, John M. Lund, Todd Pfannestiel, Paul Vickery, and Sylvie Waskiewicz. **Provided by**: OpenStax College. **Located at**: http://openstaxcollege.org/textbooks/us-history. **License**: *CC BY: Attribution*. **License Terms**: Download for free at http://cnx.org/content/col11740/latest/

New Worlds in the Americas: Labor, Commerce, and the Columbian Exchange

> ### Learning Objectives
>
> By the end of this section, you will be able to:
>
> - Describe how Europeans solved their labor problems
> - Describe the theory of mercantilism and the process of commodification
> - Analyze the effects of the Columbian Exchange

European promoters of colonization claimed the Americas overflowed with a wealth of treasures. Burnishing national glory and honor became entwined with carving out colonies, and no nation wanted to be left behind. However, the realities of life in the Americas—violence, exploitation, and particularly the need for workers—were soon driving the practice of slavery and forced labor. Everywhere in America a stark contrast existed between freedom and slavery. The Columbian Exchange, in which Europeans transported plants, animals, and diseases across the Atlantic in both directions, also left a lasting impression on the Americas.

LABOR SYSTEMS

Physical power—to work the fields, build villages, process raw materials—is a necessity for maintaining a society. During the sixteenth and seventeenth centuries, humans could derive power only from the wind, water, animals, or other humans. Everywhere in the Americas, a crushing demand for labor bedeviled Europeans because there were not enough colonists to perform the work necessary to keep the colonies going. Spain granted *encomiendas*—legal rights to native labor—to conquistadors who could prove their service to the crown. This system reflected the Spanish view of colonization: the king rewarded successful conquistadors who expanded the empire. Some native peoples who had sided with the conquistadors, like the Tlaxcalan, also gained *encomiendas*; Malintzin, the Nahua woman who helped Cortés defeat the Mexica, was granted one.

In this startling image from the Kingsborough Codex (a book written and drawn by native Mesoamericans), a well-dressed Spaniard is shown pulling the hair of a bleeding, severely injured native. The drawing was part of a complaint about Spanish abuses of their encomiendas.

The Spanish believed native peoples would work for them by right of conquest, and, in return, the Spanish would bring them Catholicism. In theory the relationship consisted of reciprocal obligations, but in practice the Spaniards ruthlessly exploited it, seeing native people as little more than beasts of burden. Convinced of their right to the land and its peoples, they sought both to control native labor and to impose what they viewed as correct religious beliefs upon the land's inhabitants. Native peoples everywhere resisted both the labor obligations and the effort to change their ancient belief systems. Indeed, many retained their religion or incorporated only the parts of Catholicism that made sense to them.

The system of *encomiendas* was accompanied by a great deal of violence. One Spaniard, Bartolomé de Las Casas, denounced the brutality of Spanish rule. A Dominican friar, Las Casas had been one of the earliest Spanish settlers in the Spanish West Indies. In his early life in the Americas, he owned Indian slaves and was the recipient of an *encomienda*. However, after witnessing the savagery with which *encomenderos* (recipients of *encomiendas*) treated the native people, he reversed his views. In 1515, Las Casas released his native slaves, gave up his *encomienda*, and began to advocate for humane treatment of native peoples. He lobbied for new legislation, eventually known as the New Laws, which would eliminate slavery and the *encomienda* system.

Las Casas's writing about the Spaniards' horrific treatment of Indians helped inspire the so-called **Black Legend**, the idea that the Spanish were bloodthirsty conquerors with no regard for human life. Perhaps not surprisingly, those who held this view of the Spanish were Spain's imperial rivals. English writers and others seized on the idea of Spain's ruthlessness to support their own colonization projects. By demonizing the Spanish, they justified their own efforts as more humane. All European colonizers, however, shared a disregard for Indians.

Bartolomé de Las Casas's *A Short Account of the Destruction of the Indies*, written in 1542 and published ten years later, detailed for Prince Philip II of Spain how Spanish colonists had been mistreating natives.

> Into and among these gentle sheep, endowed by their Maker and Creator with all the qualities aforesaid, did creep the Spaniards, who no sooner had knowledge of these people than they became like fierce wolves and tigers and lions who have gone many days without food or nourishment. And no other thing have they done for forty years until this day, and still today see fit to do, but dismember, slay, perturb, afflict, torment, and destroy the Indians by all manner of cruelty—new and divers and most singular manners such as never before seen or read or heard of—some few of which shall be recounted below, and they do this to such a degree that on the Island of Hispaniola, of the above three millions souls that we once saw, today there be no more than two hundred of those native people remaining. . . .
>
> Two principal and general customs have been employed by those, calling themselves Christians, who have passed this way, in extirpating and striking from the face of the earth those suffering nations. The first being unjust, cruel, bloody, and tyrannical warfare. The other—after having slain all those who might yearn toward or suspire after or think of freedom, or consider escaping from the torments that they are made to suffer, by which I mean all the native-born lords and adult males, for it is the Spaniards' custom in their wars to allow only young boys and females to live—being to oppress them with the hardest, harshest, and most heinous bondage to which men or beasts might ever be bound into.

How might these writings have been used to promote the "black legend" against Spain as well as subsequent English exploration and colonization?

Indians were not the only source of cheap labor in the Americas; by the middle of the sixteenth century, Africans formed an important element of the labor landscape, producing the cash crops of sugar and tobacco for European markets. Europeans viewed Africans as non-Christians, which they used as a justification for enslavement. Denied control over their lives, slaves endured horrendous conditions. At every opportunity, they resisted enslavement, and their resistance was met with violence. Indeed, physical, mental, and sexual violence formed a key strategy among European slaveholders in their effort to assert mastery and impose their will. The Portuguese led the way in the evolving transport of slaves across the Atlantic; slave "factories" on the west coast of Africa, like Elmina Castle in Ghana, served as holding pens for slaves brought from Africa's interior. In time, other European imperial powers would follow in the footsteps of the Portuguese by constructing similar outposts on the coast of West Africa.

The Portuguese traded or sold slaves to Spanish, Dutch, and English colonists in the Americas, particularly in South America and the Caribbean, where sugar was a primary export. Thousands of African slaves found themselves growing, harvesting, and processing **sugarcane** in an arduous routine of physical labor. Slaves had to cut the long cane stalks by hand and then bring them to a mill, where the cane juice was extracted. They boiled the extracted cane juice down to a brown, crystalline sugar, which then had to be cured in special curing houses to have the molasses drained from it. The result was refined sugar, while the leftover molasses could be distilled into rum. Every step was labor-intensive and often dangerous.

Las Casas estimated that by 1550, there were fifty thousand slaves on Hispaniola. However, it is a mistake to assume that during the very early years of European exploration all Africans came to America as slaves; some were free men who took part in expeditions, for example, serving as conquistadors alongside Cortés in his assault on Tenochtitlán. Nonetheless, African slavery was one of the most tragic outcomes in the emerging Atlantic World.

> Browse the PBS collection Africans in America: Part 1 to see information and primary sources for the period 1450 through 1750.

COMMERCE IN THE NEW WORLD

The economic philosophy of **mercantilism** shaped European perceptions of wealth from the 1500s to the late 1700s. Mercantilism held that only a limited amount of wealth, as measured in gold and silver bullion, existed in the world. In order to gain power, nations had to amass wealth by mining these precious raw materials from their colonial possessions. During the age of European exploration, nations employed conquest, colonization, and trade as ways to increase their share of the bounty of the New World. Mercantilists did not believe in free trade, arguing instead that the nation should control trade to create wealth. In this view, colonies existed to strengthen the colonizing nation. Mercantilists argued against allowing their nations to trade freely with other nations.

Spain's mercantilist ideas guided its economic policy. Every year, slaves or native workers loaded shipments of gold and silver aboard Spanish treasure fleets that sailed from Cuba for Spain. These ships groaned under the sheer weight of bullion, for the Spanish had found huge caches of silver and gold in the New World. In South America, for example, Spaniards discovered rich veins of silver ore in the mountain called Potosí and founded a settlement of the same name there. Throughout the sixteenth century, Potosí was a boom town, attracting settlers from many nations as well as native people from many different cultures.

Colonial mercantilism, which was basically a set of protectionist policies designed to benefit the nation, relied on several factors: colonies rich in raw materials, cheap labor, colonial loyalty to the home government, and control of the shipping trade. Under this system, the colonies sent their raw materials, harvested by slaves or native workers, back to their mother country. The mother country sent back finished materials of all sorts: textiles, tools, clothing. The colonists could purchase these goods *only* from their mother country; trade with other countries was forbidden.

The 1500s and early 1600s also introduced the process of **commodification** to the New World. American silver, tobacco, and other items, which were used by native peoples for ritual purposes, became European commodities with a monetary value that could be bought and sold. Before the arrival of the Spanish, for example, the **Inca** people of the Andes consumed *chicha*, a corn beer, for ritual purposes only. When the Spanish discovered chicha, they bought and traded for it, turning it into a commodity instead of a ritual substance. Commodification thus recast native economies and spurred the process of early commercial capitalism. New World resources, from plants to animal pelts, held the promise of wealth for European imperial powers.

THE COLUMBIAN EXCHANGE

As Europeans traversed the Atlantic, they brought with them plants, animals, and diseases that changed lives and landscapes on both sides of the ocean. These two-way exchanges between the Americas and Europe/Africa are known collectively as the **Columbian Exchange**.

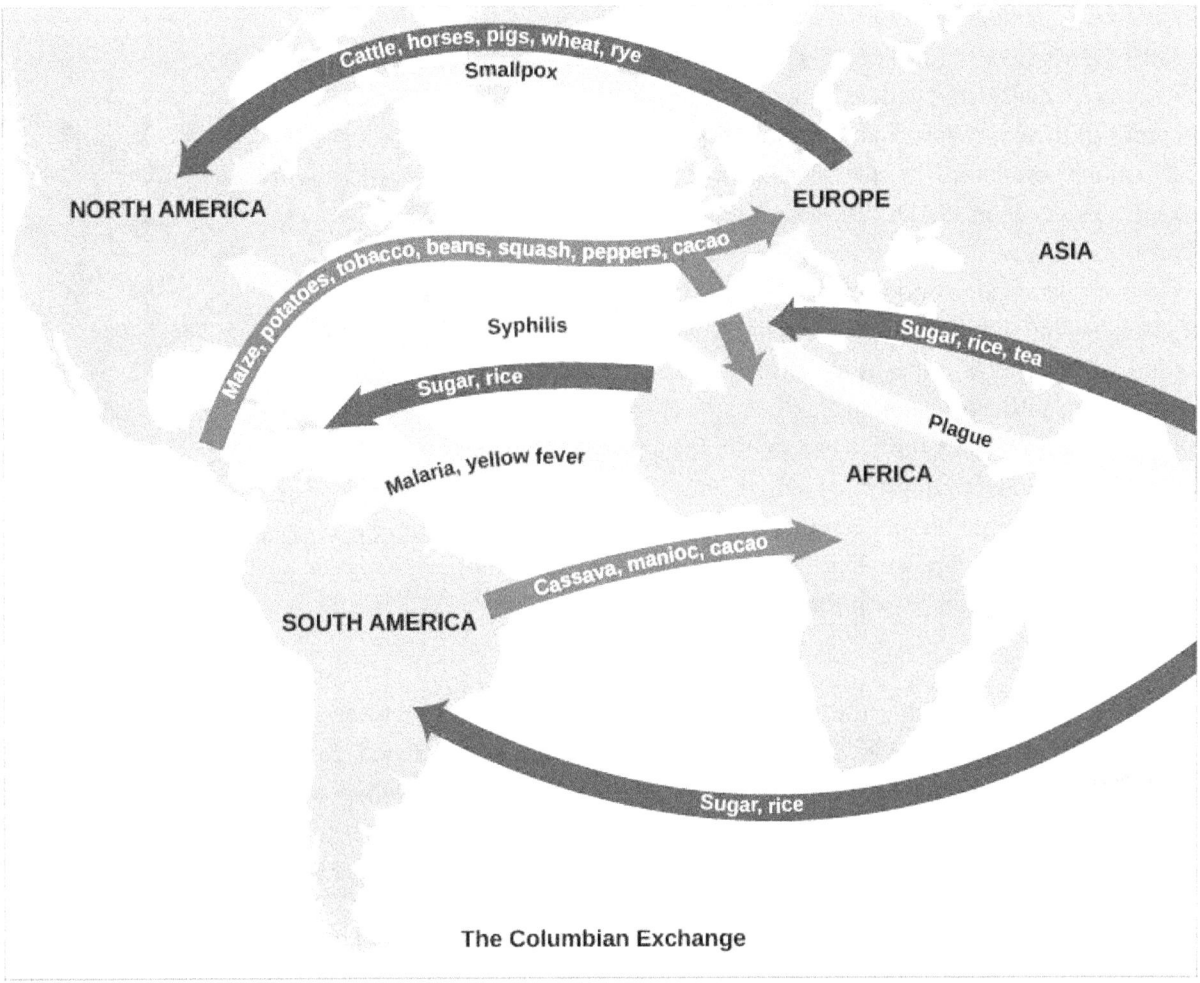

With European exploration and settlement of the New World, goods and diseases began crossing the Atlantic Ocean in both directions. This "Columbian Exchange" soon had global implications.

Of all the commodities in the Atlantic World, sugar proved to be the most important. Indeed, sugar carried the same economic importance as oil does today. European rivals raced to create sugar plantations in the Americas and fought wars for control of some of the best sugar production areas. Although refined sugar was available in the Old World, Europe's harsher climate made sugarcane difficult to grow, and it was not plentiful. Columbus brought sugar to Hispaniola in 1493, and the new crop was growing there by the end of the 1490s. By the first decades of the 1500s, the Spanish were building sugar mills on the island. Over the next century of colonization, Caribbean islands and most other tropical areas became centers of sugar production.

Though of secondary importance to sugar, tobacco achieved great value for Europeans as a cash crop as well. Native peoples had been growing it for medicinal and ritual purposes for centuries before European contact, smoking it in pipes or powdering it to use as snuff. They believed tobacco could improve concentration and enhance wisdom. To some, its use meant achieving an entranced, altered, or divine state; entering a spiritual place.

Tobacco was unknown in Europe before 1492, and it carried a negative stigma at first. The early Spanish explorers considered natives' use of tobacco to be proof of their savagery and, because of the fire and smoke produced in the consumption of tobacco, evidence of the Devil's sway in the New World. Gradually, however, European colonists became accustomed to and even took up the habit of smoking, and they brought it across the Atlantic. As did the Indians, Europeans ascribed medicinal properties to tobacco, claiming that it could cure headaches and skin irritations. Even so, Europeans did not import tobacco in great quantities until the 1590s. At that time, it became the first truly global commodity; English, French, Dutch, Spanish, and Portuguese colonists all grew it for the world market.

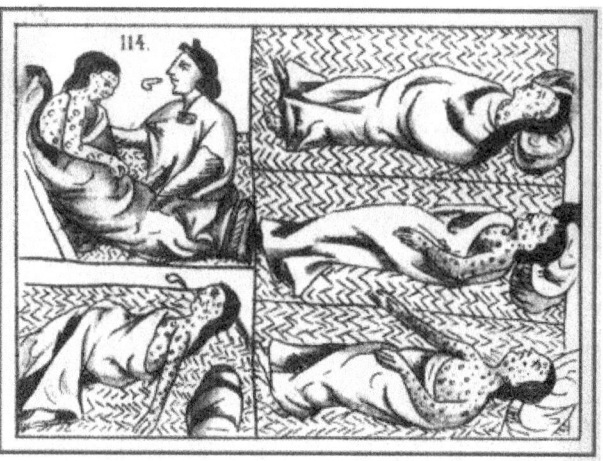

This sixteenth-century Aztec drawing shows the suffering of a typical victim of smallpox. Smallpox and other contagious diseases brought by European explorers decimated Indian populations in the Americas.

Native peoples also introduced Europeans to chocolate, made from cacao seeds and used by the Aztec in Mesoamerica as currency. Mesoamerican Indians consumed unsweetened chocolate in a drink with chili peppers, vanilla, and a spice called achiote. This chocolate drink—*xocolatl*—was part of ritual ceremonies like marriage and an everyday item for those who could afford it. Chocolate contains theobromine, a stimulant, which may be why native people believed it brought them closer to the sacred world.

Spaniards in the New World considered drinking chocolate a vile practice; one called chocolate "the Devil's vomit." In time, however, they introduced the beverage to Spain. At first, chocolate was available only in the Spanish court, where the elite mixed it with sugar and other spices. Later, as its availability spread, chocolate gained a reputation as a love potion.

> Visit Nature Transformed for a collection of scholarly essays on the environment in American history.

The crossing of the Atlantic by plants like cacao and tobacco illustrates the ways in which the discovery of the New World changed the habits and behaviors of Europeans. Europeans changed the New World in turn, not least by bringing Old World animals to the Americas. On his second voyage, Christopher Columbus brought pigs, horses, cows, and chickens to the islands of the Caribbean. Later explorers followed suit, introducing new animals or reintroducing ones that had died out (like horses). With less vulnerability to disease, these animals often fared better than humans in their new home, thriving both in the wild and in domestication.

Europeans encountered New World animals as well. Because European Christians understood the world as a place of warfare between God and Satan, many believed the Americas, which lacked Christianity, were home to the Devil and his minions. The exotic, sometimes bizarre, appearances and habits of animals in the Americas that were previously unknown to Europeans, such as manatees, sloths, and poisonous snakes, confirmed this association. Over time, however, they began to rely more on observation of the natural world than solely on scripture. This shift—from seeing the Bible as the source of all received wisdom to trusting observation or empiricism—is one of the major outcomes of the era of early globalization.

Travelers between the Americas, Africa, and Europe also included microbes: silent, invisible life forms that had profound and devastating consequences. Native peoples had no immunity to diseases from across the Atlantic, to which they had never been exposed. European explorers unwittingly brought with them chickenpox, measles, mumps, and **smallpox**, which ravaged native peoples despite their attempts to treat the diseases, decimating some populations and wholly destroying others.

In eastern North America, some native peoples interpreted death from disease as a hostile act. Some groups, including the Iroquois, engaged in raids or "**mourning wars**," taking enemy prisoners in order to assuage their grief and replace the departed. In a special ritual, the prisoners were "requickened"—assigned the identity of a dead person—and adopted by the bereaved family to take the place of their dead. As the toll from disease rose, mourning wars intensified and expanded.

Section Summary

In the minds of European rulers, colonies existed to create wealth for imperial powers. Guided by mercantilist ideas, European rulers and investors hoped to enrich their own nations and themselves, in order to gain the greatest share of what was believed to be a limited amount of wealth. In their own individual quest for riches and preeminence, European colonizers who traveled to the Americas blazed new and disturbing paths, such as the *encomienda* system of forced labor and the use of tens of thousands of Africans as slaves.

All native inhabitants of the Americas who came into contact with Europeans found their worlds turned upside down as the new arrivals introduced their religions and ideas about property and goods. Europeans gained new foods, plants, and animals in the Columbian Exchange, turning whatever they could into a commodity to be bought and sold, and Indians were introduced to diseases that nearly destroyed them. At every turn, however, Indians placed limits on European colonization and resisted the newcomers' ways.

https://www.openassessments.org/assessments/941

CRITICAL THINKING QUESTIONS

1. What were the consequences of the religious upheavals of the sixteenth and seventeenth centuries?
2. What types of labor systems were used in the Americas? Did systems of unfree labor serve more than an economic function?
3. What is meant by the Columbian Exchange? Who was affected the most by the exchange?
4. What were the various goals of the colonial European powers in the expansion of their empires? To what extent were they able to achieve these goals? Where did they fail?

5. On the whole, what was the impact of early European explorations on the New World? What was the impact of the New World on Europeans?

Glossary

Black Legend Spain's reputation as bloodthirsty conquistadors

Columbian Exchange the movement of plants, animals, and diseases across the Atlantic due to European exploration of the Americas

commodification the transformation of something—for example, an item of ritual significance—into a commodity with monetary value

encomienda legal rights to native labor as granted by the Spanish crown

mercantilism the protectionist economic principle that nations should control trade with their colonies to ensure a favorable balance of trade

mourning wars raids or wars that tribes waged in eastern North America in order to replace members lost to smallpox and other diseases

smallpox a disease that Europeans accidentally brought to the New World, killing millions of Indians, who had no immunity to the disease

sugarcane one of the primary crops of the Americas, which required a tremendous amount of labor to cultivate

Attributions

CC licensed content, Shared previously

- US History. **Authored by**: P. Scott Corbett, Volker Janssen, John M. Lund, Todd Pfannestiel, Paul Vickery, and Sylvie Waskiewicz. **Provided by**: OpenStax College. **Located at**: http://openstaxcollege.org/textbooks/us-history. **License**: *CC BY: Attribution*. **License Terms**: Download for free at http://cnx.org/content/col11740/latest/

Challenges to Spain's Supremacy

Learning Objectives

By the end of this section, you will be able to:

- Identify regions where the English, French, and Dutch explored and established settlements
- Describe the differences among the early colonies
- Explain the role of the American colonies in European nations' struggles for domination

For Europeans, the discovery of an Atlantic World meant newfound wealth in the form of gold and silver as well as valuable furs. The Americas also provided a new arena for intense imperial rivalry as different European nations jockeyed for preeminence in the New World. The religious motives for colonization spurred European expansion as well, and as the Protestant Reformation gained ground beginning in the 1520s, rivalries between Catholic and Protestant Christians spilled over into the Americas.

ENGLISH EXPLORATION

Disruptions during the Tudor monarchy—especially the creation of the Protestant Church of England by Henry VIII in the 1530s, the return of the nation to Catholicism under Queen Mary in the 1550s, and the restoration of Protestantism under Queen Elizabeth—left England with little energy for overseas projects. More important, England lacked the financial resources for such endeavors. Nonetheless, English monarchs carefully monitored developments in the new Atlantic World and took steps to assert England's claim to the Americas. As early as 1497, Henry VII of England had commissioned John Cabot, an Italian mariner, to explore new lands. Cabot sailed from England that year and made landfall somewhere along the North American coastline. For the next century, English fishermen routinely crossed the Atlantic to fish the rich waters off the North American coast. However, English colonization efforts in the 1500s were closer to home, as England devoted its energy to the colonization of Ireland.

Queen Elizabeth favored England's advance into the Atlantic World, though her main concern was blocking Spain's effort to eliminate Protestantism. Indeed, England could not commit to large-scale colonization in the Americas as long as Spain appeared ready to invade Ireland or Scotland. Nonetheless, Elizabeth approved of English **privateers**, sea captains to whom the home government had given permission to raid the enemy at will. These skilled mariners cruised the Caribbean, plundering Spanish ships whenever they could. Each year the English took more than £100,000 from Spain in this way; English privateer Francis Drake first made a name for himself when, in 1573, he looted silver, gold, and pearls worth £40,000.

Elizabeth did sanction an early attempt at colonization in 1584, when Sir Walter Raleigh, a favorite of the queen's, attempted to establish a colony at **Roanoke**, an island off the coast of present-day North Carolina. The colony was small, consisting of only 117 people, who suffered a poor relationship with the local Indians, the Croatans, and struggled to survive in their new land. Their governor, John White, returned to England in late 1587 to secure more people and supplies, but events conspired to keep him away from Roanoke for three years. By the time he returned in 1590, the entire colony had vanished. The only trace the colonists left behind was the word *Croatoan* carved into a fence surrounding the village. Governor White never knew whether the colonists had decamped for nearby Croatoan Island (now Hatteras) or whether some disaster had befallen them all. Roanoke is still called "the lost colony."

In 1588, a promoter of English colonization named Thomas Hariot published A Briefe and True Report of the New Found Land of Virginia, which contained many engravings of the native peoples who lived on the Carolina coast in the 1580s. This print, "The brovvyllinge of their fishe ouer the flame" (1590) by Theodor de Bry, shows the ingenuity and wisdom of the "savages" of the New World. (credit: UNC Chapel Hill)

English promoters of colonization pushed its commercial advantages and the religious justification that English colonies would allow the establishment of Protestantism in the Americas. Both arguments struck a chord. In the early 1600s, wealthy English merchants and the landed elite began to pool their resources to form **joint stock companies**. In this novel business arrangement, which was in many ways the precursor to the modern corporation, investors provided the capital for and assumed the risk of a venture in order to reap significant returns. The companies gained the approval of the English crown to establish colonies, and their investors dreamed of reaping great profits from the money they put into overseas colonization.

The first permanent English settlement was established by a joint stock company, the Virginia Company. Named for Elizabeth, the "virgin queen," the company gained royal approval to establish a colony on the east coast of North America, and in 1606, it sent 144 men and boys to the New World. In early 1607, this group sailed up Chesapeake Bay. Finding a river they called the James in honor of their new king, James I, they established a ramshackle settlement and named it Jamestown. Despite serious struggles, the colony survived.

Many of Jamestown's settlers were desperate men; although they came from elite families, they were younger sons who would not inherit their father's estates. The Jamestown adventurers believed they would find instant wealth in the New World and did not actually expect to have to perform work. Henry Percy, the eighth son of the Earl of Northumberland, was among them. His account, excerpted below, illustrates the hardships the English confronted in Virginia in 1607.

George Percy and the First Months at Jamestown

The 144 men and boys who started the Jamestown colony faced many hardships; by the end of the first winter, only 38 had survived. Disease, hunger, and poor relationships with local natives all contributed to the colony's high death toll. George Percy, who served twice as governor of Jamestown, kept records of the colonists' first months in the colony. These records were later published in London in 1608. This excerpt is from his account of August and September of 1607.

> The fourth day of September died Thomas Jacob Sergeant. The fifth day, there died Benjamin Beast. Our men were destroyed with cruel diseases, as Swellings, Fluxes, Burning Fevers, and by wars, and some departed suddenly, but for the most part they died of mere famine. There were never Englishmen left in a foreign Country in such misery as we were in this new discovered Virginia. . . . Our food was but a small Can of Barley sod* in water, to five men a day, our drink cold water taken out of the River, which was at a flood very salty, at a low tide full of slime and filth, which was the destruction of many of our men. Thus we lived for the space of five months in this miserable distress, not having five able men to man our Bulwarks upon any occasion. If it had not pleased God to have put a terror in the Savages' hearts, we had all perished by those wild and cruel Pagans, being in that weak estate as we were; our men night and day groaning in every corner of the Fort most pitiful to hear. If there were any conscience in men, it would make their hearts to bleed to hear the pitiful murmurings and outcries of our sick men without relief, every night and day, for the space of six weeks, some departing out of the World, many times three or four in a night; in the morning, their bodies trailed out of their Cabins like Dogs to be buried. In this sort did I see the mortality of diverse of our people.
>
> *soaked*

According to George Percy's account, what were the major problems the Jamestown settlers encountered? What kept the colony from complete destruction?

By any measure, England came late to the race to colonize. As Jamestown limped along in the 1610s, the Spanish Empire extended around the globe and grew rich from its global colonial project. Yet the English persisted, and for this reason the Jamestown settlement has a special place in history as the first permanent colony in what later became the United States.

After Jamestown's founding, English colonization of the New World accelerated. In 1609, a ship bound for Jamestown foundered in a storm and landed on Bermuda. (Some believe this incident helped inspire Shakespeare's 1611 play *The Tempest*.) The admiral of the ship, George Somers, claimed the island for the English crown. The English also began to colonize small islands in the Caribbean, an incursion into the Spanish American empire. They established themselves on small islands such as St. Christopher (1624), Barbados (1627), Nevis (1628), Montserrat (1632), and Antigua (1632).

From the start, the English West Indies had a commercial orientation, for these islands produced cash crops: first tobacco and then sugar. Very quickly, by the mid-1600s, Barbados had become one of the most important English colonies because of the sugar produced there. Barbados was the first English colony dependent on slaves, and it became a model for other English slave societies on the American mainland. These differed radically from England itself, where slavery was not practiced.

English Puritans also began to colonize the Americas in the 1620s and 1630s. These intensely religious migrants dreamed of creating communities of reformed Protestantism where the corruption of England would be eliminated. One of the first groups of Puritans to remove to North America, known as **Pilgrims** and led by William Bradford, had originally left England to live in the Netherlands. Fearing their children were losing their English identity among the Dutch, however, they sailed for North America in 1620 to settle at Plymouth, the first English settlement in New England. The Pilgrims differed from other Puritans in their insistence on separating from what they saw as the corrupt Church of England. For this reason, Pilgrims are known as **Separatists**.

Like Jamestown, Plymouth occupies an iconic place in American national memory. The tale of the 102 migrants who crossed the Atlantic aboard the *Mayflower* and their struggle for survival is a well-known narrative of the founding of the country. Their story includes the signing of the Mayflower Compact, a written agreement whereby the English voluntarily agreed to help each other. Some interpret this 1620 document as an expression of democratic spirit because of the cooperative and inclusive nature of the agreement to live and work together. In 1630, a much larger contingent of Puritans left England to escape conformity to the Church of England and founded the Massachusetts Bay Colony. In the following years, thousands more arrived to create a new life in the rocky soils and cold climates of New England.

In comparison to Catholic Spain, however, Protestant England remained a very weak imperial player in the early seventeenth century, with only a few infant colonies in the Americas in the early 1600s. The English never found treasure equal to that of the Aztec city of Tenochtitlán, and England did not quickly grow rich from its small American outposts. The English colonies also differed from each other; Barbados and Virginia had a decidedly commercial orientation from the start, while the Puritan colonies of New England were intensely religious at their inception. All English settlements in America, however, marked the increasingly important role of England in the Atlantic World.

FRENCH EXPLORATION

Spanish exploits in the New World whetted the appetite of other would-be imperial powers, including France. Like Spain, France was a Catholic nation and committed to expanding Catholicism around the globe. In the early sixteenth century, it joined the race to explore the New World and exploit the resources of the Western Hemisphere. Navigator Jacques Cartier claimed northern North America for France, naming the area New France. From 1534 to 1541, he made three voyages of discovery on the Gulf of St. Lawrence and the St. Lawrence River. Like other explorers, Cartier made exaggerated claims of mineral wealth in America, but he was unable to send great riches back to France. Due to resistance from the native peoples as well as his own lack of planning, he could not establish a permanent settlement in North America.

Explorer Samuel de Champlain occupies a special place in the history of the Atlantic World for his role in establishing the French presence in the New World. Champlain explored the Caribbean in 1601 and then the coast of New England in 1603 before traveling farther north. In 1608 he founded Quebec, and he made numerous Atlantic crossings as he worked tirelessly to promote New France. Unlike other imperial powers, France—through Champlain's efforts—fostered especially good relationships with native peoples, paving the way for French exploration further into the continent: around the Great Lakes, around Hudson Bay, and eventually to the Mississippi. Champlain made an alliance with the Huron confederacy and the Algonquins and agreed to fight with them against their enemy, the Iroquois.

In this engraving, titled Defeat of the Iroquois and based on a drawing by explorer Samuel de Champlain, Champlain is shown fighting on the side of the Huron and Algonquins against the Iroquois. He portrays himself in the middle of the battle, firing a gun, while the native people around him shoot arrows at each other. What does this engraving suggest about the impact of European exploration and settlement on the Americas?

The French were primarily interested in establishing commercially viable colonial outposts, and to that end, they created extensive trading networks in New France. These networks relied on native hunters to harvest furs, especially beaver pelts, and to exchange these items for French glass beads and other trade goods. (French fashion at the time favored broad-brimmed hats trimmed in beaver fur, so French traders had a ready market for their North American goods.) The French also dreamed of replicating the wealth of Spain by colonizing the tropical zones. After Spanish control of the Caribbean began to weaken, the French turned their attention to small islands in the West Indies, and by 1635 they had colonized two, Guadeloupe and Martinique. Though it lagged far behind Spain, France now boasted its own West Indian colonies. Both islands became lucrative sugar plantation sites that turned a profit for French planters by relying on African slave labor.

> To see how cartographers throughout history documented the exploration of the Atlantic World, browse the hundreds of digitized historical maps that make up the collection American Shores: Maps of the Middle Atlantic Region to 1850 at the New York Public Library.

DUTCH COLONIZATION

Dutch entrance into the Atlantic World is part of the larger story of religious and imperial conflict in the early modern era. In the 1500s, Calvinism, one of the major Protestant reform movements, had found adherents in the northern provinces of the Spanish Netherlands. During the sixteenth century, these provinces began a long struggle to achieve independence from Catholic Spain. Established in 1581 but not recognized as independent by Spain until 1648, the Dutch Republic, or Holland, quickly made itself a powerful force in the race for Atlantic colonies and wealth. The Dutch distinguished themselves as commercial leaders in the seventeenth century, and their mode of colonization relied on powerful corporations: the Dutch East India Company, chartered in 1602 to trade in Asia, and the Dutch West India Company, established in 1621 to colonize and trade in the Americas.

While employed by the Dutch East India Company in 1609, the English sea captain Henry Hudson explored New York Harbor and the river that now bears his name. Like many explorers of the time,

Amsterdam was the richest city in the world in the 1600s. In Courtyard of the Exchange in Amsterdam, a 1653 painting by Emanuel de Witt, merchants involved in the global trade eagerly attend to news of shipping and the prices of commodities.

Hudson was actually seeking a northwest passage to Asia and its wealth, but the ample furs harvested from the region he explored, especially the coveted beaver pelts, provided a reason to claim it for the Netherlands. The Dutch named their colony New Netherlands, and it served as a fur-trading outpost for the expanding and powerful Dutch West India Company. With headquarters in New Amsterdam on the island of Manhattan, the Dutch set up several regional trading posts, including one at Fort Orange—named for the royal Dutch House of Orange-Nassau—in present-day Albany. (The color orange remains significant to the Dutch, having become particularly associated with William of Orange, Protestantism, and the Glorious Revolution of 1688.) A brisk trade in furs with local Algonquian and Iroquois peoples brought the Dutch and native peoples together in a commercial network that extended throughout the Hudson River Valley and beyond.

The Dutch West India Company in turn established colonies on Aruba, Bonaire, and Curaçao, St. Martin, St. Eustatius, and Saba. With their outposts in New Netherlands and the Caribbean, the Dutch had established themselves in the seventeenth century as a commercially powerful rival to Spain. Amsterdam became a trade hub for all the Atlantic World.

Section Summary

By the beginning of the seventeenth century, Spain's rivals—England, France, and the Dutch Republic—had each established an Atlantic presence, with greater or lesser success, in the race for imperial power. None of the new colonies, all in the eastern part of North America, could match the Spanish possessions for gold and silver resources. Nonetheless, their presence in the New World helped these nations establish claims that they hoped could halt the runaway growth of Spain's Catholic empire. English colonists in Virginia suffered greatly, expecting riches to fall into their hands and finding reality a harsh blow. However, the colony at Jamestown survived, and the output of England's islands in the West Indies soon grew to be an important source of income for the country. New France and New Netherlands were modest colonial holdings in the northeast of the continent, but these colonies' thriving fur trade with native peoples, and their alliances with those peoples, helped to create the foundation for later shifts in the global balance of power.

https://www.openassessments.org/assessments/1094

Critical Thinking Questions

1. What were some of the main differences among the non-Spanish colonies?

Answers to Critical Thinking Questions

1. Many English colonists in Virginia were aristocrats who had never worked and didn't expect to start. They hoped to find gold and silver and were unprepared for the realities of colonial life. Farther north, the English Puritan colonies were largely founded not for profit but for religious reasons. The French and Dutch colonies were primarily trading posts. Their colonists enjoyed good relationships with many native groups because they made alliances with and traded with them.

Glossary

joint stock company a business entity in which investors provide the capital and assume the risk in order to reap significant returns

Pilgrims Separatists, led by William Bradford, who established the first English settlement in New England

privateers sea captains to whom the British government had given permission to raid Spanish ships at will

Roanoke the first English colony in Virginia, which mysteriously disappeared sometime between 1587 and 1590

Separatists a faction of Puritans who advocated complete separation from the Church of England

Attributions

CC licensed content, Shared previously

- US History. **Authored by**: P. Scott Corbett, Volker Janssen, John M. Lund, Todd Pfannestiel, Paul Vickery, and Sylvie Waskiewicz. **Provided by**: OpenStax College. **Located at**: http://openstaxcollege.org/textbooks/us-history. **License**: *CC BY: Attribution*. **License Terms**: Download for free at http://cnx.org/content/col11740/latest/

Colonial Rivalries: Dutch and French Colonial Ambitions

> **Learning Objectives**
>
> By the end of this section, you will be able to:
>
> - Compare and contrast the development and character of the French and Dutch colonies in North America
> - Discuss the economies of the French and Dutch colonies in North America

Seventeenth-century French and Dutch colonies in North America were modest in comparison to Spain's colossal global empire. New France and New Netherland remained small commercial operations focused on the fur trade and did not attract an influx of migrants. The Dutch in New Netherland confined their operations to Manhattan Island, Long Island, the Hudson River Valley, and what later became New Jersey. Dutch trade goods circulated widely among the native peoples in these areas and also traveled well into the interior of the continent along preexisting native trade routes. French *habitants*, or farmer-settlers, eked out an existence along the St. Lawrence River. French fur traders and missionaries, however, ranged far into the interior of North America, exploring the Great Lakes region and the Mississippi River. These pioneers gave France somewhat inflated imperial claims to lands that nonetheless remained firmly under the dominion of native peoples.

FUR TRADING IN NEW NETHERLAND

The Dutch Republic emerged as a major commercial center in the 1600s. Its fleets plied the waters of the Atlantic, while other Dutch ships sailed to the Far East, returning with prized spices like pepper to be sold in the bustling ports at home, especially Amsterdam. In North America, Dutch traders established themselves first on Manhattan Island.

One of the Dutch directors-general of the North American settlement, Peter Stuyvesant, served from 1647 to 1664 and expanded the fledgling outpost of New Netherland east to present-day Long Island and for many miles north along the Hudson River. The resulting elongated colony served primarily as a fur-trading post, with the powerful Dutch West India Company controlling all commerce. Fort Amsterdam, on the southern tip of Manhattan Island, defended the growing city of New Amsterdam. In 1655, Stuyvesant took over the small outpost of New Sweden along the banks of the Delaware River in present-day New Jersey, Pennsylvania, and Delaware. He also defended New Amsterdam from Indian attacks by ordering African slaves to build a protective wall on the city's northeastern border, giving present-day Wall Street its name.

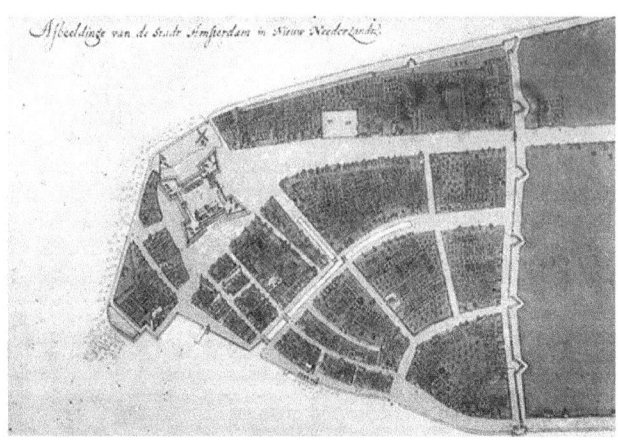

The Castello Plan is the only extant map of 1660 New Amsterdam (present-day New York City). The line with spikes on the right side of the colony is the northeastern wall for which Wall Street was named.

New Netherland failed to attract many Dutch colonists; by 1664, only nine thousand people were living there. Conflict with native peoples, as well as dissatisfaction with the Dutch West India Company's trading practices, made the Dutch outpost an undesirable place for many migrants. The small size of the population meant a severe labor shortage, and to complete the arduous tasks of early settlement, the Dutch West India Company imported some 450 African slaves between 1626 and 1664. (The company had involved itself heavily in the slave trade and in 1637 captured Elmina, the slave-trading post on the west coast of Africa, from the Portuguese.) The shortage of labor also meant that New Netherland welcomed non-Dutch immigrants, including Protestants from Germany, Sweden, Denmark, and England, and embraced a degree of religious tolerance, allowing Jewish immigrants to become residents beginning in the 1650s. Thus, a wide variety of people lived in New Netherland from the start. Indeed, one observer claimed eighteen different languages could be heard on the streets of New Amsterdam. As new settlers arrived, the colony of New Netherland stretched farther to the north and the west.

The Dutch West India Company found the business of colonization in New Netherland to be expensive. To share some of the costs, it granted Dutch merchants who invested heavily in it patroonships, or large tracts of land and the right to govern the tenants there. In return, the shareholder who gained the patroonship promised to pay for the passage of at least thirty Dutch farmers to populate the colony. One of the largest patroonships was granted to Kiliaen van Rensselaer, one of the directors of the Dutch West India Company; it covered most of present-day Albany and Rensselaer Counties. This pattern of settlement created a yawning gap in wealth and status between the tenants, who paid rent, and the wealthy patroons.

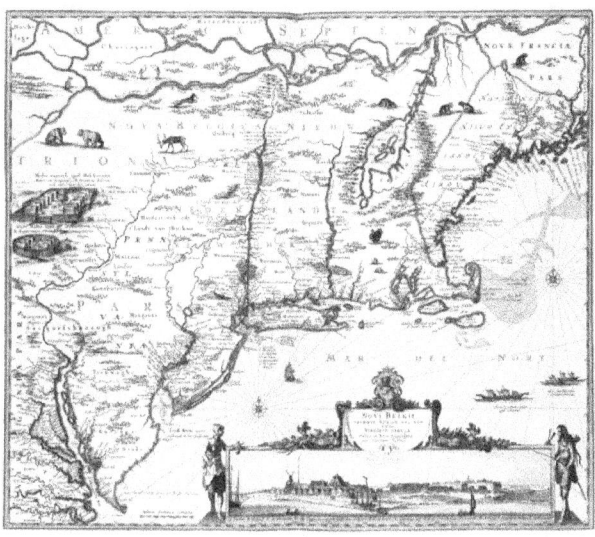

This 1684 map of New Netherland shows the extent of Dutch settlement.

During the summer trading season, Indians gathered at trading posts such as the Dutch site at Beverwijck (present-day Albany), where they exchanged furs for guns, blankets, and alcohol. The furs, especially beaver pelts destined for the lucrative European millinery market, would be sent down the Hudson River to New Amsterdam. There, slaves or workers would load them aboard ships bound for Amsterdam.

Explore an interactive map of New Amsterdam in 1660 that shows the city plan and the locations of various structures, including houses, businesses, and public buildings. Rolling over the map reveals relevant historical details, such as street names, the identities of certain buildings and businesses, and the names of residents of the houses (when known).

COMMERCE AND CONVERSION IN NEW FRANCE

After Jacques Cartier's voyages of discovery in the 1530s, France showed little interest in creating permanent colonies in North America until the early 1600s, when Samuel de Champlain established Quebec as a French fur-trading outpost. Although the fur trade was lucrative, the French saw Canada as an inhospitable frozen wasteland, and by 1640, fewer than four hundred settlers had made their home there. The sparse French presence meant that colonists depended on the local native Algonquian people; without them, the French would have perished. French fishermen, explorers, and fur traders made extensive contact with the Algonquian. The Algonquian, in turn, tolerated the French because the colonists supplied them with firearms for their ongoing war with the Iroquois. Thus, the French found themselves escalating native wars and supporting the Algonquian against the Iroquois, who received weapons from their Dutch trading partners. These seventeenth-century conflicts centered on the lucrative trade in beaver pelts, earning them the name of the Beaver Wars. In these wars, fighting between rival native peoples spread throughout the Great Lakes region.

A handful of French Jesuit priests also made their way to Canada, intent on converting the native inhabitants to Catholicism. The Jesuits were members of the Society of Jesus, an elite religious order founded in the 1540s to spread Catholicism and combat the spread of Protestantism. The first Jesuits arrived in Quebec in the 1620s, and for the next century, their numbers did not exceed forty priests. Like the Spanish Franciscan missionaries, the Jesuits in the colony called New France labored to convert the native peoples to Catholicism. They wrote detailed annual reports about their progress in bringing the faith to the Algonquian and, beginning in the 1660s, to the Iroquois. These documents are known as the *Jesuit Relations*, and they provide a rich source for understanding both the Jesuit view of the Indians and the Indian response to the colonizers.

One native convert to Catholicism, a Mohawk woman named Katherine Tekakwitha, so impressed the priests with her piety that a Jesuit named Claude Chauchetière attempted to make her a saint in the Church. However, the effort to canonize Tekakwitha faltered when leaders of the Church balked at elevating a "savage" to such a high status; she was eventually canonized in 2012. French colonizers pressured the native inhabitants of New France to convert, but they virtually never saw native peoples as their equals.

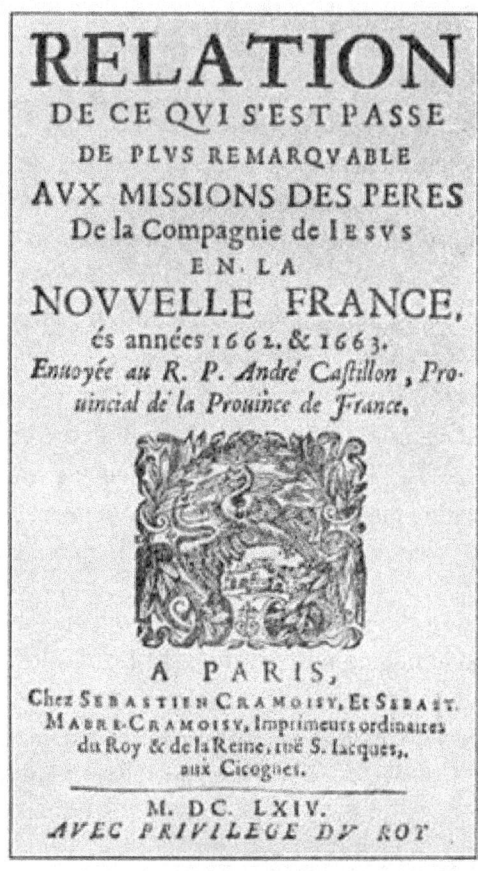

French Jesuit missionaries to New France kept detailed records of their interactions with—and observations of—the Algonquian and Iroquois that they converted to Catholicism. (credit: Project Gutenberg).

A Jesuit Priest on Indian Healing Traditions

The *Jesuit Relations* provide incredible detail about Indian life. For example, the 1636 edition, written by the Catholic priest Jean de Brébeuf, addresses the devastating effects of disease on native peoples and the efforts made to combat it.

> Let us return to the feasts. The *Aoutaerohi* is a remedy which is only for one particular kind of disease, which they call also *Aoutaerohi*, from the name of a little Demon as large as the fist, which they say is in the body of the sick man, especially in the part which pains him. They find out that they are sick of this disease, by means of a dream, or by the intervention of some Sorcerer....
>
> Of three kinds of games especially in use among these Peoples,—namely, the games of crosse [lacrosse], dish, and straw,—the first two are, they say, most healing. Is not this worthy of compassion? There is a poor sick man, fevered of body and almost dying, and a miserable Sorcerer will order for him, as a cooling remedy, a game of crosse. Or the sick man himself, sometimes, will have dreamed that he must die unless the whole country shall play crosse for his health; and, no matter how

little may be his credit, you will see then in a beautiful field, Village contending against Village, as to who will play crosse the better, and betting against one another Beaver robes and Porcelain collars, so as to excite greater interest.

According to this account, how did Indians attempt to cure disease? Why did they prescribe a game of lacrosse? What benefits might these games have for the sick?

Section Summary

The French and Dutch established colonies in the northeastern part of North America: the Dutch in present-day New York, and the French in present-day Canada. Both colonies were primarily trading posts for furs. While they failed to attract many colonists from their respective home countries, these outposts nonetheless intensified imperial rivalries in North America. Both the Dutch and the French relied on native peoples to harvest the pelts that proved profitable in Europe.

https://www.openassessments.org/assessments/943

Review Question

1. How did the French and Dutch colonists differ in their religious expectations? How did both compare to Spanish colonists?

Answer to Review Question

1. The Dutch allowed the most religious freedoms; they didn't try to convert native peoples to Christianity, and they allowed Jewish immigrants to join their colony. French Jesuit missionaries tried to convert Indians to Catholicism, but with much more acceptance of their differences than Spanish missionaries.

Glossary

Jesuits members of the Society of Jesus, an elite Catholic religious order founded in the 1540s to spread Catholicism and to combat the spread of Protestantism

patroonships large tracts of land and governing rights granted to merchants by the Dutch West India Company in order to encourage colonization

Attributions

CC licensed content, Shared previously

- US History. **Authored by**: P. Scott Corbett, Volker Janssen, John M. Lund, Todd Pfannestiel, Paul Vickery, and Sylvie Waskiewicz. **Provided by**: OpenStax College. **Located at**: http://openstaxcollege.org/textbooks/us-history. **License**: *CC BY: Attribution*. **License Terms**: Download for free at http://cnx.org/content/col11740/latest/

Primary Source Reading: Aztec Accounts of the Conquest

Introduction to the Source

In 1519 Hernan Cortés sailed from Cuba, landed in Mexico and made his way to the Aztec capital. Miguel Leon Portilla, a Mexican anthropologist, gathered accounts by the Aztecs, some of which were written shortly after the conquest.

Speeches of Motecuhzoma and Cortés

When Motecuhzoma [Montezuma] had given necklaces to each one, Cortés asked him: "Are you Motecuhzoma? Are you the king? Is it true that you are the king Motecuhzoma?"

And the king said: "Yes, I am Motecuhzoma." Then he stood up to welcome Cortés; he came forward, bowed his head low and addressed him in these words: "Our lord, you are weary. The journey has tired you, but now you have arrived on the earth. You have come to your city, Mexico. You have come here to sit on your throne, to sit under its canopy.

"The kings who have gone before, your representatives, guarded it and preserved it for your coming. The kings Itzcoatl, Motecuhzoma the Elder, Axayacatl, Tizoc and Ahuitzol ruled for you in the City of Mexico. The people were protected by their swords and sheltered by their shields.

"Do the kings know the destiny of those they left behind, their posterity? If only they are watching! If only they can see what I see!
No, it is not a dream. I am not walking in my sleep. I am not seeing you in my dreams…. I have seen you at last! I have met you face to face! I was in agony for five days, for ten days, with my eyes fixed on the Region of the Mystery. And now you have come out of the clouds and mists to sit on your throne again.
This was foretold by the kings who governed your city, and now it has taken place. You have come back to us; you have come down from the sky. Rest now, and take possession of your royal houses. Welcome to your land, my lords!"

When Motecuhzoma had finished, La Malinche translated his address into Spanish so that the Captain could understand it. Cortés replied in his strange and savage tongue, speaking first to La Malinche: "Tell Motecuhzoma that we are his friends. There is nothing to fear. We have wanted to see him for a long time, and now we have seen his face and heard his words. Tell him that we love him well and that our hearts are contented."

Then he said to Motecuhzoma: "We have come to your house in Mexico as friends. There is nothing to fear."

La Malinche translated this speech and the Spaniards grasped Motecuhzoma's hands and patted his back to show their affection for him….

Massacre in the Main Temple

During this time, the people asked Motecuhzoma how they should celebrate their god's fiesta. He said: "Dress him in all his finery, in all his sacred ornaments."

During this same time, The Sun commanded that Motecuhzoma and Itzcohuatzin, the military chief of Tlatelolco, be made prisoners. The Spaniards hanged a chief from Acolhuacan named Nezahualquentzin. They also murdered the king of Nauhtla, Cohualpopocatzin, by wounding him with arrows and then burning him alive.

For this reason, our warriors were on guard at the Eagle Gate. The sentries from Tenochtitlan stood at one side of the gate, and the sentries from Tlatelolco at the other. But messengers came to tell them to dress the figure of Huitzilopochtli. They left their posts and went to dress him in his sacred finery: his ornaments and his paper clothing.

When this had been done, the celebrants began to sing their songs. That is how they celebrated the first day of the fiesta. On the second day they began to sing again, but without warning they were all put to death. The dancers and singers were completely unarmed. They brought only their embroidered cloaks, their turquoises, their lip plugs, their necklaces, their clusters of heron feathers, their trinkets made of deer hooves. Those who played the drums, the old men, had brought their gourds of snuff and their timbrels.

The Spaniards attacked the musicians first, slashing at their hands and faces until they had killed all of them. The singers-and even the spectators- were also killed. This slaughter in the Sacred Patio went on for three hours. Then the Spaniards burst into the rooms of the temple to kill the others: those who were carrying water, or bringing fodder for the horses, or grinding meal, or sweeping, or standing watch over this work.

The king Motecuhzoma, who was accompanied by Itzcohuatzin and by those who had brought food for the Spaniards, protested: "Our lords, that is enough! What are you doing? These people are not carrying shields or macanas. Our lords, they are completely unarmed!"

The Sun had treacherously murdered our people on the twentieth day after the captain left for the coast. We allowed the Captain to return to the city in peace. But on the following day we attacked him with all our might, and that was the beginning of the war.

Attributions

Public domain content

- The Broken Spears: The Aztec Account of the Conquest of Mexico. **Authored by**: Miguel Leon Portilla. **Located at**: http://legacy.fordham.edu/Halsall/mod/aztecs1.asp. **Project**: Internet Modern History Sourcebook. **License**: *Public Domain: No Known Copyright*

Primary Source Reading: Vasco De Gama

Introduction to the Source

Vasco da Gama was born about 1460 at Sines, Portugal. Both Prince John and Prince Manuel continued the efforts of Prince Henry to find a sea route to India, and in 1497 Manuel placed Vasco da Gama, who already had some reputation as a warrior and navigator, in charge of four vessels built especially for the expedition. They set sail July 8, 1497, rounded the Cape of Good Hope four months later, and reached Calicut May 20, 1498. The Moors in Calicut instigated the Zamorin of Calicut against him, and he was compelled to return with the bare discovery and the few spices he had bought there at inflated prices [but still he made a 3000% profit!]. A force left by a second expedition under Cabral (who discovered Brazil by sailing too far west), left behind some men in a "factory" or trading station, but these were killed by the Moors in revenge for Cabral's attacks on Arab shipping in the Indian Ocean. Vasco da Gama was sent on a mission of vengeance in 1502, he bombarded Calicut (virtually destroying the port), and returned with great spoil. His expedition turned the commerce of Europe from the Mediterranean cities to the Atlantic Coast, and opened up the east to European enterprise.

Source

Vasco da Gama was born about 1460 at Sines, Portugal. Both Prince John and Prince Manuel continued the efforts of Prince Henry to find a sea route to India, and in 1497 Manuel placed Vasco da Gama, who already had some reputation as a warrior and navigator, in charge of four vessels built especially for the expedition. They set sail July 8, 1497, rounded the Cape of Good Hope four months later, and reached Calicut May 20, 1498. The Moors in Calicut instigated the Zamorin of Calicut against him, and he was compelled to return with the bare discovery and the few spices he had bought there at inflated prices [but still he made a 3000% profit!]. A force left by a second expedition under Cabral (who discovered Brazil by sailing too far west), left behind some men in a "factory" or trading station, but these were killed by the Moors in revenge for Cabral's attacks on Arab shipping in the Indian Ocean. Vasco da Gama was sent on a mission of vengeance in 1502, he bombarded Calicut (virtually destroying the port), and returned with great spoil. His expedition turned the commerce of Europe from the Mediterranean cities to the

The city of Calicut is inhabited by Christians. [The first voyagers to India mistook the Hindus for Christians.] They are of tawny complexion. Some of them have big beards and long hair, whilst others clip their hair short or shave the head, merely allowing a tuft to remain on the crown as a sign that they are Christians. They also wear moustaches. They pierce the ears and wear much gold in them. They go naked down to the waist, covering their lower extremities with very fine cotton stuffs. But it is only the most respectable who do this, for the others manage as best they are able. The women of this country, as a rule, are ugly and of small stature. They wear many jewels of gold round the neck, numerous bracelets on their arms, and rings set with precious stones on their toes. All these people are well-disposed and apparently of mild temper. At first sight they seem covetous and ignorant.

When we arrived at Calicut the king was fifteen leagues away. The captain-major sent two men to him with a message, informing him that an ambassador had arrived from the King of Portugal with letters, and that if he desired it he would take them to where the king then was. The king presented the bearers of this message with much fine cloth. He sent word to the captain-major bidding him welcome, saying that he was about to proceed to Calicut. As a matter of fact, he started at once with a large retinue. A pilot accompanied our two men, with orders to take us to a place called Pandarani, below the place (Capna) where we anchored at first. At this time we were actually in front of the city of Calicut. We were told that the anchorage at the place to which we were to go was good, whilst at the place we were then it was bad, with a stony bottom, which was quite true; and, moreover, that it was customary for the ships which came to this country to anchor there for the sake of safety. We ourselves did not feel comfortable, and the captain-major had no sooner received this royal message than he ordered the sails to be set, and we departed. We did not, however, anchor as near the shore as the king's pilot desired.

When we were at anchor, a message arrived informing the captain-major that the king was already in the city. At the same time the king sent a bale, with other men of distinction, to Pandarani, to conduct the captain-major to where the king awaited him. This bale is like an alcaide, and is always attended by two hundred men armed with swords and bucklers. As it was late when this message arrived, the captain-major deferred going.

On the following morning, which was Monday, May 28th, the captain-major set out to speak to the king, and took with him thirteen men. On landing, the captain-major was received by the alcaide, with whom were many men, armed and unarmed. The reception was friendly, as if the people were pleased to see us, though at first appearances looked threatening, for they carried naked swords in their hands. A palanquin was provided for the captain-major, such as is used by men of distinction in that country, as also by some of the merchants, who pay something to the king for this privilege. The captain-major entered the palanquin, which was carried by six men by turns. Attended by all these people we took the road of Calicut, and came first to another town, called Capna. The captain-major was there deposited at the house of a man of rank, whilst we others were provided with food, consisting of rice, with much butter, and excellent boiled fish. The captain-major did not wish to eat, and as we had done so, we embarked on a river close by, which flows between the sea end the mainland, close to the coast. The two boats in which we embarked were lashed together, so that we were not separated. There were numerous other boats, all crowded with people. As to those who were on the banks I say nothing; their number was infinite, and they had all come to see us. We went up that river for about a league, and saw many large ships drawn up high and dry on its banks, for there is no port here.

When we disembarked, the captain-major once more entered his palanquin. The road was crowded with a countless multitude anxious to see us. Even the women came out of their houses with children in their arms and followed us. When we arrived (at Calicut) they took us to a large church, and this is what we saw: The body of the church is as large as a monastery, all built of hewn stone and covered with tiles. At the main entrance rises a pillar of bronze as high as a mast, on the top of which was perched a bird, apparently a cock. In addition to this, there was another pillar as high as a man, and very stout. In the center of the body of the church rose a chapel, all built of hewn stone, with a bronze door sufficiently wide for a man to pass, and stone steps leading up to it. Within this sanctuary stood a small image which they said represented Our Lady. Along the walls, by the main entrance, hung seven small bells. In this church the captain-major said his prayers, and we with him.

We did not go within the chapel, for it is the custom that only certain servants of the church, called quafees, should enter. These quafees wore some threads passing over the left shoulder and under the right arm, in the same manner as our deacons wear the stole. They threw holy water over us, and gave us some white earth, which the Christians of this country are in the habit of putting on their foreheads, breasts, around the neck, and on the forearms. They threw holy water upon the captain-major and gave him some of the earth, which he gave in charge of someone, giving them to understand that he would put it on later. Many other saints were painted on the walls of the church, wearing crowns. They were painted variously, with teeth protruding an inch from the mouth, and four or five arms. Below this church there was a large masonry tank, similar to many others which we had seen along the road.

After we had left that place, and had arrived at the entrance to the city (of Calicut) we were shown another church, where we saw things like those described above. Here the crowd grew so dense that progress along the street became next to impossible, and for this reason they put the captain-major into a house, and us with him. The king sent a brother of the bale, who was a lord of this country, to accompany the captain-major, and he was attended by men beating drums, blowing arafils and bagpipes, and firing off matchlocks. In conducting the captain-major they showed us much respect, more than is shown in Spain to a king. The number of people was countless, for in addition to those who surrounded us, and among whom there were two thousand armed men, they crowded the roofs and houses.

The further we advanced in the direction of the king's palace, the more did they increase in number. And when we arrived there, men of much distinction and great lords came out to meet the captain-major, and joined those who were already in attendance upon him. It was then an hour before sunset. When we reached the palace we passed through a gate into a courtyard of great size, and before we arrived at where the king was, we passed four doors, through which we had to force our way, giving many blows to the people. When, at last, we reached the door where the king was, there came forth from it a little old man, who holds a position resembling that of a bishop, and whose advice the king acts upon in all affairs of the church. This man embraced the captain-major when he entered the door. Several men were wounded at this door, and we only got in by the use of much force.

Attributions

Public domain content

- **Authored by**: Oliver J. Thatcher. **Provided by**: The Library of Original Sources. **Located at**: http://legacy.fordham.edu/halsall/mod/1497degama.asp. **Project**: The Modern Internet History Sourcebook. **License**: *Public Domain: No Known Copyright*

3. English Settlements in America

Introduction

By the mid-seventeenth century, the geopolitical map of North America had become a patchwork of imperial designs and ambitions as the Spanish, Dutch, French, and English reinforced their claims to parts of the land. Uneasiness, punctuated by violent clashes, prevailed in the border zones between the Europeans' territorial claims. Meanwhile, still-powerful native peoples waged war to drive the invaders from the continent. In the Chesapeake Bay and New England colonies, conflicts erupted as the English pushed against their native neighbors.

The rise of colonial societies in the Americas brought Native Americans, Africans, and Europeans together for the first time, highlighting the radical social, cultural, and religious differences that hampered their ability to understand each other. European settlement affected every aspect of the land and its people, bringing goods, ideas, and diseases that transformed the Americas. Reciprocally, Native American practices, such as the use of tobacco, profoundly altered European habits and tastes.

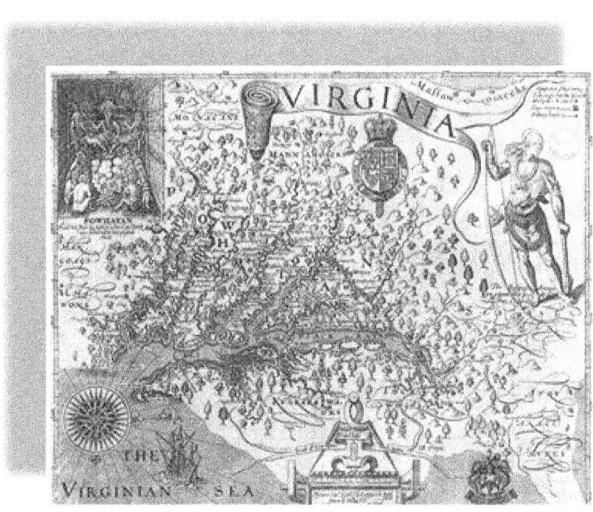

John Smith's famous map of Virginia (1622) illustrates many geopolitical features of early colonization. In the upper left, Powhatan, who governed a powerful local confederation of Algonquian communities, sits above other local chiefs, denoting his authority. Another native figure, Susquehannock, who appears in the upper right, visually reinforces the message that the English did not control the land beyond a few outposts along the Chesapeake.

Attributions

CC licensed content, Shared previously

- US History. **Authored by**: P. Scott Corbett, Volker Janssen, John M. Lund, Todd Pfannestiel, Paul Vickery, and Sylvie Waskiewicz. **Provided by**: OpenStax College. **Located at**: http://openstaxcollege.org/textbooks/us-history. **License**: *CC BY: Attribution*. **License Terms**: Download for free at http://cnx.org/content/col11740/latest/

English Settlements in America

Learning Objectives

By the end of this section, you will be able to:

- Identify the first English settlements in America
- Describe the differences between the Chesapeake Bay colonies and the New England colonies
- Compare and contrast the wars between native inhabitants and English colonists in both the Chesapeake Bay and New England colonies
- Explain the role of Bacon's Rebellion in the rise of chattel slavery in Virginia

At the start of the seventeenth century, the English had not established a permanent settlement in the Americas. Over the next century, however, they outpaced their rivals. The English encouraged emigration far more than the Spanish, French, or Dutch. They established nearly a dozen colonies, sending swarms of immigrants to populate the land. England had experienced a dramatic rise in population in the sixteenth century, and the colonies appeared a welcoming place for those who faced overcrowding and grinding poverty at home. Thousands of English migrants arrived in the Chesapeake Bay colonies of Virginia and Maryland to work in the tobacco fields. Another stream, this one of pious Puritan families, sought to live as they believed scripture demanded and established the Plymouth, Massachusetts Bay, New Haven, Connecticut, and Rhode Island colonies of New England.

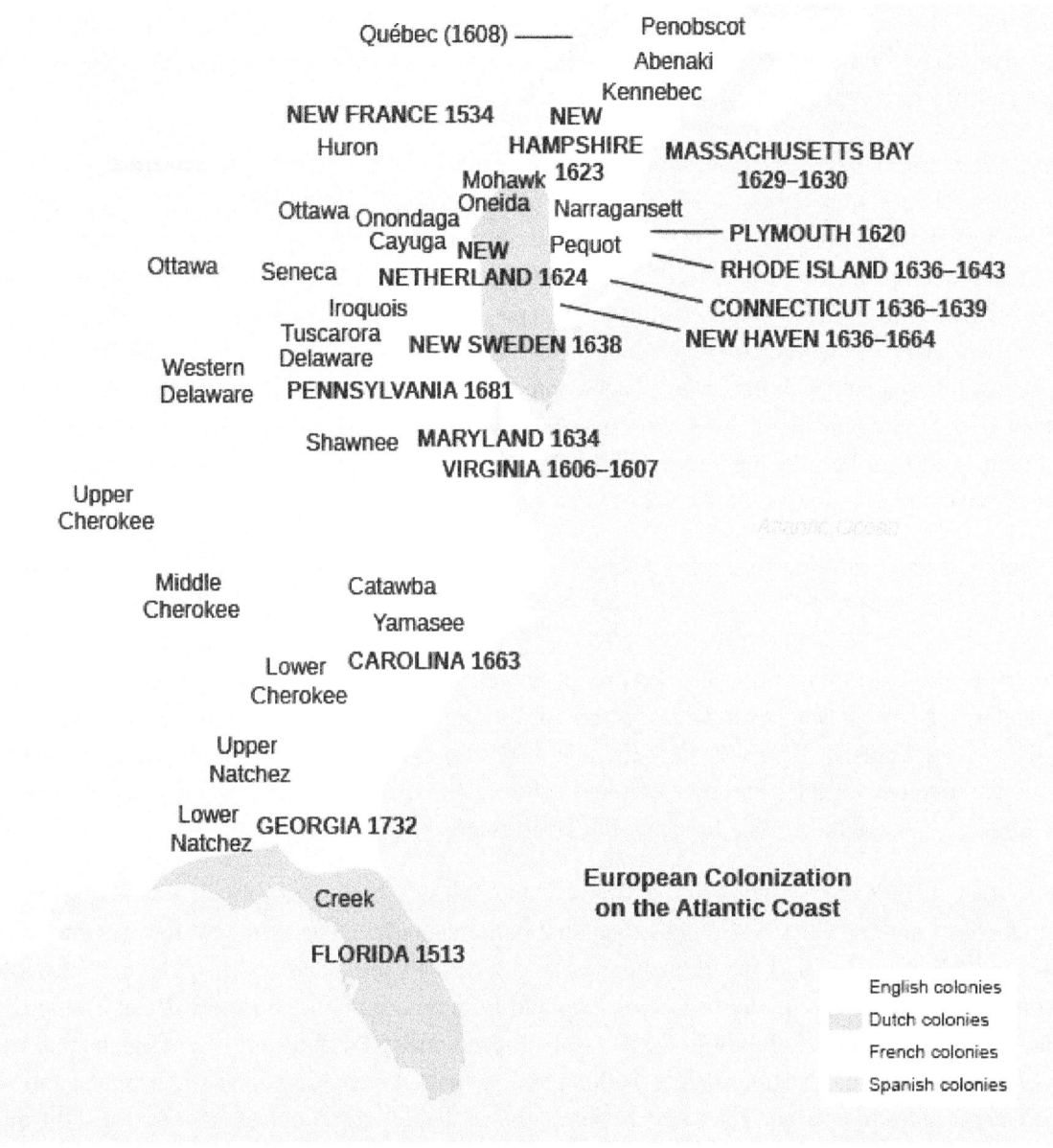

In the early seventeenth century, thousands of English settlers came to what are now Virginia, Maryland, and the New England states in search of opportunity and a better life.

THE DIVERGING CULTURES OF THE NEW ENGLAND AND CHESAPEAKE COLONIES

Promoters of English colonization in North America, many of whom never ventured across the Atlantic, wrote about the bounty the English would find there. These boosters of colonization hoped to turn a profit—whether by importing raw resources or providing new markets for English goods—and spread Protestantism. The English migrants who actually made the journey, however, had different goals. In Chesapeake Bay, English migrants established Virginia and Maryland with a decidedly commercial orientation. Though the early Virginians at Jamestown hoped to find gold, they and the settlers in Maryland quickly discovered that growing tobacco was the only sure means of making money. Thousands of unmarried, unemployed, and impatient young Englishmen, along with a few Englishwomen, pinned their hopes for a better life on the tobacco fields of these two colonies.

A very different group of English men and women flocked to the cold climate and rocky soil of New England, spurred by religious motives. Many of the Puritans crossing the Atlantic were people who brought families and children. Often they were following their ministers in a migration "beyond the seas," envisioning a new English Israel where reformed Protestantism would grow and thrive, providing a model for the rest of the Christian world and a counter to what they saw as the Catholic menace. While the English in Virginia and Maryland worked on expanding their profitable tobacco fields, the English in New England built towns focused on the church, where each congregation decided what was best for itself. The Congregational Church is the result of the Puritan enterprise in America. Many historians believe the fault lines separating what later became the North and South in the United States originated in the profound differences between the Chesapeake and New England colonies.

The source of those differences lay in England's domestic problems. Increasingly in the early 1600s, the English state church—the Church of England, established in the 1530s—demanded conformity, or compliance with its practices, but Puritans pushed for greater reforms. By the 1620s, the Church of England began to see leading Puritan ministers and their followers as outlaws, a national security threat because of their opposition to its power. As the noose of conformity tightened around them, many Puritans decided to remove to New England. By 1640, New England had a population of twenty-five thousand. Meanwhile, many loyal members of the Church of England, who ridiculed and mocked Puritans both at home and in New England, flocked to Virginia for economic opportunity.

The troubles in England escalated in the 1640s when civil war broke out, pitting Royalist supporters of King Charles I and the Church of England against Parliamentarians, the Puritan reformers and their supporters in Parliament. In 1649, the Parliamentarians gained the upper hand and, in an unprecedented move, executed Charles I. In the 1650s, therefore, England became a republic, a state without a king. English colonists in America closely followed these events. Indeed, many Puritans left New England and returned home to take part in the struggle against the king and the national church. Other English men and women in the Chesapeake colonies and elsewhere in the English Atlantic World looked on in horror at the mayhem the Parliamentarians, led by the Puritan insurgents, appeared to unleash in England. The turmoil in England made the administration and imperial oversight of the Chesapeake and New England colonies difficult, and the two regions developed divergent cultures.

THE CHESAPEAKE COLONIES: VIRGINIA AND MARYLAND

The Chesapeake colonies of Virginia and Maryland served a vital purpose in the developing seventeenth-century English empire by providing tobacco, a cash crop. However, the early history of Jamestown did not suggest the English outpost would survive. From the outset, its settlers struggled both with each other and with the native inhabitants, the powerful Powhatan, who controlled the area. Jealousies and infighting among the English destabilized the colony. One member, John Smith, whose famous map begins this chapter, took control and exercised near-dictatorial powers, which furthered aggravated the squabbling. The settlers' inability to grow their own food compounded this unstable situation. They were essentially employees of the Virginia Company of London, an English joint-stock company, in which investors provided the capital and assumed the risk in order to reap the profit, and they had to make a profit for their shareholders as well as for themselves. Most initially devoted themselves to finding gold and silver instead of finding ways to grow their own food.

Early Struggles and the Development of the Tobacco Economy

Poor health, lack of food, and fighting with native peoples took the lives of many of the original Jamestown settlers. The winter of 1609–1610, which became known as "the starving time," came close to annihilating the colony. By June 1610, the few remaining settlers had decided to abandon the area; only the last-minute arrival of a supply ship from England prevented another failed colonization effort. The supply ship brought new settlers, but only twelve hundred of the seventy-five hundred who came to Virginia between 1607 and 1624 survived.

George Percy on "The Starving Time"

George Percy, the youngest son of an English nobleman, was in the first group of settlers at the Jamestown Colony. He kept a journal describing their experiences; in the excerpt below, he reports on the privations of the colonists' third winter.

> Now all of us at James Town, beginning to feel that sharp prick of hunger which no man truly describe but he which has tasted the bitterness thereof, a world of miseries ensued as the sequel will express unto you, in so much that some to satisfy their hunger have robbed the store for the which I caused them to be executed. Then having fed upon horses and other beasts as long as they lasted, we were glad to make shift with vermin as dogs, cats, rats, and mice. All was fish that came to net to satisfy cruel hunger as to eat boots, shoes, or any other leather some could come by, and, those being spent and devoured, some were enforced to search the woods and to feed upon serpents and snakes and to dig the earth for wild and unknown roots, where many of our men were cut off of and slain by the savages. And now famine beginning to look ghastly and pale in every face that nothing was spared to maintain life and to do those things which seem incredible as to dig up dead corpses out of graves and to eat them, and some have licked up the blood which has fallen from their weak fellows.
>
> —George Percy, "A True Relation of the Proceedings and Occurances of Moment which have happened in Virginia from the Time Sir Thomas Gates shipwrecked upon the Bermudes anno 1609 until my departure out of the Country which was in anno Domini 1612," London 1624

What is your reaction to George Percy's story? How do you think Jamestown managed to survive after such an experience? What do you think the Jamestown colonists learned?

By the 1620s, Virginia had weathered the worst and gained a degree of permanence. Political stability came slowly, but by 1619, the fledgling colony was operating under the leadership of a governor, a council, and a House of Burgesses. Economic stability came from the lucrative cultivation of tobacco. Smoking tobacco was a long-standing practice among native peoples, and English and other European consumers soon adopted it. In 1614, the Virginia colony began exporting tobacco back to England, which earned it a sizable profit and saved the colony from ruin. A second tobacco colony, Maryland, was formed in 1634, when King Charles I granted its charter to the Calvert family for their loyal service to England. Cecilius Calvert, the second Lord Baltimore, conceived of Maryland as a refuge for English Catholics.

Growing tobacco proved very labor-intensive, and the Chesapeake colonists needed a steady workforce to do the hard work of clearing the land and caring for the tender young plants. The mature leaf of the plant then had to be cured (dried), which necessitated the construction of drying barns. Once cured, the tobacco had to be packaged in hogsheads (large wooden barrels) and loaded aboard ship, which also required considerable labor.

To meet these labor demands, early Virginians relied on indentured servants. An **indenture** is a labor contract that young, impoverished, and often illiterate Englishmen and occasionally Englishwomen signed in England, pledging to work for a number of years (usually between five and seven) growing tobacco in the Chesapeake colonies. In return, indentured servants received paid passage to America and food, clothing, and lodging. At the end of their indenture servants received "freedom dues," usually food and other provisions, including, in some cases, land provided by the colony. The promise of a new life in America was a strong attraction for members of England's underclass, who had few if any options at home. In the 1600s, some 100,000 indentured servants traveled to the Chesapeake Bay. Most were poor young men in their early twenties.

In this 1670 painting by an unknown artist, slaves work in tobacco-drying sheds.

Life in the colonies proved harsh, however. Indentured servants could not marry, and they were subject to the will of the tobacco planters who bought their labor contracts. If they committed a crime or disobeyed their masters, they found their terms of service lengthened, often by several years. Female indentured servants faced special dangers in what was essentially a bachelor colony. Many were exploited by unscrupulous tobacco planters who seduced them with promises of marriage. These planters would then sell their pregnant servants to other tobacco planters to avoid the costs of raising a child.

Nonetheless, those indentured servants who completed their term of service often began new lives as tobacco planters. To entice even more migrants to the New World, the Virginia Company also implemented the **headright system**, in which those who paid their own passage to Virginia received fifty acres plus an additional fifty for each servant or family member they brought with them. The headright system and the promise of a new life for servants acted as powerful incentives for English migrants to hazard the journey to the New World.

> Visit Virtual Jamestown to access a database of contracts of indentured servants. Search it by name to find an ancestor or browse by occupation, destination, or county of origin.

The Anglo-Powhatan Wars

By choosing to settle along the rivers on the banks of the Chesapeake, the English unknowingly placed themselves at the center of the Powhatan Empire, a powerful Algonquian confederacy of thirty native groups with perhaps as many as twenty-two thousand people. The territory of the equally impressive **Susquehannock** people also bordered English settlements at the north end of the Chesapeake Bay.

Tensions ran high between the English and the Powhatan, and near-constant war prevailed. The First Anglo-Powhatan War (1609–1614) resulted not only from the English colonists' intrusion onto Powhatan land, but also from their refusal to follow native protocol by giving gifts. English actions infuriated and insulted the Powhatan. In 1613, the settlers captured Pocahontas (also called Matoaka), the daughter of a Powhatan headman named Wahunsonacook, and gave her in marriage to Englishman John Rolfe. Their union, and her choice to remain with the English, helped quell the war in 1614. Pocahontas converted to Christianity, changing her name to Rebecca, and sailed with her husband and several other Powhatan to England where she was introduced to King James I. Promoters of colonization publicized Pocahontas as an example of the good work of converting the Powhatan to Christianity.

This 1616 engraving by Simon van de Passe, completed when Pocahontas and John Rolfe were presented at court in England, is the only known contemporary image of Pocahontas. Note her European garb and pose. What message did the painter likely intend to convey with this portrait of Pocahontas, the daughter of a powerful Indian chief?

> Explore the interactive exhibit Changing Images of Pocahontas on PBS's website to see the many ways artists have portrayed Pocahontas over the centuries.

Peace in Virginia did not last long. The Second Anglo-Powhatan War (1620s) broke out because of the expansion of the English settlement nearly one hundred miles into the interior, and because of the continued insults and friction caused by English activities. The Powhatan attacked in 1622 and succeeded in killing almost 350 English, about a third of the settlers. The English responded by annihilating every Powhatan village around Jamestown and from then on became even more intolerant. The Third Anglo-Powhatan War (1644–1646) began with a surprise attack in which the Powhatan killed around five hundred English colonists. However, their ultimate defeat in this conflict forced the Powhatan to acknowledge King Charles I as their sovereign. The Anglo-Powhatan Wars, spanning nearly forty years, illustrate the degree of native resistance that resulted from English intrusion into the Powhatan confederacy.

The Rise of Slavery in the Chesapeake Bay Colonies

The transition from indentured servitude to slavery as the main labor source for some English colonies happened first in the West Indies. On the small island of Barbados, colonized in the 1620s, English planters first grew tobacco as their main export crop, but in the 1640s, they converted to sugarcane and began increasingly to rely on African slaves. In 1655, England wrestled control of Jamaica from the Spanish and quickly turned it into a lucrative sugar island, run on slave labor, for its expanding empire. While slavery was slower to take hold in the Chesapeake colonies, by the end of the seventeenth century, both Virginia and Maryland had also adopted chattel slavery—which legally defined Africans as property and not people—as the dominant form of labor to grow tobacco. Chesapeake colonists also enslaved native people.

When the first Africans arrived in Virginia in 1619, slavery—which did not exist in England—had not yet become an institution in colonial America. Many Africans worked as servants and, like their white counterparts, could acquire land of their own. Some Africans who converted to Christianity became free landowners with white servants. The change in the status of Africans in the Chesapeake to that of slaves occurred in the last decades of the seventeenth century.

Bacon's Rebellion, an uprising of both whites and blacks who believed that the Virginia government was impeding their access to land and wealth and seemed to do little to clear the land of Indians, hastened the transition to African slavery in the Chesapeake colonies. The rebellion takes its name from Nathaniel Bacon, a wealthy young Englishman who arrived in Virginia in 1674. Despite an early friendship with Virginia's royal governor, William Berkeley, Bacon found himself excluded from the governor's circle of influential friends and councilors. He wanted land on the Virginia frontier, but the governor, fearing war with neighboring Indian tribes, forbade further expansion. Bacon marshaled others, especially former indentured servants who believed the governor was limiting their economic opportunities and denying them the right to own tobacco farms. Bacon's followers believed Berkeley's frontier policy didn't protect English settlers enough. Worse still in their eyes, Governor Berkeley tried to keep peace in Virginia by signing treaties with various local native peoples. Bacon and his followers, who saw all Indians as an obstacle to their access to land, pursued a policy of extermination.

Tensions between the English and the native peoples in the Chesapeake colonies led to open conflict. In 1675, war broke out when Susquehannock warriors attacked settlements on Virginia's frontier, killing English planters and destroying English plantations, including one owned by Bacon. In 1676, Bacon and other Virginians attacked the Susquehannock without the governor's approval. When Berkeley ordered Bacon's arrest, Bacon led his followers to Jamestown, forced the governor to flee to the safety of Virginia's eastern shore, and then burned the city. The civil war known as Bacon's Rebellion, a vicious struggle between supporters of the governor and those who supported Bacon, ensued. Reports of the rebellion traveled back to England, leading Charles II to dispatch both royal troops and English commissioners to restore order in the tobacco colonies. By the end of 1676, Virginians loyal to the governor gained the upper hand, executing several leaders of the rebellion. Bacon escaped the hangman's noose, instead dying of dysentery. The rebellion fizzled in 1676, but Virginians remained divided as supporters of Bacon continued to harbor grievances over access to Indian land.

Bacon's Rebellion helped to catalyze the creation of a system of racial slavery in the Chesapeake colonies. At the time of the rebellion, indentured servants made up the majority of laborers in the region. Wealthy whites worried over the presence of this large class of laborers and the relative freedom they enjoyed, as well as the alliance that black and white servants had forged in the course of the rebellion. Replacing indentured servitude with black slavery diminished these risks, alleviating the reliance on white indentured servants, who were often dissatisfied and troublesome, and creating a caste of racially defined laborers whose movements were strictly controlled. It also lessened the possibility of further alliances between black and white workers. Racial slavery even served to heal some of the divisions between wealthy and poor whites, who could now unite as members of a "superior" racial group.

While colonial laws in the tobacco colonies had made slavery a legal institution before Bacon's Rebellion, new laws passed in the wake of the rebellion severely curtailed black freedom and laid the foundation for racial slavery. Virginia passed a law in 1680 prohibiting free blacks and slaves from bearing arms, banning blacks from congregating in large numbers, and establishing harsh punishments for slaves who assaulted Christians or attempted escape. Two years later, another Virginia law stipulated that all Africans brought to the colony would be slaves for life. Thus, the increasing reliance on slaves in the tobacco colonies—and the draconian laws instituted to control them—not only helped planters meet labor demands, but also served to assuage English fears of further uprisings and alleviate class tensions between rich and poor whites.

Robert Beverley on Servants and Slaves

Robert Beverley was a wealthy Jamestown planter and slaveholder. This excerpt from his *History and Present State of Virginia*, published in 1705, clearly illustrates the contrast between white servants and black slaves.

> Their Servants, they distinguish by the Names of Slaves for Life, and Servants for a time. Slaves are the Negroes, and their Posterity, following the condition of the Mother, according to the Maxim, partus sequitur ventrem [status follows the womb]. They are call'd Slaves, in respect of the time of their Servitude, because it is for Life.
>
> Servants, are those which serve only for a few years, according to the time of their Indenture, or the Custom of the Country. The Custom of the Country takes place upon such as have no Indentures. The Law in this case is, that if such Servants be under Nineteen years of Age, they must be brought into Court, to have their Age adjudged; and from the Age they are judg'd to be of, they must serve until they reach four and twenty: But if they be adjudged upwards of Nineteen, they are then only to be Servants for the term of five Years.
>
> The Male-Servants, and Slaves of both Sexes, are employed together in Tilling and Manuring the Ground, in Sowing and Planting Tobacco, Corn, &c. Some Distinction indeed is made between them in their Cloaths, and Food; but the Work of both, is no other than what the Overseers, the Freemen, and the Planters themselves do.
>
> Sufficient Distinction is also made between the Female-Servants, and Slaves; for a White Woman is rarely or never put to work in the Ground, if she be good for any thing else: And to Discourage all Planters from using any Women so, their Law imposes the heaviest Taxes upon Female Servants working in the Ground, while it suffers all other white Women to be absolutely exempted: Whereas on the other hand, it is a common thing to work a Woman Slave out of Doors; nor does the Law make any Distinction in her Taxes, whether her Work be Abroad, or at Home.

According to Robert Beverley, what are the differences between servants and slaves? What protections did servants have that slaves did not?

PURITAN NEW ENGLAND

The second major area to be colonized by the English in the first half of the seventeenth century, New England, differed markedly in its founding principles from the commercially oriented Chesapeake tobacco colonies. Settled largely by waves of Puritan families in the 1630s, New England had a religious orientation from the start. In England, reform-minded men and women had been calling for greater changes to the English national church since the 1580s. These reformers, who followed the teachings of John Calvin and other Protestant reformers, were called Puritans because of their insistence on "purifying" the Church of England of what they believed to be un-scriptural, especially Catholic elements that lingered in its institutions and practices.

Many who provided leadership in early New England were learned ministers who had studied at Cambridge or Oxford but who, because they had questioned the practices of the Church of England, had been deprived of careers by the king and his officials in an effort to silence all dissenting voices. Other Puritan leaders, such as the first governor of the Massachusetts Bay Colony, John Winthrop, came from the privileged class of English gentry. These well-to-do Puritans and many thousands more left their English homes not to establish a land of religious freedom, but to practice their own religion without persecution. Puritan New England offered them the opportunity to live as they believed the Bible demanded. In their "New" England, they set out to create a model of reformed Protestantism, a new English Israel.

The conflict generated by Puritanism had divided English society, because the Puritans demanded reforms that undermined the traditional festive culture. For example, they denounced popular pastimes like bear-baiting—letting dogs attack a chained bear—which were often conducted on Sundays when people had a few leisure hours. In the culture where William Shakespeare had produced his masterpieces, Puritans called for an end to the theater, censuring playhouses as places of decadence. Indeed, the Bible itself became part of the struggle between Puritans and James I, who headed the Church of England. Soon after ascending the throne, James commissioned a new version of the Bible in an effort to stifle Puritan reliance on the Geneva Bible, which followed the teachings of John Calvin and placed God's authority above the monarch's. The King James Version, published in 1611, instead emphasized the majesty of kings.

During the 1620s and 1630s, the conflict escalated to the point where the state church prohibited Puritan ministers from preaching. In the Church's view, Puritans represented a national security threat, because their demands for cultural, social, and religious reforms undermined the king's authority. Unwilling to conform to the Church of England, many Puritans found refuge in the New World. Yet those who emigrated to the Americas were not united. Some called for a complete break with the Church of England, while others remained committed to reforming the national church.

Plymouth: The First Puritan Colony

The first group of Puritans to make their way across the Atlantic was a small contingent known as the Pilgrims. Unlike other Puritans, they insisted on a complete separation from the Church of England and had first migrated to the Dutch Republic seeking religious freedom. Although they found they could worship without hindrance there, they grew concerned that they were losing their Englishness as they saw their children begin to learn the Dutch language and adopt Dutch ways. In addition, the English Pilgrims (and others in Europe) feared another attack on the Dutch Republic by Catholic Spain. Therefore, in 1620, they moved on to found the Plymouth Colony in present-day Massachusetts. The governor of Plymouth, William Bradford, was a Separatist, a proponent of complete separation from the English state church. Bradford and the other Pilgrim Separatists represented a major challenge to the prevailing vision of a unified English national church and empire. On board the *Mayflower*, which was bound for Virginia but landed on the tip of Cape Cod, Bradford and forty other adult men signed the Mayflower Compact, which presented a religious (rather than an economic) rationale for colonization. The compact expressed a community ideal of working together. When a larger exodus of Puritans established the Massachusetts Bay Colony in the 1630s, the Pilgrims at Plymouth welcomed them and the two colonies cooperated with each other.

The Mayflower Compact and Its Religious Rationale

The Mayflower Compact, which forty-one Pilgrim men signed on board the *Mayflower* in Plymouth Harbor, has been called the first American governing document, predating the U.S. Constitution by over 150 years. But was the Mayflower Compact a constitution? How much authority did it convey, and to whom?

> In the name of God, Amen. We, whose names are underwritten, the loyal subjects of our dread Sovereign Lord King James, by the Grace of God, of Great Britain, France, and Ireland, King, defender of the Faith, etc.
>
> Having undertaken, for the Glory of God, and advancements of the Christian faith and honor of our King and Country, a voyage to plant the first colony in the Northern parts of Virginia, do by these presents, solemnly and mutually, in the presence of God, and one another, covenant and combine ourselves together into a civil body politic; for our better ordering, and preservation and furtherance of the ends aforesaid; and by virtue hereof to enact, constitute, and frame, such just and equal laws, ordinances, acts, constitutions, and offices, from time to time, as shall be thought most meet and convenient for the general good of the colony; unto which we promise all due submission and obedience.
>
> In witness whereof we have hereunto subscribed our names at Cape Cod the 11th of November, in the year of the reign of our Sovereign Lord King James, of England, France, and Ireland, the eighteenth, and of Scotland the fifty-fourth, 1620

Different labor systems also distinguished early Puritan New England from the Chesapeake colonies. Puritans expected young people to work diligently at their calling, and all members of their large families, including children, did the bulk of the work necessary to run homes, farms, and businesses. Very few migrants came to New England as laborers; in fact, New England towns protected their disciplined homegrown workforce by refusing to allow outsiders in, assuring their sons and daughters of steady employment. New England's labor system produced remarkable results, notably a powerful maritime-based economy with scores of oceangoing ships and the crews necessary to sail them. New England mariners sailing New England–made ships transported Virginian tobacco and West Indian sugar throughout the Atlantic World.

The original Mayflower Compact is no longer extant; only copies, such as this ca.1645 transcription by William Bradford, remain.

"A City upon a Hill"

A much larger group of English Puritans left England in the 1630s, establishing the Massachusetts Bay Colony, the New Haven Colony, the Connecticut Colony, and Rhode Island. Unlike the exodus of young males to the Chesapeake colonies, these migrants were families with young children and their university-trained ministers. Their aim, according to John Winthrop, the first governor of Massachusetts Bay, was to create a model of reformed Protestantism—a "city upon a hill," a new English Israel. The idea of a "city upon a hill" made clear the religious orientation of the New England settlement, and the charter of the Massachusetts Bay Colony stated as a goal that the colony's people "may be soe religiously, peaceablie, and civilly governed, as their good Life and orderlie Conversacon, maie wynn and incite the Natives of Country, to the Knowledg and Obedience of the onlie true God and Saulor of Mankinde, and the Christian Fayth." To illustrate this, the seal of the Massachusetts Bay Company shows a half-naked Indian who entreats more of the English to "come over and help us."

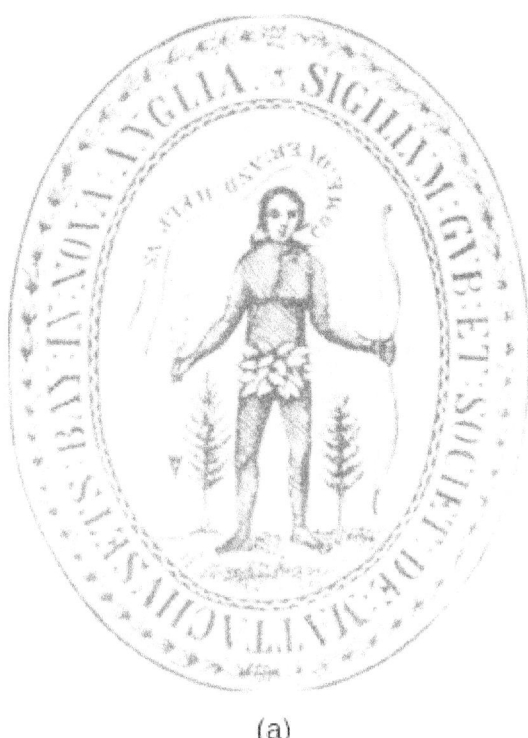 

(a)   (b)

In the 1629 seal of the Massachusetts Bay Colony (a), an Indian is shown asking colonists to "Come over and help us." This seal indicates the religious ambitions of John Winthrop (b), the colony's first governor, for his "city upon a hill."

Puritan New England differed in many ways from both England and the rest of Europe. Protestants emphasized literacy so that everyone could read the Bible. This attitude was in stark contrast to that of Catholics, who refused to tolerate private ownership of Bibles in the vernacular. The Puritans, for their part, placed a special emphasis on reading scripture, and their commitment to literacy led to the establishment of the first printing press in English America in 1636. Four years later, in 1640, they published the first book in North America, the Bay Psalm Book. As Calvinists, Puritans adhered to the doctrine of predestination, whereby a few "elect" would be saved and all others damned. No one could be sure whether they were predestined for salvation, but through introspection, guided by scripture, Puritans hoped to find a glimmer of redemptive grace. Church membership was restricted to those Puritans who were willing to provide a conversion narrative telling how they came to understand their spiritual estate by hearing sermons and studying the Bible.

Although many people assume Puritans escaped England to establish religious freedom, they proved to be just as intolerant as the English state church. When dissenters, including Puritan minister Roger Williams and Anne Hutchinson, challenged Governor Winthrop in Massachusetts Bay in the 1630s, they were banished. Roger Williams questioned the Puritans' taking of Indian land. Williams also argued for a complete separation from the Church of England, a position other Puritans in Massachusetts rejected, as well as the idea that the state could not punish individuals for their beliefs. Although he did accept that nonbelievers were destined for eternal damnation, Williams did not think the state could compel true orthodoxy. Puritan authorities found him guilty of spreading dangerous ideas, but he went on to found Rhode Island as a colony that sheltered dissenting Puritans from their brethren in Massachusetts. In Rhode Island, Williams wrote favorably about native peoples, contrasting their virtues with Puritan New England's intolerance.

Anne Hutchinson also ran afoul of Puritan authorities for her criticism of the evolving religious practices in the Massachusetts Bay Colony. In particular, she held that Puritan ministers in New England taught a shallow version of Protestantism emphasizing hierarchy and actions—a "covenant of works" rather than a "covenant of grace." Literate Puritan women like Hutchinson presented a challenge to the male ministers' authority. Indeed, her major offense was her claim of direct religious revelation, a type of spiritual experience that negated the role of ministers. Because of Hutchinson's beliefs and her defiance of authority in the colony, especially that of Governor Winthrop, Puritan authorities tried and convicted her of holding false beliefs. In 1638, she was excommunicated and banished from the colony. She went to Rhode Island and later, in 1642, sought safety among the Dutch in New Netherland. The following year, Algonquian warriors killed Hutchinson and her family. In Massachusetts, Governor Winthrop noted her death as the righteous judgment of God against a heretic.

Like many other Europeans, the Puritans believed in the supernatural. Every event appeared to be a sign of God's mercy or judgment, and people believed that witches allied themselves with the Devil to carry out evil deeds and deliberate harm such as the sickness or death of children, the loss of cattle, and other catastrophes. Hundreds were accused of witchcraft in Puritan New England, including townspeople whose habits or appearance bothered their neighbors or who appeared threatening for any reason. Women, seen as more susceptible to the Devil because of their supposedly weaker constitutions, made up the vast majority of suspects and those who were executed. The most notorious cases occurred in Salem Village in 1692. Many of the accusers who prosecuted the suspected witches had been traumatized by the Indian wars on the frontier and by unprecedented political and cultural changes in New England. Relying on their belief in witchcraft to help make sense of their changing world, Puritan authorities executed nineteen people and caused the deaths of several others.

> Explore the Salem Witchcraft Trials to learn more about the prosecution of witchcraft in seventeenth-century New England.

Puritan Relationships with Native Peoples

Like their Spanish and French Catholic rivals, English Puritans in America took steps to convert native peoples to their version of Christianity. John Eliot, the leading Puritan missionary in New England, urged natives in Massachusetts to live in "praying towns" established by English authorities for converted Indians, and to adopt the Puritan emphasis on the centrality of the Bible. In keeping with the Protestant emphasis on reading scripture, he translated the Bible into the local Algonquian language and published his work in 1663. Eliot hoped that as a result of his efforts, some of New England's native inhabitants would become preachers.

Tensions had existed from the beginning between the Puritans and the native people who controlled southern New England. Relationships deteriorated as the Puritans continued to expand their settlements aggressively and as European ways increasingly disrupted native life. These strains led to King Philip's War (1675–1676), a massive regional conflict that was nearly successful in pushing the English out of New England.

This map indicates the domains of New England's native inhabitants in 1670, a few years before King Philip's War.

When the Puritans began to arrive in the 1620s and 1630s, local Algonquian peoples had viewed them as potential allies in the conflicts already simmering between rival native groups. In 1621, the Wampanoag, led by Massasoit, concluded a peace treaty with the Pilgrims at Plymouth. In the 1630s, the Puritans in Massachusetts and Plymouth allied themselves with the Narragansett and Mohegan people against the Pequot, who had recently expanded their claims into southern New England. In May 1637, the Puritans attacked a large group of several hundred Pequot along the Mystic River in Connecticut. To the horror of their native allies, the Puritans massacred all but a handful of the men, women, and children they found.

By the mid-seventeenth century, the Puritans had pushed their way further into the interior of New England, establishing outposts along the Connecticut River Valley. There seemed no end to their expansion. Wampanoag leader Metacom or Metacomet, also known as King Philip among the English, was determined to stop the encroachment. The Wampanoag, along with the Nipmuck, Pocumtuck, and Narragansett, took up the hatchet to drive the English from the land. In the ensuing conflict, called King Philip's War, native forces succeeded in destroying half of the frontier Puritan towns; however, in the end, the English (aided by Mohegans and Christian Indians) prevailed and sold many captives into slavery in the West Indies. (The severed head of King Philip was publicly displayed in Plymouth.) The war also forever changed the English perception of native peoples; from then on, Puritan writers took great pains to vilify the natives as bloodthirsty savages. A new type of racial hatred became a defining feature of Indian-English relationships in the Northeast.

Mary Rowlandson's Captivity Narrative

Mary Rowlandson was a Puritan woman whom Indian tribes captured and imprisoned for several weeks during King Philip's War. After her release, she wrote *The Narrative of the Captivity and the Restoration of Mrs. Mary Rowlandson*, which was published in 1682. The book was an immediate sensation that was reissued in multiple editions for over a century.

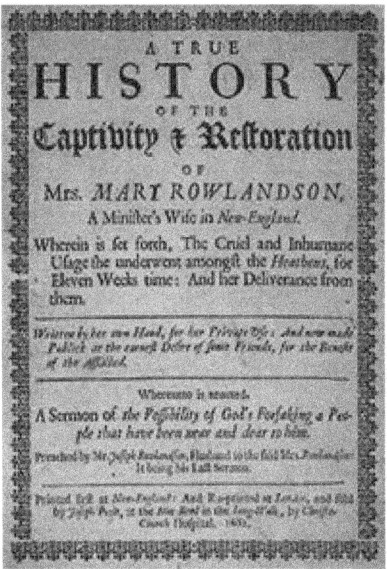 
(a) (b)

Puritan woman Mary Rowlandson wrote her captivity narrative, the front cover of which is shown here (a), after her imprisonment during King Philip's War. In her narrative, she tells of her treatment by the Indians holding her as well as of her meetings with the Wampanoag leader Metacom (b), shown in a contemporary portrait.

But now, the next morning, I must turn my back upon the town, and travel with them into the vast and desolate wilderness, I knew not whither. It is not my tongue, or pen, can express the sorrows of my heart, and bitterness of my spirit that I had at this departure: but God was with me in a wonderful manner, carrying me along, and bearing up my spirit, that it did not quite fail. One of the Indians carried my poor wounded babe upon a horse; it went moaning all along, "I shall die, I shall die." I went on foot after it, with sorrow that cannot be expressed. At length I took it off the horse, and carried it in my arms till my strength failed, and I fell down with it. Then they set me upon a horse with my wounded child in my lap, and there being no furniture upon the horse's back, as we were going down a steep hill we both fell over the horse's head, at which they, like inhumane creatures, laughed, and rejoiced to see it, though I thought we should there have ended our days, as overcome with so many difficulties. But the Lord renewed my strength still, and carried me along, that I might see more of His power; yea, so much that I could never have thought of, had I not experienced it.

What sustains Rowlandson her during her ordeal? How does she characterize her captors? What do you think made her narrative so compelling to readers?

Access the entire text of Mary Rowlandson's captivity narrative at the Gutenberg Project.

Section Summary

The English came late to colonization of the Americas, establishing stable settlements in the 1600s after several unsuccessful attempts in the 1500s. After Roanoke Colony failed in 1587, the English found more success with the founding of Jamestown in 1607 and Plymouth in 1620. The two colonies were very different in origin. The Virginia Company of London founded Jamestown with the express purpose of making money for its investors, while Puritans founded Plymouth to practice their own brand of Protestantism without interference.

Both colonies battled difficult circumstances, including poor relationships with neighboring Indian tribes. Conflicts flared repeatedly in the Chesapeake Bay tobacco colonies and in New England, where a massive uprising against the English in 1675 to 1676—King Philip's War—nearly succeeded in driving the intruders back to the sea.

https://www.openassessments.org/assessments/944

Review Question

1. How did the Chesapeake colonists solve their labor problems?

Answer to Review Question

1. They encouraged colonization by offering headrights to anyone who could pay his own way to Virginia: fifty acres for each passage. They also used the system of indenture, in which people (usually men) who didn't have enough money to pay their own passage could work for a set number of years and then gain their own land. Increasingly, they also turned to African slaves as a cheap labor source.

Glossary

headright system a system in which parcels of land were granted to settlers who could pay their own way to Virginia

indenture a labor contract that promised young men, and sometimes women, money and land after they worked for a set period of years

Attributions

CC licensed content, Shared previously

- US History. **Authored by**: P. Scott Corbett, Volker Janssen, John M. Lund, Todd Pfannestiel, Paul Vickery, and Sylvie Waskiewicz. **Provided by**: OpenStax College. **Located at**: http://openstaxcollege.org/textbooks/us-history. **License**: *CC BY: Attribution*. **License Terms**: Download for free at http://cnx.org/content/col11740/latest/

The Impact of Colonization

> *Learning Objectives*
>
> By the end of this section, you will be able to:
>
> - Explain the reasons for the rise of slavery in the American colonies
> - Describe changes to Indian life, including warfare and hunting
> - Contrast European and Indian views on property
> - Assess the impact of European settlement on the environment

As Europeans moved beyond exploration and into colonization of the Americas, they brought changes to virtually every aspect of the land and its people, from trade and hunting to warfare and personal property. European goods, ideas, and diseases shaped the changing continent.

As Europeans established their colonies, their societies also became segmented and divided along religious and racial lines. Most people in these societies were not free; they labored as servants or slaves, doing the work required to produce wealth for others. By 1700, the American continent had become a place of stark contrasts between slavery and freedom, between the haves and the have-nots.

THE INSTITUTION OF SLAVERY

Everywhere in the American colonies, a crushing demand for labor existed to grow New World cash crops, especially sugar and tobacco. This need led Europeans to rely increasingly on Africans, and after 1600, the movement of Africans across the Atlantic accelerated. The English crown chartered the Royal African Company in 1672, giving the company a monopoly over the transport of African slaves to the English colonies. Over the next four decades, the company transported around 350,000 Africans from their homelands. By 1700, the tiny English sugar island of Barbados had a population of fifty thousand slaves, and the English had encoded the institution of chattel slavery into colonial law.

This new system of African slavery came slowly to the English colonists, who did not have slavery at home and preferred to use servant labor. Nevertheless, by the end of the seventeenth century, the English everywhere in America—and particularly in the Chesapeake Bay colonies—had come to rely on African slaves. While Africans had long practiced slavery among their own people, it had not been based on race. Africans enslaved other Africans as war captives, for crimes, and to settle debts; they generally used their slaves for domestic and small-scale agricultural work, not for growing cash crops on large plantations. Additionally, African slavery was often a temporary condition rather than a lifelong sentence, and, unlike New World slavery, it was typically not heritable (passed from a slave mother to her children).

The growing slave trade with Europeans had a profound impact on the people of West Africa, giving prominence to local chieftains and merchants who traded slaves for European textiles, alcohol, guns, tobacco, and food. Africans also charged Europeans for the right to trade in slaves and imposed taxes on slave purchases. Different African groups and kingdoms even staged large-scale raids on each other to meet the demand for slaves.

Once sold to traders, all slaves sent to America endured the hellish **Middle Passage**, the transatlantic crossing, which took one to two months. By 1625, more than 325,800 Africans had been shipped to the New World, though many thousands perished during the voyage. An astonishing number, some four million, were transported to the Caribbean between 1501 and 1830. When they reached their destination in America, Africans found themselves trapped in shockingly brutal slave societies. In the Chesapeake colonies, they faced a lifetime of harvesting and processing tobacco.

Everywhere, Africans resisted slavery, and running away was common. In Jamaica and elsewhere, runaway slaves created **maroon communities**, groups that resisted recapture and eked a living from the land, rebuilding their communities as best they could. When possible, they adhered to traditional ways, following spiritual leaders such as Vodun priests.

CHANGES TO INDIAN LIFE

While the Americas remained firmly under the control of native peoples in the first decades of European settlement, conflict increased as colonization spread and Europeans placed greater demands upon the native populations, including expecting them to convert to Christianity (either Catholicism or Protestantism). Throughout the seventeenth century, the still-powerful native peoples and confederacies that retained control of the land waged war against the invading Europeans, achieving a degree of success in their effort to drive the newcomers from the continent.

At the same time, European goods had begun to change Indian life radically. In the 1500s, some of the earliest objects Europeans introduced to Indians were glass beads, copper kettles, and metal utensils. Native people often adapted these items for their own use. For example, some cut up copper kettles and refashioned the metal for other uses, including jewelry that conferred status on the wearer, who was seen as connected to the new European source of raw materials.

As European settlements grew throughout the 1600s, European goods flooded native communities. Soon native people were using these items for the same purposes as the Europeans. For example, many native inhabitants abandoned their animal-skin clothing in favor of European textiles. Similarly, clay cookware gave way to metal cooking implements, and Indians found that European flint and steel made starting fires much easier.

The abundance of European goods gave rise to new artistic objects. For example, iron awls made the creation of shell beads among the native people of the Eastern Woodlands much easier, and the result was an astonishing increase in the production of **wampum**, shell beads used in ceremonies and as jewelry and currency. Native peoples had always placed goods in the graves of their departed, and this practice escalated with the arrival of European goods. Archaeologists have found enormous caches of European trade goods in the graves of Indians on the East Coast.

In this 1681 portrait, the Niantic-Narragansett chief Ninigret wears a combination of European and Indian goods. Which elements of each culture are evident in this portrait?

Native weapons changed dramatically as well, creating an arms race among the peoples living in European colonization zones. Indians refashioned European brassware into arrow points and turned axes used for chopping wood into weapons. The most prized piece of European weaponry to obtain was a **musket**, or light, long-barreled European gun. In order to trade with Europeans for these, native peoples intensified their harvesting of beaver, commercializing their traditional practice.

The influx of European materials made warfare more lethal and changed traditional patterns of authority among tribes. Formerly weaker groups, if they had access to European metal and weapons, suddenly gained the upper hand against once-dominant groups. The Algonquian, for instance, traded with the French for muskets and gained power against their enemies, the Iroquois. Eventually, native peoples also used their new weapons against the European colonizers who had provided them.

> Explore the complexity of Indian-European relationships in the series of primary source documents on the National Humanities Center site.

ENVIRONMENTAL CHANGES

The European presence in America spurred countless changes in the environment, setting into motion chains of events that affected native animals as well as people. The popularity of beaver-trimmed hats in Europe, coupled with Indians' desire for European weapons, led to the overhunting of beaver in the Northeast. Soon, beavers were extinct in New England, New York, and other areas. With their loss came the loss of beaver ponds, which had served as habitats for fish as well as water sources for deer, moose, and other animals. Furthermore, Europeans introduced pigs, which they allowed to forage in forests and other wildlands. Pigs consumed the foods on which deer and other indigenous species depended, resulting in scarcity of the game native peoples had traditionally hunted.

European ideas about owning land as private property clashed with natives' understanding of land use. Native peoples did not believe in private ownership of land; instead, they viewed land as a resource to be held in common for the benefit of the group. The European idea of usufruct—the right to common land use and enjoyment—comes close to the native understanding, but colonists did not practice usufruct widely in America. Colonizers established fields, fences, and other means of demarcating private property. Native peoples who moved seasonally to take advantage of natural resources now found areas off limits, claimed by colonizers because of their insistence on private-property rights.

The Introduction of Disease

Perhaps European colonization's single greatest impact on the North American environment was the introduction of disease. Microbes to which native inhabitants had no immunity led to death everywhere Europeans settled. Along the New England coast between 1616 and 1618, epidemics claimed the lives of 75 percent of the native people. In the 1630s, half the Huron and Iroquois around the Great Lakes died of smallpox. As is often the case with disease, the very young and the very old were the most vulnerable and had the highest mortality rates. The loss of the older generation meant the loss of knowledge and tradition, while the death of children only compounded the trauma, creating devastating implications for future generations.

Some native peoples perceived disease as a weapon used by hostile spiritual forces, and they went to war to exorcise the disease from their midst. These "mourning wars" in eastern North America were designed to gain captives who would either be adopted ("requickened" as a replacement for a deceased loved one) or ritually tortured and executed to assuage the anger and grief caused by loss.

The Cultivation of Plants

Adriaen van Ostade, a Dutch artist, painted An Apothecary Smoking in an Interior in 1646. The large European market for American tobacco strongly influenced the development of some of the American colonies.

European expansion in the Americas led to an unprecedented movement of plants across the Atlantic. A prime example is tobacco, which became a valuable export as the habit of smoking, previously unknown in Europe, took hold. Another example is sugar. Columbus brought sugarcane to the Caribbean on his second voyage in 1494, and thereafter a wide variety of other herbs, flowers, seeds, and roots made the transatlantic voyage.

Just as pharmaceutical companies today scour the natural world for new drugs, Europeans traveled to America to discover new medicines. The task of cataloging the new plants found there helped give birth to the science of botany. Early botanists included the English naturalist Sir Hans Sloane, who traveled to Jamaica in 1687 and there recorded hundreds of new plants. Sloane also helped popularize the drinking of chocolate, made from the cacao bean, in England.

Indians, who possessed a vast understanding of local New World plants and their properties, would have been a rich source of information for those European botanists seeking to find and catalog potentially useful plants. Enslaved Africans, who had a tradition of the use of medicinal plants in their native land, adapted to their new surroundings by learning the use of New World plants through experimentation or from the native inhabitants. Native peoples and Africans employed their knowledge effectively within their own communities. One notable example was the use of the peacock flower to induce abortions: Indian and enslaved African women living in oppressive colonial regimes are said to have used this herb to prevent the birth of children into slavery. Europeans distrusted medical knowledge that came from African or native sources, however, and thus lost the benefit of this source of information.

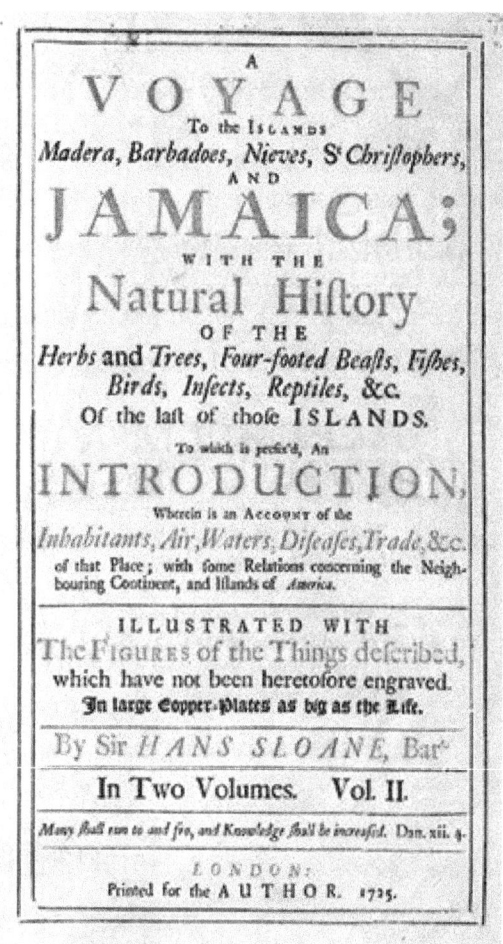

English naturalist Sir Hans Sloane traveled to Jamaica and other Caribbean islands to catalog the flora of the new world.

Section Summary

The development of the Atlantic slave trade forever changed the course of European settlement in the Americas. Other transatlantic travelers, including diseases, goods, plants, animals, and even ideas like the concept of private land ownership, further influenced life in America during the sixteenth and seventeenth centuries. The exchange of pelts for European goods including copper kettles, knives, and guns played a significant role in changing the material cultures of native peoples. During the seventeenth century, native peoples grew increasingly dependent on European trade items. At the same time, many native inhabitants died of European diseases, while survivors adopted new ways of living with their new neighbors.

- https://www.openassessments.org/assessments/945

Review Questions

1. How did European muskets change life for native peoples in the Americas?
2. Compare and contrast European and Indian views on property.

Answers to Review Questions

1. European guns started an arms race among Indian groups. Tribes with ties to Europeans had a distinct advantage in wars with other tribes because muskets were so much more effective than bows and arrows. Guns changed the balance of power among different groups and tribes and made combat more deadly.

2. Indians didn't have any concept of owning personal property and believed that land should be held in common, for use by a group. They used land as they needed, often moving from area to area to follow food sources at different times of year. Europeans saw land as something individuals could own, and they used fences and other markers to define their property.

Critical Thinking Questions

1. Compare and contrast life in the Spanish, French, Dutch, and English colonies, differentiating between the Chesapeake Bay and New England colonies. Who were the colonizers? What were their purposes in being there? How did they interact with their environments and the native inhabitants of the lands on which they settled?

2. Describe the attempts of the various European colonists to convert native peoples to their belief systems. How did these attempts compare to one another? What were the results of each effort?

3. How did chattel slavery differ from indentured servitude? How did the former system come to replace the latter? What were the results of this shift?

4. What impact did Europeans have on their New World environments—native peoples and their communities as well as land, plants, and animals? Conversely, what impact did the New World's native inhabitants, land, plants, and animals have on Europeans? How did the interaction of European and Indian societies, together, shape a world that was truly "new"?

Glossary

maroon communities groups of runaway slaves who resisted recapture and eked a living from the land

Middle Passage the perilous, often deadly transatlantic crossing of slave ships from the African coast to the New World

musket a light, long-barreled European gun

wampum shell beads used in ceremonies and as jewelry and currency

Attributions

CC licensed content, Shared previously

- US History. **Authored by**: P. Scott Corbett, Volker Janssen, John M. Lund, Todd Pfannestiel, Paul Vickery, and Sylvie Waskiewicz. **Provided by**: OpenStax College. **Located at**: http://openstaxcollege.org/textbooks/us-history. **License**: *CC BY: Attribution*. **License Terms**: Download for free at http://cnx.org/content/col11740/latest/

Primary Source Reading: Jamestown Charter

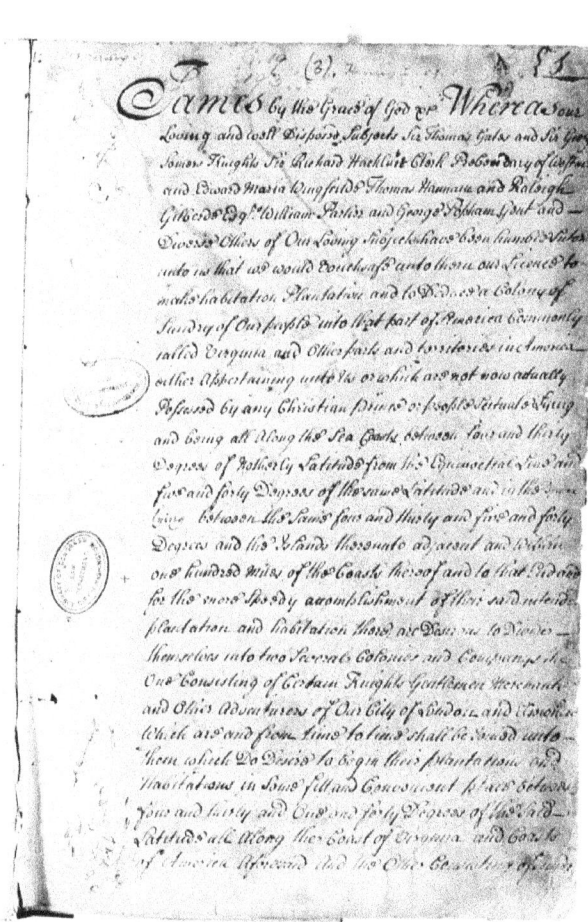

The Charter of Virginia

In case you're not an expert at reading beautiful, Old English calligraphy, you can read the text from the original Charter of Virginia below:

JAMES, by the Grace of God, King of England, Scotland, France and Ireland, Defender of the Faith, &c. WHEREAS our loving and well-disposed Subjects, Sir Thorn as Gales, and Sir George Somers, Knights, Richard Hackluit, Clerk, Prebendary of Westminster, and Edward-Maria Wingfield, Thomas Hanharm and Ralegh Gilbert, Esqrs. William Parker, and George Popham, Gentlemen, and divers others of our loving Subjects, have been humble Suitors unto us, that We would vouchsafe unto them our Licence, to make Habitation, Plantation, and to deduce a colony of sundry of our People into that part of America commonly called VIRGINIA, and other parts and Territories in America, either appertaining unto us, or which are not now actually possessed by any Christian Prince or People, situate, lying, and being all along the Sea Coasts, between four and thirty Degrees of Northerly Latitude from the Equinoctial Line, and five and forty Degrees of the same Latitude, and in the main Land between the same four and thirty and five and forty Degrees, and the Islands hereunto adjacent, or within one hundred Miles of the Coast thereof;

And to that End, and for the more speedy Accomplishment of their said intended Plantation and Habitation there, are desirous to divide themselves into two several Colonies and Companies; the one consisting of certain Knights, Gentlemen, Merchants, and other Adventurers, of our City of London and elsewhere, which are, and from time to time shall be, joined unto them, which do desire to begin their Plantation and Habitation in some fit and convenient Place, between four and thirty and one and forty Degrees of the said Latitude, alongst the Coasts of Virginia, and the Coasts of America aforesaid: And the other consisting of sundry Knights, Gentlemen, Merchants, and other Adventurers, of our Cities of Bristol and Exeter, and of our Town of Plimouth, and of other Places, which do join themselves unto that Colony, which do desire to begin their Plantation and Habitation in some fit and convenient Place, between eight and thirty Degrees and five and forty Degrees of the said Latitude, all alongst the said Coasts of Virginia and America, as that Coast lyeth:

We, greatly commending, and graciously accepting of, their Desires for the Furtherance of so noble a Work, which may, by the Providence of Almighty God, hereafter tend to the Glory of his Divine Majesty, in propagating of Christian Religion to such People, as yet live in Darkness and miserable Ignorance of the true Knowledge and Worship of God, and may in time bring the Infidels and Savages, living in those parts, to human Civility, and to a settled and quiet Government: DO, by these our Letters Patents, graciously accept of, and agree to, their humble and well-intended Desires;

And do therefore, for Us, our Heirs, and Successors, GRANT and agree, that the said Sir Thomas Gates, Sir George Somers, Richard Hackluit, and Edward-Maria Wingfield, Adventurers of and for our City of London, and all such others, as are, or shall be, joined unto them of that Colony, shall be called the first Colony; And they shall and may begin their said first Plantation and Habitation, at any Place upon the said-Coast of Virginia or America, where they shall think fit and convenient, between the said four and thirty and one and forty Degrees of the said Latitude; And that they shall have all the Lands, Woods, Soil, Grounds, Havens, Ports, Rivers, Mines, Minerals, Marshes, Waters, Fishings, Commodities, and Hereditaments, whatsoever, from the said first Seat of their Plantation and Habitation by the Space of fifty Miles of English Statute Measure, all along the said Coast of Virginia and America, towards the West and Southwest, as the Coast lyeth, with all the Islands within one hundred Miles directly over against the same Sea Coast; And also all the Lands, Soil, Grounds, Havens, Ports, Rivers, Mines, Minerals, Woods, Waters, Marshes, Fishings, Commoditites, and Hereditaments, whatsoever, from the said Place of their first Plantation and Habitation for the space of fifty like English Miles, all alongst the said Coasts of Virginia and America, towards the East and Northeast, or towards the North, as the Coast lyeth, together with all the Islands within one hundred Miles, directly over against the said Sea Coast, And also all the Lands, Woods, Soil, Grounds, Havens, Ports, Rivers, Mines, Minerals, Marshes, Waters, Fishings, Commodities, and Hereditaments, whatsoever, from the same fifty Miles every way on the Sea Coast, directly into the main Land by the Space of one hundred like English Miles; And shall and may inhabit and remain there; and shall and may also build and fortify within any the same, for their better Safeguard and Defense, according to their best Discretion, and the Discretion of the Council of that Colony; And that no other of our Subjects shall be permitted, or suffered, to plant or inhabit behind, or on the Backside of them, towards the main Land, without the Express License or Consent of the Council of that Colony, thereunto in Writing; first had and obtained.

And we do likewise, for Us, Our Heirs, and Successors, by these Presents, GRANT and agree, that the said Thomas Hanham, and Ralegh Gilbert, William Parker, and George Popham, and all others of the Town of Plimouth in the County of Devon, or elsewhere which are, or shall be, joined unto them of that Colony, shall be called the second Colony; And that they shall and may begin their said Plantation and Seat of their first Abode and Habitation, at any Place upon the said Coast of Virginia and America, where they shall think fit and convenient, between eight and thirty Degrees of the said Latitude, and five and forty Degrees of the same Latitude; And that they shall have all the Lands, Soils, Grounds, Havens, Ports, Rivers, Mines, Minerals, Woods, Marshes, Waters, Fishings, Commodities, and Hereditaments, whatsoever, from the first Seat of their Plantation and Habitation by the Space of fifty like English Miles, as is aforesaid, all alongst the said Coasts of Virginia and al raerica towards the West and Southwest, or towards the South, as the Coast lyeth, and all the Islands within one hundred Miles, directly over against the said Sea Coast; And also all the Lands, Soils, Grounds, Havens, Ports, Rivers, Mines, Minerals, Woods, Marshes, Waters, Fishings, Commodities, and Hereditaments, whatsoever, from the said Place of their first Plantation and Habitation for the Space of fifty like Miles, all alongst the said Coast of Virginia and America, towards the least and Northeast, or towards the North, as the Coast lyeth, and all the Islands also within one hundred Miles directly over against the same Sea Coast; And also all the Lands, Soils, Grounds, Havens, Ports, Rivers, Woods, Mines, Minerals, Marshes, Waters, Fishings, Commodities, and Hereditaments, whatsoever, from the same fifty Miles every way on the Sea Coast, directly into the main Land, by the Space of one hundred like English Miles; And shall and may inhabit and remain there; and shall and may also build and fortify within any the same for their better Safeguard, according to their best Discretion, and the Discretion of the Council of that Colony; And that none of our Subjects shall be permitted, or suffered, to plant or inhabit behind, or on the back of them, towards the main Land, without express Licence of the Council of that Colony, in Writing thereunto first had and obtained.

Provided always, and our Will and Pleasure herein is, that the Plantation and Habitation of such of the said Colonies, as shall last plant themselves, as aforesaid, shall not be made within one hundred like English Miles of the other of them, that first began to make their Plantation, as aforesaid.

And we do also ordain, establish, and agree, for Us, our Heirs, and Successors, that each of the said Colonies shall have a Council, which shall govern and order all Matters-and Causes, which shall arise, grow, or happen, to or within the same several Colonies, according to such Laws, Ordinances, and Instructions, as shall be, in that behalf, given and signed with Our Hand or Sign Manual, and pass under the Privy Seal of our Realm of England; Each of which Councils shall consist of thirteen Persons, to be ordained, made, and removed, from time to time, according as shall be directed and comprised in the same instructions; And shall have a several Seal, for all Matters that shall pass or concern the same several Councils; Each of which Seals, shall have the King's Arms engraver on the one Side thereof, and his Portraiture on the other; And that the Seal for the Council of the said first Colony shall have engraver round about, on the one Side, these Words; Sigillum Regis Magne Britanniae, Franciae, & Hiberniae; on the other Side this Inscription round about; Pro Concilio primae Coloniae Virginiae. And the Seal for the Council of the said second Colony shall also have engraven, round about the one Side thereof, the aforesaid Words; Sigillum Regis Magne Britanniae, Franciae, & Hiberniae; and on the other Side; Pro Concilio primae Coloniae Virginiae:

And that also there shall be a Council, established here in England, which shall, in like manner, consist of thirteen Persons, to be for that Purpose, appointed by Us, our Heirs and Successors, which shall be called our Council of Virginia; And shall, from time to time, have the superior Managing and Direction, only of and for all Matters that shall or may concern the Government, as well of the said several Colonies, as of and for any other Part or Place, within the aforesaid Precincts of four and thirty and five and forty Degrees abovementioned; Which Council shall, in like manner, have a Seal, for matters concerning the Council or Colonies, with the like Arms and Portraiture, as aforesaid, with this inscription, engraver round about on the one Side; Sigillum Regis Magne Britanniae, Franciae, & Hiberniae; and round about on the other Side, Pro Concilio fuo Virginiae.

And moreover, we do GRANT and agree, for Us, our Heirs and Successors; that that the said several Councils of and for the said several Colonies, shall and lawfully may, by Virtue hereof, from time to time, without any Interruption of Us, our Heirs or Successors, give and take Order, to dig, mine, and search for all Manner of Mines of Gold, Silver, and Copper, as well within any Part of their said several Colonies, as of the said main Lands on the Backside of the same Colonies; And to HAVE and enjoy the Gold, Silver, and Copper, to be gotten thereof, to the Use and Behoof of the same Colonies, and the Plantations thereof; YIELDING therefore to Us, our Heirs and Successors, the fifth Part only of all the same Gold and Silver, and the fifteenth Part of all the same Copper, so to be gotten or had, as is aforesaid, without any other Manner of Profit or Account, to be given or yielded to Us, our Heirs, or Successors, for or in Respect of the same:

And that they shall, or lawfully may, establish and cause to be made a Coin, to pass current there between the people of those several Colonies, for the more Ease of Traffick and Bargaining between and amongst them and the Natives there, of such Metal, and in such Manner and Form, as the said several Councils there shall limit and appoint.

And we do likewise, for Us, our Heirs, and Successors, by these Presents, give full Power and Authority to the said Sir Thomas Gates, Sir George Somers, Richard Hackluit, Edward-Maria Wingfeld, Thomas Hanham, Ralegh Gilbert, William Parker, and George Popham, and to every of them, and to the said several Companies, Plantations, and Colonies, that they, and every of them, shall and may, at all and every time and times hereafter, have, take, and lead in the said Voyage, and for and towards the said several Plantations, and Colonies, and to travel thitherward, and to abide and inhabit there, in every the said Colonies and Plantations, such and so many of our Subjects, as shall willingly accompany them or any of them, in the said Voyages and Plantations; With sufficient Shipping, and Furniture of Armour, Weapons, Ordinance, Powder, Victual, and all other things, necessary for the said Plantations, and for their Use and Defence there: PROVIDED always, that none of the said Persons be such, as shall hereafter be specially restrained by Us, our Heirs, or Successors.

Moreover, we do, by these Presents, for Us, our Heirs, and Successors, GIVE AND GRANT Licence unto the said Sir Thomas Gates, Sir George Somers, Richard Hackluit, Edward-Maria Wingfeld, Thornas Hanham, Ralegh Gilbert, William Parker, and George Popham, and to every of the said Colonies, that they, and every of them, shall and may, from time to time, and at all times forever hereafter, for their several Defences, encounter, expulse, repel, and resist, as well by Sea as by Land, by all Ways and Means whatsoever, all and every such Person or Persons, as without the especial Licence of the said several Colonies and Plantations, shall attempt to inhabit within the said several Precincts and Limits of the said several Colonies and Plantations, or any of them, or that shall enterprise or attempt, at any time hereafter, the Hurt, Detriment, or Annoyance, of the said several Colonies or Plantations:

Giving and granting, by these Presents, unto the said Sir Thomas Gates, Sir George Somers, Richard Hackluit, Edward-Maria Wingfield, Thornas Hanham, Ralegh Gilbert, William Parker, and George Popham, and their Associates of the said second Colony, arid to every of them, from time to time, and at all times for ever hereafter, Power and Authority to take and surprise, by all Ways and Means whatsoever, all and every Person and Persons, with their Ships, Vessels, Goods, and other Furniture, which shall be found trafficking, into any Harbour or Harbours, Creek or Creeks, or Place, within the Limits ok Precincts of the said several Colonies and Plantations, not being of the same Colony, until such time, as they, being of any Realms, or Dominions under our Obedience, shall pay, or agree to pay, to the Hands of the Treasurer of that Colony, within whose Limits and Precincts they shall so traffick, two and a half upon every Hundred, of any thing so by them trafficked, bought, or sold; And being Strangers, and not Subjects under our Obeysance, until they shall pay five upon every Hundred, of such Wares and Merchandises, as they shall traffick, buy, or sell, within the Precincts of the said several Colonies, wherein they shall so traffick, buy, or sell, as aforesaid; WHICH Sums of Money, or Benefit, as aforesaid, for and during the Space of one and twenty Years, next ensuing the Date hereof, shall be wholly emploied to the Use, Benefit, and Behoof of the said several Plantations, where such Traffick shall be made; And after the said one and twenty Years ended, the same shall be taken to the Use of Us, our Heires, and Successors, by such Officers and Ministers as by Us, our Heirs, and Successors, shall be thereunto assigned or appointed.

And we do further, by these Presents, for Us, our Heirs and Successors, GIVE AND GRANT unto the said Sir Thomas Gates, Sir George Sommers, Richard Hackluit, and Edward-Maria Wingfield, and to their Associates of the said first Colony and Plantation, and to the said Thomas Hanham, Ralegh Gilbert, William Parker, and George Popham, and their Associates of the said second Colony and Plantation, that they, and every of them, by their Deputies, Ministers, and Factors, may transport the Goods, Chattels, Armour, Munition, and Furniture, needful to be used by them, for their said Apparel, Food, Defence, or otherwise in Respect of the said Plantations, out of our Realms of England and Ireland, and all other our Dominions, from time to time, for and during the Time of seven Years, next ensuing the Date hereof, for the better Relief of the said several Colonies and Plantations, without any Customs, Subsidy, or other Duty, unto Us, our Heirs, or Successors, to be yielded or payed for the same.

Also we do, for Us, our Heirs, and Successors, DECLARE, by these Presents, that all and every the Persons being our Subjects, which shall dwell and inhabit within every or any of the said several Colonies and Plantations, and every of their children, which shall happen to be born within any of the Limits and Precincts of the said several Colonies and Plantations, shall HAVE and enjoy all Liberties, Franchises, and Immunities, within any of our other Dominions, to all Intents and Purposes, as if they had been abiding and born, within this our Realm of England, or any other of our said Dominions.

Moreover, our gracious Will and Pleasure is, and we do, by these Presents, for Us, our Heirs, and Successors, declare and set forth, that if any Person or Persons, which shall be of any of the said Colonies and Plantations, or any other, which shall trick to the said Colonies and Plantations, or any of them, shall, at any time or times hereafter, transport any Wares, Merchandises, or Commodities, out of any of our Dominions, with a Pretence to land, sell, or otherwise dispose of the same, within any the Limits and Precincts of any of the said Colonies and Plantations, and yet nevertheless, being at Sea, or after he hath landed the same within any of the said Colonies and Plantations, shall carry the same into any other Foreign Country, with a Purpose there to sell or dispose of the same, without the Licence of Us, our Heirs, and Successors, in that Behalf first had and obtained; That then, all the Goods and Chattels of such Person or Persons, so offending and transporting together with the said Ship or Vessel, wherein such Transportation was made, shall be forfeited to Us, our Heirs, and Successors.

Provided always, and our Will and Pleasure is, and we do hereby declare to all Christian Kings, Princes, and States, that if any Person or Persons which shall hereafter be of any of the said several Colonies and Plantations, or any other, by his, their, or any of their Licence and Appointment, shall, at any Time or Times hereafter, rob or spoil, by Sea or Land, or do any Act of unjust and unlawful Hostility to any the Subjects of Us, our Heirs, or Successors, or any the Subjects of any King, Prince, Ruler, Governor, or State, being then in League or Amitie with Us, our Heirs, or Successors, and that upon such Injury, or upon just Complaint of such Prince, Ruler, Governor, or State, or their Subjects, We, our Heirs, or Successors, shall make open Proclamation, within any of the Ports of our Realm of England, commodious for that purpose, That the said Person or Persons, having committed any such robbery, or Spoil, shall, within the term to be limited by such Proclamations, make full Restitution or Satisfaction of all such Injuries done, so as the said Princes, or others so complaining, may hold themselves fully satisfied and contented; And, that if the said Person or Persons, having committed such Robery or Spoil, shall not make, or cause to be made Satisfaction accordingly, within such Time so to be limited, That then it shall be lawful to Us, our Heirs, and Successors, to put the said Person or Persons, having committed such Robbery or Spoil, and their Procurers, Abettors, and Comforters, out of our Allegiance and Protection; And that it shall be lawful and free, for all Princes, and others to pursue with hostility the said offenders, and every of them, and their and every of their Procurers, Aiders, abettors, and comforters, in that behalf.

And finally, we do for Us, our Heirs, and Successors, and agree, to and with the said Sir Thomas Gates, Sir George Somers, Richard Hackluit, Edward-Maria Wingfield, and all others of the said first colony, that We, our Heirs and Successors, upon Petition in that Behalf to be made, shall, by Letters Patent under the Great Seal of England, GIVE and GRANT unto such Persons, their Heirs and Assigns, as the Council of that Colony, or the most part of then, shall, for that Purpose, nominate and assign all the lands, Tenements, and Hereditaments, which shall be within the Precincts limited for that Colony, as is aforesaid, To BE HOLDEN of Us, our heirs and Successors, as of our Manor at East-Greenwich, in the County of Kent, in free and common Soccage only, and not in Capite:

And do in like Manner, Grant and Agree, for Us, our Heirs and Successors, to and with the said Thomas Hanham, Ralegh Gilbert, William Parker, and George Popham, and all others of the said second Colony, That We, our Heirs, and Successors, upon Petition in that Behalf to be made, shall, by Letters-Patent, under the Great Seal of England, GIVE and GRANT, unto such Persons, their Heirs and Assigns, as the Council of that Colony, or the most Part of them, shall for that Purpose nominate and assign, all the Lands, Tenements, and Hereditaments, which shall be within the Precincts limited for that Colony, as is aforesaid, To BE nodded of Us, our Heires, and Successors, as of our Manor of East-Greenwich, in the County of Kent, in free and common Soccage only, and not in Capite.

All which Lands, Tenements, and Hereditaments, so to be passed by the said several Letters-Patent, shall be sufficient Assurance from the said Patentees, so distributed and divided amongst the Undertakers for the Plantation of the said several Colonies, and such as shall make their Plantations in either of the said several Colonies, in such Manner and Form, and for such Estates, as shall be ordered and set down by the Council of the said Colony, or the most part of them, respectively, within which the same Lands, Tenements, and Hereditaments shall lye or be; Although express Mention of the true yearly Value or Certainty of the Premises, or any of them, or of any other Gifts or Grants, by Us or any of our Progenitors or Predecessors, to the aforesaid Sir Thomas Gates, Knt. Sir George Somers, Knt. Richard Hackluit, Edward-Maria Wingfield, Thomas Hanham, Ralegh Gilbert, William Parker, and George Popham, or any of them, heretofore made, in these Presents, is not made; Or any Statute, Act, Ordinance, or Provision, Proclamation, or Restraint, to the contrary hereof had, made, ordained, or any other Thing, Cause, or Matter whatsoever, in any wise notwithstanding. IN Wetness whereof, we have caused these our Letters to be made Patent; Witness Ourself at Westminster, the tenth Day of April, in the fourth Year of our Reign of England, France, and Ireland, and of Scotland the nine and thirtieth.

Attributions

CC licensed content, Shared previously

- Charter of Virginia, 1606. **Provided by**: Wikipedia. **Located at**: https://en.wikisource.org/wiki/Charter_of_Virginia,_1606. **License**: *CC BY-SA: Attribution-ShareAlike*

Public domain content

- Jamestown Charter. **Provided by**: Library of Congress. **Located at**: http://memory.loc.gov/cgi-bin/ampage?collId=mtj8&fileName=mtj8page062.db&recNum=3. **License**: *Public Domain: No Known Copyright*

Primary Source Reading: Bradford, History of Plymouth Plantation

Bradford was one of the leaders of the English Puritan Separatists who we now call "The Pilgrims." This history was his personal journal, completed around 1650, after he had served some 35 years as governor of the colony. The first excerpt describes his feelings as he is on The Mayflower in 1620, on the night before they land to start their puritan colony, the first utopian experiment in the Americas.

- On the Mayflower (1620)
- How they sought a place of habitation (1620)
- The Mayflower Compact (1620)
- Treaty with the Indians (1621)

On the Mayflower (1620)

Being thus arrived in a good harbor, and brought safe to land, they fell upon their knees and blessed the God of Heaven who had brought them over the fast and furious ocean, and delivered them from all the perils and miseries thereof, again to set their feet on the firm and stable earth, their proper element. And no marvel if they were thus joyful, seeing wise Seneca was so affected with sailing a few miles on the coast of his own Italy, as he affirmed, that he had rather remain twenty years on his way by land than pass by sea to any place in a short time, so tedious and dreadful was the same unto him.

But here I cannot but stay and make a pause, and stand half amazed at this poor people's present condition; and so I think will the reader, too, when he well considers the same. Being thus passed the vast ocean, and a sea of troubles before in their preparation (as may be remembered by that which went before), they had now no friends to welcome them nor inns to entertain or refresh their weatherbeaten bodies; no houses or much less towns to repair to, to seek for succor. It is recorded in Scripture as a mercy to the Apostle and his shipwrecked company, that the barbarians showed them no small kindness in refreshing them, but these savage barbarians, when they met with them (as after will appear) were readier to fill their sides full of arrows than otherwise. And for the season it was winter, and they know that the winters of that country know them to be sharp and violent, and subject to cruel and fierce storms, dangerous to travel to known places, much more to search an unknown coast. Besides, what could they see but a hideous and desolate wilderness, full of wild beasts and wild men–and what multitudes there might be of them they knew not. Neither could they, as it were, go up to the top of Pisgah to view from this wilderness a more goodly country to feed their hopes; for which way soever they turned their eyes (save upward to the heavens) they could have little solace or content in respect of any outward objects. For summer being done, all things stand upon them with a weatherbeaten face, and the whole country, full of woods and thickets, represented a wild and savage hue. If they looked behind them, there was the mighty ocean which they had passed and was now as a main bar and gulf to separate them from all the civil parts of the world. If it be said they had a ship to succor them, it is true; but what heard they daily from the master and company? But that with speed they should look out a place (with their shallop) where they would be, at some near distance; for the season was such that he would not stir from thence till a safe harbor was discovered by them, where they would be, and he might go without danger; and that victuals consumed space but he must and would keep sufficient for themselves and their return. Yea, it was muttered by some that if they got not a place in time, they would turn them and their goods ashore and leave them. Let it also be considered what weak hopes of supply and succor they left behind them, that might bear up their minds in this sad condition and trials they were under; and they could not but be very small. It is true, indeed, the affections and love of their brethren at Leyden was cordial and entire towards them, but they had little power to help them or themselves; and how the case stood between them and the merchants at their coming away hath already been declared.

What could now sustain them but the Spirit of God and His grace? May not and ought not the children of these fathers rightly say: "Our fathers were Englishmen which came over this great ocean, and were ready to perish in this wilderness; but they cried unto the Lord, and He heard their voice and looked on their adversity," etc. "Let them therefore praise the Lord, because He is good: and his mercies endure forever. Yea, let them which have been redeemed of the Lord, show how He hath delivered them from the hand of the oppressor. When they wandered in the desert wilderness out of the way, and found no city to dwell in, both hungry and thirsty, their soul was overwhelmed in them." "Let them confess before the Lord His lovingkindness and His wonderful works before the sons of men."

How they sought a place of habitation (1620)

Being thus arrived at Cape Cod the 11th of November, and necessity calling them to look out a place for habitation (as well as the master's and mariner's importunity); they having brought a large shallop with them out of England, stowed in quarters in the ship, they now got her out and set their carpenters to work to trim her up; but being much bruised and shattered in the ship with foul weather, they saw she would be long in mending. Whereupon a few of them tendered themselves to go by land and discover those nearest places, whilst the shallop was in mending; and the rather because as they went into that harbor there seemed to be an opening some two or three leagues off, which the master judged to be a river. It was conceived there might be some danger in the attempt, yet seeing them resolute, they were permitted to go, being sixteen of them well armed under the conduct of Captain Standish, having such instructions given them as was thought meet.

They set forth the 15 of November; and when they had marched about the space of a mile by the seaside, they espied five or six persons with a dog coming towards them, who were savages; but they fled from them and ran up into the woods, and the English followed them, partly to see if they could speak with them, and partly to discover if there might not be more of them lying in ambush. But the Indians seeing themselves thus followed, they again forsook the woods and ran away on the sands as hard as they could, so as they could not come near them but followed them by the track of their feet sundry miles and saw that they had come the same way. So, night coming on, they made their rendezvous and set out their sentinels, and rested in quiet that night; and the next morning followed their track till they had headed a great creek and so left the sands, and turned another way into the woods. But they still followed them by guess, hoping to find their dwellings; but they soon lost both them and themselves, falling into such thickets as were ready to tear their clothes and armor in pieces; but were most distressed for want of drink. But at length they found water and refreshed themselves, being the first New England water they drunk of, and was now in great thirst as pleasant unto them as wine or beer had been in foretimes.

Afterwards, they directed their course to come to the other shore, for they knew it was a neck of land they were to cross over, and so at length got to the seaside and marched to this supposed river, and by the way found a pond of clear, fresh water, and shortly after a good quantity of clear ground where the Indians had formerly set corn, and some of their graves. And proceeding further they saw new stubble where corn had been set the same year; also they found where lately a house had been, where some planks and a great kettle was remaining, and heaps of sand newly paddled with their hands. Which, they digging up, found in them divers fair Indian baskets filled with corn, and some in ears, fair and good, of divers colors, which seemed to them a very goodly sight (having never seen any such before). This was near the place of that supposed river they came to seek, unto which they went and found it to open itself into two arms with a high cliff of sand in the entrance but more like to be creeks of salt water than any fresh, for aught they saw; and that there was good harborage for their shallop, leaving it further to be discovered by their shallop, when she was ready. So, their time limited them being expired, they returned to the ship lest they should be in fear of their safety; and took with them part of the corn and buried up the rest. And so, like the men from Eshcol, carried with them of the fruits of the land and showed their brethren; of which, and their return, they were marvelously glad and their hearts encouraged.

After this, the shallop being got ready, they set out again for the better discovery of this place, and the master of the ship desired to go himself. So there went some thirty men but found it to be no harbor for ships but only for boats. There was also found two of their houses covered with mats, and sundry of their implements in them, but the people were run away and could not be seen. Also there was found more of their corn and of their beans of various colors; the corn and beans they brought away, purposing to give them full satisfaction when they should meet with any of them as, about some six months afterward they did, to their good content.

And here is to be noted a special providence of God, and a great mercy to this poor people, that here they got seed to plant them corn the next year, or else they might have starved, for they had none nor any likelihood to get any till the season had been past, as the sequel did manifest. Neither is it likely they had had this, if the first voyage had not been made, for the ground was now all covered with snow and hard frozen; but the Lord is never wanting unto His in their greatest needs; let His holy name have all the praise. . . .

The Mayflower Compact (1620)

I shall a little return back, and begin with a combination of made by them before they came ashore; being the first foundation of their government in this place. Occasioned partly by the discontented and mutinous speeches that some of the strangers amongst them had let fall from them in the ship: That when they came ashore they would use their own liberty, for none had power to command them, the patent they had being for Virginia and not for New England, which belonged to another government, with which the Virginia Company had nothing to do. And partly that such an act by them done, this their condition considered, might be as firm as any patent and in some respects more sure.

The form was as followeth:

IN THE NAME OF GOD, AMEN.

We whose names are underwritten, the loyal subjects of our dread Sovereign Lord King James, by the Grace of God of Great Britain, France, and Ireland King, Defender of the faith, etc.

Having undertaken, for the Glory of God and advancement of the Christian Faith and Honor of our King and Country, a Voyage to plant the First Colony in the Northern Parts of Virginia, do by these presents solemnly and mutually in the presence of God and one of another, Covenant and Combine ourselves together into a Civil Body Politic, for our better ordering and preservation and furtherance of the ends aforesaid; and by virtue hereof to enact, constitute and frame such just and equal Laws, Ordinances, Acts, Constitutions and Offices, from time to time, as shall be thought most meet and convenient for the general good of the Colony, unto which we promise all due submission and obedience. In witness whereof we have hereunder subscribed our names at Cape Cod, the 11th of November, in the year of the reign of our Sovereign Lord King James, of England, France and Ireland the eighteenth, and of Scotland the fifty-fourth. Anno Domini 1620.

After this they chose, or rather confirmed, Mr. John Carver (a man godly and well approved amongst them) their Governor for that year. And after they had provided a place for their goods, or common store (which were long in unlading for want of boats, foulness of the winter weather and sickness of divers) and begun some small cottages for their habitation; as time would admit, they met and consulted of laws and orders, both for their civil and military government as the necessity of their condition did require, still adding thereunto as urgent occasion in several times, and as cases did require.

In these hard and difficult beginnings they found some discontents and murmurings arise amongst some, and mutinous speeches and carriages in other; but they were soon quelled and overcome by the wisdom, patience, and just and equal carriage of things, by the Governor and better part, which clave faithfully together in the main.

Treaty with the Indians (1621)

All this while the Indians came skulking about them, and would sometimes show themselves aloof off, but when any approached near them, they would run away; and once they stole away their tools where they had been at work and were gone to dinner. But about the 16th of March, a certain Indian came boldly amongst them and spoke to them in broken English, which they could well understand but marveled at it. At length they understood by discourse with him, that he was not of these parts, but belonged to the eastern parts where some English ships came to fish, with whom he was acquainted and could name sundry of them by their names, amongst whom he had got his language. He became profitable to them in acquainting them with many things concerning the state of the country in the east parts where he lived, which was afterwards profitable unto them; as also of the people here, of their names, number and strength, of their situation and distance from this place, and who was chief amongst them. His name was Samoset. He told them also of another Indian whose name was Sguanto, a native of this place, who had been in England and could speak better English than himself.

Being after some time of entertainment and gifts dismissed, a while after he came again, and five more with him, and they brought again all the tools that were stolen away before, and made way for the coming of their great Sachem, called Massasoit. Who, about four or five days after, came with the chief of his friends and other attendance, with the aforesaid Squanto. With whom, after friendly entertainment and some gifts given him, they made a peace with him (which hath now continued this 24 years) in these terms:

- That neither he nor any of his should injure or do hurt to any of their people.
- That if any of his did hurt to any of theirs, he should send the offender, that they might punish him.
- That if anything were taken away from any of theirs, he should cause it to be restored; and they should do the like to his.
- If any did unjustly war against him, they would aid him; if any did war against them, he should aid them.
- He should send to his neighbors confederates to certify them of this, that they might not wrong them, but might be likewise comprised in the conditions of peace.
- That when their men came to them, they should leave their bows and arrows behind them.

After these thing he returned to his place called Sowams, some 40 miles from this place, but Squanto continued with them and was their interpreter and was a special instrument sent of God for their good beyond their expectation. He directed them how to set their corn, where to take fish, and to procure other commodities, and was also their pilot to bring them to unknown places for their profit, and never left them till he died. He was a native of this place, and scarce any left alive besides himself. He we carried away with divers others by one Hunt, a master of a ship, who thought to sell them for slaves in Spain. But he got away for England and was entertained by a merchant in London, and employed to Newfoundland and other parts, and lastly brought hither into these parts by one Mr. Dermer, a gentleman employed by Sir Ferdinando Gorges and others for discovery and other designs in these parts.

Source: William Bradford: History of Plymouth Plantation, c. 1650

Attributions

Public domain content

- History of Plymouth Plantation, c. 1650. **Authored by**: William Bradford. **Located at**: http://legacy.fordham.edu/halsall/mod/1650bradford.asp#On%20the%20Mayflower. **Project**: Internet Modern History Sourcebook. **License**: *Public Domain: No Known Copyright*

4. Rule Britannia! The English Empire, 1660-1763

Introduction

The eighteenth century witnessed the birth of Great Britain (after the union of England and Scotland in 1707) and the expansion of the British Empire. By the mid-1700s, Great Britain had developed into a commercial and military powerhouse; its economic sway ranged from India, where the British East India Company had gained control over both trade and territory, to the West African coast, where British slave traders predominated, and to the British West Indies, whose lucrative sugar plantations, especially in Barbados and Jamaica, provided windfall profits for British planters. Meanwhile, the population rose dramatically in Britain's North American colonies. In the early 1700s the population in the colonies had reached 250,000. By 1750, however, over a million British migrants and African slaves had established a near-continuous zone of settlement on the Atlantic coast from Maine to Georgia.

Isaac Royall and his family, seen here in a 1741 portrait by Robert Feke, moved to Medford, Massachusetts, from the West Indian island of Antigua, bringing their slaves with them. They were an affluent British colonial family, proud of their success and the success of the British Empire.

During this period, the ties between Great Britain and the American colonies only grew stronger. Anglo-American colonists considered themselves part of the British Empire in all ways: politically, militarily, religiously (as Protestants), intellectually, and racially. The portrait of the Royall family exemplifies the colonial American gentry of the eighteenth century. Successful and well-to-do, they display fashions, hairstyles, and furnishings that all speak to their identity as proud and loyal British subjects.

Attributions

CC licensed content, Shared previously

- US History. **Authored by**: P. Scott Corbett, Volker Janssen, John M. Lund, Todd Pfannestiel, Paul Vickery, and Sylvie Waskiewicz. **Provided by**: OpenStax College. **Located at**: http://openstaxcollege.org/textbooks/us-history. **License**: CC BY: Attribution. **License Terms**: Download for free at http://cnx.org/content/col11740/latest/

Charles II and the Restoration Colonies

Learning Objectives

By the end of this section, you will be able to:

- Analyze the causes and consequences of the Restoration
- Identify the Restoration colonies and their role in the expansion of the Empire

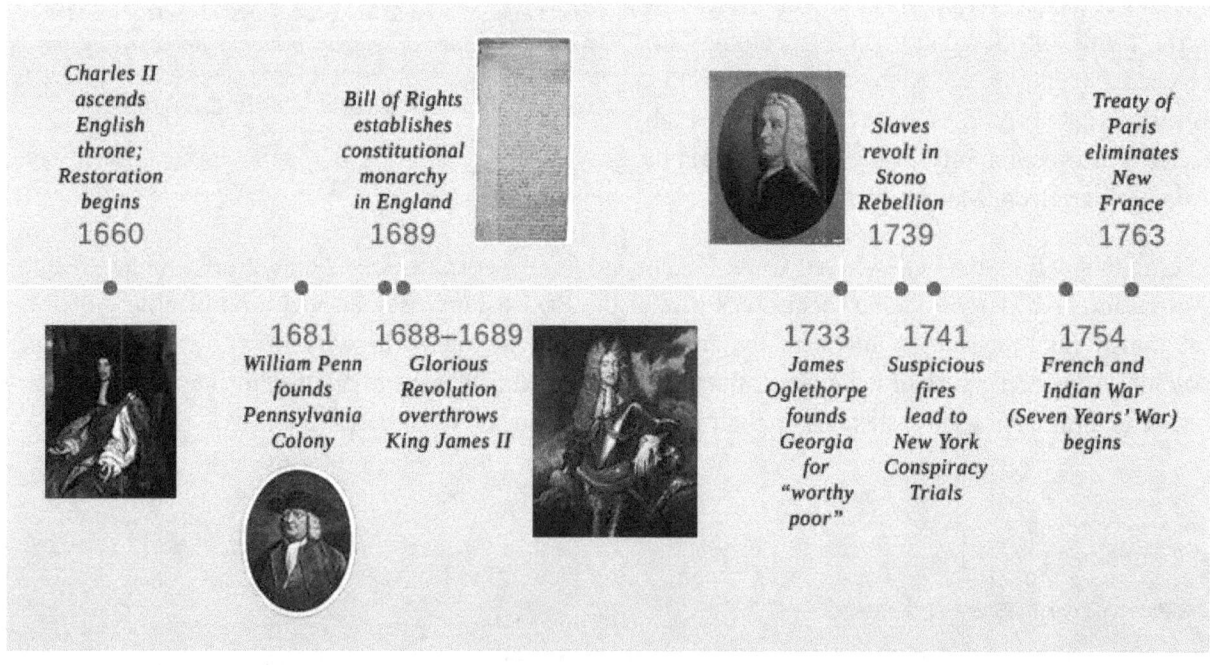

When Charles II ascended the throne in 1660, English subjects on both sides of the Atlantic celebrated the restoration of the English monarchy after a decade of living without a king as a result of the English Civil

Wars. Charles II lost little time in strengthening England's global power. From the 1660s to the 1680s, Charles II added more possessions to England's North American holdings by establishing the Restoration colonies of New York and New Jersey (taking these areas from the Dutch) as well as Pennsylvania and the Carolinas. In order to reap the greatest economic benefit from England's overseas possessions, Charles II enacted the mercantilist Navigation Acts, although many colonial merchants ignored them because enforcement remained lax.

CHARLES II

The chronicle of Charles II begins with his father, Charles I. Charles I ascended the English throne in 1625 and soon married a French Catholic princess, Henrietta Maria, who was not well liked by English Protestants because she openly practiced Catholicism during her husband's reign. The most outspoken Protestants, the Puritans, had a strong voice in Parliament in the 1620s, and they strongly opposed the king's marriage and his ties to Catholicism. When Parliament tried to contest his edicts, including the king's efforts to impose taxes without Parliament's consent, Charles I suspended Parliament in 1629 and ruled without one for the next eleven years.

The ensuing struggle between the king and Parliament led to the outbreak of war. The English Civil War lasted from 1642 to 1649 and pitted the king and his Royalist supporters against Oliver Cromwell and his Parliamentary forces. After years of fighting, the Parliamentary forces gained the upper hand, and in 1649, they charged Charles I with treason and beheaded him. The monarchy was dissolved, and England became a republic: a state without a king. Oliver Cromwell headed the new English Commonwealth, and the period known as the **English interregnum**, or the time between kings, began.

Though Cromwell enjoyed widespread popularity at first, over time he appeared to many in England to be taking on the powers of a military dictator. Dissatisfaction with Cromwell grew. When he died in 1658 and control passed to his son Richard, who lacked the political skills of his father, a majority of the English people feared an alternate hereditary monarchy in the making. They had had enough and asked Charles II to be king. In 1660, they welcomed the son of the executed king Charles I back to the throne to resume the English monarchy and bring the interregnum to an end. The return of Charles II is known as the Restoration.

The monarchy and Parliament fought for control of England during the seventeenth century. Though Oliver Cromwell (a), shown here in a 1656 portrait by Samuel Cooper, appeared to offer England a better mode of government, he assumed broad powers for himself and disregarded cherished English liberties established under Magna Carta in 1215. As a result, the English people welcomed Charles II (b) back to the throne in 1660. This portrait by John Michael Wright was painted ca. 1660–1665, soon after the new king gained the throne.

Charles II was committed to expanding England's overseas possessions. His policies in the 1660s through the 1680s established and supported the **Restoration colonies**: the Carolinas, New Jersey, New York, and Pennsylvania. All the Restoration colonies started as **proprietary colonies**, that is, the king gave each colony to a trusted individual, family, or group.

THE CAROLINAS

Charles II hoped to establish English control of the area between Virginia and Spanish Florida. To that end, he issued a royal charter in 1663 to eight trusted and loyal supporters, each of whom was to be a feudal-style proprietor of a region of the province of Carolina.

The port of colonial Charles Towne, depicted here on a 1733 map of North America, was the largest in the South and played a significant role in the Atlantic slave trade.

These proprietors did not relocate to the colonies, however. Instead, English plantation owners from the tiny Caribbean island of Barbados, already a well-established English sugar colony fueled by slave labor, migrated to the southern part of Carolina to settle there. In 1670, they established Charles Town (later Charleston), named in honor of Charles II, at the junction of the Ashley and Cooper Rivers. As the settlement around Charles Town grew, it began to produce livestock for export to the West Indies. In the northern part of Carolina, settlers turned sap from pine trees into turpentine used to waterproof wooden ships. Political disagreements between settlers in the northern and southern parts of Carolina escalated in the 1710s through the 1720s and led to the creation, in 1729, of two colonies, North and South Carolina. The southern part of Carolina had been producing rice and indigo (a plant that yields a dark blue dye used by English royalty) since the 1700s, and South Carolina continued to depend on these main crops. North Carolina continued to produce items for ships, especially turpentine and tar, and its population increased as Virginians moved there to expand their tobacco holdings. Tobacco was the primary export of both Virginia and North Carolina, which also traded in deerskins and slaves from Africa.

Slavery developed quickly in the Carolinas, largely because so many of the early migrants came from Barbados, where slavery was well established. By the end of the 1600s, a very wealthy class of rice planters who relied on slaves had attained dominance in the southern part of the Carolinas, especially around Charles Town. By 1715, South Carolina had a black majority because of the number of slaves in the colony. The legal basis for slavery was established in the early 1700s as the Carolinas began to pass slave laws based on the Barbados slave codes of the late 1600s. These laws reduced Africans to the status of property to be bought and sold as other commodities.

> Visit the Charleston Museum's interactive exhibit The Walled City to learn more about the history of Charleston.

As in other areas of English settlement, native peoples in the Carolinas suffered tremendously from the introduction of European diseases. Despite the effects of disease, Indians in the area endured and, following the pattern elsewhere in the colonies, grew dependent on European goods. Local Yamasee and Creek tribes built up a trade deficit with the English, trading deerskins and captive slaves for European guns. English settlers exacerbated tensions with local Indian tribes, especially the Yamasee, by expanding their rice and tobacco fields into Indian lands. Worse still, English traders took native women captive as payment for debts.

The outrages committed by traders, combined with the seemingly unstoppable expansion of English settlement onto native land, led to the outbreak of the Yamasee War (1715–1718), an effort by a coalition of local tribes to drive away the European invaders. This native effort to force the newcomers back across the Atlantic nearly succeeded in annihilating the Carolina colonies. Only when the Cherokee allied themselves with the English did the coalition's goal of eliminating the English from the region falter. The Yamasee War demonstrates the key role native peoples played in shaping the outcome of colonial struggles and, perhaps most important, the disunity that existed between different native groups.

NEW YORK AND NEW JERSEY

Charles II also set his sights on the Dutch colony of New Netherland. The English takeover of New Netherland originated in the imperial rivalry between the Dutch and the English. During the Anglo-Dutch wars of the 1650s and 1660s, the two powers attempted to gain commercial advantages in the Atlantic World. During the Second Anglo-Dutch War (1664–1667), English forces gained control of the Dutch fur trading colony of New Netherland, and in 1664, Charles II gave this colony (including present-day New Jersey) to his brother James, Duke of York (later James II). The colony and city were renamed New York in his honor. The Dutch in New York chafed under English rule. In 1673, during the Third Anglo-Dutch War (1672–1674), the Dutch recaptured the colony. However, at the end of the conflict, the English had regained control.

"View of New Amsterdam" (ca. 1665), a watercolor by Johannes Vingboons, was painted during the Anglo-Dutch wars of the 1660s and 1670s. New Amsterdam was officially reincorporated as New York City in 1664, but alternated under Dutch and English rule until 1674.

The Duke of York had no desire to govern locally or listen to the wishes of local colonists. It wasn't until 1683, therefore, almost 20 years after the English took control of the colony, that colonists were able to convene a local representative legislature. The assembly's 1683 Charter of Liberties and Privileges set out the traditional rights of Englishmen, like the right to trial by jury and the right to representative government.

The English continued the Dutch patroonship system, granting large estates to a favored few families. The largest of these estates, at 160,000 acres, was given to Robert Livingston in 1686. The Livingstons and the other manorial families who controlled the Hudson River Valley formed a formidable political and economic force. Eighteenth-century New York City, meanwhile, contained a variety of people and religions—as well as Dutch and English people, it held French Protestants (Huguenots), Jews, Puritans, Quakers, Anglicans, and a large population of slaves. As they did in other zones of colonization, native peoples played a key role in shaping the history of colonial New York. After decades of war in the 1600s, the powerful Five Nations of the Iroquois, composed of the Mohawk, Oneida, Onondaga, Cayuga, and Seneca, successfully pursued a policy of neutrality with both the English and, to the north, the French in Canada during the first half of the 1700s. This native policy meant that the Iroquois continued to live in their own villages under their own government while enjoying the benefits of trade with both the French and the English.

PENNSYLVANIA

The Restoration colonies also included Pennsylvania, which became the geographic center of British colonial America. Pennsylvania (which means "Penn's Woods" in Latin) was created in 1681, when Charles II bestowed the largest proprietary colony in the Americas on William Penn to settle the large debt he owed the Penn family. William Penn's father, Admiral William Penn, had served the English crown by helping take Jamaica from the Spanish in 1655. The king personally owed the Admiral money as well.

Like early settlers of the New England colonies, Pennsylvania's first colonists migrated mostly for religious reasons. William Penn himself was a Quaker, a member of a new Protestant denomination called the Society of Friends. George Fox had founded the Society of Friends in England in the late 1640s, having grown dissatisfied with Puritanism and the idea of predestination. Rather, Fox and his followers stressed that everyone had an "inner light" inside him or her, a spark of divinity. They gained the name Quakers because they were said to quake when the inner light moved them. Quakers rejected the idea of worldly rank, believing instead in a new and radical form of social equality. Their speech reflected this belief in that they addressed all others as equals, using "thee" and "thou" rather than terms like "your lordship" or "my lady" that were customary for privileged individuals of the hereditary elite.

Charles II granted William Penn the land that eventually became the Commonwealth of Pennsylvania in order to settle a debt the English crown owed to Penn's father.

The English crown persecuted Quakers in England, and colonial governments were equally harsh; Massachusetts even executed several early Quakers who had gone to proselytize there. To avoid such persecution, Quakers and their families at first created a community on the sugar island of Barbados. Soon after its founding, however, Pennsylvania became the destination of choice. Quakers flocked to Pennsylvania as well as New Jersey, where they could preach and practice their religion in peace. Unlike New England, whose official religion was Puritanism, Pennsylvania did not establish an official church. Indeed, the colony allowed a degree of religious tolerance found nowhere else in English America. To help encourage immigration to his colony, Penn promised fifty acres of land to people who agreed to come to Pennsylvania and completed their term of service. Not surprisingly, those seeking a better life came in large numbers, so much so that Pennsylvania relied on indentured servants more than any other colony.

One of the primary tenets of Quakerism is pacifism, leading William Penn to establish friendly relationships with local native peoples. He formed a covenant of friendship with the Lenni Lenape (Delaware) tribe, buying their land for a fair price instead of taking it by force. In 1701, he also signed a treaty with the Susquehannocks to avoid war. Unlike other colonies, Pennsylvania did not experience war on the frontier with native peoples during its early history.

As an important port city, Philadelphia grew rapidly. Quaker merchants there established contacts throughout the Atlantic world and participated in the thriving African slave trade. Some Quakers, who were deeply troubled by the contradiction between their belief in the "inner light" and the practice of slavery, rejected the practice and engaged in efforts to abolish it altogether. Philadelphia also acted as a magnet for immigrants, who came not only from England, but from all over Europe by the hundreds of thousands. The city, and indeed all of Pennsylvania, appeared to be the best country for poor men and women, many of whom arrived as servants and dreamed of owning land. A very few, like the fortunate Benjamin Franklin, a runaway from Puritan Boston, did extraordinarily well. Other immigrant groups in the colony, most notably Germans and Scotch-Irish (families from Scotland and England who had first lived in Ireland before moving to British America), greatly improved their lot in Pennsylvania. Of course, Africans imported into the colony to labor for white masters fared far worse.

John Wilson Offers Reward for Escaped Prisoners

The *American Weekly Mercury*, published by William Bradford, was Philadelphia's first newspaper. This advertisement from "John Wilson, *Goaler*" (jailer) offers a reward for anyone capturing several men who escaped from the jail.

> *BROKE out of the Common Goal of Philadelphia, the 15th of this Instant February, 1721, the following Persons:*
>
> John Palmer, also Plumly, *alias* Paine, *Servant to Joseph Jones, run away and was lately taken up at New-York. He is fully described in the* American Mercury, *Novem. 23, 1721. He has a Cinnamon coloured Coat on, a middle sized fresh coloured Man. His Master will give a Pistole Reward to any who Shall Secure him, besides what is here offered.*
>
> Daniel Oughtopay, *A Dutchman, aged about 24 Years, Servant to Dr. Johnston in Amboy. He is a thin Spare man, grey Drugget Waistcoat and Breeches and a light-coloured Coat on.*
>
> Ebenezor Mallary, *a New-England, aged about 24 Years, is a middle-sized thin Man, having on a Snuff colour'd Coat, and ordinary Ticking Waistcoat and Breeches. He has dark brown strait Hair.*
>
> Matthew Dulany, *an Irish Man, down-look'd Swarthy Complexion, and has on an Olive-coloured Cloth Coat and Waistcoat with Cloth Buttons.*
>
> John Flemming, *an Irish Lad, aged about 18, belonging to Mr. Miranda, Merchant in this City. He has no Coat, a grey Drugget Waistcoat, and a narrow brim'd Hat on.*
>
> John Corbet, *a Shropshire Man, a Runaway Servant from Alexander Faulkner of Maryland, broke out on the 12th Instant. He has got a double-breasted Sailor's Jacket on lined with red Bays, pretends to be a Sailor, and once taught School at Josephs Collings's in the Jerseys.*
>
> *Whoever takes up and secures all, or any One of these Felons, shall have a Pistole Reward for each of them and reasonable Charges, paid them by* John Wilson, *Goaler*

—Advertisement from the *American Weekly Mercury*, 1722

What do the descriptions of the men tell you about life in colonial Philadelphia?

> Browse a number of issues of the *American Weekly Mercury* that were digitized by New Jersey's Stockton University. Read through several to get a remarkable flavor of life in early eighteenth-century Philadelphia.

THE NAVIGATION ACTS

Creating wealth for the Empire remained a primary goal, and in the second half of the seventeenth century, especially during the Restoration, England attempted to gain better control of trade with the American colonies. The mercantilist policies by which it tried to achieve this control are known as the **Navigation Acts**.

The 1651 Navigation Ordnance, a product of Cromwell's England, required that only English ships carry goods between England and the colonies, and that the captain and three-fourths of the crew had to be English. The ordnance further listed "enumerated articles" that could be transported only to England or to English colonies, including the most lucrative commodities like sugar and tobacco as well as indigo, rice, molasses, and naval stores such as turpentine. All were valuable goods not produced in England or in demand by the British navy. After ascending the throne, Charles II approved the 1660 Navigation Act, which restated the 1651 act to ensure a monopoly on imports from the colonies.

Other Navigation Acts included the 1663 Staple Act and the 1673 Plantation Duties Act. The Staple Act barred colonists from importing goods that had not been made in England, creating a profitable monopoly for English exporters and manufacturers. The Plantation Duties Act taxed enumerated articles exported from one colony to another, a measure aimed principally at New Englanders, who transported great quantities of molasses from the West Indies, including smuggled molasses from French-held islands, to make into rum.

In 1675, Charles II organized the Lords of Trade and Plantation, commonly known as the Lords of Trade, an administrative body intended to create stronger ties between the colonial governments and the crown. However, the 1696 Navigation Act created the Board of Trade, replacing the Lords of Trade. This act, meant to strengthen enforcement of customs laws, also established vice-admiralty courts where the crown could prosecute customs violators without a jury. Under this act, customs officials were empowered with warrants known as "writs of assistance" to board and search vessels suspected of containing smuggled goods.

Despite the Navigation Acts, however, Great Britain exercised lax control over the English colonies during most of the eighteenth century because of the policies of Prime Minister Robert Walpole. During his long term (1721–1742), Walpole governed according to his belief that commerce flourished best when it was not encumbered with restrictions. Historians have described this lack of strict enforcement of the Navigation Acts as **salutary neglect**. In addition, nothing prevented colonists from building their own fleet of ships to engage in trade. New England especially benefited from both salutary neglect and a vibrant maritime culture made possible by the scores of trading vessels built in the northern colonies. The case of the 1733 Molasses Act illustrates the weaknesses of British mercantilist policy. The 1733 act placed a sixpence-per-gallon duty on raw sugar, rum, and molasses from Britain's competitors, the French and the Dutch, in order to give an advantage to British West Indian producers. Because the British did not enforce the 1733 law, however, New England mariners routinely smuggled these items from the French and Dutch West Indies more cheaply than they could buy them on English islands.

Section Summary

After the English Civil War and interregnum, England began to fashion a stronger and larger empire in North America. In addition to wresting control of New York and New Jersey from the Dutch, Charles II established the Carolinas and Pennsylvania as proprietary colonies. Each of these colonies added immensely to the Empire, supplying goods not produced in England, such as rice and indigo. The Restoration colonies also contributed to the rise in population in English America as many thousands of Europeans made their way to the colonies. Their numbers were further augmented by the forced migration of African slaves. Starting in 1651, England pursued mercantilist policies through a series of Navigation Acts designed to make the most of England's overseas possessions. Nonetheless, without proper enforcement of Parliament's acts and with nothing to prevent colonial traders from commanding their own fleets of ships, the Navigation Acts did not control trade as intended.

https://www.openassessments.org/assessments/946

Review Question

1. What sorts of labor systems were used in the Restoration colonies?

Answer to Review Question

1. Since the proprietors of the Carolina colonies were absent, English planters from Barbados moved in and gained political power, establishing slave labor as the predominant form of labor. In Pennsylvania, where prospective servants were offered a bounty of fifty acres of land for emigrating and finishing their term of labor, indentured servitude abounded.

Glossary

English interregnum the period from 1649 to 1660 when England had no king

Navigation Acts a series of English mercantilist laws enacted between 1651 and 1696 in order to control trade with the colonies

proprietary colonies colonies granted by the king to a trusted individual, family, or group

Restoration colonies the colonies King Charles II established or supported during the Restoration (the Carolinas, New York, New Jersey, and Pennsylvania)

salutary neglect the laxness with which the English crown enforced the Navigation Acts in the eighteenth century

Attributions

CC licensed content, Shared previously

- US History. **Authored by**: P. Scott Corbett, Volker Janssen, John M. Lund, Todd Pfannestiel, Paul Vickery, and Sylvie Waskiewicz. **Provided by**: OpenStax College. **Located at**: http://openstaxcollege.org/textbooks/us-history. **License**: *CC BY: Attribution*. **License Terms**: Download for free at http://cnx.org/content/col11740/latest/

The Glorious Revolution and the English Empire

> ### Learning Objectives
>
> By the end of this section, you will be able to:
>
> - Identify the causes of the Glorious Revolution
> - Explain the outcomes of the Glorious Revolution

During the brief rule of King James II, many in England feared the imposition of a Catholic absolute monarchy by the man who modeled his rule on that of his French Catholic cousin, Louis XIV. Opposition to James II, spearheaded by the English Whig party, overthrew the king in the Glorious Revolution of 1688–1689. This paved the way for the Protestant reign of William of Orange and his wife Mary (James's Protestant daughter).

JAMES II AND THE GLORIOUS REVOLUTION

James II (shown here in a painting ca. 1690) worked to centralize the English government. The Catholic king of France, Louis XIV, provided a template for James's policies.

King James II, the second son of Charles I, ascended the English throne in 1685 on the death of his brother, Charles II. James then worked to model his rule on the reign of the French Catholic King Louis XIV, his cousin. This meant centralizing English political strength around the throne, giving the monarchy absolute power. Also like Louis XIV, James II practiced a strict and intolerant form of Roman Catholicism after he converted from Protestantism in the late 1660s. He had a Catholic wife, and when they had a son, the potential for a Catholic heir to the English throne became a threat to English Protestants. James also worked to modernize the English army and navy. The fact that the king kept a standing army in times of peace greatly alarmed the English, who believed that such a force would be used to crush their liberty. As James's strength grew, his opponents feared their king would turn England into a Catholic monarchy with absolute power over her people.

In 1686, James II applied his concept of a centralized state to the colonies by creating an enormous colony called the **Dominion of New England**. The Dominion included all the New England colonies (Massachusetts, New Hampshire, Plymouth, Connecticut, New Haven, and Rhode Island) and in 1688 was enlarged by the addition of New York and New Jersey. James placed in charge Sir Edmund Andros, a former colonial governor of New York. Loyal to James II and his family, Andros had little sympathy for New Englanders. His regime caused great uneasiness among New England Puritans when it called into question the many land titles that did not acknowledge the king and imposed fees for their reconfirmation. Andros also committed himself to enforcing the Navigation Acts, a move that threatened to disrupt the region's trade, which was based largely on smuggling.

In England, opponents of James II's efforts to create a centralized Catholic state were known as Whigs. The Whigs worked to depose James, and in late 1688 they succeeded, an event they celebrated as the **Glorious Revolution** while James fled to the court of Louis XIV in France. William III (William of Orange) and his wife Mary II ascended the throne in 1689.

This broadside, signed by several citizens, demands the surrender of Sir Edmund (spelled here "Edmond") Andros, James II's hand-picked leader of the Dominion of New England.

The Glorious Revolution spilled over into the colonies. In 1689, Bostonians overthrew the government of the Dominion of New England and jailed Sir Edmund Andros as well as other leaders of the regime. The removal of Andros from power illustrates New England's animosity toward the English overlord who had, during his tenure, established Church of England worship in Puritan Boston and vigorously enforced the Navigation Acts, to the chagrin of those in port towns. In New York, the same year that Andros fell from power, Jacob Leisler led a group of Protestant New Yorkers against the dominion government. Acting on his own authority, Leisler assumed the role of King William's governor and organized intercolonial military action independent of British authority. Leisler's actions usurped the crown's prerogative and, as a result, he was tried for treason and executed. In 1691, England restored control over the Province of New York.

The Glorious Revolution provided a shared experience for those who lived through the tumult of 1688 and 1689. Subsequent generations kept the memory of the Glorious Revolution alive as a heroic defense of English liberty against a would-be tyrant.

ENGLISH LIBERTY

The Glorious Revolution led to the establishment of an English nation that limited the power of the king and provided protections for English subjects. In October 1689, the same year that William and Mary took the throne, the 1689 Bill of Rights established a constitutional monarchy. It stipulated Parliament's independence from the monarchy and protected certain of Parliament's rights, such as the right to freedom of speech, the right to regular elections, and the right to petition the king. The 1689 Bill of Rights also guaranteed certain rights to all English subjects, including trial by jury and habeas corpus (the requirement that authorities bring an imprisoned person before a court to demonstrate the cause of the imprisonment).

John Locke (1632–1704), a doctor and educator who had lived in exile in Holland during the reign of James II and returned to England after the Glorious Revolution, published his *Two Treatises of Government* in 1690. In it, he argued that government was a form of contract between the leaders and the people, and that representative government existed to protect "life, liberty and property." Locke rejected the divine right of kings and instead advocated for the central role of Parliament with a limited monarchy. Locke's political philosophy had an enormous impact on future generations of colonists and established the paramount importance of representation in government.

> Visit the Digital Locke Project to read more of John Locke's writings. This digital collection contains over thirty of his philosophical texts.

The Glorious Revolution also led to the English Toleration Act of 1689, a law passed by Parliament that allowed for greater religious diversity in the Empire. This act granted religious tolerance to **nonconformist** Trinitarian Protestants (those who believed in the Holy Trinity of God the Father, Son, and Holy Ghost), such as Baptists (those who advocated adult baptism) and Congregationalists (those who followed the Puritans' lead in creating independent churches). While the Church of England remained the official state religious establishment, the Toleration Act gave much greater religious freedom to nonconformists. However, this tolerance did not extend to Catholics, who were routinely excluded from political power. The 1689 Toleration Act extended to the British colonies, where several colonies—Pennsylvania, Rhode Island, Delaware, and New Jersey—refused to allow the creation of an established colonial church, a major step toward greater religious diversity.

Section Summary

The threat of a Catholic absolute monarchy prompted not only the overthrow of James II but also the adoption of laws and policies that changed English government. The Glorious Revolution restored a Protestant monarchy and at the same time limited its power by means of the 1689 Bill of Rights. Those who lived through the events preserved the memory of the Glorious Revolution and the defense of liberty that it represented. Meanwhile, thinkers such as John Locke provided new models and inspirations for the evolving concept of government.

- https://www.openassessments.org/assessments/947

Review Question

1. What was the outcome of the Glorious Revolution?

> ### Answer to Review Question
>
> 1. James II was overthrown, and William III and Mary II took his place. The 1689 Bill of Rights limited the future power of the monarchy and outlined the rights of Parliament and Englishmen. In Massachusetts, Bostonians overthrew royal governor Edmund Andros.

> ### Glossary
>
> **Dominion of New England** James II's consolidated New England colony, made up of all the colonies from New Haven to Massachusetts and later New York and New Jersey
>
> **Glorious Revolution** the overthrow of James II in 1688
>
> **nonconformists** Protestants who did not conform to the doctrines or practices of the Church of England

Attributions

CC licensed content, Shared previously

- US History. **Authored by**: P. Scott Corbett, Volker Janssen, John M. Lund, Todd Pfannestiel, Paul Vickery, and Sylvie Waskiewicz. **Provided by**: OpenStax College. **Located at**: http://openstaxcollege.org/textbooks/us-history. **License**: *CC BY: Attribution*. **License Terms**: Download for free at http://cnx.org/content/col11740/latest/

An Empire of Slavery and the Consumer Revolution

Learning Objectives

By the end of this section, you will be able to:

- Analyze the role slavery played in the history and economy of the British Empire
- Explain the effects of the 1739 Stono Rebellion and the 1741 New York Conspiracy Trials
- Describe the consumer revolution and its effect on the life of the colonial gentry and other settlers

Slavery formed a cornerstone of the British Empire in the eighteenth century. Every colony had slaves, from the southern rice plantations in Charles Town, South Carolina, to the northern wharves of Boston. Slavery was more than a labor system; it also influenced every aspect of colonial thought and culture. The uneven relationship it engendered gave white colonists an exaggerated sense of their own status. English liberty gained greater meaning and coherence for whites when they contrasted their status to that of the unfree class of black slaves in British America. African slavery provided whites in the colonies with a shared racial bond and identity.

SLAVERY AND THE STONO REBELLION

The transport of slaves to the American colonies accelerated in the second half of the seventeenth century. In 1660, Charles II created the Royal African Company to trade in slaves and African goods. His brother, James II, led the company before ascending the throne. Under both these kings, the Royal African Company enjoyed a monopoly to transport slaves to the English colonies. Between 1672 and 1713, the company bought 125,000 captives on the African coast, losing 20 percent of them to death on the Middle Passage, the journey from the African coast to the Americas.

The Royal African Company's monopoly ended in 1689 as a result of the Glorious Revolution. After that date, many more English merchants engaged in the slave trade, greatly increasing the number of slaves being transported. Africans who survived the brutal Middle Passage usually arrived in the West Indies, often in Barbados. From there, they were transported to the mainland English colonies on company ships. While merchants in London, Bristol, and Liverpool lined their pockets, Africans trafficked by the company endured a nightmare of misery, privation, and dislocation.

The 1686 English guinea shows the logo of the Royal African Company, an elephant and castle, beneath a bust of King James II. The coins were commonly called guineas because most British gold came from Guinea in West Africa.

Slaves strove to adapt to their new lives by forming new communities among themselves, often adhering to traditional African customs and healing techniques. Indeed, the development of families and communities formed the most important response to the trauma of being enslaved. Other slaves dealt with the trauma of their situation by actively resisting their condition, whether by defying their masters or running away. Runaway slaves formed what were called "maroon" communities, groups that successfully resisted recapture and formed their own autonomous groups. The most prominent of these communities lived in the interior of Jamaica, controlling the area and keeping the British away.

Slaves everywhere resisted their exploitation and attempted to gain freedom. They fully understood that rebellions would bring about massive retaliation from whites and therefore had little chance of success. Even so, rebellions occurred frequently. One notable uprising that became known as the Stono Rebellion took place in South Carolina in September 1739. A literate slave named Jemmy led a large group of slaves in an armed insurrection against white colonists, killing several before militia stopped them. The militia suppressed the rebellion after a battle in which both slaves and militiamen were killed, and the remaining slaves were executed or sold to the West Indies.

Jemmy is believed to have been taken from the Kingdom of Kongo, an area where the Portuguese had introduced Catholicism. Other slaves in South Carolina may have had a similar background: Africa-born and familiar with whites. If so, this common background may have made it easier for Jemmy to communicate with the other slaves, enabling them to work together to resist their enslavement even though slaveholders labored to keep slaves from forging such communities.

In the wake of the Stono Rebellion, South Carolina passed a new slave code in 1740 called An Act for the Better Ordering and Governing of Negroes and Other Slaves in the Province, also known as the Negro Act of 1740. This law imposed new limits on slaves' behavior, prohibiting slaves from assembling, growing their own food, learning to write, and traveling freely.

THE NEW YORK CONSPIRACY TRIALS OF 1741

Eighteenth-century New York City contained many different ethnic groups, and conflicts among them created strain. In addition, one in five New Yorkers was a slave, and tensions ran high between slaves and the free population, especially in the aftermath of the Stono Rebellion. These tensions burst forth in 1741.

That year, thirteen fires broke out in the city, one of which reduced the colony's Fort George to ashes. Ever fearful of an uprising among enslaved New Yorkers, the city's whites spread rumors that the fires were part of a massive slave revolt in which slaves would murder whites, burn the city, and take over the colony. The Stono Rebellion was only a few years in the past, and throughout British America, fears of similar incidents were still fresh. Searching for solutions, and convinced slaves were the principal danger, nervous British authorities interrogated almost two hundred slaves and accused them of conspiracy. Rumors that Roman Catholics had joined the suspected conspiracy and planned to murder Protestant inhabitants of the city only added to the general hysteria. Very quickly, two hundred people were arrested, including a large number of the city's slave population.

In the wake of a series of fires throughout New York City, rumors of a slave revolt led authorities to convict and execute thirty people, including thirteen black men who were publicly burned at the stake.

After a quick series of trials at City Hall, known as the New York Conspiracy Trials of 1741, the government executed seventeen New Yorkers. Thirteen black men were publicly burned at the stake, while the others (including four whites) were hanged. Seventy slaves were sold to the West Indies. Little evidence exists to prove that an elaborate conspiracy, like the one white New Yorkers imagined, actually existed.

The events of 1741 in New York City illustrate the racial divide in British America, where panic among whites spurred great violence against and repression of the feared slave population. In the end, the Conspiracy Trials furthered white dominance and power over enslaved New Yorkers.

> View the map of New York in the 1740s at the New York Public Library's digital gallery, which allows you to zoom in and see specific events. Look closely at numbers 55 and 56 just north of the city limits to see illustrations depicting the executions.

COLONIAL GENTRY AND THE CONSUMER REVOLUTION

British Americans' reliance on indentured servitude and slavery to meet the demand for colonial labor helped give rise to a wealthy colonial class—the gentry—in the Chesapeake tobacco colonies and elsewhere. To be "genteel," that is, a member of the gentry, meant to be refined, free of all rudeness. The British American gentry modeled themselves on the English aristocracy, who embodied the ideal of refinement and gentility. They built elaborate mansions to advertise their status and power. William Byrd II of Westover, Virginia, exemplifies the colonial gentry; a wealthy planter and slaveholder, he is known for founding Richmond and for his diaries documenting the life of a gentleman planter.

William Byrd's Secret Diary

The diary of William Byrd, a Virginia planter, provides a unique way to better understand colonial life on a plantation. What does it show about daily life for a gentleman planter? What does it show about slavery?

This painting by Hans Hysing, ca. 1724, depicts William Byrd II. Byrd was a wealthy gentleman planter in Virginia and a member of the colonial gentry.

> August 27, 1709
>
> I rose at 5 o'clock and read two chapters in Hebrew and some Greek in Josephus. I said my prayers and ate milk for breakfast. I danced my dance. I had like to have whipped my maid Anaka for her laziness but I forgave her. I read a little geometry. I denied my man G-r-l to go to a horse race because there was nothing but swearing and drinking there. I ate roast mutton for dinner. In the afternoon I played at piquet with my own wife and made her out of humor by cheating her. I read some Greek in Homer. Then I walked about the plantation. I lent John H-ch £7 [7 English pounds] in his distress. I said my prayers and had good health, good thoughts, and good humor, thanks be to God Almighty.
>
> September 6, 1709About one o'clock this morning my wife was happily delivered of a son, thanks be to God Almighty. I was awake in a blink and rose and my cousin Harrison met me on the stairs and told me it was a boy. We drank some French wine and went to bed again and rose at 7 o'clock. I read a chapter in Hebrew and then drank chocolate with the women for breakfast. I returned God humble thanks for so great a blessing and recommended my young son to His divine protection. . . .
>
> September 15, 1710I rose at 5 o'clock and read two chapters in Hebrew and some Greek in Thucydides. I said my prayers and ate milk and pears for breakfast. About 7 o'clock the negro boy [*or* Betty] that ran away was brought home. My wife against my will caused little Jenny to be burned with a hot iron, for which I quarreled with her. . . .

This photograph shows the view down the stairway from the third floor of Westover Plantation, home of William Byrd II. What does this image suggest about the lifestyle of the inhabitants—masters and servants—of this house?

One of the ways in which the gentry set themselves apart from others was through their purchase, consumption, and display of goods. An increased supply of consumer goods from England that became available in the eighteenth century led to a phenomenon called the consumer revolution. These products linked the colonies to Great Britain in real and tangible ways. Indeed, along with the colonial gentry, ordinary settlers in the colonies also participated in the frenzy of consumer spending on goods from Great Britain. Tea, for example, came to be regarded as the drink of the Empire, with or without fashionable tea sets.

The consumer revolution also made printed materials more widely available. Before 1680, for instance, no newspapers had been printed in colonial America. In the eighteenth century, however, a flood of journals, books, pamphlets, and other publications became available to readers on both sides of the Atlantic. This shared trove of printed matter linked members of the Empire by creating a community of shared tastes and ideas.

Cato's Letters, by Englishmen John Trenchard and Thomas Gordon, was one popular series of 144 pamphlets. These Whig circulars were published between 1720 and 1723 and emphasized the glory of England, especially its commitment to liberty. However, the pamphlets cautioned readers to be ever vigilant and on the lookout for attacks upon that liberty. Indeed, *Cato's Letters* suggested that there were constant efforts to undermine and destroy it.

Another very popular publication was the English gentlemen's magazine the *Spectator*, published between 1711 and 1714. In each issue, "Mr. Spectator" observed and commented on the world around him. What made the *Spectator* so wildly popular was its style; the essays were meant to persuade, and to cultivate among readers a refined set of behaviors, rejecting deceit and intolerance and focusing instead on the polishing of genteel taste and manners.

Novels, a new type of literature, made their first appearance in the eighteenth century and proved very popular in the British Atlantic. Daniel Defoe's *Robinson Crusoe* and Samuel Richardson's *Pamela: Or, Virtue*

Rewarded found large and receptive audiences. Reading also allowed female readers the opportunity to interpret what they read without depending on a male authority to tell them what to think. Few women beyond the colonial gentry, however, had access to novels.

Section Summary

The seventeenth and eighteenth centuries saw the expansion of slavery in the American colonies from South Carolina to Boston. The institution of slavery created a false sense of superiority in whites, while simultaneously fueling fears of slave revolt. White response to such revolts, or even the threat of them, led to gross overreactions and further constraints on slaves' activities. The development of the Atlantic economy also allowed colonists access to more British goods than ever before. The buying habits of both commoners and the rising colonial gentry fueled the consumer revolution, creating even stronger ties with Great Britain by means of a shared community of taste and ideas.

https://www.openassessments.org/assessments/948

Attributions

CC licensed content, Shared previously

- US History. **Authored by**: P. Scott Corbett, Volker Janssen, John M. Lund, Todd Pfannestiel, Paul Vickery, and Sylvie Waskiewicz. **Provided by**: OpenStax College. **Located at**: http://openstaxcollege.org/textbooks/us-history. **License**: *CC BY: Attribution*. **License Terms**: Download for free at http://cnx.org/content/col11740/latest/

Great Awakening and Enlightenment

> **Learning Objectives**
>
> By the end of this section, you will be able to:
>
> - Explain the significance of the Great Awakening
> - Describe the genesis, central ideas, and effects of the Enlightenment in British North America

Two major cultural movements further strengthened Anglo-American colonists' connection to Great Britain: the Great Awakening and the Enlightenment. Both movements began in Europe, but they advocated very different ideas: the Great Awakening promoted a fervent, emotional religiosity, while the Enlightenment encouraged the pursuit of reason in all things. On both sides of the Atlantic, British subjects grappled with these new ideas.

THE FIRST GREAT AWAKENING

During the eighteenth century, the British Atlantic experienced an outburst of Protestant revivalism known as the **First Great Awakening**. (A Second Great Awakening would take place in the 1800s.) During the First Great Awakening, evangelists came from the ranks of several Protestant denominations: Congregationalists, Anglicans (members of the Church of England), and Presbyterians. They rejected what appeared to be sterile, formal modes of worship in favor of a vigorous emotional religiosity. Whereas Martin Luther and John Calvin had preached a doctrine of predestination and close reading of scripture, new evangelical ministers spread a message of personal and experiential faith that rose above mere book learning. Individuals could bring about their own salvation by accepting Christ, an especially welcome message for those who had felt excluded by traditional Protestantism: women, the young, and people at the lower end of the social spectrum.

The Great Awakening caused a split between those who followed the evangelical message (the "New Lights") and those who rejected it (the "Old Lights"). The elite ministers in British America were firmly Old Lights, and they censured the new revivalism as chaos. Indeed, the revivals did sometimes lead to excess. In one notorious incident in 1743, an influential New Light minister named James Davenport urged his listeners to burn books. The next day, he told them to burn their clothes as a sign of their casting off the sinful trappings of the world. He then took off his own pants and threw them into the fire, but a woman saved them and tossed them back to Davenport, telling him he had gone too far.

This image shows the frontispiece of Sinners in the Hands of an Angry God, A Sermon Preached at Enfield, July 8, 1741 by Jonathan Edwards. Edwards was an evangelical preacher who led a Protestant revival in New England. This was his most famous sermon, the text of which was reprinted often and distributed widely.

Another outburst of Protestant revivalism began in New Jersey, led by a minister of the Dutch Reformed Church named Theodorus Frelinghuysen. Frelinghuysen's example inspired other ministers, including Gilbert Tennent, a Presbyterian. Tennant helped to spark a Presbyterian revival in the Middle Colonies (Pennsylvania, New York, and New Jersey), in part by founding a seminary to train other evangelical clergyman. New Lights also founded colleges in Rhode Island and New Hampshire that would later become Brown University and Dartmouth College.

In Northampton, Massachusetts, Jonathan Edwards led still another explosion of evangelical fervor. Edwards's best-known sermon, "Sinners in the Hands of an Angry God," used powerful word imagery to describe the terrors of hell and the possibilities of avoiding damnation by personal conversion. One passage reads: "The wrath of God burns against them [sinners], their damnation don't slumber, the pit is prepared, the fire is made ready, the furnace is now hot, ready to receive them, the flames do now rage and glow. The glittering sword is whet, and held over them, and the pit hath opened her mouth under them." Edwards's revival spread along the Connecticut River Valley, and news of the event spread rapidly through the frequent reprinting of his famous sermon.

The foremost evangelical of the Great Awakening was an Anglican minister named George Whitefield. Like many evangelical ministers, Whitefield was itinerant, traveling the countryside instead of having his own church and congregation. Between 1739 and 1740, he electrified colonial listeners with his brilliant oratory.

Two Opposing Views of George Whitefield

Not everyone embraced George Whitefield and other New Lights. Many established Old Lights decried the way the new evangelical religions appealed to people's passions, rather than to traditional religious values. The two illustrations below present two very different visions of George Whitefield.

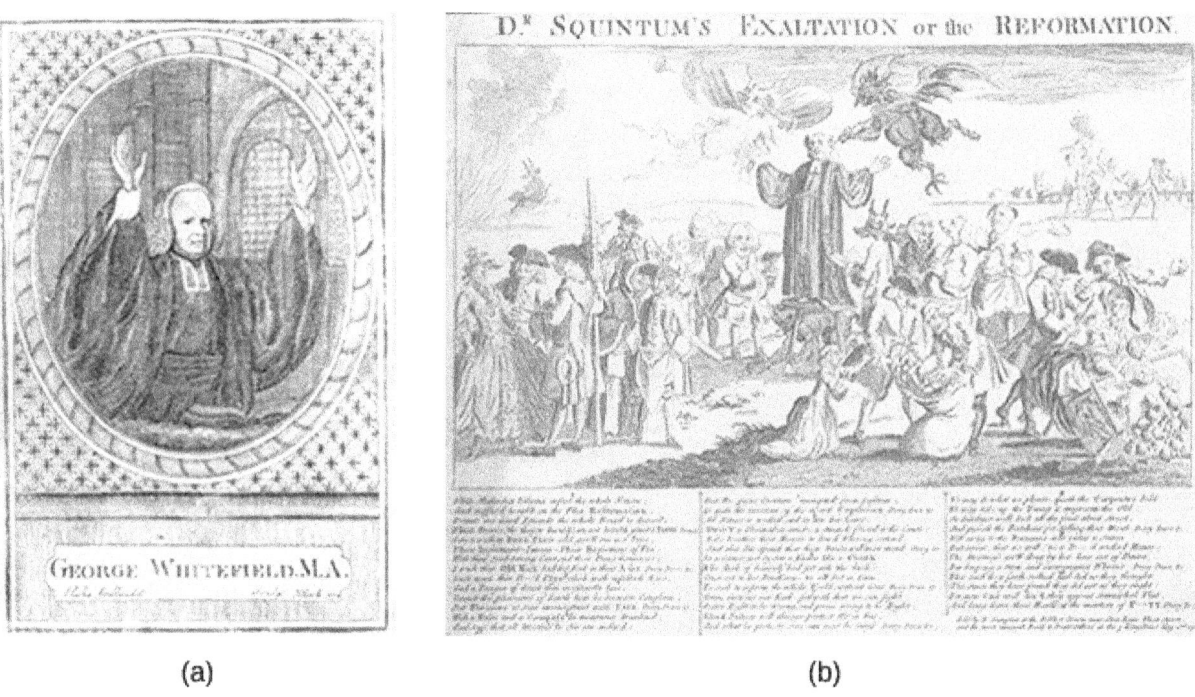

In the 1774 portrait of George Whitefield by engraver Elisha Gallaudet (a), Whitefield appears with a gentle expression on his face. Although his hands are raised in exultation or entreaty, he does not look particularly roused or rousing. In the 1763 British political cartoon to the right, "Dr. Squintum's Exaltation or the Reformation" (b), Whitefield's hands are raised in a similar position, but there the similarities end.

Compare the two images above. On the left is an illustration for Whitefield's memoirs, while on the right is a cartoon satirizing the circus-like atmosphere that his preaching seemed to attract (Dr. Squintum was a nickname for Whitefield, who was cross-eyed). How do these two artists portray the same man? What emotions are the illustration for his memoirs intended to evoke? What details can you find in the cartoon that indicate the artist's distaste for the preacher?

The Great Awakening saw the rise of several Protestant denominations, including Methodists, Presbyterians, and Baptists (who emphasized adult baptism of converted Christians rather than infant baptism). These new churches gained converts and competed with older Protestant groups like Anglicans (members of the

Church of England), Congregationalists (the heirs of Puritanism in America), and Quakers. The influence of these older Protestant groups, such as the New England Congregationalists, declined because of the Great Awakening. Nonetheless, the Great Awakening touched the lives of thousands on both sides of the Atlantic and provided a shared experience in the eighteenth-century British Empire.

THE ENLIGHTENMENT

The **Enlightenment**, or the Age of Reason, was an intellectual and cultural movement in the eighteenth century that emphasized reason over superstition and science over blind faith. Using the power of the press, Enlightenment thinkers like John Locke, Isaac Newton, and Voltaire questioned accepted knowledge and spread new ideas about openness, investigation, and religious tolerance throughout Europe and the Americas. Many consider the Enlightenment a major turning point in Western civilization, an age of light replacing an age of darkness.

Several ideas dominated Enlightenment thought, including rationalism, empiricism, progressivism, and cosmopolitanism. Rationalism is the idea that humans are capable of using their faculty of reason to gain knowledge. This was a sharp turn away from the prevailing idea that people needed to rely on scripture or church authorities for knowledge. Empiricism promotes the idea that knowledge comes from experience and observation of the world. Progressivism is the belief that through their powers of reason and observation, humans could make unlimited, linear progress over time; this belief was especially important as a response to the carnage and upheaval of the English Civil Wars in the seventeenth century. Finally, cosmopolitanism reflected Enlightenment thinkers' view of themselves as citizens of the world and actively engaged in it, as opposed to being provincial and close-minded. In all, Enlightenment thinkers endeavored to be ruled by reason, not prejudice.

In this 1748 portrait by Robert Feke, a forty-year-old Franklin wears a stylish British wig, as befitted a proud and loyal member of the British Empire.

The **Freemasons** were a fraternal society that advocated Enlightenment principles of inquiry and tolerance. Freemasonry originated in London coffeehouses in the early eighteenth century, and Masonic lodges (local units) soon spread throughout Europe and the British colonies. One prominent Freemason, Benjamin Franklin, stands as the embodiment of the Enlightenment in British America. Born in Boston in 1706 to a large Puritan family, Franklin loved to read, although he found little beyond religious publications in his father's house. In 1718 he was apprenticed to his brother to work in a print shop, where he learned how to be a good writer by copying the style he found in the *Spectator*, which his brother printed. At the age of seventeen, the independent-minded Franklin ran away, eventually ending up in Quaker Philadelphia. There he began publishing the *Pennsylvania Gazette* in the late 1720s, and in 1732 he started his annual publication *Poor Richard: An Almanack*, in which he gave readers much practical advice, such as "Early to bed, early to rise, makes a man healthy, wealthy, and wise."

Franklin subscribed to **deism**, an Enlightenment-era belief in a God who created, but has no continuing involvement in, the world and the events within it. Deists also advanced the belief that personal morality—an individual's moral compass, leading to good works and actions—is more important than strict church doctrines. Franklin's deism guided his many philanthropic projects. In 1731, he established a reading library that became the Library Company of Philadelphia. In 1743, he founded the American Philosophical Society to encourage the spirit of inquiry. In 1749, he provided the foundation for the University of Pennsylvania, and in 1751, he helped found Pennsylvania Hospital.

His career as a printer made Franklin wealthy and well-respected. When he retired in 1748, he devoted himself to politics and scientific experiments. His most famous work, on electricity, exemplified Enlightenment principles. Franklin observed that lightning strikes tended to hit metal objects and reasoned that he could therefore direct lightning through the placement of metal objects during an electrical storm. He used this knowledge to advocate the use of lightning rods: metal poles connected to wires directing lightning's electrical charge into the ground and saving wooden homes in cities like Philadelphia from catastrophic fires. He published his findings in 1751, in *Experiments and Observations on Electricity*.

Franklin also wrote of his "rags to riches" tale, his *Memoir*, in the 1770s and 1780s. This story laid the foundation for the American Dream of upward social mobility.

> Visit the Worldly Ways section of PBS's Benjamin Franklin site to see an interactive map showing Franklin's overseas travels and his influence around the world. His diplomatic, political, scientific, and business achievements had great effects in many countries.

THE FOUNDING OF GEORGIA

The reach of Enlightenment thought was both broad and deep. In the 1730s, it even prompted the founding of a new colony. Having witnessed the terrible conditions of debtors' prison, as well as the results of releasing penniless debtors onto the streets of London, James Oglethorpe, a member of Parliament and advocate of social reform, petitioned King George II for a charter to start a new colony. George II, understanding the strategic advantage of a British colony standing as a buffer between South Carolina and Spanish Florida, granted the charter to Oglethorpe and twenty like-minded proprietors in 1732. Oglethorpe led the settlement of the colony, which was called Georgia in honor of the king. In 1733, he and 113 immigrants arrived on the ship *Anne*. Over the next decade, Parliament funded the migration of twenty-five hundred settlers, making Georgia the only government-funded colonial project.

Oglethorpe's vision for Georgia followed the ideals of the **Age of Reason**, seeing it as a place for England's "worthy poor" to start anew. To encourage industry, he gave each male immigrant fifty acres of land, tools, and a year's worth of supplies. In Savannah, the Oglethorpe Plan provided for a utopia: "an agrarian model of sustenance while sustaining egalitarian values holding all men as equal."

Oglethorpe's vision called for alcohol and slavery to be banned. However, colonists who relocated from other colonies, especially South Carolina, disregarded these prohibitions. Despite its proprietors' early vision of a colony guided by Enlightenment ideals and free of slavery, by the 1750s, Georgia was producing quantities of rice grown and harvested by slaves.

Section Summary

The eighteenth century saw a host of social, religious, and intellectual changes across the British Empire. While the Great Awakening emphasized vigorously emotional religiosity, the Enlightenment promoted the power of reason and scientific observation. Both movements had lasting impacts on the colonies. The beliefs of the New Lights of the First Great Awakening competed with the religions of the first colonists, and the religious fervor in Great Britain and her North American colonies bound the eighteenth-century British Atlantic together in a shared, common experience. The British colonist Benjamin Franklin gained fame on both sides of the Atlantic as a printer, publisher, and scientist. He embodied Enlightenment ideals in the British Atlantic with his scientific experiments and philanthropic endeavors. Enlightenment principles even guided the founding of the colony of Georgia, although those principles could not stand up to the realities of colonial life, and slavery soon took hold in the colony.

https://www.openassessments.org/assessments/949

Review Question

1. Who were the Freemasons, and why were they significant?

Answer to Review Question

1. The Freemasons were a fraternal society that originated in London coffeehouses in the early eighteenth century. They advocated Enlightenment principles of inquiry and tolerance. Masonic lodges soon spread throughout Europe and the British colonies, creating a shared experience on both sides of the Atlantic and spreading Enlightenment intellectual currents throughout the British Empire. Benjamin Franklin was a prominent Freemason.

Glossary

deism an Enlightenment-era belief in the existence of a supreme being—specifically, a creator who does not intervene in the universe—representing a rejection of the belief in a supernatural deity who interacts with humankind

Enlightenment an eighteenth-century intellectual and cultural movement that emphasized reason and science over superstition, religion, and tradition

First Great Awakening an eighteenth-century Protestant revival that emphasized individual, experiential faith over church doctrine and the close study of scripture

Freemasons a fraternal society founded in the early eighteenth century that advocated Enlightenment principles of inquiry and tolerance

Attributions

CC licensed content, Shared previously

- US History. **Authored by**: P. Scott Corbett, Volker Janssen, John M. Lund, Todd Pfannestiel, Paul Vickery, and Sylvie Waskiewicz. **Provided by**: OpenStax College. **Located at**: http://openstaxcollege.org/textbooks/us-history. **License**: *CC BY: Attribution*. **License Terms**: Download for free at http://cnx.org/content/col11740/latest/

Wars for Empire

> ### Learning Objectives
>
> By the end of this section, you will be able to:
>
> - Describe the wars for empire
> - Analyze the significance of these conflicts

Wars for empire composed a final link connecting the Atlantic sides of the British Empire. Great Britain fought four separate wars against Catholic France from the late 1600s to the mid-1700s. Another war, the War of Jenkins' Ear, pitted Britain against Spain. These conflicts for control of North America also helped colonists forge important alliances with native peoples, as different tribes aligned themselves with different European powers.

GENERATIONS OF WARFARE

Generations of British colonists grew up during a time when much of North America, especially the Northeast, engaged in war. Colonists knew war firsthand. In the eighteenth century, fighting was seasonal. Armies mobilized in the spring, fought in the summer, and retired to winter quarters in the fall. The British army imposed harsh discipline on its soldiers, who were drawn from the poorer classes, to ensure they did not step out of line during engagements. If they did, their officers would kill them. On the battlefield, armies dressed in bright uniforms to advertise their bravery and lack of fear. They stood in tight formation and exchanged volleys with the enemy. They often feared their officers more than the enemy.

> Read the diary of a provincial soldier who fought in the French and Indian War on the Captain David Perry Web Site hosted by Rootsweb. David Perry's journal, which includes a description of the 1758 campaign, provides a glimpse of warfare in the eighteenth century.

Most imperial conflicts had both American and European fronts, leaving us with two names for each war. For instance, King William's War (1688–1697) is also known as the War of the League of Augsburg. In America, the bulk of the fighting in this conflict took place between New England and New France. The war proved inconclusive, with no clear victor.

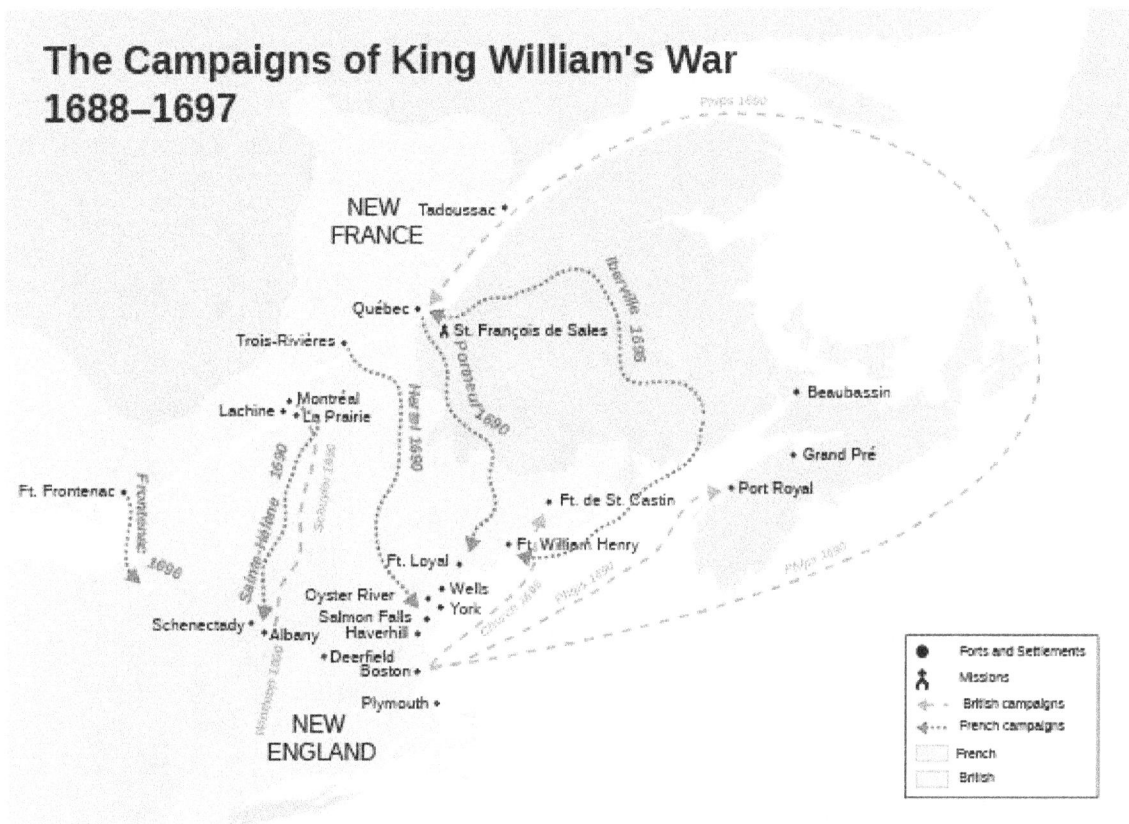

This map shows the French and British armies' movements during King William's War, in which there was no clear victor.

Queen Anne's War (1702–1713) is also known as the War of Spanish Succession. England fought against both Spain and France over who would ascend the Spanish throne after the last of the Hapsburg rulers died. In North America, fighting took place in Florida, New England, and New France. In Canada, the French prevailed but lost Acadia and Newfoundland; however, the victory was again not decisive because the English failed to take Quebec, which would have given them control of Canada.

This conflict is best remembered in the United States for the French and Indian raid against Deerfield, Massachusetts, in 1704. A small French force, combined with a native group made up of Catholic Mohawks and Abenaki (Pocumtucs), attacked the frontier outpost of Deerfield, killing scores and taking 112 prisoners. Among the captives was the seven-year-old daughter of Deerfield's minister John Williams, named Eunice. She was held by the Mohawks for years as her family tried to get her back, and became assimilated into the tribe. To the horror of the Puritan leaders, when she grew up Eunice married a Mohawk and refused to return to New England.

In North America, possession of Georgia and trade with the interior was the focus of the War of Jenkins' Ear (1739–1742), a conflict between Britain and Spain over contested claims to the land occupied by the fledgling colony between South Carolina and Florida. The war got its name from an incident in 1731 in which a Spanish Coast Guard captain severed the ear of British captain Robert Jenkins as punishment for raiding Spanish ships in Panama. Jenkins fueled the growing animosity between England and Spain by presenting his ear to Parliament and stirring up British public outrage. More than anything else, the War of Jenkins' Ear disrupted the Atlantic trade, a situation that hurt both Spain and Britain and was a major reason the war came to a close in 1742. Georgia, founded six years earlier, remained British and a buffer against Spanish Florida.

King George's War (1744–1748), known in Europe as the War of Austrian Succession (1740–1748), was fought in the northern colonies and New France. In 1745, the British took the massive French fortress at Louisbourg on Cape Breton Island, Nova Scotia. However, three years later, under the terms of the Treaty of Aix-la-Chapelle, Britain relinquished control of the fortress to the French. Once again, war resulted in an incomplete victory for both Britain and France.

In this 1747 painting by J. Stevens, View of the landing of the New England forces in ye expedition against Cape Breton, *British forces land on the island of Cape Breton to capture Fort Louisbourg.*

THE FRENCH AND INDIAN WAR

The final imperial war, the **French and Indian War** (1754–1763), known as the Seven Years' War in Europe, proved to be the decisive contest between Britain and France in America. It began over rival claims along the frontier in present-day western Pennsylvania. Well-connected planters from Virginia faced stagnant tobacco prices and hoped expanding into these western lands would stabilize their wealth and status. Some of them established the Ohio Company of Virginia in 1748, and the British crown granted the company half a million acres in 1749. However, the French also claimed the lands of the Ohio Company, and to protect the region they established Fort Duquesne in 1754, where the Ohio, Monongahela, and Allegheny Rivers met.

The war began in May 1754 because of these competing claims between Britain and France. Twenty-two-year-old Virginian George Washington, a surveyor whose family helped to found the Ohio Company, gave the command to fire on French soldiers near present-day Uniontown, Pennsylvania. This incident on the Pennsylvania frontier proved to be a decisive event that led to imperial war. For the next decade, fighting took place along the frontier of New France and British America from Virginia to Maine. The war also spread to Europe as France and Britain looked to gain supremacy in the Atlantic World.

The British fared poorly in the first years of the war. In 1754, the French and their native allies forced Washington to surrender at Fort Necessity, a hastily built fort constructed after his attack on the French. In 1755, Britain dispatched General Edward Braddock to the colonies to take Fort Duquesne. The French, aided by the Potawotomis, Ottawas, Shawnees, and Delawares, ambushed the fifteen hundred British soldiers and Virginia militia who marched to the fort. The attack sent panic through the British force, and hundreds of British soldiers and militiamen died, including General Braddock. The campaign of 1755 proved to be a disaster for the British. In fact, the only British victory that year was the capture of Nova Scotia. In 1756 and 1757, Britain suffered further defeats with the fall of Fort Oswego and Fort William Henry.

This schematic map depicts the events of the French and Indian War. Note the scarcity of British victories.

The war began to turn in favor of the British in 1758, due in large part to the efforts of William Pitt, a very popular member of Parliament. Pitt pledged huge sums of money and resources to defeating the hated Catholic French, and Great Britain spent part of the money on bounties paid to new young recruits in the colonies, helping invigorate the British forces. In 1758, the Iroquois, Delaware, and Shawnee signed the Treaty of Easton, aligning themselves with the British in return for some contested land around Pennsylvania and Virginia. In 1759, the British took Quebec, and in 1760, Montreal. The French empire in North America had crumbled.

The war continued until 1763, when the French signed the **Treaty of Paris**. This treaty signaled a dramatic reversal of fortune for France. Indeed, New France, which had been founded in the early 1600s, ceased to exist. The British Empire had now gained mastery over North America. The Empire not only gained New France under the treaty; it also acquired French sugar islands in the West Indies, French trading posts in India, and French-held posts on the west coast of Africa. Great Britain's victory in the French and Indian War meant that it had become a truly global empire. British colonists joyously celebrated, singing the refrain of "Rule, Britannia! / Britannia, rule the waves! / Britons never, never, never shall be slaves!"

In the American colonies, ties with Great Britain were closer than ever. Professional British soldiers had fought alongside Anglo-American militiamen, forging a greater sense of shared identity. With Great Britain's victory, colonial pride ran high as colonists celebrated their identity as British subjects.

This last of the wars for empire, however, also sowed the seeds of trouble. The war led Great Britain deeply into debt, and in the 1760s and 1770s, efforts to deal with the debt through imperial reforms would have the unintended consequence of causing stress and strain that threatened to tear the Empire apart.

Section Summary

From 1688 to 1763, Great Britain engaged in almost continuous power struggles with France and Spain. Most of these conflicts originated in Europe, but their engagements spilled over into the colonies. For almost eighty years, Great Britain and France fought for control of eastern North America. During most of that time, neither force was able to win a decisive victory, though each side saw occasional successes with the crucial help of native peoples. It was not until halfway through the French and Indian War (1754–1763), when Great Britain swelled its troops with more volunteers and native allies, that the balance of power shifted toward the British. With the 1763 Treaty of Paris, New France was eliminated, and Great Britain gained control of all the lands north of Florida and east of the Mississippi. British subjects on both sides of the Atlantic rejoiced.

- https://www.openassessments.org/assessments/950

Review Question

1. What prompted the French and Indian War?

Answer to Review Question

1. Virginia planters, pinched by stagnant tobacco prices, wanted to expand westward. However, France contested Britain's claim to that land and built Fort Duquesne to defend it. The battle over this land sparked the war that eventually ended France's presence in North America.

Critical Thinking Questions

1. How did Pennsylvania's Quaker beginnings distinguish it from other colonies in British America?

2. What were the effects of the consumer revolution on the colonies?

3. How did the ideas of the Enlightenment and the Great Awakening offer opposing outlooks to British Americans? What similarities were there between the two schools of thought?

4. What was the impact of the wars for empire in North America, Europe, and the world?

5. What role did Indians play in the wars for empire?

6. What shared experiences, intellectual currents, and cultural elements drew together British subjects on both sides of the Atlantic during this period? How did these experiences, ideas, and goods serve to strengthen those bonds?

Glossary

French and Indian War the last eighteenth-century imperial struggle between Great Britain and France, leading to a decisive British victory; this war lasted from 1754 to 1763 and was also called the Seven Years' War

Attributions

CC licensed content, Shared previously

- US History. **Authored by**: P. Scott Corbett, Volker Janssen, John M. Lund, Todd Pfannestiel, Paul Vickery, and Sylvie Waskiewicz. **Provided by**: OpenStax College. **Located at**: http://openstaxcollege.org/textbooks/us-history. **License**: CC BY: Attribution. **License Terms**: Download for free at http://cnx.org/content/col11740/latest/

Primary Source Reading: The Social Contract

Jean Jacques Rousseau: The Social Contract, 1763

Introduction to the Source

In moral and political philosophy, the social contract or political contract is a theory or model, originating during the Age of Enlightenment, that typically addresses the questions of the origin of society and the legitimacy of the authority of the state over the individual. Social contract arguments typically posit that individuals have consented, either explicitly or tacitly, to surrender some of their freedoms and submit to the authority of the ruler or magistrate (or to the decision of a majority), in exchange for protection of their remaining rights. The question of the relation between natural and legal rights, therefore, is often an aspect of social contract theory. The Social Contract (Du contrat social ou Principes du droit politique) is also the title of a 1762 book by Jean-Jacques Rousseau on this topic.

Although the antecedents of social contract theory are found in antiquity, in Greek and Stoic philosophy and Roman and Canon Law, as well as in the Biblical idea of the covenant, the heyday of the social contract was the mid-17th to early 19th centuries, when it emerged as the leading doctrine of political legitimacy. The starting point for most social contract theories is a heuristic examination of the human condition absent from any political order that Thomas Hobbes termed the "state of nature".[2] In this condition, individuals' actions are bound only by their personal power and conscience. From this shared starting point, social contract theorists seek to demonstrate, in different ways, why a rational individual would voluntarily consent to give up his or her natural freedom to obtain the benefits of political order.

Hugo Grotius (1625), Thomas Hobbes (1651), Samuel Pufendorf (1673), John Locke (1689), Jean-Jacques Rousseau (1762), and Immanuel Kant (1797) are among the most prominent of 17th- and 18th-century theorists of social contract and natural rights. Each solved the problem of political authority in a different way.

Origin and Terms of the Social Contract

Man was born free, but everywhere he is in chains. This man believes that he is the master of others, and still he is more of a slave than they are. How did that transformation take place? I don't know. How may the restraints on man become legitimate? I do believe I can answer that question....

At a point in the state of nature when the obstacles to human preservation have become greater than each individual with his own strength can cope with . . ., an adequate combination of forces must be the result of men coming together. Still, each man's power and freedom are his main means of selfpreservation. How is he to put them under the control of others without damaging himself . . . ?

This question might be rephrased: "How is a method of associating to be found which will defend and protect-using the power of all-the person and property of each member and still enable each member of the group to obey only himself and to remain as free as before?" This is the fundamental problem; the social contract offers a solution to it.

The very scope of the action dictates the terms of this contract and renders the least modification of them inadmissible, something making them null and void. Thus, although perhaps they have never been stated in so man) words, they are the same everywhere and tacitly conceded and recognized everywhere. And so it follows that each individual immediately recovers hi primitive rights and natural liberties whenever any violation of the social contract occurs and thereby loses the contractual freedom for which he renounced them.

The social contract's terms, when they are well understood, can be reduced to a single stipulation: the individual member alienates himself totally to the whole community together with all his rights. This is first because conditions will be the same for everyone when each individual gives himself totally, and secondly, because no one will be tempted to make that condition of shared equality worse for other men....

Once this multitude is united this way into a body, an offense against one of its members is an offense against the body politic. It would be even less possible to injure the body without its members feeling it. Duty and interest thus equally require the two contracting parties to aid each other mutually. The individual people should be motivated from their double roles as individuals and members of the body, to combine all the advantages which mutual aid offers them....

Source: From Jean Jacques Rousseau, *Contrat social ou Principes du droit politique* (Paris: Garnier Frères 1800), pp. 240332, passim. Translated by Henry A. Myers.

Attributions

CC licensed content, Shared previously

- Introduction to the Source: Social Contracts. **Provided by**: Wikipedia. **Located at**: https://en.wikipedia.org/wiki/Social_contract. **License**: *CC BY-SA: Attribution-ShareAlike*

Public domain content

- Contrat social ou Principes du droit politique, 1763. **Authored by**: Jean Jacques Rousseau. **Located at**: http://legacy.fordham.edu/halsall/mod/rousseau-soccon.asp. **Project**: Internet Modern History Sourcebook.. **License**: *Public Domain: No Known Copyright*

Primary Source Reading: A Treatise on Tolerance

Follow this link to read Voltaire's A Treatise on Toleration (1763): http://public.wsu.edu/~brians/world_civ/worldcivreader/world_civ_reader_2/voltaire.html

Attributions

Public domain content

- Voltaire: A Treatise on Toleration (1763). **Authored by**: Paul Brians. **Located at**: http://public.wsu.edu/~brians/world_civ/worldcivreader/world_civ_reader_2/voltaire.html. **Project**: Reading About the World, Volume 2. **License**: *Public Domain: No Known Copyright*

5. Imperial Reforms and Colonial Protests, 1763-1774

Introduction

The Bostonians Paying the Excise-man, or Tarring and Feathering, shows five Patriots tarring and feathering the Commissioner of Customs, John Malcolm, a sea captain, army officer, and staunch **Loyalist**. The print shows the Boston Tea Party, a protest against the Tea Act of 1773, and the Liberty Tree, an elm tree near Boston Common that became a rallying point against the Stamp Act of 1765. When the crowd threatened to hang Malcolm if he did not renounce his position as a royal customs officer, he reluctantly agreed and the protestors allowed him to go home. The scene represents the animosity toward those who supported royal authority and illustrates the high tide of unrest in the colonies after the British government imposed a series of imperial reform measures during the years 1763–1774.

The Bostonians Paying the Excise-man, or Tarring and Feathering (1774), attributed to Philip Dawe, depicts the most publicized tarring and feathering incident of the American Revolution. The victim is John Malcolm, a customs official loyal to the British crown.

The government's formerly lax oversight of the colonies ended as the architects of the British Empire put these new reforms in place. The British hoped to gain greater control over colonial trade and frontier settlement as well as to reduce the administrative cost of the colonies and the enormous debt left by the French and Indian War. Each step the British took, however, generated a backlash. Over time, imperial reforms pushed many colonists toward separation from the British Empire.

Attributions

CC licensed content, Shared previously

- US History. **Authored by**: P. Scott Corbett, Volker Janssen, John M. Lund, Todd Pfannestiel, Paul Vickery, and Sylvie Waskiewicz. **Provided by**: OpenStax College. **Located at**: http://openstaxcollege.org/textbooks/us-history. **License**: *CC BY: Attribution*. **License Terms**: Download for free at http://cnx.org/content/col11740/latest/

Confronting the National Debt: The Aftermath of the French and Indian War

Learning Objectives

By the end of this section, you will be able to:

- Discuss the status of Great Britain's North American colonies in the years directly following the French and Indian War
- Describe the size and scope of the British debt at the end of the French and Indian War
- Explain how the British Parliament responded to the debt crisis
- Outline the purpose of the Proclamation Line, the Sugar Act, and the Currency Act

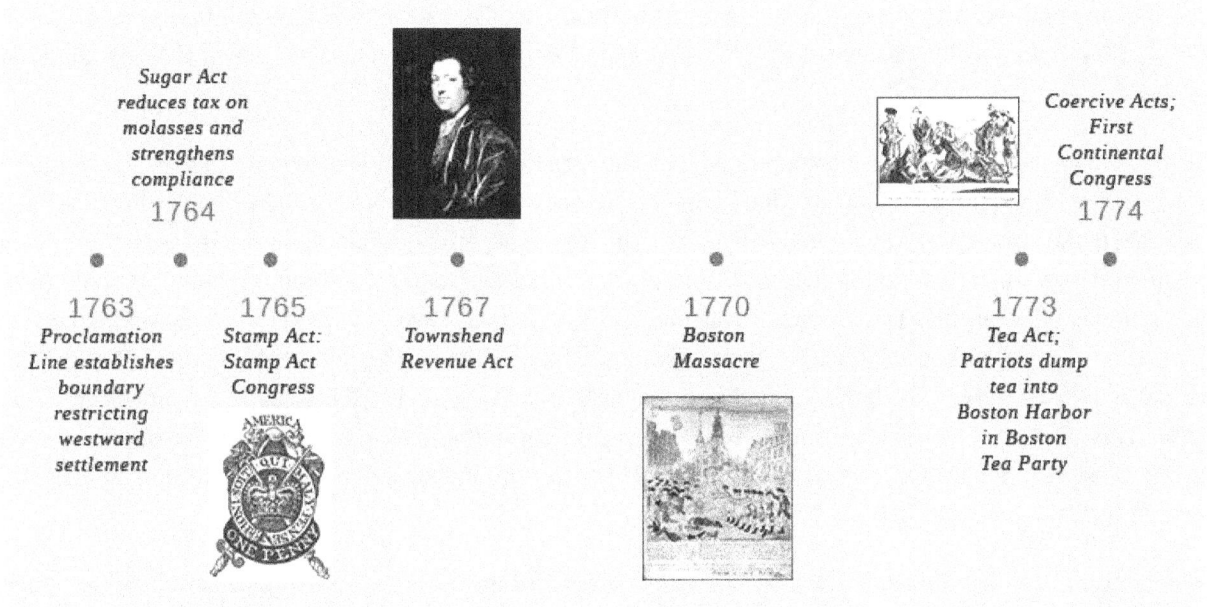

(credit "1765": modification of work by the United Kingdom Government)

Great Britain had much to celebrate in 1763. The long and costly war with France had finally ended, and Great Britain had emerged victorious. British subjects on both sides of the Atlantic celebrated the strength of the British Empire. Colonial pride ran high; to live under the British Constitution and to have defeated the hated French Catholic menace brought great joy to British Protestants everywhere in the Empire. From Maine to Georgia, British colonists joyously celebrated the victory and sang the refrain of "Rule, Britannia! Britannia, rule the waves! Britons never, never, never shall be slaves!"

Despite the celebratory mood, the victory over France also produced major problems within the British Empire, problems that would have serious consequences for British colonists in the Americas. During the war, many Indian tribes had sided with the French, who supplied them with guns. After the 1763 Treaty of Paris that ended the French and Indian War (or the Seven Years' War), British colonists had to defend the frontier, where French colonists and their tribal allies remained a powerful force. The most organized resistance, Pontiac's Rebellion, highlighted tensions the settlers increasingly interpreted in racial terms.

The massive debt the war generated at home, however, proved to be the most serious issue facing Great Britain. The frontier had to be secure in order to prevent another costly war. Greater enforcement of imperial trade laws had to be put into place. Parliament had to find ways to raise revenue to pay off the crippling debt from the war. Everyone would have to contribute their expected share, including the British subjects across the Atlantic.

PROBLEMS ON THE AMERICAN FRONTIER

With the end of the French and Indian War, Great Britain claimed a vast new expanse of territory, at least on paper. Under the terms of the Treaty of Paris, the French territory known as New France had ceased to exist. British territorial holdings now extended from Canada to Florida, and British military focus shifted to maintaining peace in the king's newly enlarged lands. However, much of the land in the American British Empire remained under the control of powerful native confederacies, which made any claims of British mastery beyond the Atlantic coastal settlements hollow. Great Britain maintained ten thousand troops in North America after the war ended in 1763 to defend the borders and repel any attack by their imperial rivals.

British colonists, eager for fresh land, poured over the Appalachian Mountains to stake claims. The western frontier had long been a "middle ground" where different imperial powers (British, French, Spanish) had interacted and compromised with native peoples. That era of accommodation in the "middle ground" came to an end after the French and Indian War. Virginians (including George Washington) and other land-hungry colonists had already raised tensions in the 1740s with their quest for land. Virginia landowners in particular eagerly looked to diversify their holdings beyond tobacco, which had stagnated in price and exhausted the fertility of the lands along the Chesapeake Bay. They invested heavily in the newly available land. This westward movement brought the settlers into conflict as never before with Indian tribes, such as the Shawnee, Seneca-Cayuga, Wyandot, and Delaware, who increasingly held their ground against any further intrusion by white settlers.

The treaty that ended the war between France and Great Britain proved to be a significant blow to native peoples, who had viewed the conflict as an opportunity to gain additional trade goods from both sides. With the French defeat, many Indians who had sided with France lost a valued trading partner as well as bargaining power over the British. Settlers' encroachment on their land, as well as the increased British military presence, changed the situation on the frontier dramatically. After the war, British troops took over the former French forts but failed to court favor with the local tribes by distributing ample gifts, as the French had done. They also significantly reduced the amount of gunpowder and ammunition they sold to the Indians, worsening relationships further.

Indians' resistance to colonists drew upon the teachings of Delaware (Lenni Lenape) prophet Neolin and the leadership of Ottawa war chief Pontiac. Neolin was a spiritual leader who preached a doctrine of shunning European culture and expelling Europeans from native lands. Neolin's beliefs united Indians from many villages. In a broad-based alliance that came to be known as Pontiac's Rebellion, Pontiac led a loose coalition of these native tribes against the colonists and the British army.

Pontiac started bringing his coalition together as early as 1761, urging Indians to "drive [the Europeans] out and make war upon them." The conflict began in earnest in 1763, when Pontiac and several hundred Ojibwas, Potawatomis, and Hurons laid siege to Fort Detroit. At the same time, Senecas, Shawnees, and Delawares laid siege to Fort Pitt. Over the next year, the war spread along the backcountry from Virginia to Pennsylvania. Pontiac's Rebellion (also known as Pontiac's War) triggered horrific violence on both sides. Firsthand reports of Indian attacks tell of murder, scalping, dismemberment, and burning at the stake. These stories incited a deep racial hatred among colonists against all Indians.

The actions of a group of Scots-Irish settlers from Paxton (or Paxtang), Pennsylvania, in December 1763, illustrates the deadly situation on the frontier. Forming a mob known as the Paxton Boys, these frontiersmen attacked a nearby group of Conestoga of the Susquehannock tribe. The Conestoga had lived peacefully with local settlers, but the Paxton Boys viewed all Indians as savages and they brutally murdered the six Conestoga they found at home and burned their houses. When Governor John Penn put the remaining fourteen Conestoga in protective custody in Lancaster, Pennsylvania, the Paxton Boys broke into the building and killed and scalped the Conestoga they found there. Although Governor Penn offered a reward for the capture of any Paxton Boys involved in the murders, no one ever identified the attackers. Some colonists reacted to the incident with outrage. Benjamin Franklin described the Paxton Boys as "the barbarous Men who committed the atrocious act, in Defiance of Government, of all Laws human and divine, and to the eternal Disgrace of their Country and Colour," stating that "the Wickedness cannot be covered, the Guilt will lie on the whole Land, till Justice is done on the Murderers. The blood of the innocent will cry to heaven for vengeance." Yet, as the inability to bring the perpetrators to justice clearly indicates, the Paxton Boys had many more supporters than critics.

This nineteenth-century lithograph depicts the massacre of Conestoga in 1763 at Lancaster, Pennsylvania, where they had been placed in protective custody. None of the attackers, members of the Paxton Boys, were ever identified.

> Visit Explore PAhistory.com to read the full text of Benjamin Franklin's "Benjamin Franklin, An Account of the Paxton Boys' Murder of the Conestoga Indians, 1764."

Pontiac's Rebellion and the Paxton Boys' actions were examples of early American race wars, in which both sides saw themselves as inherently different from the other and believed the other needed to be eradicated. The prophet Neolin's message, which he said he received in a vision from the Master of Life, was: "Wherefore do you suffer the whites to dwell upon your lands? Drive them away; wage war against them." Pontiac echoed this idea in a meeting, exhorting tribes to join together against the British: "It is important for us, my brothers, that we exterminate from our lands this nation which seeks only to destroy us." In his letter suggesting "gifts" to the natives of smallpox-infected blankets, Field Marshal Jeffrey Amherst said, "You will do well to inoculate the Indians by means of blankets, as well as every other method that can serve to extirpate this execrable race." Pontiac's Rebellion came to an end in 1766, when it became clear that the French, whom Pontiac had hoped would side with his forces, would not be returning. The repercussions, however, would last much longer. Race relations between Indians and whites remained poisoned on the frontier.

Well aware of the problems on the frontier, the British government took steps to try to prevent bloodshed and another costly war. At the beginning of Pontiac's uprising, the British issued the Proclamation of 1763, which forbade white settlement west of the **Proclamation Line**, a borderline running along the spine of the Appalachian Mountains. The Proclamation Line aimed to forestall further conflict on the frontier, the clear flashpoint of tension in British North America. British colonists who had hoped to move west after the war chafed at this restriction, believing the war had been fought and won to ensure the right to settle west. The Proclamation Line therefore came as a setback to their vision of westward expansion.

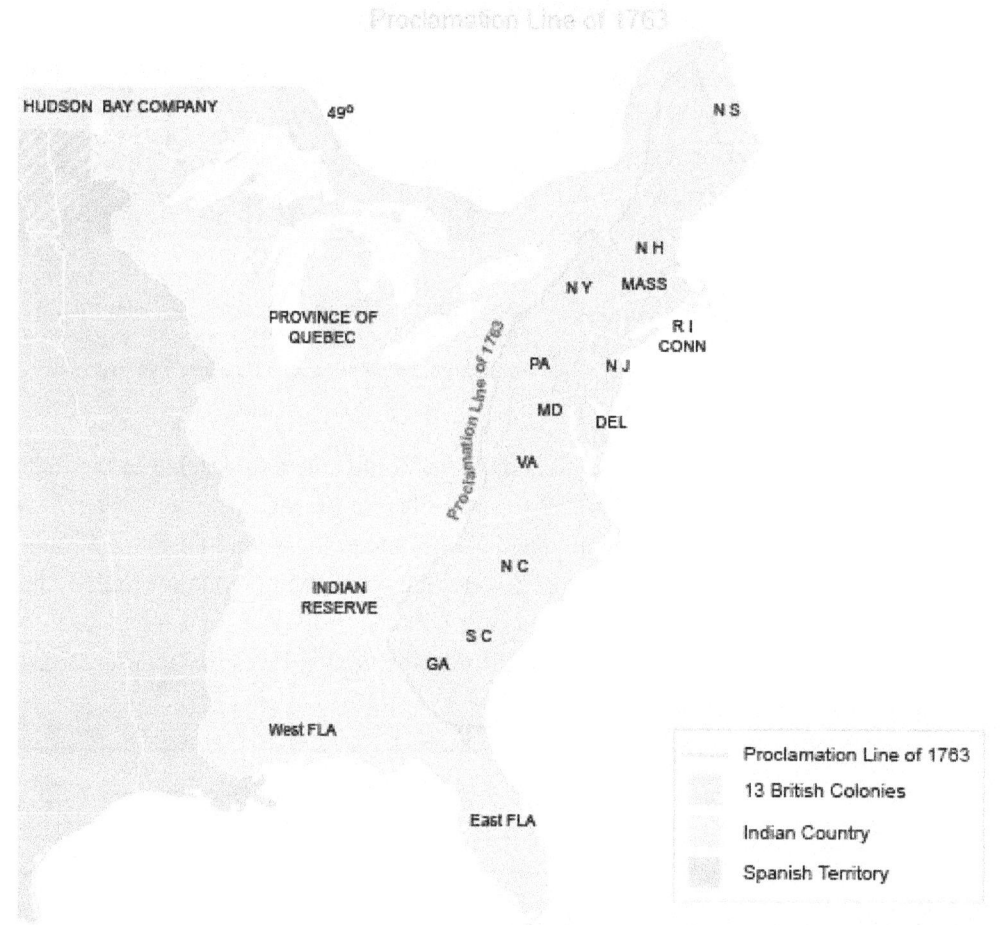

This map shows the status of the American colonies in 1763, after the end of the French and Indian War. Although Great Britain won control of the territory east of the Mississippi, the Proclamation Line of 1763 prohibited British colonists from settling west of the Appalachian Mountains. (credit: modification of work by the National Atlas of the United States)

THE BRITISH NATIONAL DEBT

Great Britain's newly enlarged empire meant a greater financial burden, and the mushrooming debt from the war was a major cause of concern. The war nearly doubled the British national debt, from £75 million in 1756 to £133 million in 1763. Interest payments alone consumed over half the national budget, and the continuing military presence in North America was a constant drain. The Empire needed more revenue to replenish its dwindling coffers. Those in Great Britain believed that British subjects in North America, as the major beneficiaries of Great Britain's war for global supremacy, should certainly shoulder their share of the financial burden.

The British government began increasing revenues by raising taxes at home, even as various interest groups lobbied to keep their taxes low. Powerful members of the aristocracy, well represented in Parliament, successfully convinced Prime Minister John Stuart, third earl of Bute, to refrain from raising taxes on land. The greater tax burden, therefore, fell on the lower classes in the form of increased import duties, which raised the prices of imported goods such as sugar and tobacco. George Grenville succeeded Bute as prime minister in 1763. Grenville determined to curtail government spending and make sure that, as subjects of the British Empire, the American colonists did their part to pay down the massive debt.

IMPERIAL REFORMS

The new era of greater British interest in the American colonies through imperial reforms picked up in pace in the mid-1760s. In 1764, Prime Minister Grenville introduced the Currency Act of 1764, prohibiting the colonies from printing additional paper money and requiring colonists to pay British merchants in gold and silver instead of the colonial paper money already in circulation. The Currency Act aimed to standardize the currency used in Atlantic trade, a logical reform designed to help stabilize the Empire's economy. This rule brought American economic activity under greater British control. Colonists relied on their own paper currency to conduct trade and, with gold and silver in short supply, they found their finances tight. Not surprisingly, they grumbled about the new imperial currency regulations.

Grenville also pushed Parliament to pass the Sugar Act of 1764, which actually lowered duties on British molasses by half, from six pence per gallon to three. Grenville designed this measure to address the problem of rampant colonial smuggling with the French sugar islands in the West Indies. The act attempted to make it easier for colonial traders, especially New England mariners who routinely engaged in illegal trade, to comply with the imperial law.

To give teeth to the 1764 Sugar Act, the law intensified enforcement provisions. Prior to the 1764 act, colonial violations of the Navigation Acts had been tried in local courts, where sympathetic colonial juries refused to convict merchants on trial. However, the Sugar Act required violators to be tried in **vice-admiralty courts**. These crown-sanctioned tribunals, which settled disputes that occurred at sea, operated without juries. Some colonists saw this feature of the 1764 act as dangerous. They argued that trial by jury had long been honored as a basic right of Englishmen under the British Constitution. To deprive defendants of a jury, they contended, meant reducing liberty-loving British subjects to political slavery. In the British Atlantic world, some colonists perceived this loss of liberty as parallel to the enslavement of Africans.

As loyal British subjects, colonists in America cherished their Constitution, an unwritten system of government that they celebrated as the best political system in the world. The British Constitution prescribed the roles of the King, the House of Lords, and the House of Commons. Each entity provided a check and balance against the worst tendencies of the others. If the King had too much power, the result would be tyranny. If the Lords had too much power, the result would be oligarchy. If the Commons had the balance of power, democracy or mob rule would prevail. The British Constitution promised representation of the will of British subjects, and without such representation, even the **indirect tax** of the Sugar Act was considered a threat to the settlers' rights as British subjects. Furthermore, some American colonists felt the colonies were on equal political footing with Great Britain. The Sugar Act meant they were secondary, mere adjuncts to the Empire. All subjects of the British crown knew they had liberties under the constitution. The Sugar Act suggested that some in Parliament labored to deprive them of what made them uniquely British.

Section Summary

The British Empire had gained supremacy in North America with its victory over the French in 1763. Almost all of the North American territory east of the Mississippi fell under Great Britain's control, and British leaders took this opportunity to try to create a more coherent and unified empire after decades of lax oversight. Victory over the French had proved very costly, and the British government attempted to better regulate their expanded empire in North America. The initial steps the British took in 1763 and 1764 raised suspicions among some colonists about the intent of the home government. These suspicions would grow and swell over the coming years.

https://www.openassessments.org/assessments/951

Review Question

1. What did British colonists find so onerous about the acts that Prime Minister Grenville passed?

Answer to Review Question

1. The Currency Act required colonists to pay British merchants in gold and silver instead of colonial paper money. With gold and silver in short supply, this put a strain on colonists' finances. The Sugar Act curtailed smuggling, angering merchants, and imposed stricter enforcement. Many colonists feared the loss of liberty with trials without juries as mandated by the Sugar Act.

Glossary

indirect tax a tax imposed on businesses, rather than directly on consumers

Loyalists colonists in America who were loyal to Great Britain

Proclamation Line a line along the Appalachian Mountains, imposed by the Proclamation of 1763, west of which British colonists could not settle

vice-admiralty courts British royal courts without juries that settled disputes occurring at sea

Attributions

CC licensed content, Shared previously

- US History. **Authored by**: P. Scott Corbett, Volker Janssen, John M. Lund, Todd Pfannestiel, Paul Vickery, and Sylvie Waskiewicz. **Provided by**: OpenStax College. **Located at**: http://openstaxcollege.org/textbooks/us-history. **License**: *CC BY: Attribution*.

License Terms: Download for free at http://cnx.org/content/col11740/latest/

The Stamp Act and the Sons and Daughters of Liberty

> *Learning Objectives*
>
> By the end of this section, you will be able to:
>
> - Explain the purpose of the 1765 Stamp Act
> - Describe the colonial responses to the Stamp Act

In 1765, the British Parliament moved beyond the efforts during the previous two years to better regulate westward expansion and trade by putting in place the Stamp Act. As a **direct tax** on the colonists, the Stamp Act imposed an internal tax on almost every type of printed paper colonists used, including newspapers, legal documents, and playing cards. While the architects of the Stamp Act saw the measure as a way to defray the costs of the British Empire, it nonetheless gave rise to the first major colonial protest against British imperial control as expressed in the famous slogan "no taxation without representation." The Stamp Act reinforced the sense among some colonists that Parliament was not treating them as equals of their peers across the Atlantic.

THE STAMP ACT AND THE QUARTERING ACT

Prime Minister Grenville, author of the Sugar Act of 1764, introduced the **Stamp Act** in the early spring of 1765. Under this act, anyone who used or purchased anything printed on paper had to buy a revenue stamp for it. In the same year, 1765, Parliament also passed the Quartering Act, a law that attempted to solve the problems of stationing troops in North America. The Parliament understood the Stamp Act and the Quartering Act as an assertion of their power to control colonial policy.

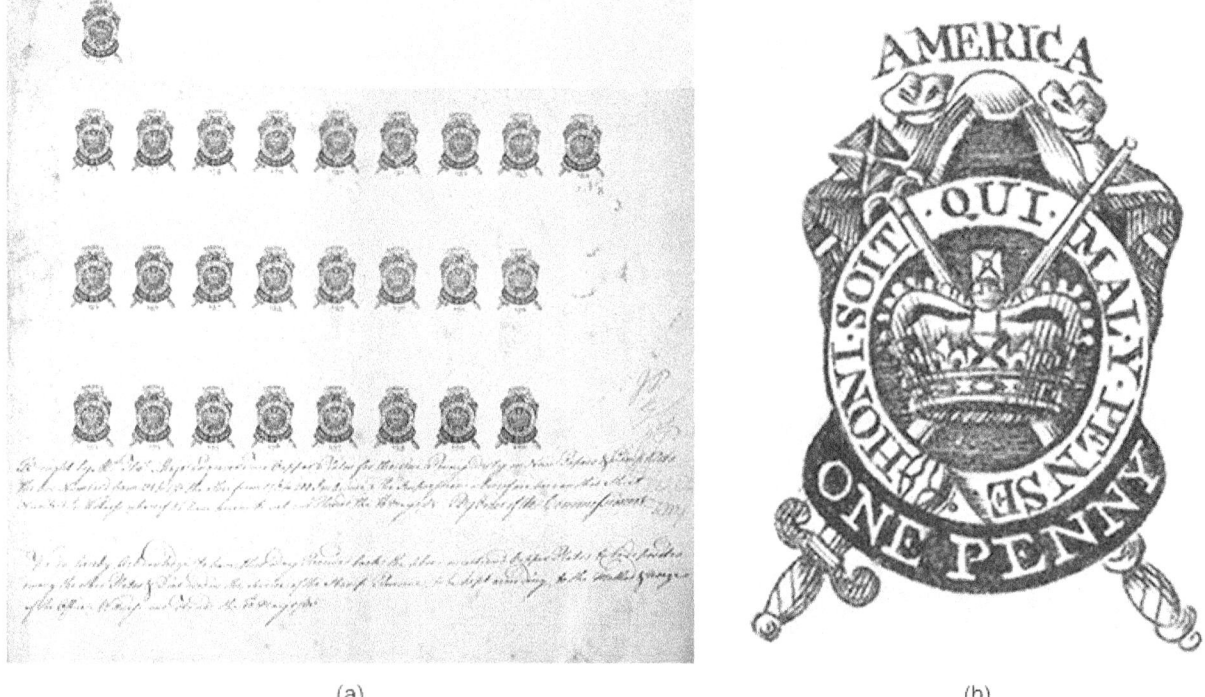

(a) (b)

Under the Stamp Act, anyone who used or purchased anything printed on paper had to buy a revenue stamp for it. Image (a) shows a partial proof sheet of one-penny stamps. Image (b) provides a close-up of a one-penny stamp. (credit a: modification of work by the United Kingdom Government; credit b: modification of work by the United Kingdom Government)

The Stamp Act signaled a shift in British policy after the French and Indian War. Before the Stamp Act, the colonists had paid taxes to their colonial governments or indirectly through higher prices, not directly to the Crown's appointed governors. This was a time-honored liberty of representative legislatures of the colonial governments. The passage of the Stamp Act meant that starting on November 1, 1765, the colonists would contribute £60,000 per year—17 percent of the total cost—to the upkeep of the ten thousand British soldiers in North America. Because the Stamp Act raised constitutional issues, it triggered the first serious protest against British imperial policy.

The announcement of the Stamp Act, seen in this newspaper publication (a), raised numerous concerns among colonists in America. Protests against British imperial policy took many forms, such as this mock stamp (b) whose text reads "An Emblem of the Effects of the STAMP. O! the Fatal STAMP."

Parliament also asserted its prerogative in 1765 with the **Quartering Act**. The Quartering Act of 1765 addressed the problem of housing British soldiers stationed in the American colonies. It required that they be provided with barracks or places to stay in public houses, and that if extra housing were necessary, then troops could be stationed in barns and other uninhabited private buildings. In addition, the costs of the troops' food and lodging fell to the colonists. Since the time of James II, who ruled from 1685 to 1688, many British subjects had mistrusted the presence of a standing army during peacetime, and having to pay for the soldiers' lodging and food was especially burdensome. Widespread evasion and disregard for the law occurred in almost all the colonies, but the issue was especially contentious in New York, the headquarters of British forces. When fifteen hundred troops arrived in New York in 1766, the New York Assembly refused to follow the Quartering Act.

COLONIAL PROTEST: GENTRY, MERCHANTS, AND THE STAMP ACT CONGRESS

For many British colonists living in America, the Stamp Act raised many concerns. As a direct tax, it appeared to be an unconstitutional measure, one that deprived freeborn British subjects of their liberty, a concept they defined broadly to include various rights and privileges they enjoyed as British subjects, including the right to representation. According to the unwritten British Constitution, only representatives for whom British subjects voted could tax them. Parliament was in charge of taxation, and although it was a representative body, the colonies did not have "actual" (or direct) representation in it. Parliamentary members who supported the Stamp Act argued that the colonists had virtual representation, because the architects of the British Empire knew best how to maximize returns from its possessions overseas. However, this argument did not satisfy the protesters, who viewed themselves as having the same right as all British subjects to avoid taxation without their consent. With no representation in the House of Commons, where bills of taxation originated, they felt themselves deprived of this inherent right.

Patrick Henry Before the Virginia House of Burgesses (1851), painted by Peter F. Rothermel, offers a romanticized depiction of Henry's speech denouncing the Stamp Act of 1765. Supporters and opponents alike debated the stark language of the speech, which quickly became legendary.

The British government knew the colonists might object to the Stamp Act's expansion of parliamentary power, but Parliament believed the relationship of the colonies to the Empire was one of dependence, not equality. However, the Stamp Act had the unintended and ironic consequence of drawing colonists from very different areas and viewpoints together in protest. In Massachusetts, for instance, James Otis, a lawyer and defender of British liberty, became the leading voice for the idea that "Taxation without representation is tyranny." In the Virginia House of Burgesses, firebrand and slaveholder Patrick Henry introduced the Virginia Stamp Act Resolutions, which denounced the Stamp Act and the British crown in language so strong that some conservative Virginians accused him of treason. Henry replied that Virginians were subject only to taxes that they themselves—or their representatives—imposed. In short, there could be **no taxation without representation**.

The colonists had never before formed a unified political front, so Grenville and Parliament did not fear true revolt. However, this was to change in 1765. In response to the Stamp Act, the Massachusetts Assembly sent letters to the other colonies, asking them to attend a meeting, or congress, to discuss how to respond to the act. Many American colonists from very different colonies found common cause in their opposition to the Stamp Act. Representatives from nine colonial legislatures met in New York in the fall of 1765 to reach a consensus. Could Parliament impose taxation without representation? The members of this first congress, known as the Stamp Act Congress, said no. These nine representatives had a vested interest in repealing the tax. Not only did it weaken their businesses and the colonial economy, but it also threatened their liberty under the British Constitution. They drafted a rebuttal to the Stamp Act, making clear that they desired only to protect their liberty as loyal subjects of the Crown. The document, called the Declaration of Rights and Grievances, outlined the unconstitutionality of taxation without representation and trials without juries. Meanwhile, popular protest was also gaining force.

Browse the collection of the Massachusetts Historical Society to examine digitized primary sources of the documents that paved the way to the fight for liberty.

MOBILIZATION: POPULAR PROTEST AGAINST THE STAMP ACT

The Stamp Act Congress was a gathering of landowning, educated white men who represented the political elite of the colonies and was the colonial equivalent of the British landed aristocracy. While these gentry were drafting their grievances during the Stamp Act Congress, other colonists showed their distaste for the new act by boycotting British goods and protesting in the streets. Two groups, the **Sons of Liberty** and the **Daughters of Liberty**, led the popular resistance to the Stamp Act. Both groups considered themselves British patriots defending their liberty, just as their forebears had done in the time of James II.

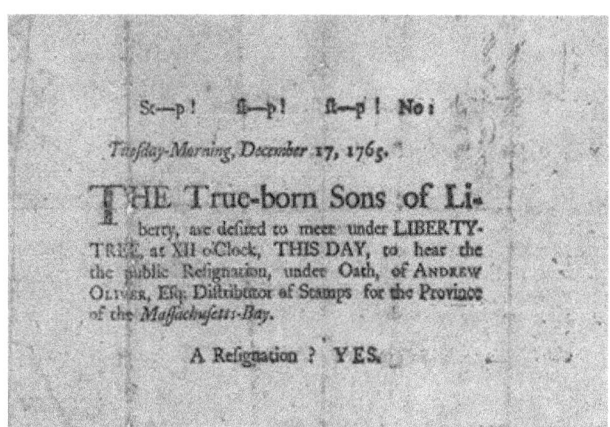

With this broadside of December 17, 1765, the Sons of Liberty call for the resignation of Andrew Oliver, the Massachusetts Distributor of Stamps.

Forming in Boston in the summer of 1765, the Sons of Liberty were artisans, shopkeepers, and small-time merchants willing to adopt extralegal means of protest. Before the act had even gone into effect, the Sons of Liberty began protesting. On August 14, they took aim at Andrew Oliver, who had been named the Massachusetts Distributor of Stamps. After hanging Oliver in effigy—that is, using a crudely made figure as a representation of Oliver—the unruly crowd stoned and ransacked his house, finally beheading the effigy and burning the remains. Such a brutal response shocked the royal governmental officials, who hid until the violence had spent itself. Andrew Oliver resigned the next day. By that time, the mob had moved on to the home of Lieutenant Governor Thomas Hutchinson who, because of his support of Parliament's actions, was considered an enemy of English liberty. The Sons of Liberty barricaded Hutchinson in his home and demanded that he renounce the Stamp Act; he refused, and the protesters looted and burned his house. Furthermore, the Sons (also called "True Sons" or "True-born Sons" to make clear their commitment to liberty and distinguish them from the likes of Hutchinson) continued to lead violent protests with the goal of securing the resignation of all appointed stamp collectors.

Starting in early 1766, the Daughters of Liberty protested the Stamp Act by refusing to buy British goods and encouraging others to do the same. They avoided British tea, opting to make their own teas with local herbs and berries. They built a community—and a movement—around creating homespun cloth instead of buying British linen. Well-born women held "spinning bees," at which they competed to see who could spin the most and the finest linen. An entry in *The Boston Chronicle* of April 7, 1766, states that on March 12, in Providence, Rhode Island, "18 Daughters of Liberty, young ladies of good reputation, assembled at the house of Doctor Ephraim Bowen, in this town. . . . There they exhibited a fine example of industry, by spinning from sunrise until dark, and displayed a spirit for saving their sinking country rarely to be found among persons of more age and experience." At dinner, they "cheerfully agreed to omit tea, to render their conduct consistent. Besides this instance of their patriotism, before they separated, they unanimously resolved that the Stamp Act was unconstitutional, that they would purchase no more British manufactures unless it be repealed, and that they would not even admit the addresses of any gentlemen should they have the opportunity, without they determined to oppose its execution to the last extremity, if the occasion required."

The Daughters' **non-importation movement** broadened the protest against the Stamp Act, giving women a new and active role in the political dissent of the time. Women were responsible for purchasing goods for the home, so by exercising the power of the purse, they could wield more power than they had in the past. Although they could not vote, they could mobilize others and make a difference in the political landscape.

From a local movement, the protests of the Sons and Daughters of Liberty soon spread until there was a chapter in every colony. The Daughters of Liberty promoted the boycott on British goods while the Sons enforced it, threatening retaliation against anyone who bought imported goods or used stamped paper. In the protest against the Stamp Act, wealthy, lettered political figures like John Adams supported the goals of the Sons and Daughters of Liberty, even if they did not engage in the Sons' violent actions. These men, who were lawyers, printers, and merchants, ran a propaganda campaign parallel to the Sons' campaign of violence. In newspapers and pamphlets throughout the colonies, they published article after article outlining the reasons the Stamp Act was unconstitutional and urging peaceful protest. They officially condemned violent actions but did not have the protesters arrested; a degree of cooperation prevailed, despite the groups' different economic backgrounds. Certainly, all the protesters saw themselves as acting in the best British tradition, standing up against the corruption (especially the extinguishing of their right to representation) that threatened their liberty.

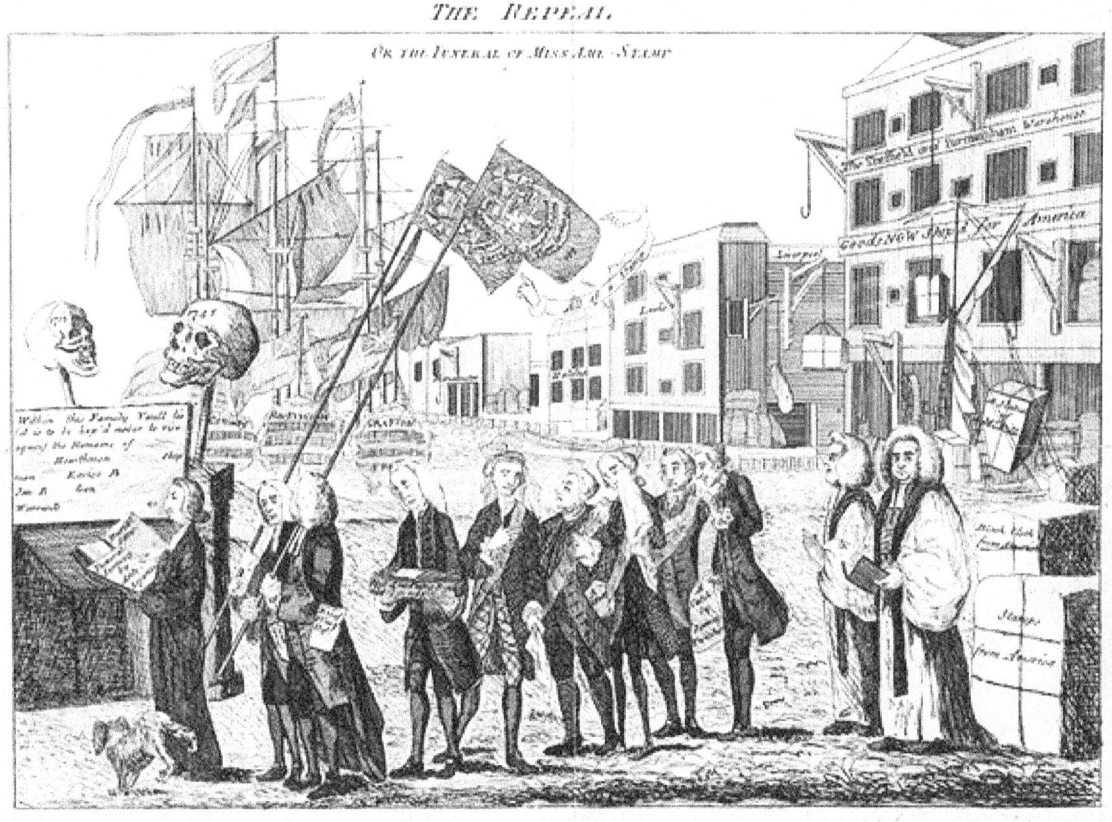

This 1766 illustration shows a funeral procession for the Stamp Act. Reverend William Scott leads the procession of politicians who had supported the act, while a dog urinates on his leg. George Grenville, pictured fourth in line, carries a small coffin. What point do you think this cartoon is trying to make?

THE DECLARATORY ACT

Back in Great Britain, news of the colonists' reactions worsened an already volatile political situation. Grenville's imperial reforms had brought about increased domestic taxes and his unpopularity led to his dismissal by King George III. While many in Parliament still wanted such reforms, British merchants argued strongly for their repeal. These merchants had no interest in the philosophy behind the colonists' desire for liberty; rather, their motive was that the non-importation of British goods by North American colonists was hurting their business. Many of the British at home were also appalled by the colonists' violent reaction to the Stamp Act. Other Britons cheered what they saw as the manly defense of liberty by their counterparts in the colonies.

In March 1766, the new prime minister, Lord Rockingham, compelled Parliament to repeal the Stamp Act. Colonists celebrated what they saw as a victory for their British liberty; in Boston, merchant John Hancock treated the entire town to drinks. However, to appease opponents of the repeal, who feared that it would weaken parliamentary power over the American colonists, Rockingham also proposed the Declaratory Act. This stated in no uncertain terms that Parliament's power was supreme and that any laws the colonies may have passed to govern and tax themselves were null and void if they ran counter to parliamentary law.

> Visit USHistory.org to read the full text of the Declaratory Act, in which Parliament asserted the supremacy of parliamentary power.

Section Summary

Though Parliament designed the 1765 Stamp Act to deal with the financial crisis in the Empire, it had unintended consequences. Outrage over the act created a degree of unity among otherwise unconnected American colonists, giving them a chance to act together both politically and socially. The crisis of the Stamp Act allowed colonists to loudly proclaim their identity as defenders of British liberty. With the repeal of the Stamp Act in 1766, liberty-loving subjects of the king celebrated what they viewed as a victory.

https://www.openassessments.org/assessments/952

> ### Glossary
>
> **Daughters of Liberty** well-born British colonial women who led a non-importation movement against British goods
>
> **direct tax** a tax that consumers pay directly, rather than through merchants' higher prices
>
> **no taxation without representation** the principle, first articulated in the Virginia Stamp Act Resolutions, that the colonists needed to be represented in Parliament if they were to be taxed
>
> **non-importation movement** a widespread colonial boycott of British goods

Sons of Liberty artisans, shopkeepers, and small-time merchants who opposed the Stamp Act and considered themselves British patriots

Attributions

CC licensed content, Shared previously

- US History. **Authored by**: P. Scott Corbett, Volker Janssen, John M. Lund, Todd Pfannestiel, Paul Vickery, and Sylvie Waskiewicz. **Provided by**: OpenStax College. **Located at**: http://openstaxcollege.org/textbooks/us-history. **License**: *CC BY: Attribution*. **License Terms**: Download for free at http://cnx.org/content/col11740/latest/

The Townshend Acts and Colonial Protest

> ### Learning Objectives
>
> By the end of this section, you will be able to:
>
> - Describe the purpose of the 1767 Townshend Acts
> - Explain why many colonists protested the 1767 Townshend Acts and the consequences of their actions

Colonists' joy over the repeal of the Stamp Act and what they saw as their defense of liberty did not last long. The Declaratory Act of 1766 had articulated Great Britain's supreme authority over the colonies, and Parliament soon began exercising that authority. In 1767, with the passage of the Townshend Acts, a tax on consumer goods in British North America, colonists believed their liberty as loyal British subjects had come under assault for a second time.

THE TOWNSHEND ACTS

Lord Rockingham's tenure as prime minister was not long (1765–1766). Rich landowners feared that if he were not taxing the colonies, Parliament would raise their taxes instead, sacrificing them to the interests of merchants and colonists. George III duly dismissed Rockingham. William Pitt, also sympathetic to the colonists, succeeded him. However, Pitt was old and ill with gout. His chancellor of the exchequer, Charles **Townshend**, whose job was to manage the Empire's finances, took on many of his duties. Primary among these was raising the needed revenue from the colonies.

Townshend's first act was to deal with the unruly New York Assembly, which had voted not to pay for supplies for the garrison of British soldiers that the Quartering Act required. In response, Townshend proposed the Restraining Act of 1767, which disbanded the New York Assembly until it agreed to pay for the garrison's supplies, which it eventually agreed to do.

The Townshend Revenue Act of 1767 placed duties on various consumer items like paper, paint, lead, tea, and glass. These British goods had to be imported, since the colonies did not have the manufacturing base to produce them. Townshend hoped the new duties would not anger the colonists because they were external taxes, not internal ones like the Stamp Act. In 1766, in arguing before Parliament for the repeal of the Stamp Act, Benjamin Franklin had stated, "I never heard any objection to the right of laying duties to regulate commerce; but a right to lay internal taxes was never supposed to be in parliament, as we are not represented there."

Charles Townshend, chancellor of the exchequer, shown here in a 1765 painting by Joshua Reynolds, instituted the Townshend Revenue Act of 1767 in order to raise money to support the British military presence in the colonies.

The Indemnity Act of 1767 exempted tea produced by the British East India Company from taxation when it was imported into Great Britain. When the tea was re-exported to the colonies, however, the colonists had to pay taxes on it because of the Revenue Act. Some critics of Parliament on both sides of the Atlantic saw this tax policy as an example of corrupt politicians giving preferable treatment to specific corporate interests, creating a monopoly. The sense that corruption had become entrenched in Parliament only increased colonists' alarm.

In fact, the revenue collected from these duties was only nominally intended to support the British army in America. It actually paid the salaries of some royally appointed judges, governors, and other officials whom the colonial assemblies had traditionally paid. Thanks to the Townshend Revenue Act of 1767, however, these officials no longer relied on colonial leadership for payment. This change gave them a measure of independence from the assemblies, so they could implement parliamentary acts without fear that their pay would be withheld in retaliation. The Revenue Act thus appeared to sever the relationship between governors and assemblies, drawing royal officials closer to the British government and further away from the colonial legislatures.

The Revenue Act also gave the customs board greater powers to counteract smuggling. It granted "writs of assistance"—basically, search warrants—to customs commissioners who suspected the presence of contraband goods, which also opened the door to a new level of bribery and trickery on the waterfronts of colonial America. Furthermore, to ensure compliance, Townshend introduced the Commissioners of Customs Act of 1767, which created an American Board of Customs to enforce trade laws. Customs enforcement had been based in Great Britain, but rules were difficult to implement at such a distance, and smuggling was rampant. The new customs board was based in Boston and would severely curtail smuggling in this large colonial seaport.

Townshend also orchestrated the Vice-Admiralty Court Act, which established three more vice-admiralty courts, in Boston, Philadelphia, and Charleston, to try violators of customs regulations without a jury. Before this, the only colonial vice-admiralty court had been in far-off Halifax, Nova Scotia, but with three local courts, smugglers could be tried more efficiently. Since the judges of these courts were paid a percentage of the worth of the goods they recovered, leniency was rare. All told, the Townshend Acts resulted in higher taxes and stronger British power to enforce them. Four years after the end of the French and Indian War, the Empire continued to search for solutions to its debt problem and the growing sense that the colonies needed to be brought under control.

REACTIONS: THE NON-IMPORTATION MOVEMENT

Like the Stamp Act, the Townshend Acts produced controversy and protest in the American colonies. For a second time, many colonists resented what they perceived as an effort to tax them without representation and thus to deprive them of their liberty. The fact that the revenue the Townshend Acts raised would pay royal governors only made the situation worse, because it took control away from colonial legislatures that otherwise had the power to set and withhold a royal governor's salary. The Restraining Act, which had been intended to isolate New York without angering the other colonies, had the opposite effect, showing the rest of the colonies how far beyond the British Constitution some members of Parliament were willing to go.

The Townshend Acts generated a number of protest writings, including "Letters from a Pennsylvania Farmer" by John Dickinson. In this influential pamphlet, which circulated widely in the colonies, Dickinson conceded that the Empire could regulate trade but argued that Parliament could not impose either internal taxes, like stamps, on goods or external taxes, like customs duties, on imports.

"Address to the Ladies" Verse from *The Boston Post-Boy and Advertiser*

This verse, which ran in a Boston newspaper in November 1767, highlights how women were encouraged to take political action by boycotting British goods. Notice that the writer especially encourages women to avoid British tea (Bohea and Green Hyson) and linen, and to manufacture their own homespun cloth. Building on the protest of the 1765 Stamp Act by the Daughters of Liberty, the non-importation movement of 1767–1768 mobilized women as political actors.

> Young ladies in town, and those that live round,
>
> Let a friend at this season advise you:
>
> Since money's so scarce, and times growing worse
>
> Strange things may soon hap and surprize you:
>
> First then, throw aside your high top knots of pride

Wear none but your own country linnen;

of economy boast, let your pride be the most

What, if homespun they say is not quite so gay

As brocades, yet be not in a passion,

For when once it is known this is much wore in town,

One and all will cry out, 'tis the fashion!

And as one, all agree that you'll not married be

To such as will wear London Fact'ry:

But at first sight refuse, tell 'em such you do chuse

As encourage our own Manufact'ry.

No more Ribbons wear, nor in rich dress appear,

Love your country much better than fine things,

Begin without passion, 'twill soon be the fashion

To grace your smooth locks with a twine string.

Throw aside your Bohea, and your Green Hyson Tea,

And all things with a new fashion duty;

Procure a good store of the choice Labradore,

For there'll soon be enough here to suit ye;

These do without fear and to all you'll appear

Fair, charming, true, lovely, and cleaver;

Tho' the times remain darkish, young men may be sparkish.

And love you much stronger than ever. !O!

In Massachusetts in 1768, Samuel Adams wrote a letter that became known as the **Massachusetts Circular**. Sent by the Massachusetts House of Representatives to the other colonial legislatures, the letter laid out the unconstitutionality of taxation without representation and encouraged the other colonies to again protest the taxes by boycotting British goods. Adams wrote, "It is, moreover, [the Massachusetts House of Representatives] humble opinion, which they express with the greatest deference to the wisdom of the Parliament, that the acts made there, imposing duties on the people of this province, with the sole and express purpose of raising a revenue, are infringements of their natural and constitutional rights; because, as they are not represented in the Parliament, his Majesty's Commons in Britain, by those acts, grant their property without their consent." Note that even in this letter of protest, the humble and submissive tone shows the Massachusetts Assembly's continued deference to parliamentary authority. Even in that hotbed of political protest, it is a clear expression of allegiance and the hope for a restoration of "natural and constitutional rights."

Great Britain's response to this threat of disobedience served only to unite the colonies further. The colonies' initial response to the Massachusetts Circular was lukewarm at best. However, back in Great Britain, the secretary of state for the colonies—Lord Hillsborough—demanded that Massachusetts retract the letter, promising that any colonial assemblies that endorsed it would be dissolved. This threat had the effect of pushing the other colonies to Massachusetts's side. Even the city of Philadelphia, which had originally opposed the Circular, came around.

The Daughters of Liberty once again supported and promoted the boycott of British goods. Women resumed spinning bees and again found substitutes for British tea and other goods. Many colonial merchants signed non-importation agreements, and the Daughters of Liberty urged colonial women to shop only with those merchants. The Sons of Liberty used newspapers and circulars to call out by name those merchants who refused to sign such agreements; sometimes they were threatened by violence. For instance, a broadside from 1769–1770 reads:

> WILLIAM JACKSON,
>
> an IMPORTER;
>
> at the BRAZEN HEAD,
>
> North Side of the TOWN-HOUSE,
>
> and Opposite the Town-Pump, [in]
>
> Corn-hill, BOSTON
>
> It is desired that the SONS
>
> and DAUGHTERS of LIBERTY,
>
> would not buy any one thing of
>
> him, for in so doing they will bring
>
> disgrace upon themselves, and their
>
> Posterity, for ever and ever, AMEN.

The boycott in 1768–1769 turned the purchase of consumer goods into a political gesture. It mattered what you consumed. Indeed, the very clothes you wore indicated whether you were a defender of liberty in homespun or a protector of parliamentary rights in superfine British attire.

> For examples of the types of luxury items that many American colonists favored, visit the National Humanities Center to see pictures and documents relating to home interiors of the wealthy.

TROUBLE IN BOSTON

The Massachusetts Circular got Parliament's attention, and in 1768, Lord Hillsborough sent four thousand British troops to Boston to deal with the unrest and put down any potential rebellion there. The troops were a constant reminder of the assertion of British power over the colonies, an illustration of an unequal relationship between members of the same empire. As an added aggravation, British soldiers moonlighted as dockworkers, creating competition for employment. Boston's labor system had traditionally been closed, privileging native-born laborers over outsiders, and jobs were scarce. Many Bostonians, led by the Sons of Liberty, mounted a campaign of harassment against British troops. The Sons of Liberty also helped protect the smuggling actions of the merchants; smuggling was crucial for the colonists' ability to maintain their boycott of British goods.

John Hancock was one of Boston's most successful merchants and prominent citizens. While he maintained too high a profile to work actively with the Sons of Liberty, he was known to support their aims, if not their means of achieving them. He was also one of the many prominent merchants who had made their fortunes by smuggling, which was rampant in the colonial seaports. In 1768, customs officials seized the *Liberty*, one of his ships, and violence erupted. Led by the Sons of Liberty, Bostonians rioted against customs officials, attacking the customs house and chasing out the officers, who ran to safety at Castle William, a British fort on a Boston harbor island. British soldiers crushed the riots, but over the next few years, clashes between British officials and Bostonians became common.

Conflict turned deadly on March 5, 1770, in a confrontation that came to be known as the **Boston Massacre**. On that night, a crowd of Bostonians from many walks of life started throwing snowballs, rocks, and sticks at the British soldiers guarding the customs house. In the resulting scuffle, some soldiers, goaded by the mob who hectored the soldiers as "lobster backs" (the reference to lobster equated the soldiers with bottom feeders, i.e., aquatic animals that feed on the lowest organisms in the food chain), fired into the crowd, killing five people. Crispus Attucks, the first man killed—and, though no one could have known it then, the first official casualty in the war for independence—was of Wampanoag and African descent. The bloodshed illustrated the level of hostility that had developed as a result of Boston's occupation by British troops, the competition for scarce jobs between Bostonians and the British soldiers stationed in the city, and the larger question of Parliament's efforts to tax the colonies.

The Sons of Liberty immediately seized on the event, characterizing the British soldiers as murderers and their victims as martyrs. Paul Revere, a silversmith and member of the Sons of Liberty, circulated an engraving that showed a line of grim redcoats firing ruthlessly into a crowd of unarmed, fleeing civilians. Among colonists who resisted British power, this view of the "massacre" confirmed their fears of a tyrannous government using its armies to curb the freedom of British subjects. But to others, the attacking mob was equally to blame for pelting the British with rocks and insulting them.

It was not only British Loyalists who condemned the unruly mob. John Adams, one of the city's strongest supporters of peaceful protest against Parliament, represented the British soldiers at their murder trial. Adams argued that the mob's lawlessness required the soldiers' response, and that without law and order, a society was nothing. He argued further that the soldiers were the tools of a much broader program, which transformed a street brawl into the injustice of imperial policy. Of the eight soldiers on trial, the jury acquitted six, convicting the other two of the reduced charge of manslaughter.

Adams argued: "Facts are stubborn things; and whatever may be our wishes, our inclinations, or the dictates of our passions, they cannot alter the state of facts and evidence: nor is the law less stable than the fact; if an assault was made to endanger their lives, the law is clear, they had a right to kill in their own defense; if it was not so severe as to endanger their lives, yet if they were assaulted at all, struck and abused by blows of any sort, by snow-balls, oyster-shells, cinders, clubs, or sticks of any kind; this was a provocation, for which the law reduces the offence of killing, down to manslaughter, in consideration of those passions in our nature, which cannot be eradicated. To your candour and justice I submit the prisoners and their cause."

Propaganda and the Sons of Liberty

Long after the British soldiers had been tried and punished, the Sons of Liberty maintained a relentless propaganda campaign against British oppression. Many of them were printers or engravers, and they were able to use public media to sway others to their cause. Shortly after the incident outside the customs house, Paul Revere created "The bloody massacre perpetrated in King Street Boston on March 5th 1770 by a party of the 29th Regt.", based on an image by engraver Henry Pelham. The picture—which represents only the protesters' point of view—shows the ruthlessness of the British soldiers and the helplessness of the crowd of civilians. Notice the subtle details Revere uses to help convince the viewer of the civilians' innocence and the soldiers' cruelty. Although eyewitnesses said the crowd started the fight by throwing snowballs and rocks, in the engraving they are innocently standing by. Revere also depicts the crowd as well dressed and well-to-do, when in fact they were laborers and probably looked quite a bit rougher.

The Sons of Liberty circulated this sensationalized version of the events of March 5, 1770, in order to promote the rightness of their cause. The verses below the image begin as follows: "Unhappy Boston! see thy Sons deplore, Thy hallowed Walks besmeared with guiltless Gore."

Newspaper articles and pamphlets that the Sons of Liberty circulated implied that the "massacre" was a planned murder. In the *Boston Gazette* on March 12, 1770, an article describes the soldiers as striking first. It goes on to discuss this version of the events: "On hearing the noise, one Samuel Atwood came up to see what was the matter; and entering the alley from dock square, heard the latter part of the combat; and when the boys had dispersed he met the ten or twelve soldiers aforesaid rushing down the alley towards the square and asked them if they intended to murder people? They answered Yes, by God, root and branch! With that one of them struck Mr. Atwood with a club which was repeated by another; and being unarmed, he turned to go off and received a wound on the left shoulder which reached the bone and gave him much pain."

What do you think most people in the United States think of when they consider the Boston Massacre? How does the propaganda of the Sons of Liberty still affect the way we think of this event?

PARTIAL REPEAL

As it turned out, the Boston Massacre occurred after Parliament had partially repealed the Townshend Acts. By the late 1760s, the American boycott of British goods had drastically reduced British trade. Once again, merchants who lost money because of the boycott strongly pressured Parliament to loosen its restrictions on the colonies and break the non-importation movement. Charles Townshend died suddenly in 1767 and was replaced by Lord North, who was inclined to look for a more workable solution with the colonists. North convinced Parliament to drop all the Townshend duties except the tax on tea. The administrative and enforcement provisions under the Townshend Acts—the American Board of Customs Commissioners and the vice-admiralty courts—remained in place.

To those who had protested the Townshend Acts for several years, the partial repeal appeared to be a major victory. For a second time, colonists had rescued liberty from an unconstitutional parliamentary measure. The hated British troops in Boston departed. The consumption of British goods skyrocketed after the partial repeal, an indication of the American colonists' desire for the items linking them to the Empire.

Section Summary

Like the Stamp Act in 1765, the Townshend Acts led many colonists to work together against what they perceived to be an unconstitutional measure, generating the second major crisis in British Colonial America. The experience of resisting the Townshend Acts provided another shared experience among colonists from diverse regions and backgrounds, while the partial repeal convinced many that liberty had once again been defended. Nonetheless, Great Britain's debt crisis still had not been solved.

https://www.openassessments.org/assessments/953

Review Question

1. What factors contributed to the Boston Massacre?

Answer to Review Question

1. Tensions between colonists and the redcoats had been simmering for some time. British soldiers had been moonlighting as dockworkers, taking needed jobs away from colonists. Many British colonists were also wary of standing armies during peacetime, so skirmishes were common. Finally, the Sons of Liberty promoted tensions with their propaganda.

Glossary

Boston Massacre a confrontation between a crowd of Bostonians and British soldiers on March 5, 1770, which resulted in the deaths of five people, including Crispus Attucks, the first official casualty in the war for independence

Massachusetts Circular a letter penned by Son of Liberty Samuel Adams that laid out the unconstitutionality of taxation without representation and encouraged the other colonies to boycott British goods

Attributions

CC licensed content, Shared previously

- US History. **Authored by**: P. Scott Corbett, Volker Janssen, John M. Lund, Todd Pfannestiel, Paul Vickery, and Sylvie Waskiewicz. **Provided by**: OpenStax College. **Located at**: http://openstaxcollege.org/textbooks/us-history. **License**: *CC BY: Attribution*. **License Terms**: Download for free at http://cnx.org/content/col11740/latest/

The Destruction of the Tea and the Coercive Acts

Learning Objectives

By the end of this section, you will be able to:

- Describe the socio-political environment in the colonies in the early 1770s
- Explain the purpose of the Tea Act of 1773 and discuss colonial reactions to it
- Identify and describe the Coercive Acts

The Tea Act of 1773 triggered a reaction with far more significant consequences than either the 1765 Stamp Act or the 1767 Townshend Acts. Colonists who had joined in protest against those earlier acts renewed their efforts in 1773. They understood that Parliament had again asserted its right to impose taxes without representation, and they feared the Tea Act was designed to seduce them into conceding this important principle by lowering the price of tea to the point that colonists might abandon their scruples. They also deeply resented the East India Company's monopoly on the sale of tea in the American colonies; this resentment sprang from the knowledge that some members of Parliament had invested heavily in the company.

SMOLDERING RESENTMENT

Even after the partial repeal of the Townshend duties, however, suspicion of Parliament's intentions remained high. This was especially true in port cities like Boston and New York, where British customs agents were a daily irritant and reminder of British power. In public houses and squares, people met and discussed politics. Philosopher John Locke's *Two Treatises of Government*, published almost a century earlier, influenced political thought about the role of government to protect life, liberty, and property. The Sons of Liberty issued propaganda ensuring that colonists remained aware when Parliament overreached itself.

Violence continued to break out on occasion, as in 1772, when Rhode Island colonists boarded and burned the British revenue ship *Gaspée* in Narragansett Bay. Colonists had attacked or burned British customs ships in the past, but after the Gaspée Affair, the British government convened a Royal Commission of Inquiry. This Commission had the authority to remove the colonists, who were charged with treason, to Great Britain for trial. Some colonial protestors saw this new ability as another example of the overreach of British power.

This 1883 engraving, which appeared in Harper's New Monthly Magazine, depicts the burning of the Gaspée. This attack provoked the British government to convene a Royal Commission of Inquiry; some regarded the Commission as an example of excessive British power and control over the colonies.

Samuel Adams, along with Joseph Warren and James Otis, re-formed the Boston **Committee of Correspondence**, which functioned as a form of shadow government, to address the fear of British overreach. Soon towns all over Massachusetts had formed their own committees, and many other colonies followed suit. These committees, which had between seven and eight thousand members in all, identified enemies of the movement and communicated the news of the day. Sometimes they provided a version of events that differed from royal interpretations, and slowly, the committees began to supplant royal governments as sources of information. They later formed the backbone of communication among the colonies in the rebellion against the Tea Act, and eventually in the revolt against the British crown.

THE TEA ACT OF 1773

Parliament did not enact the **Tea Act of 1773** in order to punish the colonists, assert parliamentary power, or even raise revenues. Rather, the act was a straightforward order of economic protectionism for a British tea firm, the East India Company, that was on the verge of bankruptcy. In the colonies, tea was the one remaining consumer good subject to the hated Townshend duties. Protest leaders and their followers still avoided British tea, drinking smuggled Dutch tea as a sign of patriotism.

The Tea Act of 1773 gave the British East India Company the ability to export its tea directly to the colonies without paying import or export duties and without using middlemen in either Great Britain or the colonies. Even with the Townshend tax, the act would allow the East India Company to sell its tea at lower prices than the smuggled Dutch tea, thus undercutting the smuggling trade.

This act was unwelcome to those in British North America who had grown displeased with the pattern of imperial measures. By granting a monopoly to the East India Company, the act not only cut out colonial merchants who would otherwise sell the tea themselves; it also reduced their profits from smuggled foreign tea. These merchants were among the most powerful and influential people in the colonies, so their dissatisfaction carried some weight. Moreover, because the tea tax that the Townshend Acts imposed remained in place, tea had intense power to symbolize the idea of "no taxation without representation."

COLONIAL PROTEST: THE DESTRUCTION OF THE TEA

The 1773 act reignited the worst fears among the colonists. To the Sons and Daughters of Liberty and those who followed them, the act appeared to be proof positive that a handful of corrupt members of Parliament were violating the British Constitution. Veterans of the protest movement had grown accustomed to interpreting British actions in the worst possible light, so the 1773 act appeared to be part of a large conspiracy against liberty.

As they had done to protest earlier acts and taxes, colonists responded to the Tea Act with a boycott. The Committees of Correspondence helped to coordinate resistance in all of the colonial port cities, so up and down the East Coast, British tea-carrying ships were unable to come to shore and unload their wares. In Charlestown, Boston, Philadelphia, and New York, the equivalent of millions of dollars' worth of tea was held hostage, either locked in storage warehouses or rotting in the holds of ships as they were forced to sail back to Great Britain.

In Boston, Thomas Hutchinson, now the royal governor of Massachusetts, vowed that radicals like Samuel Adams would not keep the ships from unloading their cargo. He urged the merchants who would have accepted the tea from the ships to stand their ground and receive the tea once it had been unloaded. When the *Dartmouth* sailed into Boston Harbor in November 1773, it had twenty days to unload its cargo of tea and pay the duty before it had to return to Great Britain. Two more ships, the *Eleanor* and the *Beaver*, followed soon after. Samuel Adams and the Sons of Liberty tried to keep the captains of the ships from paying the duties and posted groups around the ships to make sure the tea would not be unloaded.

On December 16, just as the *Dartmouth*'s deadline approached, townspeople gathered at the Old South Meeting House determined to take action. From this gathering, a group of Sons of Liberty and their followers approached the three ships. Some were disguised as Mohawks. Protected by a crowd of spectators, they systematically dumped all the tea into the harbor, destroying goods worth almost $1 million in today's dollars, a very significant loss. This act soon inspired further acts of resistance up and down the East Coast. However, not all colonists, and not even all Patriots, supported the dumping of the tea. The wholesale destruction of property shocked people on both sides of the Atlantic.

> To learn more about the Boston Tea Party, explore the extensive resources in the Boston Tea Party Ships and Museum collection of articles, photos, and video. At the museum itself, you can board replicas of the *Eleanor* and the *Beaver* and experience a recreation of the dumping of the tea.

PARLIAMENT RESPONDS: THE COERCIVE ACTS

In London, response to the destruction of the tea was swift and strong. The violent destruction of property infuriated King George III and the prime minister, Lord North, who insisted the loss be repaid. Though some American merchants put forward a proposal for restitution, the Massachusetts Assembly refused to make payments. Massachusetts's resistance to British authority united different factions in Great Britain against the colonies. North had lost patience with the unruly British subjects in Boston. He declared: "The Americans have tarred and feathered your subjects, plundered your merchants, burnt your ships, denied all obedience to your laws and authority; yet so clement and so long forbearing has our conduct been that it is incumbent on us now to take a different course. Whatever may be the consequences, we must risk something; if we do not, all is over." Both Parliament and the king agreed that Massachusetts should be forced to both pay for the tea and yield to British authority.

Lord North, seen here in Portrait of Frederick North, Lord North (1773–1774), painted by Nathaniel Dance, was prime minister at the time of the destruction of the tea and insisted that Massachusetts make good on the loss.

In early 1774, leaders in Parliament responded with a set of four measures designed to punish Massachusetts, commonly known at the **Coercive Acts**. The Boston Port Bill shut down Boston Harbor until the East India Company was repaid. The Massachusetts Government Act placed the colonial government under the direct control of crown officials and made traditional town meetings subject to the governor's approval. The Administration of Justice Act allowed the royal governor to unilaterally move any trial of a crown officer out of Massachusetts, a change designed to prevent hostile Massachusetts juries from deciding these cases. This act was especially infuriating to John Adams and others who emphasized the time-honored rule of law. They saw this part of the Coercive Acts as striking at the heart of fair and equitable justice. Finally, the Quartering Act encompassed all the colonies and allowed British troops to be housed in occupied buildings.

At the same time, Parliament also passed the Quebec Act, which expanded the boundaries of Quebec westward and extended religious tolerance to Roman Catholics in the province. For many Protestant colonists, especially Congregationalists in New England, this forced tolerance of Catholicism was the most objectionable provision of the act. Additionally, expanding the boundaries of Quebec raised troubling questions for many colonists who eyed the West, hoping to expand the boundaries of their provinces. The Quebec Act appeared gratuitous, a slap in the face to colonists already angered by the Coercive Acts.

American Patriots renamed the Coercive and Quebec measures the **Intolerable Acts**. Some in London also thought the acts went too far; see the cartoon "The Able Doctor, or America Swallowing the Bitter Draught" for one British view of what Parliament was doing to the colonies. Meanwhile, punishments designed to hurt only one colony (Massachusetts, in this case) had the effect of mobilizing all the colonies to its side. The Committees of Correspondence had already been active in coordinating an approach to the Tea Act. Now the talk would turn to these new, intolerable assaults on the colonists' rights as British subjects.

The artist of "The Able Doctor, or America Swallowing the Bitter Draught" (London Magazine, May 1, 1774) targets select members of Parliament as the perpetrators of a devilish scheme to overturn the constitution; this is why Mother Britannia weeps. Note that this cartoon came from a British publication; Great Britain was not united in support of Parliament's policies toward the American colonies.

Section Summary

The colonial rejection of the Tea Act, especially the destruction of the tea in Boston Harbor, recast the decade-long argument between British colonists and the home government as an intolerable conspiracy against liberty and an excessive overreach of parliamentary power. The Coercive Acts were punitive in nature, awakening the worst fears of otherwise loyal members of the British Empire in America.

https://www.openassessments.org/assessments/954

Review Question

1. What was the significance of the Committees of Correspondence?

Answer to Review Question

1. The Committees of Correspondence provided a crucial means of communication among the colonies. They also set the foundation for a colonial government by breaking away from royal governmental structures. Finally, they promoted a sense of colonial unity.

Glossary

Coercive Acts four acts (Administration of Justice Act, Massachusetts Government Act, Port Bill, Quartering Act) that Lord North passed to punish Massachusetts for destroying the tea and refusing to pay for the damage

Committees of Correspondence colonial extralegal shadow governments that convened to coordinate plans of resistance against the British

Intolerable Acts the name American Patriots gave to the Coercive Acts and the Quebec Act

Attributions

CC licensed content, Shared previously

- US History. **Authored by**: P. Scott Corbett, Volker Janssen, John M. Lund, Todd Pfannestiel, Paul Vickery, and Sylvie Waskiewicz. **Provided by**: OpenStax College. **Located at**: http://openstaxcollege.org/textbooks/us-history. **License**: *CC BY: Attribution*. **License Terms**: Download for free at http://cnx.org/content/col11740/latest/

Disaffection: The First Continental Congress and American Identity

> **Learning Objectives**
>
> By the end of this section, you will be able to:
> - Describe the state of affairs between the colonies and the home government in 1774
> - Explain the purpose and results of the First Continental Congress

Disaffection—the loss of affection toward the home government—had reached new levels by 1774. Many colonists viewed the Intolerable Acts as a turning point; they now felt they had to take action. The result was the First Continental Congress, a direct challenge to Lord North and British authority in the colonies. Still, it would be a mistake to assume there was a groundswell of support for separating from the British Empire and creating a new, independent nation. Strong ties still bound the Empire together, and colonists did not agree about the proper response. Loyalists tended to be property holders, established residents who feared the loss of their property. To them the protests seemed to promise nothing but mob rule, and the violence and disorder they provoked were shocking. On both sides of the Atlantic, opinions varied.

After the passage of the Intolerable Acts in 1774, the Committees of Correspondence and the Sons of Liberty went straight to work, spreading warnings about how the acts would affect the liberty of all colonists, not just urban merchants and laborers. The Massachusetts Government Act had shut down the colonial government there, but resistance-minded colonists began meeting in extralegal assemblies. One of these assemblies, the Massachusetts Provincial Congress, passed the **Suffolk Resolves** in September 1774, which laid out a plan of resistance to the Intolerable Acts. Meanwhile, the First Continental Congress was convening to discuss how to respond to the acts themselves.

The First Continental Congress was made up of elected representatives of twelve of the thirteen American colonies. (Georgia's royal governor blocked the move to send representatives from that colony, an indication of the continued strength of the royal government despite the crisis.) The representatives met in Philadelphia from September 5 through October 26, 1774, and at first they did not agree at all about the appropriate response to the Intolerable Acts. Joseph Galloway of Pennsylvania argued for a conciliatory approach; he proposed that an elected Grand Council in America, like the Parliament in Great Britain, should be paired with a royally appointed President General, who would represent the authority of the Crown. More radical factions argued for a move toward separation from the Crown.

In the end, Paul Revere rode from Massachusetts to Philadelphia with the Suffolk Resolves, which became the basis of the Declaration and Resolves of the First Continental Congress. In the Declaration and Resolves, adopted on October 14, the colonists demanded the repeal of all repressive acts passed since 1773 and agreed to a non-importation, non-exportation, and non-consumption pact against all British goods until the acts were repealed. In the "Petition of Congress to the King" on October 24, the delegates adopted a further recommendation of the Suffolk Resolves and proposed that the colonies raise and regulate their own militias.

The representatives at the First Continental Congress created a Continental Association to ensure that the full boycott was enforced across all the colonies. The Continental Association served as an umbrella group for colonial and local committees of observation and inspection. By taking these steps, the First Continental Congress established a governing network in opposition to royal authority.

> **Visit the** Massachusetts Historical Society **to see a digitized copy and read the transcript of the First Continental Congress's petition to King George.**

The First List of Un-American Activities

In her book *Toward A More Perfect Union: Virtue and the Formation of American Republics*, historian Ann Fairfax Withington explores actions the delegates to the First Continental Congress took during the weeks they were together. Along with their efforts to bring about the repeal of the Intolerable Acts, the delegates also banned certain activities they believed would undermine their fight against what they saw as British corruption.

In particular, the delegates prohibited horse races, cockfights, the theater, and elaborate funerals. The reasons for these prohibitions provide insight into the state of affairs in 1774. Both horse races and cockfights encouraged gambling and, for the delegates, gambling threatened to prevent the unity of action and purpose they desired. In addition, cockfighting appeared immoral and corrupt because the roosters were fitted with razors and fought to the death.

Cockfights, as depicted in The Cockpit *(1759) by British artist and engraver William Hogarth, were among the entertainments the First Continental Congress sought to outlaw, considering them un-American.*

The ban on the theater aimed to do away with another corrupt British practice. Critics had long believed that theatrical performances drained money from working people. Moreover, they argued, theatergoers learned to lie and deceive from what they saw on stage. The delegates felt banning the theater would demonstrate their resolve to act honestly and without pretence in their fight against corruption.

Finally, eighteenth-century mourning practices often required lavish spending on luxury items and even the employment of professional mourners who, for a price, would shed tears at the grave. Prohibiting these practices reflected the idea that luxury bred corruption, and the First Continental Congress wanted to demonstrate that the colonists would do without British vices. Congress emphasized the need to be frugal and self-sufficient when confronted with corruption.

The First Continental Congress banned all four activities—horse races, cockfights, the theater, and elaborate funerals—and entrusted the Continental Association with enforcement. Rejecting what they saw as corruption coming from Great Britain, the delegates were also identifying themselves as standing apart from their British relatives. They cast themselves as virtuous defenders of liberty against a corrupt Parliament.

In the Declaration and Resolves and the Petition of Congress to the King, the delegates to the First Continental Congress refer to George III as "Most Gracious Sovereign" and to themselves as "inhabitants of the English colonies in North America" or "inhabitants of British America," indicating that they still considered themselves British subjects of the king, not American citizens. At the same time, however, they were slowly moving away from British authority, creating their own de facto government in the First Continental Congress. One of the provisions of the Congress was that it meet again in one year to mark its progress; the Congress was becoming an elected government.

Section Summary

The First Continental Congress, which comprised elected representatives from twelve of the thirteen American colonies, represented a direct challenge to British authority. In its Declaration and Resolves, colonists demanded the repeal of all repressive acts passed since 1773. The delegates also recommended that the colonies raise militias, lest the British respond to the Congress's proposed boycott of British goods with force. While the colonists still considered themselves British subjects, they were slowly retreating from British authority, creating their own de facto government via the First Continental Congress.

https://www.openassessments.org/assessments/955

Critical Thinking Questions

1. Was reconciliation between the American colonies and Great Britain possible in 1774? Why or why not?

2. Look again at the painting that opened this chapter: *The Bostonians Paying the Excise-man, or Tarring and Feathering*. How does this painting represent the relationship between Great Britain and the American colonies in the years from 1763 to 1774?

3. Why did the colonists react so much more strongly to the Stamp Act than to the Sugar Act? How did the principles that the Stamp Act raised continue to provide points of contention between colonists and the British government?

4. History is filled with unintended consequences. How do the British government's attempts to control and regulate the colonies during this tumultuous era provide a case in point? How did the aims of the British measure up against the results of their actions?

5. What evidence indicates that colonists continued to think of themselves as British subjects throughout this era? What evidence suggests that colonists were beginning to forge a separate, collective "American" identity? How would you explain this shift?

Glossary

Suffolk Resolves a Massachusetts plan of resistance to the Intolerable Acts that formed the basis of the eventual plan adopted by the First Continental Congress for resisting the British, including the arming of militias and the adoption of a widespread non-importation, non-exportation, and non-consumption agreement

Attributions

CC licensed content, Shared previously

- US History. **Authored by**: P. Scott Corbett, Volker Janssen, John M. Lund, Todd Pfannestiel, Paul Vickery, and Sylvie Waskiewicz.

Provided by: OpenStax College. **Located at**: http://openstaxcollege.org/textbooks/us-history. **License**: CC BY: Attribution.
License Terms: Download for free at http://cnx.org/content/col11740/latest/

Primary Source Reading: Common Sense

Common Sense by Thomas Paine

Introduction

Common Sense is a pamphlet written by Thomas Paine in 1775–76 that inspired people in the Thirteen Colonies to declare and fight for independence from Great Britain in the summer of 1776. The pamphlet explained the advantages of and the need for immediate independence in clear, simple language. It was published anonymously on January 10, 1776, at the beginning of the American Revolution and became an immediate sensation. It was sold and distributed widely and read aloud at taverns and meeting places.

Washington had it read to all his troops, which at the time had surrounded the British army in Boston. In proportion to the population of the colonies at that time (2.5 million), it had the largest sale and circulation of any book published in American history. As of 2006, it remains the all-time best selling American title.

Common Sense presented the American colonists with an argument for freedom from British rule at a time when the question of whether or not to seek independence was the central issue of the day. Paine wrote and reasoned in a style that common people understood. Forgoing the philosophical and Latin references used by Enlightenment era writers, he structured Common Sense as if it were a sermon, and relied on Biblical references to make his case to the people. He connected independence with common dissenting Protestant beliefs as a means to present a distinctly American political identity. Historian Gordon S. Wood described Common Sense as "the most incendiary and popular pamphlet of the entire revolutionary era".

Source (Selection)

Thoughts of the present state of American Affairs

The sun never shined on a cause of greater worth. 'Tis not the affair of a city, a country, a province, or a kingdom, but of a continent— of at least one eighth part of the habitable globe. 'Tis not the concern of a day, a year, or an age; posterity are virtually involved in the contest, and will be more or less affected, even to the end of time, by the proceedings now. Now is the seed time of continental union, faith and honor. The least fracture now will be like a name engraved with the point of a pin on the tender rind of a young oak; The wound will enlarge with the tree, and posterity read it in full grown characters.

By referring the matter from argument to arms, a new æra for politics is struck; a new method of thinking hath arisen. All plans, proposals, &c. prior to the nineteenth of April, i. e. to the commencement of hostilities, are like the almanacks of the last year; which, though proper then, are superceded and useless now. Whatever was advanced by the advocates on either side of the question then, terminated in one and the same point, viz. a union with Great-Britain; the only difference between the parties was the method of effecting it; the one proposing force, the other friendship; but it hath so far happened that the first hath failed, and the second hath withdrawn her influence.

As much hath been said of the advantages of reconciliation, which, like an agreeable dream, hath passed away and left us as we were, it is but right, that we should examine the contrary side of the argument, and inquire into some of the many material injuries which these colonies sustain, and always will sustain, by being connected with, and dependant on Great-Britain. To examine that connexion and dependance, on the principles of nature and common sense, to see what we have to trust to, if separated, and what we are to expect, if dependant.

I have heard it asserted by some, that as America hath flourished under her former connexion with Great-Britain, that the same connexion is necessary towards her future happiness, and will always have the same effect. Nothing can be more fallacious than this kind of argument. We may as well assert that because a child has thrived upon milk, that it is never to have meat, or that the first twenty years of our lives is to become a precedent for the next twenty. But even this is admitting more than is true, for I answer roundly, that America would have flourished as much, and probably much more, had no European power had any thing to do with her. The commerce, by which she hath enriched herself are the necessaries of life, and will always have a market while eating is the custom of Europe.

But she has protected us, say some. That she hath engrossed us is true, and defended the continent at our expence as well as her own is admitted, and she would have defended Turkey from the same motive, viz. the sake of trade and dominion.

Alas, we have been long led away by ancient prejudices, and made large sacrifices to superstition. We have boasted the protection of Great-Britain, without considering, that her motive was interest not attachment; that she did not protect us from our enemies on our account, but from her enemies on her own account, from those who had no quarrel with us on any other account, and who will always be our enemies on the same account. Let Britain wave her pretensions to the continent, or the continent throw off the dependance, and we should be at peace with France and Spain were they at war with Britain. The miseries of Hanover last war ought to warn us against connexions.

It hath lately been asserted in parliament, that the colonies have no relation to each other but through the parent country, i. e. that Pennsylvania and the Jerseys, and so on for the rest, are sister colonies by the way of England; this is certainly a very round-about way of proving relationship, but it is the nearest and only true way of proving enemyship, if I may so call it. France and Spain never were, nor perhaps ever will be our enemies as Americans, but as our being the subjects of Great-Britain.

But Britain is the parent country, say some. Then the more shame upon her conduct. Even brutes do not devour their young, nor savages make war upon their families; wherefore the assertion, if true, turns to her reproach; but it happens not to be true, or only partly so, and the phrase parent or mother country hath been jesuitically adopted by the king and his parasites, with a low papistical design of gaining an unfair bias on the credulous weakness of our minds. Europe, and not England, is the parent country of America. This new world hath been the asylum for the persecuted lovers of civil and religious liberty from every part of Europe. Hither have they fled, not from the tender embraces of the mother, but from the cruelty of the monster; and it is so far true of England, that the same tyranny which drove the first emigrants from home, pursues their descendants still.

In this extensive quarter of the globe, we forget the narrow limits of three hundred and sixty miles (the extent of England) and carry our friendship on a larger scale; we claim brotherhood with every European Christian, and triumph in the generosity of the sentiment.

It is pleasant to observe by what regular gradations we surmount the force of local prejudice, as we enlarge our acquaintance with the world. A man born in any town in England divided into parishes, will naturally associate most with his fellow parishioners (because their interests in many cases will be common) and distinguish him by the name of neighbour; if he meet him but a few miles from home, he drops the narrow idea of a street, and salutes him by the name of townsman; if he travel out of the county, and meet him in any other, he forgets the minor divisions of street and town, and calls him countryman; i. e. county-man; but if in their foreign excursions they should associate in France or any other part of Europe, their local remembrance would be enlarged into that of Englishmen. And by a just parity of reasoning, all Europeans meeting in America, or any other quarter of the globe, are countrymen; for England, Holland, Germany, or Sweden, when compared with the whole, stand in the same places on the larger scale, which the divisions of street, town, and county do on the smaller ones; distinctions too limited for continental minds. Not one third of the inhabitants, even of this province, are of English descent. Wherefore I reprobate the phrase of parent or mother country applied to England only, as being false, selfish, narrow and ungenerous.

But admitting, that we were all of English descent, what does it amount to? Nothing. Britain, being now an open enemy, extinguishes every other name and title: And to say that reconciliation is our duty, is truly farcical. The first king of England, of the present line (William the Conqueror) was a Frenchman, and half the Peers of England are descendants from the same country; wherefore, by the same method of reasoning, England ought to be governed by France.

Much hath been said of the united strength of Britain and the colonies, that in conjunction they might bid defiance to the world. But this is mere presumption; the fate of war is uncertain, neither do the expressions mean any thing; for this continent would never suffer itself to be drained of inhabitants, to support the British arms in either Asia, Africa, or Europe.

Besides, what have we to do with setting the world at defiance? Our plan is commerce, and that, well attended to, will secure us the peace and friendship of all Europe; because, it is the interest of all Europe to have America a free port. Her trade will always be a protection, and her barrenness of gold and silver secure her from invaders.

I challenge the warmest advocate for reconciliation, to shew, a single advantage that this continent can reap, by being connected with Great Britain. I repeat the challenge, not a single advantage is derived. Our corn will fetch its price in any market in Europe, and our imported goods must be paid for buy them where we will.

But the injuries and disadvantages we sustain by that connection, are without number; and our duty to mankind at large, as well as to ourselves, instruct us to renounce the alliance: Because, any submission to, or dependance on Great-Britain, tends directly to involve this continent in European wars and quarrels; and sets us at variance with nations, who would otherwise seek our friendship, and against whom, we have neither anger nor complaint. As Europe is our market for trade, we ought to form no partial connection with any part of it. It is the true interest of America to steer clear of European contentions, which she never can do, while by her dependance on Britain, she is made the make-weight in the scale on British politics.

Europe is too thickly planted with kingdoms to be long at peace, and whenever a war breaks out between England and any foreign power, the trade of America goes to ruin, because of her connection with Britain. The next war may not turn out like the last, and should it not, the advocates for reconciliation now will be wishing for separation then, because, neutrality in that case, would be a safer convoy than a man of war. Every thing that is right or natural pleads for separation. The blood of the slain, the weeping voice of nature cries, 'TIS TIME TO PART. Even the distance at which the Almighty hath placed England and America, is a strong and natural proof, that the authority of the one, over the other, was never the design of Heaven. The time likewise at which the continent was discovered, adds weight to the argument, and the manner in which it was peopled encreases the force of it. The Reformation was preceded by the discovery of America, as if the Almighty graciously meant to open a sanctuary to the persecuted in future years, when home should afford neither friendship nor safety.

The authority of Great-Britain over this continent, is a form of government, which sooner or later must have an end: And a serious mind can draw no true pleasure by looking forward, under the painful and positive conviction, that what he calls "the present constitution" is merely temporary. As parents, we can have no joy, knowing that this government is not sufficiently lasting to ensure any thing which we may bequeath to posterity: And by a plain method of argument, as we are running the next generation into debt, we ought to do the work of it, otherwise we use them meanly and pitifully. In order to discover the line of our duty rightly, we should take our children in our hand, and fix our station a few years farther into life; that eminence will present a prospect, which a few present fears and prejudices conceal from our sight.

Attributions

CC licensed content, Shared previously

- Introduction to Common Sense. **Provided by**: Wikipedia. **Located at**: http://en.wikipedia.org/wiki/Common_Sense_%28pamphlet%29. **License**: *CC BY-SA: Attribution-ShareAlike*

Public domain content

- Excerpt from Common Sense. **Provided by**: Wikisource. **Located at**: https://en.wikisource.org/wiki/Common_Sense. **License**: *Public Domain: No Known Copyright*

Primary Source Reading: "Give Me Liberty or Give Me Death!"

Introduction

"Give me liberty, or give me death!" is a quotation attributed to Patrick Henry from a speech he made to the Virginia Convention in 1775, at St. John's Church in Richmond, Virginia, he is credited with having swung the balance in convincing the Virginia House of Burgesses to pass a resolution delivering the Virginia troops to the Revolutionary War. Among the delegates to the convention were future U.S. Presidents Thomas Jefferson and George Washington. (http://en.wikipedia.org/wiki/Give_me_liberty,_or_give_me_death!)

The Speech

No man thinks more highly than I do of the patriotism, as well as abilities, of the very worthy gentlemen who have just addressed the House. But different men often see the same subject in different lights; and, therefore, I hope it will not be thought disrespectful to those gentlemen if, entertaining as I do opinions of a character very opposite to theirs, I shall speak forth my sentiments freely and without reserve. This is no time for ceremony.

The question before the House is one of awful moment to this country. For my own part, I consider it as nothing less than a question of freedom or slavery; and in proportion to the magnitude of the subject ought to be the freedom of the debate. It is only in this way that we can hope to arrive at truth, and fulfill the great responsibility which we hold to God and our country. Should I keep back my opinions at such a time, through fear of giving offense, I should consider myself as guilty of treason towards my country, and of an act of disloyalty toward the Majesty of Heaven, which I revere above all earthly kings.

Mr. President, it is natural to man to indulge in the illusions of hope. We are apt to shut our eyes against a painful truth, and listen to the song of that siren till she transforms us into beasts. Is this the part of wise men, engaged in a great and arduous struggle for liberty? Are we disposed to be of the number of those who, having eyes, see not, and, having ears, hear not, the things which so nearly concern their temporal salvation? For my part, whatever anguish of spirit it may cost, I am willing to know the whole truth; to know the worst, and to provide for it.

I have but one lamp by which my feet are guided, and that is the lamp of experience. I know of no way of judging of the future but by the past. And judging by the past, I wish to know what there has been in the conduct of the British ministry for the last ten years to justify those hopes with which gentlemen have been pleased to solace themselves and the House. Is it that insidious smile with which our petition has been lately received? Trust it not, sir; it will prove a snare to your feet. Suffer not yourselves to be betrayed with a kiss.

Ask yourselves how this gracious reception of our petition comports with those warlike preparations which cover our waters and darken our land. Are fleets and armies necessary to a work of love and reconciliation? Have we shown ourselves so unwilling to be reconciled that force must be called in to win back our love? Let us not deceive ourselves, sir. These are the implements of war and subjugation; the last arguments to which kings resort.

I ask gentlemen, sir, what means this martial array, if its purpose be not to force us to submission? Can gentlemen assign any other possible motive for it? Has Great Britain any enemy, in this quarter of the world, to call for all this accumulation of navies and armies? No, sir, she has none. They are meant for us: they can be meant for no other. They are sent over to bind and rivet upon us those chains which the British ministry have been so long forging.

And what have we to oppose to them? Shall we try argument? Sir, we have been trying that for the last ten years. Have we anything new to offer upon the subject? Nothing. We have held the subject up in every light of which it is capable; but it has been all in vain. Shall we resort to entreaty and humble supplication? What terms shall we find which have not been already exhausted? Let us not, I beseech you, sir, deceive ourselves longer.

Sir, we have done everything that could be done to avert the storm which is now coming on. We have petitioned; we have remonstrated; we have supplicated; we have prostrated ourselves before the throne, and have implored its interposition to arrest the tyrannical hands of the ministry and Parliament. Our petitions have been slighted; our remonstrances have produced additional violence and insult; our supplications have been disregarded; and we have been spurned, with contempt, from the foot of the throne!

In vain, after these things, may we indulge the fond hope of peace and reconciliation. There is no longer any room for hope. If we wish to be free—if we mean to preserve inviolate those inestimable privileges for which we have been so long contending—if we mean not basely to abandon the noble struggle in which we have been so long engaged, and which we have pledged ourselves never to abandon until the glorious object of our contest shall be obtained—we must fight! I repeat it, sir, we must fight! An appeal to arms and to the God of hosts is all that is left us!

They tell us, sir, that we are weak; unable to cope with so formidable an adversary. But when shall we be stronger? Will it be the next week, or the next year? Will it be when we are totally disarmed, and when a British guard shall be stationed in every house? Shall we gather strength by irresolution and inaction? Shall we acquire the means of effectual resistance by lying supinely on our backs and hugging the delusive phantom of hope, until our enemies shall have bound us hand and foot?

Sir, we are not weak if we make a proper use of those means which the God of nature hath placed in our power. Three millions of people, armed in the holy cause of liberty, and in such a country as that which we possess, are invincible by any force which our enemy can send against us.

Besides, sir, we shall not fight our battles alone. There is a just God who presides over the destinies of nations, and who will raise up friends to fight our battles for us. The battle, sir, is not to the strong alone; it is to the vigilant, the active, the brave. Besides, sir, we have no election. If we were base enough to desire it, it is now too late to retire from the contest. There is no retreat but in submission and slavery! Our chains are forged! Their clanking may be heard on the plains of Boston! The war is inevitable—and let it come! I repeat it, sir, let it come.

It is in vain, sir, to extenuate the matter. Gentlemen may cry, peace, peace—but there is no peace. The war is actually begun! The next gale that sweeps from the north will bring to our ears the clash of resounding arms! Our brethren are already in the field! Why stand we here idle? What is it that gentlemen wish? What would they have? Is life so dear, or peace so sweet, as to be purchased at the price of chains and slavery?

Forbid it, Almighty God! I know not what course others may take; but as for me, give me liberty or give me death!

Attributions

CC licensed content, Shared previously

- Introduction . **Provided by**: Wikipedia. **Located at**: https://en.wikipedia.org/wiki/Give_me_liberty,_or_give_me_death!. **License**: *CC BY-SA: Attribution-ShareAlike*

Public domain content

- Speech. **Provided by**: Wikisource. **Located at**: https://en.wikisource.org/wiki/Give_me_liberty_or_give_me_death. **License**: *Public Domain: No Known Copyright*

Primary Source Reading: The Declaration of Independence

The Declaration of Independence is the usual name of a statement adopted by the Continental Congress on July 4, 1776, which announced that the thirteen American colonies, then at war with Great Britain, regarded themselves as 13 newly independent sovereign states, and no longer a part of the British Empire. Instead they formed a new nation—the United States of America. John Adams was a leader in pushing for independence, which was unanimously approved on July 2. A committee had already drafted the formal declaration, to be ready when Congress voted on independence. The term "Declaration of Independence" is not used in the document itself.

Adams persuaded the committee to select Thomas Jefferson to compose the original draft of the document, which congress would edit to produce the final version. The Declaration was ultimately a formal explanation of why Congress had voted on July 2 to declare independence from Great Britain, more than a year after the outbreak of the American Revolutionary War. The national birthday, the Independence Day is celebrated on July 4, although Adams wanted July 2.

After ratifying the text on July 4, Congress issued the Declaration of Independence in several forms. It was initially published as the printed Dunlap broadside that was widely distributed and read to the public. The source copy used for this printing has been lost, and may have been a copy in Thomas Jefferson's hand. Jefferson's original draft, complete with changes made by John Adams and Benjamin Franklin, and Jefferson's notes of changes made by Congress, is preserved at the Library of Congress. The most famous version of the Declaration, a signed copy that is popularly regarded as the official document, is displayed at the National Archives in Washington, D.C. This engrossed copy was ordered by Congress on July 19, and signed primarily on August 2.

The Declaration

In CONGRESS, July 4, 1776.
A DECLARATION
By the REPRESENTATIVES of the
UNITED STATES OF AMERICA,
In GENERAL CONGRESS assembled.

When in the course of human Events, it becomes necessary for one People to dissolve the Political Bands which have connected them with another, and to assume among the Powers of the Earth, the separate and equal Station to which the Laws of Nature and of Nature's God entitle them, a decent Respect to the Opinions of Mankind requires that they should declare the causes which impel them to the Separation.

We hold these Truths to be self-evident, that all Men are created equal, that they are endowed by their Creator with certain unalienable Rights, that among these are Life, Liberty, and the pursuit of Happiness—That to secure these Rights, Governments are instituted among Men, deriving their just Powers from the Consent of the Governed, that whenever any Form of Government becomes destructive of these Ends, it is the Right of the People to alter or abolish it, and to institute a new Government, laying its Foundation on such Principles, and organizing its Powers in such Form, as to them shall seem most likely to effect their Safety and Happiness. Prudence, indeed, will dictate that Governments long established should not be changed for light and transient Causes; and accordingly all Experience hath shewn, that Mankind are more disposed to suffer, while Evils are sufferable, than to right themselves by abolishing the Forms to which they are accustomed. But when a long Train of Abuses and Usurpations, pursuing invariably the same Object, evinces a Design to reduce them under absolute Despotism, it is their Right, it is their Duty, to throw off such Government, and to provide new Guards for their future Security. Such has been the patient Sufferance of these Colonies; and such is now the Necessity which constrains them to alter their former Systems of Government. The History of the Present King of Great-Britain is a History of repeated Injuries and Usurpations, all having in direct Object the Establishment of an absolute Tyranny over these States. To prove this, let Facts be submitted to a candid World.

He has refused his Assent to Laws, the most wholesome and necessary for the public Good.

He has forbidden his Governors to pass Laws of immediate and pressing Importance, unless suspended in their Operation till his Assent should be obtained; and when so suspended, he has utterly neglected to attend to them.

He has refused to pass other Laws for the Accommodation of large Districts of People; unless those People would relinquish the Right of Representation in the Legislature, a Right inestimable to them, and formidable to Tyrants only.

He has called together Legislative Bodies at Places unusual, uncomfortable, and distant from the Depository of their public Records, for the sole Purpose of fatiguing them into Compliance with his Measures.

He has dissolved Representative Houses repeatedly, for opposing with manly Firmness his Invasions on the Rights of the People.

He has refused for a long Time, after such Dissolutions, to cause others to be elected; whereby the Legislative Powers, incapable of Annihilation, have returned to the People at large for their exercise; the State remaining in the mean time exposed to all the Dangers of Invasion from without, and Convulsions within.

He has endeavoured to prevent the Population of these States; for that Purpose obstructing the Laws for Naturalization of Foreigners; refusing to pass others to encourage their Migrations hither, and raising the Conditions of new Appropriations of Lands.

He has obstructed the Administration of Justice, by refusing his Assent to Laws for establishing Judiciary Powers.

He has made Judges dependent on his Will alone, for the Tenure of their Offices, and Amount and Payment of their Salaries.

He has erected a Multitude of new Offices, and sent hither Swarms of Officers to harass our People, and eat out their Substance.

He has kept among us, in Times of Peace, Standing Armies, without the consent of our Legislature.

He has affected to render the Military independent of and superior to the Civil Power.

He has combined with others to subject us to a Jurisdiction foreign to our Constitution, and unacknowledged by our Laws; giving his Assent to their Acts of pretended Legislation:

For quartering large Bodies of Armed Troops among us:

For protecting them, by a mock Trial, from Punishment for any Murders which they should commit on the Inhabitants of these States:

For cutting off our Trade with all Parts of the World:

For imposing taxes on us without our Consent:

For depriving us, in many Cases, of the Benefits of Trial by Jury:

For transporting us beyond Seas to be tried for pretended Offences:

For abolishing the free System of English Laws in a neighbouring Province, establishing therein an arbitrary Government, and enlarging its Boundaries, so as to render it at once an Example and fit Instrument for introducing the same absolute Rule in these Colonies:

For taking away our Charters, abolishing our most valuable Laws, and altering fundamentally the Forms of our Governments:

For suspending our own Legislatures, and declaring themselves invested with Powers to legislate for us in all Cases whatsoever.

He has abdicated Government here, by declaring us out of his Protection and waging War against us.

He has plundered our Seas, ravaged our Coasts, burnt our Towns, and destroyed the Lives of our People.

He is, at this Time, transporting large Armies of foreign Mercenaries to compleat the Works of Death, Desolation, and Tyranny, already begun with circumstances of Cruelty and Perfidy, scarcely paralleled in the most barbarous Ages, and totally unworthy the Head of a civilized Nation.

He has constrained our fellow Citizens taken Captive on the high Seas to bear Arms against their Country, to become the Executioners of their Friends and Brethren, or to fall themselves by their Hands.

He has excited domestic Insurrections among us, and has endeavoured to bring on the Inhabitants of our Frontiers, the merciless Indian Savages, whose known Rule of Warfare, is an undistinguished Destruction, of all Ages, Sexes and Conditions.

In every stage of these Oppressions we have Petitioned for Redress in the most humble Terms: Our repeated Petitions have been answered only by repeated Injury. A Prince, whose Character is thus marked by every act which may define a Tyrant, is unfit to be the Ruler of a free People.

Nor have we been wanting in Attentions to our British Brethren. We have warned them from Time to Time of Attempts by their Legislature to extend an unwarrantable Jurisdiction over us. We have reminded them of the Circumstances of our Emigration and Settlement here. We have appealed to their native Justice and Magnanimity, and we have conjured them by the Ties of our common Kindred to disavow these Usurpations, which, would inevitably interrupt our Connections and Correspondence. They too have been deaf to the Voice of Justice and of Consanguinity. We must, therefore, acquiesce in the Necessity, which denounces our Separation, and hold them, as we hold the rest of Mankind, Enemies in War, in Peace, Friends.

We, therefore, the Representatives of the United States of America, in General Congress, Assembled, appealing to the Supreme Judge of the World for the Rectitude of our Intentions, do, in the Name, and by the Authority of the good People of these Colonies, solemnly Publish and Declare, That these United Colonies are, and of Right ought to be, Free and Independent States; that they are absolved from all Allegiance to the British Crown, and that all political Connection between them and the State of Great-Britain, is and ought to be totally dissolved; and that as Free and Independent States, they have full Power to levy War, conclude Peace, contract Alliances, establish Commerce, and to do all other Acts and Things which Independent States may of right do. And for the support of this Declaration, with a firm Reliance on the Protection of the divine Providence, we mutually pledge to each other our Lives, our Fortunes, and our sacred Honor.

Signed by Order and in Behalf of the Congress,

John Hancock, President.

Attest.

Charles Thomson, Secretary.

Attributions

CC licensed content, Shared previously

- Introduction: United States Declaration of Independence. **Provided by**: Wikipedia. **Located at**: https://en.wikipedia.org/wiki/United_States_Declaration_of_Independence. **License**: *CC BY-SA: Attribution-ShareAlike*

Public domain content

- United States Declaration of Independence. **Provided by**: Wikisource. **Located at**: https://en.wikisource.org/wiki/United_States_Declaration_of_Independence. **License**: *Public Domain: No Known Copyright*

6. America's War for Independence, 1775-1783

Introduction

This famous 1819 painting by John Trumbull shows members of the committee entrusted with drafting the Declaration of Independence presenting their work to the Continental Congress in 1776. Note the British flags on the wall. Separating from the British Empire proved to be very difficult as the colonies and the Empire were linked with strong cultural, historical, and economic bonds forged over several generations.

By the 1770s, Great Britain ruled a vast empire, with its American colonies producing useful raw materials and profitably consuming British goods. From Britain's perspective, it was inconceivable that the colonies would wage a successful war for independence; in 1776, they appeared weak and disorganized, no match for the Empire. Yet, although the Revolutionary War did indeed drag on for eight years, in 1783, the thirteen colonies, now the United States, ultimately prevailed against the British.

The Revolution succeeded because colonists from diverse economic and social backgrounds united in their opposition to Great Britain. Although thousands of colonists remained loyal to the crown and many others preferred to remain neutral, a sense of community against a common enemy prevailed among Patriots. The signing of the Declaration of Independence exemplifies the spirit of that common cause. Representatives asserted: "That these United Colonies are, and of Right ought to be Free and Independent States; that they are Absolved from all Allegiance to the British Crown, . . . And for the support of this Declaration, . . . we mutually pledge to each other our Lives, our Fortunes and our sacred Honor."

Attributions

CC licensed content, Shared previously

- US History. **Authored by**: P. Scott Corbett, Volker Janssen, John M. Lund, Todd Pfannestiel, Paul Vickery, and Sylvie Waskiewicz. **Provided by**: OpenStax College. **Located at**: http://openstaxcollege.org/textbooks/us-history. **License**: *CC BY: Attribution*. **License Terms**: Download for free at http://cnx.org/content/col11740/latest/

Britain's Law-and-Order Strategy and Its Consequences

Learning Objectives

By the end of this section, you will be able to:

- Explain how Great Britain's response to the destruction of a British shipment of tea in Boston Harbor in 1773 set the stage for the Revolution
- Describe the beginnings of the American Revolution

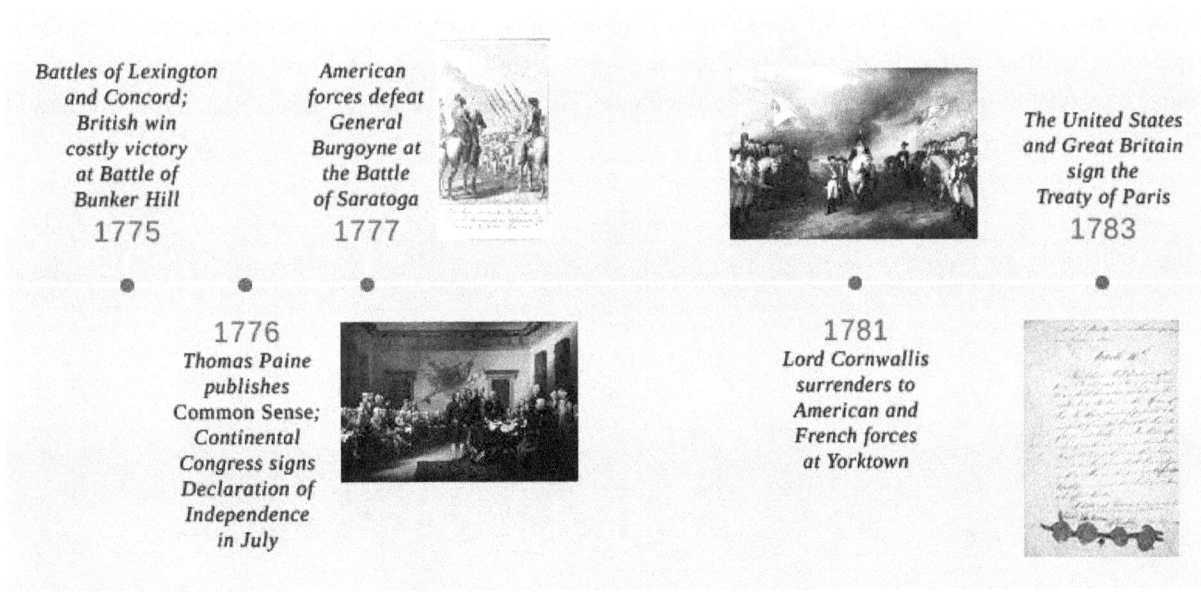

Great Britain pursued a policy of law and order when dealing with the crises in the colonies in the late 1760s and 1770s. Relations between the British and many American Patriots worsened over the decade, culminating in an unruly mob destroying a fortune in tea by dumping it into **Boston Harbor** in December

1773 as a protest against British tax laws. The harsh British response to this act in 1774, which included sending British troops to Boston and closing Boston Harbor, caused tensions and resentments to escalate further. The British tried to disarm the insurgents in Massachusetts by confiscating their weapons and ammunition and arresting the leaders of the patriotic movement. However, this effort faltered on April 19, when Massachusetts militias and British troops fired on each other as British troops marched to Lexington and Concord, an event immortalized by poet Ralph Waldo Emerson as the "shot heard round the world." The American Revolution had begun.

ON THE EVE OF REVOLUTION

The decade from 1763 to 1774 was a difficult one for the British Empire. Although Great Britain had defeated the French in the French and Indian War, the debt from that conflict remained a stubborn and seemingly unsolvable problem for both Great Britain and the colonies. Great Britain tried various methods of raising revenue on both sides of the Atlantic to manage the enormous debt, including instituting a tax on tea and other goods sold to the colonies by British companies, but many subjects resisted these taxes. In the colonies, Patriot groups like the Sons of Liberty led boycotts of British goods and took violent measures that stymied British officials.

Boston proved to be the epicenter of protest. In December 1773, a group of Patriots protested the Tea Act passed that year—which, among other provisions, gave the East India Company a monopoly on tea—by boarding British tea ships docked in Boston Harbor and dumping tea worth over $1 million (in current prices) into the water. The destruction of the tea radically escalated the crisis between Great Britain and the American colonies. When the Massachusetts Assembly refused to pay for the tea, Parliament enacted a series of laws called the Coercive Acts, which some colonists called the Intolerable Acts. Parliament designed these laws, which closed the port of Boston, limited the meetings of the colonial assembly, and disbanded all town meetings, to punish Massachusetts and bring the colony into line. However, many British Americans in other colonies were troubled and angered by Parliament's response to Massachusetts. In September and October 1774, all the colonies except Georgia participated in the First Continental Congress in Philadelphia. The Congress advocated a boycott of all British goods and established the Continental Association to enforce local adherence to the boycott. The Association supplanted royal control and shaped resistance to Great Britain.

Joining the Boycott

Many British colonists in Virginia, as in the other colonies, disapproved of the destruction of the tea in Boston Harbor. However, after the passage of the Coercive Acts, the Virginia House of Burgesses declared its solidarity with Massachusetts by encouraging Virginians to observe a day of fasting and prayer on May 24 in sympathy with the people of Boston. Almost immediately thereafter, Virginia's colonial governor dissolved the House of Burgesses, but many of its members met again in secret on May 30 and adopted a resolution stating that "the Colony of Virginia will concur with the other Colonies in such Measures as shall be judged most effectual for the preservation of the Common Rights and Liberty of British America."

After the First Continental Congress in Philadelphia, Virginia's Committee of Safety ensured that all merchants signed the non-importation agreements that the Congress had proposed. This British cartoon shows a Virginian signing the Continental Association boycott agreement.

In "The Alternative of Williams-Burg" (1775), a merchant has to sign a non-importation agreement or risk being covered with the tar and feathers suspended behind him.

Note the tar and feathers hanging from the gallows in the background of this image and the demeanor of the people surrounding the signer. What is the message of this engraving? Where are the sympathies of the artist? What is the meaning of the title "The Alternative of Williams-Burg?"

In an effort to restore law and order in Boston, the British dispatched General Thomas Gage to the New England seaport. He arrived in Boston in May 1774 as the new royal governor of the Province of Massachusetts, accompanied by several regiments of British troops. As in 1768, the British again occupied the town. Massachusetts delegates met in a Provincial Congress and published the Suffolk Resolves, which officially rejected the Coercive Acts and called for the raising of colonial militias to take military action if needed. The Suffolk Resolves signaled the overthrow of the royal government in Massachusetts.

Both the British and the rebels in New England began to prepare for conflict by turning their attention to supplies of weapons and gunpowder. General Gage stationed thirty-five hundred troops in Boston, and from there he ordered periodic raids on towns where guns and gunpowder were stockpiled, hoping to impose law and order by seizing them. As Boston became the headquarters of British military operations, many residents fled the city.

Gage's actions led to the formation of local rebel militias that were able to mobilize in a minute's time. These **minutemen**, many of whom were veterans of the French and Indian War, played an important role in the war for independence. In one instance, General Gage seized munitions in Cambridge and Charlestown, but when he arrived to do the same in Salem, his troops were met by a large crowd of minutemen and had to leave empty-handed. In New Hampshire, minutemen took over Fort William and Mary and confiscated weapons and cannons there. New England readied for war.

THE OUTBREAK OF FIGHTING

Throughout late 1774 and into 1775, tensions in New England continued to mount. General Gage knew that a powder magazine was stored in Concord, Massachusetts, and on April 19, 1775, he ordered troops to seize these munitions. Instructions from London called for the arrest of rebel leaders Samuel Adams and John Hancock. Hoping for secrecy, his troops left Boston under cover of darkness, but riders from Boston let the militias know of the British plans. (Paul Revere was one of these riders, but the British captured him and he never finished his ride. Henry Wadsworth Longfellow memorialized Revere in his 1860 poem, "Paul Revere's Ride," incorrectly implying that he made it all the way to Concord.) Minutemen met the British troops and skirmished with them, first at Lexington and then at Concord. The British retreated to Boston, enduring ambushes from several other militias along the way. Over four thousand militiamen took part in these skirmishes with British soldiers. Seventy-three British soldiers and forty-nine Patriots died during the British retreat to Boston. The famous confrontation is the basis for Emerson's "Concord Hymn" (1836), which begins with the description of the "shot heard round the world." Although propagandists on both sides pointed fingers, it remains unclear who fired that shot.

Amos Doolittle was an American printmaker who volunteered to fight against the British. His engravings of the battles of Lexington and Concord—such as this detail from The Battle of Lexington, April 19th 1775—are the only contemporary American visual records of the events there.

After the battles of Lexington and Concord, New England fully mobilized for war. Thousands of militias from towns throughout New England marched to Boston, and soon the city was besieged by a sea of rebel forces. In May 1775, Ethan Allen and Colonel Benedict Arnold led a group of rebels against Fort Ticonderoga in New York. They succeeded in capturing the fort, and cannons from Ticonderoga were brought to Massachusetts and used to bolster the Siege of Boston.

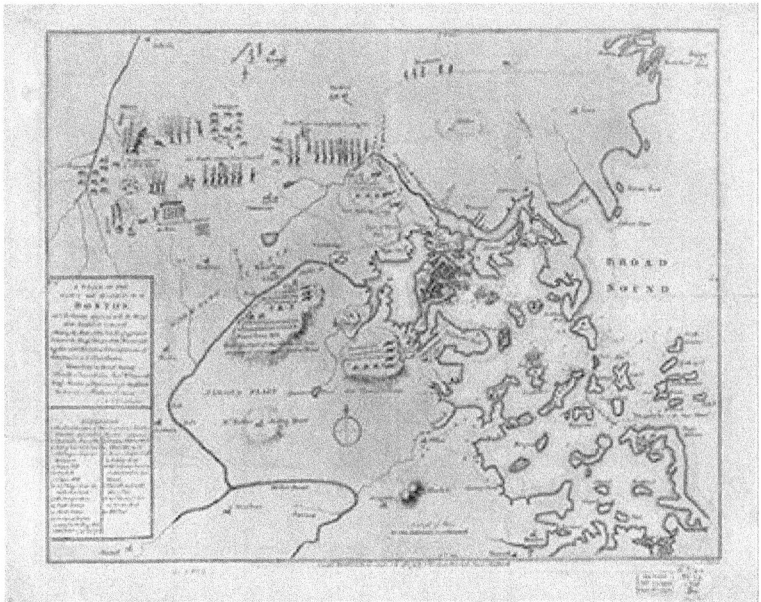

This 1779 map shows details of the British and Patriot troops in and around Boston, Massachusetts, at the beginning of the war.

In June, General Gage resolved to take Breed's Hill and **Bunker Hill**, the high ground across the Charles River from Boston, a strategic site that gave the rebel militias an advantage since they could train their cannons on the British. In the Battle of Bunker Hill, on June 17, the British launched three assaults on the hills, gaining control only after the rebels ran out of ammunition. British losses were very high—over two hundred were killed and eight hundred wounded—and, despite his victory, General Gage was unable to break the colonial forces' siege of the city. In August, King George III declared the colonies to be in a state of rebellion. Parliament and many in Great Britain agreed with their king. Meanwhile, the British forces in Boston found themselves in a terrible predicament, isolated in the city and with no control over the countryside.

(a) (b)

The British cartoon "Bunkers Hill or America's Head Dress" (a) depicts the initial rebellion as an elaborate colonial coiffure. The illustration pokes fun at both the colonial rebellion and the overdone hairstyles for women that had made their way from France and Britain to the American colonies. Despite gaining control of the high ground after the colonial militias ran out of ammunition, General Thomas Gage (b), shown here in a painting made in 1768–1769 by John Singleton Copley, was unable to break the siege of the city.

In the end, General George Washington, commander in chief of the Continental Army since June 15, 1775, used the Fort Ticonderoga cannons to force the evacuation of the British from Boston. Washington had positioned these cannons on the hills overlooking both the fortified positions of the British and Boston Harbor, where the British supply ships were anchored. The British could not return fire on the colonial positions because they could not elevate their cannons. They soon realized that they were in an untenable position and had to withdraw from Boston. On March 17, 1776, the British evacuated their troops to Halifax, Nova Scotia, ending the nearly year-long siege.

By the time the British withdrew from Boston, fighting had broken out in other colonies as well. In May 1775, Mecklenburg County in North Carolina issued the **Mecklenburg Resolves**, stating that a rebellion against Great Britain had begun, that colonists did not owe any further allegiance to Great Britain, and that governing authority had now passed to the Continental Congress. The resolves also called upon the formation of militias to be under the control of the Continental Congress. Loyalists and Patriots clashed in North Carolina in February 1776 at the Battle of Moore's Creek Bridge.

In Virginia, the royal governor, Lord Dunmore, raised Loyalist forces to combat the rebel colonists and also tried to use the large slave population to put down the rebellion. In November 1775, he issued a decree, known as **Dunmore's Proclamation**, promising freedom to slaves and indentured servants of rebels who remained loyal to the king and who pledged to fight with the Loyalists against the insurgents. Dunmore's Proclamation exposed serious problems for both the Patriot cause and for the British. In order for the British to put down the rebellion, they needed the support of Virginia's landowners, many of whom owned slaves. (While Patriot slaveholders in Virginia and elsewhere proclaimed they acted in defense of liberty, they kept thousands in bondage, a fact the British decided to exploit.) Although a number of slaves did join Dunmore's side, the proclamation had the unintended effect of galvanizing Patriot resistance to Britain.

From the rebels' point of view, the British looked to deprive them of their slave property and incite a race war. Slaveholders feared a slave uprising and increased their commitment to the cause against Great Britain, calling for independence. Dunmore fled Virginia in 1776.

COMMON SENSE

With the events of 1775 fresh in their minds, many colonists reached the conclusion in 1776 that the time had come to secede from the Empire and declare independence. Over the past ten years, these colonists had argued that they deserved the same rights as Englishmen enjoyed in Great Britain, only to find themselves relegated to an intolerable subservient status in the Empire. The groundswell of support for their cause of independence in 1776 also owed much to the appearance of an anonymous pamphlet, first published in January 1776, entitled *Common Sense*. Thomas Paine, who had emigrated from England to Philadelphia in 1774, was the author. Arguably the most radical pamphlet of the revolutionary era, *Common Sense* made a powerful argument for independence.

Paine's pamphlet rejected the monarchy, calling King George III a "royal brute" and questioning the right of an island (England) to rule over America. In this way, Paine helped to channel colonial discontent toward the king himself and not, as had been the case, toward the British Parliament—a bold move that signaled the desire to create a new political order disavowing monarchy entirely. He argued for the creation of an American republic, a state without a king, and extolled the blessings of **republicanism**, a political philosophy that held that elected representatives, not a hereditary monarch, should govern states. The vision of an American republic put forward by Paine included the idea of **popular sovereignty**: citizens in the republic would determine who would represent them, and decide other issues, on the basis of majority rule. Republicanism also served as a social philosophy guiding the conduct of the Patriots in their struggle against the British Empire. It demanded adherence to a code of virtue, placing the public good and community above narrow self-interest.

Paine wrote *Common Sense* in simple, direct language aimed at ordinary people, not just the learned elite. The pamphlet proved immensely popular and was soon available in all **thirteen colonies**, where it helped convince many to reject monarchy and the British Empire in favor of independence and a republican form of government.

Thomas Paine's Common Sense (a) helped convince many colonists of the need for independence from Great Britain. Paine, shown here in a portrait by Laurent Dabos (b), was a political activist and revolutionary best known for his writings on both the American and French Revolutions.

THE DECLARATION OF INDEPENDENCE

In the summer of 1776, the Continental Congress met in Philadelphia and agreed to sever ties with Great Britain. Virginian Thomas Jefferson and John Adams of Massachusetts, with the support of the Congress, articulated the justification for liberty in the Declaration of Independence. The Declaration, written primarily by Jefferson, included a long list of grievances against King George III and laid out the foundation of American government as a republic in which the consent of the governed would be of paramount importance.

The preamble to the Declaration began with a statement of Enlightenment principles about universal human rights and values: "We hold these Truths to be self-evident, that all Men are created equal, that they are endowed by their Creator with certain unalienable Rights, that among these are Life, Liberty, and the pursuit of Happiness—That to secure these Rights, Governments are instituted among Men, deriving their just Powers from the Consent of the Governed, that whenever any Form of Government becomes destructive of these Ends, it is the Right of the People to alter or abolish it." In addition to this statement of principles, the document served another purpose: Patriot leaders sent copies to France and Spain in hopes of winning their support and aid in the contest against Great Britain. They understood how important foreign recognition and aid would be to the creation of a new and independent nation.

The Dunlap Broadsides, one of which is shown here, are considered the first published copies of the Declaration of Independence. This one was printed on July 4, 1776.

The Declaration of Independence has since had a global impact, serving as the basis for many subsequent movements to gain independence from other colonial powers. It is part of America's civil religion, and thousands of people each year make pilgrimages to see the original document in Washington, DC.

The Declaration also reveals a fundamental contradiction of the American Revolution: the conflict between the existence of slavery and the idea that "all men are created equal." One-fifth of the population in 1776 was enslaved, and at the time he drafted the Declaration, Jefferson himself owned more than one hundred slaves. Further, the Declaration framed equality as existing only among white men; women and nonwhites were entirely left out of a document that referred to native peoples as "merciless Indian savages" who indiscriminately killed men, women, and children. Nonetheless, the promise of equality for all planted the seeds for future struggles waged by slaves, women, and many others to bring about its full realization. Much of American history is the story of the slow realization of the promise of equality expressed in the Declaration of Independence.

> Visit Digital History to view "The Female Combatants." In this 1776 engraving by an anonymous artist, Great Britain is depicted on the left as a staid, stern matron, while America, on the right, is shown as a half-dressed American Indian. Why do you think the artist depicted the two opposing

sides this way?

Section Summary

Until Parliament passed the Coercive Acts in 1774, most colonists still thought of themselves as proud subjects of the strong British Empire. However, the Coercive (or Intolerable) Acts, which Parliament enacted to punish Massachusetts for failing to pay for the destruction of the tea, convinced many colonists that Great Britain was indeed threatening to stifle their liberty. In Massachusetts and other New England colonies, militias like the minutemen prepared for war by stockpiling weapons and ammunition. After the first loss of life at the battles of Lexington and Concord in April 1775, skirmishes continued throughout the colonies. When Congress met in Philadelphia in July 1776, its members signed the Declaration of Independence, officially breaking ties with Great Britain and declaring their intention to be self-governing.

- https://www.openassessments.org/assessments/956

Review Question

1. What are the main arguments that Thomas Paine makes in his pamphlet *Common Sense*? Why was this pamphlet so popular?

Answer to Review Question

1. In *Common Sense*, Paine rejects the monarchy, calling into question both the right of any king to rule any people and Great Britain's right to rule America. He argues for the creation of an American republic and the adoption of a philosophy of republicanism, which would extend to both the structure of the government—composed of representatives, rather than a monarch—and the conduct of the Patriots, who must place the public good and community above their own self-interest. Paine wrote his pamphlet simply, appealing to the "common sense" of ordinary citizens, which helped to increase its popularity.

Glossary

Dunmore's Proclamation the decree signed by Lord Dunmore, the royal governor of Virginia, which proclaimed that any slaves or indentured servants who fought on the side of the British would be rewarded with their freedom

Mecklenburg Resolves North Carolina's declaration of rebellion against Great Britain

minutemen colonial militias prepared to mobilize and fight the British with a minute's notice

popular sovereignty the practice of allowing the citizens of a state or territory to decide issues based on the principle of majority rule

republicanism a political philosophy that holds that states should be governed by representatives, not a monarch; as a social philosophy, republicanism required civic virtue of its citizens

thirteen colonies the British colonies in North America that declared independence from Great Britain in 1776, which included Connecticut, Delaware, Georgia, Maryland, the province of Massachusetts Bay, New Hampshire, New Jersey, New York, North Carolina, Pennsylvania, Rhode Island and Providence Plantations, South Carolina, and Virginia

Attributions

CC licensed content, Shared previously

- US History. **Authored by**: P. Scott Corbett, Volker Janssen, John M. Lund, Todd Pfannestiel, Paul Vickery, and Sylvie Waskiewicz. **Provided by**: OpenStax College. **Located at**: http://openstaxcollege.org/textbooks/us-history. **License**: *CC BY: Attribution*. **License Terms**: Download for free at http://cnx.org/content/col11740/latest/

The Early Years of the Revolution

Learning Objectives

By the end of this section, you will be able to:

- Explain the British and American strategies of 1776 through 1778
- Identify the key battles of the early years of the Revolution

---

After the British quit Boston, they slowly adopted a strategy to isolate New England from the rest of the colonies and force the insurgents in that region into submission, believing that doing so would end the conflict. At first, British forces focused on taking the principal colonial centers. They began by easily capturing New York City in 1776. The following year, they took over the American capital of Philadelphia. The larger British effort to isolate New England was implemented in 1777. That effort ultimately failed when the British surrendered a force of over five thousand to the Americans in the fall of 1777 at the Battle of Saratoga.

The major campaigns over the next several years took place in the middle colonies of New York, New Jersey, and Pennsylvania, whose populations were sharply divided between Loyalists and Patriots. Revolutionaries faced many hardships as British superiority on the battlefield became evident and the difficulty of funding the war caused strains.

THE BRITISH STRATEGY IN THE MIDDLE COLONIES

After evacuating Boston in March 1776, British forces sailed to Nova Scotia to regroup. They devised a strategy, successfully implemented in 1776, to take New York City. The following year, they planned to end the rebellion by cutting New England off from the rest of the colonies and starving it into submission. Three British armies were to move simultaneously from New York City, Montreal, and Fort Oswego to converge along the Hudson River; British control of that natural boundary would isolate New England.

General William Howe, commander in chief of the British forces in America, amassed thirty-two thousand troops on Staten Island in June and July 1776. His brother, Admiral Richard Howe, controlled New York Harbor. Command of New York City and the Hudson River was their goal. In August 1776, General Howe landed his forces on Long Island and easily routed the American Continental Army there in the Battle of Long Island (August 27). The Americans were outnumbered and lacked both military experience and discipline. Sensing victory, General and Admiral Howe arranged a peace conference in September 1776, where Benjamin Franklin, John Adams, and South Carolinian John Rutledge represented the Continental Congress. Despite the Howes' hopes, however, the Americans demanded recognition of their independence, which the Howes were not authorized to grant, and the conference disbanded.

General William Howe, shown here in a 1777 portrait by Richard Purcell, led British forces in America in the first years of the war.

On September 16, 1776, George Washington's forces held up against the British at the Battle of Harlem Heights. This important American military achievement, a key reversal after the disaster on Long Island, occurred as most of Washington's forces retreated to New Jersey. A few weeks later, on October 28, General Howe's forces defeated Washington's at the Battle of White Plains and New York City fell to the British. For the next seven years, the British made the city the headquarters for their military efforts to defeat the rebellion, which included raids on surrounding areas. In 1777, the British burned Danbury, Connecticut, and in July 1779, they set fire to homes in Fairfield and Norwalk. They held American prisoners aboard ships in the waters around New York City; the death toll was shocking, with thousands perishing in the holds. Meanwhile, New York City served as a haven for Loyalists who disagreed with the effort to break away from the Empire and establish an American republic.

GEORGE WASHINGTON AND THE CONTINENTAL ARMY

When the Second Continental Congress met in Philadelphia in May 1775, members approved the creation of a professional Continental Army with Washington as commander in chief. Although sixteen thousand volunteers enlisted, it took several years for the Continental Army to become a truly professional force. In 1775 and 1776, militias still composed the bulk of the Patriots' armed forces, and these soldiers returned home after the summer fighting season, drastically reducing the army's strength.

This 1775 etching shows George Washington taking command of the Continental Army at Cambridge, Massachusetts, just two weeks after his appointment by the Continental Congress.

That changed in late 1776 and early 1777, when Washington broke with conventional eighteenth-century military tactics that called for fighting in the summer months only. Intent on raising revolutionary morale after the British captured New York City, he launched surprise strikes against British forces in their winter quarters. In Trenton, New Jersey, he led his soldiers across the Delaware River and surprised an encampment of **Hessians**, German mercenaries hired by Great Britain to put down the American rebellion. Beginning the night of December 25, 1776, and continuing into the early hours of December 26, Washington moved on Trenton where the Hessians were encamped. Maintaining the element of surprise by attacking at Christmastime, he defeated them, taking over nine hundred captive. On January 3, 1777, Washington achieved another much-needed victory at the Battle of Princeton. He again broke with eighteenth-century military protocol by attacking unexpectedly after the fighting season had ended.

THOMAS PAINE ON "THE AMERICAN CRISIS"

During the American Revolution, following the publication of *Common Sense* in January 1776, Thomas Paine began a series of sixteen pamphlets known collectively as *The American Crisis*. He wrote the first volume in 1776, describing the dire situation facing the revolutionaries at the end of that hard year.

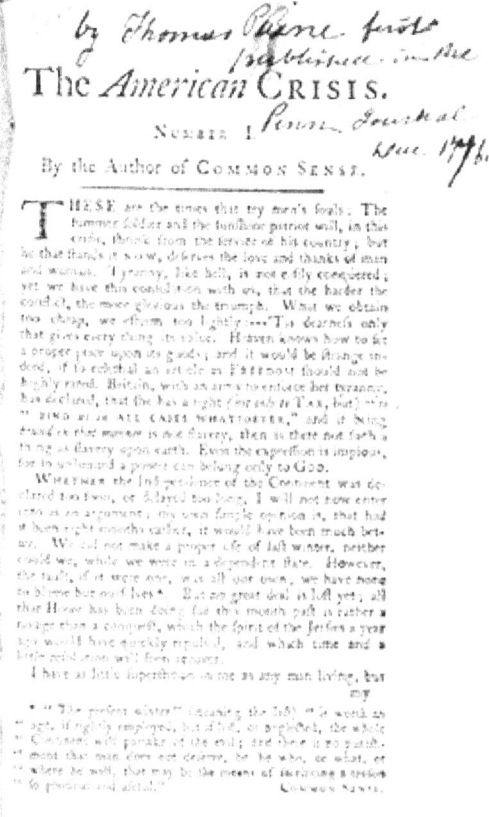

Thomas Paine wrote the pamphlet The American Crisis, the first page of which is shown here, in 1776.

These are the times that try men's souls. The summer soldier and the sunshine patriot will, in this crisis, shrink from the service of their country; but he that stands it now, deserves the love and thanks of man and woman. . . . Britain, with an army to enforce her tyranny, has declared that she has a right (not only to tax) but "to bind us in all cases whatsoever," and if being bound in that manner, is not slavery, then is there not such a thing as slavery upon earth. Even the expression is impious; for so unlimited a power can belong only to God. . . .

I shall conclude this paper with some miscellaneous remarks on the state of our affairs; and shall begin with asking the following question, Why is it that the enemy have left the New England provinces, and made these middle ones the seat of war? The answer is easy: New England is not infested with Tories, and we are. I have been tender in raising the cry against these men, and used numberless arguments to show them their danger, but it will not do to sacrifice a world either to their folly or their baseness. The period is now arrived, in which either they or we must change our sentiments, or one or both must fall. . . .

By perseverance and fortitude we have the prospect of a glorious issue; by cowardice and submission, the sad choice of a variety of evils—a ravaged country—a depopulated city—habitations without safety, and slavery without hope—our homes turned into barracks and bawdy-houses for Hessians, and a future race to provide for, whose fathers we shall doubt of. Look on this picture and weep over it! and if there yet remains one thoughtless wretch who believes it not, let him suffer it unlamented.

—Thomas Paine, "The American Crisis," December 23, 1776

What topics does Paine address in this pamphlet? What was his purpose in writing? What does he write about Tories (Loyalists), and why does he consider them a problem?

> Visit Wikisource to read the rest of Thomas Paine's first *American Crisis* pamphlet, as well as the other fifteen in the series

PHILADELPHIA AND SARATOGA: BRITISH AND AMERICAN VICTORIES

In August 1777, General Howe brought fifteen thousand British troops to Chesapeake Bay as part of his plan to take Philadelphia, where the Continental Congress met. That fall, the British defeated Washington's soldiers in the Battle of Brandywine Creek and took control of Philadelphia, forcing the Continental Congress to flee. During the winter of 1777–1778, the British occupied the city, and Washington's army camped at Valley Forge, Pennsylvania.

Prussian soldier Friedrich Wilhelm von Steuben, shown here in a 1786 portrait by Ralph Earl, was instrumental in transforming Washington's Continental Army into a professional armed force.

Washington's winter at Valley Forge was a low point for the American forces. A lack of supplies weakened the men, and disease took a heavy toll. Amid the cold, hunger, and sickness, soldiers deserted in droves. On February 16, Washington wrote to George Clinton, governor of New York: "For some days past, there has been little less than a famine in camp. A part of the army has been a week without any kind of flesh & the rest three or four days. Naked and starving as they are, we cannot enough admire the incomparable patience and fidelity of the soldiery, that they have not been ere [before] this excited by their sufferings to a general mutiny and dispersion." Of eleven thousand soldiers encamped at Valley Forge, twenty-five hundred died of starvation, malnutrition, and disease. As Washington feared, nearly one hundred soldiers deserted every week. (Desertions continued, and by 1780, Washington was executing recaptured deserters every Saturday.) The low morale extended all the way to Congress, where some wanted to replace Washington with a more seasoned leader.

Assistance came to Washington and his soldiers in February 1778 in the form of the Prussian soldier Friedrich Wilhelm von Steuben. Baron von Steuben was an experienced military man, and he implemented a thorough training course for Washington's ragtag troops. By drilling a small corps of soldiers and then having them train others, he finally transformed the Continental Army into a force capable of standing up to the professional British and Hessian soldiers. His drill manual—*Regulations for the Order and Discipline of the Troops of the United States*—informed military practices in the United States for the next several decades.

> Explore Friedrich Wilhelm von Steuben's Revolutionary War Drill Manual to understand how von Steuben was able to transform the Continental Army into a professional fighting force. Note the tremendous amount of precision and detail in von Steuben's descriptions.

Meanwhile, the campaign to sever New England from the rest of the colonies had taken an unexpected turn during the fall of 1777. The British had attempted to implement the plan, drawn up by Lord George Germain and Prime Minister Lord North, to isolate New England with the combined forces of three armies. One army, led by General John Burgoyne, would march south from Montreal. A second force, led by Colonel Barry St. Leger and made up of British troops and Iroquois, would march east from Fort Oswego on the banks of Lake Ontario. A third force, led by General Sir Henry Clinton, would march north from New York City. The armies would converge at Albany and effectively cut the rebellion in two by isolating New England. This northern campaign fell victim to competing strategies, however, as General Howe had meanwhile decided to take Philadelphia. His decision to capture that city siphoned off troops that would have been vital to the overall success of the campaign in 1777.

The British plan to isolate New England ended in disaster. St. Leger's efforts to bring his force of British regulars, Loyalist fighters, and Iroquois allies east to link up with General Burgoyne failed, and he retreated to Quebec. Burgoyne's forces encountered ever-stiffer resistance as he made his way south from Montreal, down Lake Champlain and the upper Hudson River corridor. Although they did capture Fort Ticonderoga when American forces retreated, Burgoyne's army found themselves surrounded by a sea of colonial militias in Saratoga, New York. In the meantime, the small British force under Clinton that left New York City to aid Burgoyne advanced slowly up the Hudson River, failing to provide the much-needed support for the troops at Saratoga. On October 17, 1777, Burgoyne surrendered his five thousand soldiers to the Continental Army.

This German engraving, created by Daniel Chodowiecki in 1784, shows British soldiers laying down their arms before the American forces.

The American victory at the Battle of Saratoga was the major turning point in the war. This victory convinced the French to recognize American independence and form a military alliance with the new nation, which changed the course of the war by opening the door to badly needed military support from France. Still smarting from their defeat by Britain in the Seven Years' War, the French supplied the United States with gunpowder and money, as well as soldiers and naval forces that proved decisive in the defeat of Great Britain. The French also contributed military leaders, including the Marquis de Lafayette, who arrived in America in 1777 as a volunteer and served as Washington's aide-de-camp.

The war quickly became more difficult for the British, who had to fight the rebels in North America as well as the French in the Caribbean. Following France's lead, Spain joined the war against Great Britain in 1779, though it did not recognize American independence until 1783. The Dutch Republic also began to support the American revolutionaries and signed a treaty of commerce with the United States in 1782.

Great Britain's effort to isolate New England in 1777 failed. In June 1778, the occupying British force in Philadelphia evacuated and returned to New York City in order to better defend that city, and the British then turned their attention to the southern colonies.

Section Summary

The British successfully implemented the first part of their strategy to isolate New England when they took New York City in the fall of 1776. For the next seven years, they used New York as a base of operations, expanding their control to Philadelphia in the winter of 1777. After suffering through a terrible winter in 1777–1778 in Valley Forge, Pennsylvania, American forces were revived with help from Baron von Steuben, a Prussian military officer who helped transform the Continental Army into a professional fighting force. The effort to cut off New England from the rest of the colonies failed with the General Burgoyne's surrender at Saratoga in October 1777. After Saratoga, the struggle for independence gained a powerful ally when France agreed to recognize the United States as a new nation and began to send much-needed military support. The entrance of France—Britain's archrival in the contest of global empire—into the American fight helped to turn the tide of the war in favor of the revolutionaries.

https://www.openassessments.org/assessments/957

Review Questions

1. Describe the British strategy in the early years of the war and explain whether or not it succeeded.
2. How did George Washington's military tactics help him to achieve success?

Answers to Review Questions

1. The British strategy in the period from 1776 to 1778 was to isolate the New England colonies, where the rebellion was concentrated. They succeeded in the beginning by taking first New York and then Philadelphia. However, they stalled there, and after the British defeat at Saratoga, they were not able to complete their plan to isolate New England.
2. In the eighteenth century, militaries typically fought only in the summer months. On December 25 and 26, 1776, Washington triumphed over the Hessians encamped at Trenton by surprising them as they celebrated Christmas. Shortly thereafter, he used this same tactic to achieve victory at the Battle of Princeton.

Glossary

Hessians German mercenaries hired by Great Britain to put down the American rebellion

Attributions

CC licensed content, Shared previously

- US History. **Authored by**: P. Scott Corbett, Volker Janssen, John M. Lund, Todd Pfannestiel, Paul Vickery, and Sylvie Waskiewicz. **Provided by**: OpenStax College. **Located at**: http://openstaxcollege.org/textbooks/us-history. **License**: *CC BY: Attribution*. **License Terms**: Download for free at http://cnx.org/content/col11740/latest/

War in the South

> ### Learning Objectives
>
> By the end of this section, you will be able to:
>
> - Outline the British southern strategy and its results
> - Describe key American victories and the end of the war
> - Identify the main terms of the Treaty of Paris (1783)

By 1778, the war had turned into a stalemate. Although some in Britain, including Prime Minister Lord North, wanted peace, King George III demanded that the colonies be brought to obedience. To break the deadlock, the British revised their strategy and turned their attention to the southern colonies, where they could expect more support from Loyalists. The southern colonies soon became the center of the fighting. The **southern strategy** brought the British success at first, but thanks to the leadership of George Washington and General Nathanael Greene and the crucial assistance of French forces, the Continental Army defeated the British at Yorktown, effectively ending further large-scale operations during the war.

GEORGIA AND SOUTH CAROLINA

The British architect of the war strategy, Lord George Germain, believed Britain would gain the upper hand with the support of Loyalists, slaves, and Indian allies in the South, and indeed, this southern strategy initially achieved great success. The British began their southern campaign by capturing Savannah, the capital of Georgia, in December 1778. In Georgia, they found support from thousands of slaves who ran to the British side to escape their bondage. As the British regained political control in Georgia, they forced the inhabitants to swear allegiance to the king and formed twenty Loyalist regiments. The Continental Congress had suggested that slaves be given freedom if they joined the Patriot army against the British, but revolutionaries in Georgia and South Carolina refused to consider this proposal. Once again, the Revolution served to further divisions over race and slavery.

After taking Georgia, the British turned their attention to South Carolina. Before the Revolution, South Carolina had been starkly divided between the backcountry, which harbored revolutionary partisans, and the coastal regions, where Loyalists remained a powerful force. Waves of violence rocked the backcountry from the late 1770s into the early 1780s. The Revolution provided an opportunity for residents to fight over their local resentments and antagonisms with murderous consequences. Revenge killings and the destruction of property became mainstays in the savage civil war that gripped the South.

In April 1780, a British force of eight thousand soldiers besieged American forces in Charleston. After six weeks of the Siege of Charleston, the British triumphed. General Benjamin Lincoln, who led the effort for the revolutionaries, had to surrender his entire force, the largest American loss during the entire war. Many of the defeated Americans were placed in jails or in British prison ships anchored in Charleston Harbor. The British established a military government in Charleston under the command of General Sir Henry Clinton. From this base, Clinton ordered General Charles Cornwallis to subdue the rest of South Carolina.

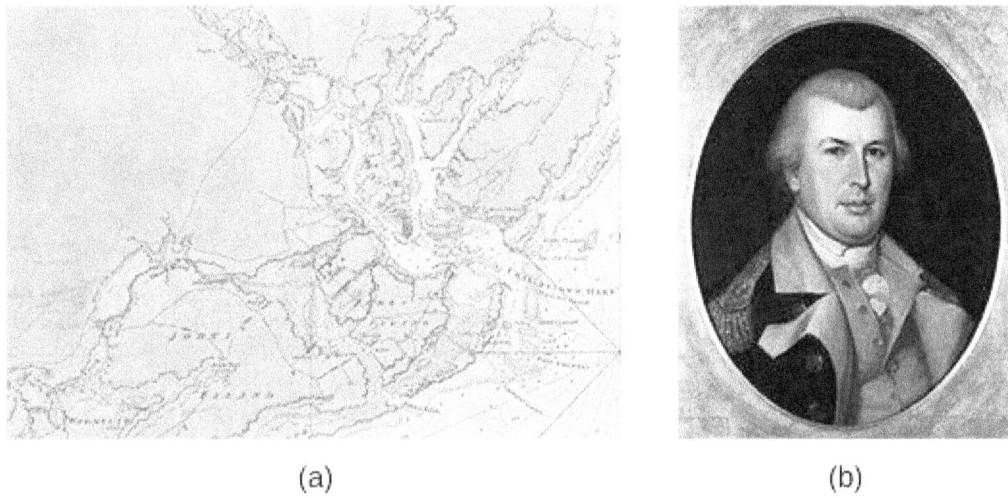

(a) (b)

This 1780 map of Charleston (a), which shows details of the Continental defenses, was probably drawn by British engineers in anticipation of the attack on the city. The Siege of Charleston was one of a series of defeats for the Continental forces in the South, which led the Continental Congress to place General Nathanael Greene (b), shown here in a 1783 portrait by Charles Wilson Peale, in command in late 1780. Greene led his troops to two crucial victories.

The disaster at Charleston led the Continental Congress to change leadership by placing General Horatio Gates in charge of American forces in the South. However, General Gates fared no better than General Lincoln; at the Battle of Camden, South Carolina, in August 1780, Cornwallis forced General Gates to retreat into North Carolina. Camden was one of the worst disasters suffered by American armies during the entire Revolutionary War. Congress again changed military leadership, this time by placing General Nathanael Greene ([link]) in command in December 1780.

As the British had hoped, large numbers of Loyalists helped ensure the success of the southern strategy, and thousands of slaves seeking freedom arrived to aid Cornwallis's army. However, the war turned in the Americans' favor in 1781. General Greene realized that to defeat Cornwallis, he did not have to win a single battle. So long as he remained in the field, he could continue to destroy isolated British forces. Greene therefore made a strategic decision to divide his own troops to wage war—and the strategy worked. American forces under General Daniel Morgan decisively beat the British at the Battle of Cowpens in South Carolina. General Cornwallis now abandoned his strategy of defeating the backcountry rebels in South Carolina. Determined to destroy Greene's army, he gave chase as Greene strategically retreated north into

North Carolina. At the Battle of Guilford Courthouse in March 1781, the British prevailed on the battlefield but suffered extensive losses, an outcome that paralleled the Battle of Bunker Hill nearly six years earlier in June 1775.

YORKTOWN

In the summer of 1781, Cornwallis moved his army to **Yorktown**, Virginia. He expected the Royal Navy to transport his army to New York, where he thought he would join General Sir Henry Clinton. Yorktown was a tobacco port on a peninsula, and Cornwallis believed the British navy would be able to keep the coast clear of rebel ships. Sensing an opportunity, a combined French and American force of sixteen thousand men swarmed the peninsula in September 1781. Washington raced south with his forces, now a disciplined army, as did the Marquis de Lafayette and the Comte de Rochambeau with their French troops. The French Admiral de Grasse sailed his naval force into Chesapeake Bay, preventing Lord Cornwallis from taking a seaward escape route.

In October 1781, the American forces began the battle for Yorktown, and after a siege that lasted eight days, Lord Cornwallis capitulated on October 19. Tradition says that during the surrender of his troops, the British band played "The World Turned Upside Down," a song that befitted the Empire's unexpected reversal of fortune.

The 1820 painting above, by John Trumbull, is titled Surrender of Lord Cornwallis, but Cornwallis actually sent his general, Charles O'Hara, to perform the ceremonial surrendering of the sword. The painting depicts General Benjamin Lincoln holding out his hand to receive the sword. General George Washington is in the background on the brown horse, since he refused to accept the sword from anyone but Cornwallis himself.

"The World Turned Upside Down"

"The World Turned Upside Down," reputedly played during the surrender of the British at Yorktown, was a traditional English ballad from the seventeenth century. It was also the theme of a popular British print that circulated in the 1790s.

In many of the images in this popular print, entitled "The World Turned Upside Down or the Folly of Man," animals and humans have switched places. In one, children take care of their parents, while in another, the sun, moon, and stars appear below the earth.

Why do you think these images were popular in Great Britain in the decade following the Revolutionary War? What would these images imply to Americans?

> **Visit the** Public Domain Review **to explore the images in an eighteenth-century British chapbook (a pamphlet for tracts or ballads) titled "The World Turned Upside Down." The chapbook is illustrated with woodcuts similar to those in the popular print mentioned above.**

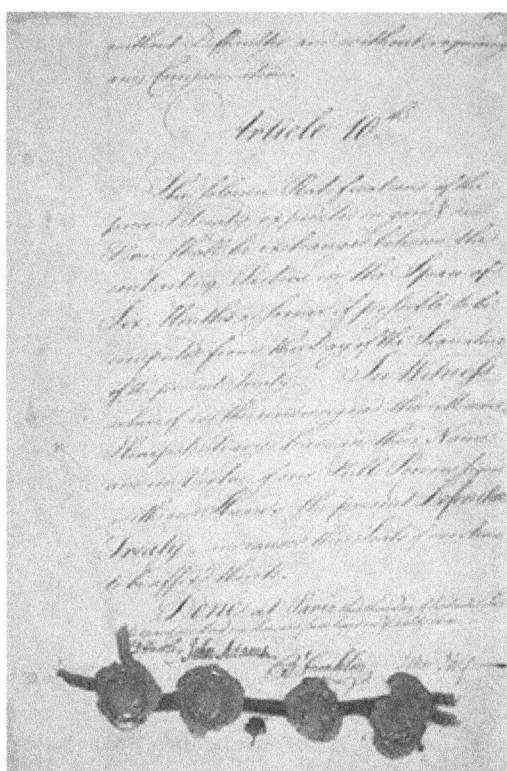

The last page of the Treaty of Paris, signed on September 3, 1783, contained the signatures and seals of representatives for both the British and the Americans. From right to left, the seals pictured belong to David Hartley, who represented Great Britain, and John Adams, Benjamin Franklin, and John Jay for the Americans.

THE TREATY OF PARIS

The British defeat at Yorktown made the outcome of the war all but certain. In light of the American victory, the Parliament of Great Britain voted to end further military operations against the rebels and to begin peace negotiations. Support for the war effort had come to an end, and British military forces began to evacuate the former American colonies in 1782. When hostilities had ended, Washington resigned as commander in chief and returned to his Virginia home.

In April 1782, Benjamin Franklin, John Adams, and John Jay had begun informal peace negotiations in Paris. Officials from Great Britain and the United States finalized the treaty in 1783, signing the Treaty of Paris in September of that year. The treaty recognized the independence of the United States; placed the western, eastern, northern, and southern boundaries of the nation at the Mississippi River, the Atlantic Ocean, Canada, and Florida, respectively; and gave New Englanders fishing rights in the waters off Newfoundland. Under the terms of the treaty, individual states were encouraged to refrain from persecuting Loyalists and to return their confiscated property.

Section Summary

The British gained momentum in the war when they turned their military efforts against the southern colonies. They scored repeated victories in the coastal towns, where they found legions of supporters, including slaves escaping bondage. As in other colonies, however, control of major seaports did not mean the British could control the interior. Fighting in the southern colonies devolved into a merciless civil war as the Revolution opened the floodgates of pent-up anger and resentment between frontier residents and those along the coastal regions. The southern campaign came to an end at Yorktown when Cornwallis surrendered to American forces.

https://www.openassessments.org/assessments/958

Review Question

1. Describe the British southern strategy and its results.

Answer to Review Question

1. The British southern strategy was to move the military theater to the southern colonies where there were more Loyalist colonists. Slaves and Indian allies, the British hoped, would also swell their ranks. This strategy worked at first, allowing the British to take Charleston. However, British fortunes changed after Nathanael Greene took command of the southern Continental Army and scored decisive victories at the battles of Cowpens and Guilford. This set the stage for the final American victory at Yorktown, Virginia. The southern strategy had failed.

Glossary

Yorktown the Virginia port where British General Cornwallis surrendered to American forces

Attributions

CC licensed content, Shared previously

- US History. **Authored by**: P. Scott Corbett, Volker Janssen, John M. Lund, Todd Pfannestiel, Paul Vickery, and Sylvie Waskiewicz. **Provided by**: OpenStax College. **Located at**: http://openstaxcollege.org/textbooks/us-history. **License**: *CC BY: Attribution*. **License Terms**: Download for free at http://cnx.org/content/col11740/latest/

Identity during the American Revolution

> **Learning Objectives**
>
> By the end of this section, you will be able to:
>
> - Explain Loyalist and Patriot sentiments
> - Identify different groups that participated in the Revolutionary War

The American Revolution in effect created multiple civil wars. Many of the resentments and antagonisms that fed these conflicts predated the Revolution, and the outbreak of war acted as the catalyst they needed to burst forth. In particular, the middle colonies of New York, New Jersey, and Pennsylvania had deeply divided populations. Loyalty to Great Britain came in many forms, from wealthy elites who enjoyed the prewar status quo to runaway slaves who desired the freedom that the British offered.

LOYALISTS

Historians disagree on what percentage of colonists were Loyalists; estimates range from 20 percent to over 30 percent. In general, however, of British America's population of 2.5 million, roughly one-third remained loyal to Great Britain, while another third committed themselves to the cause of independence. The remaining third remained apathetic, content to continue with their daily lives as best they could and preferring not to engage in the struggle.

Many Loyalists were royal officials and merchants with extensive business ties to Great Britain, who viewed themselves as the rightful and just defenders of the British constitution. Others simply resented local business and political rivals who supported the Revolution, viewing the rebels as hypocrites and schemers who selfishly used the break with the Empire to increase their fortunes. In New York's Hudson Valley, animosity among the tenants of estates owned by Revolutionary leaders turned them to the cause of King and Empire.

During the war, all the states passed **confiscation acts**, which gave the new revolutionary governments in the former colonies the right to seize Loyalist land and property. To ferret out Loyalists, revolutionary governments also passed laws requiring the male population to take oaths of allegiance to the new states. Those who refused lost their property and were often imprisoned or made to work for the new local revolutionary order.

The Coming of the Loyalists, a ca. 1880 work that artist Henry Sandham created at least a century after the Revolution, shows Anglo-American colonists arriving by ship in New Brunswick, Canada.

William Franklin, Benjamin Franklin's only surviving son, remained loyal to Crown and Empire and served as royal governor of New Jersey, a post he secured with his father's help. During the war, revolutionaries imprisoned William in Connecticut; however, he remained steadfast in his allegiance to Great Britain and moved to England after the Revolution. He and his father never reconciled.

As many as nineteen thousand colonists served the British in the effort to put down the rebellion, and after the Revolution, as many as 100,000 colonists left, moving to England or north to Canada rather than staying in the new United States. Eight thousand whites and five thousand free blacks went to Britain. Over thirty thousand went to Canada, transforming that nation from predominately French to predominantly British. Another sizable group of Loyalists went to the British West Indies, taking their slaves with them.

Hannah Ingraham on Removing to Nova Scotia

Hannah Ingraham was eleven years old in 1783, when her Loyalist family removed from New York to Ste. Anne's Point in the colony of Nova Scotia. Later in life, she compiled her memories of that time.

> [Father] said we were to go to Nova Scotia, that a ship was ready to take us there, so we made all haste to get ready.... Then on Tuesday, suddenly the house was surrounded by rebels and father was taken prisoner and carried away.... When morning came, they said he was free to go.
>
> We had five wagon loads carried down the Hudson in a sloop and then we went on board the transport that was to bring us to Saint John. I was just eleven years old when we left our farm to come here. It was the last transport of the season and had on board all those who could not come sooner. The first transports had come in May so the people had all the summer before them to get settled....

> We lived in a tent at St. Anne's until father got a house ready.... There was no floor laid, no windows, no chimney, no door, but we had a roof at least. A good fire was blazing and mother had a big loaf of bread and she boiled a kettle of water and put a good piece of butter in a pewter bowl. We toasted the bread and all sat around the bowl and ate our breakfast that morning and mother said: "Thank God we are no longer in dread of having shots fired through our house. This is the sweetest meal I ever tasted for many a day."

What do these excerpts tell you about life as a Loyalist in New York or as a transplant to Canada?

SLAVES AND INDIANS

While some slaves who fought for the Patriot cause received their freedom, revolutionary leaders—unlike the British—did not grant such slaves their freedom as a matter of course. Washington, the owner of more than two hundred slaves during the Revolution, refused to let slaves serve in the army, although he did allow free blacks. (In his will, Washington did free his slaves.) In the new United States, the Revolution largely reinforced a racial identity based on skin color. Whiteness, now a national identity, denoted freedom and stood as the key to power. Blackness, more than ever before, denoted servile status. Indeed, despite their class and ethnic differences, white revolutionaries stood mostly united in their hostility to both blacks and Indians.

Boyrereau Brinch and Boston King on the Revolutionary War

In the Revolutionary War, some blacks, both free and enslaved, chose to fight for the Americans. Others chose to fight for the British, who offered them freedom for joining their cause. Read the excerpts below for the perspective of a black veteran from each side of the conflict.

Boyrereau Brinch was captured in Africa at age sixteen and brought to America as a slave. He joined the Patriot forces and was honorably discharged and emancipated after the war. He told his story to Benjamin Prentiss, who published it as *The Blind African Slave* in 1810.

Jean-Baptiste-Antoine de Verger created this 1781 watercolor, which depicts American soldiers at the Siege of Yorktown. Verger was an officer in Rochambeau's army, and his diary holds firsthand accounts of his experiences in the campaigns of 1780 and 1781. This image contains one of the earliest known representations of a black Continental soldier.

> Finally, I was in the battles at Cambridge, White Plains, Monmouth, Princeton, Newark, Frog's Point, Horseneck where I had a ball pass through my knapsack. All which battels [sic] the reader can obtain a more perfect account of in history, than I can give. At last we returned to West Point and were discharged [1783], as the war was over. Thus was I, a slave for five years fighting for liberty. After we were disbanded, I returned to my old master at Woodbury [Connecticut], with whom I lived one year, my services in the American war, having emancipated me from further slavery, and from being bartered or sold.... Here I enjoyed the pleasures of a freeman; my food was sweet, my labor pleasure: and one bright gleam of life seemed to shine upon me.

Boston King was a Charleston-born slave who escaped his master and joined the Loyalists. He made his way to Nova Scotia and later Sierra Leone, where he published his memoirs in 1792. The excerpt below describes his experience in New York after the war.

> When I arrived at New-York, my friends rejoiced to see me once more restored to liberty, and joined me in praising the Lord for his mercy and goodness.... [In 1783] the horrors and devastation of war happily terminated, and peace was restored between America and Great Britain, which diffused universal joy among all parties, except us, who had escaped from slavery and taken refuge in the English army; for a report prevailed at New-York, that all the slaves, in number 2000, were to be delivered up to their masters, altho' some of them had been three or four years among the English. This dreadful rumour filled us all with inexpressible anguish and terror, especially when we saw our old masters coming from Virginia, North-Carolina, and other parts, and seizing upon their slaves in the streets of New-York, or even dragging them out of their beds. Many of the slaves had very cruel masters, so that the thoughts of returning home with them embittered life to us. For some days we lost our appetite for food, and sleep departed from our eyes. The English had compassion upon us in the day of distress, and issued out a Proclamation, importing, That all slaves should be free, who had taken refuge in the British lines, and claimed the sanction and privileges of the Proclamations respecting the security and protection of Negroes. In consequence of this, each of us received a certificate from the commanding officer at New-York, which dispelled all our fears, and filled us with joy and gratitude.

What do these two narratives have in common, and how are they different? How do the two men describe freedom?

For slaves willing to run away and join the British, the American Revolution offered a unique occasion to escape bondage. Of the half a million slaves in the American colonies during the Revolution, twenty thousand joined the British cause. At Yorktown, for instance, thousands of black troops fought with Lord Cornwallis. Slaves belonging to George Washington, Thomas Jefferson, Patrick Henry, and other revolutionaries seized the opportunity for freedom and fled to the British side. Between ten and twenty thousand slaves gained their freedom because of the Revolution; arguably, the Revolution created the largest slave uprising and the greatest emancipation until the Civil War. After the Revolution, some of these African Loyalists emigrated to Sierra Leone on the west coast of Africa. Others removed to Canada and England. It is also true that people of color made heroic contributions to the cause of American independence. However, while the British offered slaves freedom, most American revolutionaries clung to notions of black inferiority.

Powerful Indian peoples who had allied themselves with the British, including the Mohawk and the Creek, also remained loyal to the Empire. A Mohawk named Joseph Brant, whose given name was Thayendanegea, rose to prominence while fighting for the British during the Revolution. He joined forces with Colonel Barry St. Leger during the 1777 campaign, which ended with the surrender of General Burgoyne at Saratoga. After the war, Brant moved to the Six Nations reserve in Canada. From his home on the shores of Lake Ontario, he remained active in efforts to restrict white encroachment onto Indian lands. After their defeat, the British did not keep promises they'd made to help their Indian allies keep their territory; in fact, the Treaty of Paris granted the United States huge amounts of supposedly British-owned regions that were actually Indian lands.

(a) (b)

What similarities can you see in these two portraits of Joseph Brant, one by Gilbert Stuart in 1786 (a) and one by Charles Wilson Peale in 1797 (b)? What are the differences? Why do you think the artists made the specific choices they did?

PATRIOTS

The American revolutionaries (also called Patriots or Whigs) came from many different backgrounds and included merchants, shoemakers, farmers, and sailors. What is extraordinary is the way in which the struggle for independence brought a vast cross-section of society together, animated by a common cause.

During the war, the revolutionaries faced great difficulties, including massive supply problems; clothing, ammunition, tents, and equipment were all hard to come by. After an initial burst of enthusiasm in 1775 and 1776, the shortage of supplies became acute in 1777 through 1779, as Washington's difficult winter at Valley Forge demonstrates.

Funding the war effort also proved very difficult. Whereas the British could pay in gold and silver, the American forces relied on paper money, backed by loans obtained in Europe. This first American money was called **Continental currency**; unfortunately, it quickly fell in value. "Not worth a Continental" soon became a shorthand term for something of no value. The new revolutionary government printed a great amount of this paper money, resulting in runaway inflation. By 1781, inflation was such that 146 Continental dollars were worth only one dollar in gold. The problem grew worse as each former colony, now a revolutionary state, printed its own currency.

WOMEN

In colonial America, women shouldered enormous domestic and child-rearing responsibilities. The war for independence only increased their workload and, in some ways, solidified their roles. Rebel leaders required women to produce articles for war—everything from clothing to foodstuffs—while also keeping their homesteads going. This was not an easy task when their husbands and sons were away fighting. Women were also expected to provide food and lodging for armies and to nurse wounded soldiers.

The Revolution opened some new doors for women, however, as they took on public roles usually reserved for men. The Daughters of Liberty, an informal organization formed in the mid-1760s to oppose British revenue-raising measures, worked tirelessly to support the war effort. Esther DeBerdt Reed of Philadelphia, wife of Governor Joseph Reed, formed the Ladies Association of Philadelphia and led a fundraising drive to provide sorely needed supplies to the Continental Army. In "The Sentiments of an American Woman" (1780), she wrote to other women, "The time is arrived to display the same sentiments which animated us at the beginning of the Revolution, when we renounced the use of teas, however agreeable to our taste, rather than receive them from our persecutors; when we made it appear to them that we placed former necessaries in the rank of superfluities, when our liberty was interested; when our republican and laborious hands spun the flax, prepared the linen intended for the use of our soldiers; when exiles and fugitives we supported with courage all the evils which are the concomitants of war." Reed and other elite women in Philadelphia raised almost $300,000 in Continental money for the war.

> Read the entire text of Esther Reed's "The Sentiments of "The Sentiments of an American Woman" on a page hosted by the University of Michigan-Dearborn.

Women who did not share Reed's elite status nevertheless played key economic roles by producing homespun cloth and food. During shortages, some women formed mobs and wrested supplies from those who hoarded them. Crowds of women beset merchants and demanded fair prices for goods; if a merchant refused, a riot would ensue. Still other women accompanied the army as "camp followers," serving as cooks, washerwomen, and nurses. A few also took part in combat and proved their equality with men through violence against the hated British.

> ### Section Summary
>
> The American Revolution divided the colonists as much as it united them, with Loyalists (or Tories) joining the British forces against the Patriots (or revolutionaries). Both sides included a broad cross-section of the population. However, Great Britain was able to convince many slaves to join its forces by promising them freedom, something the southern revolutionaries would not agree to do. The war provided new opportunities, as well as new challenges, for slaves, free blacks, women, and Indians. After the war, many Loyalists fled the American colonies, heading across the Atlantic to England, north to Canada, or south to the West Indies.

- https://www.openassessments.org/assessments/959

Critical Thinking Questions

1. How did the colonists manage to triumph in their battle for independence despite Great Britain's military might? If any of these factors had been different, how might it have affected the outcome of the war?

2. How did the condition of certain groups, such as women, blacks, and Indians, reveal a contradiction in the Declaration of Independence?

3. What was the effect and importance of Great Britain's promise of freedom to slaves who joined the British side?

4. How did the Revolutionary War provide both new opportunities and new challenges for slaves and free blacks in America?

5. Describe the ideology of republicanism. As a political philosophy, how did republicanism compare to the system that prevailed in Great Britain?

6. Describe the backgrounds and philosophies of Patriots and Loyalists. Why did colonists with such diverse individual interests unite in support of their respective causes? What might different groups of Patriots and Loyalists, depending upon their circumstances, have hoped to achieve by winning the war?

Glossary

confiscation acts state-wide acts that made it legal for state governments to seize Loyalists' property

Continental currency the paper currency that the Continental government printed to fund the Revolution

Attributions

CC licensed content, Shared previously

- US History. **Authored by**: P. Scott Corbett, Volker Janssen, John M. Lund, Todd Pfannestiel, Paul Vickery, and Sylvie Waskiewicz. **Provided by**: OpenStax College. **Located at**: http://openstaxcollege.org/textbooks/us-history. **License**: *CC BY: Attribution*. **License Terms**: Download for free at http://cnx.org/content/col11740/latest/

7. Creating Republican Governments, 1776-1783

Introduction

After the Revolutionary War, the ideology that "all men are created equal" failed to match up with reality, as the revolutionary generation could not solve the contradictions of freedom and slavery in the new United States. Trumbull's 1780 painting of George Washington hints at some of these contradictions. What attitude do you think Trumbull was trying to convey? Why did Trumbull include Washington's slave Billy Lee, and what does Lee represent in this painting?

During the 1770s and 1780s, Americans took bold steps to define American equality. Each state held constitutional conventions and crafted state constitutions that defined how government would operate and who could participate in political life. Many elite revolutionaries recoiled in horror from the idea of majority rule—the basic principle of democracy—fearing that it would effectively create a "mob rule" that would bring about the ruin of the hard-fought struggle for independence. Statesmen everywhere believed that a republic should replace the British monarchy: a government where the important affairs would be entrusted only to representative men of learning and refinement.

John Trumbull, Washington's aide-de-camp, painted this wartime image of Washington on a promontory above the Hudson River. Just behind Washington, his slave William "Billy" Lee has his eyes firmly fixed on his master. In the far background, British warships fire on an American fort.

Attributions

CC licensed content, Shared previously

- US History. **Authored by**: P. Scott Corbett, Volker Janssen, John M. Lund, Todd Pfannestiel, Paul Vickery, and Sylvie Waskiewicz. **Provided by**: OpenStax College. **Located at**: http://openstaxcollege.org/textbooks/us-history. **License**: *CC BY: Attribution*. **License Terms**: Download for free at http://cnx.org/content/col11740/latest/

Common Sense: From Monarchy to an American Republic

Learning Objectives

By the end of this section, you will be able to:

- Compare and contrast monarchy and republican government
- Describe the tenets of republicanism

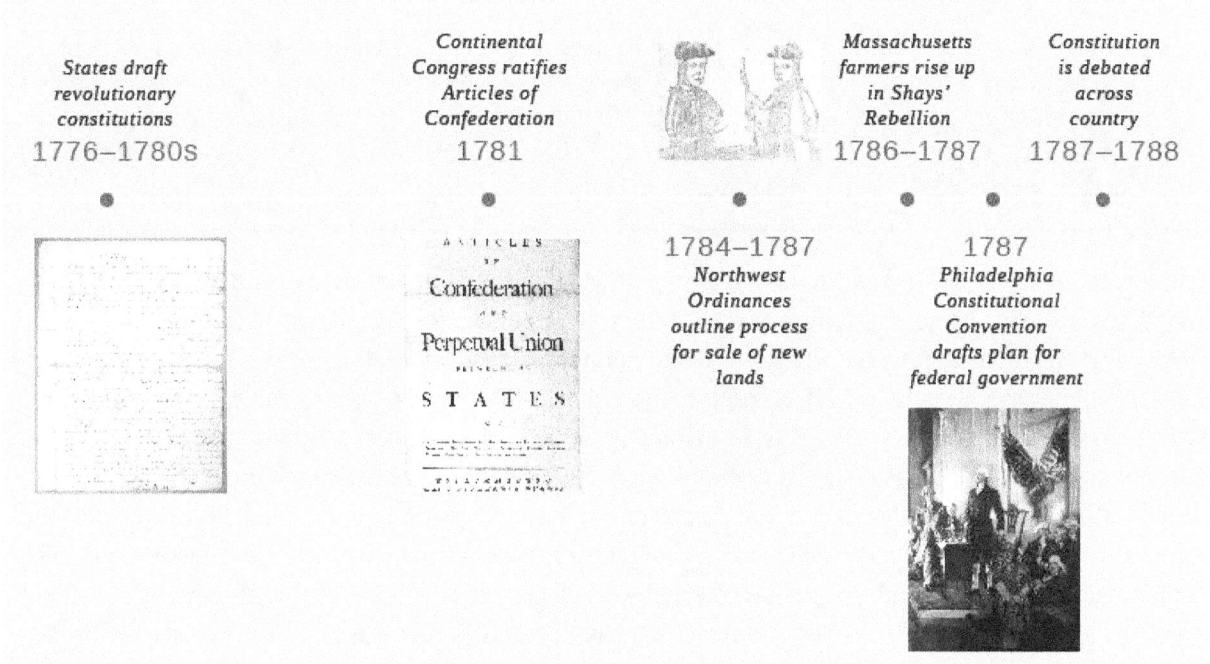

While monarchies dominated eighteenth-century Europe, American revolutionaries were determined to find an alternative to this method of government. Radical pamphleteer Thomas Paine, whose enormously popular essay *Common Sense* was first published in January 1776, advocated a republic: a state without a king. Six months later, Jefferson's Declaration of Independence affirmed the break with England but did not suggest what form of government should replace monarchy, the only system most English colonists had ever known. In the late eighteenth century, republics were few and far between. Genoa, Venice, and the Dutch Republic provided examples of states without monarchs, but many European Enlightenment thinkers questioned the stability of a republic. Nonetheless, after their break from Great Britain, Americans turned to republicanism for their new government.

REPUBLICANISM AS A POLITICAL PHILOSOPHY

Monarchy rests on the practice of dynastic succession, in which the monarch's child or other relative inherits the throne. Contested dynastic succession produced chronic conflict and warfare in Europe. In the eighteenth century, well-established monarchs ruled most of Europe and, according to tradition, were obligated to protect and guide their subjects. However, by the mid-1770s, many American colonists believed that George III, the king of Great Britain, had failed to do so. Patriots believed the British monarchy under George III had been corrupted and the king turned into a tyrant who cared nothing for the traditional liberties afforded to members of the British Empire. The disaffection from monarchy explains why a republic appeared a better alternative to the revolutionaries.

American revolutionaries looked to the past for inspiration for their break with the British monarchy and their adoption of a republican form of government. The Roman Republic provided guidance. Much like the Americans in their struggle against Britain, Romans had thrown off monarchy and created a republic in which Roman citizens would appoint or select the leaders who would represent them.

> Visit the Metropolitan Museum of Art to see a Roman-style bust of George Washington, complete with toga. In 1791, Italian sculptor Giuseppe Ceracchi visited Philadelphia, hoping the government might commission a monument of his creation. He did not succeed, but the bust of Washington, one of the ones he produced to demonstrate his skill, illustrates the connection between the American and Roman republics that revolutionaries made.

While republicanism offered an alternative to monarchy, it was also an alternative to **democracy**, a system of government characterized by **majority rule**, where the majority of citizens have the power to make decisions binding upon the whole. To many revolutionaries, especially wealthy landowners, merchants, and planters, democracy did not offer a good replacement for monarchy. Indeed, **conservative Whigs** defined themselves in opposition to democracy, which they equated with anarchy. In the tenth in a series of essays later known as *The Federalist Papers*, Virginian James Madison wrote: "Democracies have ever been spectacles of turbulence and contention; have ever been found incompatible with personal security or the rights of property; and have in general been as short in their lives as they have been violent in their deaths." Many shared this perspective and worked hard to keep democratic tendencies in check. It is easy to understand why democracy seemed threatening: majority rule can easily overpower minority rights, and the wealthy few had reason to fear that a hostile and envious majority could seize and redistribute their wealth.

While many now assume the United States was founded as a democracy, history, as always, is more complicated. Conservative Whigs believed in government by a patrician class, a ruling group composed of a small number of privileged families. **Radical Whigs** favored broadening the popular participation in political life and pushed for democracy. The great debate after independence was secured centered on this question: Who should rule in the new American republic?

REPUBLICANISM AS A SOCIAL PHILOSOPHY

According to political theory, a republic requires its citizens to cultivate virtuous behavior; if the people are virtuous, the republic will survive. If the people become corrupt, the republic will fall. Whether republicanism succeeded or failed in the United States would depend on civic virtue and an educated citizenry. Revolutionary leaders agreed that the ownership of property provided one way to measure an individual's virtue, arguing that property holders had the greatest stake in society and therefore could be trusted to make decisions for it. By the same token, non-property holders, they believed, should have very little to do with government. In other words, unlike a democracy, in which the mass of non-property holders could exercise the political right to vote, a republic would limit political rights to property holders. In this way, republicanism exhibited a bias toward the elite, a preference that is understandable given the colonial legacy. During colonial times, wealthy planters and merchants in the American colonies had looked to the British ruling class, whose social order demanded deference from those of lower rank, as a model of behavior. Old habits died hard.

Benjamin Franklin's Thirteen Virtues for Character Development

In the 1780s, Benjamin Franklin carefully defined thirteen virtues to help guide his countrymen in maintaining a virtuous republic. His choice of thirteen is telling since he wrote for the citizens of the thirteen new American republics. These virtues were:

1. *Temperance*. Eat not to dullness; drink not to elevation.
2. *Silence*. Speak not but what may benefit others or yourself; avoid trifling conversation.
3. *Order*. Let all your things have their places; let each part of your business have its time.
4. *Resolution*. Resolve to perform what you ought; perform without fail what you resolve.
5. *Frugality*. Make no expense but to do good to others or yourself; i.e., waste nothing.
6. *Industry*. Lose no time; be always employ'd in something useful; cut off all unnecessary actions.
7. *Sincerity*. Use no hurtful deceit; think innocently and justly, and, if you speak, speak accordingly.
8. *Justice*. Wrong none by doing injuries, or omitting the benefits that are your duty.
9. *Moderation*. Avoid extremes; forbear resenting injuries so much as you think they deserve.
10. *Cleanliness*. Tolerate no uncleanliness in body, cloaths, or habitation.
11. *Tranquillity*. Be not disturbed at trifles, or at accidents common or unavoidable.
12. *Chastity*. Rarely use venery but for health or offspring, never to dullness, weakness, or the injury of your own or another's peace or reputation.
13. *Humility*. Imitate Jesus and Socrates.

Franklin's thirteen virtues suggest that hard work and good behavior will bring success. What factors does Franklin ignore? How would he likely address a situation in which children inherit great wealth rather than working for it? How do Franklin's values help to define the notion of republican virtue?

> Check how well you are demonstrating all thirteen of Franklin's virtues on thirteenvirtues.com, where you can register to track your progress.

George Washington served as a role model par excellence for the new republic, embodying the exceptional talent and public virtue prized under the political and social philosophy of republicanism. He did not seek to become the new king of America; instead he retired as commander in chief of the Continental Army and returned to his Virginia estate at Mount Vernon to resume his life among the planter elite. Washington modeled his behavior on that of the Roman aristocrat Cincinnatus, a representative of the patrician or ruling class, who had also retired from public service in the Roman Republic and returned to his estate to pursue agricultural life.

The aristocratic side of republicanism—and the belief that the true custodians of public virtue were those who had served in the military—found expression in the Society of the Cincinnati, of which Washington was the first president general. Founded in 1783, the society admitted only officers of the Continental Army and the French forces, not militia members or minutemen. Following the rule of primogeniture, the eldest sons of members inherited their fathers' memberships. The society still exists today and retains the motto *Omnia relinquit servare rempublicam* ("He relinquished everything to save the Republic").

This membership certificate for the Society of the Cincinnati commemorates "the great Event which gave Independence to North America."

Section Summary

The guiding principle of republicanism was that the people themselves would appoint or select the leaders who would represent them. The debate over how much democracy (majority rule) to incorporate in the governing of the new United States raised questions about who was best qualified to participate in government and have the right to vote. Revolutionary leaders argued that property holders had the greatest stake in society and favored a republic that would limit political rights to property holders. In this way, republicanism exhibited a bias toward the elite. George Washington served as a role model for the new republic, embodying the exceptional talent and public virtue prized in its political and social philosophy.

https://www.openassessments.org/assessments/960

Review Question

1. What defined republicanism as a social philosophy?

Answer to Review Question

1. Citizenship within a republic meant accepting certain rights and responsibilities as well as cultivating virtuous behavior. This philosophy was based on the notion that the success or failure of the republic depended upon the virtue or corruption of its citizens.

Glossary

conservative Whigs the politically and economically elite revolutionary class that wanted to limit political participation to a few powerful families

democracy a system of government in which the majority rules

majority rule a fundamental principle of democracy, providing that the majority should have the power to make decisions binding upon the whole

monarchy a form of government with a monarch at its head

radical Whigs revolutionaries who favored broadening participation in the political process

Attributions

CC licensed content, Shared previously

- US History. **Authored by**: P. Scott Corbett, Volker Janssen, John M. Lund, Todd Pfannestiel, Paul Vickery, and Sylvie Waskiewicz. **Provided by**: OpenStax College. **Located at**: http://openstaxcollege.org/textbooks/us-history. **License**: *CC BY: Attribution*. **License Terms**: Download for free at http://cnx.org/content/col11740/latest/

How Much Revolutionary Change?

> **Learning Objectives**
>
> By the end of this section, you will be able to:
>
> - Describe the status of women in the new republic
> - Describe the status of nonwhites in the new republic

Elite republican revolutionaries did not envision a completely new society; traditional ideas and categories of race and gender, order and decorum remained firmly entrenched among members of their privileged class. Many Americans rejected the elitist and aristocratic republican order, however, and advocated radical changes. Their efforts represented a groundswell of sentiment for greater equality, a part of the democratic impulse unleashed by the Revolution.

THE STATUS OF WOMEN

In eighteenth-century America, as in Great Britain, the legal status of married women was defined as **coverture**, meaning a married woman (or *feme covert*) had no legal or economic status independent of her husband. She could not conduct business or buy and sell property. Her husband controlled any property she brought to the marriage, although he could not sell it without her agreement. Married women's status as *femes covert* did not change as a result of the Revolution, and wives remained economically dependent on their husbands. The women of the newly independent nation did not call for the right to vote, but some, especially the wives of elite republican statesmen, began to agitate for equality under the law between husbands and wives, and for the same educational opportunities as men.

Some women hoped to overturn coverture. From her home in Braintree, Massachusetts, Abigail Adams wrote to her husband, Whig leader John Adams, in 1776, "In the new code of laws which I suppose it will be necessary for you to make, I desire you would remember the ladies and be more generous and favorable to them than your ancestor. Do not put such unlimited power in the husbands. Remember, all men would be tyrants if they could." Abigail Adams ran the family homestead during the Revolution, but she did not have the ability to conduct business without her husband's consent. Elsewhere in the famous 1776 letter quoted above, she speaks of the difficulties of running the homestead when her husband is away. Her frustration grew when her husband responded in an April 1776 letter: "As to your extraordinary Code of Laws, I cannot but laugh. We have been told that our Struggle has loosened the bands of Government every where. That Children and Apprentices were disobedient—that schools and Colledges were grown turbulent—that Indians slighted their Guardians and Negroes grew insolent to their Masters. But your Letter was the first Intimation that another Tribe more numerous and powerfull than all the rest were grown discontented. . . . Depend on it, We know better than to repeal our Masculine systems."

Abigail Adams (a), shown here in a 1766 portrait by Benjamin Blythe, is best remembered for her eloquent letters to her husband, John Adams (b), who would later become the second president of the United States.

Another privileged member of the revolutionary generation, Mercy Otis Warren, also challenged gender assumptions and traditions during the revolutionary era. Born in Massachusetts, Warren actively opposed British reform measures before the outbreak of fighting in 1775 by publishing anti-British works. In 1812, she published a three-volume history of the Revolution, a project she had started in the late 1770s. By publishing her work, Warren stepped out of the female sphere and into the otherwise male-dominated sphere of public life.

Inspired by the Revolution, Judith Sargent Murray of Massachusetts advocated women's economic independence and equal educational opportunities for men and women. Murray, who came from a well-to-do family in Gloucester, questioned why boys were given access to education as a birthright while girls had very limited educational opportunities. She began to publish her ideas about educational equality beginning in the 1780s, arguing that God had made the minds of women and men equal.

John Singleton Copley's 1772 portrait of Judith Sargent Murray (a) and 1763 portrait of Mercy Otis Warren (b) show two of America's earliest advocates for women's rights. Notice how their fine silk dresses telegraph their privileged social status.

Murray's more radical ideas championed woman's economic independence. She argued that a woman's education should be extensive enough to allow her to maintain herself—and her family—if there was no male breadwinner. Indeed, Murray was able to make money of her own from her publications. Her ideas were both radical and traditional, however: Murray also believed that women were much better at raising children and maintaining the morality and virtue of the family than men.

Adams, Murray, and Warren all came from privileged backgrounds. All three were fully literate, while many women in the American republic were not. Their literacy and station allowed them to push for new roles for women in the atmosphere of unique possibility created by the Revolution and its promise of change. Female authors who published their work provide evidence of how women in the era of the American Revolution challenged traditional gender roles.

Overall, the Revolution reconfigured women's roles by undermining the traditional expectations of wives and mothers, including subservience. In the home, the separate domestic sphere assigned to women, women were expected to practice republican virtues, especially frugality and simplicity. Republican motherhood meant that women, more than men, were responsible for raising good children, instilling in them all the virtue necessary to ensure the survival of the republic. The Revolution also opened new doors to educational opportunities for women. Men understood that the republic needed women to play a substantial role in upholding republicanism and ensuring the survival of the new nation. Benjamin Rush, a Whig educator and physician from Philadelphia, strongly advocated for the education of girls and young women as part of the larger effort to ensure that republican virtue and republican motherhood would endure.

THE MEANING OF RACE

By the time of the Revolution, slavery had been firmly in place in America for over one hundred years. In many ways, the Revolution served to reinforce the assumptions about race among white Americans. They viewed the new nation as a white republic; blacks were slaves, and Indians had no place. Racial hatred of blacks increased during the Revolution because many slaves fled their white masters for the freedom offered by the British. The same was true for Indians who allied themselves with the British; Jefferson wrote in the Declaration of Independence that separation from the Empire was necessary because George III had incited "the merciless Indian savages" to destroy the white inhabitants on the frontier. Similarly, Thomas Paine argued in *Common Sense* that Great Britain was guilty of inciting "the Indians and Negroes to destroy us." For his part, Benjamin Franklin wrote in the 1780s that, in time, alcoholism would wipe out the Indians, leaving the land free for white settlers.

Phillis Wheatley: "On Being Brought from Africa to America"

Phillis Wheatley was born in Africa in 1753 and sold as a slave to the Wheatley family of Boston; her African name is lost to posterity. Although most slaves in the eighteenth century had no opportunities to learn to read and write, Wheatley achieved full literacy and went on to become one of the best-known poets of the time, although many doubted her authorship of her poems because of her race.

This portrait of Phillis Wheatley from the frontispiece of Poems on various subjects, religious and moral shows the writer at work. Despite her status as a slave, her poems won great renown in America and in Europe.

Wheatley's poems reflected her deep Christian beliefs. In the poem below, how do her views on Christianity affect her views on slavery?

Twas mercy brought me from my Pagan land,

> Taught my benighted soul to understand
> That there's a God, that there's a Saviour too:
> Once I redemption neither sought nor knew.
> Some view our sable race with scornful eye,
> "Their colour is a diabolic dye."
> Remember, Christians, Negroes, black as Cain,
> May be refin'd, and join th' angelic train.—Phillis Wheatley, "On Being Brought from Africa to America"

Slavery

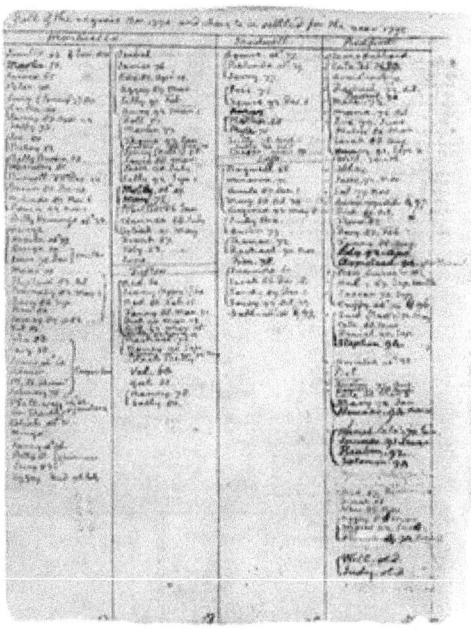

This page, taken from one of Thomas Jefferson's record books from 1795, lists his slaves.

Slavery offered the most glaring contradiction between the idea of equality stated in the Declaration of Independence ("all men are created equal") and the reality of race relations in the late eighteenth century.

Racism shaped white views of blacks. Although he penned the Declaration of Independence, Thomas Jefferson owned more than one hundred slaves, of whom he freed only a few either during his lifetime or in his will. He thought blacks were inferior to whites, dismissing Phillis Wheatley by arguing, "Religion indeed has produced a Phillis Wheatley; but it could not produce a poet." White slaveholders took their female slaves as mistresses, as most historians agree that Jefferson did with one of his slaves, Sally Hemings. Together, they had several children.

> Browse the Thomas Jefferson Papers at the Massachusetts Historical Society to examine Jefferson's "farm books," in which he kept records of his land holdings, animal husbandry, and slaves, including specific references to Sally Hemings.

Jefferson understood the contradiction fully, and his writings reveal hard-edged racist assumptions. In his *Notes on the State of Virginia* in the 1780s, Jefferson urged the end of slavery in Virginia and the removal of blacks from that state. He wrote: "It will probably be asked, Why not retain and incorporate the blacks into the state, and thus save the expense of supplying, by importation of white settlers, the vacancies they will leave? Deep rooted prejudices entertained by the whites; ten thousand recollections, by the blacks, of the injuries they have sustained; new provocations; the real distinctions which nature has made; and many other circumstances, will divide us into parties, and produce convulsions which will probably never end but in the extermination of the one or the other race. —To these objections, which are political, may be added others, which are physical and moral." Jefferson envisioned an "empire of liberty" for white farmers and relied on the argument of sending blacks out of the United States, even if doing so would completely destroy the slaveholders' wealth in their human property.

Southern planters strongly objected to Jefferson's views on abolishing slavery and removing blacks from America. When Jefferson was a candidate for president in 1796, an anonymous "Southern Planter" wrote, "If this wild project succeeds, under the auspices of Thomas Jefferson, President of the United States, and three hundred thousand slaves are set free in Virginia, farewell to the safety, prosperity, the importance, perhaps the very existence of the Southern States." Slaveholders and many other Americans protected and defended the institution.

This 1796 broadside to "the Citizens of the Southern States" by "a Southern Planter" argued that Thomas Jefferson's advocacy of the emancipation of slaves in his Notes on the State of Virginia posed a threat to the safety, the prosperity, and even the existence of the southern states.

Freedom

While racial thinking permeated the new country, and slavery existed in all the new states, the ideals of the Revolution generated a movement toward the abolition of slavery. Private **manumissions**, by which slaveholders freed their slaves, provided one pathway from bondage. Slaveholders in Virginia freed some ten thousand slaves. In Massachusetts, the Wheatley family manumitted Phillis in 1773 when she was twenty-one. Other revolutionaries formed societies dedicated to abolishing slavery. One of the earliest efforts began in 1775 in Philadelphia, where Dr. Benjamin Rush and other Philadelphia Quakers formed what became the Pennsylvania Abolition Society. Similarly, wealthy New Yorkers formed the New York Manumission Society in 1785. This society worked to educate black children and devoted funds to protect free blacks from kidnapping.

Slavery persisted in the North, however, and the example of Massachusetts highlights the complexity of the situation. The 1780 Massachusetts constitution technically freed all slaves. Nonetheless, several hundred individuals remained enslaved in the state. In the 1780s, a series of court decisions undermined slavery in Massachusetts when several slaves, citing assault by their masters, successfully sought their freedom in court. These individuals refused to be treated as slaves in the wake of the American Revolution. Despite these legal victories, about eleven hundred slaves continued to be held in the New England states in 1800. The contradictions illustrate the difference between the letter and the spirit of the laws abolishing slavery in Massachusetts. In all, over thirty-six thousand slaves remained in the North, with the highest concentrations in New Jersey and New York. New York only gradually phased out slavery, with the last slaves emancipated in the late 1820s.

Indians

The 1783 Treaty of Paris, which ended the war for independence, did not address Indians at all. All lands held by the British east of the Mississippi and south of the Great Lakes (except Spanish Florida) now belonged to the new American republic. Though the treaty remained silent on the issue, much of the territory now included in the boundaries of the United States remained under the control of native peoples. Earlier in the eighteenth century, a "middle ground" had existed between powerful native groups in the West and British and French imperial zones, a place where the various groups interacted and accommodated each other. As had happened in the French and Indian War and Pontiac's Rebellion, the Revolutionary War turned the middle ground into a battle zone that no one group controlled.

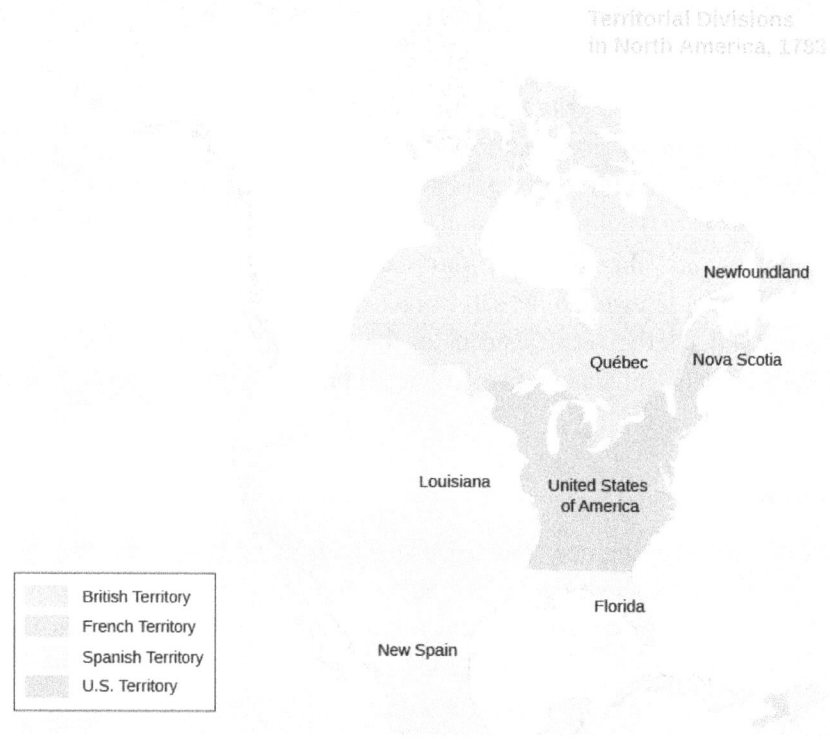

The 1783 Treaty of Paris divided North America into territories belonging to the United States and several European countries, but it failed to address Indian lands at all.

During the Revolution, a complex situation existed among Indians. Many villages remained neutral. Some native groups, such as the Delaware, split into factions, with some supporting the British while other Delaware maintained their neutrality. The Iroquois Confederacy, a longstanding alliance of tribes, also split up: the Mohawk, Cayuga, Onondaga, and Seneca fought on the British side, while the Oneida and Tuscarora supported the revolutionaries. Ohio River Valley tribes such as the Shawnee, Miami, and Mungo had been fighting for years against colonial expansion west; these groups supported the British. Some native peoples who had previously allied with the French hoped the conflict between the colonies and Great Britain might lead to French intervention and the return of French rule. Few Indians sided with the American revolutionaries, because almost all revolutionaries in the middle ground viewed them as an enemy to be destroyed. This racial hatred toward native peoples found expression in the American massacre of ninety-six Christian Delawares in 1782. Most of the dead were women and children.

After the war, the victorious Americans turned a deaf ear to Indian claims to what the revolutionaries saw as their hard-won land, and they moved aggressively to assert control over western New York and Pennsylvania. In response, Mohawk leader Joseph Brant helped to form the Western Confederacy, an alliance of native peoples who pledged to resist American intrusion into what was then called the Northwest. The Northwest Indian War (1785–1795) ended with the defeat of the Indians and their claims. Under the Treaty of Greenville (1795), the United States gained dominion over land in Ohio.

RELIGION AND THE STATE

Prior to the Revolution, several colonies had official, tax-supported churches. After the Revolution, some questioned the validity of state-authorized churches; the limitation of public office-holding to those of a particular faith; and the payment of taxes to support churches. In other states, especially in New England where the older Puritan heritage cast a long shadow, religion and state remained intertwined.

During the colonial era in Virginia, the established church had been the Church of England, which did not tolerate Catholics, Baptists, or followers or other religions. In 1786, as a revolutionary response against the privileged status of the Church of England, Virginia's lawmakers approved the Virginia Statute for Religious Freedom, which ended the Church of England's hold and allowed religious liberty. Under the statute, no one could be forced to attend or support a specific church or be prosecuted for his or her beliefs.

Pennsylvania's original constitution limited officeholders in the state legislature to those who professed a belief in both the Old and the New Testaments. This religious test prohibited Jews from holding that office, as the New Testament is not part of Jewish belief. In 1790, however, Pennsylvania removed this qualification from its constitution.

The New England states were slower to embrace freedom of religion. In the former Puritan colonies, the Congregational Church (established by seventeenth-century Puritans) remained the church of most inhabitants. Massachusetts, Connecticut, and New Hampshire all required the public support of Christian churches. Article III of the Massachusetts constitution blended the goal of republicanism with the goal of promoting Protestant Christianity. It reads:

> As the happiness of a people, and the good order and preservation of civil government, essentially depend upon piety, religion and morality; and as these cannot be generally diffused through a community, but by the institution of the public worship of GOD, and of public instructions in piety, religion and morality: Therefore, to promote their happiness and to secure the good order and preservation of their government, the people of this Commonwealth have a right to invest their legislature with power to authorize and require, and the legislature shall, from time to time, authorize and require, the several towns, parishes, precincts, and other bodies-politic, or religious societies, to make suitable

provision, at their own expense, for the institution of the public worship of GOD, and for the support and maintenance of public protestant teachers of piety, religion and morality, in all cases where such provision shall not be made voluntarily. . . .

And every denomination of Christians, demeaning themselves peaceably, and as good subjects of the Commonwealth, shall be equally under the protection of the law: And no subordination of any one sect or denomination to another shall ever be established by law.

Read more about religion and state governments at the Religion and the Founding of the American Republic exhibition page on the Library of Congress site. What was the meaning of the term "nursing fathers" of the church?

Section Summary

After the Revolution, the balance of power between women and men and between whites, blacks, and Indians remained largely unchanged. Yet revolutionary principles, including the call for universal equality in the Declaration of Independence, inspired and emboldened many. Abigail Adams and others pressed for greater rights for women, while the Pennsylvania Abolition Society and New York Manumission Society worked toward the abolition of slavery. Nonetheless, for blacks, women, and native peoples, the revolutionary ideals of equality fell far short of reality. In the new republic, full citizenship—including the right to vote—did not extend to nonwhites or to women.

- https://www.openassessments.org/assessments/961

Review Question

1. How would you characterize Thomas Jefferson's ideas on race and slavery?

Answer to Review Question

1. Although he owned hundreds of slaves in his lifetime and fathered several children with his slave Sally Hemings, Jefferson opposed slavery. He argued that the institution should be abolished and slaves returned to Africa, believing that blacks and whites could not live together in a free society without the result of a race war.

Glossary

coverture the legal status of married women in the United States, which included complete legal and economic dependence on husbands

manumission the freeing of a slave by his or her owner

Attributions

CC licensed content, Shared previously

- US History. **Authored by**: P. Scott Corbett, Volker Janssen, John M. Lund, Todd Pfannestiel, Paul Vickery, and Sylvie Waskiewicz. **Provided by**: OpenStax College. **Located at**: http://openstaxcollege.org/textbooks/us-history. **License**: *CC BY: Attribution*. **License Terms**: Download for free at http://cnx.org/content/col11740/latest/

Debating Democracy

> ### Learning Objectives
>
> By the end of this section, you will be able to:
>
> - Explain the development of state constitutions
> - Describe the features of the Articles of Confederation
> - Analyze the causes and consequences of Shays' Rebellion

The task of creating republican governments in each of the former colonies, now independent states, presented a new opportunity for American revolutionaries to define themselves anew after casting off British control. On the state and national levels, citizens of the new United States debated who would hold the keys to political power. The states proved to be a laboratory for how much democracy, or majority rule, would be tolerated.

THE STATE CONSTITUTIONS

In 1776, John Adams urged the thirteen independent colonies—soon to be states—to write their own state constitutions. Enlightenment political thought profoundly influenced Adams and other revolutionary leaders seeking to create viable republican governments. The ideas of the French philosopher **Montesquieu**, who had advocated the separation of powers in government, guided Adams's thinking. Responding to a request for advice on proper government from North Carolina, Adams wrote *Thoughts on Government*, which influenced many state legislatures. Adams did not advocate democracy; rather, he wrote, "there is no good government but what is republican." Fearing the potential for tyranny with only one group in power, he suggested a system of **checks and balances** in which three separate branches of government—executive, legislative, and judicial—would maintain a balance of power. He also proposed that each state remain sovereign, as its own republic. The state constitutions of the new United States illustrate different approaches to addressing the question of how much democracy would prevail in the thirteen republics. Some states embraced democratic practices, while others adopted far more aristocratic and republican ones.

> Visit the Avalon Project to read the constitutions of the seven states (Virginia, New Jersey, North Carolina, Maryland, Connecticut, Pennsylvania, and Delaware) that had written constitutions by the end of 1776.

The 1776 Pennsylvania constitution, the first page of which is shown here, adhered to more democratic principles than some other states' constitutions did initially.

The 1776 Pennsylvania constitution and the 1784 New Hampshire constitution both provide examples of democratic tendencies. In Pennsylvania, the requirement to own property in order to vote was eliminated, and if a man was twenty-one or older, had paid taxes, and had lived in the same location for one year, he could vote. This opened voting to most free white male citizens of Pennsylvania. The 1784 New Hampshire constitution allowed every small town and village to send representatives to the state government, making the lower house of the legislature a model of democratic government.

Conservative Whigs, who distrusted the idea of majority rule, recoiled from the abolition of property qualifications for voting and office holding in Pennsylvania. Conservative Whig John Adams reacted with horror to the 1776 Pennsylvania constitution, declaring that it was "so democratical that it must produce confusion and every evil work." In his mind and those of other conservative Whigs, this constitution simply put too much power in the hands of men who had no business exercising the right to vote. Pennsylvania's constitution also eliminated the executive branch (there was no governor) and the upper house. Instead, Pennsylvania had a one-house—a **unicameral**—legislature.

The Maryland and South Carolina constitutions provide examples of efforts to limit the power of a democratic majority. Maryland's, written in 1776, restricted office holding to the wealthy planter class. A man had to own at least £5,000 worth of personal property to be the governor of Maryland, and possess an estate worth £1,000 to be a state senator. This latter qualification excluded over 90 percent of the white males in Maryland from political office. The 1778 South Carolina constitution also sought to protect the interests of the wealthy. Governors and lieutenant governors of the state had to have "a settled plantation or freehold in their and each of their own right of the value of at least ten thousand pounds currency, clear of debt." This provision limited high office in the state to its wealthiest inhabitants. Similarly, South Carolina state senators had to own estates valued at £2,000.

John Adams wrote much of the 1780 Massachusetts constitution, which reflected his fear of too much democracy. It therefore created two legislative chambers, an upper and lower house, and a strong governor with broad veto powers. Like South Carolina, Massachusetts put in place office-holding requirements: To be governor under the new constitution, a candidate had to own an estate worth at least £1,000. To serve in the state senate, a man had to own an estate worth at least £300 and have at least £600 in total wealth. To vote, he had to be worth at least sixty pounds. To further keep democracy in check, judges were appointed, not elected. One final limit was the establishment of the state capitol in the commercial center of Boston, which made it difficult for farmers from the western part of the state to attend legislative sessions.

THE ARTICLES OF CONFEDERATION

Most revolutionaries pledged their greatest loyalty to their individual states. Recalling the experience of British reform efforts imposed in the 1760s and 1770s, they feared a strong national government and took some time to adopt the **Articles of Confederation**, the first national constitution. In June 1776, the Continental Congress prepared to announce independence and began to think about the creation of a new government to replace royal authority. Reaching agreement on the Articles of Confederation proved difficult as members of the Continental Congress argued over western land claims. Connecticut, for example, used its colonial charter to assert its claim to western lands in Pennsylvania and the Ohio Territory.

Members of the Continental Congress also debated what type of representation would be best and tried to figure out how to pay the expenses of the new government. In lieu of creating a new federal government, the Articles of Confederation created a "league of friendship" between the states. Congress readied the Articles in 1777 but did not officially approve them until 1781. The delay of four years illustrates the difficulty of getting the thirteen states to agree on a plan of national government. Citizens viewed their respective states as sovereign republics and guarded their prerogatives against other states.

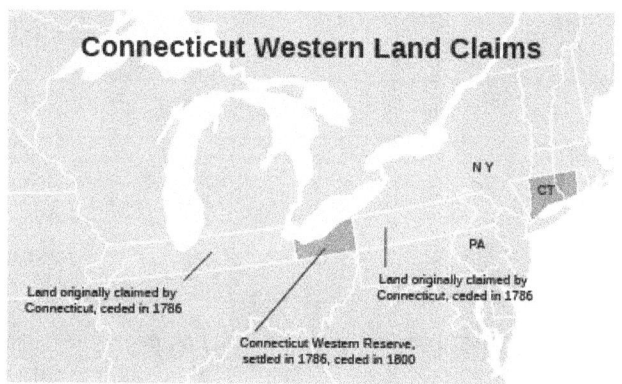

Connecticut, like many other states, used its state constitution to stake claims to uncharted western lands.

The Articles of Confederation authorized a unicameral legislature, a continuation of the earlier Continental Congress. The people could not vote directly for members of the national Congress; rather, state legislatures decided who would represent the state. In practice, the national Congress was composed of state delegations. There was no president or executive office of any kind, and there was no national judiciary (or Supreme Court) for the United States.

Passage of any law under the Articles of Confederation proved difficult. It took the consensus of nine states for any measure to pass, and amending the Articles required the consent of all the states, also extremely difficult to achieve. Further, any acts put forward by the Congress were non-binding; states had the option to enforce them or not. This meant that while the Congress had power over Indian affairs and foreign policy, individual states could choose whether or not to comply.

The Congress did not have the power to tax citizens of the United States, a fact that would soon have serious consequences for the republic. During the Revolutionary War, the Continental Congress had sent requisitions for funds to the individual former colonies (now revolutionary states). These states already had an enormous financial burden because they had to pay for militias as well as supply them. In the end, the states failed to provide even half the funding requested by the Congress during the war, which led to a national debt in the tens of millions by 1784.

The first page of the 1777 Articles of Confederation, printed by Alexander Purdie, emphasized the "perpetual union" between the states.

By the 1780s, some members of the Congress were greatly concerned about the financial health of the republic, and they argued that the national government needed greater power, especially the power to tax. This required amending the Articles of Confederation with the consent of all the states. Those who called for a stronger federal government were known as nationalists. The nationalist group that pushed for the power to tax included Washington's chief of staff, Alexander Hamilton; Virginia planter James Madison; Pennsylvania's wealthy merchant Robert Morris (who served under the Confederation government as superintendent of finance in the early 1780s); and Pennsylvania lawyer James Wilson. Two New Yorkers, Gouverneur Morris and James Duane, also joined the effort to address the debt and the weakness of the Confederation government.

These men proposed a 5 percent tax on imports coming into the United States, a measure that would have yielded enough revenue to clear the debt. However, their proposal failed to achieve unanimous support from the states when Rhode Island rejected it. Plans for a national bank also failed to win unanimous support. The lack of support illustrates the Americans' deep suspicion of a powerful national government, a suspicion that originated from the unilateral and heavy-handed reform efforts that the British Parliament imposed on the colonies in the 1760s and 1770s. Without revenue, the Congress could not pay back American creditors who had lent it money. However, it did manage to make interest payments to foreign creditors in France and the Dutch Republic, fearful that defaulting on those payments would destroy the republic's credit and leave it unable to secure loans.

One soldier in the Continental Army, Joseph Plumb Martin, recounted how he received no pay in paper money after 1777 and only one month's payment in specie, or hard currency, in 1781. Like thousands of other soldiers, Martin had fought valiantly against the British and helped secure independence, but had not been paid for his service. In the 1780s and beyond, men like Martin would soon express their profound dissatisfaction with their treatment. Their anger found expression in armed uprisings and political divisions.

Establishing workable foreign and commercial policies under the Articles of Confederation also proved difficult. Each state could decide for itself whether to comply with treaties between the Congress and foreign countries, and there were no means of enforcement. Both Great Britain and Spain understood the weakness of the Confederation Congress, and they refused to make commercial agreements with the United States because they doubted they would be enforced. Without stable commercial policies, American exporters found it difficult to do business, and British goods flooded U.S. markets in the 1780s, in a repetition of the economic imbalance that existed before the Revolutionary War.

The Confederation Congress under the Articles did achieve success through a series of directives called land ordinances, which established rules for the settlement of western lands in the public domain and the admission of new states to the republic. The ordinances were designed to prepare the land for sale to citizens and raise revenue to boost the failing economy of the republic. In the land ordinances, the Confederation Congress created the Mississippi and Southwest Territories and stipulated that slavery would be permitted there. The system of dividing the vast domains of the United States stands as a towering achievement of the era, a blueprint for American western expansion.

The Ordinance of 1784, written by Thomas Jefferson and the first of what were later called the Northwest Ordinances, directed that new states would be formed from a huge area of land below the Great Lakes, and these new states would have equal standing with the original states. The Ordinance of 1785 called for the division of this land into rectangular plots in order to prepare for the government sale of land. Surveyors would divide the land into townships of six square miles, and the townships would be subdivided into thirty-six plots of 640 acres each, which could be further subdivided. The price of an acre of land was set at a minimum of one dollar, and the land was to be sold at public auction under the direction of the Confederation.

The Ordinance of 1787 officially turned the land into an incorporated territory called the Northwest Territory and prohibited slavery north of the Ohio River. The map of the 1787 Northwest Territory shows how the public domain was to be divided by the national government for sale. Townships of thirty-six square miles were to be surveyed. Each had land set aside for schools and other civic purposes. Smaller parcels could then be made: a 640-acre section could be divided into quarter-sections of 160 acres, and then again into sixteen sections of 40 acres. The geometric grid pattern established by the ordinance is still evident today on the American landscape. Indeed, much of the western United States, when viewed from an airplane, is composed of an orderly grid system.

- Territory divided into 3–5 states
- Eligible for statehood with 60,000 settlers
- Religious freedom, the right of trial by jury, free access to the major rivers of the region
- Banned slavery north of the Ohio River
- Township = 6 miles square
- 6 miles square = 36 plots
- 1 plot = 640 acres (1 mile square)
- The Northwest Territory eventually became the states of Ohio, Indiana, Illinois, Michigan, and Wisconsin

The Northwest Ordinance of 1787 created territories and an orderly method for the admission of new states.

> Visit Window Seat to explore aerial views of the grid system established by the Northwest Ordinance of 1787, which is still evident in much of the Midwest.

The land ordinances proved to be the great triumph of the Confederation Congress. The Congress would appoint a governor for the territories, and when the population in the territory reached five thousand free adult settlers, those citizens could create their own legislature and begin the process of moving toward statehood. When the population reached sixty thousand, the territory could become a new state.

SHAYS' REBELLION

Despite Congress's victory in creating an orderly process for organizing new states and territories, land sales failed to produce the revenue necessary to deal with the dire economic problems facing the new country in the 1780s. Each state had issued large amounts of paper money and, in the aftermath of the Revolution, widespread internal devaluation of that currency occurred as many lost confidence in the value of state paper money and the Continental dollar. A period of extreme inflation set in. Added to this dilemma was American citizens' lack of specie (gold and silver currency) to conduct routine business. Meanwhile, demobilized soldiers, many of whom had spent their formative years fighting rather than learning a peacetime trade, searched desperately for work.

The economic crisis came to a head in 1786 and 1787 in western Massachusetts, where farmers were in a difficult position: they faced high taxes and debts, which they found nearly impossible to pay with the worthless state and Continental paper money. For several years after the peace in 1783, these indebted citizens had petitioned the state legislature for redress. Many were veterans of the Revolutionary War who had returned to their farms and families after the fighting ended and now faced losing their homes.

Their petitions to the state legislature raised economic and political issues for citizens of the new state. How could people pay their debts and state taxes when paper money proved unstable? Why was the state government located in Boston, the center of the merchant elite? Why did the 1780 Massachusetts constitution cater to the interests of the wealthy? To the indebted farmers, the situation in the 1780s seemed hauntingly familiar; the revolutionaries had routed the British, but a new form of seemingly corrupt and self-serving government had replaced them.

In 1786, when the state legislature again refused to address the petitioners' requests, Massachusetts citizens took up arms and closed courthouses across the state to prevent foreclosure (seizure of land in lieu of overdue loan payments) on farms in debt. The farmers wanted their debts forgiven, and they demanded that the 1780 constitution be revised to address citizens beyond the wealthy elite who could serve in the legislature.

This woodcut, from Bickerstaff's Boston Almanack of 1787, depicts Daniel Shays and Job Shattuck. Shays and Shattuck were two of the leaders of the rebels who rose up against the Massachusetts government in 1786 to 1787. As Revolutionary War veterans, both men wear the uniform of officers of the Continental Army.

Many of the rebels were veterans of the war for independence, including Captain Daniel Shays from Pelham. Although Shays was only one of many former officers in the Continental Army who took part in the revolt, authorities in Boston singled him out as a ringleader, and the uprising became known as Shays' Rebellion. The Massachusetts legislature responded to the closing of the courthouses with a flurry of legislation, much of it designed to punish the rebels. The government offered the rebels clemency if they took an oath of allegiance. Otherwise, local officials were empowered to use deadly force against them without fear of prosecution. Rebels would lose their property, and if any militiamen refused to defend the state, they would be executed.

Despite these measures, the rebellion continued. To address the uprising, Governor James Bowdoin raised a private army of forty-four hundred men, funded by wealthy Boston merchants, without the approval of the legislature. The climax of Shays' Rebellion came in January 1787, when the rebels attempted to seize the federal armory in Springfield, Massachusetts. A force loyal to the state defeated them there, although the rebellion continued into February.

Shays' Rebellion resulted in eighteen deaths overall, but the uprising had lasting effects. To men of property, mostly conservative Whigs, Shays' Rebellion strongly suggested the republic was falling into anarchy and chaos. The other twelve states had faced similar economic and political difficulties, and continuing problems seemed to indicate that on a national level, a democratic impulse was driving the population. Shays' Rebellion convinced George Washington to come out of retirement and lead the convention called for by Alexander Hamilton to amend the Articles of Confederation in order to deal with insurgencies like the one in Massachusetts and provide greater stability in the United States.

Section Summary

The late 1770s and 1780s witnessed one of the most creative political eras as each state drafted its own constitution. The Articles of Confederation, a weak national league among the states, reflected the dominant view that power should be located in the states and not in a national government. However, neither the state governments nor the Confederation government could solve the enormous economic problems resulting from the long and costly Revolutionary War. The economic crisis led to Shays' Rebellion by residents of western Massachusetts, and to the decision to revise the Confederation government.

https://www.openassessments.org/assessments/962

Review Question

1. What were the primary causes of Shays' Rebellion?

Answer to Review Question

1. A group of farmers in western Massachusetts, including Daniel Shays, rebelled against the Massachusetts government, which they saw as unresponsive to their needs. Many were veterans of the Revolutionary War and faced tremendous debts and high taxes, which they couldn't pay with their worthless paper money. They felt that they didn't have a voice in the Massachusetts government, which seemed to cater to wealthy Boston merchants. They wanted their debts to be forgiven and the Massachusetts constitution to be rewritten to address their needs, and when these demands weren't met, they rebelled.

Glossary

checks and balances the system that ensures a balance of power among the branches of government

unicameral having a single house (of legislative government)

Attributions

CC licensed content, Shared previously

- US History. **Authored by**: P. Scott Corbett, Volker Janssen, John M. Lund, Todd Pfannestiel, Paul Vickery, and Sylvie Waskiewicz. **Provided by**: OpenStax College. **Located at**: http://openstaxcollege.org/textbooks/us-history. **License**: *CC BY: Attribution*. **License Terms**: Download for free at http://cnx.org/content/col11740/latest/

The Constitutional Convention and Federal Constitution

> *Learning Objectives*
>
> By the end of this section, you will be able to:
>
> - Identify the central issues of the 1787 Constitutional Convention and their solutions
> - Describe the conflicts over the ratification of the federal constitution

The economic problems that plagued the thirteen states of the Confederation set the stage for the creation of a strong central government under a federal constitution. Although the original purpose of the convention was to amend the Articles of Confederation, some—though not all—delegates moved quickly to create a new framework for a more powerful national government. This proved extremely controversial. Those who attended the convention split over the issue of robust, centralized government and questions of how Americans would be represented in the federal government. Those who opposed the proposal for a stronger federal government argued that such a plan betrayed the Revolution by limiting the voice of the American people.

THE CONSTITUTIONAL CONVENTION

There had been earlier efforts to address the Confederation's perilous state. In early 1786, Virginia's James Madison advocated a meeting of states to address the widespread economic problems that plagued the new nation. Heeding Madison's call, the legislature in Virginia invited all thirteen states to meet in Annapolis, Maryland, to work on solutions to the issue of commerce between the states. Eight states responded to the invitation. But the resulting 1786 Annapolis Convention failed to provide any solutions because only five states sent delegates. These delegates did, however, agree to a plan put forward by Alexander Hamilton for a second convention to meet in May 1787 in Philadelphia. Shays' Rebellion gave greater urgency to the planned convention. In February 1787, in the wake of the uprising in western Massachusetts, the Confederation Congress authorized the Philadelphia convention. This time, all the states except Rhode Island sent delegates to Philadelphia to confront the problems of the day.

The stated purpose of the Philadelphia Convention in 1787 was to amend the Articles of Confederation. Very quickly, however, the attendees decided to create a new framework for a national government. That framework became the United States Constitution, and the Philadelphia convention became known as the Constitutional Convention of 1787. Fifty-five men met in Philadelphia in secret; historians know of the proceedings only because James Madison kept careful notes of what transpired. The delegates knew that what they were doing would be controversial; Rhode Island refused to send delegates, and New Hampshire's delegates arrived late. Two delegates from New York, Robert Yates and John Lansing, left the convention when it became clear that the Articles were being put aside and a new plan of national government was being drafted. They did not believe the delegates had the authority to create a strong national government.

> **Read** "Reasons for Dissent from the Proposed Constitution" in order to understand why Robert Yates and John Lansing, New York's delegates to the 1787 Philadelphia Convention, didn't believe the convention should draft a new plan of national government.

THE QUESTION OF REPRESENTATION

One issue that the delegates in Philadelphia addressed was the way in which representatives to the new national government would be chosen. Would individual citizens be able to elect representatives? Would representatives be chosen by state legislatures? How much representation was appropriate for each state?

James Madison put forward a proposition known as the **Virginia Plan**, which called for a strong national government that could overturn state laws. The plan featured a **bicameral** or two-house legislature, with an upper and a lower house. The people of the states would elect the members of the lower house, whose numbers would be determined by the population of the state. State legislatures would send delegates to the upper house. The number of representatives in the upper chamber would also be based on the state's population. This **proportional representation** gave the more populous states, like Virginia, more political power. The Virginia Plan also called for an executive branch and a judicial branch, both of which were absent under the Articles of Confederation. The lower and upper house together were to appoint members to the executive and judicial branches. Under this plan, Virginia, the most populous state, would dominate national political power and ensure its interests, including slavery, would be safe

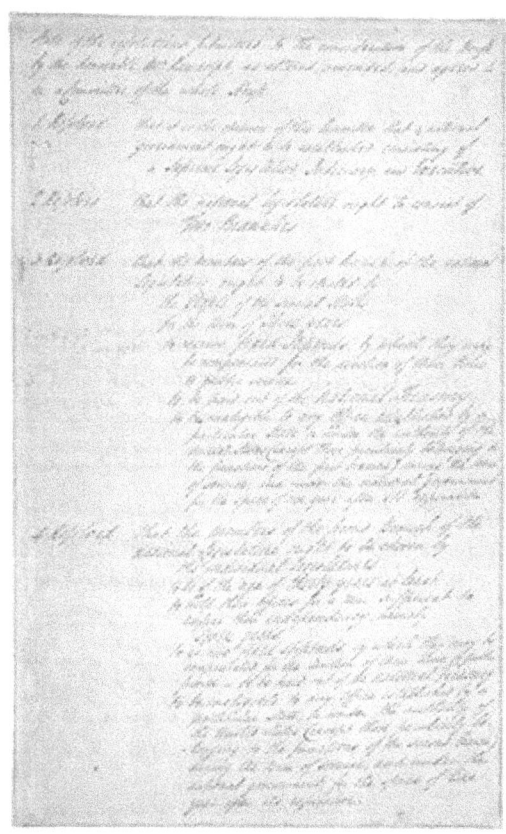

James Madison's Virginia Plan, shown here, proposed a strong national government with proportional state representation.

The Virginia Plan's call for proportional representation alarmed the representatives of the smaller states. William Paterson introduced a **New Jersey Plan** to counter Madison's scheme, proposing that all states have equal votes in a unicameral national legislature. He also addressed the economic problems of the day by calling for the Congress to have the power to regulate commerce, to raise revenue though taxes on imports and through postage, and to enforce Congressional requisitions from the states.

Roger Sherman from Connecticut offered a compromise to break the deadlock over the thorny question of representation. His **Connecticut Compromise**, also known as the Great Compromise, outlined a different bicameral legislature in which the upper house, the Senate, would have equal representation for all states; each state would be represented by two senators chosen by the state legislatures. Only the lower house, the House of Representatives, would have proportional representation.

THE QUESTION OF SLAVERY

The question of slavery stood as a major issue at the Constitutional Convention because slaveholders wanted slaves to be counted along with whites, termed "free inhabitants," when determining a state's total population. This, in turn, would augment the number of representatives accorded to those states in the lower house. Some northerners, however, such as New York's Gouverneur Morris, hated slavery and did not even want the term included in the new national plan of government. Slaveholders argued that slavery imposed great burdens upon them and that, because they carried this liability, they deserved special consideration; slaves needed to be counted for purposes of representation.

The issue of counting or not counting slaves for purposes of representation connected directly to the question of taxation. Beginning in 1775, the Second Continental Congress asked states to pay for war by collecting taxes and sending the tax money to the Congress. The amount each state had to deliver in tax revenue was determined by a state's total population, including both free and enslaved individuals. States routinely fell far short of delivering the money requested by Congress under the plan. In April 1783, the Confederation Congress amended the earlier system of requisition by having slaves count as three-fifths of the white population. In this way, slaveholders gained a significant tax break. The delegates in Philadelphia adopted this same three-fifths formula in the summer of 1787.

Under the **three-fifths compromise** in the 1787 Constitution, each slave would be counted as three-fifths of a white person. Article 1, Section 2 stipulated that "Representatives and direct Taxes shall be apportioned among the several states . . . according to their respective Number, which shall be determined by adding to the whole number of free Persons, including those bound for service for a Term of Years [white servants], and excluding Indians not taxed, three fifths of all other persons." Since representation in the House of Representatives was based on the population of a state, the three-fifths compromise gave extra political power to slave states, although not as much as if the total population, both free and slave, had been used. Significantly, no direct federal income tax was immediately imposed. (The Sixteenth Amendment, ratified in 1913, put in place a federal income tax.) Northerners agreed to the three-fifths compromise because the Northwest Ordinance of 1787, passed by the Confederation Congress, banned slavery in the future states of the northwest. Northern delegates felt this ban balanced political power between states with slaves and those without. The three-fifths compromise gave an advantage to slaveholders; they added three-fifths of their human property to their state's population, allowing them to send representatives based in part on the number of slaves they held.

THE QUESTION OF DEMOCRACY

Many of the delegates to the Constitutional Convention had serious reservations about democracy, which they believed promoted anarchy. To allay these fears, the Constitution blunted democratic tendencies that appeared to undermine the republic. Thus, to avoid giving the people too much direct power, the delegates made certain that senators were chosen by the state legislatures, not elected directly by the people (direct elections of senators came with the Seventeenth Amendment to the Constitution, ratified in 1913). As an additional safeguard, the delegates created the **Electoral College**, the mechanism for choosing the president. Under this plan, each state has a certain number of electors, which is its number of senators (two) plus its number of representatives in the House of Representatives. Critics, then as now, argue that this process prevents the direct election of the president.

THE FIGHT OVER RATIFICATION

The draft constitution was finished in September 1787. The delegates decided that in order for the new national government to be implemented, each state must first hold a special ratifying convention. When nine of the thirteen had approved the plan, the constitution would go into effect.

When the American public learned of the new constitution, opinions were deeply divided, but most people were opposed. To salvage their work in Philadelphia, the architects of the new national government began a campaign to sway public opinion in favor of their blueprint for a strong central government. In the fierce debate that erupted, the two sides articulated contrasting visions of the American republic and of democracy. Supporters of the 1787 Constitution, known as **Federalists**, made the case that a centralized republic provided the best solution for the future. Those who opposed it, known as **Anti-Federalists**, argued that the Constitution would consolidate all power in a national government, robbing the states of the power to make their own decisions. To them, the Constitution appeared to mimic the old corrupt and centralized British regime, under which a far-off government made the laws. Anti-Federalists argued that wealthy aristocrats would run the new national government, and that the elite would not represent ordinary citizens; the rich would monopolize power and use the new government to formulate policies that benefited their class—a development that would also undermine local state elites. They also argued that the Constitution did not contain a bill of rights.

New York's ratifying convention illustrates the divide between the Federalists and Anti-Federalists. When one Anti-Federalist delegate named Melancton Smith took issue with the scheme of representation as being too limited and not reflective of the people, Alexander Hamilton responded:

> It has been observed by an honorable gentleman [Smith], that a pure democracy, if it were practicable, would be the most perfect government. Experience has proven, that no position in politics is more false than this. The ancient democracies, in which the people themselves deliberated, never possessed one feature of good government. Their very character was tyranny; their figure deformity: When they assembled, the field of debate presented an ungovernable mob, not only incapable of deliberation, but prepared for every enormity. In these assemblies, the enemies of the people brought forward their plans of ambition systematically. They were opposed by their enemies of another party; and it became a matter of contingency, whether the people subjected themselves to be led blindly by one tyrant or by another.

The Federalists, particularly John Jay, Alexander Hamilton, and James Madison, put their case to the public in a famous series of essays known as *The Federalist Papers*. These were first published in New York and subsequently republished elsewhere in the United States.

James Madison on the Benefits of Republicanism

The tenth essay in *The Federalist Papers*, often called Federalist No. 10, is one of the most famous. Written by James Madison, it addresses the problems of political parties ("factions"). Madison argued that there were two approaches to solving the problem of political parties: a republican government and a democracy. He argued that a large republic provided the best defense against what he viewed as the tumult of direct democracy. Compromises would be reached in a large republic and citizens would be represented by representatives of their own choosing.

John Vanderlyn's 1816 portrait depicts James Madison, one of the leading Federalists who supported the 1787 Constitution.

From this view of the subject, it may be concluded, that a pure Democracy, by which I mean a Society consisting of a small number of citizens, who assemble and administer the Government in person, can admit of no cure for the mischiefs of faction. A common passion or interest will, in almost every case, be felt by a majority of the whole; a communication and concert result from the form of Government itself; and there is nothing to check the inducements to sacrifice the weaker party, or an obnoxious individual. Hence it is, that such Democracies have ever been spectacles of turbulence and contention; have ever been found incompatible with personal security, or the rights of property; and have in general been as short in their lives, as they have been violent in their deaths. Theoretic politicians, who have patronized this species of Government, have erroneously supposed, that by reducing mankind to a perfect equality in their political rights, they would, at the same time, be perfectly equalized and assimilated in their possessions, their opinions, and their passions.

A Republic, by which I mean a Government in which the scheme of representation takes place, opens a different prospect, and promises the cure for which we are seeking. Let us examine the points in which it varies from pure Democracy, and we shall comprehend both the nature of the cure, and the efficacy which it must derive from the Union.

The two great points of difference, between a Democracy and a Republic, are, first, the delegation of the Government, in the latter, to a small number of citizens elected by the rest: Secondly, the greater number of citizens, and greater sphere of country, over which the latter may be extended.

Does Madison recommend republicanism or democracy as the best form of government? What arguments does he use to prove his point?

Read the full text of Federalist No. 10 on Wikisource. What do you think are Madison's most and least compelling arguments? How would different members of the new United States view his arguments?

Including all the state ratifying conventions around the country, a total of fewer than two thousand men voted on whether to adopt the new plan of government. In the end, the Constitution only narrowly won approval. In New York, the vote was thirty in favor to twenty-seven opposed. In Massachusetts, the vote to approve was 187 to 168, and some claim supporters of the Constitution resorted to bribes in order to ensure approval. Virginia ratified by a vote of eighty-nine to seventy-nine, and Rhode Island by thirty-four to thirty-two. The opposition to the Constitution reflected the fears that a new national government, much like the British monarchy, created too much centralized power and, as a result, deprived citizens in the various states of the ability to make their own decisions.

The first page of the 1787 United States Constitution, shown here, begins: "We the People of the United States, in Order to form a more perfect Union, establish Justice, insure domestic Tranquility, provide for the common defence, promote the general Welfare, and secure the Blessings of Liberty to ourselves and our Posterity, do ordain and establish this Constitution for the United States of America."

Section Summary

The economic crisis of the 1780s, shortcomings of the Articles of Confederation, and outbreak of Shays' Rebellion spurred delegates from twelve of the thirteen states to gather for the Constitutional Convention of 1787. Although the stated purpose of the convention was to modify the Articles of Confederation, their mission shifted to the building of a new, strong federal government. Federalists like James Madison and Alexander Hamilton led the charge for a new United States Constitution, the document that endures as the oldest written constitution in the world, a testament to the work done in 1787 by the delegates in Philadelphia.

https://www.openassessments.org/assessments/963

Review Question

1. Explain the argument that led to the three-fifths rule and the consequences of that rule.

Answer to Review Question

1. Southern slaveholders wanted slaves to count for the purposes of representation, while people from northern states feared that counting slaves would give the southern states too much power. Their fears were valid; the three-fifths rule, which stated that each slave counted as three-fifths of a white person for purposes of representation, gave the southern states the balance of political power.

Critical Thinking Questions

1. Describe the state constitutions that were more democratic and those that were less so. What effect would these different constitutions have upon those states? Who could participate in government, whether by voting or by holding public office? Whose interests were represented, and whose were compromised?

2. In what ways does the United States Constitution manifest the principles of both republican and democratic forms of government? In what ways does it deviate from those principles?

3. In this chapter's discussion of New York's ratifying convention, Alexander Hamilton takes issue with Anti-Federalist delegate Melancton Smith's assertion that (as Hamilton says) "a pure democracy, if it were practicable, would be the most perfect government." What did Smith—and Hamilton—mean by "a pure democracy"? How does this compare to the type of democracy that represents the modern United States?

4. Describe popular attitudes toward African Americans, women, and Indians in the wake of the Revolution. In what ways did the established social and political order depend upon keeping members of these groups in their circumscribed roles? If those roles were to change, how would American society and politics have had to adjust?

5. How did the process of creating and ratifying the Constitution, and the language of the Constitution itself, confirm the positions of African Americans, women, and Indians in the new republic? How did these roles compare to the stated goals of the republic?

6. What were the circumstances that led to Shays' Rebellion? What was the government's response? Would this response have confirmed or negated the grievances of the participants in the uprising? Why?

> ## Glossary
>
> **Anti-Federalists** those who opposed the 1787 Constitution and favored stronger individual states
>
> **bicameral** having two legislative houses, an upper and a lower house
>
> **Connecticut Compromise** also known as the Great Compromise, Roger Sherman's proposal at the Constitutional Convention for a bicameral legislature, with the upper house having equal representation for all states and the lower house having proportional representation
>
> **Electoral College** the mechanism by which electors, based on the number of representatives from each state, choose the president
>
> **Federalists** those who supported the 1787 Constitution and a strong central government; these advocates of the new national government formed the ruling political party in the 1790s
>
> **proportional representation** representation that gives more populous states greater political power by allowing them more representatives
>
> **three-fifths compromise** the agreement at the Constitutional Convention that each slave would count as three-fifths of a white person for purposes of representation

Attributions

CC licensed content, Shared previously

- US History. **Authored by**: P. Scott Corbett, Volker Janssen, John M. Lund, Todd Pfannestiel, Paul Vickery, and Sylvie Waskiewicz. **Provided by**: OpenStax College. **Located at**: http://openstaxcollege.org/textbooks/us-history. **License**: *CC BY: Attribution*. **License Terms**: Download for free at http://cnx.org/content/col11740/latest/

Primary Source Reading: The U.S. Constitution

Introduction

The Constitution of the United States is the supreme law of the United States of America. The Constitution, originally comprising seven articles, delineates the national frame of government. Its first three articles entrench the doctrine of the separation of powers, whereby the federal government is divided into three branches: the legislative, consisting of the bicameral Congress; the executive, consisting of the President; and the judicial, consisting of the Supreme Court and other federal courts. Articles Four, Five and Six entrench concepts of federalism, describing the rights and responsibilities of state governments and of the states in relationship to the federal government. Article Seven establishes the procedure subsequently used by the thirteen States to ratify it.

Since the Constitution came into force in 1789, it has been amended twenty-seven times. In general, the first ten amendments, known collectively as the Bill of Rights, offer specific protections of individual liberty and justice and place restrictions on the powers of government. The majority of the seventeen later amendments expand individual civil rights. Others address issues related to federal authority or modify government processes and procedures. Amendments to the US Constitution, unlike ones made to many constitutions world-wide, are appended to the end of the document. At seven articles and twenty-seven amendments, it is the shortest written constitution in force.

The Constitution is interpreted, supplemented, and implemented by a large body of constitutional law. The Constitution of the United States was the first constitution of its kind, and has influenced the constitutions of other nations.

The Constitution

We the People of the United States, in Order to form a more perfect Union, establish Justice, insure domestic Tranquility, provide for the common defence, promote the general Welfare, and secure the Blessings of Liberty to ourselves and our Posterity, do ordain and establish this Constitution for the United States of America.

Article. I.

Section. 1.
All legislative Powers herein granted shall be vested in a Congress of the United States, which shall consist of a Senate and House of Representatives.

Section. 2.The House of Representatives shall be composed of Members chosen every second Year by the People of the several States, and the Electors in each State shall have the Qualifications requisite for Electors of the most numerous Branch of the State Legislature.No Person shall be a Representative who shall not have attained to the age of twenty five Years, and been seven Years a Citizen of the United States, and who shall not, when elected, be an Inhabitant of that State in which he shall be chosen.Representatives and direct Taxes shall be apportioned among the several States which may be included within this Union, according to their respective Numbers, which shall be determined by adding to the whole Number of free Persons, including those bound to Service for a Term of Years, and excluding Indians not taxed, three fifths of all other Persons. The actual Enumeration shall be made within three Years after the first Meeting of the Congress of the United States, and within every subsequent Term of ten Years, in such Manner as they shall by Law direct. The Number of Representatives shall not exceed one for every thirty Thousand, but each State shall have at Least one Representative; and until such enumeration shall be made, the State of New Hampshire shall be entitled to chuse three, Massachusetts eight, Rhode-Island and Providence Plantations one,Connecticut five, New-York six, New Jersey four, Pennsylvania eight, Delaware one, Maryland six, Virginia ten, North Carolinafive, South Carolina five, and Georgia three.When vacancies happen in the Representation from any State, the Executive Authority thereof shall issue Writs of Election to fill such Vacancies.The House of Representatives shall chuse their Speaker and other Officers; and shall have the sole Power of Impeachment.

Section. 3.The Senate of the United States shall be composed of two Senators from each State, chosen by the Legislature thereof, for six Years; and each Senator shall have one Vote.Immediately after they shall be assembled in Consequence of the first Election, they shall be divided as equally as may be into three Classes. The Seats of the Senators of the first Class shall be vacated at the Expiration of the second Year, of the second Class at the Expiration of the fourth Year, and of the third Class at the Expiration of the sixth Year, so that one third may be chosen every second Year; and if Vacancies happen by Resignation, or otherwise, during the Recess of the Legislature of any State, the Executive thereof may make temporary Appointments until the next Meeting of the Legislature, which shall then fill such Vacancies.No Person shall be a Senator who shall not have attained to the Age of thirty Years, and been nine Years a Citizen of the United States, and who shall not, when elected, be an Inhabitant of that State for which he shall be chosen.The Vice President of the United States shall be President of the Senate but shall have no Vote, unless they be equally divided.The Senate shall chuse their other Officers, and also a President pro tempore, in the Absence of the Vice President, or when he shall exercise the Office of President of the United States.The Senate shall have the sole Power to try all Impeachments. When sitting for that Purpose, they shall be on Oath or Affirmation. When the President of the United States is tried the Chief Justice shall preside: And no Person shall be convicted without the Concurrence of two thirds of the Members present.Judgment in Cases of Impeachment shall not extend further than to removal from Office, and disqualification to hold and enjoy any Office of honor, Trust or Profit under the United States: but the Party convicted shall nevertheless be liable and subject to Indictment, Trial, Judgment and Punishment, according to Law.

Section. 4.The Times, Places and Manner of holding Elections for Senators and Representatives, shall be prescribed in each State by the Legislature thereof; but the Congress may at any time by Law make or alter such Regulations, except as to the Places of chusing Senators.The Congress shall assemble at least once in every Year, and such Meeting shall be on the first Monday in December, unless they shall by Law appoint a different Day.

Section. 5.Each House shall be the Judge of the Elections, Returns and Qualifications of its own Members, and a Majority of each shall constitute a Quorum to do Business; but a smaller Number may adjourn from day to day, and may be authorized to compel the Attendance of absent Members, in such Manner, and under such Penalties as each House may provide.Each House may determine the Rules of its Proceedings, punish its Members for disorderly Behaviour, and, with the Concurrence of two thirds, expel a Member.Each House shall keep a Journal of its Proceedings, and from time to time publish the same, excepting such Parts as may in their Judgment require Secrecy; and the Yeas and Nays of the Members of either House on any question shall, at the Desire of one fifth of those Present, be entered on the Journal.Neither House, during the Session of Congress, shall, without the Consent of the other, adjourn for more than three days, nor to any other Place than that in which the two Houses shall be sitting.

Section. 6.The Senators and Representatives shall receive a Compensation for their Services, to be ascertained by Law, and paid out of the Treasury of the United States. They shall in all Cases, except Treason, Felony and Breach of the Peace, be privileged from Arrest during their Attendance at the Session of their respective Houses, and in going to and returning from the same; and for any Speech or Debate in either House, they shall not be questioned in any other Place.No Senator or Representative shall, during the Time for which he was elected, be appointed to any civil Office under the Authority of the United States, which shall have been created, or the Emoluments whereof shall have been encreased during such time; and no Person holding any Office under the United States, shall be a Member of either House during his Continuance in Office.

Section. 7.All Bills for raising Revenue shall originate in the House of Representatives; but the Senate may propose or concur with amendments as on other Bills.Every Bill which shall have passed the House of Representatives and the Senate, shall, before it become a law, be presented to the President of theUnited States: If he approve he shall sign it, but if not he shall return it, with his Objections to that House in which it shall have originated, who shall enter the Objections at large on their Journal, and proceed to reconsider it. If after such Reconsideration two thirds of that House shall agree to pass the Bill, it shall be sent, together with the Objections, to the other House, by which it shall likewise be reconsidered, and if approved by two thirds of that House, it shall become a Law. But in all such Cases the Votes of both Houses shall be determined by Yeas and Nays, and the Names of the Persons voting for and against the Bill shall be entered on the Journal of each House respectively. If any Bill shall not be returned by the President within ten Days (Sundays excepted) after it shall have been presented to him, the Same shall be a Law, in like Manner as if he had signed it, unless the Congress by their Adjournment prevent its Return, in which Case it shall not be a Law.Every Order, Resolution, or Vote to which the Concurrence of the Senate and House of Representatives may be necessary (except on a question of Adjournment) shall be presented to the President of the United States; and before the Same shall take Effect, shall be approved by him, or being disapproved by him, shall be repassed by two thirds of the Senate and House of Representatives, according to the Rules and Limitations prescribed in the Case of a Bill.

Section. 8.The Congress shall have Power To lay and collect Taxes, Duties, Imposts and Excises, to pay the Debts and provide for the common Defence and general Welfare of the United States; but all Duties, Imposts and Excises shall be uniform throughout the United States;To borrow Money on the credit of the United States;To regulate Commerce with foreign Nations, and among the several States, and with the

Indian Tribes;To establish an uniform Rule of Naturalization, and uniform Laws on the subject of Bankruptcies throughout the United States;To coin Money, regulate the Value thereof, and of foreign Coin, and fix the Standard of Weights and Measures;To provide for the Punishment of counterfeiting the Securities and current Coin of the United States;To establish Post Offices and post Roads;To promote the Progress of Science and useful Arts, by securing for limited Times to Authors and Inventors the exclusive Right to their respective Writings and Discoveries;To constitute Tribunals inferior to the supreme Court;To define and punish Piracies and Felonies committed on the high Seas, and Offences against the Law of Nations;To declare War, grant Letters of Marque and Reprisal, and make Rules concerning Captures on Land and Water;To raise and support Armies, but no Appropriation of Money to that Use shall be for a longer Term than two Years;To provide and maintain a Navy;To make Rules for the Government and Regulation of the land and naval Forces;To provide for calling forth the Militia to execute the Laws of the Union, suppress Insurrections and repel Invasions;To provide for organizing, arming, and disciplining, the Militia, and for governing such Part of them as may be employed in the Service of the United States, reserving to the States respectively, the Appointment of the Officers, and the Authority of training the Militia according to the discipline prescribed by Congress;To exercise exclusive Legislation in all Cases whatsoever, over such District (not exceeding ten Miles square) as may, by Cession of Particular States, and the Acceptance of Congress, become the Seat of the Government of the United States, and to exercise like Authority over all Places purchased by the Consent of the Legislature of the State in which the Same shall be, for the Erection of Forts, Magazines, Arsenals, dock-Yards and other needful Buildings;—AndTo make all Laws which shall be necessary and proper for carrying into Execution the foregoing Powers and all other Powers vested by this Constitution in the Government of the United States, or in any Department or Officer thereof.

Section. 9.The Migration or Importation of such Persons as any of the States now existing shall think proper to admit, shall not be prohibited by the Congress prior to the Year one thousand eight hundred and eight, but a Tax or duty may be imposed on such Importation, not exceeding ten dollars for each Person.The Privilege of the Writ of Habeas Corpus shall not be suspended, unless when in Cases of Rebellion or Invasion the public Safety may require it.No Bill of Attainder or ex post facto Law shall be passed.No Capitation, or other direct, Tax shall be laid, unless in Proportion to the Census or Enumeration herein before directed to be taken.No Tax or Duty shall be laid on Articles exported from any State.No Preference shall be given by any Regulation of Commerce or Revenue to the Ports of one State over those of another: nor shall Vessels bound to, or from, one State, be obliged to enter, clear or pay Duties in another.No Money shall be drawn from the Treasury, but in Consequence of Appropriations made by Law; and a regular Statement and Account of the Receipts and Expenditures of all public Money shall be published from time to time.No Title of Nobility shall be granted by the United States: And no Person holding any Office of Profit or Trust under them, shall, without the Consent of the Congress, accept of any present, Emolument, Office, or Title, of any kind whatever, from any King, Prince or foreign State.

Section. 10.No State shall enter into any Treaty, Alliance, or Confederation; grant Letters of Marque and Reprisal; coin Money; emit Bills of Credit; make any Thing but gold and silver Coin a Tender in Payment of Debts; pass any Bill of Attainder, ex post facto Law, or Law impairing the Obligation of Contracts, or grant any Title of Nobility.No State shall, without the Consent of the Congress, lay any Imposts or Duties on Imports or Exports, except what may be absolutely necessary for executing it's inspection Laws: and the net Produce of all Duties and Imposts, laid by any State on Imports or Exports, shall be for the Use of the Treasury of the United States; and all such Laws shall be subject to the Revision and Controul of the Congress.No State shall, without the Consent of Congress, lay any Duty of Tonnage, keep Troops, or Ships of War in time of Peace, enter into any Agreement or Compact with another State, or with a foreign Power, or engage in War, unless actually invaded, or in such imminent Danger as will not admit of delay.

Article. II.

Section. 1.

The executive Power shall be vested in a President of the United States of America. He shall hold his Office during the Term of four Years, and, together with the Vice President, chosen for the same Term, be elected, as follows:

Each State shall appoint, in such Manner as the Legislature thereof may direct, a Number of Electors, equal to the whole Number of Senators and Representatives to which the State may be entitled in the Congress: but no Senator or Representative, or Person holding an Office of Trust or Profit under the United States, shall be appointed an Elector.

The Electors shall meet in their respective States, and vote by Ballot for two Persons, of whom one at least shall not be an Inhabitant of the same State with themselves. And they shall make a List of all the Persons voted for, and of the Number of Votes for each; which List they shall sign and certify, and transmit sealed to the Seat of the Government of the United States, directed to the President of the Senate. The President of the Senate shall, in the Presence of the Senate and House of Representatives, open all the Certificates, and the Votes shall then be counted. The Person having the greatest Number of Votes shall be the President, if such Number be a Majority of the whole Number of Electors appointed; and if there be more than one who have such Majority, and have an equal Number of Votes, then the House of Representatives shall immediately chuse by Ballot one of them for President; and if no Person have a Majority, then from the five highest on the List the said House shall in like Manner chuse the President. But in chusing the President, the Votes shall be taken by States, the Representatives from each State having one Vote; a quorum for this Purpose shall consist of a Member or Members from two thirds of the States, and a Majority of all the States shall be necessary to a Choice. In every Case, after the Choice of the President, the Person having the greatest Number of Votes of the Electors shall be the Vice President. But if there should remain two or more who have equal Votes, the Senate shall chuse from them by Ballot the Vice President.

The Congress may determine the Time of chusing the Electors, and the Day on which they shall give their Votes; which Day shall be the same throughout the United States.

No Person except a natural born Citizen, or a Citizen of the United States, at the time of the Adoption of this Constitution, shall be eligible to the Office of President; neither shall any person be eligible to that Office who shall not have attained to the Age of thirty five Years, and been fourteen Years a Resident within the United States.

In Case of the Removal of the President from Office, or of his Death, Resignation, or Inability to discharge the Powers and Duties of the said Office, the Same shall devolve on the Vice President, and the Congress may by Law provide for the Case of Removal, Death, Resignation or Inability, both of the President and Vice President, declaring what Officer shall then act as President, and such Officer shall act accordingly, until the Disability be removed, or a President shall be elected.

The President shall, at stated Times, receive for his Services, a Compensation, which shall neither be encreased nor diminished during the Period for which he shall have been elected, and he shall not receive within that Period any other Emolument from the United States, or any of them.

Before he enter on the Execution of his Office, he shall take the following Oath or Affirmation:—"I do solemnly swear (or affirm) that I will faithfully execute the Office of President of the United States, and will to the best of my Ability, preserve, protect and defend the Constitution of the United States."

Section. 2. The President shall be Commander in Chief of the Army and Navy of the United States, and of the Militia of the several States, when called into the actual Service of the United States; he may require the

Opinion, in writing, of the principal Officer in each of the executive Departments, upon any Subject relating to the Duties of their respective Offices, and he shall have Power to Grant Reprieves and Pardons for Offences against the United States, except in Cases of Impeachment.He shall have Power, by and with the Advice and Consent of the Senate, to make Treaties, provided two thirds of the Senators present concur; and he shall nominate, and by and with the Advice and Consent of the Senate, shall appoint Ambassadors, other public Ministers and Consuls, Judges of the supreme Court, and all other Officers of the United States, whose Appointments are not herein otherwise provided for, and which shall be established by Law: but the Congress may by Law vest the Appointment of such inferior Officers, as they think proper, in the President alone, in the Courts of Law, or in the Heads of Departments.The President shall have Power to fill up all Vacancies that may happen during the Recess of the Senate, by granting Commissions which shall expire at the End of their next Session.

Section. 3.He shall from time to time give to the Congress Information on the State of the Union, and recommend to their Consideration such Measures as he shall judge necessary and expedient; he may, on extraordinary Occasions, convene both Houses, or either of them, and in Case of Disagreement between them, with Respect to the Time of Adjournment, he may adjourn them to such Time as he shall think proper; he shall receive Ambassadors and other public Ministers; he shall take Care that the Laws be faithfully executed, and shall Commission all the Officers of the United States.

Section. 4.The President, Vice President and all Civil Officers of the United States, shall be removed from Office on Impeachment for and Conviction of, Treason, Bribery, or other high Crimes and Misdemeanors.

Article. III.

Section. 1.
The judicial Power of the United States, shall be vested in one supreme Court, and in such inferior Courts as the Congress may from time to time ordain and establish. The Judges, both of the supreme and inferior Courts, shall hold their Offices during good Behaviour, and shall, at stated Times, receive for their Services, a Compensation, which shall not be diminished during their Continuance in Office.

Section. 2.The judicial Power shall extend to all Cases, in Law and Equity, arising under this Constitution, the Laws of the United States, and Treaties made, or which shall be made, under their Authority;—to all Cases affecting Ambassadors, other public ministers and Consuls;—to all Cases of admiralty and maritime Jurisdiction;—to Controversies to which the United States shall be a Party;—to Controversies between two or more States;—between a State and Citizens of another State;—between Citizens of different States;—between Citizens of the same State claiming Lands under Grants of different States, and between a State, or the Citizens thereof, and foreign States, Citizens or Subjects.In all Cases affecting Ambassadors, other public Ministers and Consuls, and those in which a State shall be Party, the supreme Court shall have original Jurisdiction. In all the other Cases before mentioned, the supreme Court shall have appellate Jurisdiction, both as to Law and Fact, with such Exceptions, and under such Regulations as the Congress shall make.The Trial of all Crimes, except in Cases of Impeachment, shall be by Jury; and such Trial shall be held in the State where the said Crimes shall have been committed; but when not committed within any State, the Trial shall be at such Place or Places as the Congress may by Law have directed.

Section. 3.Treason against the United States, shall consist only in levying War against them, or in adhering to their Enemies, giving them Aid and Comfort. No Person shall be convicted of Treason unless on the Testimony of two Witnesses to the same overt Act, or on Confession in open Court.The Congress shall have Power to declare the Punishment of Treason, but no Attainder of Treason shall work Corruption of Blood, or Forfeiture except during the Life of the Person attainted.

Article. IV.

Section. 1.
Full Faith and Credit shall be given in each State to the public Acts, Records, and judicial Proceedings of every other State. And the Congress may by general Laws prescribe the Manner in which such Acts, Records and Proceedings shall be proved, and the Effect thereof.

Section. 2.The Citizens of each State shall be entitled to all Privileges and Immunities of Citizens in the several States.A Person charged in any State with Treason, Felony, or other Crime, who shall flee from Justice, and be found in another State, shall on Demand of the executive Authority of the State from which he fled, be delivered up, to be removed to the State having Jurisdiction of the Crime.No Person held to Service or Labour in one State, under the Laws thereof, escaping into another, shall, in Consequence of any Law or Regulation therein, be discharged from such Service or Labour, but shall be delivered up on Claim of the Party to whom such Service or Labour may be due.

Section. 3.New States may be admitted by the Congress into this Union; but no new State shall be formed or erected within the Jurisdiction of any other State; nor any State be formed by the Junction of two or more States, or Parts of States, without the Consent of the Legislatures of the States concerned as well as of the Congress.The Congress shall have Power to dispose of and make all needful Rules and Regulations respecting the Territory or other Property belonging to the United States; and nothing in this Constitution shall be so construed as to Prejudice any Claims of the United States, or of any particular State.

Section. 4.The United States shall guarantee to every State in this Union a Republican Form of Government, and shall protect each of them against Invasion; and on Application of the Legislature, or of the Executive (when the Legislature cannot be convened) against domestic Violence.

Article. V.

The Congress, whenever two thirds of both Houses shall deem it necessary, shall propose Amendments to this Constitution, or, on the Application of the Legislatures of two thirds of the several States, shall call a Convention for proposing Amendments, which, in either Case, shall be valid to all Intents and Purposes, as Part of this Constitution, when ratified by the Legislatures of three fourths of the several States, or by Conventions in three fourths thereof, as the one or the other Mode of Ratification may be proposed by the Congress; Provided that no Amendment which may be made prior to the Year One thousand eight hundred and eight shall in any Manner affect the first and fourth Clauses in the Ninth Section of the first Article; and that no State, without its Consent, shall be deprived of its equal Suffrage in the Senate.

Article. VI.

All Debts contracted and Engagements entered into, before the Adoption of this Constitution, shall be as valid against the United States under this Constitution, as under the Confederation.

This Constitution, and the Laws of the United States which shall be made in Pursuance thereof; and all Treaties made, or which shall be made, under the Authority of the United States, shall be the supreme Law of the Land; and the Judges in every State shall be bound thereby, any Thing in the Constitution or Laws of any state to the Contrary notwithstanding.

The Senators and Representatives before mentioned, and the Members of the several State Legislatures, and all executive and judicial Officers, both of the United States and of the several States, shall be bound by Oath or Affirmation, to support this Constitution; but no religious Test shall ever be required as a Qualification to any Office or public Trust under the United States.

Article. VII.

The Ratification of the Conventions of nine States, shall be sufficient for the Establishment of this Constitution between the States so ratifying the same.

done in Convention by the Unanimous Consent of the States present the Seventeenth Day of September in the Year of our Lord one thousand seven hundred and Eighty seven and of the Independance of the United States of America the Twelfth In Witness whereof We have hereunto subscribed our Names,
G⁰. Washington—Presid^t.
and deputy from Virginia

Delaware	Geo: Read Gunning Bedford jun John Dickinson Richard Bassett Jaco: Broom
Maryland	James McHenry Dan of St Thos Jenifer Danl Carroll
Virginia	John Blair— James Madison Jr.
North Carolina	Wm Blount Richd Dobbs Spaight Hu Williamson
South Carolina	J. Rutledge Charles Cotesworth Pinckney Charles Pinckney Pierce Butler
Georgia	William Few Abr Baldwin

New Hampshire	John Langdon Nicholas Gilman
Massachusetts	Nathaniel Gorham Rufus King
Connecticut	Wm Saml Johnson Roger Sherman
New York . . .	Alexander Hamilton

New Jersey	{	Wil: Livingston David Brearley. Wm Paterson. Jona: Dayton
Pensylvania	{	B Franklin Thomas Mifflin Robt Morris Geo. Clymer Thos FitzSimons Jared Ingersol James Wilson Gouv Morris

Attributions

CC licensed content, Shared previously

- Introduction to the Constitution. **Provided by**: Wikipedia. **Located at**: https://en.wikipedia.org/wiki/United_States_Constitution. **License**: *CC BY-SA: Attribution-ShareAlike*

Public domain content

- Constitution of the United States of America. **Provided by**: Wikisource. **Located at**: https://en.wikisource.org/wiki/Constitution_of_the_United_States_of_America. **License**: *Public Domain: No Known Copyright*

8. Growing Pains: The New Republic, 1790-1820

Introduction

"The happy Effects of the Grand Systom [sic] of shutting Ports against the English!!" appeared in 1808. Less than a year earlier, Thomas Jefferson had recommended (and Congress had passed) the Embargo Act of 1807, which barred American ships from leaving their ports.

The partisan political cartoon above lampoons Thomas Jefferson's 1807 Embargo Act, a move that had a devastating effect on American commerce. American farmers and merchants complain to President Jefferson, while the French emperor Napoleon Bonaparte whispers to him, "You shall be King hereafter." This image illustrates one of many political struggles in the years after the fight for ratification of the Constitution. In the nation's first few years, no organized political parties existed. This began to change as U.S. citizens argued bitterly about the proper size and scope of the new national government. As a result, the 1790s witnessed the rise of opposing political parties: the Federalists and the Democratic-Republicans. Federalists saw unchecked democracy as a dire threat to the republic, and they pointed to the excesses of the French Revolution as proof of what awaited. Democratic-Republicans opposed the Federalists' notion that only the wellborn and well educated were able to oversee the republic; they saw it as a pathway to oppression by an aristocracy.

Attributions

CC licensed content, Shared previously

- US History. **Authored by**: P. Scott Corbett, Volker Janssen, John M. Lund, Todd Pfannestiel, Paul Vickery, and Sylvie Waskiewicz. **Provided by**: OpenStax College. **Located at**: http://openstaxcollege.org/textbooks/us-history. **License**: *CC BY: Attribution*. **License Terms**: Download for free at http://cnx.org/content/col11740/latest/

Competing Visions: Federalists and Democratic-Republicans

Learning Objectives

By the end of this section, you will be able to:

- Describe the competing visions of the Federalists and the Democratic-Republicans
- Identify the protections granted to citizens under the Bill of Rights
- Explain Alexander Hamilton's financial programs as secretary of the treasury

---

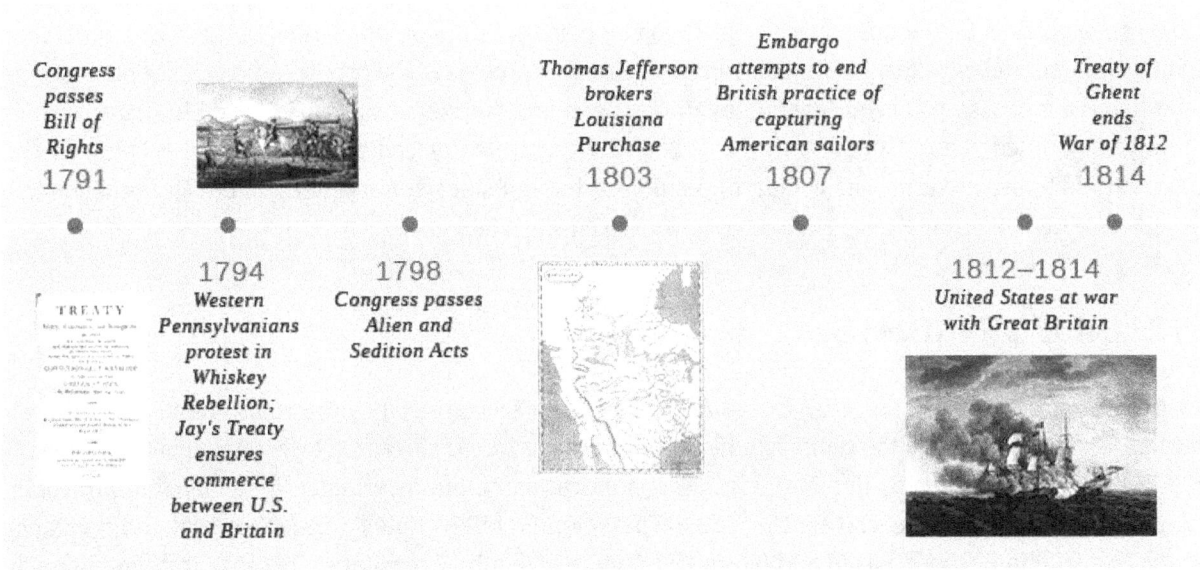

In June 1788, New Hampshire became the ninth state to ratify the federal Constitution, and the new plan for a strong central government went into effect. Elections for the first U.S. Congress were held in 1788 and 1789, and members took their seats in March 1789. In a reflection of the trust placed in him as the personification of republican virtue, George Washington became the first president in April 1789. John Adams served as his vice president; the pairing of a representative from Virginia (Washington) with one from Massachusetts (Adams) symbolized national unity. Nonetheless, political divisions quickly became apparent. Washington and Adams represented the Federalist Party, which generated a backlash among those who resisted the new government's assertions of federal power.

FEDERALISTS IN POWER

Though the Revolution had overthrown British rule in the United States, supporters of the 1787 federal constitution, known as Federalists, adhered to a decidedly British notion of social hierarchy. The Federalists did not, at first, compose a political party. Instead, Federalists held certain shared assumptions. For them, political participation continued to be linked to property rights, which barred many citizens from voting or holding office. Federalists did not believe the Revolution had changed the traditional social roles between women and men, or between whites and other races. They did believe in clear distinctions in rank and intelligence. To these supporters of the Constitution, the idea that all were equal appeared ludicrous. Women, blacks, and native peoples, they argued, had to know their place as secondary to white male citizens. Attempts to impose equality, they feared, would destroy the republic. The United States was not created to be a democracy.

The architects of the Constitution committed themselves to leading the new republic, and they held a majority among the members of the new national government. Indeed, as expected, many assumed the new executive posts the first Congress created. Washington appointed Alexander Hamilton, a leading Federalist, as secretary of the treasury. For secretary of state, he chose Thomas Jefferson. For secretary of war, he appointed Henry Knox, who had served with him during the Revolutionary War. Edmond Randolph, a Virginia delegate to the Constitutional Convention, was named attorney general. In July 1789, Congress also passed the Judiciary Act, creating a Supreme Court of six justices headed by those who were committed to the new national government.

Congress passed its first major piece of legislation by placing a duty on imports under the 1789 Tariff Act. Intended to raise revenue to address the country's economic problems, the act was a victory for nationalists, who favored a robust, powerful federal government and had worked unsuccessfully for similar measures during the Confederation Congress in the 1780s. Congress also placed a fifty-cent-per-ton duty (based on materials transported, not the weight of a ship) on foreign ships coming into American ports, a move designed to give the commercial advantage to American ships and goods.

THE BILL OF RIGHTS

Many Americans opposed the 1787 Constitution because it seemed a dangerous concentration of centralized power that threatened the rights and liberties of ordinary U.S. citizens. These opponents, known collectively as Anti-Federalists, did not constitute a political party, but they united in demanding protection for individual rights, and several states made the passing of a bill of rights a condition of their acceptance of the Constitution. Rhode Island and North Carolina rejected the Constitution because it did not already have this specific bill of rights.

Federalists followed through on their promise to add such a bill in 1789, when Virginia Representative James Madison introduced and Congress approved the **Bill of Rights**. Adopted in 1791, the bill consisted of the first ten amendments to the Constitution and outlined many of the personal rights state constitutions already guaranteed.

Rights Protected by the First Ten Amendments

Amendment 1	Right to freedoms of religion and speech; right to assemble and to petition the government for redress of grievances
Amendment 2	Right to keep and bear arms to maintain a well-regulated militia
Amendment 3	Right not to house soldiers during time of war
Amendment 4	Right to be secure from unreasonable search and seizure
Amendment 5	Rights in criminal cases, including to due process and indictment by grand jury for capital crimes, as well as the right not to testify against oneself
Amendment 6	Right to a speedy trial by an impartial jury
Amendment 7	Right to a jury trial in civil cases
Amendment 8	Right not to face excessive bail or fines, or cruel and unusual punishment
Amendment 9	Rights retained by the people, even if they are not specifically enumerated by the Constitution
Amendment 10	States' rights to powers not specifically delegated to the federal government

The adoption of the Bill of Rights softened the Anti-Federalists' opposition to the Constitution and gave the new federal government greater legitimacy among those who otherwise distrusted the new centralized power created by men of property during the secret 1787 Philadelphia Constitutional Convention.

> Visit the National Archives to consider the first ten amendments to the Constitution as an expression of the fears many citizens harbored about the powers of the new federal government. What were these fears? How did the Bill of Rights calm them?

ALEXANDER HAMILTON'S PROGRAM

Alexander Hamilton, Washington's secretary of the treasury, was an ardent nationalist who believed a strong federal government could solve many of the new country's financial ills. Born in the West Indies, Hamilton had worked on a St. Croix plantation as a teenager and was in charge of the accounts at a young age. He knew the Atlantic trade very well and used that knowledge in setting policy for the United States. In the early 1790s, he created the foundation for the U.S. financial system. He understood that a robust federal government would provide a solid financial foundation for the country.

The United States began mired in debt. In 1789, when Hamilton took up his post, the federal debt was over $53 million. The states had a combined debt of around $25 million, and the United States had been unable to pay its debts in the 1780s and was therefore considered a credit risk by European countries. Hamilton wrote three reports offering solutions to the economic crisis brought on by these problems. The first addressed public credit, the second addressed banking, and the third addressed raising revenue.

The Report on Public Credit

For the national government to be effective, Hamilton deemed it essential to have the support of those to whom it owed money: the wealthy, domestic creditor class as well as foreign creditors. In January 1790, he delivered his "**Report on Public Credit**", addressing the pressing need of the new republic to become creditworthy. He recommended that the new federal government honor all its debts, including all paper money issued by the Confederation and the states during the war, at face value. Hamilton especially wanted wealthy American creditors who held large amounts of paper money to be invested, literally, in the future and welfare of the new national government. He also understood the importance of making the new United States financially stable for creditors abroad. To pay these debts, Hamilton proposed that the federal government sell bonds—federal interest-bearing notes—to the public. These bonds would have the backing of the government and yield interest payments. Creditors could exchange their old notes for the new government bonds. Hamilton wanted to give the paper money that states had issued during the war the same status as government bonds; these federal notes would begin to yield interest payments in 1792.

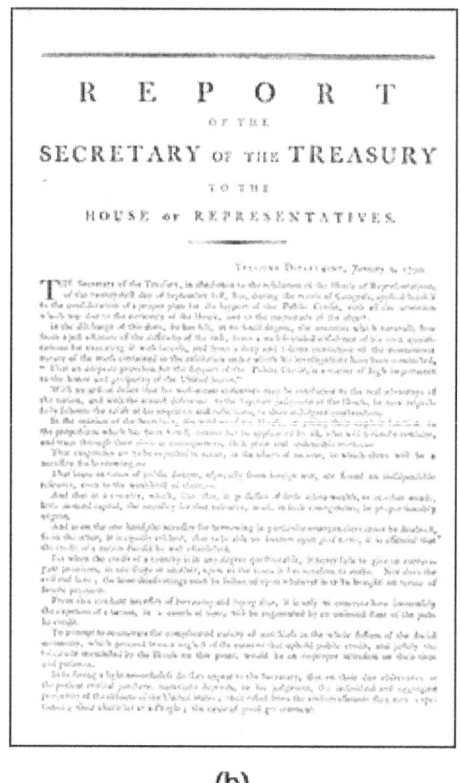

(a) (b)

As the first secretary of the treasury, Alexander Hamilton (a), shown here in a 1792 portrait by John Trumbull, released the "Report on Public Credit" (b) in January 1790.

Hamilton designed his "Report on Public Credit" (later called "First Report on Public Credit") to ensure the survival of the new and shaky American republic. He knew the importance of making the United States financially reliable, secure, and strong, and his plan provided a blueprint to achieve that goal. He argued that his plan would satisfy creditors, citing the goal of "doing justice to the creditors of the nation." At the same time, the plan would work "to promote the increasing respectability of the American name; to answer the calls for justice; to restore landed property to its due value; to furnish new resources both to agriculture and commerce; to cement more closely the union of the states; to add to their security against foreign attack; to establish public order on the basis of upright and liberal policy."

Hamilton's program ignited a heated debate in Congress. A great many of both Confederation and state notes had found their way into the hands of speculators, who had bought them from hard-pressed veterans in the 1780s and paid a fraction of their face value in anticipation of redeeming them at full value at a later date. Because these speculators held so many notes, many in Congress objected that Hamilton's plan would benefit them at the expense of the original note-holders. One of those who opposed Hamilton's 1790 report was James Madison, who questioned the fairness of a plan that seemed to cheat poor soldiers.

Not surprisingly, states with a large debt, like South Carolina, supported Hamilton's plan, while states with less debt, like North Carolina, did not. To gain acceptance of his plan, Hamilton worked out a compromise with Virginians Madison and Jefferson, whereby in return for their support he would give up New York City as the nation's capital and agree on a more southern location, which they preferred. In July 1790, a site along the Potomac River was selected as the new "federal city," which became the District of Columbia.

Hamilton's plan to convert notes to bonds worked extremely well to restore European confidence in the U.S. economy. It also proved a windfall for creditors, especially those who had bought up state and Confederation notes at far less than face value. But it immediately generated controversy about the size and scope of the government. Some saw the plan as an unjust use of federal power, while Hamilton argued that Article 1, Section 8 of the Constitution granted the government "implied powers" that gave the green light to his program.

The Report on a National Bank

As secretary of the treasury, Hamilton hoped to stabilize the American economy further by establishing a national bank. The United States operated with a flurry of different notes from multiple state banks and no coherent regulation. By proposing that the new **national bank** buy up large volumes of state bank notes and demanding their conversion into gold, Hamilton especially wanted to discipline those state banks that issued paper money irresponsibly. To that end, he delivered his "Report on a National Bank" in December 1790, proposing a Bank of the United States, an institution modeled on the Bank of England. The bank would issue loans to American merchants and bills of credit (federal bank notes that would circulate as money) while serving as a repository of government revenue from the sale of land. Stockholders would own the bank, along with the federal government.

Like the recommendations in his "Report on Public Credit," Hamilton's bank proposal generated opposition. Jefferson, in particular, argued that the Constitution did not permit the creation of a national bank. In response, Hamilton again invoked the Constitution's implied powers. President Washington backed Hamilton's position and signed legislation creating the bank in 1791.

The Report on Manufactures

The third report Hamilton delivered to Congress, known as the "Report on Manufactures," addressed the need to raise revenue to pay the interest on the national debt. Using the power to tax as provided under the Constitution, Hamilton put forth a proposal to tax American-made whiskey. He also knew the importance of promoting domestic manufacturing so the new United States would no longer have to rely on imported manufactured goods. To break from the old colonial system, Hamilton therefore advocated tariffs on all foreign imports to stimulate the production of American-made goods. To promote domestic industry further, he proposed federal subsidies to American industries. Like all of Hamilton's programs, the idea of government involvement in the development of American industries was new.

With the support of Washington, the entire Hamiltonian economic program received the necessary support in Congress to be implemented. In the long run, Hamilton's financial program helped to rescue the United States from its state of near-bankruptcy in the late 1780s. His initiatives marked the beginning of an American capitalism, making the republic creditworthy, promoting commerce, and setting for the nation a solid financial foundation. His policies also facilitated the growth of the stock market, as U.S. citizens bought and sold the federal government's interest-bearing certificates.

THE DEMOCRATIC-REPUBLICAN PARTY AND THE FIRST PARTY SYSTEM

James Madison and Thomas Jefferson felt the federal government had overstepped its authority by adopting the treasury secretary's plan. Madison found Hamilton's scheme immoral and offensive. He argued that it turned the reins of government over to the class of speculators who profited at the expense of hardworking citizens.

Jefferson, who had returned to the United States in 1790 after serving as a diplomat in France, tried unsuccessfully to convince Washington to block the creation of a national bank. He also took issue with what he perceived as favoritism given to commercial classes in the principal American cities. He thought urban life widened the gap between the wealthy few and an underclass of landless poor workers who, because of their oppressed condition, could never be good republican property owners. Rural areas, in contrast, offered far more opportunities for property ownership and virtue. In 1783 Jefferson wrote, "Those who labor in the earth are the chosen people of God, if ever he had a chosen people." Jefferson believed that self-sufficient, property-owning republican citizens or yeoman farmers held the key to the success and longevity of the American republic. (As a creature of his times, he did not envision a similar role for either women or nonwhite men.) To him, Hamilton's program seemed to encourage economic inequalities and work against the ordinary American yeoman.

Opposition to Hamilton, who had significant power in the new federal government, including the ear of President Washington, began in earnest in the early 1790s. Jefferson turned to his friend Philip Freneau to help organize the effort through the publication of the *National Gazette* as a counter to the Federalist press, especially the *Gazette of the United States*. From 1791 until 1793, when it ceased publication, Freneau's partisan paper attacked Hamilton's program and Washington's administration. "Rules for Changing a Republic into a Monarchy," written by Freneau, is an example of the type of attack aimed at the national government, and especially at the elitism of the Federalist Party. Newspapers in the 1790s became enormously important in American culture as partisans like Freneau attempted to sway public opinion. These newspapers did not aim to be objective; instead, they served to broadcast the views of a particular party.

(a) (b)

Here, the front page of the Federalist Gazette of the United States from September 9, 1789 (a), is shown beside that of the oppositional National Gazette from November 14, 1791 (b). The Gazette of the United States featured articles, sometimes written pseudonymously or anonymously, from leading Federalists like Alexander Hamilton and John Adams. The National Gazette was founded two years later to counter their political influence.

Visit Lexrex.com to read Philip Freneau's essay and others from the *National Gazette*. Can you identify three instances of persuasive writing against the Federalist Party or the government?

Opposition to the Federalists led to the formation of Democratic-Republican societies, composed of men who felt the domestic policies of the Washington administration were designed to enrich the few while ignoring everyone else. **Democratic-Republicans** championed limited government. Their fear of centralized power originated in the experience of the 1760s and 1770s when the distant, overbearing, and seemingly corrupt British Parliament attempted to impose its will on the colonies. The 1787 federal constitution, written in secret by fifty-five wealthy men of property and standing, ignited fears of a similar menacing plot. To opponents, the Federalists promoted aristocracy and a monarchical government—a betrayal of what many believed to be the goal of the American Revolution.

While wealthy merchants and planters formed the core of the Federalist leadership, members of the Democratic-Republican societies in cities like Philadelphia and New York came from the ranks of artisans. These citizens saw themselves as acting in the spirit of 1776, this time not against the haughty British but by what they believed to have replaced them—a commercial class with no interest in the public good. Their political efforts against the Federalists were a battle to preserve republicanism, to promote the public good against private self-interest. They published their views, held meetings to voice their opposition, and sponsored festivals and parades. In their strident newspapers attacks, they also worked to undermine the traditional forms of deference and subordination to aristocrats, in this case the Federalist elites. Some members of northern Democratic-Republican clubs denounced slavery as well.

DEFINING CITIZENSHIP

While questions regarding the proper size and scope of the new national government created a divide among Americans and gave rise to political parties, a consensus existed among men on the issue of who qualified and who did not qualify as a citizen. The 1790 Naturalization Act defined citizenship in stark racial terms. To be a citizen of the American republic, an immigrant had to be a "free white person" of "good character." By excluding slaves, free blacks, Indians, and Asians from citizenship, the act laid the foundation for the United States as a republic of white men.

Full citizenship that included the right to vote was restricted as well. Many state constitutions directed that only male property owners or taxpayers could vote. For women, the right to vote remained out of reach except in the state of New Jersey. In 1776, the fervor of the Revolution led New Jersey revolutionaries to write a constitution extending the right to vote to unmarried women who owned property worth £50. Federalists and Democratic-Republicans competed for the votes of New Jersey women who met the requirements to cast ballots. This radical innovation continued until 1807, when New Jersey restricted voting to free white males.

Section Summary

While they did not yet constitute distinct political parties, Federalists and Anti-Federalists, shortly after the Revolution, found themselves at odds over the Constitution and the power that it concentrated in the federal government. While many of the Anti-Federalists' fears were assuaged by the adoption of the Bill of Rights in 1791, the early 1790s nevertheless witnessed the rise of two political parties: the Federalists and the Democratic-Republicans. These rival political factions began by defining themselves in relationship to Hamilton's financial program, a debate that exposed contrasting views of the proper role of the federal government. By championing Hamilton's bold financial program, Federalists, including President Washington, made clear their intent to use the federal government to stabilize the national economy and overcome the financial problems that had plagued it since the 1780s. Members of the Democratic-Republican opposition, however, deplored the expanded role of the new national government. They argued that the Constitution did not permit the treasury secretary's expansive program and worried that the new national government had assumed powers it did not rightfully possess. Only on the question of citizenship was there broad agreement: only free, white males who met taxpayer or property qualifications could cast ballots as full citizens of the republic.

https://www.openassessments.org/assessments/964

Review Question

1. What were the fundamental differences between the Federalist and Democratic-Republican visions?

Answer to Review Question

1. Federalists believed in a strong federal republican government led by learned, public-spirited men of property. They believed that too much democracy would threaten the republic. The Democratic-Republicans, alternatively, feared too much federal government power and focused more on the rural areas of the country, which they thought were underrepresented and underserved. Democratic-Republicans felt that the spirit of true republicanism, which meant virtuous living for the common good, depended on farmers and agricultural areas.

Glossary

Bill of Rights the first ten amendments to the United States Constitution, which guarantee individual rights

Democratic-Republicans advocates of limited government who were troubled by the expansive domestic policies of Washington's administration and opposed the Federalists

Attributions

CC licensed content, Shared previously

- US History. **Authored by**: P. Scott Corbett, Volker Janssen, John M. Lund, Todd Pfannestiel, Paul Vickery, and Sylvie Waskiewicz. **Provided by**: OpenStax College. **Located at**: http://openstaxcollege.org/textbooks/us-history. **License**: *CC BY: Attribution*. **License Terms**: Download for free at http://cnx.org/content/col11740/latest/

The New American Republic

> ### Learning Objectives
>
> By the end of this section, you will be able to:
>
> - Identify the major foreign and domestic uprisings of the early 1790s
> - Explain the effect of these uprisings on the political system of the United States

The colonies' alliance with France, secured after the victory at Saratoga in 1777, proved crucial in their victory against the British, and during the 1780s France and the new United States enjoyed a special relationship. Together they had defeated their common enemy, Great Britain. But despite this shared experience, American opinions regarding France diverged sharply in the 1790s when France underwent its own revolution. Democratic-Republicans seized on the French revolutionaries' struggle against monarchy as the welcome harbinger of a larger republican movement around the world. To the Federalists, however, the French Revolution represented pure anarchy, especially after the execution of the French king in 1793. Along with other foreign and domestic uprisings, the French Revolution helped harden the political divide in the United States in the early 1790s.

THE FRENCH REVOLUTION

The French Revolution, which began in 1789, further split American thinkers into different ideological camps, deepening the political divide between Federalists and their Democratic-Republican foes. At first, in 1789 and 1790, the revolution in France appeared to most in the United States as part of a new chapter in the rejection of corrupt monarchy, a trend inspired by the American Revolution. A constitutional monarchy replaced the absolute monarchy of Louis XVI in 1791, and in 1792, France was declared a republic. Republican liberty, the creed of the United States, seemed to be ushering in a new era in France. Indeed, the American Revolution served as an inspiration for French revolutionaries.

An image from a 1791 Hungarian journal depicts the beheading of Louis XVI during the French Revolution. The violence of the revolutionary French horrified many in the United States—especially Federalists, who saw it as an example of what could happen when the mob gained political control and instituted direct democracy.

The events of 1793 and 1794 challenged the simple interpretation of the French Revolution as a happy chapter in the unfolding triumph of republican government over monarchy. The French king was executed in January 1793, and the next two years became known as **the Terror**, a period of extreme violence against perceived enemies of the revolutionary government. Revolutionaries advocated direct representative democracy, dismantled Catholicism, replaced that religion with a new philosophy known as the Cult of the Supreme Being, renamed the months of the year, and relentlessly employed the guillotine against their enemies. Federalists viewed these excesses with growing alarm, fearing that the radicalism of the French Revolution might infect the minds of citizens at home. Democratic-Republicans interpreted the same events with greater optimism, seeing them as a necessary evil of eliminating the monarchy and aristocratic culture that supported the privileges of a hereditary class of rulers.

The controversy in the United States intensified when France declared war on Great Britain and Holland in February 1793. France requested that the United States make a large repayment of the money it had borrowed from France to fund the Revolutionary War. However, Great Britain would judge any aid given to France as a hostile act. Washington declared the United States neutral in 1793, but Democratic-Republican groups denounced neutrality and declared their support of the French republicans. The Federalists used the violence of the French revolutionaries as a reason to attack Democratic-Republicanism in the United States, arguing that Jefferson and Madison would lead the country down a similarly disastrous path.

> Visit Liberty, Equality, Fraternity for images, texts, and songs relating to the French Revolution. This momentous event's impact extended far beyond Europe, influencing politics in the United States and elsewhere in the Atlantic World.

THE CITIZEN GENÊT AFFAIR AND JAY'S TREATY

In 1793, the revolutionary French government sent Edmond-Charles Genêt to the United States to negotiate an alliance with the U.S. government. France empowered Genêt to issue **letters of marque**—documents authorizing ships and their crews to engage in piracy—to allow him to arm captured British ships in American ports with U.S. soldiers. Genêt arrived in Charleston, South Carolina, amid great Democratic-Republican fanfare. He immediately began commissioning American privateer ships and organizing volunteer American militias to attack Spanish holdings in the Americas, then traveled to Philadelphia, gathering support for the French cause along the way. President Washington and Hamilton denounced Genêt, knowing his actions threatened to pull the United States into a war with Great Britain. The **Citizen Genêt affair**, as it became known, spurred Great Britain to instruct its naval commanders in the West Indies to seize all ships trading with the French. The British captured hundreds of American ships and their cargoes, increasing the possibility of war between the two countries.

In this tense situation, Great Britain worked to prevent a wider conflict by ending its seizure of American ships and offered to pay for captured cargoes. Hamilton saw an opportunity and recommended to Washington that the United States negotiate. Supreme Court Justice John Jay was sent to Britain, instructed by Hamilton to secure compensation for captured American ships; ensure the British leave the Northwest outposts they still occupied despite the 1783 Treaty of Paris; and gain an agreement for American trade in the West Indies. Even though Jay personally disliked slavery, his mission also required him to seek compensation from the British for slaves who left with the British at the end of the Revolutionary War.

The resulting 1794 agreement, known as Jay's Treaty, fulfilled most of his original goals. The British would turn over the frontier posts in the Northwest, American ships would be allowed to trade freely in the West Indies, and the United States agreed to assemble a commission charged with settling colonial debts U.S. citizens owed British merchants. The treaty did not address the important issue of **impressment**, however—the British navy's practice of forcing or "impressing" American sailors to work and fight on British warships. Jay's Treaty led the Spanish, who worried that it signaled an alliance between the United States and Great Britain, to negotiate a treaty of their own—Pinckney's Treaty—that allowed American commerce to flow through the Spanish port of New Orleans. Pinckney's Treaty allowed American farmers, who were moving in greater numbers to the Ohio River Valley, to ship their products down the Ohio and Mississippi Rivers to New Orleans, where they could be transported to East Coast markets.

Jay's Treaty confirmed the fears of Democratic-Republicans, who saw it as a betrayal of republican France, cementing the idea that the Federalists favored aristocracy and monarchy. Partisan American newspapers tried to sway public opinion, while the skillful writing of Hamilton, who published a number of essays on the subject, explained the benefits of commerce with Great Britain.

THE FRENCH REVOLUTION'S CARIBBEAN LEGACY

Unlike the American Revolution, which ultimately strengthened the institution of slavery and the powers of American slaveholders, the French Revolution inspired slave rebellions in the Caribbean, including a 1791 slave uprising in the French colony of Saint-Domingue (modern-day Haiti). Thousands of slaves joined together to overthrow the brutal system of slavery. They took control of a large section of the island, burning sugar plantations and killing the white planters who had forced them to labor under the lash.

In 1794, French revolutionaries abolished slavery in the French empire, and both Spain and England attacked Saint-Domingue, hoping to add the colony to their own empires. Toussaint L'Ouverture, a former domestic slave, emerged as the leader in the fight against Spain and England to secure a Haiti free of slavery and further European colonialism. Because revolutionary France had abolished slavery, Toussaint aligned himself with France, hoping to keep Spain and England at bay.

An 1802 portrait shows Toussaint L'Ouverture, "Chef des Noirs Insurgés de Saint Domingue" ("Leader of the Black Insurgents of Saint Domingue"), mounted and armed in an elaborate uniform.

Events in Haiti further complicated the partisan wrangling in the United States. White refugee planters from Haiti and other French West Indian islands, along with slaves and free people of color, left the Caribbean for the United States and for Louisiana, which at the time was held by Spain. The presence of these French migrants raised fears, especially among Federalists, that they would bring the contagion of French radicalism to the United States. In addition, the idea that the French Revolution could inspire a successful slave uprising just off the American coastline filled southern whites and slaveholders with horror.

THE WHISKEY REBELLION

While the wars in France and the Caribbean divided American citizens, a major domestic test of the new national government came in 1794 over the issue of a tax on whiskey, an important part of Hamilton's financial program. In 1791, Congress had authorized a tax of 7.5 cents per gallon of whiskey and rum. Although most citizens paid without incident, trouble erupted in four western Pennsylvania counties in an uprising known as the Whiskey Rebellion.

Farmers in the western counties of Pennsylvania produced whiskey from their grain for economic reasons. Without adequate roads or other means to transport a bulky grain harvest, these farmers distilled their grains into gin and whiskey, which were more cost-effective to transport. Since these farmers depended on the sale of whiskey, some citizens in western Pennsylvania (and elsewhere) viewed the new tax as further proof that the new national government favored the commercial classes on the eastern seaboard at the expense of farmers in the West. On the other hand, supporters of the tax argued that it helped stabilize the economy and its cost could easily be passed on to the consumer, not the farmer-distiller. However, in the spring and summer months of 1794, angry citizens rebelled against the federal officials in charge of enforcing the federal excise law. Like the Sons of Liberty before the American Revolution, the whiskey rebels used violence and intimidation to protest policies they saw as unfair. They tarred and feathered federal officials, intercepted the federal mail, and intimidated wealthy citizens. The extent of their discontent found expression in their plan to form an independent western commonwealth, and they even began negotiations with British and Spanish representatives, hoping to secure their support for independence from the United States. The rebels also contacted their backcountry neighbors in Kentucky and South Carolina, circulating the idea of secession.

This painting, attributed to Frederick Kemmelmeyer ca. 1795, depicts the massive force George Washington led to put down the Whiskey Rebellion of the previous year. Federalists made clear they would not tolerate mob action.

With their emphasis on personal freedoms, the whiskey rebels aligned themselves with the Democratic-Republican Party. They saw the tax as part of a larger Federalist plot to destroy their republican liberty and, in its most extreme interpretation, turn the United States into a monarchy. The federal government lowered the tax, but when federal officials tried to subpoena those distillers who remained intractable, trouble escalated. Washington responded by creating a thirteen-thousand-man militia, drawn from several states, to put down the rebellion. This force made it known, both domestically and to the European powers that looked on in anticipation of the new republic's collapse, that the national government would do everything in its power to ensure the survival of the United States.

Alexander Hamilton: "Shall the majority govern or be governed?"

Alexander Hamilton frequently wrote persuasive essays under pseudonyms, like "Tully," as he does here. In this 1794 essay, Hamilton denounces the whiskey rebels and majority rule.

> It has been observed that the means most likely to be employed to turn the insurrection in the western country to the detriment of the government, would be artfully calculated among other things 'to divert your attention from the true question to be decided.'
>
> Let us see then what is this question. It is plainly this—shall the majority govern or be governed? shall the nation rule, or be ruled? shall the general will prevail, or the will of a faction? shall there be government, or no government? . . .

The Constitution *you* have ordained for yourselves and your posterity contains this express clause, 'The Congress *shall have power* to lay and collect taxes, duties, imposts, and *Excises*, to pay the debts, and provide for the common defence and general welfare of the United States.' You have then, by a solemn and deliberate act, the most important and sacred that a nation can perform, pronounced and decreed, that your Representatives in Congress shall have power to lay Excises. You have done nothing since to reverse or impair that decree. . . .

But the four western counties of Pennsylvania, undertake to rejudge and reverse your decrees, you have said, 'The Congress *shall have power* to lay *Excises*.' They say, 'The Congress *shall not have* this power.' . . .

There is no road to *despotism* more sure or more to be dreaded than that which begins at *anarchy*."

—Alexander Hamilton's "Tully No. II" for the *American Daily Advertiser*, Philadelphia, August 26, 1794

What are the major arguments put forward by Hamilton in this document? Who do you think his audience is?

WASHINGTON'S INDIAN POLICY

Relationships with Indians were a significant problem for Washington's administration, but one on which white citizens agreed: Indians stood in the way of white settlement and, as the 1790 Naturalization Act made clear, were not citizens. After the War of Independence, white settlers poured into lands west of the Appalachian Mountains. As a result, from 1785 to 1795, a state of war existed on the frontier between these settlers and the Indians who lived in the Ohio territory. In both 1790 and 1791, the Shawnee and Miami had defended their lands against the whites who arrived in greater and greater numbers from the East. In response, Washington appointed General Anthony Wayne to bring the Western Confederacy—a loose alliance of tribes—to heel. In 1794, at the Battle of Fallen Timbers, Wayne was victorious. With the 1795 Treaty of Greenville, the Western Confederacy gave up their claims to Ohio.

Notice the contrasts between the depictions of federal and native representatives in this painting of the signing of the Treaty of Greenville in 1795. What message or messages did the artist intend to convey?

Section Summary

Federalists and Democratic-Republicans interpreted the execution of the French monarch and the violent establishment of a French republic in very different ways. Revolutionaries' excesses in France and the slaves' revolt in the French colony of Haiti raised fears among Federalists of similar radicalism and slave uprisings on American shores. They looked to better relationships with Great Britain through Jay's Treaty. Pinckney's Treaty, which came about as a result of Jay's Treaty, improved U.S. relations with the Spanish and opened the Spanish port of New Orleans to American commerce. Democratic-Republicans took a more positive view of the French Revolution and grew suspicious of the Federalists when they brokered Jay's Treaty. Domestically, the partisan divide came to a dramatic head in western Pennsylvania when distillers of whiskey, many aligned with the Democratic-Republicans, took action against the federal tax on their product. Washington led a massive force to put down the uprising, demonstrating Federalist intolerance of mob action. Though divided on many issues, the majority of white citizens agreed on the necessity of eradicating the Indian presence on the frontier.

- https://www.openassessments.org/assessments/965

Review Question

1. How did the French Revolution in the early 1790s influence the evolution of the American political system?

Answer to Review Question

1. In the United States, the French Revolution hardened differences between the Federalists and the Democratic-Republicans. The Federalists feared the anarchy of the French Revolution and worried that Democratic-Republicanism would bring that kind of disorder to the United States. The Democratic-Republicans supported the goals of the French Revolution, even if they didn't support the means, and believed that siding with Great Britain instead of France meant a return to a system of monarchy.

Glossary

Citizen Genêt affair the controversy over the French representative who tried to involve the United States in France's war against Great Britain

impressment the practice of capturing sailors and forcing them into military service

letters of marque French warrants allowing ships and their crews to engage in piracy

the Terror a period during the French Revolution characterized by extreme violence and the execution of numerous enemies of the revolutionary government, from 1793 through 1794

Attributions

CC licensed content, Shared previously

- US History. **Authored by**: P. Scott Corbett, Volker Janssen, John M. Lund, Todd Pfannestiel, Paul Vickery, and Sylvie Waskiewicz. **Provided by**: OpenStax College. **Located at**: http://openstaxcollege.org/textbooks/us-history. **License**: *CC BY: Attribution*. **License Terms**: Download for free at http://cnx.org/content/col11740/latest/

Partisan Politics

> ### Learning Objectives
>
> By the end of this section, you will be able to:
>
> - Identify key examples of partisan wrangling between the Federalists and Democratic-Republicans
> - Describe how foreign relations affected American politics
> - Assess the importance of the Louisiana Purchase

George Washington, who had been reelected in 1792 by an overwhelming majority, refused to run for a third term, thus setting a precedent for future presidents. In the presidential election of 1796, the two parties—Federalist and Democratic-Republican—competed for the first time. Partisan rancor over the French Revolution and the Whiskey Rebellion fueled the divide between them, and Federalist John Adams defeated his Democratic-Republican rival Thomas Jefferson by a narrow margin of only three electoral votes. In 1800, another close election swung the other way, and Jefferson began a long period of Democratic-Republican government.

THE PRESIDENCY OF JOHN ADAMS

The war between Great Britain and France in the 1790s shaped U.S. foreign policy. As a new and, in comparison to the European powers, extremely weak nation, the American republic had no control over European events, and no real leverage to obtain its goals of trading freely in the Atlantic. To Federalist president John Adams, relations with France posed the biggest problem. After the Terror, the French Directory ruled France from 1795 to 1799. During this time, Napoleon rose to power.

The Art of Ralph Earl

Ralph Earl was an eighteenth-century American artist, born in Massachusetts, who remained loyal to the British during the Revolutionary War. He fled to England in 1778, but he returned to New England in the mid-1780s and began painting portraits of leading Federalists.

His portrait of Connecticut Federalist Oliver Ellsworth and his wife Abigail conveys the world as Federalists liked to view it: an orderly landscape administered by men of property and learning. His portrait of dry goods merchant Elijah Boardman shows Boardman as well-to-do and highly cultivated; his books include the works of Shakespeare and Milton.

(a)

(b)

Ralph Earl's portraits are known for placing their subjects in an orderly world, as seen here in the 1801 portrait of Oliver and Abigail Wolcott Ellsworth (a) and the 1789 portrait of Elijah Boardman (b).

What similarities do you see in the two portraits by Ralph Earl? What do the details of each portrait reveal about the sitters? About the artist and the 1790s?

Because France and Great Britain were at war, the French Directory issued decrees stating that any ship carrying British goods could be seized on the high seas. In practice, this meant the French would target American ships, especially those in the West Indies, where the United States conducted a brisk trade with the British. France declared its 1778 treaty with the United States null and void, and as a result, France and the United States waged an undeclared war—or what historians refer to as the Quasi-War—from 1796 to 1800. Between 1797 and 1799, the French seized 834 American ships, and Adams urged the buildup of the U.S. Navy, which consisted of only a single vessel at the time of his election in 1796.

This 1799 print, entitled "Preparation for WAR to defend Commerce," shows the construction of a naval ship, part of the effort to ensure the United States had access to free trade in the Atlantic world.

In 1797, Adams sought a diplomatic solution to the conflict with France and dispatched envoys to negotiate terms. The French foreign minister,

Charles-Maurice de Talleyrand, sent emissaries who told the American envoys that the United States must repay all outstanding debts owed to France, lend France 32 million guilders (Dutch currency), and pay a £50,000 bribe before any negotiations could take place. News of the attempt to extract a bribe, known as the **XYZ affair** because the French emissaries were referred to as X, Y, and Z in letters that President Adams released to Congress, outraged the American public and turned public opinion decidedly against France. In the court of public opinion, Federalists appeared to have been correct in their interpretation of France, while the pro-French Democratic-Republicans had been misled.

This anonymous 1798 cartoon, Property Protected à la Françoise, satirizes the XYZ affair. Five Frenchmen are shown plundering the treasures of a woman representing the United States. One man holds a sword labeled "French Argument" and a sack of gold and riches labeled "National Sack and Diplomatic Perquisites," while the others collect her valuables. A group of other Europeans look on and commiserate that France treated them the same way.

> Read the "transcript" of the above cartoon in the America in Caricature, 1765–1865 collection at Indiana University's Lilly Library.

The complicated situation in Haiti, which remained a French colony in the late 1790s, also came to the attention of President Adams. The president, with the support of Congress, had created a U.S. Navy that now included scores of vessels. Most of the American ships cruised the Caribbean, giving the United States the edge over France in the region. In Haiti, the rebellion leader Toussaint, who had to contend with various domestic rivals seeking to displace him, looked to end an U.S. embargo on France and its colonies, put in place in 1798, so that his forces would receive help to deal with the civil unrest. In early 1799, in order to capitalize upon trade in the lucrative West Indies and undermine France's hold on the island, Congress ended the ban on trade with Haiti—a move that acknowledged Toussaint's leadership, to the horror of American slaveholders. Toussaint was able to secure an independent black republic in Haiti by 1804.

THE ALIEN AND SEDITION ACTS

The surge of animosity against France during the Quasi-War led Congress to pass several measures that in time undermined Federalist power. These 1798 war measures, known as the Alien and Sedition Acts, aimed to increase national security against what most had come to regard as the French menace. The Alien Act and the Alien Enemies Act took particular aim at French immigrants fleeing the West Indies by giving the president the power to deport new arrivals who appeared to be a threat to national security. The act expired in 1800 with no immigrants having been deported. The Sedition Act imposed harsh penalties—up to five years' imprisonment and a massive fine of $5,000 in 1790 dollars—on those convicted of speaking or writing "in a scandalous or malicious" manner against the government of the United States. Twenty-five men, all Democratic-Republicans, were indicted under the act, and ten were convicted. One of these was Congressman Matthew Lyon, representative from Vermont, who had launched his own newspaper, *The Scourge Of Aristocracy and Repository of Important Political Truth*.

This 1798 cartoon, "Congressional Pugilists," shows partisan chaos in the U.S. House of Representatives as Matthew Lyon, a Democratic-Republican from Vermont, holds forth against his opponent, Federalist Roger Griswold.

The Alien and Sedition Acts raised constitutional questions about the freedom of the press provided under the First Amendment. Democratic-Republicans argued that the acts were evidence of the Federalists' intent to squash individual liberties and, by enlarging the powers of the national government, crush states' rights. Jefferson and Madison mobilized the response to the acts in the form of statements known as the Virginia and Kentucky Resolutions, which argued that the acts were illegal and unconstitutional. The resolutions introduced the idea of nullification, the right of states to nullify acts of Congress, and advanced the argument of states' rights. The resolutions failed to rally support in other states, however. Indeed, most other states rejected them, citing the necessity of a strong national government.

The Quasi-War with France came to an end in 1800, when President Adams was able to secure the Treaty of Mortefontaine. His willingness to open talks with France divided the Federalist Party, but the treaty reopened trade between the two countries and ended the French practice of taking American ships on the high seas.

THE REVOLUTION OF 1800 AND THE PRESIDENCY OF THOMAS JEFFERSON

The **Revolution of 1800** refers to the first transfer of power from one party to another in American history, when the presidency passed to Democratic-Republican Thomas Jefferson in the 1800 election. The peaceful transition calmed contemporary fears about possible violent reactions to a new party's taking the reins of government. The passing of political power from one political party to another without bloodshed also set an important precedent.

The election did prove even more divisive than the 1796 election, however, as both the Federalist and Democratic-Republican Parties waged a mudslinging campaign unlike any seen before. Because the Federalists were badly divided, the Democratic-Republicans gained political ground. Alexander Hamilton, who disagreed with President Adams's approach to France, wrote a lengthy letter, meant for people within his party, attacking his fellow Federalist's character and judgment and ridiculing his handling of foreign affairs. Democratic-Republicans got hold of and happily reprinted the letter.

Thomas Jefferson's victory in 1800 signaled the ascendency of the Democratic-Republicans and the decline of Federalist power.

Jefferson viewed participatory democracy as a positive force for the republic, a direct departure from Federalist views. His version of participatory democracy only extended, however, to the white yeoman farmers in whom Jefferson placed great trust. While Federalist statesmen, like the architects of the 1787 federal constitution, feared a pure democracy, Jefferson was far more optimistic that the common American farmer could be trusted to make good decisions. He believed in majority rule, that is, that the majority of yeoman should have the power to make decisions binding upon the whole. Jefferson had cheered the French Revolution, even when the French republic instituted the Terror to ensure the monarchy would not return. By 1799, however, he had rejected the cause of France because of his opposition to Napoleon's seizure of power and creation of a dictatorship.

Over the course of his two terms as president—he was reelected in 1804—Jefferson reversed the policies of the Federalist Party by turning away from urban commercial development. Instead, he promoted agriculture through the sale of western public lands in small and affordable lots. Perhaps Jefferson's most lasting legacy is his vision of an "empire of liberty." He distrusted cities and instead envisioned a rural republic of land-owning white men, or yeoman republican farmers. He wanted the United States to be the breadbasket of the world, exporting its agricultural commodities without suffering the ills of urbanization and industrialization. Since American yeomen would own their own land, they could stand up against those who might try to buy their votes with promises of property. Jefferson championed the rights of states and insisted on limited federal government as well as limited taxes. This stood in stark contrast to the Federalists' insistence on a strong, active federal government. Jefferson also believed in fiscal austerity. He pushed for—and Congress approved—the end of all internal taxes, such as those on whiskey and rum. The most significant trimming of the federal budget came at the expense of the military; Jefferson did not believe in maintaining a costly military, and he slashed the size of the navy Adams had worked to build up. Nonetheless, Jefferson responded to the capture of American ships and sailors by pirates off the coast of North Africa by leading the United States into war against the Muslim Barbary States in 1801, the first conflict fought by Americans overseas.

The slow decline of the Federalists, which began under Jefferson, led to a period of one-party rule in national politics. Historians call the years between 1815 and 1828 the "Era of Good Feelings" and highlight the "Virginia dynasty" of the time, since the two presidents who followed Jefferson—James Madison and James Monroe—both hailed from his home state. Like him, they owned slaves and represented the Democratic-Republican Party. Though Federalists continued to enjoy popularity, especially in the Northeast, their days of prominence in setting foreign and domestic policy had ended.

PARTISAN ACRIMONY

The earliest years of the nineteenth century were hardly free of problems between the two political parties. Early in Jefferson's term, controversy swirled over President Adams's judicial appointments of many Federalists during his final days in office. When Jefferson took the oath of office, he refused to have the commissions for these Federalist justices delivered to the appointed officials.

One of Adams's appointees, William Marbury, had been selected to be a justice of the peace in the District of Columbia, and when his commission did not arrive, he petitioned the Supreme Court for an explanation from Jefferson's secretary of state, James Madison. In deciding the case, **Marbury v. Madison**, in 1803, Chief Justice John Marshall agreed that Marbury had the right to a legal remedy, establishing that individuals had rights even the president of the United States could not abridge. However, Marshall also found that Congress's Judicial Act of 1789, which would have given the Supreme Court the power to grant Marbury remedy, was unconstitutional because the Constitution did not allow for cases like Marbury's to come directly before the Supreme Court. Thus, Marshall established the principle of judicial review, which strengthened the court by asserting its power to review (and possibly nullify) the actions of Congress and the president. Jefferson was not pleased, but neither did Marbury get his commission.

The animosity between the political parties exploded into open violence in 1804, when Aaron Burr, Jefferson's first vice president, and Alexander Hamilton engaged in a duel. When Democratic-Republican Burr lost his bid for the office of governor of New York, he was quick to blame Hamilton, who had long hated him and had done everything in his power to discredit him. On July 11, the two antagonists met in Weehawken, New Jersey, to exchange bullets in a duel in which Burr shot and mortally wounded Hamilton.

THE LOUISIANA PURCHASE

Jefferson, who wanted to expand the United States to bring about his "empire of liberty," realized his greatest triumph in 1803 when the United States bought the Louisiana territory from France. For $15 million—a bargain price, considering the amount of land involved—the United States doubled in size. Perhaps the greatest real estate deal in American history, the **Louisiana Purchase** greatly enhanced the Jeffersonian vision of the United States as an agrarian republic in which yeomen farmers worked the land. Jefferson also wanted to bolster trade in the West, seeing the port of New Orleans and the Mississippi River (then the western boundary of the United States) as crucial to American agricultural commerce. In his mind, farmers would send their produce down the Mississippi River to New Orleans, where it would be sold to European traders.

The purchase of Louisiana came about largely because of circumstances beyond Jefferson's control, though he certainly recognized the implications of the transaction. Until 1801, Spain had controlled New Orleans and had given the United States the right to traffic goods in the port without paying customs duties. That year, however, the Spanish had ceded Louisiana (and New Orleans) to France. In 1802, the United States lost its right to deposit goods free in the port, causing outrage among many, some of whom called for war with France.

Jefferson instructed Robert Livingston, the American envoy to France, to secure access to New Orleans, sending James Monroe to France to add additional pressure. The timing proved advantageous. Because black slaves in the French colony of Haiti had successfully overthrown the brutal plantation regime, Napoleon could no longer hope to restore the empire lost with France's defeat in the French and Indian War (1754–1763). His vision of Louisiana and the Mississippi Valley as the source for food for Haiti, the most profitable sugar island in the world, had failed. The emperor therefore agreed to the sale in early 1803.

> Explore the collected maps and documents relating to the Louisiana Purchase and its history at the Library of Congress site.

The true extent of the United States' new territory remained unknown. Would it provide the long-sought quick access to Asian markets? Geographical knowledge was limited; indeed, no one knew precisely what lay to the west or how long it took to travel from the Mississippi to the Pacific. Jefferson selected two fellow Virginians, Meriwether Lewis and William Clark, to lead an expedition to the new western lands. Their purpose was to discover the commercial possibilities of the new land and, most importantly, potential trade routes. From 1804 to 1806, Lewis and Clark traversed the West.

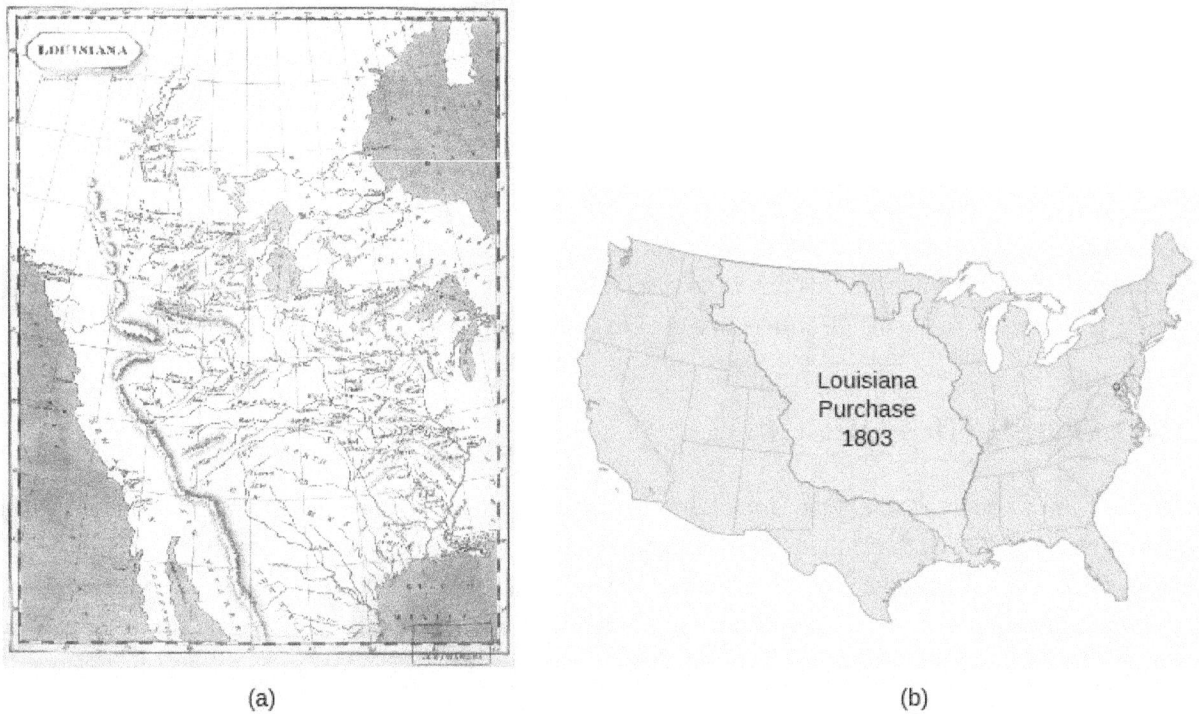

This 1804 map (a) shows the territory added to the United States in the Louisiana Purchase of 1803. Compare this depiction to the contemporary map (b). How does the 1804 version differ from what you know of the geography of the United States?

The Louisiana Purchase helped Jefferson win reelection in 1804 by a landslide. Of 176 electoral votes cast, all but 14 were in his favor. The great expansion of the United States did have its critics, however, especially northerners who feared the addition of more slave states and a corresponding lack of representation of their interests in the North. And under a strict interpretation of the Constitution, it remained unclear whether the president had the power to add territory in this fashion. But the vast majority of citizens cheered the increase in the size of the republic. For slaveholders, new western lands would be a boon; for slaves, the Louisiana Purchase threatened to entrench their suffering further.

Section Summary

Partisan politics dominated the American political scene at the close of the eighteenth century. The Federalists' and Democratic-Republicans' views of the role of government were in direct opposition to each other, and the close elections of 1796 and 1801 show how the nation grappled with these opposing visions. The high tide of the Federalist Party came after the election of 1796, when the United States engaged in the Quasi-War with France. The issues arising from the Quasi-War gave Adams and the Federalists license to expand the powers of the federal government. However, the tide turned with the close election of 1800, when Jefferson began an administration based on Democratic-Republican ideals. A major success of Jefferson's administration was the Louisiana Purchase of 1803, which helped to fulfill his vision of the United States as an agrarian republic.

https://www.openassessments.org/assessments/966

Review Questions

1. How did U.S. relations with France influence events at the end of the eighteenth century?
2. Why do historians refer to the election of Thomas Jefferson as the Revolution of 1800?

Answers to Review Questions

1. Relations with France were strongly tied to political events in the United States. Whereas the Federalists had roundly condemned the French revolutionaries for their excesses, the Democratic-Republicans applauded the rallying cries of liberty and equality. Relations with the French also led the Federalists to pass the Alien and Sedition Acts during the Adams administration, which many saw as a violation of the First Amendment.

2. The election was considered a revolution because, for the first time in American history, political power passed from one party to another. Jefferson's presidency was a departure from the Federalist administrations of Washington and Adams, who had favored the commercial class and urban centers of the country. The Democratic-Republican vision increased states' rights and limited the power of the federal government, lowering taxes and slashing the military, which Adams had built up.

Glossary

Louisiana Purchase the U.S. purchase of the large territory of Louisiana from France in 1803

Marbury v. Madison the landmark 1803 case establishing the Supreme Court's powers of judicial review, specifically the power to review and possibly nullify actions of Congress and the president

Revolution of 1800 the peaceful transfer of power from the Federalists to the Democratic-Republicans with the election of 1800

XYZ affair the French attempt to extract a bribe from the United States during the Quasi-War of 1798–1800

Attributions

CC licensed content, Shared previously

- US History. **Authored by**: P. Scott Corbett, Volker Janssen, John M. Lund, Todd Pfannestiel, Paul Vickery, and Sylvie Waskiewicz. **Provided by**: OpenStax College. **Located at**: http://openstaxcollege.org/textbooks/us-history. **License**: *CC BY: Attribution*. **License Terms**: Download for free at http://cnx.org/content/col11740/latest/

The United States Goes Back to War

> **Learning Objectives**
>
> By the end of this section, you will be able to:
> - Describe the causes and consequences of the War of 1812
> - Identify the important events of the War of 1812 and explain their significance

The origins of the War of 1812, often called the Second War of American Independence, are found in the unresolved issues between the United States and Great Britain. One major cause was the British practice of impressment, whereby American sailors were taken at sea and forced to fight on British warships; this issue was left unresolved by Jay's Treaty in 1794. In addition, the British in Canada supported Indians in their fight against further U.S. expansion in the Great Lakes region. Though Jefferson wanted to avoid what he called "entangling alliances," staying neutral proved impossible.

THE EMBARGO OF 1807

France and England, engaged in the Napoleonic Wars, which raged between 1803 and 1815, both declared open season on American ships, which they seized on the high seas. England was the major offender, since the Royal Navy, following a time-honored practice, "impressed" American sailors by forcing them into its service. The issue came to a head in 1807 when the HMS *Leopard*, a British warship, fired on a U.S. naval ship, the *Chesapeake*, off the coast of Norfolk, Virginia. The British then boarded the ship and took four sailors. Jefferson chose what he thought was the best of his limited options and responded to the crisis through the economic means of a sweeping ban on trade, the **Embargo Act of 1807**. This law prohibited American ships from leaving their ports until Britain and France stopped seizing them on the high seas. As a result of the embargo, American commerce came to a near-total halt.

The logic behind the embargo was that cutting off all trade would so severely hurt Britain and France that the seizures at sea would end. However, while the embargo did have some effect on the British economy, it was American commerce that actually felt the brunt of the impact. The embargo hurt American farmers, who could no longer sell their goods overseas, and seaport cities experienced a huge increase in unemployment and an uptick in bankruptcies. All told, American business activity declined by 75 percent from 1808 to 1809.

In this political cartoon from 1807, a snapping turtle (holding a shipping license) grabs a smuggler in the act of sneaking a barrel of sugar to a British ship. The smuggler cries, "Oh, this cursed Ograbme!" ("Ograbme" is "embargo" spelled backwards.)

Enforcement of the embargo proved very difficult, especially in the states bordering British Canada. Smuggling was widespread; Smugglers' Notch in Vermont, for example, earned its name from illegal trade with British Canada. Jefferson attributed the problems with the embargo to lax enforcement.

At the very end of his second term, Jefferson signed the Non-Intercourse Act of 1808, lifting the unpopular embargoes on trade except with Britain and France. In the election of 1808, American voters elected another Democratic-Republican, James Madison. Madison inherited Jefferson's foreign policy issues involving Britain and France. Most people in the United States, especially those in the West, saw Great Britain as the major problem.

TECUMSEH AND THE WESTERN CONFEDERACY

Another underlying cause of the War of 1812 was British support for native resistance to U.S. western expansion. For many years, white settlers in the American western territories had besieged the Indians living there. Under Jefferson, two Indian policies existed: forcing Indians to adopt American ways of agricultural life, or aggressively driving Indians into debt in order to force them to sell their lands.

In 1809, Tecumseh, a Shawnee war chief, rejuvenated the Western Confederacy. His brother, Tenskwatawa, was a prophet among the Shawnee who urged a revival of native ways and rejection of Anglo-American culture, including alcohol. In 1811, William Henry Harrison, the governor of the Indiana Territory, attempted to eliminate the native presence by attacking Prophetstown, a Shawnee settlement named in honor of Tenskwatawa. In the ensuing Battle of Tippecanoe, U.S. forces led by Harrison destroyed the settlement. They also found ample evidence that the British had supplied the Western Confederacy with weapons, despite the stipulations of earlier treaties.

(a)   (b)

Portrait (a), painted by Charles Bird King in 1820, is a depiction of Shawnee prophet Tenskwatawa. Portrait (b) is Rembrandt Peele's 1813 depiction of William Henry Harrison. What are the significant similarities and differences between the portraits? What was each artist trying to convey?

THE WAR OF 1812

The seizure of American ships and sailors, combined with the British support of Indian resistance, led to strident calls for war against Great Britain. The loudest came from the "war hawks," led by Henry Clay from Kentucky and John C. Calhoun from South Carolina, who would not tolerate British insults to American honor. Opposition to the war came from Federalists, especially those in the Northeast, who knew war would disrupt the maritime trade on which they depended. In a narrow vote, Congress authorized the president to declare war against Britain in June 1812.

The war went very badly for the United States at first. In August 1812, the United States lost Detroit to the British and their Indian allies, including a force of one thousand men led by Tecumseh. By the end of the year, the British controlled half the Northwest. The following year, however, U.S. forces scored several victories. Captain Oliver Hazard Perry and his naval force defeated the British on Lake Erie. At the Battle of the Thames in Ontario, the United States defeated the British and their native allies, and Tecumseh was counted among the dead. Indian resistance began to ebb, opening the Indiana and Michigan territories for white settlement.

These victories could not turn the tide of the war, however. With the British gaining the upper hand during the Napoleonic Wars and Napoleon's French army on the run, Great Britain now could divert skilled combat troops from Europe to fight in the United States. In July 1814, forty-five hundred hardened British soldiers sailed up the Chesapeake Bay and burned Washington, DC, to the ground, forcing President Madison and his wife to run for their lives. According to one report, they left behind a dinner the British officers ate. That summer, the British shelled Baltimore, hoping for another victory. However, they failed to dislodge the U.S. forces, whose survival of the bombardment inspired Francis Scott Key to write "The Star-Spangled Banner."

George Munger painted The President's House shortly after the War of 1812, ca. 1814–1815. The painting shows the result of the British burning of Washington, DC.

Francis Scott Key's "In Defense of Fort McHenry"

After the British bombed Baltimore's Fort McHenry in 1814 but failed to overcome the U.S. forces there, Francis Scott Key was inspired by the sight of the American flag, which remained hanging proudly in the aftermath. He wrote the poem "In Defense of Fort McHenry," which was later set to the tune of a British song called "The Anacreontic Song" and eventually became the U.S. national anthem, "The Star-Spangled Banner."

> Oh, say, can you see, by the dawn's early light,
> What so proudly we hailed at the twilight's last gleaming?
> Whose broad stripes and bright stars, thru the perilous fight,
> O'er the ramparts we watched, were so gallantly streaming?
> And the rockets' red glare, the bombs bursting in air,
> Gave proof through the night that our flag was still there.
> O say, does that star-spangled banner yet wave
> O'er the land of the free and the home of the brave?
>
> On the shore dimly seen through the mists of the deep,
> Where the foe's haughty host in dread silence reposes,
> What is that which the breeze, o'er the towering steep,
> As it fitfully blows, half conceals, half discloses?
> Now it catches the gleam of the morning's first beam,
> In full glory reflected, now shines on the stream:
> Tis the star-spangled banner: O, long may it wave
> O'er the land of the free and the home of the brave!
>
> And where is that band who so vauntingly swore
> That the havoc of war and the battle's confusion

A home and a country should leave us no more?
Their blood has washed out their foul footsteps' pollution.
No refuge could save the hireling and slave
From the terror of flight or the gloom of the grave:
And the star-spangled banner in triumph doth wave
O'er the land of the free and the home of the brave.

O, thus be it ever when freemen shall stand,
Between their loved home and the war's desolation!
Blest with victory and peace, may the heav'n-rescued land
Praise the Power that hath made and preserved us a nation!
Then conquer we must, when our cause it is just,
And this be our motto: "In God is our trust"
And the star-spangled banner in triumph shall wave
O'er the land of the free and the home of the brave!

—Francis Scott Key, "In Defense of Fort McHenry," 1814

What images does Key use to describe the American spirit? Most people are familiar with only the first verse of the song; what do you think the last three verses add?

> Visit the Smithsonian Institute to explore an interactive feature on the flag that inspired "The Star-Spangled Banner," where clickable "hot spots" on the flag reveal elements of its history.

With the end of the war in Europe, Britain was eager to end the conflict in the Americas as well. In 1814, British and U.S. diplomats met in Flanders, in northern Belgium, to negotiate the Treaty of Ghent, signed in December. The boundaries between the United States and British Canada remained as they were before the war, an outcome welcome to those in the United States who feared a rupture in the country's otherwise steady expansion into the West.

The War of 1812 was very unpopular in New England because it inflicted further economic harm on a region dependent on maritime commerce. This unpopularity caused a resurgence of the Federalist Party in New England. Many Federalists deeply resented the power of the slaveholding Virginians (Jefferson and then Madison), who appeared indifferent to their region. The depth of the Federalists' discontent is illustrated by the proceedings of the December 1814 Hartford Convention, a meeting of twenty-six Federalists in Connecticut, where some attendees issued calls for New England to secede from the United States. These arguments for disunion during wartime, combined with the convention's condemnation of the government, made Federalists appear unpatriotic. The convention forever discredited the Federalist Party and led to its downfall.

EPILOGUE: THE BATTLE OF NEW ORLEANS

Due to slow communication, the last battle in the War of 1812 happened after the Treaty of Ghent had been signed ending the war. Andrew Jackson had distinguished himself in the war by defeating the Creek Indians in March 1814 before invading Florida in May of that year. After taking Pensacola, he moved his force of Tennessee fighters to New Orleans to defend the strategic port against British attack.

On January 8, 1815 (despite the official end of the war), a force of battle-tested British veterans of the Napoleonic Wars attempted to take the port. Jackson's forces devastated the British, killing over two thousand. New Orleans and the vast Mississippi River Valley had been successfully defended, ensuring the future of American settlement and commerce. The **Battle of New Orleans** immediately catapulted Jackson to national prominence as a war hero, and in the 1820s, he emerged as the head of the new Democratic Party.

Section Summary

The United States was drawn into its "Second War of Independence" against Great Britain when the British, engaged in the Napoleonic Wars against France, took liberties with the fledgling nation by impressing (capturing) its sailors on the high seas and arming its Indian enemies. The War of 1812 ended with the boundaries of the United Stated remaining as they were before the war. The Indians in the Western Confederacy suffered a significant defeat, losing both their leader Tecumseh and their fight for contested land in the Northwest. The War of 1812 proved to be of great importance because it generated a surge of national pride, with expressions of American identity such as the poem by Francis Scott Key. The United States was unequivocally separate from Britain and could now turn as never before to expansion in the West.

https://www.openassessments.org/assessments/967

Critical Thinking Questions

1. Describe Alexander Hamilton's plans to address the nation's financial woes. Which aspects proved most controversial, and why? What elements of the foundation Hamilton laid can still be found in the system today?
2. Describe the growth of the first party system in the United States. How did these parties come to develop? How did they define themselves, both independently and in opposition to one another? Where did they find themselves in agreement?
3. What led to the passage of the Alien and Sedition Acts? What made them so controversial?
4. What was the most significant impact of the War of 1812?
5. In what ways did the events of this era pose challenges to the U.S. Constitution? What constitutional issues were raised, and how were they addressed?

Attributions

CC licensed content, Shared previously

- US History. **Authored by**: P. Scott Corbett, Volker Janssen, John M. Lund, Todd Pfannestiel, Paul Vickery, and Sylvie Waskiewicz. **Provided by**: OpenStax College. **Located at**: http://openstaxcollege.org/textbooks/us-history. **License**: *CC BY: Attribution*. **License Terms**: Download for free at http://cnx.org/content/col11740/latest/

Primary Source Reading: The Alien and Sedition Acts

The Alien and Sedition Acts were four bills that were passed by the Federalists in the 5th United States Congress and signed into law by President John Adams in 1798, the result of the French Revolution and during an undeclared naval war with France, later known as the Quasi-War. Authored by the Federalists, the laws were purported to strengthen national security, but critics argued that they were primarily an attempt to suppress voters who disagreed with the Federalist party.

The Naturalization Act increased the residency requirement for American citizenship from 5 to 14 years. The Alien Friends Act allowed the president to imprison or deport aliens considered "dangerous to the peace and safety of the United States" at any time, while the Alien Enemies Act authorized the president to do the same to any male citizen of a hostile nation, above the age of 14, during times of war. (At the time, the majority of immigrants supported Thomas Jefferson and the Democratic-Republicans, the political opponents of the Federalists.) Lastly, the controversial Sedition Act restricted speech which was critical of the federal government.

The acts were denounced by Democratic-Republicans and ultimately helped them to victory in the 1800 election, when Thomas Jefferson defeated the incumbent President Adams. The Sedition Act and the Alien Friends Act were allowed to expire in 1800 and 1801, respectively. The Alien Enemies Act, however, remains in effect as 50 USC Sections 21–24. During World War II, it was used to detain, deport and confiscate the property of Japanese, German, Italian, and other Axis nation citizens residing in the United States.

The Sedition Act

Chap. LXXIV.—*An Act in addition to the act, entitled "An act for the punishment of certain crimes against the United States."*

Section 1. *Be it enacted by the Senate and House of Representatives of the United States of America, in Congress assembled*, Penalty on unlawful combinations to oppose the measures of government, &c.
Ante, p. 112.That if any persons shall unlawfully combine or conspire together, with intent to oppose any measure or measures of the government of the United States, which are or shall be directed by proper authority, or to impede the operation of any law of the United States, or to intimidate or prevent any person holding a place or office in or under the government of the United States, from undertaking, performing or executing his trust or duty; And with such intent counselling &c. insurrections, riots, &c.and if any person or persons, with intent as aforesaid, shall counsel, advise or attempt to procure any insurrection, riot, unlawful assembly, or combination, whether such conspiracy, threatening, counsel, advice, or attempt shall have the proposed effect or not, he or they shall be deemed guilty of a high misdemeanor, and on conviction, before any court of the United States having jurisdiction thereof; shall be punished by a fine not exceeding five thousand dollars, and by imprisonment during a term not less than six months nor exceeding five years; and further, at the discretion of the court may be holden to find sureties for his good behaviour in such sum, and for such time, as the said court may direct.

The Sedition Act.

Sec. 2. *And be it further enacted*, Penalty on libelling the governmentThat if any person shall write, print, utter or publish, or shall cause or procure to be written, printed, uttered or published, or shall knowingly and willingly assist or aid in writing, printing, uttering or publishing any false, scandalous and malicious writing or writings against the government of the United States, or either house of the Congress of the United States, or the President of the United States, with intent to defame the said government, or either house of the said Congress, or the said President, or to bring them, or either of them, into contempt or disrepute; or to excite against them, or either or any of them, the hatred of the good people of the United States, or to stir up sedition within the United States, or to excite any unlawful combinations therein, for opposing or resisting any law of the United States, or any act of the President of the United States, done in pursuance of any such law, or of the powers in him vested by the constitution of the United States, or to resist, oppose, or defeat any such law or act, or to aid, encourage or abet any hostile designs of any foreign nation against the United States, their people or government, then such person, being thereof convicted before any court of the United States having jurisdiction thereof, shall be punished by a fine not exceeding two thousand dollars, and by imprisonment not exceeding two years.

Sec. 3. *And be it further enacted and declared*, Truth of the matter may be given in evidence. The jury shall determine the law and the fact, under the court's direction.

Limitation.That if any person shall be prosecuted under this act, for the writing or publishing any libel aforesaid, it shall be lawful for the defendant, upon the trial of the cause, to give in evidence in his defence, the truth of the matter contained in the publication charged as a libel. And the jury who shall try the cause, shall have a right to determine the law and the fact, under the direction of the court, as in other cases.

Sec. 4. *And be it further enacted*, That this act shall continue and be in force until the third day of March, one thousand eight hundred and one, and no longer: *Provided*, that the expiration of the act shall not prevent or defeat a prosecution and punishment of any offence against the law, during the time it shall be in force.

Approved, July 14, 1798.

Attributions

CC licensed content, Shared previously

- Alien and Sedition Acts. **Provided by**: Wikipedia. **Located at**: https://en.wikipedia.org/wiki/Alien_and_Sedition_Acts. **License**: *CC BY-SA: Attribution-ShareAlike*

Public domain content

- United States Statutes at Large/Volume 1/5th Congress/2nd Session/Chapter 74. **Provided by**: Wikisource. **Located at**: https://en.wikisource.org/wiki/United_States_Statutes_at_Large/Volume_1/5th_Congress/2nd_Session/Chapter_74. **License**: *Public Domain: No Known Copyright*

Primary Source Reading: The Star-Spangled Banner

"The Star-Spangled Banner" is the national anthem of the United States of America. The lyrics come from "Defence of Fort M'Henry", a poem written in 1814 by the 35-year-old lawyer and amateur poet Francis Scott Key after witnessing the bombardment of Fort McHenry by British ships of the Royal Navy in the Chesapeake Bay during the Battle of Fort McHenry in the War of 1812.

The poem was set to the tune of a popular British song written by John Stafford Smith for the Anacreontic Society, a men's social club in London. "To Anacreon in Heaven" (or "The Anacreontic Song"), with various lyrics, was already popular in the United States. Set to Key's poem and renamed "The Star-Spangled Banner", it would soon become a well-known American patriotic song. With a range of one octave and one fifth (a semitone more than an octave and a half), it is known for being difficult to sing. Although the poem has four stanzas, only the first is commonly sung today.

"The Star-Spangled Banner" was recognized for official use by the U.S. Navy in 1889, and by U.S. President Woodrow Wilson in 1916, and was made the national anthem by a congressional resolution on March 3, 1931 (46 Stat. 1508, codified at 36 U.S.C. § 301), which was signed by President Herbert Hoover.

Before 1931, other songs served as the hymns of American officialdom. "Hail, Columbia" served this purpose at official functions for most of the 19th century. "My Country, 'Tis of Thee", whose melody is identical to "God Save the Queen", the British national anthem,[2] also served as a de facto anthem.[3] Following the War of 1812 and subsequent American wars, other songs emerged to compete for popularity at public events, among them "The Star-Spangled Banner".

One of two surviving copies of the 1812 broadside printing of the Defense of Fort McHenry, a poem that later became the national anthem of the United States.

Text of the Star-Spangled Banner

O! say can you see by the dawn's early light,

What so proudly we hailed at the twilight's last gleaming,

Whose broad stripes and bright stars through the perilous fight,

O'er the ramparts we watch'd, were so gallantly streaming?

And the Rockets' red glare, the Bombs bursting in air,

Gave proof through the night that our Flag was still there;

O! say does that star-spangled Banner yet wave,

O'er the Land of the free and the home of the brave?

On the shore dimly seen through the mists of the deep,

Where the foe's haughty host in dread silence reposes,

What is that which the breeze, o'er the towering steep,

As it fitfully blows, half conceals, half discloses?

Now it catches the gleam of the morning's first beam,

In full glory reflected now shines on the stream,

'Tis the star-spangled banner, O! long may it wave

O'er the land of the free and the home of the brave.

And where is that band who so vauntingly swore

That the havoc of war and the battle's confusion,

A home and a country should leave us no more?

Their blood has washed out their foul footsteps pollution.

No refuge could save the hireling and slave,

From the terror of flight, or the gloom of the grave,

And the star-spangled banner in triumph doth wave,

O'er the Land of the Free and the Home of the Brave.

O! thus be it ever, when freemen shall stand,

Between their lov'd home and the war's desolation,

Blest with vict'ry and peace, may the Heav'n rescued land,

Praise the Power that hath made and preserv'd us a nation!

Then conquer we must, when our cause it is just,

And this be our motto—"In God is our Trust;"

And the star-spangled Banner in triumph shall wave,

O'er the Land of the Free and the Home of the Brave.

This *1814 copy of "The Star-Spangled Banner"* was the first printed edition to combine the words and sheet music.

Attributions

CC licensed content, Shared previously

- The Star-Spangled Banner. **Provided by**: Wikipedia. **Located at**: *https://en.wikipedia.org/wiki/The_Star-Spangled_Banner*. **License**: *CC BY-SA: Attribution-ShareAlike*

9. Industrial Transformation in the North: 1800-1850

Introduction

By the 1830s, the United States had developed a thriving industrial and commercial sector in the Northeast. Farmers embraced regional and distant markets as the primary destination for their products. Artisans witnessed the methodical division of the labor process in factories. Wage labor became an increasingly common experience. These industrial and market revolutions, combined with advances in transportation, transformed the economic and social landscape. Americans could now quickly produce larger amounts of goods for a nationwide, and sometimes an international, market and rely less on foreign imports than in colonial times.

As American economic life shifted rapidly and modes of production changed, new class divisions emerged and solidified, resulting in previously unknown economic and social inequalities. This image of the Five Points district in New York City

Five Points (1827), by George Catlin, depicts the infamous Five Points neighborhood of New York City, so called because it was centered at the intersection of five streets. Five Points was home to a polyglot mix of recent immigrants, freed slaves, and other members of the working class.

captures the turbulence of the time. Five Points began as a settlement for freed slaves, but it soon became a crowded urban world of American day laborers and low-wage workers who lived a precarious existence that the economic benefits of the new economy largely bypassed. An influx of immigrant workers swelled and diversified an already crowded urban population. By the 1830s, the area had become a slum, home to widespread poverty, crime, and disease. Advances in industrialization and the market revolution came at a human price.

Attributions

CC *licensed content, Shared previously*

- US History. **Authored by**: P. Scott Corbett, Volker Janssen, John M. Lund, Todd Pfannestiel, Paul Vickery, and Sylvie Waskiewicz. **Provided by**: OpenStax College. **Located at**: http://openstaxcollege.org/textbooks/us-history. **License**: CC BY: Attribution. **License Terms**: Download for free at http://cnx.org/content/col11740/latest/

Early Industrialization in the Northeast

Learning Objectives

By the end of this section, you will be able to:

- Explain the role of the putting-out system in the rise of industrialization
- Understand industrialization's impact on the nature of production and work
- Describe the effect of industrialization on consumption
- Identify the goals of workers' organizations like the Working Men's Party

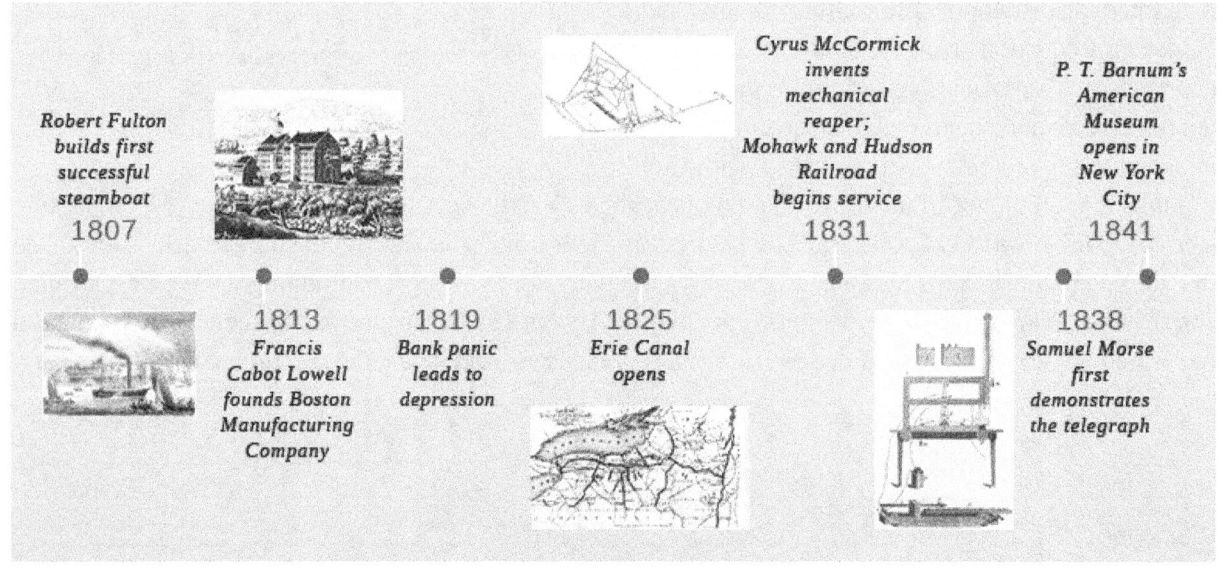

(credit "1807 photo": Project Gutenberg Archives)

Northern industrialization expanded rapidly following the War of 1812. Industrialized manufacturing began in New England, where wealthy merchants built water-powered textile mills (and mill towns to support them) along the rivers of the Northeast. These mills introduced new modes of production centralized within the confines of the mill itself. As never before, production relied on mechanized sources with water power, and later steam, to provide the force necessary to drive machines. In addition to the mechanization and centralization of work in the mills, specialized, repetitive tasks assigned to wage laborers replaced earlier modes of handicraft production done by artisans at home. The operations of these mills irrevocably changed the nature of work by deskilling tasks, breaking down the process of production to its most basic, elemental parts. In return for their labor, the workers, who at first were young women from rural New England farming families, received wages. From its origin in New England, manufacturing soon spread to other regions of the United States.

FROM ARTISANS TO WAGE WORKERS

During the seventeenth and eighteenth centuries, **artisans**—skilled, experienced craft workers—produced goods by hand. The production of shoes provides a good example. In colonial times, people bought their shoes from master shoemakers, who achieved their status by living and working as apprentices under the rule of an older master artisan. An apprenticeship would be followed by work as a journeyman (a skilled worker without his own shop). After sufficient time as a journeyman, a shoemaker could at last set up his own shop as a master artisan. People came to the shop, usually attached to the back of the master artisan's house, and there the shoemaker measured their feet in order to cut and stitch together an individualized product for each customer.

In the late eighteenth and early nineteenth century, merchants in the Northeast and elsewhere turned their attention as never before to the benefits of using unskilled wage labor to make a greater profit by reducing labor costs. They used the **putting-out system**, which the British had employed at the beginning of their own Industrial Revolution, whereby they hired farming families to perform specific tasks in the production process for a set wage. In the case of shoes, for instance, American merchants hired one group of workers to cut soles into standardized sizes. A different group of families cut pieces of leather for the uppers, while still another was employed to stitch the standardized parts together.

This process proved attractive because it whittled production costs. The families who participated in the putting-out system were not skilled artisans. They had not spent years learning and perfecting their craft and did not have ambitious journeymen to pay. Therefore, they could not demand—and did not receive—high wages. Most of the year they tended fields and orchards, ate the food that they produced, and sold the surplus. Putting-out work proved a welcome source of extra income for New England farm families who saw their profits dwindle from new competition from midwestern farms with higher-yield lands.

Much of this part-time production was done under contract to merchants. Some farming families engaged in shoemaking (or shoe assemblage), as noted above. Many made brooms, plaited hats from straw or palm leaves (which merchants imported from Cuba and the West Indies), crafted furniture, made pottery, or wove baskets. Some, especially those who lived in Connecticut, made parts for clocks. The most common part-time occupation, however, was the manufacture of textiles. Farm women spun woolen thread and wove fabric. They also wove blankets, made rugs, and knit stockings. All this manufacturing took place on the farm, giving farmers and their wives control over the timing and pace of their labor. Their domestic productivity increased the quantity of goods available for sale in country towns and nearby cities.

THE RISE OF MANUFACTURING

In the late 1790s and early 1800s, Great Britain boasted the most advanced textile mills and machines in the world, and the United States continued to rely on Great Britain for finished goods. Great Britain hoped to maintain its economic advantage over its former colonies in North America. So, in an effort to prevent the knowledge of advanced manufacturing from leaving the Empire, the British banned the emigration of mechanics, skilled workers who knew how to build and repair the latest textile machines.

Some skilled British mechanics, including Samuel Slater, managed to travel to the United States in the hopes of profiting from their knowledge and experience with advanced textile manufacturing. Slater understood the workings of the latest water-powered textile mills, which British industrialist Richard Arkwright had pioneered. In the 1790s in Pawtucket, Rhode Island, Slater convinced several American merchants, including the wealthy Providence industrialist Moses Brown, to finance and build a water-powered cotton mill based on the British models. Slater's knowledge of both technology and mill organization made him the founder of the first truly successful cotton mill in the United States.

Samuel Slater (a) was a British migrant who brought plans for English textile mills to the United States and built the nation's first successful water-powered mill in Pawtucket, Massachusetts (b).

The success of Slater and his partners Smith Brown and William Almy, relatives of Moses Brown, inspired others to build additional mills in Rhode Island and Massachusetts. By 1807, thirteen more mills had been established. President Jefferson's embargo on British manufactured goods from late 1807 to early 1809 (discussed in a previous chapter) spurred more New England merchants to invest in industrial enterprises. By 1812, seventy-eight new textile mills had been built in rural New England towns. More than half turned out woolen goods, while the rest produced cotton cloth.

Slater's mills and those built in imitation of his were fairly small, employing only seventy people on average. Workers were organized the way that they had been in English factories, in family units. Under the **"Rhode Island system,"** families were hired. The father was placed in charge of the family unit, and he directed the labor of his wife and children. Instead of being paid in cash, the father was given "credit" equal to the extent of his family's labor that could be redeemed in the form of rent (of company-owned housing) or goods from the company-owned store.

The Embargo of 1807 and the War of 1812 played a pivotal role in spurring industrial development in the United States. Jefferson's embargo prevented American merchants from engaging in the Atlantic trade, severely cutting into their profits. The War of 1812 further compounded the financial woes of American merchants. The acute economic problems led some New England merchants, including Francis Cabot Lowell, to cast their gaze on manufacturing. Lowell had toured English mills during a stay in Great Britain. He returned to Massachusetts having memorized the designs for the advanced textile machines he had seen in his travels, especially the power loom, which replaced individual hand weavers. Lowell convinced other wealthy merchant families to invest in the creation of new mill towns. In 1813, Lowell and these wealthy investors, known as the Boston Associates, created the Boston Manufacturing Company. Together they raised $400,000 and, in 1814, established a textile mill in Waltham and a second one in the same town shortly thereafter.

At Waltham, cotton was carded and drawn into coarse strands of cotton fibers called rovings. The rovings were then spun into yarn, and the yarn woven into cotton cloth. Yarn no longer had to be put out to farm families for further processing. All the work was now performed at a central location—the factory.

The work in Lowell's mills was both mechanized and specialized. Specialization meant the work was broken down into specific tasks, and workers repeatedly did the one task assigned to them in the course of a day. As machines took over labor from humans and people increasingly found themselves confined to the same repetitive step, the process of **deskilling** began.

The Boston Manufacturing Company, shown in this engraving made in 1813–1816, was headquartered in Waltham, Massachusetts. The company started the northeastern textile industry by building water-powered textile mills along suitable rivers and developing mill towns around them.

The Boston Associates' mills, which each employed hundreds of workers, were located in company towns, where the factories and worker housing were owned by a single company. This gave the owners and their agents control over their workers. The most famous of these company towns was Lowell, Massachusetts. The new town was built on land the Boston Associates purchased in 1821 from the village of East Chelmsford at the falls of the Merrimack River, north of Boston. The mill buildings themselves were constructed of red brick with large windows to let in light. Company-owned boarding houses to shelter employees were constructed near the mills. The mill owners planted flowers and trees to maintain the appearance of a rural New England town and to forestall arguments, made by many, that factory work was unnatural and unwholesome.

In contrast to many smaller mills, the Boston Associates' enterprises avoided the Rhode Island system, preferring individual workers to families. These employees were not difficult to find. The competition New England farmers faced from farmers now settling in the West, and the growing scarcity of land in population-dense New England, had important implications for farmers' children. Realizing their chances of inheriting a large farm or receiving a substantial dowry were remote, these teenagers sought other employment opportunities, often at the urging of their parents. While young men could work at a variety of occupations, young women had more limited options. The textile mills provided suitable employment for the daughters of Yankee farm families.

Needing to reassure anxious parents that their daughters' virtue would be protected and hoping to avoid what they viewed as the problems of industrialization—filth and vice—the Boston Associates established strict rules governing the lives of these young workers. The women lived in company-owned boarding houses to which they paid a portion of their wages. They woke early at the sound of a bell and worked a twelve-hour day during which talking was forbidden. They could not swear or drink alcohol, and they were required to attend church on Sunday. Overseers at the mills and boarding-house keepers kept a close eye on the young women's behavior; workers who associated with people of questionable reputation or acted in ways that called their virtue into question lost their jobs and were evicted.

Michel Chevalier on Mill Worker Rules and Wages

In the 1830s, the French government sent engineer and economist Michel Chevalier to study industrial and financial affairs in Mexico and the United States. In 1839, he published *Society, Manners, and Politics in the United States*, in which he recorded his impressions of the Lowell textile mills. In the excerpt below, Chevalier describes the rules and wages of the Lawrence Company in 1833.

> All persons employed by the Company must devote themselves assiduously to their duty during working-hours. They must be capable of doing the work which they undertake, or use all their efforts to this effect. They must on all occasions, both in their words and in their actions, show that they are penetrated by a laudable love of temperance and virtue, and animated by a sense of their moral and social obligations. The Agent of the Company shall endeavour to set to all a good example in this respect. Every individual who shall be notoriously dissolute, idle, dishonest, or intemperate, who shall be in the practice of absenting himself from divine service, or shall violate the Sabbath, or shall be addicted to gaming, shall be dismissed from the service of the Company. . . . All ardent spirits are banished from the Company's grounds, except when prescribed by a physician. All games of hazard and cards are prohibited within their limits and in the boarding-houses.
>
> Weekly wages were as follows:
> For picking and carding, $2.78 to $3.10
> For spinning, $3.00
> For weaving, $3.10 to $3.12
> For warping and sizing, $3.45 to $4.00
> For measuring and folding, $3.12

What kind of world were the factory owners trying to create with these rules? How do you think those who believed all white people were born free and equal would react to them?

> Visit the Textile Industry History site to explore the mills of New England through its collection of history, images, and ephemera.

The mechanization of formerly handcrafted goods, and the removal of production from the home to the factory, dramatically increased output of goods. For example, in one nine-month period, the numerous Rhode Island women who spun yarn into cloth on hand looms in their homes produced a total of thirty-four thousand yards of fabrics of different types. In 1855, the women working in just one of Lowell's mechanized mills produced more than forty-three thousand yards.

The Boston Associates' cotton mills quickly gained a competitive edge over the smaller mills established by Samuel Slater and those who had imitated him. Their success prompted the Boston Associates to expand. In Massachusetts, in addition to Lowell, they built new mill towns in Chicopee, Lawrence, and Holyoke. In New Hampshire, they built them in Manchester, Dover, and Nashua. And in Maine, they built a large mill in Saco on the Saco River. Other entrepreneurs copied them. By the time of the Civil War, 878 textile factories had been built in New England. All together, these factories employed more than 100,000 people and produced more than 940 million yards of cloth.

Success in New England was repeated elsewhere. Small mills, more like those in Rhode Island than those in northern Massachusetts, New Hampshire, and Maine, were built in New York, Delaware, and Pennsylvania. By midcentury, three hundred textile mills were located in and near Philadelphia. Many produced specialty goods, such as silks and printed fabrics, and employed skilled workers, including people working in their own homes. Even in the South, the region that otherwise relied on slave labor to produce the very cotton that fed the northern factory movement, more than two hundred textile mills were built. Most textiles, however, continued to be produced in New England before the Civil War.

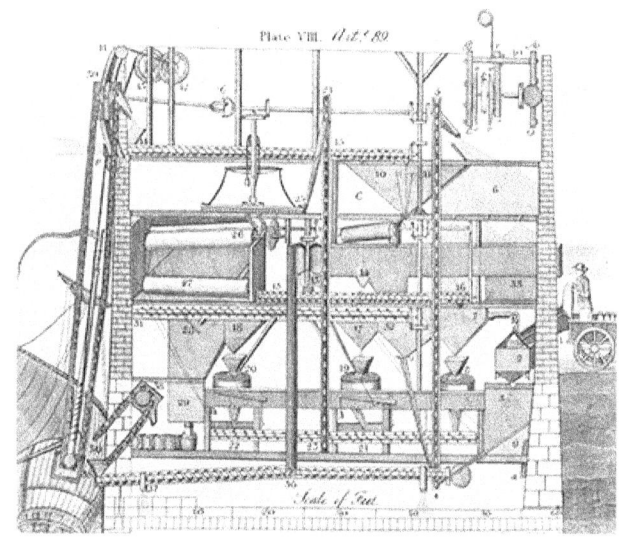

Oliver Evans was an American engineer and inventor, best known for developing ways to automate the flour milling process, which is illustrated here in a drawing from a 1785 instructional book called The Young Mill-Wright & Miller's Guide.

Alongside the production of cotton and woolen cloth, which formed the backbone of the Industrial Revolution in the United States as in Britain, other crafts increasingly became mechanized and centralized in factories in the first half of the nineteenth century. Shoe making, leather tanning, papermaking, hat making, clock making, and gun making had all become mechanized to one degree or another by the time of the Civil War. Flour milling, because of the inventions of Oliver Evans, had become almost completely automated and centralized by the early decades of the nineteenth century. So efficient were Evans-style mills that two employees were able to do work that had originally required five, and mills using Evans's system spread throughout the mid-Atlantic states.

THE RISE OF CONSUMERISM

At the end of the eighteenth century, most American families lived in candlelit homes with bare floors and unadorned walls, cooked and warmed themselves over fireplaces, and owned few changes of clothing. All manufactured goods were made by hand and, as a result, were usually scarce and fairly expensive.

The automation of the manufacturing process changed that, making consumer goods that had once been thought of as luxury items widely available for the first time. Now all but the very poor could afford the necessities and some of the small luxuries of life. Rooms were lit by oil lamps, which gave brighter light than candles. Homes were heated by parlor stoves, which allowed for more privacy; people no longer needed to huddle together around the hearth. Iron cookstoves with multiple burners made it possible for housewives to prepare more elaborate meals. Many people could afford carpets and upholstered furniture, and even farmers could decorate their homes with curtains and wallpaper. Clocks, which had once been quite expensive, were now within the reach of most ordinary people.

THE WORK EXPERIENCE TRANSFORMED

As production became mechanized and relocated to factories, the experience of workers underwent significant changes. Farmers and artisans had controlled the pace of their labor and the order in which things were done. If an artisan wanted to take the afternoon off, he could. If a farmer wished to rebuild his fence on Thursday instead of on Wednesday, he could. They conversed and often drank during the workday. Indeed, journeymen were often promised alcohol as part of their wages. One member of the group might be asked to read a book or a newspaper aloud to the others. In the warm weather, doors and windows might be opened to the outside, and work stopped when it was too dark to see.

Work in factories proved to be quite different. Employees were expected to report at a certain time, usually early in the morning, and to work all day. They could not leave when they were tired or take breaks other than at designated times. Those who arrived late found their pay docked; five minutes' tardiness could result in several hours' worth of lost pay, and repeated tardiness could result in dismissal. The monotony of repetitive tasks made days particularly long. Hours varied according to the factory, but most factory employees toiled ten to twelve hours a day, six days a week. In the winter, when the sun set early, oil lamps were used to light the factory floor, and employees strained their eyes to see their work and coughed as the rooms filled with smoke from the lamps. In the spring, as the days began to grow longer, factories held "blowing-out" celebrations to mark the extinguishing of the oil lamps. These "blow-outs" often featured processions and dancing.

Freedom within factories was limited. Drinking was prohibited. Some factories did not allow employees to sit down. Doors and windows were kept closed, especially in textile factories where fibers could be easily disturbed by incoming breezes, and mills were often unbearably hot and humid in the summer. In the winter, workers often shivered in the cold. In such environments, workers' health suffered.

The workplace posed other dangers as well. The presence of cotton bales alongside the oil used to lubricate machines made fire a common problem in textile factories. Workplace injuries were also common. Workers' hands and fingers were maimed or severed when they were caught in machines; in some cases, their limbs or entire bodies were crushed. Workers who didn't die from such injuries almost certainly lost their jobs, and with them, their income. Corporal punishment of both children and adults was common in factories; where abuse was most extreme, children sometimes died as a result of injuries suffered at the hands of an overseer.

As the decades passed, working conditions deteriorated in many mills. Workers were assigned more machines to tend, and the owners increased the speed at which the machines operated. Wages were cut in many factories, and employees who had once labored for an hourly wage now found themselves reduced to piecework, paid for the amount they produced and not for the hours they toiled. Owners also reduced compensation for piecework. Low wages combined with regular periods of unemployment to make the lives of workers difficult, especially for those with families to support. In New York City in 1850, for example, the average male worker earned $300 a year; it cost approximately $600 a year to support a family of five.

WORKERS AND THE LABOR MOVEMENT

Many workers undoubtedly enjoyed some of the new wage opportunities factory work presented. For many of the young New England women who ran the machines in Waltham, Lowell, and elsewhere, the experience of being away from the family was exhilarating and provided a sense of solidarity among them. Though most sent a large portion of their wages home, having even a small amount of money of their own was a liberating experience, and many used their earnings to purchase clothes, ribbons, and other consumer goods for themselves.

The long hours, strict discipline, and low wages, however, soon led workers to organize to protest their working conditions and pay. In 1821, the young women employed by the Boston Manufacturing Company in Waltham went on strike for two days when their wages were cut. In 1824, workers in Pawtucket struck to protest reduced pay rates and longer hours, the latter of which had been achieved by cutting back the amount of time allowed for meals. Similar strikes occurred at Lowell and in other mill towns like Dover, New Hampshire, where the women employed by the Cocheco Manufacturing Company ceased working in December 1828 after their wages were reduced. In the 1830s, female mill operatives in Lowell formed the Lowell Factory Girls Association to organize strike activities in the face of wage cuts and, later, established the Lowell Female Labor Reform Association to protest the twelve-hour workday. Even though strikes were rarely successful and workers usually were forced to accept reduced wages and increased hours, work stoppages as a form of labor protest represented the beginnings of the labor movement in the United States.

New England mill workers were often young women, as seen in this early tintype made ca. 1870 (a). When management proposed rent increases for those living in company boarding houses, female textile workers in Lowell responded by forming the Lowell Factory Girls Association—its constitution is shown in image (b)—in 1836 and organizing a "turn-out" or strike.

Critics of industrialization blamed it for the increased concentration of wealth in the hands of the few: the factory owners made vast profits while the workers received only a small fraction of the revenue from what they produced. Under the **labor theory of value**, said critics, the value of a product should accurately reflect the labor needed to produce it. Profits from the sale of goods produced by workers should be distributed so laborers recovered in the form of wages the value their effort had added to the finished product. While factory owners, who contributed the workspace, the machinery, and the raw materials needed to create a product, should receive a share of the profits, their share should not be greater than the value of their contribution. Workers should thus receive a much larger portion of the profits than they currently did, and factory owners should receive less.

In Philadelphia, New York, and Boston—all cities that experienced dizzying industrial growth during the nineteenth century—workers united to form political parties. Thomas Skidmore, from Connecticut, was the outspoken organizer of the **Working Men's Party**, which lodged a radical protest against the exploitation of workers that accompanied industrialization. Skidmore took his cue from Thomas Paine and the American Revolution to challenge the growing inequity in the United States. He argued that inequality originated in the unequal distribution of property through inheritance laws. In his 1829 treatise, *The Rights of Man to Property*, Skidmore called for the abolition of inheritance and the redistribution of property. The Working Men's Party also advocated the end of imprisonment for debt, a common practice whereby the debtor who could not pay was put in jail and his tools and property, if any, were confiscated. Skidmore's vision of radical equality extended to all; women and men, no matter their race, should be allowed to vote and receive property, he believed. Skidmore died in 1832 when a cholera epidemic swept New York City, but the state of New York did away with imprisonment for debt in the same year.

Worker activism became less common in the late 1840s and 1850s. As German and Irish immigrants poured into the United States in the decades preceding the Civil War, native-born laborers found themselves competing for jobs with new arrivals who were willing to work longer hours for less pay. In Lowell, Massachusetts, for example, the daughters of New England farmers encountered competition from the daughters of Irish farmers suffering the effects of the potato famine; these immigrant women were willing to work for far less and endure worse conditions than native-born women. Many of these native-born "daughters of freemen," as they referred to themselves, left the factories and returned to their families. Not all wage workers had this luxury, however. Widows with children to support and girls from destitute families had no choice but to stay and accept the faster pace and lower pay. Male German and Irish immigrants competed with native-born men. Germans, many of whom were skilled workers, took jobs in furniture making. The Irish provided a ready source of unskilled labor needed to lay railroad track and dig canals. American men with families to support grudgingly accepted low wages in order to keep their jobs. As work became increasingly deskilled, no worker was irreplaceable, and no one's job was safe.

Section Summary

Industrialization led to radical changes in American life. New industrial towns, like Waltham, Lowell, and countless others, dotted the landscape of the Northeast. The mills provided many young women an opportunity to experience a new and liberating life, and these workers relished their new freedom. Workers also gained a greater appreciation of the value of their work and, in some instances, began to question the basic fairness of the new industrial order. The world of work had been fundamentally reorganized.

https://www.openassessments.org/assessments/968

Review Question

1. What effect did industrialization have on consumers?

Answer to Review Question

1. Industrialization made manufactured goods more abundant and more widely available. All but the poorest Americans were able to equip their homes with cookstoves, parlor stoves, upholstered furniture, and decorations such as wallpaper and window curtains. Even such formerly expensive goods as clocks were now affordable for most.

Glossary

artisan skilled, experienced worker who produces specialized goods by hand

deskilling breaking an artisanal production process into smaller steps that unskilled workers can perform

labor theory of value an economic theory holding that profits from the sale of the goods produced by workers should be equitably distributed to those workers

putting-out system a labor system whereby a merchant hired different families to perform specific tasks in a production process

Working Men's Party a political group that radically opposed what they viewed as the exploitation of workers

Attributions

CC licensed content, Shared previously

- US History. **Authored by**: P. Scott Corbett, Volker Janssen, John M. Lund, Todd Pfannestiel, Paul Vickery, and Sylvie Waskiewicz. **Provided by**: OpenStax College. **Located at**: http://openstaxcollege.org/textbooks/us-history. **License**: *CC BY: Attribution*. **License Terms**: Download for free at http://cnx.org/content/col11740/latest/

A Vibrant Capitalist Republic

> **Learning Objectives**
>
> By the end of this section, you will be able to:
>
> - Explain the process of selling western land
> - Discuss the causes of the Panic of 1819
> - Identify key American innovators and inventors

By the 1840s, the United States economy bore little resemblance to the import-and-export economy of colonial days. It was now a market economy, one in which the production of goods, and their prices, were unregulated by the government. Commercial centers, to which job seekers flocked, mushroomed. New York City's population skyrocketed. In 1790, it was 33,000; by 1820, it had reached 200,000; and by 1825, it had swelled to 270,000. New opportunities for wealth appeared to be available to anyone.

However, the expansion of the American economy made it prone to the boom-and-bust cycle. Market economies involve fluctuating prices for labor, raw materials, and consumer goods and depend on credit and financial instruments—any one of which can be the source of an imbalance and an economic downturn in which businesses and farmers default, wage workers lose their employment, and investors lose their assets. This happened for the first time in the United States in 1819, when waves of enthusiastic speculation (expectations of rapidly rising prices) in land and commodities gave way to drops in prices.

THE LAND OFFICE BUSINESS

In the early nineteenth century, people poured into the territories west of the long-settled eastern seaboard. Among them were speculators seeking to buy cheap parcels from the federal government in anticipation of a rise in prices. The Ohio Country in the Northwest Territory appeared to offer the best prospects for many in the East, especially New Englanders. The result was "Ohio fever," as thousands traveled there to reap the benefits of settling in this newly available territory.

The federal government oversaw the orderly transfer of public land to citizens at public auctions. The Land Law of 1796 applied to the territory of Ohio after it had been wrested from Indians. Under this law, the United States would sell a minimum parcel of 640 acres for $2 an acre. The Land Law of 1800 further encouraged land sales in the Northwest Territory by reducing the minimum parcel size by half and enabling sales on credit, with the goal of stimulating settlement by ordinary farmers.

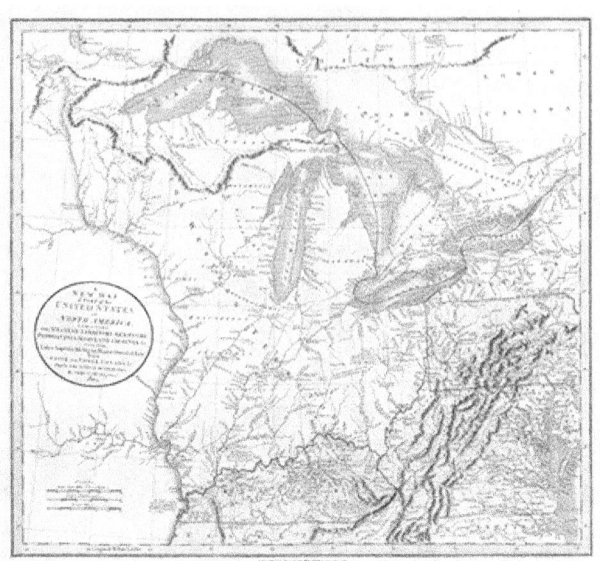

Cartographer John Cary drew this map "exhibiting The Western Territory, Kentucky, Pennsylvania, Maryland, Virginia &c" for his 1808 atlas; it depicted the huge western territory that fascinated settlers in the early nineteenth century.

The government created **land offices** to handle these sales and established them in the West within easy reach of prospective landowners. They could thus purchase land directly from the government, at the price the government had set. Buyers were given low interest rates, with payments that could be spread over four years. Surveyors marked off the parcels in straight lines, creating a landscape of checkerboard squares.

The future looked bright for those who turned their gaze on the land in the West. Surveying, settling, and farming, turning the wilderness into a profitable commodity, gave purchasers a sense of progress. A uniquely American story of settling the land developed: hardy individuals wielding an axe cleared it, built a log cabin, and turned the frontier into a farm that paved the way for mills and towns.

Thomas Cole, who painted Home in the Woods in 1847, was an American artist. Cole founded the Hudson River School, a style renowned for portrayals of landscapes and wilderness influenced by the emotional aesthetic known as romanticism. In what ways is this image realistic, and how is it idealized or romanticized?

A New Englander Heads West

A native of Vermont, Gershom Flagg was one of thousands of New Englanders who caught "Ohio fever." In this letter to his brother, Azariah Flagg, dated August 3, 1817, he describes the hustle and bustle of the emerging commercial town of Cincinnati.

> DEAR BROTHER,
>
> Cincinnati is an incorporated City. It contained in 1815, 1,100 buildings of different descriptions among which are above 20 of Stone 250 of brick & 800 of Wood. The population in 1815 was 6,500. There are about 60 Mercantile stores several of which are wholesale. Here are a great share of Mechanics of all kinds.
>
> Here is one Woolen Factory four Cotton factories but not now in operation. A most stupendously large building of Stone is likewise erected immediately on the bank of the River for a steam Mill. It is nine stories high at the Waters edge & is 87 by 62 feet. It drives four pair of Stones besides various other Machinery as Wool carding &c &c. There is also a valuable Steam Saw Mill driving four saws also an inclined Wheel ox Saw Mill with two saws, one Glass Factory. The town is Rapidly increasing in Wealth & population. Here is a Branch of the United States Bank and three other banks & two Printing offices. The country around is rich. . . .
>
> That you may all be prospered in the world is the anxious wish of your affectionate Brother
>
> GERSHOM FLAGG

What caught Flagg's attention? From your reading of this letter and study of the engraving below, what impression can you take away of Cincinnati in 1817?

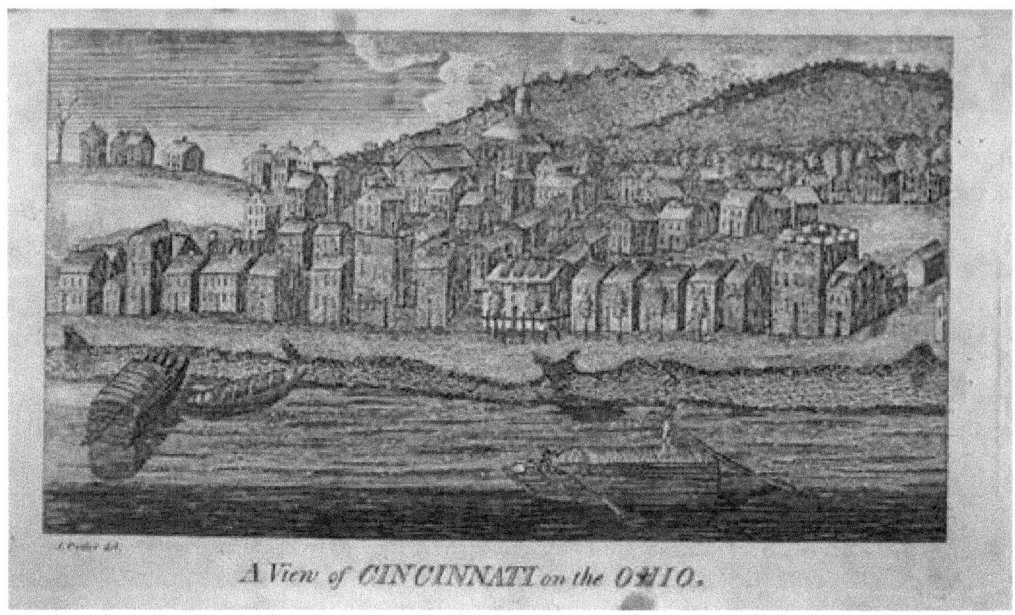

This engraving from A Topographical Description of the State of Ohio, Indiana Territory, and Louisiana (1812), by Jervis Cutler, presents a view of Cincinnati as it may have looked to Gershom Flagg.

> Learn more about settlement of and immigration to the Northwest Territory by exploring the National Park Service's Historic Resource Study related to the Lincoln Boyhood National Memorial. According to the guide's maps, what lands were available for purchase?

THE PANIC OF 1819

The first major economic crisis in the United States after the War of 1812 was due, in large measure, to factors in the larger Atlantic economy. It was made worse, however, by land speculation and poor banking practices at home. British textile mills voraciously consumed American cotton, and the devastation of the Napoleonic Wars made Europe reliant on other American agricultural commodities such as wheat. This drove up both the price of American agricultural products and the value of the land on which staples such as cotton, wheat, corn, and tobacco were grown.

Many Americans were struck with "**land fever**." Farmers strove to expand their acreage, and those who lived in areas where unoccupied land was scarce sought holdings in the West. They needed money to purchase this land, however. Small merchants and factory owners, hoping to take advantage of this boom time, also sought to borrow money to expand their businesses. When existing banks refused to lend money to small farmers and others without a credit history, state legislatures chartered new banks to meet the demand. In one legislative session, Kentucky chartered forty-six. As loans increased, paper money from new state banks flooded the country, creating inflation that drove the price of land and goods still higher. This, in turn, encouraged even more people to borrow money with which to purchase land or to expand or start their own businesses. Speculators took advantage of this boom in the sale of land by purchasing property not to live on, but to buy cheaply and resell at exorbitant prices.

During the War of 1812, the Bank of the United States had suspended payments in **specie**, "hard money" usually in the form of gold and silver coins. When the war ended, the bank continued to issue only paper banknotes and to redeem notes issued by state banks with paper only. The newly chartered banks also adopted this practice, issuing banknotes in excess of the amount of specie in their vaults. This shaky economic scheme worked only so long as people were content to conduct business with paper money and refrain from demanding that banks instead give them the gold and silver that was supposed to back it. If large numbers of people, or banks that had loaned money to other banks, began to demand specie payments, the banking system would collapse, because there was no longer enough specie to support the amount of paper money the banks had put into circulation. So terrified were bankers that customers would demand gold and silver that an irate bank employee in Ohio stabbed a customer who had the audacity to ask for specie in exchange for the banknotes he held.

In an effort to bring stability to the nation's banking system, Congress chartered the Second Bank of the United States (a revival of Alexander Hamilton's national bank) in 1816. But this new institution only compounded the problem by making risky loans, opening branches in the South and West where land fever was highest, and issuing a steady stream of Bank of the United States notes, a move that increased inflation and speculation.

The inflated economic bubble burst in 1819, resulting in a prolonged economic depression or severe downturn in the economy called the Panic of 1819. It was the first economic depression experienced by the American public, who panicked as they saw the prices of agricultural products fall and businesses fail. Prices had already begun falling in 1815, at the end of the Napoleonic Wars, when Britain began to "dump" its surplus manufactured goods, the result of wartime overproduction, in American ports, where they were sold for low prices and competed with American-manufactured goods. In 1818, to make the economic situation worse, prices for American agricultural products began to fall both in the United States and in Europe; the overproduction of staples such as wheat and cotton coincided with the recovery of European agriculture, which reduced demand for American crops. Crop prices tumbled by as much 75 percent.

This dramatic decrease in the value of agricultural goods left farmers unable to pay their debts. As they defaulted on their loans, banks seized their property. However, because the drastic fall in agricultural prices had greatly reduced the value of land, the banks were left with farms they were unable to sell. Land speculators lost the value of their investments. As the countryside suffered, hard-hit farmers ceased to purchase manufactured goods. Factories responded by cutting wages or firing employees.

In 1818, the Second Bank of the United States needed specie to pay foreign investors who had loaned money to the United States to enable the country to purchase Louisiana. The bank began to call in the loans it had made and required that state banks pay their debts in gold and silver. State banks that could not collect loan payments from hard-pressed farmers could not, in turn, meet their obligations to the Second Bank of the United States. Severe consequences followed as banks closed their doors and businesses failed. Three-quarters of the work force in Philadelphia was unemployed, and charities were swamped by thousands of newly destitute people needing assistance. In states with imprisonment for debt, the prison population swelled. As a result, many states drafted laws to provide relief for debtors. Even those at the top of the social ladder were affected by the Panic of 1819. Thomas Jefferson, who had cosigned a loan for a friend, nearly lost Monticello when his acquaintance defaulted, leaving Jefferson responsible for the debt.

In an effort to stimulate the economy in the midst of the economic depression, Congress passed several acts modifying land sales. The Land Law of 1820 lowered the price of land to $1.25 per acre and allowed small parcels of eighty acres to be sold. The Relief Act of 1821 allowed Ohioans to return land to the government if they could not afford to keep it. The money they received in return was credited toward their debt. The act also extended the credit period to eight years. States, too, attempted to aid those faced with economic hard times by passing laws to prevent mortgage foreclosures so buyers could keep their homes. Americans made the best of the opportunities presented in business, in farming, or on the frontier, and by 1823 the Panic of 1819 had ended. The recovery provided ample evidence of the vibrant and resilient nature of the American people.

ENTREPRENEURS AND INVENTORS

The volatility of the U.S. economy did nothing to dampen the creative energies of its citizens in the years before the Civil War. In the 1800s, a frenzy of entrepreneurship and invention yielded many new products and machines. The republic seemed to be a laboratory of innovation, and technological advances appeared unlimited.

The First Cotton-Gin, an 1869 drawing by William L. Sheppard, shows the first use of a cotton gin "at the close of the last century." African American slaves handle the gin while white men conduct business in the background. What do you think the artist was trying to convey with this image? (credit: Library of Congress)

One of the most influential advancements of the early nineteenth century was the cotton engine or gin, invented by Eli Whitney and patented in 1794. Whitney, who was born in Massachusetts, had spent time in the South and knew that a device to speed up the production of cotton was desperately needed so cotton farmers could meet the growing demand for their crop. He hoped the cotton gin would render slavery obsolete. Whitney's seemingly simple invention cleaned the seeds from the raw cotton far more quickly and efficiently than could slaves working by hand. The raw cotton with seeds was placed in the cotton gin, and with the use of a hand crank, the seeds were extracted through a carding device that aligned the cotton fibers in strands for spinning.

Whitney also worked on **machine tools**, devices that cut and shaped metal to make standardized, interchangeable parts for other mechanical devices like clocks and guns. Whitney's machine tools to manufacture parts for muskets enabled guns to be manufactured and repaired by people other than skilled gunsmiths. His creative genius served as a source of inspiration for many other American inventors.

Another influential new technology of the early 1800s was the steamship engine, invented by Robert Fulton in 1807. Fulton's first steamship, the *Clermont*, used paddle wheels to travel the 150 miles from New York City to Albany in a record time of only thirty-two hours. Soon, a fleet of steamboats was traversing the Hudson River and New York Harbor, later expanding to travel every major American river including the mighty Mississippi. By the 1830s there were over one thousand of these vessels, radically changing water transportation by ending its dependence on the wind. Steamboats could travel faster and more cheaply than sailing vessels or keelboats, which floated downriver and had to be poled or towed upriver on the return voyage. Steamboats also arrived with much greater dependability. The steamboat facilitated the rapid economic development of the massive Mississippi River Valley and the settlement of the West.

Fulton's steamboat the Clermont transformed the speed, cost, and dependability of water transportation in the United States. (credit: Project Gutenberg Archives)

Virginia-born Cyrus McCormick wanted to replace the laborious process of using a scythe to cut and gather wheat for harvest. In 1831, he and the slaves on his family's plantation tested a horse-drawn mechanical reaper, and over the next several decades, he made constant improvements to it. More farmers began using it in the 1840s, and greater demand for the McCormick reaper led McCormick and his brother to establish the McCormick Harvesting Machine Company in Chicago, where labor was more readily available. By the 1850s, McCormick's mechanical reaper had enabled farmers to vastly increase their output. McCormick—and also John Deere, who improved on the design of plows—opened the prairies to agriculture. McCormick's bigger machine could harvest grain faster, and Deere's plow could cut through the thick prairie sod. Agriculture north of the Ohio River became the pantry that would lower food prices and feed the major cities in the East. In short order, Ohio, Indiana, and Illinois all become major agricultural states.

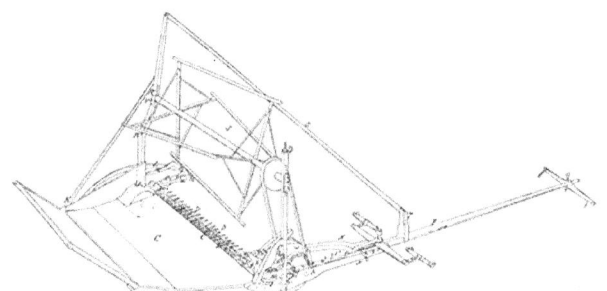

This sketch is from the 1845 patent for an improved grain reaper invented by Cyrus Hall McCormick. The reaper mechanized the labor-intensive use of scythes to harvest wheat.

Samuel Morse added the telegraph to the list of American innovations introduced in the years before the Civil War. Born in Massachusetts in 1791, Morse first gained renown as a painter before turning his attention to the development of a method of rapid communication in the 1830s. In 1838, he gave the first public demonstration of his method of conveying electric pulses over a wire, using the basis of what became known as Morse code. In 1843, Congress agreed to help fund the new technology by allocating $30,000 for a telegraph line to connect Washington, DC, and Baltimore along the route of the Baltimore and Ohio Railroad. In 1844, Morse sent the first telegraph message on the new link. Improved communication systems fostered the development of business, economics, and politics by allowing for dissemination of news at a speed previously unknown.

Section Summary

The selling of the public domain was one of the key features of the early nineteenth century in the United States. Thousands rushed west to take part in the bounty. In the wild frenzy of land purchases and speculation in land, state banks advanced risky loans and created unstable paper money not backed by gold or silver, ultimately leading to the Panic of 1819. The ensuing economic depression was the first in U.S. history. Recovery came in the 1820s, followed by a period of robust growth. In this age of entrepreneurship, in which those who invested their money wisely in land, business ventures, or technological improvements reaped vast profits, inventors produced new wonders that transformed American life.

https://www.openassessments.org/assessments/969

Review Question

1. What did federal and state governments do to help people who were hurt in the Panic of 1819?

Answer to Review Question

1. The federal government passed laws allowing people to sell back land they could not pay for and use the money to pay their debt. States made it more difficult to foreclose on mortgages and tried to make it easier for people to declare bankruptcy.

Glossary

land offices sites where prospective landowners could buy public land from the government

machine tools machines that cut and shape metal to produce standardized, interchangeable parts for mechanical devices such as clocks or guns

specie "hard" money, usually in the form of gold and silver coins

Attributions

CC licensed content, Shared previously

- US History. **Authored by**: P. Scott Corbett, Volker Janssen, John M. Lund, Todd Pfannestiel, Paul Vickery, and Sylvie Waskiewicz. **Provided by**: OpenStax College. **Located at**: http://openstaxcollege.org/textbooks/us-history. **License**: *CC BY: Attribution*. **License Terms**: Download for free at http://cnx.org/content/col11740/latest/

On the Move: The Transportation Revolution

> ### Learning Objectives
>
> By the end of this section, you will be able to:
>
> - Describe the development of improved methods of nineteenth-century domestic transportation
> - Identify the ways in which roads, canals, and railroads impacted Americans' lives in the nineteenth century

Americans in the early 1800s were a people on the move, as thousands left the eastern coastal states for opportunities in the West. Unlike their predecessors, who traveled by foot or wagon train, these settlers had new transport options. Their trek was made possible by the construction of roads, canals, and railroads, projects that required the funding of the federal government and the states.

New technologies, like the steamship and railroad lines, had brought about what historians call the transportation revolution. States competed for the honor of having the most advanced transport systems. People celebrated the transformation of the wilderness into an orderly world of improvement demonstrating the steady march of progress and the greatness of the republic. In 1817, John C. Calhoun of South Carolina looked to a future of rapid internal improvements, declaring, "Let us . . . bind the Republic together with a perfect system of roads and canals." Americans agreed that internal transportation routes would promote progress. By the eve of the Civil War, the United States had moved beyond roads and canals to a well-established and extensive system of railroads.

ROADS AND CANALS

One key part of the transportation revolution was the widespread building of roads and turnpikes. In 1811, construction began on the **Cumberland Road**, a national highway that provided thousands with a route from Maryland to Illinois. The federal government funded this important artery to the West, beginning the creation of a transportation infrastructure for the benefit of settlers and farmers. Other entities built turnpikes, which (as today) charged fees for use. New York State, for instance, chartered turnpike companies that dramatically increased the miles of state roads from one thousand in 1810 to four thousand by 1820. New York led the way in building turnpikes.

Canal mania swept the United States in the first half of the nineteenth century. Promoters knew these artificial rivers could save travelers immense amounts of time and money. Even short waterways, such as the two-and-a-half-mile canal going around the rapids of the Ohio River near Louisville, Kentucky, proved a huge leap forward, in this case by opening a water route from Pittsburgh to New Orleans. The preeminent example was the **Erie Canal**, which linked the Hudson River, and thus New York City and the Atlantic seaboard, to the Great Lakes and the Mississippi River Valley.

Although the Erie Canal was primarily used for commerce and trade, in Pittsford on the Erie Canal (1837), George Harvey portrays it in a pastoral, natural setting. Why do you think the painter chose to portray the canal this way?

With its central location, large harbor, and access to the hinterland via the Hudson River, New York City already commanded the lion's share of commerce. Still, the city's merchants worried about losing ground to their competitors in Philadelphia and Baltimore. Their search for commercial advantage led to the dream of creating a water highway connecting the city's Hudson River to Lake Erie and markets in the West. The result was the Erie Canal. Chartered in 1817 by the state of New York, the canal took seven years to complete. When it opened in 1825, it dramatically decreased the cost of shipping while reducing the time to travel to the West. Soon $15 million worth of goods (more than $200 million in today's money) was being transported on the 363-mile waterway every year.

> Explore the Erie Canal on ErieCanal.org via an interactive map. Click throughout the map for images of and artifacts from this historic waterway.

The success of the Erie Canal led to other, similar projects. The Wabash and Erie Canal, which opened in the early 1840s, stretched over 450 miles, making it the longest canal in North America. Canals added immensely to the country's sense of progress. Indeed, they appeared to be the logical next step in the process of transforming wilderness into civilization.

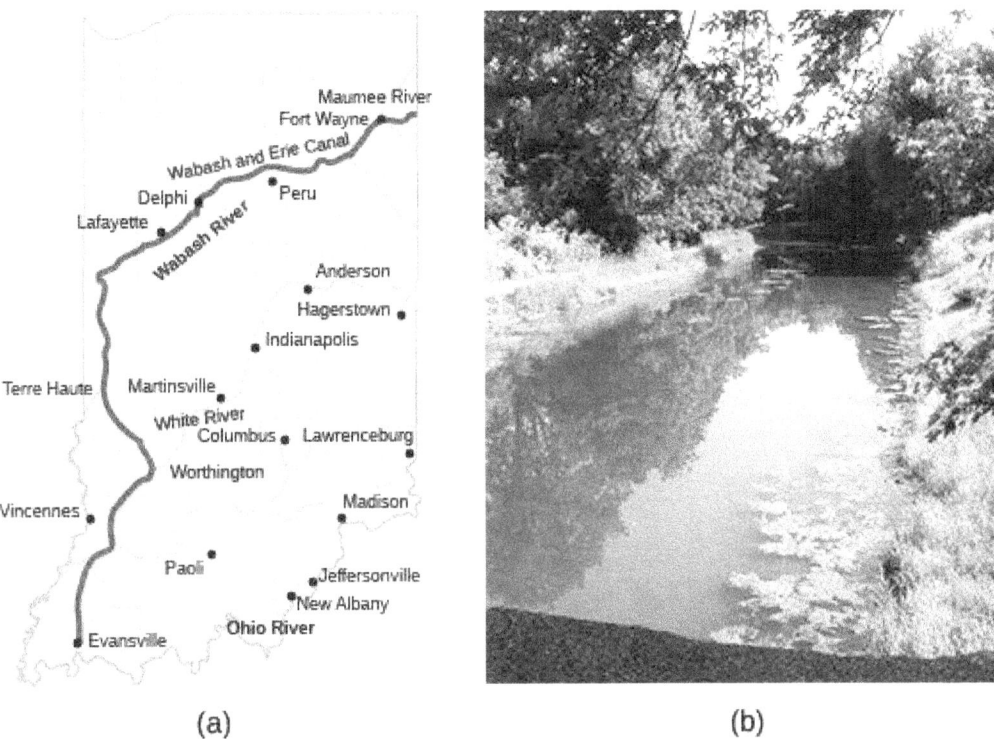

This map (a) shows the route taken by the Wabash and Erie Canal through the state of Indiana. The canal began operation in 1843 and boats operated on it until the 1870s. Sections have since been restored, as shown in this 2007 photo (b) from Delphi, Indiana.

> Visit Southern Indiana Trails to see historic photographs of the Wabash and Erie Canal:

As with highway projects such as the Cumberland Road, many canals were federally sponsored, especially during the presidency of John Quincy Adams in the late 1820s. Adams, along with Secretary of State Henry Clay, championed what was known as the American System, part of which included plans for a broad range of internal transportation improvements. Adams endorsed the creation of roads and canals to facilitate commerce and develop markets for agriculture as well as to advance settlement in the West.

RAILROADS

Starting in the late 1820s, steam locomotives began to compete with horse-drawn locomotives. The railroads with steam locomotives offered a new mode of transportation that fascinated citizens, buoying their optimistic view of the possibilities of technological progress. The **Mohawk and Hudson Railroad** was the first to begin service with a steam locomotive. Its inaugural train ran in 1831 on a track outside Albany and covered twelve miles in twenty-five minutes. Soon it was traveling regularly between Albany and Schenectady.

Toward the middle of the century, railroad construction kicked into high gear, and eager investors quickly formed a number of railroad companies. As a railroad grid began to take shape, it stimulated a greater demand for coal, iron, and steel. Soon, both railroads and canals crisscrossed the states, providing a transportation infrastructure that fueled the growth of American commerce. Indeed, the transportation revolution led to development in the coal, iron, and steel industries, providing many Americans with new job opportunities.

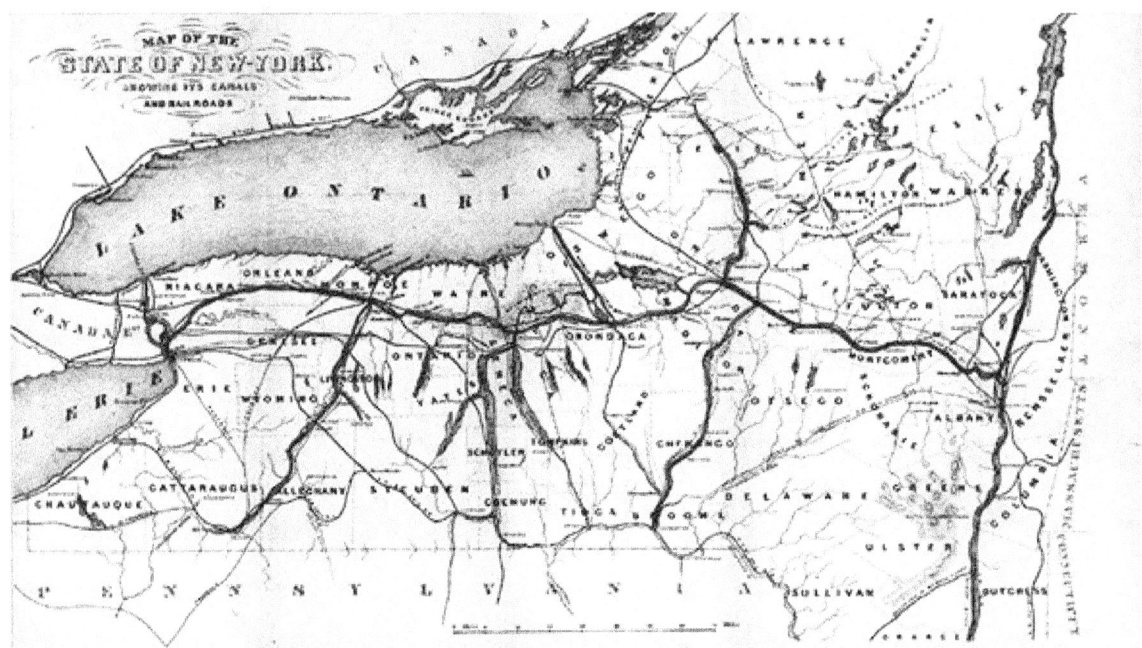

This 1853 map of the "Empire State" shows the extent of New York's canal and railroad networks. The entire country's transportation infrastructure grew dramatically during the first half of the nineteenth century.

AMERICANS ON THE MOVE

The expansion of roads, canals, and railroads changed people's lives. In 1786, it had taken a minimum of four days to travel from Boston, Massachusetts, to Providence, Rhode Island. By 1840, the trip took half a day on a train. In the twenty-first century, this may seem intolerably slow, but people at the time were amazed by the railroad's speed. Its average of twenty miles per hour was twice as fast as other available modes of transportation.

By 1840, more than three thousand miles of canals had been dug in the United States, and thirty thousand miles of railroad track had been laid by the beginning of the Civil War. Together with the hundreds of steamboats that plied American rivers, these advances in transportation made it easier and less expensive to ship agricultural products from the West to feed people in eastern cities, and to send manufactured goods from the East to people in the West. Without this ability to transport goods, the market revolution would not have been possible. Rural families also became less isolated as a result of the transportation revolution. Traveling circuses, menageries, peddlers, and itinerant painters could now more easily make their way into rural districts, and people in search of work found cities and mill towns within their reach.

Section Summary

A transportation infrastructure rapidly took shape in the 1800s as American investors and the government began building roads, turnpikes, canals, and railroads. The time required to travel shrank vastly, and people marveled at their ability to conquer great distances, enhancing their sense of the steady advance of progress. The transportation revolution also made it possible to ship agricultural and manufactured goods throughout the country and enabled rural people to travel to towns and cities for employment opportunities.

https://www.openassessments.org/assessments/970

Review Question

1. What were the benefits of the transportation revolution?

Answer to Review Question

1. The Cumberland Road made transportation to the West easier for new settlers. The Erie Canal facilitated trade with the West by connecting the Hudson River to Lake Erie. Railroads shortened transportation times throughout the country, making it easier and less expensive to move people and goods.

Glossary

Cumberland Road a national highway that provided thousands with a route from Maryland to Illinois

Erie Canal a canal that connected the Hudson River to Lake Erie and markets in the West

Mohawk and Hudson Railroad the first steam-powered locomotive railroad in the United States

Attributions

CC licensed content, Shared previously

- US History. **Authored by**: P. Scott Corbett, Volker Janssen, John M. Lund, Todd Pfannestiel, Paul Vickery, and Sylvie Waskiewicz. **Provided by**: OpenStax College. **Located at**: http://openstaxcollege.org/textbooks/us-history. **License**: *CC BY: Attribution*. **License Terms**: Download for free at http://cnx.org/content/col11740/latest/

A New Social Order: Class Divisions

Learning Objectives

By the end of this section, you will be able to:

- Identify the shared perceptions and ideals of each social class
- Assess different social classes' views of slavery

The profound economic changes sweeping the United States led to equally important social and cultural transformations. The formation of distinct classes, especially in the rapidly industrializing North, was one of the most striking developments. The unequal distribution of newly created wealth spurred new divisions along class lines. Each class had its own specific culture and views on the issue of slavery.

THE ECONOMIC ELITE

Economic elites gained further social and political ascendance in the United States due to a fast-growing economy that enhanced their wealth and allowed distinctive social and cultural characteristics to develop among different economic groups. In the major northern cities of Boston, New York, and Philadelphia, leading merchants formed an industrial capitalist elite. Many came from families that had been deeply engaged in colonial trade in tea, sugar, pepper, slaves, and other commodities and that were familiar with trade networks connecting the United States with Europe, the West Indies, and the Far East. These colonial merchants had passed their wealth to their children.

Junius Spencer Morgan of Boston was one of the fathers of the American private banking system. (credit: Project Gutenberg Archives)

After the War of 1812, the new generation of merchants expanded their economic activities. They began to specialize in specific types of industry, spearheading the development of industrial capitalism based on factories they owned and on specific commercial services such as banking, insurance, and shipping. Junius Spencer Morgan, for example, rose to prominence as a banker. His success began in Boston, where he worked in the import business in the 1830s. He then formed a partnership with a London banker, George Peabody, and created Peabody, Morgan & Co. In 1864, he renamed the enterprise J. S. Morgan & Co. His son, J. P. Morgan, became a noted financier in the later nineteenth and early twentieth century.

> Visit the Internet Archive to see scanned pages from *Hunt's Merchant's Magazine and Commercial Review*. This monthly business review provided the business elite with important information about issues pertaining to trade and finance: commodity prices, new laws affecting business, statistics regarding imports and exports, and similar content. Choose three articles and decide how they might have been important to the northern business elite.

Members of the northern business elite forged close ties with each other to protect and expand their economic interests. Marriages between leading families formed a crucial strategy to advance economic advantage, and the homes of the northern elite became important venues for solidifying social bonds. Exclusive neighborhoods started to develop as the wealthy distanced themselves from the poorer urban residents, and cities soon became segregated by class.

Industrial elites created chambers of commerce to advance their interests; by 1858 there were ten in the United States. These networking organizations allowed top bankers and merchants to stay current on the economic activities of their peers and further strengthen the bonds among themselves. The elite also established social clubs to forge and maintain ties. The first of these, the Philadelphia Club, came into being in 1834. Similar clubs soon formed in other cities and hosted a range of social activities designed to further bind together the leading economic families. Many northern elites worked hard to ensure the transmission of their inherited wealth from one generation to the next. Politically, they exercised considerable power in local and state elections. Most also had ties to the cotton trade, so they were strong supporters of slavery.

The Industrial Revolution led some former artisans to reinvent themselves as manufacturers. These enterprising leaders of manufacturing differed from the established commercial elite in the North and South because they did not inherit wealth. Instead, many came from very humble working-class origins and embodied the dream of achieving upward social mobility through hard work and discipline. As the beneficiaries of the economic transformations sweeping the republic, these newly established manufacturers formed a new economic elite that thrived in the cities and cultivated its own distinct sensibilities. They created a culture that celebrated hard work, a position that put them at odds with southern planter elites who prized leisure and with other elite northerners who had largely inherited their wealth and status.

Peter Cooper provides one example of the new northern manufacturing class. Ever inventive, Cooper dabbled in many different moneymaking enterprises before gaining success in the glue business. He opened his Manhattan glue factory in the 1820s and was soon using his profits to expand into a host of other activities, including iron production. One of his innovations was the steam locomotive, which he invented in 1827. Despite becoming one of the wealthiest men in New York City, Cooper lived simply. Rather than buying an ornate bed, for example, he built his own. He believed respectability came through hard work, not family pedigree.

Peter Cooper, who would go on to found the Cooper Union for the Advancement of Science and Art in New York City, designed and built the Tom Thumb, the first American-built steam locomotive, a replica of which is shown here.

Those who had inherited their wealth derided self-made men like Cooper, and he and others like him were excluded from the social clubs established by the merchant and financial elite of New York City. Self-made northern manufacturers, however, created their own organizations that aimed to promote upward mobility. The Providence Association of Mechanics and Manufacturers was formed in 1789 and promoted both industrial arts and education as a pathway to economic success. In 1859, Peter Cooper established the Cooper Union for the Advancement of Science and Art, a school in New York City dedicated to providing education in technology. Merit, not wealth, mattered most according to Cooper, and admission to the school was based solely on ability; race, sex, and family connections had no place. The best and brightest could attend Cooper Union tuition-free, a policy that remained in place until 2014.

THE MIDDLE CLASS

Not all enterprising artisans were so successful that they could rise to the level of the elite. However, many artisans and small merchants, who owned small factories and stores, did manage to achieve and maintain respectability in an emerging middle class. Lacking the protection of great wealth, members of the middle class agonized over the fear that they might slip into the ranks of wage laborers; thus they strove to maintain or improve their middle-class status and that of their children.

To this end, the middle class valued cleanliness, discipline, morality, hard work, education, and good manners. Hard work and education enabled them to rise in life. Middle-class children, therefore, did not work in factories. Instead they attended school and in their free time engaged in "self-improving" activities, such as reading or playing the piano, or they played with toys and games that would teach them the skills and values they needed to succeed in life. In the early nineteenth century, members of the middle class began to limit the number of children they had. Children no longer contributed economically to the household, and raising them "correctly" required money and attention. It therefore made sense to have fewer of them.

Middle-class women did not work for wages. Their job was to care for the children and to keep the house in a state of order and cleanliness, often with the help of a servant. They also performed the important tasks of cultivating good manners among their children and their husbands and of purchasing consumer goods; both activities proclaimed to neighbors and prospective business partners that their families were educated, cultured, and financially successful.

Northern business elites, many of whom owned or had invested in businesses like cotton mills that profited from slave labor, often viewed the institution of slavery with ambivalence. Most members of the middle class took a dim view of it, however, since it promoted a culture of leisure. Slavery stood as the antithesis of the middle-class view that dignity and respectability were achieved through work, and many members of this class became active in efforts to end it.

This class of upwardly mobile citizens promoted temperance, or abstinence from alcohol. They also gave their support to Protestant ministers like George Grandison Finney, who preached that all people possessed **free moral agency**, meaning they could change their lives and bring about their own salvation, a message that resonated with members of the middle class, who already believed their worldly efforts had led to their economic success.

THE WORKING CLASS

The Industrial Revolution in the United States created a new class of wage workers, and this working class also developed its own culture. They formed their own neighborhoods, living away from the oversight of bosses and managers. While industrialization and the market revolution brought some improvements to the lives of the working class, these sweeping changes did not benefit laborers as much as they did the middle class and the elites. The working class continued to live an often precarious existence. They suffered greatly during economic slumps, such as the Panic of 1819.

Although most working-class men sought to emulate the middle class by keeping their wives and children out of the work force, their economic situation often necessitated that others besides the male head of the family contribute to its support. Thus, working-class children might attend school for a few years or learn to read and write at Sunday school, but education was sacrificed when income was needed, and many working-class children went to work in factories. While the wives of wage laborers usually did not work for wages outside the home, many took in laundry or did piecework at home to supplement the family's income.

Although the urban working class could not afford the consumer goods that the middle class could, its members did exercise a great deal of influence over popular culture. Theirs was a festive public culture of release and escape from the drudgery of factory work, catered to by the likes of Phineas Taylor Barnum, the celebrated circus promoter and showman. Taverns also served an important function as places to forget the long hours and uncertain wages of the factories. Alcohol consumption was high among the working class, although many workers did take part in the temperance movement. It is little wonder that middle-class manufacturers attempted to abolish alcohol.

P. T. Barnum and the Feejee Mermaid

The Connecticut native P. T. Barnum catered to the demand for escape and cheap amusements among the working class. His American Museum in New York City opened in 1841 and achieved great success. Millions flocked to see Barnum's exhibits, which included a number of fantastic human and animal oddities, almost all of which were hoaxes. One exhibit in the 1840s featured the "Feejee Mermaid," which Barnum presented as proof of the existence of the mythical mermaids of the deep. In truth, the mermaid was a half-monkey, half-fish stitched together.

(a)

(b)

Spurious though they were, attractions such as the Feejee mermaid (a) from P. T. Barnum's American Museum in New York City (b) drew throngs of working-class wage earners in the middle of the nineteenth century.

Visit The Lost Museum to take a virtual tour of P. T. Barnum's incredible museum.

Wage workers in the North were largely hostile to the abolition of slavery, fearing it would unleash more competition for jobs from free blacks. Many were also hostile to immigration. The pace of immigration to the United States accelerated in the 1840s and 1850s as Europeans were drawn to the promise of employment and land in the United States. Many new members of the working class came from the ranks of these immigrants, who brought new foods, customs, and religions. The Roman Catholic population of the United States, fairly small before this period, began to swell with the arrival of the Irish and the Germans.

Section Summary

The creation of distinctive classes in the North drove striking new cultural developments. Even among the wealthy elites, northern business families, who had mainly inherited their money, distanced themselves from the newly wealthy manufacturing leaders. Regardless of how they had earned their money, however, the elite lived and socialized apart from members of the growing middle class. The middle class valued work, consumption, and education and dedicated their energies to maintaining or advancing their social status. Wage workers formed their own society in industrial cities and mill villages, though lack of money and long working hours effectively prevented the working class from consuming the fruits of their labor, educating their children, or advancing up the economic ladder.

https://www.openassessments.org/assessments/971

Review Question

1. What did Peter Cooper envision for the United States, and how did he work to bring his vision to life?

Answer to Review Question

1. A successful northern manufacturer and inventor, Cooper valued hard work, thrift, and simplicity. He lived according to these values, choosing utilitarian, self-made furnishings rather than luxurious goods. Cooper's vision of hard work leading to respectability led him to found the Cooper Union for the Advancement of Science and Art; admission to this college, which was dedicated to the pursuit of technology, was based solely on merit.

Critical Thinking Questions

1. Industrialization in the Northeast produced great benefits and also major problems. What were they? Who benefited and who suffered? Did the benefits outweigh the problems, or

vice versa?

2. What factors led to the Panic of 1819? What government regulations might have prevented it?

3. Would the Industrial Revolution have been possible without the use of slave labor? Why or why not?

4. What might have been the advantages and disadvantages of railroads for the people who lived along the routes or near the stations?

5. What were the values of the middle class? How did they differ from the values of those above and below them on the socioeconomic ladder? In what ways are these values similar to or different from those held by the middle class today?

Glossary

free moral agency the freedom to change one's own life and bring about one's own salvation

Attributions

CC licensed content, Shared previously

- US History. **Authored by**: P. Scott Corbett, Volker Janssen, John M. Lund, Todd Pfannestiel, Paul Vickery, and Sylvie Waskiewicz. **Provided by**: OpenStax College. **Located at**: http://openstaxcollege.org/textbooks/us-history. **License**: *CC BY: Attribution*. **License Terms**: Download for free at http://cnx.org/content/col11740/latest/

10. Jacksonian Democracy, 1820-1840

Introduction

The most extraordinary political development in the years before the Civil War was the rise of American democracy. Whereas the founders envisioned the United States as a republic, not a democracy, and had placed safeguards such as the Electoral College in the 1787 Constitution to prevent simple majority rule, the early 1820s saw many Americans embracing majority rule and rejecting old forms of deference that were based on elite ideas of virtue, learning, and family lineage.

A new breed of politicians learned to harness the magic of the many by appealing to the resentments, fears, and passions of ordinary citizens to win elections. The charismatic Andrew Jackson gained a reputation as a fighter and defender of American expansion, emerging as the quintessential figure leading the rise of American democracy. In the image above, crowds flock to the White House to celebrate his inauguration as president.

In *President's Levee, or all Creation going to the White House, Washington* (1841), by Robert Cruikshank, the artist depicts Andrew Jackson's inauguration in 1829, with crowds surging into the White House to join the celebrations. Rowdy revelers destroyed many White House furnishings in their merriment. A new political era of democracy had begun, one characterized by the rule of the majority.

While earlier inaugurations had been reserved for Washington's political elite, Jackson's was an event for the people, so much so that the pushing throngs caused thousands of dollars of damage to White House property. Characteristics of modern American democracy, including the turbulent nature of majority rule, first appeared during the Age of Jackson.

Attributions

CC licensed content, Shared previously

- US History. **Authored by**: P. Scott Corbett, Volker Janssen, John M. Lund, Todd Pfannestiel, Paul Vickery, and Sylvie Waskiewicz. **Provided by**: OpenStax College. **Located at**: http://openstaxcollege.org/textbooks/us-history. **License**: *CC BY: Attribution*. **License Terms**: Download for free at http://cnx.org/content/col11740/latest/

A New Political Style: From John Quincy Adams to Andrew Jackson

Learning Objectives

By the end of this section, you will be able to:

- Explain and illustrate the new style of American politics in the 1820s
- Describe the policies of John Quincy Adams's presidency and explain the political divisions that resulted

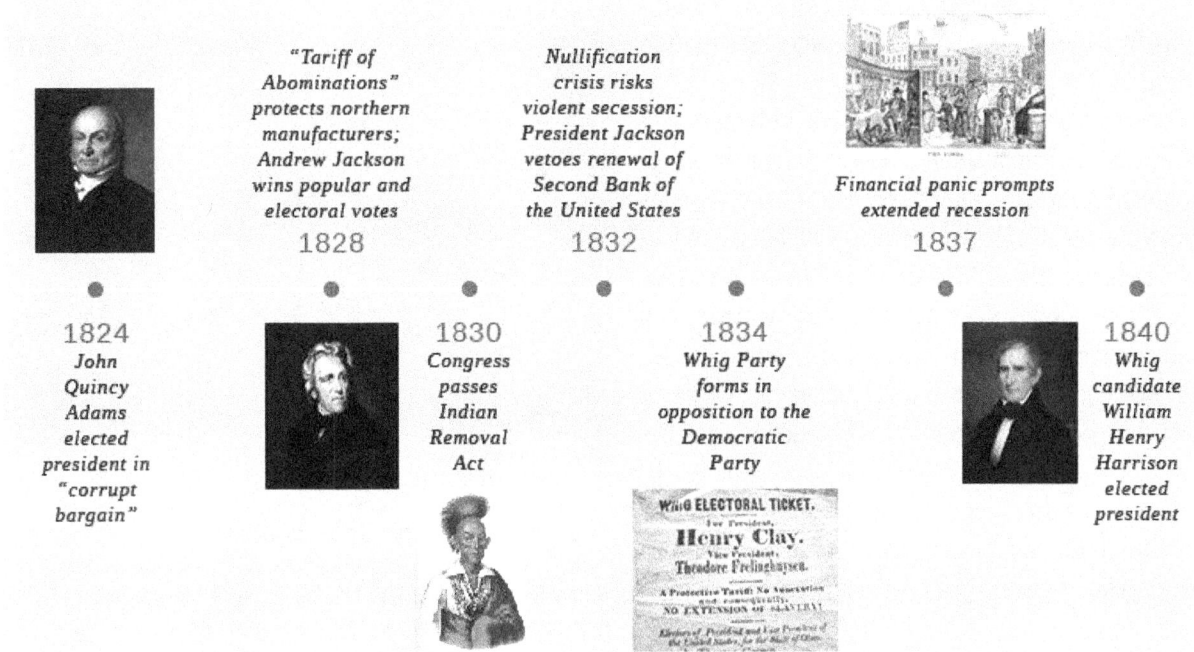

In the 1820s, American political culture gave way to the democratic urges of the citizenry. Political leaders and parties rose to popularity by championing the will of the people, pushing the country toward a future in which a wider swath of citizens gained a political voice. However, this expansion of political power was limited to white men; women, free blacks, and Indians remained—or grew increasingly—disenfranchised by the American political system.

THE DECLINE OF FEDERALISM

The first party system in the United States shaped the political contest between the Federalists and the Democratic-Republicans. The Federalists, led by Washington, Hamilton, and Adams, dominated American politics in the 1790s. After the election of Thomas Jefferson—the Revolution of 1800—the Democratic-Republicans gained ascendance. The gradual decline of the Federalist Party is evident in its losses in the presidential contests that occurred between 1800 and 1820. After 1816, in which Democratic-Republican James Monroe defeated his Federalist rival Rufus King, the Federalists never ran another presidential candidate.

Before the 1820s, a **code of deference** had underwritten the republic's political order. Deference was the practice of showing respect for individuals who had distinguished themselves through military accomplishments, educational attainment, business success, or family pedigree. Such individuals were members of what many Americans in the early republic agreed was a natural aristocracy. Deference shown to them dovetailed with republicanism and its emphasis on virtue, the ideal of placing the common good above narrow self-interest. Republican statesmen in the 1780s and 1790s expected and routinely received deferential treatment from others, and ordinary Americans deferred to their "social betters" as a matter of course.

For the generation who lived through the American Revolution, for instance, George Washington epitomized republican virtue, entitling him to great deference from his countrymen. His judgment and decisions were considered beyond reproach. An Anglican minister named Mason Locke Weems wrote the classic tale of Washington's unimpeachable virtue in his 1800 book, *The Life of Washington*. Generations of nineteenth-century American children read its fictional story of a youthful Washington chopping down one of his father's cherry trees and, when confronted by his father, confessing: "I cannot tell a lie." The story spoke to Washington's unflinching honesty and integrity, encouraging readers to remember the deference owed to such towering national figures.

"Father, I Can Not Tell a Lie: I Cut the Tree" (1867) by John McRae, after a painting by George Gorgas White, illustrates Mason Locke Weems's tale of Washington's honesty and integrity as revealed in the incident of the cherry tree. Although it was fiction, this story about Washington taught generations of children about the importance of virtue.

Washington and those who celebrated his role as president established a standard for elite, virtuous leadership that cast a long shadow over subsequent presidential administrations. The presidents who followed Washington shared the first president's pedigree. With the exception of John Adams, who was from Massachusetts, all the early presidents—Thomas Jefferson, James Madison, and James Monroe—were members of Virginia's elite slaveholder aristocracy.

DEMOCRATIC REFORMS

In the early 1820s, deference to pedigree began to wane in American society. A new type of deference—to the will of the majority and not to a ruling class—took hold. The spirit of democratic reform became most evident in the widespread belief that all white men, regardless of whether they owned property, had the right to participate in elections.

Before the 1820s, many state constitutions had imposed property qualifications for voting as a means to keep democratic tendencies in check. However, as Federalist ideals fell out of favor, ordinary men from the middle and lower classes increasingly questioned the idea that property ownership was an indication of virtue. They argued for **universal manhood suffrage**, or voting rights for all white male adults.

New states adopted constitutions that did not contain property qualifications for voting, a move designed to stimulate migration across their borders. Vermont and Kentucky, admitted to the Union in 1791 and 1792 respectively, granted the right to vote to all white men regardless of whether they owned property or paid taxes. Ohio's state constitution placed a minor taxpaying requirement on voters but otherwise allowed for expansive white male suffrage. Alabama, admitted to the Union in 1819, eliminated property qualifications for voting in its state constitution. Two other new states, Indiana (1816) and Illinois (1818), also extended the right to vote to white men regardless of property. Initially, the new state of Mississippi (1817) restricted voting to white male property holders, but in 1832 it eliminated this provision.

In Connecticut, Federalist power largely collapsed in 1818 when the state held a constitutional convention. The new constitution granted the right to vote to all white men who paid taxes or served in the militia. Similarly, New York amended its state constitution in 1821–1822 and removed the property qualifications for voting.

Expanded voting rights did not extend to women, Indians, or free blacks in the North. Indeed, race replaced property qualifications as the criterion for voting rights. American democracy had a decidedly racist orientation; a white majority limited the rights of black minorities. New Jersey explicitly restricted the right to vote to white men only. Connecticut passed a law in 1814 taking the right to vote away from free black men and restricting suffrage to white men only. By the 1820s, 80 percent of the white male population could vote in New York State elections. No other state had expanded suffrage so dramatically. At the same time, however, New York effectively disenfranchised free black men in 1822 (black men had had the right to vote under the 1777 constitution) by requiring that "men of color" must possess property over the value of $250.

PARTY POLITICS AND THE ELECTION OF 1824

In addition to expanding white men's right to vote, democratic currents also led to a new style of political party organization, most evident in New York State in the years after the War of 1812. Under the leadership of Martin Van Buren, New York's "Bucktail" Republican faction (so named because members wore a deer's tail on their hats, a symbol of membership in the Tammany Society) gained political power by cultivating loyalty to the will of the majority, not to an elite family or renowned figure. The **Bucktails** emphasized a pragmatic approach. For example, at first they opposed the Erie Canal project, but when the popularity of the massive transportation venture became clear, they supported it.

One of the Bucktails' greatest achievements in New York came in the form of revisions to the state constitution in the 1820s. Under the original constitution, a Council of Appointments selected local officials such as sheriffs and county clerks. The Bucktails replaced this process with a system of direct elections, which meant thousands of jobs immediately became available to candidates who had the support of the majority. In practice, Van Buren's party could nominate and support their own candidates based on their loyalty to the party. In this way, Van Buren helped create a political machine of disciplined party members who prized loyalty above all else, a harbinger of future patronage politics in the United States. This system of rewarding party loyalists is known as the **spoils system** (from the expression, "To the victor belong the spoils"). Van Buren's political machine helped radically transform New York politics.

Party politics also transformed the national political landscape, and the election of 1824 proved a turning point in American politics. With tens of thousands of new voters, the older system of having members of Congress form congressional caucuses to determine who would run no longer worked. The new voters had regional interests and voted on them. For the first time, the popular vote mattered in a presidential election. Electors were chosen by popular vote in eighteen states, while the six remaining states used the older system in which state legislatures chose electors.

With the caucus system defunct, the presidential election of 1824 featured five candidates, all of whom ran as Democratic-Republicans (the Federalists having ceased to be a national political force). The crowded field included John Quincy Adams, the son of the second president, John Adams. Candidate Adams had broken with the Federalists in the early 1800s and served on various diplomatic missions, including the mission to secure peace with Great Britain in 1814. He represented New England. A second candidate, John C. Calhoun from South Carolina, had served as secretary of war and represented the slaveholding South. He dropped out of the presidential race to run for vice president. A third candidate, Henry Clay, the Speaker of the House of Representatives, hailed from Kentucky and represented the western states. He favored an active federal government committed to internal improvements, such as roads and canals, to bolster national economic development and settlement of the West. William H. Crawford, a slaveholder from Georgia, suffered a stroke in 1823 that left him largely incapacitated, but he ran nonetheless and had the backing of the New York machine headed by Van Buren. Andrew Jackson, the famed "hero of New Orleans," rounded out the field. Jackson had very little formal education, but he was popular for his military victories in the War of 1812 and in wars against the Creek and the Seminole. He had been elected to the Senate in 1823, and his popularity soared as pro-Jackson newspapers sang the praises of the courage and daring of the Tennessee slaveholder.

The two most popular presidential candidates in the election of 1824 were Andrew Jackson (a), who won the popular vote but failed to secure the requisite number of votes in the Electoral College, and John Quincy Adams (b), who emerged victorious after a contentious vote in the U.S. House of Representatives.

Results from the eighteen states where the popular vote determined the electoral vote gave Jackson the election, with 152,901 votes to Adams's 114,023, Clay's 47,217, and Crawford's 46,979. The Electoral College, however, was another matter. Of the 261 electoral votes, Jackson needed 131 or better to win but secured only 99. Adams won 84, Crawford 41, and Clay 37. Because Jackson did not receive a majority vote from the Electoral College, the election was decided following the terms of the Twelfth Amendment, which stipulated that when a candidate did not receive a majority of electoral votes, the election went to the House of Representatives, where each state would provide one vote. House Speaker Clay did not want to see his rival, Jackson, become president and therefore worked within the House to secure the presidency for Adams, convincing many to cast their vote for the New Englander. Clay's efforts paid off; despite not having won the popular vote, John Quincy Adams was certified by the House as the next president. Once in office, he elevated Henry Clay to the post of secretary of state.

John C. Calhoun (a) believed that the assistance Henry Clay (b) gave to John Quincy Adams in the U.S. House of Representatives' vote to decide the presidential election of 1824 indicated that a "corrupt bargain" had been made.

Jackson and his supporters cried foul. To them, the election of Adams reeked of anti-democratic corruption. So too did the appointment of Clay as secretary of state. John C. Calhoun labeled the whole affair a "**corrupt bargain.**" Everywhere, Jackson supporters vowed revenge against the anti-majoritarian result of 1824.

THE PRESIDENCY OF JOHN QUINCY ADAMS

Secretary of State Clay championed what was known as the **American System** of high tariffs, a national bank, and federally sponsored internal improvements of canals and roads. Once in office, President Adams embraced Clay's American System and proposed a national university and naval academy to train future leaders of the republic. The president's opponents smelled elitism in these proposals and pounced on what they viewed as the administration's catering to a small privileged class at the expense of ordinary citizens.

Clay also envisioned a broad range of internal transportation improvements. Using the proceeds from land sales in the West, Adams endorsed the creation of roads and canals to facilitate commerce and the advance of settlement in the West. Many in Congress vigorously opposed federal funding of internal improvements, citing among other reasons that the Constitution did not give the federal government the power to fund these projects. However, in the end, Adams succeeded in extending the Cumberland Road into Ohio (a federal highway project). He also broke ground for the Chesapeake and Ohio Canal on July 4, 1828.

> Visit the Cumberland Road Project and the Chesapeake and Ohio Canal National Historic Park to learn more about transportation developments in the first half of the nineteenth century. How were these two projects important for westward expansion?

Tariffs, which both Clay and Adams promoted, were not a novel idea; since the birth of the republic they had been seen as a way to advance domestic manufacturing by making imports more expensive. Congress had approved a tariff in 1789, for instance, and Alexander Hamilton had proposed a protective tariff in 1790. Congress also passed tariffs in 1816 and 1824. Clay spearheaded the drive for the federal government to impose high tariffs to help bolster domestic manufacturing. If imported goods were more expensive than domestic goods, then people would buy American-made goods.

President Adams wished to promote manufacturing, especially in his home region of New England. To that end, in 1828 he proposed a high tariff on imported goods, amounting to 50 percent of their value. The tariff raised questions about how power should be distributed, causing a fiery debate between those who supported states' rights and those who supported the expanded power of the federal government. Those who championed states' rights denounced the 1828 measure as the **Tariff of Abominations**, clear evidence that the federal government favored one region, in this case the North, over another, the South. They made their case by pointing out that the North had an expanding manufacturing base while the South did not. Therefore, the South imported far more manufactured goods than the North, causing the tariff to fall most heavily on the southern states.

The Monkey System or 'Every one for himself at the expense of his neighbor!!!!!!!!' (1831) critiqued Henry Clay's proposed tariff and system of internal improvements. In this political cartoon by Edward Williams Clay, four caged monkeys labeled "Home," "Consumption," "Internal," and "Improv" (improvements)—different parts of the nation's economy—steal each other's food while Henry Clay, in the foreground, extols the virtues of his "grand original American System." (credit: Project Gutenberg Archives)

The 1828 tariff generated additional fears among southerners. In particular, it suggested to them that the federal government would unilaterally take steps that hurt the South. This line of reasoning led some southerners to fear that the very foundation of the South—slavery—could come under attack from a hostile northern majority in Congress. The spokesman for this southern view was President Adams's vice president, John C. Calhoun.

John C. Calhoun on the Tariff of 1828

Vice President John C. Calhoun, angry about the passage of the Tariff of 1828, anonymously wrote a report titled "South Carolina Exposition and Protest" (later known as "Calhoun's Exposition") for the South Carolina legislature. As a native of South Carolina, Calhoun articulated the fear among many southerners that the federal government could exercise undue power over the states.

> If it be conceded, as it must be by every one who is the least conversant with our institutions, that the sovereign powers delegated are divided between the General and State Governments, and that the latter hold their portion by the same tenure as the former, it would seem impossible to deny to the States the right of deciding on the infractions of their powers, and the proper remedy to be applied for their correction. The right of judging, in such cases, is an essential attribute of sovereignty, of which the States cannot be divested without losing their sovereignty itself, and being reduced to a subordinate corporate condition. In fact, to divide power, and to give to one of the parties the exclusive right of judging of the portion allotted to each, is, in reality, not to divide it at all; and to reserve such exclusive right to the General Government (it matters not by what department) to be exercised,

is to convert it, in fact, into a great consolidated government, with unlimited powers, and to divest the States, in reality, of all their rights, It is impossible to understand the force of terms, and to deny so plain a conclusion.

—John C. Calhoun, "South Carolina Exposition and Protest," 1828

What is Calhoun's main point of protest? What does he say about the sovereignty of the states?

Section Summary

The early 1800s saw an age of deference give way to universal manhood suffrage and a new type of political organization based on loyalty to the party. The election of 1824 was a fight among Democratic-Republicans that ended up pitting southerner Andrew Jackson against northerner John Quincy Adams. When Adams won through political negotiations in the House of Representatives, Jackson's supporters derided the election as a "corrupt bargain." The Tariff of 1828 further stirred southern sentiment, this time against a perceived bias in the federal government toward northeastern manufacturers. At the same time, the tariff stirred deeper fears that the federal government might take steps that could undermine the system of slavery.

https://www.openassessments.org/assessments/972

Review Questions

1. Why did Andrew Jackson and his supporters consider the election of John Quincy Adams to be a "corrupt bargain"?
2. Who stood to gain from the Tariff of Abominations, and who expected to lose by it?

Answers to Review Questions

1. Jackson and his supporters resented Speaker Henry Clay's maneuvering in the House of Representatives, which gave Adams the election even though Jackson had won the popular vote. When Adams, after taking office, gave Clay the post of secretary of state, it seemed that Adams was rewarding Clay—perhaps even fulfilling the terms of a secret bargain.
2. Northern manufacturers were expected to gain from the tariff because it made competing goods from abroad more expensive than those they made. Southern plantation owners expected the tariff would be costly for them, because it raised the price of goods they could only import. Southerners also feared the tariff represented an unwelcome expansion of federal power over the states.

Glossary

American System the program of federally sponsored roads and canals, protective tariffs, and a national bank advocated by Henry Clay and enacted by President Adams

code of deference the practice of showing respect for individuals who had distinguished themselves through accomplishments or birth

corrupt bargain the term that Andrew Jackson's supporters applied to John Quincy Adams's 1824 election, which had occurred through the machinations of Henry Clay in the U.S. House of Representatives

spoils system the political system of rewarding friends and supporters with political appointments

Tariff of Abominations a federal tariff introduced in 1828 that placed a high duty on imported goods in order to help American manufacturers, which southerners viewed as unfair and harmful to their region

universal manhood suffrage voting rights for all male adults

Attributions

CC licensed content, Shared previously

- US History. **Authored by**: P. Scott Corbett, Volker Janssen, John M. Lund, Todd Pfannestiel, Paul Vickery, and Sylvie Waskiewicz. **Provided by**: OpenStax College. **Located at**: http://openstaxcollege.org/textbooks/us-history. **License**: *CC BY: Attribution*. **License Terms**: Download for free at http://cnx.org/content/col11740/latest/

The Rise of American Democracy

> **Learning Objectives**
>
> By the end of this section, you will be able to:
>
> - Describe the key points of the election of 1828
> - Explain the scandals of Andrew Jackson's first term in office

A turning point in American political history occurred in 1828, which witnessed the election of Andrew Jackson over the incumbent John Quincy Adams. While democratic practices had been in ascendance since 1800, the year also saw the further unfolding of a democratic spirit in the United States. Supporters of Jackson called themselves Democrats or the Democracy, giving birth to the Democratic Party. Political authority appeared to rest with the majority as never before.

THE CAMPAIGN AND ELECTION OF 1828

During the 1800s, democratic reforms made steady progress with the abolition of property qualifications for voting and the birth of new forms of political party organization. The 1828 campaign pushed new democratic practices even further and highlighted the difference between the Jacksonian expanded electorate and the older, exclusive Adams style. A slogan of the day, "Adams who can write/Jackson who can fight," captured the contrast between Adams the aristocrat and Jackson the frontiersman.

The 1828 campaign differed significantly from earlier presidential contests because of the party organization that promoted Andrew Jackson. Jackson and his supporters reminded voters of the "corrupt bargain" of 1824. They framed it as the work of a small group of political elites deciding who would lead the nation, acting in a self-serving manner and ignoring the will of the majority. From Nashville, Tennessee, the Jackson campaign organized supporters around the nation through editorials in partisan newspapers and other publications. Pro-Jackson newspapers heralded the "hero of New Orleans" while denouncing Adams. Though he did not wage an election campaign filled with public appearances, Jackson did give one major campaign speech in New Orleans on January 8, the anniversary of the defeat of the British in 1815. He also engaged in rounds of discussion with politicians who came to his home, the Hermitage, in Nashville.

The bitter rivalry between Andrew Jackson and Henry Clay was exacerbated by the "corrupt bargain" of 1824, which Jackson made much of during his successful presidential campaign in 1828. This drawing, published in the 1830s during the debates over the future of the Second Bank of the United States, shows Clay sewing up Jackson's mouth while the "cure for calumny [slander]" protrudes from his pocket.

At the local level, Jackson's supporters worked to bring in as many new voters as possible. Rallies, parades, and other rituals further broadcast the message that Jackson stood for the common man against the corrupt elite backing Adams and Clay. Democratic organizations called Hickory Clubs, a tribute to Jackson's nickname, Old Hickory, also worked tirelessly to ensure his election.

In November 1828, Jackson won an overwhelming victory over Adams, capturing 56 percent of the popular vote and 68 percent of the electoral vote. As in 1800, when Jefferson had won over the Federalist incumbent John Adams, the presidency passed to a new political party, the Democrats. The election was the climax of several decades of expanding democracy in the United States and the end of the older politics of deference.

> Visit The Hermitage to explore a timeline of Andrew Jackson's life and career. How do you think the events of his younger life affected the trajectory of his political career?

SCANDAL IN THE PRESIDENCY

Amid revelations of widespread fraud, including the disclosure that some $300,000 was missing from the Treasury Department, Jackson removed almost 50 percent of appointed civil officers, which allowed him to handpick their replacements. This replacement of appointed federal officials is called **rotation in office**. Lucrative posts, such as postmaster and deputy postmaster, went to party loyalists, especially in places where Jackson's support had been weakest, such as New England. Some Democratic newspaper editors who had supported Jackson during the campaign also gained public jobs.

Jackson's opponents were angered and took to calling the practice the spoils system, after the policies of Van Buren's Bucktail Republican Party. The rewarding of party loyalists with government jobs resulted in spectacular instances of corruption. Perhaps the most notorious occurred in New York City, where a Jackson appointee made off with over $1 million. Such examples seemed proof positive that the Democrats were disregarding merit, education, and respectability in decisions about the governing of the nation.

Peggy O'Neal was so well known that advertisers used her image to sell products to the public. In this anonymous nineteenth-century cigar-box lid, her portrait is flanked by vignettes showing her scandalous past. On the left, President Andrew Jackson presents her with flowers. On the right, two men fight a duel for her.

In addition to dealing with rancor over rotation in office, the Jackson administration became embroiled in a personal scandal known as the **Petticoat affair**. This incident exacerbated the division between the president's team and the insider class in the nation's capital, who found the new arrivals from Tennessee lacking in decorum and propriety. At the center of the storm was Margaret ("Peggy") O'Neal, a well-known socialite in Washington, DC. O'Neal cut a striking figure and had connections to the republic's most powerful men. She married John Timberlake, a naval officer, and they had three children. Rumors abounded, however, about her involvement with John Eaton, a U.S. senator from Tennessee who had come to Washington in 1818.

Timberlake committed suicide in 1828, setting off a flurry of rumors that he had been distraught over his wife's reputed infidelities. Eaton and Mrs. Timberlake married soon after, with the full approval of President Jackson. The so-called Petticoat affair divided Washington society. Many Washington socialites snubbed the new Mrs. Eaton as a woman of low moral character. Among those who would have nothing to do with her was Vice President John C. Calhoun's wife, Floride. Calhoun fell out of favor with President Jackson, who defended Peggy Eaton and derided those who would not socialize with her, declaring she was "as chaste as a virgin." (Jackson had personal reasons for defending Eaton: he drew a parallel between Eaton's treatment and that of his late wife, Rachel, who had been subjected to attacks on her reputation related to her first marriage, which had ended in divorce.) Martin Van Buren, who defended the Eatons and organized social gatherings with them, became close to Jackson, who came to rely on a group of informal advisers that included Van Buren and was dubbed the **Kitchen Cabinet**. This select group of presidential supporters highlights the importance of party loyalty to Jackson and the Democratic Party.

Section Summary

The Democratic-Republicans' "corrupt bargain" that brought John Quincy Adams and Henry Clay to office in 1824 also helped to push them out of office in 1828. Jackson used it to highlight the cronyism of Washington politics. Supporters presented him as a true man of the people fighting against the elitism of Clay and Adams. Jackson rode a wave of populist fervor all the way to the White House, ushering in the ascendency of a new political party: the Democrats. Although Jackson ran on a platform of clearing the corruption out of Washington, he rewarded his own loyal followers with plum government jobs, thus continuing and intensifying the cycle of favoritism and corruption.

https://www.openassessments.org/assessments/973

Review Questions

1. What were the planks of Andrew Jackson's campaign platform in 1828?
2. What was the significance of the Petticoat affair?

Answers to Review Questions

1. Jackson campaigned as a man of the people, intent on sweeping away the corrupt elite by undoing the "corrupt bargain" of Adams's election, making new federal appointments, and elevating officials whose election actually reflected the will of the majority of voters.
2. The Petticoat affair divided those loyal to President Jackson from Washington, DC, insiders. When Washington socialite Peggy O'Neal's husband committed suicide and O'Neal then married John Eaton, a Tennessee senator with whom she was reportedly unfaithful to her husband, Jackson and those loyal to him defended Peggy Eaton against other Washington, DC, socialites and politicians. Martin Van Buren, in particular, supported the Eatons and became an important figure in Jackson's "Kitchen Cabinet" of select supporters and advisers.

Glossary

Kitchen Cabinet a nickname for Andrew Jackson's informal group of loyal advisers

rotation in office originally, simply the system of having term limits on political appointments; in the Jackson era, this came to mean the replacement of officials with party loyalists

Attributions

CC licensed content, Shared previously

- US History. **Authored by**: P. Scott Corbett, Volker Janssen, John M. Lund, Todd Pfannestiel, Paul Vickery, and Sylvie Waskiewicz. **Provided by**: OpenStax College. **Located at**: http://openstaxcollege.org/textbooks/us-history. **License**: *CC BY: Attribution*. **License Terms**: Download for free at http://cnx.org/content/col11740/latest/

The Nullification Crisis and the Bank War

> ### Learning Objectives
>
> By the end of this section, you will be able to:
>
> - Explain the factors that contributed to the Nullification Crisis
> - Discuss the origins and creation of the Whig Party

The crisis over the Tariff of 1828 continued into the 1830s and highlighted one of the currents of democracy in the Age of Jackson: namely, that many southerners believed a democratic majority could be harmful to their interests. These southerners saw themselves as an embattled minority and claimed the right of states to nullify federal laws that appeared to threaten state sovereignty. Another undercurrent was the resentment and anger of the majority against symbols of elite privilege, especially powerful financial institutions like the Second Bank of the United States.

THE NULLIFICATION CRISIS

The Tariff of 1828 had driven Vice President Calhoun to pen his "South Carolina Exposition and Protest," in which he argued that if a national majority acted against the interest of a regional minority, then individual states could void—or nullify—federal law. By the early 1830s, the battle over the tariff took on new urgency as the price of cotton continued to fall. In 1818, cotton had been thirty-one cents per pound. By 1831, it had sunk to eight cents per pound. While production of cotton had soared during this time and this increase contributed to the decline in prices, many southerners blamed their economic problems squarely on the tariff for raising the prices they had to pay for imported goods while their own income shrank.

Resentment of the tariff was linked directly to the issue of slavery, because the tariff demonstrated the use of federal power. Some southerners feared the federal government would next take additional action against the South, including the abolition of slavery. The theory of **nullification**, or the voiding of unwelcome federal laws, provided wealthy slaveholders, who were a minority in the United States, with an argument for resisting the national government if it acted contrary to their interests. James Hamilton, who served as governor of South Carolina in the early 1830s, denounced the "despotic majority that oppresses us." Nullification also raised the specter of secession; aggrieved states at the mercy of an aggressive majority would be forced to leave the Union.

On the issue of nullification, South Carolina stood alone. Other southern states backed away from what they saw as the extremism behind the idea. President Jackson did not make the repeal of the 1828 tariff a priority and denied the nullifiers' arguments. He and others, including former President Madison, argued that Article 1, Section 8 of the Constitution gave Congress the power to "lay and collect taxes, duties, imposts, and excises." Jackson pledged to protect the Union against those who would try to tear it apart over the tariff issue. "The union shall be preserved," he declared in 1830.

To deal with the crisis, Jackson advocated a reduction in tariff rates. The Tariff of 1832, passed in the summer, lowered the rates on imported goods, a move designed to calm southerners. It did not have the desired effect, however, and Calhoun's nullifiers still claimed their right to override federal law. In November, South Carolina passed the Ordinance of Nullification, declaring the 1828 and 1832 tariffs null and void in the Palmetto State. Jackson responded, however, by declaring in the December 1832 Nullification Proclamation that a state did not have the power to void a federal law.

With the states and the federal government at an impasse, civil war seemed a real possibility. The next governor of South Carolina, Robert Hayne, called for a force of ten thousand volunteers to defend the state against any federal action. At the same time, South Carolinians who opposed the nullifiers told Jackson that eight thousand men stood ready to defend the Union. Congress passed the Force Bill of 1833, which gave the federal government the right to use federal troops to ensure compliance with federal law. The crisis—or at least the prospect of armed conflict in South Carolina—was defused by the Compromise Tariff of 1833, which reduced tariff rates considerably. Nullifiers in South Carolina accepted it, but in a move that demonstrated their inflexibility, they nullified the Force Bill.

The governor of South Carolina, Robert Hayne, elected in 1832, was a strong proponent of states' rights and the theory of nullification.

The Nullification Crisis illustrated the growing tensions in American democracy: an aggrieved minority of elite, wealthy slaveholders taking a stand against the will of a democratic majority; an emerging sectional divide between South and North over slavery; and a clash between those who believed in free trade and those who believed in protective tariffs to encourage the nation's economic growth. These tensions would color the next three decades of politics in the United States.

THE BANK WAR

Congress established the Bank of the United States in 1791 as a key pillar of Alexander Hamilton's financial program, but its twenty-year charter expired in 1811. Congress, swayed by the majority's hostility to the bank as an institution catering to the wealthy elite, did not renew the charter at that time. In its place, Congress approved a new national bank—the Second Bank of the United States—in 1816. It too had a twenty-year charter, set to expire in 1836.

The Second Bank of the United States was created to stabilize the banking system. More than two hundred banks existed in the United States in 1816, and almost all of them issued paper money. In other words, citizens faced a bewildering welter of paper money with no standard value. In fact, the problem of paper money had contributed significantly to the Panic of 1819.

In the 1820s, the national bank moved into a magnificent new building in Philadelphia. However, despite Congress's approval of the Second Bank of the United States, a great many people continued to view it as tool of the wealthy, an anti-democratic force. President Jackson was among them; he had faced economic crises of his own during his days speculating in land, an experience that had made him uneasy about paper money. To Jackson, hard currency—that is, gold or silver—was the far better alternative. The president also personally disliked the bank's director, Nicholas Biddle.

A large part of the allure of mass democracy for politicians was the opportunity to capture the anger and resentment of ordinary Americans against what they saw as the privileges of a few. One of the leading opponents of the bank was Thomas Hart Benton, a senator from Missouri, who declared that the bank served "to make the rich richer, and the poor poorer." The self-important statements of Biddle, who claimed to have more power that President Jackson, helped fuel sentiments like Benton's.

In the reelection campaign of 1832, Jackson's opponents in Congress, including Henry Clay, hoped to use their support of the bank to their advantage. In January 1832, they pushed for legislation that would re-charter it, even though its charter was not scheduled to expire until 1836. When the bill for re-chartering passed and came to President Jackson, he used his executive authority to veto the measure.

The defeat of the Second Bank of the United States demonstrates Jackson's ability to focus on the specific issues that aroused the democratic majority. Jackson understood people's anger and distrust toward the bank, which stood as an emblem of special privilege and big government. He skillfully used that perception to his advantage, presenting the bank issue as a struggle of ordinary people against a rapacious elite class who cared nothing for the public and pursued only their own selfish ends. As Jackson portrayed it, his was a battle for small government and ordinary Americans. His stand against what bank opponents called the **"monster bank"** proved very popular, and the Democratic press lionized him for it. In the election of 1832, Jackson received nearly 53 percent of the popular vote against his opponent Henry Clay.

In *General Jackson Slaying the Many Headed Monster (1836)*, the artist, Henry R. Robinson, depicts President Jackson using a cane marked "Veto" to battle a many-headed snake representing state banks, which supported the national bank. Battling alongside Martin Van Buren and Jack Downing, Jackson addresses the largest head, that of Nicholas Biddle, the director of the national bank: "Biddle thou Monster Avaunt [go away]!! . . ."

Jackson's veto was only one part of the war on the "monster bank." In 1833, the president removed the deposits from the national bank and placed them in state banks. Biddle, the bank's director, retaliated by restricting loans to the state banks, resulting in a reduction of the money supply. The financial turmoil only increased when Jackson issued an executive order known as the Specie Circular, which required that western land sales be conducted using gold or silver only. Unfortunately, this policy proved a disaster when the Bank of England, the source of much of the hard currency borrowed by American businesses, dramatically cut back on loans to the United States. Without the flow of hard currency from England, American depositors drained the gold and silver from their own domestic banks, making hard currency scarce. Adding to the economic distress of the late 1830s, cotton prices plummeted, contributing to a financial crisis called the Panic of 1837. This economic panic would prove politically useful for Jackson's opponents in the coming years and Van Buren, elected president in 1836, would pay the price for Jackson's hard-currency preferences.

WHIGS

Jackson's veto of the bank and his Specie Circular helped galvanize opposition forces into a new political party, the **Whigs**, a faction that began to form in 1834. The name was significant; opponents of Jackson saw him as exercising tyrannical power, so they chose the name Whig after the eighteenth-century political party that resisted the monarchical power of King George III. One political cartoon dubbed the president "King Andrew the First" and displayed Jackson standing on the Constitution, which has been ripped to shreds.

This anonymous 1833 political caricature (a) represents President Andrew Jackson as a despotic ruler, holding a scepter in one hand and a veto in the other. Contrast the image of "King Andrew" with a political cartoon from 1831 (b) of Jackson overseeing a scene of uncontrollable chaos as he falls from a hickory chair "coming to pieces at last."

Whigs championed an active federal government committed to internal improvements, including a national bank. They made their first national appearance in the presidential election of 1836, a contest that pitted Jackson's handpicked successor, Martin Van Buren, against a field of several Whig candidates. Indeed, the large field of Whig candidates indicated the new party's lack of organization compared to the Democrats. This helped Van Buren, who carried the day in the Electoral College. As the effects of the Panic of 1837 continued to be felt for years afterward, the Whig press pinned the blame for the economic crisis on Van Buren and the Democrats.

> Explore a Library of Congress collection of 1830s political cartoons from the pages of *Harper's Weekly* to learn more about how Andrew Jackson was viewed by the public in that era.

Section Summary

Andrew Jackson's election in 1832 signaled the rise of the Democratic Party and a new style of American politics. Jackson understood the views of the majority, and he skillfully used the popular will to his advantage. He adroitly navigated through the Nullification Crisis and made headlines with what his supporters viewed as his righteous war against the bastion of money, power, and entrenched insider interests, the Second Bank of the United States. His actions, however, stimulated opponents to fashion an opposition party, the Whigs.

https://www.openassessments.org/assessments/974

Review Questions

1. Why did the Second Bank of the United States make such an inviting target for President Jackson?
2. What were the philosophies and policies of the new Whig Party?

Answers to Review Questions

1. Many people saw the Second Bank of the United States, the "monster bank," as a tool for the privileged few, not for the public good. To Jackson, who saw himself as a spokesman for the common people against a powerful minority elite, it represented the elites' self-serving policies. Fighting to dismantle the bank increased his popularity among many American voters.
2. Whigs opposed what they viewed as the tyrannical rule of Andrew Jackson. For this reason, they named themselves after the eighteenth-century British-American Whigs, who stood in opposition to King George. Whigs believed in an active federal government committed to internal improvements, including the establishment of a national bank.

Glossary

monster bank the term Democratic opponents used to denounce the Second Bank of the United States as an emblem of special privilege and big government

nullification the theory, advocated in response to the Tariff of 1828, that states could void federal law at their discretion

Whigs a political party that emerged in the early 1830s to oppose what members saw as President Andrew Jackson's abuses of power

Attributions

CC licensed content, Shared previously

- US History. **Authored by**: P. Scott Corbett, Volker Janssen, John M. Lund, Todd Pfannestiel, Paul Vickery, and Sylvie Waskiewicz. **Provided by**: OpenStax College. **Located at**: http://openstaxcollege.org/textbooks/us-history. **License**: *CC BY: Attribution*. **License Terms**: Download for free at http://cnx.org/content/col11740/latest/

Indian Removal

> **Learning Objectives**
>
> By the end of this section, you will be able to:
>
> - Explain the legal wrangling that surrounded the Indian Removal Act
> - Describe how depictions of Indians in popular culture helped lead to Indian removal

Pro-Jackson newspapers touted the president as a champion of opening land for white settlement and moving native inhabitants beyond the boundaries of "American civilization." In this effort, Jackson reflected majority opinion: most Americans believed Indians had no place in the white republic. Jackson's animosity toward Indians ran deep. He had fought against the Creek in 1813 and against the Seminole in 1817, and his reputation and popularity rested in large measure on his firm commitment to remove Indians from states in the South. The 1830 Indian Removal Act and subsequent displacement of the Creek, Choctaw, Chickasaw, Seminole, and Cherokee tribes of the Southeast fulfilled the vision of a white nation and became one of the identifying characteristics of the Age of Jackson.

INDIANS IN POPULAR CULTURE

Popular culture in the first half of the nineteenth century reflected the aversion to Indians that was pervasive during the Age of Jackson. Jackson skillfully played upon this racial hatred to engage the United States in a policy of ethnic cleansing, eradicating the Indian presence from the land to make way for white civilization.

In an age of mass democracy, powerful anti-Indian sentiments found expression in mass culture, shaping popular perceptions. James Fenimore Cooper's very popular historical novel, *The Last of the Mohicans*, published in 1826 as part of his Leatherstocking series, told the tale of Nathaniel "Natty" Bumppo (aka Hawkeye), who lived among Indians but had been born to white parents. Cooper provides a romantic version of the French and Indian War in which Natty helps the British against the French and the feral, bloodthirsty Huron. Natty endures even as his Indian friends die, including the noble Uncas, the last Mohican, in a narrative that dovetailed with most people's approval of Indian removal.

Indians also made frequent appearances in art. George Catlin produced many paintings of native peoples, which he offered as true representations despite routinely emphasizing their supposed savage nature. *The Cutting Scene, Mandan O-kee-pa Ceremony* is one example. Scholars have long questioned the accuracy of this portrayal of a rite of passage among the Mandan people. Accuracy aside, the painting captured the imaginations of white viewers, reinforcing their disgust at the savagery of Indians.

The Cutting Scene, Mandan O-kee-pa Ceremony, an 1832 painting by George Catlin, depicts a rite-of-passage ceremony that Catlin said he witnessed. It featured wooden splints inserted into the chest and back muscles of young men. Such paintings increased Indians' reputation as savages.

The Paintings of George Catlin

George Catlin seized upon the public fascination with the supposedly exotic and savage Indian, seeing an opportunity to make money by painting them in a way that conformed to popular white stereotypes. In the late 1830s, he toured major cities with his Indian Gallery, a collection of paintings of native peoples. Though he hoped his exhibition would be profitable, it did not bring him financial security.

(a)   (b)

In Attacking the Grizzly Bear (a), painted in 1844, Catlin focused on the Indians' own vanishing culture, while in Wi-jún-jon, Pigeon's Egg Head (The Light) Going To and Returning From Washington (b), painted in 1837–1839, he contrasted their ways with those of whites by showing an Assiniboine chief transformed by a visit to Washington, DC.

Catlin routinely painted Indians in a supposedly aboriginal state. In *Attacking the Grizzly Bear*, the hunters do not have rifles and instead rely on spears. Such a portrayal stretches credibility as native peoples had long been exposed to and adopted European weapons. Indeed, the painting's depiction of Indians riding horses, which were introduced by the Spanish, makes clear that, as much as Catlin and white viewers wanted to believe in the primitive and savage native, the reality was otherwise.

In *Wi-jún-jon, Pigeon's Egg Head (The Light) Going To and Returning From Washington*, the viewer is shown a before and after portrait of Wi-jún-jon, who tried to emulate white dress and manners after going to Washington, DC. What differences do you see between these two representations of Wi-jún-jon? Do you think his attempt to imitate whites was successful? Why or why not? What do you think Catlin was trying to convey with this depiction of Wi-jún-jon's assimilation?

THE INDIAN REMOVAL ACT

In his first message to Congress, Jackson had proclaimed that Indian groups living independently within states, as sovereign entities, presented a major problem for state sovereignty. This message referred directly to the situation in Georgia, Mississippi, and Alabama, where the Creek, Choctaw, Chickasaw, Seminole, and Cherokee peoples stood as obstacles to white settlement. These groups were known as the **Five Civilized Tribes**, because they had largely adopted Anglo-American culture, speaking English and practicing Christianity. Some held slaves like their white counterparts.

Whites especially resented the Cherokee in Georgia, coveting the tribe's rich agricultural lands in the northern part of the state. The impulse to remove the Cherokee only increased when gold was discovered on their lands. Ironically, while whites insisted the Cherokee and other native peoples could never be good citizens because of their savage ways, the Cherokee had arguably gone farther than any other indigenous group in adopting white culture. The *Cherokee Phoenix*, the newspaper of the Cherokee, began publication in 1828 in English and the Cherokee language. Although the Cherokee followed the lead of their white neighbors by farming and owning property, as well as embracing Christianity and owning their own slaves, this proved of little consequence in an era when whites perceived all Indians as incapable of becoming full citizens of the republic.

This image depicts the front page of the Cherokee Phoenix newspaper from May 21, 1828. The paper was published in both English and the Cherokee language.

Jackson's anti-Indian stance struck a chord with a majority of white citizens, many of whom shared a hatred of nonwhites that spurred Congress to pass the 1830 **Indian Removal Act**. The act called for the removal of the Five Civilized Tribes from their home in the southeastern United States to land in the West, in present-day Oklahoma. Jackson declared in December 1830, "It gives me pleasure to announce to Congress that the benevolent policy of the Government, steadily pursued for nearly thirty years, in relation to the removal of the Indians beyond the white settlements is approaching to a happy consummation. Two important tribes have accepted the provision made for their removal at the last session of Congress, and it is believed that their example will induce the remaining tribes also to seek the same obvious advantages."

The Cherokee decided to fight the federal law, however, and took their case to the Supreme Court. Their legal fight had the support of anti-Jackson members of Congress, including Henry Clay and Daniel Webster, and they retained the legal services of former attorney general William Wirt. In *Cherokee Nation v. Georgia*, Wirt argued that the Cherokee constituted an independent foreign nation, and that an injunction (a stop) should be placed on Georgia laws aimed at eradicating them. In 1831, the Supreme Court found the Cherokee did not meet the criteria for being a foreign nation.

Another case involving the Cherokee also found its way to the highest court in the land. This legal struggle—*Worcester v. Georgia*—asserted the rights of non-natives to live on Indian lands. Samuel Worcester was a Christian missionary and federal postmaster of New Echota, the capital of the Cherokee nation. A Congregationalist, he had gone to live among the Cherokee in Georgia to further the spread of Christianity, and he strongly opposed Indian removal.

By living among the Cherokee, Worcester had violated a Georgia law forbidding whites, unless they were agents of the federal government, to live in Indian territory. Worcester was arrested, but because his federal job as postmaster gave him the right to live there, he was released. Jackson supporters then succeeded in taking away Worcester's job, and he was re-arrested. This time, a court sentenced him and nine others for violating the Georgia state law banning whites from living on Indian land. Worcester was sentenced to four years of hard labor. When the case of *Worcester v. Georgia* came before the Supreme Court in 1832, Chief Justice John Marshall ruled in favor of Worcester, finding that the Cherokee constituted "distinct political communities" with sovereign rights to their own territory.

Chief Justice John Marshall's Ruling in *Worcester v. Georgia*

In 1832, Chief Justice of the Supreme Court John Marshall ruled in favor of Samuel Worcester in *Worcester v. Georgia*. In doing so, he established the principle of tribal sovereignty. Although this judgment contradicted *Cherokee Nation v. Georgia*, it failed to halt the Indian Removal Act. In his opinion, Marshall wrote the following:

> From the commencement of our government Congress has passed acts to regulate trade and intercourse with the Indians; which treat them as nations, respect their rights, and manifest a firm purpose to afford that protection which treaties stipulate. All these acts, and especially that of 1802, which is still in force, manifestly consider the several Indian nations as distinct political communities, having territorial boundaries, within which their authority is exclusive, and having a right to all the lands within those boundaries, which is not only acknowledged, but guaranteed by the United States. . . .
>
> The Cherokee Nation, then, is a distinct community, occupying its own territory, with boundaries accurately described, in which the laws of Georgia can have no force, and which the citizens of Georgia have no right to enter but with the assent of the Cherokees themselves or in conformity with treaties and with the acts of Congress. The whole intercourse between the United States and this nation is, by our Constitution and laws, vested in the government of the United States.
>
> The act of the State of Georgia under which the plaintiff in error was prosecuted is consequently void, and the judgment a nullity. . . . The Acts of Georgia are repugnant to the Constitution, laws, and treaties of the United States.

How does this opinion differ from the outcome of *Cherokee Nation v. Georgia* just one year earlier? Why do you think the two outcomes were different?

The Supreme Court did not have the power to enforce its ruling in *Worcester v. Georgia*, however, and it became clear that the Cherokee would be compelled to move. Those who understood that the only option was removal traveled west, but the majority stayed on their land. In order to remove them, the president relied on the U.S. military. In a series of forced marches, some fifteen thousand Cherokee were finally relocated to Oklahoma. This forced migration, known as the **Trail of Tears**, caused the deaths of as many as four thousand Cherokee. The Creek, Choctaw, Chickasaw, and Seminole peoples were also compelled to go. The removal of the Five Civilized Tribes provides an example of the power of majority opinion in a democracy.

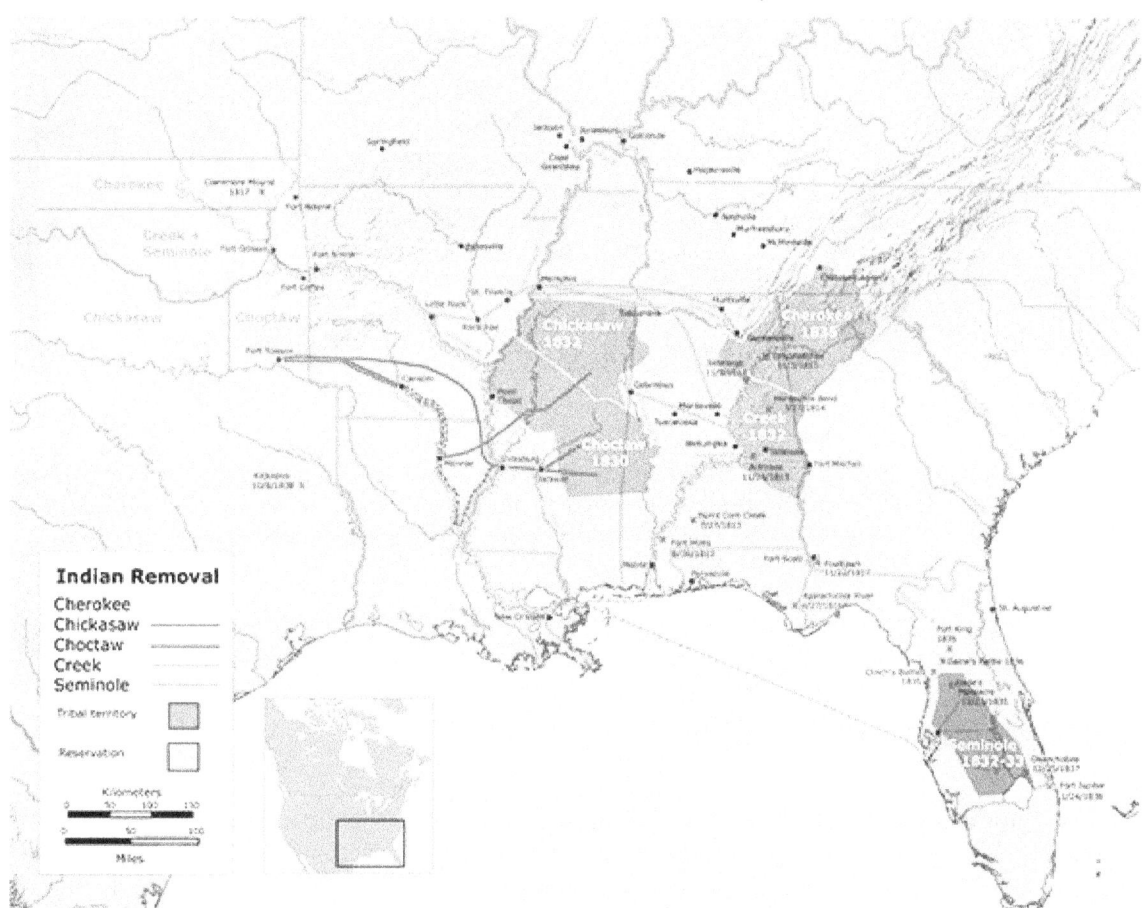

After the passage of the Indian Removal Act, the U.S. military forced the Cherokee, Creek, Choctaw, Chickasaw, and Seminole to relocate from the Southeast to an area in the western territory (now Oklahoma), marching them along the routes shown here.

Explore the interactive Trail of Tears map at PBS.org to see the routes the Five Civilized Tribes traveled when they were expelled from their lands. Then listen to a collection of Cherokee oral histories including verses of a Cherokee-language song about the Trail of Tears. What do you think is the importance of oral history in documenting the Cherokee experience?

BLACK HAWK'S WAR

The policy of removal led some Indians to actively resist. In 1832, the Fox and the Sauk, led by Sauk chief Black Hawk (Makataimeshekiakiah), moved back across the Mississippi River to reclaim their ancestral home in northern Illinois. A brief war in 1832, Black Hawk's War, ensued. White settlers panicked at the return of the native peoples, and militias and federal troops quickly mobilized. At the Battle of Bad Axe (also known as the Bad Axe Massacre), they killed over two hundred men, women, and children. Some seventy white settlers and soldiers also lost their lives in the conflict. The war, which lasted only a matter of weeks, illustrates how much whites on the frontier hated and feared Indians during the Age of Jackson.

Charles Bird King's 1837 portrait Sauk Chief Makataimeshekiakiah, or Black Hawk (a), depicts the Sauk chief who led the Fox and Sauk peoples in an ill-fated effort to return to their native lands in northern Illinois. This engraving depicting the Battle of Bad Axe (b) shows U.S. soldiers on a steamer firing on Indians aboard a raft. (credit b: modification of work by Library of Congress)

Section Summary

Popular culture in the Age of Jackson emphasized the savagery of the native peoples and shaped domestic policy. Popular animosity found expression in the Indian Removal Act. Even the U.S. Supreme Court's ruling in favor of the Cherokee in Georgia offered no protection against the forced removal of the Five Civilized Tribes from the Southeast, mandated by the 1830 Indian Removal Act and carried out by the U.S. military.

https://www.openassessments.org/assessments/975

Review Question

1. What was the Trail of Tears?

Answer to Review Question

1. The Trail of Tears was the route of the forced removal of the Cherokee and other Indian tribes from their ancestral lands in the southeastern United States to what is now Oklahoma. The expulsion was carried out by the U.S. military, and thousands of Indians perished on the way.

> ### Glossary
>
> **Five Civilized Tribes** the five tribes—Cherokee, Seminole, Creek, Choctaw, and Chickasaw—who had most thoroughly adopted Anglo-American culture; they also happened to be the tribes that were believed to stand in the way of western settlement in the South
>
> **Trail of Tears** the route of the forced removal of the Cherokee and other tribes from the southeastern United States to the territory that is now Oklahoma

Attributions

CC licensed content, Shared previously

- US History. **Authored by**: P. Scott Corbett, Volker Janssen, John M. Lund, Todd Pfannestiel, Paul Vickery, and Sylvie Waskiewicz. **Provided by**: OpenStax College. **Located at**: http://openstaxcollege.org/textbooks/us-history. **License**: *CC BY: Attribution*. **License Terms**: Download for free at http://cnx.org/content/col11740/latest/

The Tyranny and Triumph of the Majority

> ### Learning Objectives
>
> By the end of this section, you will be able to:
>
> - Explain Alexis de Tocqueville's analysis of American democracy
> - Describe the election of 1840 and its outcome

To some observers, the rise of democracy in the United States raised troubling questions about the new power of the majority to silence minority opinion. As the will of the majority became the rule of the day, everyone outside of mainstream, white American opinion, especially Indians and blacks, were vulnerable to the wrath of the majority. Some worried that the rights of those who opposed the will of the majority would never be safe. Mass democracy also shaped political campaigns as never before. The 1840 presidential election marked a significant turning point in the evolving style of American democratic politics.

ALEXIS DE TOCQUEVILLE

Perhaps the most insightful commentator on American democracy was the young French aristocrat Alexis de Tocqueville, whom the French government sent to the United States to report on American prison reforms. Tocqueville marveled at the spirit of democracy that pervaded American life. Given his place in French society, however, much of what he saw of American democracy caused him concern.

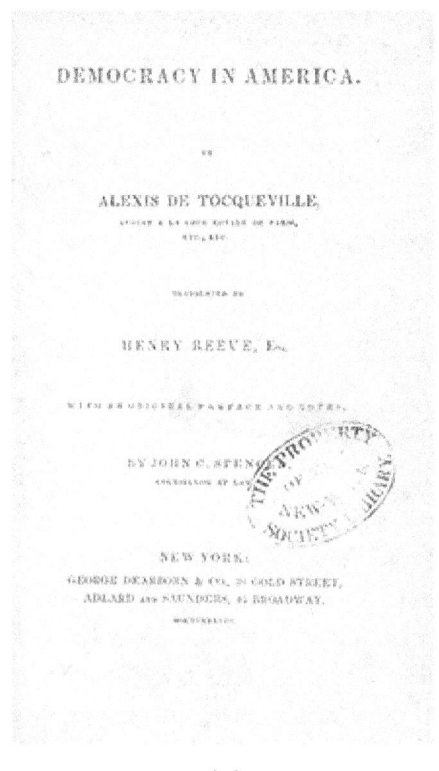 

(a) (b)

Alexis de Tocqueville is best known for his insightful commentary on American democracy found in De la démocratie en Amérique. The first volume of Tocqueville's two-volume work was immediately popular throughout Europe. The first English translation, by Henry Reeve and titled Democracy in America (a), was published in New York in 1838. Théodore Chassériau painted this portrait of Alexis de Tocqueville in 1850 (b).

Tocqueville's experience led him to believe that democracy was an unstoppable force that would one day overthrow monarchy around the world. He wrote and published his findings in 1835 and 1840 in a two-part work entitled *Democracy in America*. In analyzing the democratic revolution in the United States, he wrote that the major benefit of democracy came in the form of equality before the law. A great deal of the social revolution of democracy, however, carried negative consequences. Indeed, Tocqueville described a new type of tyranny, the **tyranny of the majority**, which overpowers the will of minorities and individuals and was, in his view, unleashed by democracy in the United States.

In this excerpt from *Democracy in America*, Alexis de Tocqueville warns of the dangers of democracy when the majority will can turn to tyranny:

> When an individual or a party is wronged in the United States, to whom can he apply for redress? If to public opinion, public opinion constitutes the majority; if to the legislature, it represents the majority, and implicitly obeys its injunctions; if to the executive power, it is appointed by the majority, and remains a passive tool in its hands; the public troops consist of the majority under arms; the jury is the majority invested with the right of hearing judicial cases; and in certain States even the judges are elected by the majority. However iniquitous or absurd the evil of which you complain may be, you must submit to it as well as you can.
>
> The authority of a king is purely physical, and it controls the actions of the subject without subduing his private will; but the majority possesses a power which is physical and moral at the same time;

it acts upon the will as well as upon the actions of men, and it represses not only all contest, but all controversy. I know no country in which there is so little true independence of mind and freedom of discussion as in America.

> Take the Alexis de Tocqueville Tour to experience nineteenth-century America as Tocqueville did, by reading his journal entries about the states and territories he visited with fellow countryman Gustave de Beaumont. What regional differences can you draw from his descriptions?

THE 1840 ELECTION

The presidential election contest of 1840 marked the culmination of the democratic revolution that swept the United States. By this time, the **second party system** had taken hold, a system whereby the older Federalist and Democratic-Republican Parties had been replaced by the new Democratic and Whig Parties. Both Whigs and Democrats jockeyed for election victories and commanded the steady loyalty of political partisans. Large-scale presidential campaign rallies and emotional propaganda became the order of the day. Voter turnout increased dramatically under the second party system. Roughly 25 percent of eligible voters had cast ballots in 1828. In 1840, voter participation surged to nearly 80 percent.

The differences between the parties were largely about economic policies. Whigs advocated accelerated economic growth, often endorsing federal government projects to achieve that goal. Democrats did not view the federal government as an engine promoting economic growth and advocated a smaller role for the national government. The membership of the parties also differed: Whigs tended to be wealthier; they were prominent planters in the South and wealthy urban northerners—in other words, the beneficiaries of the market revolution. Democrats presented themselves as defenders of the common people against the elite.

In the 1840 presidential campaign, taking their cue from the Democrats who had lionized Jackson's military accomplishments, the Whigs promoted William Henry Harrison as a war hero based on his 1811 military service against the Shawnee chief Tecumseh at the Battle of Tippecanoe. John Tyler of Virginia ran as the vice presidential candidate, leading the Whigs to trumpet, "Tippecanoe and Tyler too!" as a campaign slogan.

The campaign thrust Harrison into the national spotlight. Democrats tried to discredit him by declaring, "Give him a barrel of hard [alcoholic] cider and settle a pension of two thousand a year on him, and take my word for it, he will sit the remainder of his days in his log cabin." The Whigs turned the slur to their advantage by presenting Harrison as a man of the people who had been born in a log cabin (in fact, he came from a privileged background in Virginia), and the contest became known as the **log cabin campaign**. At Whig political rallies, the faithful were treated to whiskey made by the E. C. Booz Company, leading to the introduction of the word "booze" into the American lexicon. Tippecanoe Clubs, where booze flowed freely, helped in the marketing of the Whig candidate.

 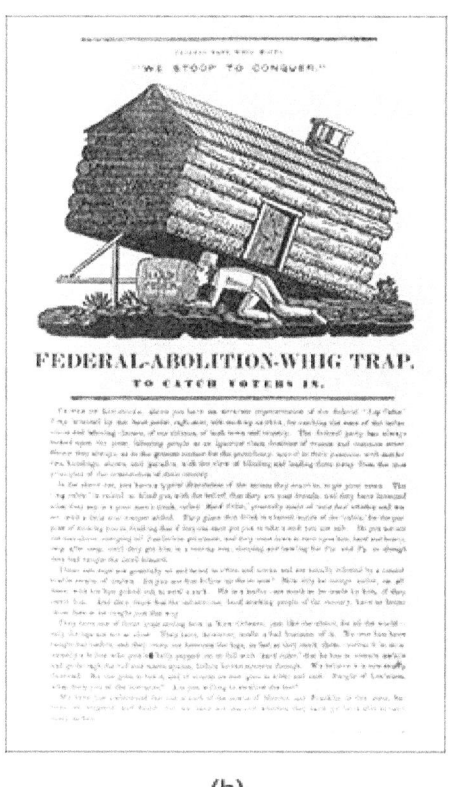

The Whig campaign song "Tippecanoe and Tyler Too!" (a) and the anti-Whig flyers (b) that were circulated in response to the "log cabin campaign" illustrate the partisan fervor of the 1840 election.

The Whigs' efforts, combined with their strategy of blaming Democrats for the lingering economic collapse that began with the hard-currency Panic of 1837, succeeded in carrying the day. A mass campaign with political rallies and party mobilization had molded a candidate to fit an ideal palatable to a majority of American voters, and in 1840 Harrison won what many consider the first modern election.

Section Summary

American culture of the 1830s reflected the rise of democracy. The majority exercised a new type of power that went well beyond politics, leading Alexis de Tocqueville to write about the "tyranny of the majority." Very quickly, politicians among the Whigs and Democrats learned to master the magic of the many by presenting candidates and policies that catered to the will of the majority. In the 1840 "log cabin campaign," both sides engaged in the new democratic electioneering. The uninhibited expression during the campaign inaugurated a new political style.

https://www.openassessments.org/assessments/976

Review Question

1. How did Alexis de Tocqueville react to his visit to the United States? What impressed and what worried him?

Answer to Review Question

1. Tocqueville came to believe that democracy was an unstoppable force whose major benefit was equality before the law. However, he also described the tyranny of the majority, which overpowers the will of minorities and individuals.

Critical Thinking Questions

1. What were some of the social and cultural beliefs that became widespread during the Age of Jackson? What lay behind these beliefs, and do you observe any of them in American culture today?
2. Were the political changes of the early nineteenth century positive or negative? Explain your opinion.
3. If you were defending the Cherokee and other native nations before the U.S. Supreme Court in the 1830s, what arguments would you make? If you were supporting Indian removal, what arguments would you make?
4. How did depictions of Indians in popular culture help to sway popular opinion? Does modern popular culture continue to wield this kind of power over us? Why or why not?
5. Does Alexis de Tocqueville's argument about the tyranny of the majority reflect American democracy today? Provide examples to support your answer.

Glossary

log cabin campaign the 1840 election, in which the Whigs painted William Henry Harrison as a man of the people

second party system the system in which the Democratic and Whig Parties were the two main political parties after the decline of the Federalist and Democratic-Republican Parties

tyranny of the majority Alexis de Tocqueville's phrase warning of the dangers of American democracy

Attributions

CC licensed content, Shared previously

- US History. **Authored by**: P. Scott Corbett, Volker Janssen, John M. Lund, Todd Pfannestiel, Paul Vickery, and Sylvie Waskiewicz. **Provided by**: OpenStax College. **Located at**: http://openstaxcollege.org/textbooks/us-history. **License**: *CC BY: Attribution*. **License Terms**: Download for free at http://cnx.org/content/col11740/latest/

Primary Source Reading: "An Address to the Whites"

Elias Boudinot, "An Address to the Whites," Philadelphia, May 26, 1826

Introduction

Elias Boudinot (born Gallegina Uwati, also known as Buck Watie[1]) (1802 – June 22, 1839), was a member of a prominent family of the Cherokee Nation who was born in and grew up in present-day Georgia. His Cherokee name reportedly means either 'male deer' or 'turkey.' Educated at a missionary school in Connecticut, he became one of several leaders who believed that acculturation was critical to Cherokee survival; he was influential in the period of removal to Indian Territory. In 1828 Boudinot became the editor of the Cherokee Phoenix, the first Native American newspaper. It published in Cherokee and English, to showcase Cherokee achievements as well as to build unity within the Nation while under United States pressure for Indian Removal.

Boudinot delivered this speech in the First Presbyterian Church in Philadelphia on May 26, 1826. He described the similarities between the Cherokee and the whites, and ways in which the Cherokee were adopting aspects of white culture. He was fundraising for a Cherokee national academy and printing equipment for the newspaper, support for "civilizing" the Cherokee. Following the speech, he published his speech in a pamphlet by the same title. "An Address to the Whites" was well received and "proved to be remarkably effective at fund-raising".

Text

Download and read the speech HERE: nationalhumanitiescenter.org/pds/triumphnationalism/expansion/text3/addresswhites.pdf (From the National Humanities Center).

Attributions

CC licensed content, Shared previously

- Elias Boudinot. **Provided by**: Wikipedia. **Located at**: https://en.wikipedia.org/wiki/Elias_Boudinot_%28Cherokee%29. **License**: *CC BY-SA: Attribution-ShareAlike*

Primary Source Reading: Speech to Congress on India Removal

Introduction

The Indian Removal Act was passed by Congress on May 28, 1830, during the presidency of Andrew Jackson. The law authorized the president to negotiate with Indian tribes in the Southern United States for their removal to federal territory west of the Mississippi River in exchange for their ancestral homelands.

The act enjoyed strong support from the non-native peoples of the South, who were eager to gain access to lands inhabited by the Five Civilized Tribes. Christian missionaries, such as Jeremiah Evarts, protested against the law's passage.

Andrew Jackson's Speech to Congress on Indian Removal

"It gives me pleasure to announce to Congress that the benevolent policy of the Government, steadily pursued for nearly thirty years, in relation to the removal of the Indians beyond the white settlements is approaching to a happy consummation. Two important tribes have accepted the provision made for their removal at the last session of Congress, and it is believed that their example will induce the remaining tribes also to seek the same obvious advantages.

The consequences of a speedy removal will be important to the United States, to individual States, and to the Indians themselves. The pecuniary advantages which it promises to the Government are the least of its recommendations. It puts an end to all possible danger of collision between the authorities of the General and State Governments on account of the Indians. It will place a dense and civilized population in large tracts of country now occupied by a few savage hunters. By opening the whole territory between Tennessee on the north and Louisiana on the south to the settlement of the whites it will incalculably strengthen the southwestern frontier and render the adjacent States strong enough to repel future invasions without remote aid. It will relieve the whole State of Mississippi and the western part of Alabama of Indian occupancy, and enable those States to advance rapidly in population, wealth, and power. It will separate the Indians from immediate contact with settlements of whites; free them from the power of the States; enable them to pursue happiness in their own way and under their own rude institutions; will retard the progress of decay, which is lessening their numbers, and perhaps cause them gradually, under the protection of the Government and through the influence of good counsels, to cast off their savage habits and become an interesting, civilized, and Christian community.

What good man would prefer a country covered with forests and ranged by a few thousand savages to our extensive Republic, studded with cities, towns, and prosperous farms embellished with all the improvements which art can devise or industry execute, occupied by more than 12,000,000 happy people, and filled with all the blessings of liberty, civilization and religion?

The present policy of the Government is but a continuation of the same progressive change by a milder process. The tribes which occupied the countries now constituting the Eastern States were annihilated or have melted away to make room for the whites. The waves of population and civilization are rolling to the westward, and we now propose to acquire the countries occupied by the red men of the South and West by a fair exchange, and, at the expense of the United States, to send them to land where their existence may be prolonged and perhaps made perpetual. Doubtless it will be painful to leave the graves of their fathers; but what do they more than our ancestors did or than our children are now doing? To better their condition in an unknown land our forefathers left all that was dear in earthly objects. Our children by thousands yearly leave the land of their birth to seek new homes in distant regions. Does Humanity weep at these painful separations from everything, animate and inanimate, with which the young heart has become entwined? Far from it. It is rather a source of joy that our country affords scope where our young population may range unconstrained in body or in mind, developing the power and facilities of man in their highest perfection. These remove hundreds and almost thousands of miles at their own expense, purchase the lands they occupy, and support themselves at their new homes from the moment of their arrival. Can it be cruel in this Government when, by events which it cannot control, the Indian is made discontented in his ancient home to purchase his lands, to give him a new and extensive territory, to pay the expense of his removal, and support him a year in his new abode? How many thousands of our own people would gladly embrace National Park Service, Park Museum Management Program Teaching with Museum Collections the opportunity of removing to the West on such conditions! If the offers made to the Indians were extended to them, they would be hailed with gratitude and joy.

And is it supposed that the wandering savage has a stronger attachment to his home than the settled, civilized Christian? Is it more afflicting to him to leave the graves of his fathers than it is to our brothers and children? Rightly considered, the policy of the General Government toward the red man is not only liberal, but generous. He is unwilling to submit to the laws of the States and mingle with their population. To save him from this alternative, or perhaps utter annihilation, the General Government kindly offers him a new home, and proposes to pay the whole expense of his removal and settlement."

Citation: President Jackson's Message to Congress "On Indian Removal", December 6, 1830; Records of the United States Senate, 1789-1990; Record Group 46; Records of the United States Senate, 1789-1990; National Archives and Records Administration (NARA]

Attributions

Public domain content

- President Jackson's Message to Congress On Indian Removal. **Located at**: http://www.nps.gov/museum/tmc/manz/handouts/andrew_jackson_annual_message.pdf. **License**: *Public Domain: No Known Copyright*

Primary Source Reading: Jackson and the Bank of the U.S.

President Jackson's Veto Message Regarding the Bank of the United States; July 10, 1832

VETO MESSAGE.

WASHINGTON, July 10, 1832.

To the Senate.

The bill " to modify and continue " the act entitled "An act to incorporate the subscribers to the Bank of the United States " was presented to me on the 4th July instant. Having considered it with that solemn regard to the principles of the Constitution which the day was calculated to inspire, and come to the conclusion that it ought not to become a law, I herewith return it to the Senate, in which it originated, with my objections.

A bank of the United States is in many respects convenient for the Government and useful to the people. Entertaining this opinion, and deeply impressed with the belief that some of the powers and privileges possessed by the existing bank are unauthorized by the Constitution, subversive of the rights of the States, and dangerous to the liberties of the people, I felt it my duty at an early period of my Administration to call the attention of Congress to the practicability of organizing an institution combining all its advantages and obviating these objections. I sincerely regret that in the act before me I can perceive none of those modifications of the bank charter which are necessary, in my opinion, to make it compatible with justice, with sound policy, or with the Constitution of our country.

The present corporate body, denominated the president, directors, and company of the Bank of the United States, will have existed at the time this act is intended to take effect twenty years. It enjoys an exclusive privilege of banking under the authority of the General Government, a monopoly of its favor and support, and, as a necessary consequence, almost a monopoly of the foreign and domestic exchange. The powers, privileges, and favors bestowed upon it in the original charter, by increasing the value of the stock far above its par value, operated as a gratuity of many millions to the stockholders.

An apology may be found for the failure to guard against this result in the consideration that the effect of the original act of incorporation could not be certainly foreseen at the time of its passage. The act before me proposes another gratuity to the holders of the same stock, and in many cases to the same men, of at least seven millions more. This donation finds no apology in any uncertainty as to the effect of the act. On all hands it is conceded that its passage will increase at least so or 30 per cent more the market price of the stock, subject to the payment of the annuity of $200,000 per year secured by the act, thus adding in a moment one-fourth to its par value. It is not our own citizens only who are to receive the bounty of our Government. More than eight millions of the stock of this bank are held by foreigners. By this act the American Republic proposes virtually to make them a present of some millions of dollars. For these gratuities to foreigners and to some of our own opulent citizens the act secures no equivalent whatever. They are the certain gains of the present stockholders under the operation of this act, after making full allowance for the payment of the bonus.

Every monopoly and all exclusive privileges are granted at the expense of the public, which ought to receive a fair equivalent. The many millions which this act proposes to bestow on the stockholders of the existing bank must come directly or indirectly out of the earnings of the American people. It is due to them, therefore, if their Government sell monopolies and exclusive privileges, that they should at least exact for them as much as they are worth in open market. The value of the monopoly in this case may be correctly ascertained. The twenty-eight millions of stock would probably be at an advance of 50 per cent, and command in market at least $42,000,000, subject to the payment of the present bonus. The present value of the monopoly, therefore, is $17,000,000, and this the act proposes to sell for three millions, payable in fifteen annual installments of $200,000 each.

It is not conceivable how the present stockholders can have any claim to the special favor of the Government. The present corporation has enjoyed its monopoly during the period stipulated in the original contract. If we must have such a corporation, why should not the Government sell out the whole stock and thus secure to the people the full market value of the privileges granted? Why should not Congress create and sell twenty-eight millions of stock, incorporating the purchasers with all the powers and privileges secured in this act and putting the premium upon the sales into the Treasury?

But this act does not permit competition in the purchase of this monopoly. It seems to be predicated on the erroneous idea that the present stockholders have a prescriptive right not only to the favor but to the bounty of Government. It appears that more than a fourth part of the stock is held by foreigners and the residue is held by a few hundred of our own citizens, chiefly of the richest class. For their benefit does this act exclude the whole American people from competition in the purchase of this monopoly and dispose of it for many millions less than it is worth. This seems the less excusable because some of our citizens not now stockholders petitioned that the door of competition might be opened, and offered to take a charter on terms much more favorable to the Government and country.

But this proposition, although made by men whose aggregate wealth is believed to be equal to all the private stock in the existing bank, has been set aside, and the bounty of our Government is proposed to be again bestowed on the few who have been fortunate enough to secure the stock and at this moment wield the power of the existing institution. I can not perceive the justice or policy of this course. If our Government must sell monopolies, it would seem to be its duty to take nothing less than their full value, and if gratuities must be made once in fifteen or twenty years let them not be bestowed on the subjects of a foreign government nor upon a designated and favored class of men in our own country. It is but justice and good policy, as far as the nature of the case will admit, to confine our favors to our own fellow-citizens, and let each in his turn enjoy an opportunity to profit by our bounty. In the bearings of the act before me upon these points I find ample reasons why it should not become a law.

…

I have now done my duty to my country. If sustained by my fellow citizens, I shall be grateful and happy; if not, I shall find in the motives which impel me ample grounds for contentment and peace. In the difficulties which surround us and the dangers which threaten our institutions there is cause for neither dismay nor alarm. For relief and deliverance let us firmly rely on that kind Providence which I am sure watches with peculiar care over the destinies of our Republic, and on the intelligence and wisdom of our countrymen. Through His abundant goodness and heir patriotic devotion our liberty and Union will be preserved.

ANDREW JACKSON.

Source:

A Compilation of the Messages and Papers of the Presidents
Prepared under the direction of the Joint Committee on printing, of the House and Senate
Pursuant to an Act of the Fifty-Second Congress of the United States.
New York: Bureau of National Literature, Inc., 1897

Attributions

Public domain content

- President Jackson's Veto Message Regarding the Bank of the United States; July 10, 1832. **Located at**: http://avalon.law.yale.edu/19th_century/ajveto01.asp. **Project**: The Avalon Project. **License**: *Public Domain: No Known Copyright*

11. A Nation on the Move: Westward Expansion, 1800-1860

Introduction

After 1800, the United States militantly expanded westward across North America, confident of its right and duty to gain control of the continent and spread the benefits of its "superior" culture. In John Gast's *American Progress*, the white, blonde figure of Columbia—a historical personification of the United States—strides triumphantly westward with the Star of Empire on her head. She brings education, symbolized by the schoolbook, and modern technology, represented by the telegraph wire. White settlers follow her lead, driving the helpless natives away and bringing successive waves of technological progress in their wake. In the first half of the nineteenth century, the quest for control of the West led to the Louisiana Purchase, the annexation of Texas, and the Mexican-American War. Efforts to seize western territories from native peoples and expand the republic by warring with Mexico succeeded beyond expectations. Few nations ever expanded so quickly. Yet, this expansion led to debates about the fate of slavery in the West, creating tensions between North and South that ultimately led to the collapse of American democracy and a brutal civil war.

In the first half of the nineteenth century, settlers began to move west of the Mississippi River in large numbers. In John Gast's American Progress (ca. 1872), the figure of Columbia, representing the United States and the spirit of democracy, makes her way westward, literally bringing light to the darkness as she advances.

Attributions

CC licensed content, Shared previously

- US History. **Authored by**: P. Scott Corbett, Volker Janssen, John M. Lund, Todd Pfannestiel, Paul Vickery, and Sylvie Waskiewicz. **Provided by**: OpenStax College. **Located at**: http://openstaxcollege.org/textbooks/us-history. **License**: CC BY: Attribution. **License Terms**: Download for free at http://cnx.org/content/col11740/latest/

Lewis and Clark

> ### Learning Objectives
>
> By the end of this section, you will be able to:
>
> - Explain the significance of the Louisiana Purchase
> - Describe the terms of the Adams-Onís Treaty
> - Describe the role played by the filibuster in American expansion

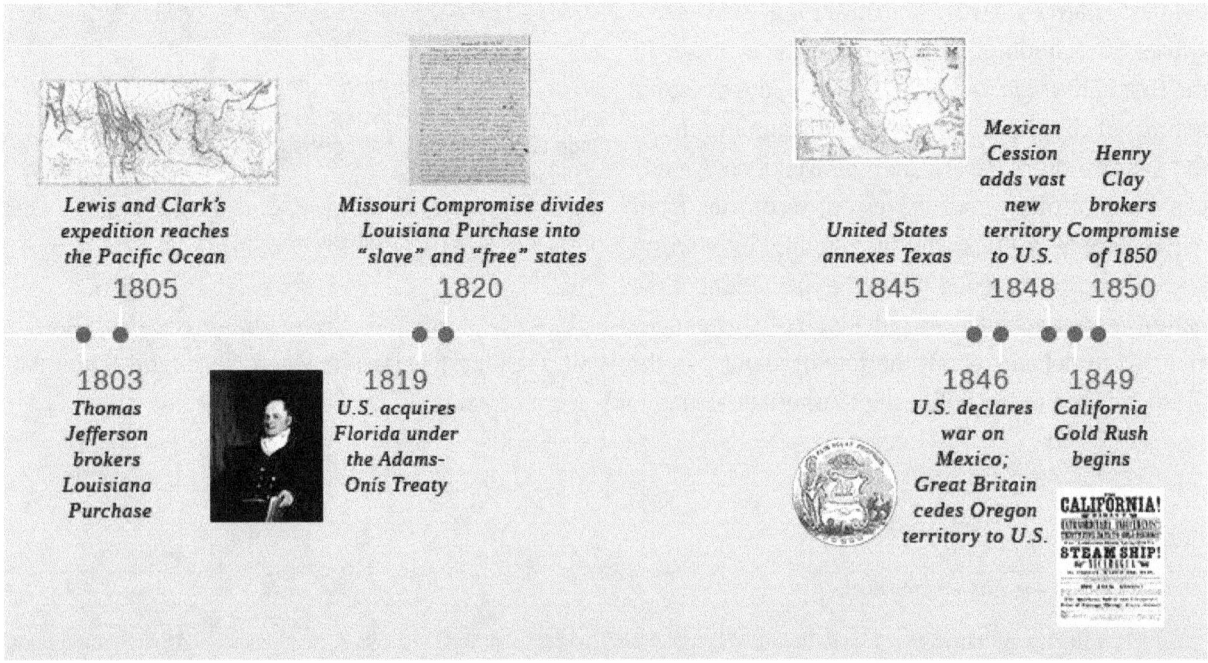

For centuries Europeans had mistakenly believed an all-water route across the North American continent existed. This **"Northwest Passage"** would afford the country that controlled it not only access to the interior of North America but also—more importantly—a relatively quick route to the Pacific Ocean and to trade with Asia. The Spanish, French, and British searched for years before American explorers took up the challenge of finding it. Indeed, shortly before Lewis and Clark set out on their expedition for the U.S. government, Alexander Mackenzie, an officer of the British North West Company, a fur trading outfit, had attempted to discover the route. Mackenzie made it to the Pacific and even believed (erroneously) he had discovered the headwaters of the Columbia River, but he could not find an easy water route with a minimum of difficult portages, that is, spots where boats must be carried overland.

Many Americans also dreamed of finding a Northwest Passage and opening the Pacific to American commerce and influence, including President Thomas Jefferson. In April 1803, Jefferson achieved his goal of purchasing the Louisiana Territory from France, effectively doubling the size of the United States. The purchase was made possible due to events outside the nation's control. With the success of the Haitian Revolution, an uprising of slaves against the French, France's Napoleon abandoned his quest to re-establish an extensive French Empire in America. As a result, he was amenable to selling off the vast Louisiana territory. President Jefferson quickly set out to learn precisely what he had bought and to assess its potential for commercial exploitation. Above all else, Jefferson wanted to exert U.S. control over the territory, an area already well known to French and British explorers. It was therefore vital for the United States to explore and map the land to pave the way for future white settlement.

JEFFERSON'S CORPS OF DISCOVERY HEADS WEST

To head the expedition into the Louisiana territory, Jefferson appointed his friend and personal secretary, twenty-nine-year-old army captain Meriwether Lewis, who was instructed to form a **Corps of Discovery**. Lewis in turn selected William Clark, who had once been his commanding officer, to help him lead the group.

Jefferson wanted to improve the ability of American merchants to access the ports of China. Establishing a river route from St. Louis to the Pacific Ocean was crucial to capturing a portion of the fur trade that had proven so profitable to Great Britain. He also wanted to legitimize American claims to the land against rivals, such as Great Britain and Spain. Lewis and Clark were thus instructed to map the territory through which they would pass and to explore all tributaries of the Missouri River. This part of the expedition struck fear into Spanish officials, who believed that Lewis and Clark would encroach on New Mexico, the northern part of New Spain. Spain dispatched four unsuccessful expeditions from Santa Fe to intercept the explorers. Lewis and Clark also had directives to estab-

(a)   (b)

Charles Willson Peale, celebrated portraitist of the American Revolution, painted both William Clark (a) and Meriwether Lewis (b) in 1810 and 1807, respectively, after they returned from their expedition west.

lish friendly relationships with the western tribes, introducing them to American trade goods and encouraging warring groups to make peace. Establishing an overland route to the Pacific would bolster U.S. claims to the Pacific Northwest, first established in 1792 when Captain Robert Gray sailed his ship *Columbia* into the mouth of the river that now bears his vessel's name and forms the present-day border between Oregon and Washington. Finally, Jefferson, who had a keen interest in science and nature, ordered Lewis and Clark to take extensive notes on the geography, plant life, animals, and natural resources of the region into which they would journey.

After spending the winter of 1803–1804 encamped at the mouth of the Missouri River while the men prepared for their expedition, the corps set off in May 1804. Although the thirty-three frontiersmen, boatmen, and hunters took with them Alexander Mackenzie's account of his explorations and the best maps they could find, they did not have any real understanding of the difficulties they would face. Fierce storms left them drenched and freezing. Enormous clouds of gnats and mosquitos swarmed about their heads as they made their way up the Missouri River. Along the way they encountered (and killed) a variety of animals including elk, buffalo, and grizzly bears. One member of the expedition survived a rattlesnake bite. As the men collected minerals and specimens of plants and animals, the overly curious Lewis sampled minerals by tasting them and became seriously ill at one point. What they did not collect, they sketched and documented in the journals they kept. They also noted the customs of the Indian tribes who controlled the land and attempted to establish peaceful relationships with them in order to ensure that future white settlement would not be impeded.

> Read the journals of Lewis and Clark on the University of Virginia website or on the University of Nebraska–Lincoln website, which also has footnotes, maps, and commentary. According to their writings, what challenges did the explorers confront?

The corps spent their first winter in the wilderness, 1804–1805, in a Mandan village in what is now North Dakota. There they encountered a reminder of France's former vast North American empire when they met a French fur trapper named Toussaint Charbonneau. When the corps left in the spring of 1805, Charbonneau accompanied them as a guide and interpreter, bringing his teenage Shoshone wife Sacagawea and their newborn son. Charbonneau knew the land better than the Americans, and Sacagawea proved invaluable in many ways, not least of which was that the presence of a young woman and her infant convinced many groups that the men were not a war party and meant no harm.

The corps set about making friends with native tribes while simultaneously attempting to assert American power over the territory. Hoping to overawe the people of the land, Lewis would let out a blast of his air rifle, a relatively new piece of technology the Indians had never seen. The corps also followed native custom by distributing gifts, including shirts, ribbons, and kettles, as a sign of goodwill. The explorers presented native leaders with medallions, many of which bore Jefferson's image, and invited them to visit their new "ruler" in the East. These medallions or peace medals were meant to allow future explorers to identify friendly native groups. Not all efforts to assert U.S. control went peacefully; some Indians rejected the explorers' intrusion onto their land. An encounter with the Blackfoot turned hostile, for example, and members of the corps killed two Blackfoot men.

In this idealized image, Sacagawea leads Lewis and Clark through the Montana wilderness. In reality, she was still a teenager at the time and served as interpreter; she did not actually guide the party, although legend says she did. Kidnapped as a child, she would not likely have retained detailed memories about the place where she grew up.

After spending eighteen long months on the trail and nearly starving to death in the Bitterroot Mountains of Montana, the Corps of Discovery finally reached the Pacific Ocean in 1805 and spent the winter of 1805–1806 in Oregon. They returned to St. Louis later in 1806 having lost only one man, who had died of appendicitis. Upon their return, Meriwether Lewis was named governor of the Louisiana Territory. Unfortunately, he died only three years later in circumstances that are still disputed, before he could write a complete account of what the expedition had discovered.

Although the Corps of Discovery failed to find an all-water route to the Pacific Ocean (for none existed), it nevertheless accomplished many of the goals Jefferson had set. The men traveled across the North American continent and established relationships with many Indian tribes, paving the way for fur traders like John Jacob Astor who later established trading posts solidifying U.S. claims to Oregon. Delegates of several tribes did go to Washington to meet the president. Hundreds of plant and animal specimens were collected, several of which were named for Lewis and Clark in recognition of their efforts. And the territory was now more accurately mapped and legally claimed by the United States. Nonetheless, most of the vast territory, home to a variety of native peoples, remained unknown to Americans.

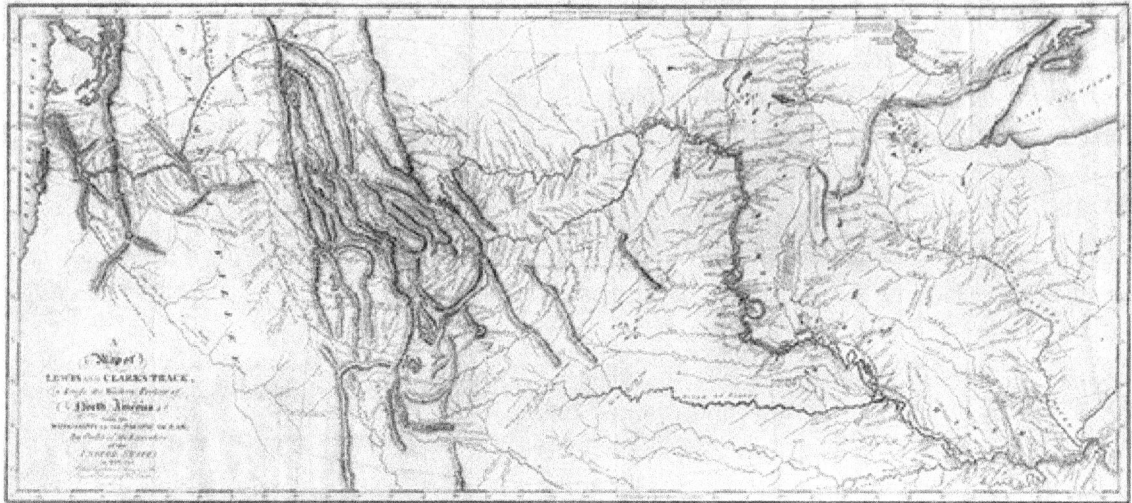

This 1814 map of Lewis and Clark's path across North America from the Missouri River to the Pacific Ocean was based on maps and notes made by William Clark. Although most of the West still remained unknown, the expedition added greatly to knowledge of what lay west of the Mississippi. Most important, it allowed the United States to solidify its claim to the immense territory.

A Selection of Hats for the Fashionable Gentleman

Beaver hats were popular apparel in the eighteenth and nineteenth centuries in both Europe and the United States because they were naturally waterproof and bore a glossy sheen. Demand for beaver pelts (and for the pelts of sea otters, foxes, and martens) by hat makers, dressmakers, and tailors led many fur trappers into the wilderness in pursuit of riches. Beaver hats fell out of fashion in the 1850s when silk hats became the rage and beaver became harder to find. In some parts of the West, the animals had been hunted nearly to extinction.

Are there any contemporary fashions or fads that likewise promise to alter the natural world?

SPANISH FLORIDA AND THE ADAMS-ONÍS TREATY

Despite the Lewis and Clark expedition, the boundaries of the Louisiana Purchase remained contested. Expansionists chose to believe the purchase included vast stretches of land, including all of Spanish Texas. The Spanish government disagreed, however. The first attempt to resolve this issue took place in February 1819 with the signing of the Adams-Onís Treaty, which was actually intended to settle the problem of Florida.

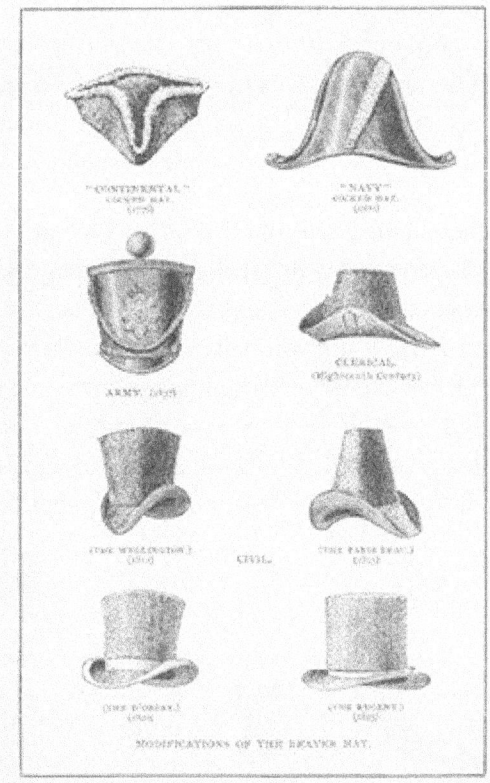

This illustration from Castrologia, Or, The History and Traditions of the Canadian Beaver shows a variety of beaver hat styles. Beaver pelts were also used to trim women's bonnets.

Spanish Florida had presented difficulties for its neighbors since the settlement of the original North American colonies, first for England and then for the United States. By 1819, American settlers no longer feared attack by Spanish troops garrisoned in Florida, but hostile tribes like the Creek and Seminole raided Georgia and then retreated to the relative safety of the Florida wilderness. These tribes also sheltered runaway slaves, often intermarrying with them and making them members of their tribes. Sparsely populated by Spanish colonists and far from both Mexico City and Madrid, the frontier in Florida proved next to impossible for the Spanish government to control.

In March 1818, General Andrew Jackson, frustrated by his inability to punish Creek and Seminole raiders, pursued them across the international border into Spanish Florida. Under Jackson's command, U.S. troops defeated the Creek and Seminole, occupied several Florida settlements, and executed two British citizens accused of acting against the United States. Outraged by the U.S. invasion of its territory, the Spanish government demanded that Jackson and his troops withdraw. In agreeing to the withdrawal, however, U.S. Secretary of State John Quincy Adams also offered to purchase the colony. Realizing that conflict between the United States and the Creeks and Seminoles would continue, Spain opted to cede the Spanish colony to its northern neighbor. The Adams-Onís Treaty, named for Adams and the Spanish ambassador, Luís de Onís, made the cession of Florida official while also setting the boundary between the United States and Mexico at the Sabine River. In exchange, Adams gave up U.S. claims to lands west of the Sabine and forgave Spain's $5 million debt to the United States.

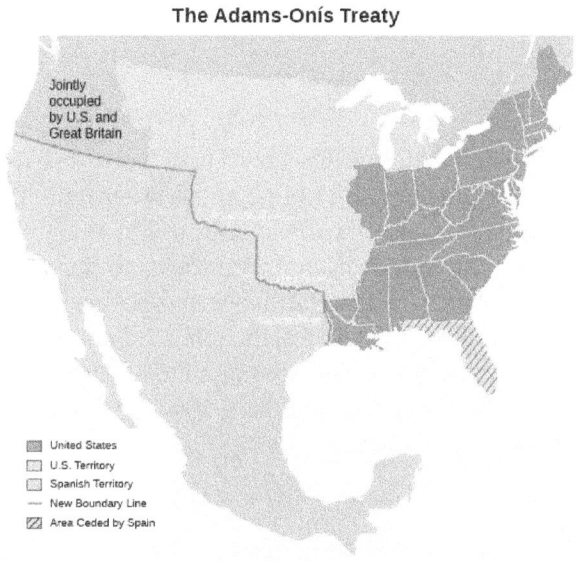

The red line indicates the border between U.S. and Spanish territory established by the Adams-Onís Treaty of 1819.

The Adams-Onís Treaty upset many American expansionists, who criticized Adams for not laying claim to all of Texas, which they believed had been included in the Louisiana Purchase. In the summer of 1819, James Long, a planter from Natchez, Mississippi, became a **filibuster**, or a private, unauthorized military adventurer, when he led three hundred men on an expedition across the Sabine River to take control of Texas. Long's men succeeded in capturing Nacogdoches, writing a Declaration of Independence (see below), and setting up a republican government. Spanish troops drove them out a month later. Returning in 1820 with a much smaller force, Long was arrested by the Spanish authorities, imprisoned, and killed. Long was but one of many nineteenth-century American filibusters who aimed at seizing territory in the Caribbean and Central America.

The Long Expedition's Declaration of Independence

The Long Expedition's short-lived Republic of Texas was announced with the drafting of a Declaration of Independence in 1819. The declaration named settlers' grievances against the limits put on expansion by the Adams-Onís treaty and expressed their fears of Spain:

> The citizens of Texas have long indulged the hope, that in the adjustment of the boundaries of the Spanish possessions in America, and of the territories of the United States, that they should be included within the limits of the latter. The claims of the United States, long and strenuously urged, encouraged the hope. The recent [Adams-Onís] treaty between Spain and the United States of America has dissipated an illusion too long fondly cherished, and has roused the citizens of Texas... They have seen themselves... literally abandoned to the dominion of the crown of Spain and left a prey... to all those exactions which Spanish rapacity is fertile in devising. The citizens of Texas would have proved themselves unworthy of the age... unworthy of their ancestry, of the kindred of the republics of the American continent, could they have hesitated in this emergency... Spurning the fetters of colonial vassalage, disdaining to submit to the most atrocious despotism that ever disgraced the annals of Europe, they have resolved under the blessing of God to be free.

How did the filibusters view Spain? What do their actions say about the nature of American society and of U.S. expansion?

Section Summary

In 1803, Thomas Jefferson appointed Meriwether Lewis to organize an expedition into the Louisiana Territory to explore and map the area but also to find an all-water route from the Missouri River to the Pacific Coast. The Louisiana Purchase and the journey of Lewis and Clark's Corps of Discovery captured the imagination of many, who dedicated themselves to the economic exploitation of the western lands and the expansion of American influence and power. In the South, the Adams-Onís treaty legally secured Florida for the United States, though it did nothing to end the resistance of the Seminoles against American expansionists. At the same time, the treaty frustrated those Americans who considered Texas a part of the Louisiana Purchase. Taking matters into their own hands, some American settlers tried to take Texas by force.

- https://www.openassessments.org/assessments/977

Review Question

1. For what purposes did Thomas Jefferson send Lewis and Clark to explore the Louisiana Territory? What did he want them to accomplish?

Answer to Review Question

1. Jefferson wanted Lewis and Clark to find an all-water route to the Pacific Ocean, strengthen U.S. claims to the Pacific Northwest by reaching it through an overland route, explore and map the territory, make note of its natural resources and wildlife, and make contact with Indian tribes with the intention of establishing trade with them.

Glossary

Corps of Discovery the group led by Meriwether Lewis and William Clark on the expedition to explore and map the territory acquired in the Louisiana Purchase

filibuster a person who engages in an unofficial military operation intended to seize land from foreign countries or foment revolution there

Northwest Passage the nonexistent all-water route across the North American continent sought by European and American explorers

Attributions

CC licensed content, Shared previously

- US History. **Authored by**: P. Scott Corbett, Volker Janssen, John M. Lund, Todd Pfannestiel, Paul Vickery, and Sylvie Waskiewicz. **Provided by**: OpenStax College. **Located at**: http://openstaxcollege.org/textbooks/us-history. **License**: *CC BY: Attribution*. **License Terms**: Download for free at http://cnx.org/content/col11740/latest/

The Missouri Crisis

Learning Objectives

By the end of this section, you will be able to:

- Explain why the North and South differed over the admission of Missouri as a state
- Explain how the admission of new states to the Union threatened to upset the balance between free and slave states in Congress

Another stage of U.S. expansion took place when inhabitants of Missouri began petitioning for statehood beginning in 1817. The Missouri territory had been part of the Louisiana Purchase and was the first part of that vast acquisition to apply for statehood. By 1818, tens of thousands of settlers had flocked to Missouri, including slaveholders who brought with them some ten thousand slaves. When the status of the Missouri territory was taken up in earnest in the U.S. House of Representatives in early 1819, its admission to the Union proved to be no easy matter, since it brought to the surface a violent debate over whether slavery would be allowed in the new state.

Politicians had sought to avoid the issue of slavery ever since the 1787 Constitutional Convention arrived at an uneasy compromise in the form of the "three-fifths clause." This provision stated that the entirety of a state's free population and 60 percent of its enslaved population would be counted in establishing the number of that state's members in the House of Representatives and the size of its federal tax bill. Although slavery existed in several northern states at the time, the compromise had angered many northern politicians because, they argued, the "extra" population of slaves would give southern states more votes than they deserved in both the House and the Electoral College. Admitting Missouri as a slave state also threatened the tenuous balance between free and slave states in the Senate by giving slave states a two-vote advantage.

The debate about representation shifted to the morality of slavery itself when New York representative James Tallmadge, an opponent of slavery, attempted to amend the statehood bill in the House of Representatives. Tallmadge proposed that Missouri be admitted as a free state, that no more slaves be allowed to enter Missouri after it achieved statehood, and that all enslaved children born there after its admission be freed at age twenty-five. The amendment shifted the terms of debate by presenting slavery as an evil to be stopped.

Northern representatives supported the **Tallmadge Amendment**, denouncing slavery as immoral and opposed to the nation's founding principles of equality and liberty. Southerners in Congress rejected the amendment as an attempt to gradually abolish slavery—not just in Missouri but throughout the Union—by violating the property rights of slaveholders and their freedom to take their property wherever they wished. Slavery's apologists, who had long argued that slavery was a necessary evil, now began to perpetuate the idea that slavery was a positive good for the United States. They asserted that it generated wealth and left white men free to exercise their true talents instead of toiling in the soil, as the descendants of Africans were better suited to do. Slaves were cared for, supporters argued, and were better off exposed to the teachings of Christianity as slaves than living as free heathens in uncivilized Africa. Above all, the United States had a destiny, they argued, to create an empire of slavery throughout the Americas. These proslavery arguments were to be made repeatedly and forcefully as expansion to the West proceeded.

Most disturbing for the unity of the young nation, however, was that debaters divided along sectional lines, not party lines. With only a few exceptions, northerners supported the Tallmadge Amendment regardless of party affiliation, and southerners opposed it despite having party differences on other matters. It did not pass, and the crisis over Missouri led to strident calls of disunion and threats of civil war.

Congress finally came to an agreement, called the **Missouri Compromise**, in 1820. Missouri and Maine (which had been part of Massachusetts) would enter the Union at the same time, Maine as a free state, Missouri as a slave state. The Tallmadge Amendment was narrowly rejected, the balance between free and slave states was maintained in the Senate, and southerners did not have to fear that Missouri slaveholders would be deprived of their human property. To prevent similar conflicts each time a territory applied for statehood, a line coinciding with the southern border of Missouri (at latitude 36° 30′) was drawn across the remainder of the Louisiana Territory. Slavery could exist south of this line but was forbidden north of it, with the obvious exception of Missouri.

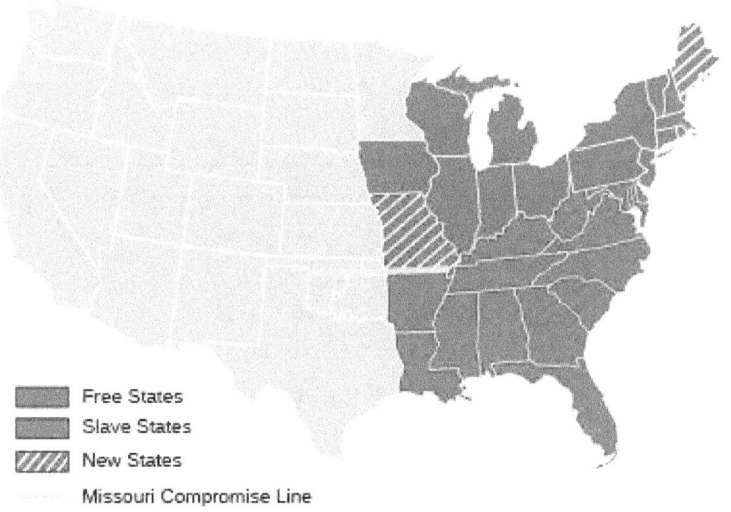

The Missouri Compromise resulted in the District of Maine, which had originally been settled in 1607 by the Plymouth Company and was a part of Massachusetts, being admitted to the Union as a free state and Missouri being admitted as a slave state.

Thomas Jefferson on the Missouri Crisis

On April 22, 1820, Thomas Jefferson wrote to John Holmes to express his reaction to the Missouri Crisis, especially the open threat of disunion and war:

> I thank you, Dear Sir, for the copy you have been so kind as to send me of the letter to your constituents on the Missouri question. it is a perfect justification to them. I had for a long time ceased to read the newspapers or pay any attention to public affairs, confident they were in good hands, and content to be a passenger in our bark to the shore from which I am not distant. but this momentous question [over slavery in Missouri], like a fire bell in the night, awakened and filled me with terror. I considered it at once as the knell of the Union. it is hushed indeed for the moment. but this is a reprieve only, not a final sentence. a geographical line, coinciding with a marked principle, moral and political, once concieved [sic] and held up to the angry passions of men, will never be obliterated; and every new irritation will mark it deeper and deeper. I can say with conscious truth that there is not a man on earth who would sacrifice more than I would, to relieve us from this heavy reproach, in any practicable way. . . .
>
> I regret that I am now to die in the belief that the useless sacrifice of themselves, by the generation of 76. to acquire self government and happiness to their country, is to be thrown away by the unwise and unworthy passions of their sons, and that my only consolation is to be that I live not to weep over it. if they would but dispassionately weigh the blessings they will throw away against an abstract principle more likely to be effected by union than by scission, they would pause before they would perpetuate this act of suicide themselves and of treason against the hopes of the world. to yourself as the faithful advocate of union I tender the offering of my high esteem and respect.
>
> Th. Jefferson

How would you characterize the former president's reaction? What do you think he means by writing that the Missouri Compromise line "is a reprieve only, not a final sentence"?

> Access a collection of primary documents relating to the Missouri Compromise, including Missouri's application for admission into the Union and Jefferson's correspondence on the Missouri question, at the Library of Congress website.

Section Summary

The Missouri Crisis created a division over slavery that profoundly and ominously shaped sectional identities and rivalries as never before. Conflict over the uneasy balance between slave and free states in Congress came to a head when Missouri petitioned to join the Union as a slave state in 1819, and the debate broadened from simple issues of representation to a critique of the morality of slavery. The debates also raised the specter of disunion and civil war, leading many, including Thomas Jefferson, to fear for the future of the republic. Under the Missouri Compromise, Missouri and Maine entered the Union at the same time, Maine as a free state, Missouri as a slave state, and a line was drawn across the remainder of the Louisiana territory north of which slavery was forbidden.

https://www.openassessments.org/assessments/978

Review Question

1. Why did the Missouri Crisis trigger threats of disunion and war? Identify the positions of both southern slaveholders and northern opponents of the spread of slavery.

Answer to Review Question

1. Northern politicians disliked the terms of the Missouri Compromise because it allowed the expansion of slavery into the lands acquired in the Louisiana Purchase. They feared this would lead to the West being dominated by slaveholders. Southerners disliked the compromise because it prohibited people from taking their slaves into the territory north of 36° 30′ latitude, which they believed was a violation of their property rights.

Glossary

Missouri Compromise an agreement reached in Congress in 1820 that allowed Missouri to enter the Union as a slave state, brought Maine into the Union as a free state, and prohibited slavery north of 36° 30′ latitude

Tallmadge Amendment an amendment (which did not pass) proposed by representative James Tallmadge in 1819 that called for Missouri to be admitted as a free state and for all slaves there to be gradually emancipated

Attributions

CC licensed content, Shared previously

- US History. **Authored by**: P. Scott Corbett, Volker Janssen, John M. Lund, Todd Pfannestiel, Paul Vickery, and Sylvie Waskiewicz. **Provided by**: OpenStax College. **Located at**: http://openstaxcollege.org/textbooks/us-history. **License**: CC BY: Attribution. **License Terms**: Download for free at http://cnx.org/content/col11740/latest/

Independence for Texas

> *Learning Objectives*
>
> By the end of this section, you will be able to:
>
> - Explain why American settlers in Texas sought independence from Mexico
> - Discuss early attempts to make Texas independent of Mexico
> - Describe the relationship between Anglo-Americans and Tejanos in Texas before and after independence

As the incursions of the earlier filibusters into Texas demonstrated, American expansionists had desired this area of Spain's empire in America for many years. After the 1819 Adams-Onís treaty established the boundary between Mexico and the United States, more American expansionists began to move into the northern portion of Mexico's province of Coahuila y Texas. Following Mexico's independence from Spain in 1821, American settlers immigrated to Texas in even larger numbers, intent on taking the land from the new and vulnerable Mexican nation in order to create a new American slave state.

AMERICAN SETTLERS MOVE TO TEXAS

After the 1819 Adams-Onís Treaty defined the U.S.-Mexico boundary, Spain began actively encouraging Americans to settle their northern province. Texas was sparsely settled, and the few Mexican farmers and ranchers who lived there were under constant threat of attack by hostile Indian tribes, especially the **Comanche**, who supplemented their hunting with raids in pursuit of horses and cattle.

To increase the non-Indian population in Texas and provide a buffer zone between its hostile tribes and the rest of Mexico, Spain began to recruit *empresarios*. An ***empresario*** was someone who brought settlers to the region in exchange for generous grants of land. Moses Austin, a once-prosperous entrepreneur reduced to poverty by the **Panic of 1819**, requested permission to settle three hundred English-speaking American residents in Texas. Spain agreed on the condition that the resettled people convert to Roman Catholicism.

On his deathbed in 1821, Austin asked his son Stephen to carry out his plans, and Mexico, which had won independence from Spain the same year, allowed Stephen to take control of his father's grant. Like Spain, Mexico also wished to encourage settlement in the state of Coahuila y Texas and passed colonization laws to encourage immigration. Thousands of Americans, primarily from slave states, flocked to Texas and quickly came to outnumber the **Tejanos**, the Mexican residents of the region. The soil and climate offered good opportunities to expand slavery and the cotton kingdom. Land was plentiful and offered at generous terms. Unlike the U.S. government, Mexico allowed buyers to pay for their land in installments and did not require a minimum purchase. Furthermore, to many whites, it seemed not only their God-given right but also their patriotic duty to populate the lands beyond the Mississippi River, bringing with them American slavery, culture, laws, and political traditions.

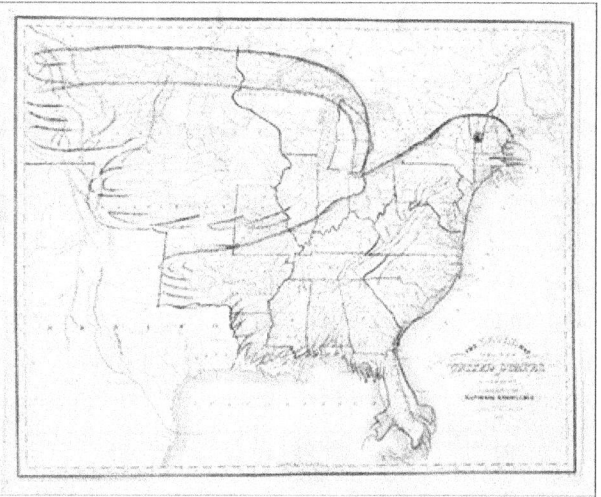

By the early 1830s, all the lands east of the Mississippi River had been settled and admitted to the Union as states. The land west of the river, though in this contemporary map united with the settled areas in the body of an eagle symbolizing the territorial ambitions of the United States, remained largely unsettled by white Americans. Texas (just southwest of the bird's tail feathers) remained outside the U.S. border.

THE TEXAS WAR FOR INDEPENDENCE

Many Americans who migrated to Texas at the invitation of the Mexican government did not completely shed their identity or loyalty to the United States. They brought American traditions and expectations with them (including, for many, the right to own slaves). For instance, the majority of these new settlers were Protestant, and though they were not required to attend the Catholic mass, Mexico's prohibition on the public practice of other religions upset them and they routinely ignored it.

Accustomed to representative democracy, jury trials, and the defendant's right to appear before a judge, the Anglo-American settlers in Texas also disliked the Mexican legal system, which provided for an initial hearing by an *alcalde*, an administrator who often combined the duties of mayor, judge, and law enforcement officer. The *alcalde* sent a written record of the proceeding to a judge in Saltillo, the state capital, who decided the outcome. Settlers also resented that at most two Texas representatives were allowed in the state legislature.

Their greatest source of discontent, though, was the Mexican government's 1829 abolition of slavery. Most American settlers were from southern states, and many had brought slaves with them. Mexico tried to accommodate them by maintaining the fiction that the slaves were indentured servants. But American slaveholders in Texas distrusted the Mexican government and wanted Texas to be a new U.S. slave state. The dislike of most for Roman Catholicism (the prevailing religion of Mexico) and a widely held belief in American racial superiority led them generally to regard Mexicans as dishonest, ignorant, and backward.

Belief in their own superiority inspired some Texans to try to undermine the power of the Mexican government. When *empresario* Haden Edwards attempted to evict people who had settled his land grant before he gained title to it, the Mexican government nullified its agreement with him. Outraged, Edwards and a small party of men took prisoner the *alcalde* of Nacogdoches. The Mexican army marched to the town, and Edwards and his troop then declared the formation of the **Republic of Fredonia** between the Sabine and Rio Grande Rivers. To demonstrate loyalty to their adopted country, a force led by Stephen Austin hastened to Nacogdoches to support the Mexican army. Edwards's revolt collapsed, and the revolutionaries fled Texas.

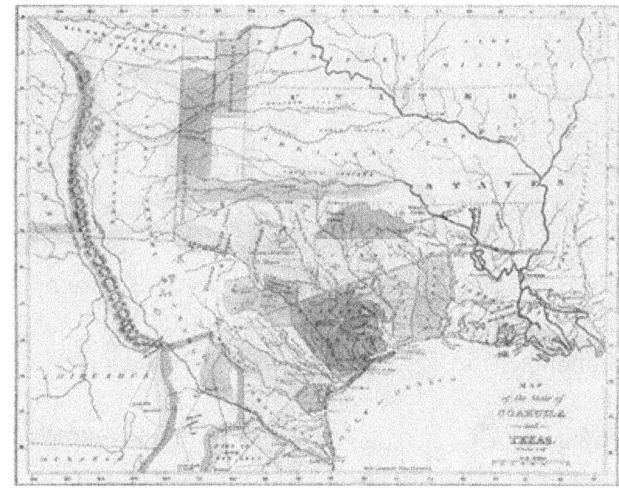

This 1833 map shows the extent of land grants made by Mexico to American settlers in Texas. Nearly all are in the eastern portion of the state, one factor that led to war with Mexico in 1846.

The growing presence of American settlers in Texas, their reluctance to abide by Mexican law, and their desire for independence caused the Mexican government to grow wary. In 1830, it forbade future U.S. immigration and increased its military presence in Texas. Settlers continued to stream illegally across the long border; by 1835, after immigration resumed, there were twenty thousand Anglo-Americans in Texas.

Fifty-five delegates from the Anglo-American settlements gathered in 1831 to demand the suspension of customs duties, the resumption of immigration from the United States, better protection from Indian tribes, the granting of promised land titles, and the creation of an independent state of Texas separate from Coahuila. Ordered to disband, the delegates reconvened in early April 1833 to write a constitution for an independent Texas. Surprisingly, General Antonio Lopez de Santa Anna, Mexico's new president, agreed to all demands, except the call for statehood. Coahuila y Texas made provisions for jury trials, increased Texas's representation in the state legislature, and removed restrictions on commerce.

Texans' hopes for independence were quashed in 1834, however, when Santa Anna dismissed the Mexican Congress and abolished all state governments, including that of Coahuila y Texas. In January 1835, reneging on earlier promises, he dispatched troops to the town of Anahuac to collect customs duties. Lawyer and soldier William B. Travis and a small force marched on Anahuac in June, and the fort surrendered. On October 2, Anglo-American forces met Mexican troops at the town of Gonzales; the Mexican troops fled and the Americans moved on to take San Antonio. Now more cautious, delegates to the Consultation of 1835 at San Felipe de Austin voted against declaring independence, instead drafting a statement, which became known as the Declaration of Causes, promising continued loyalty if Mexico returned to a constitutional form of government. They selected Henry Smith, leader of the Independence Party, as governor of Texas and placed Sam Houston, a former soldier who had been a congressman and governor of Tennessee, in charge of its small military force.

This portrait of General Antonio Lopez de Santa Anna depicts the Mexican president and general in full military regalia.

The Consultation delegates met again in March 1836. They declared their independence from Mexico and drafted a constitution calling for an American-style judicial system and an elected president and legislature. Significantly, they also established that slavery would not be prohibited in Texas. Many wealthy Tejanos supported the push for independence, hoping for liberal governmental reforms and economic benefits.

REMEMBER THE ALAMO!

Mexico had no intention of losing its northern province. Santa Anna and his army of four thousand had besieged San Antonio in February 1836. Hopelessly outnumbered, its two hundred defenders, under Travis, fought fiercely from their refuge in an old mission known as the Alamo. After ten days, however, the mission was taken and all but a few of the defenders were dead, including Travis and James Bowie, the famed frontiersman who was also a land speculator and slave trader. A few male survivors, possibly including the frontier legend and former Tennessee congressman Davy Crockett, were led outside the walls and executed. The few women and children inside the mission were allowed to leave with the only adult male survivor, a slave owned by Travis who was then freed by the Mexican Army. Terrified, they fled.

Although hungry for revenge, the Texas forces under Sam Houston nevertheless withdrew across Texas, gathering recruits as they went. Coming upon Santa Anna's encampment on the banks of San Jacinto River on April 21, 1836, they waited as the Mexican troops settled for an afternoon nap. Assured by Houston that "Victory is certain!" and told to "Trust in God and fear not!" the seven hundred men descended on a sleeping force nearly twice their number with cries of "Remember the Alamo!" Within fifteen minutes the Battle of San Jacinto was over. Approximately half the Mexican troops were killed, and the survivors, including Santa Anna, taken prisoner.

The Fall of the Alamo, painted by Theodore Gentilz fewer than ten years after this pivotal moment in the Texas Revolution, depicts the 1836 assault on the Alamo complex.

Santa Anna grudgingly signed a peace treaty and was sent to Washington, where he met with President Andrew Jackson and, under pressure, agreed to recognize an independent Texas with the Rio Grande River as its southwestern border. By the time the agreement had been signed, however, Santa Anna had been removed from power in Mexico. For that reason, the Mexican Congress refused to be bound by Santa Anna's promises and continued to insist that the renegade territory still belonged to Mexico.

> Visit the official Alamo website to learn more about the battle of the Alamo and take a virtual tour of the old mission.

THE LONE STAR REPUBLIC

In September 1836, military hero Sam Houston was elected president of Texas, and, following the relentless logic of U.S. expansion, Texans voted in favor of annexation to the United States. This had been the dream of many settlers in Texas all along. They wanted to expand the United States west and saw Texas as the next logical step. Slaveholders there, such as Sam Houston, William B. Travis and James Bowie (the latter two of whom died at the Alamo), believed too in the destiny of slavery. Mindful of the vicious debates over Missouri that had led to talk of disunion and war, American politicians were reluctant to annex Texas or, indeed, even to recognize it as a sovereign nation. Annexation would almost certainly mean war with Mexico, and the admission of a state with a large slave population, though permissible under the Missouri Compromise, would bring the issue of slavery once again to the fore. Texas had no choice but to organize itself as the independent Lone Star Republic. To protect itself from Mexican attempts to reclaim it, Texas sought and received recognition from France, Great Britain, Belgium, and the Netherlands. The United States did not officially recognize Texas as an independent nation until March 1837, nearly a year after the final victory over the Mexican army at San Jacinto.

Uncertainty about its future did not discourage Americans committed to expansion, especially slaveholders, from rushing to settle in the Lone Star Republic, however. Between 1836 and 1846, its population nearly tripled. By 1840, nearly twelve thousand enslaved Africans had been brought to Texas by American slaveholders. Many new settlers had suffered financial losses in the severe financial depression of 1837 and hoped for a new start in the new nation. According to folklore, across the United States, homes and farms were deserted overnight, and curious neighbors found notes reading only "GTT" ("Gone to Texas"). Many Europeans, especially Germans, also immigrated to Texas during this period.

In keeping with the program of ethnic cleansing and white racial domination, as illustrated by the image at the beginning of this chapter, Americans in Texas generally treated both Tejano and Indian residents with utter contempt, eager to displace and dispossess them. Anglo-American leaders failed to return the support their Tejano neighbors had extended during the rebellion and repaid them by seizing their lands. In 1839, the republic's militia attempted to drive out the Cherokee and Comanche.

The impulse to expand did not lay dormant, and Anglo-American settlers and leaders in the newly formed Texas republic soon cast their gaze on the Mexican province of New Mexico as well. Repeating the tactics of earlier filibusters, a Texas force set out in 1841 intent on taking Santa Fe. Its members encountered an army of New Mexicans and were taken prisoner and sent to Mexico City. On Christmas Day, 1842, Texans avenged a Mexican assault on San Antonio by attacking the Mexican town of Mier. In August, another Texas army was sent to attack Santa Fe, but Mexican troops forced them to retreat. Clearly, hostilities between Texas and Mexico had not ended simply because Texas had declared its independence.

Section Summary

The establishment of the Lone Star Republic formed a new chapter in the history of U.S. westward expansion. In contrast to the addition of the Louisiana Territory through diplomacy with France, Americans in Texas employed violence against Mexico to achieve their goals. Orchestrated largely by slaveholders, the acquisition of Texas appeared the next logical step in creating an American empire that included slavery. Nonetheless, with the Missouri Crisis in mind, the United States refused the Texans' request to enter the United States as a slave state in 1836. Instead, Texas formed an independent republic where slavery was legal. But American settlers there continued to press for more land. The strained relationship between expansionists in Texas and Mexico in the early 1840s hinted of things to come.

https://www.openassessments.org/assessments/979

Review Question

1. How did Texas settlers' view of Mexico and its people contribute to the history of Texas in the 1830s?

Answer to Review Question

1. American slaveholders in Texas distrusted the Mexican government's reluctant tolerance of slavery and wanted Texas to be a new U.S. slave state. Most also disliked Mexicans' Roman

> Catholicism and regarded them as dishonest, ignorant, and backward. Belief in their own superiority inspired some Texans to try to undermine the power of the Mexican government.

Glossary

alcalde a Mexican official who often served as combined civil administrator, judge, and law enforcement officer

empresario a person who brought new settlers to Texas in exchange for a grant of land

Tejanos Mexican residents of Texas

Attributions

CC licensed content, Shared previously

- US History. **Authored by**: P. Scott Corbett, Volker Janssen, John M. Lund, Todd Pfannestiel, Paul Vickery, and Sylvie Waskiewicz. **Provided by**: OpenStax College. **Located at**: http://openstaxcollege.org/textbooks/us-history. **License**: *CC BY: Attribution*. **License Terms**: Download for free at http://cnx.org/content/col11740/latest/

The Mexican-American War, 1846–1848

Learning Objectives

By the end of this section, you will be able to:

- Identify the causes of the Mexican-American War
- Describe the outcomes of the war in 1848, especially the Mexican Cession
- Describe the effect of the California Gold Rush on westward expansion

Tensions between the United States and Mexico rapidly deteriorated in the 1840s as American expansionists eagerly eyed Mexican land to the west, including the lush northern Mexican province of California. Indeed, in 1842, a U.S. naval fleet, incorrectly believing war had broken out, seized Monterey, California, a part of Mexico. Monterey was returned the next day, but the episode only added to the uneasiness with which Mexico viewed its northern neighbor. The forces of expansion, however, could not be contained, and American voters elected James Polk in 1844 because he promised to deliver more lands. President Polk fulfilled his promise by gaining Oregon and, most spectacularly, provoking a war with Mexico that ultimately fulfilled the wildest fantasies of expansionists. By 1848, the United States encompassed much of North America, a republic that stretched from the Atlantic to the Pacific.

JAMES K. POLK AND THE TRIUMPH OF EXPANSION

A fervent belief in expansion gripped the United States in the 1840s. In 1845, a New York newspaper editor, John O'Sullivan, introduced the concept of "manifest destiny" to describe the very popular idea of the special role of the United States in overspreading the continent—the divine right and duty of white Americans to seize and settle the American West, thus spreading Protestant, democratic values. In this climate of opinion, voters in 1844 elected James K. Polk, a slaveholder from Tennessee, because he vowed to annex Texas as a new slave state and take Oregon.

Annexing Oregon was an important objective for U.S. foreign policy because it appeared to be an area rich in commercial possibilities. Northerners favored U.S. control of Oregon because ports in the Pacific Northwest would be gateways for trade with Asia. Southerners hoped that, in exchange for their support of expansion into the northwest, northerners would not oppose plans for expansion into the southwest.

President Polk—whose campaign slogan in 1844 had been "Fifty-four forty or fight!"—asserted the United States' right to gain full control of what was known as Oregon Country, from its southern border at 42° latitude (the current boundary with California) to its northern border at 54° 40′ latitude. According to an 1818 agreement, Great Britain and the United States held joint ownership of this territory, but the 1827 Treaty of Joint Occupation opened the land to settlement by both countries. Realizing that the British were not willing to cede all claims to the territory, Polk proposed the land be divided at 49° latitude (the current border between Washington and Canada). The British, however, denied U.S. claims to land north of the Columbia River (Oregon's current northern border). Indeed, the British foreign secretary refused even to relay Polk's proposal to London. However, reports of the difficulty Great Britain would face defending Oregon in the event of a U.S. attack, combined with concerns over affairs at home and elsewhere in its empire, quickly changed the minds

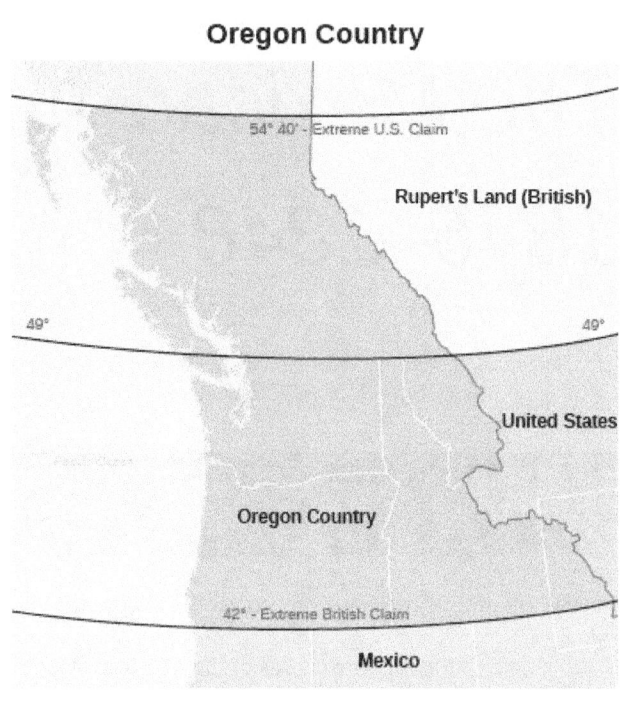

This map of the Oregon territory during the period of joint occupation by the United States and Great Britain shows the area whose ownership was contested by the two powers.

of the British, and in June 1846, Queen Victoria's government agreed to a division at the forty-ninth parallel.

In contrast to the diplomatic solution with Great Britain over Oregon, when it came to Mexico, Polk and the American people proved willing to use force to wrest more land for the United States. In keeping with voters' expectations, President Polk set his sights on the Mexican state of California. After the mistaken capture of Monterey, negotiations about purchasing the port of San Francisco from Mexico broke off until September 1845. Then, following a revolt in California that left it divided in two, Polk attempted to purchase Upper California and New Mexico as well. These efforts went nowhere. The Mexican government, angered by U.S. actions, refused to recognize the independence of Texas.

Finally, after nearly a decade of public clamoring for the annexation of Texas, in December 1845 Polk officially agreed to the annexation of the former Mexican state, making the Lone Star Republic an additional slave state. Incensed that the United States had annexed Texas, however, the Mexican government refused to discuss the matter of selling land to the United States. Indeed, Mexico refused even to acknowledge Polk's emissary, John Slidell, who had been sent to Mexico City to negotiate. Not to be deterred, Polk encouraged Thomas O. Larkin, the U.S. consul in Monterey, to assist any American settlers and any **Californios**, the Mexican residents of the state, who wished to proclaim their independence from Mexico.

By the end of 1845, having broken diplomatic ties with the United States over Texas and having grown alarmed by American actions in California, the Mexican government warily anticipated the next move. It did not have long to wait.

WAR WITH MEXICO, 1846–1848

Expansionistic fervor propelled the United States to war against Mexico in 1846. The United States had long argued that the Rio Grande was the border between Mexico and the United States, and at the end of the Texas war for independence Santa Anna had been pressured to agree. Mexico, however, refused to be bound by Santa Anna's promises and insisted the border lay farther north, at the Nueces River. To set it at the Rio Grande would, in effect, allow the United States to control land it had never occupied. In Mexico's eyes, therefore, President Polk violated its sovereign territory when he ordered U.S. troops into the disputed lands in 1846. From the Mexican perspective, it appeared the United States had invaded their nation.

In January 1846, the U.S. force that was ordered to the banks of the Rio Grande to build a fort on the "American" side encountered a Mexican cavalry unit on patrol. Shots rang out, and sixteen U.S. soldiers were killed or wounded. Angrily declaring that Mexico "has invaded our territory and shed American blood upon American soil," President Polk demanded the United States declare war on Mexico. On May 12, Congress obliged.

In 1845, when Texas joined the United States, Mexico insisted the United States had a right only to the territory northeast of the Nueces River. The United States argued in turn that it should have title to all land between the Nueces and the Rio Grande as well.

The small but vocal antislavery faction decried the decision to go to war, arguing that Polk had deliberately provoked hostilities so the United States could annex more slave territory. Illinois representative Abraham Lincoln and other members of Congress issued the "Spot Resolutions" in which they demanded to know the precise spot on U.S. soil where American blood had been spilled. Many Whigs also denounced the war. Democrats, however, supported Polk's decision, and volunteers for the army came forward in droves from every part of the country except New England, the seat of abolitionist activity. Enthusiasm for the war was aided by the widely held belief that Mexico was a weak, impoverished country and that the Mexican people, perceived as ignorant, lazy, and controlled by a corrupt Roman Catholic clergy, would be easy to defeat.

U.S. military strategy had three main objectives: 1) Take control of northern Mexico, including New Mexico; 2) seize California; and 3) capture Mexico City. General Zachary Taylor and his Army of the Center were assigned to accomplish the first goal, and with superior weapons they soon captured the Mexican city of Monterrey. Taylor quickly became a hero in the eyes of the American people, and Polk appointed him commander of all U.S. forces.

General Stephen Watts Kearny, commander of the Army of the West, accepted the surrender of Santa Fe, New Mexico, and moved on to take control of California, leaving Colonel Sterling Price in command. Despite Kearny's assurances that New Mexicans need not fear for their lives or their property, and in fact the region's residents rose in revolt in January 1847 in an effort to drive the Americans away. Although Price managed to put an end to the rebellion, tensions remained high.

Anti-Catholic sentiment played an important role in the Mexican-American War. The American public widely regarded Roman Catholics as cowardly and vice-ridden, like the clergy in this ca. 1846 lithograph who are shown fleeing the Mexican town of Matamoros accompanied by pretty women and baskets full of alcohol. (credit: Library of Congress)

Kearny, meanwhile, arrived in California to find it already in American hands through the joint efforts of California settlers, U.S. naval commander John D. Sloat, and John C. Fremont, a former army captain and son-in-law of Missouri senator Thomas Benton. Sloat, at anchor off the coast of Mazatlan, learned that war had begun and quickly set sail for California. He seized the town of Monterey in July 1846, less than a month after a group of American settlers led by William B. Ide had taken control of Sonoma and declared California a republic. A week after the fall of Monterey, the navy took San Francisco with no resistance. Although some Californios staged a short-lived rebellion in September 1846, many others submitted to the U.S. takeover. Thus Kearny had little to do other than take command of California as its governor.

Leading the Army of the South was General Winfield Scott. Both Taylor and Scott were potential competitors for the presidency, and believing—correctly—that whoever seized Mexico City would become a hero, Polk assigned Scott the campaign to avoid elevating the more popular Taylor, who was affectionately known as "Old Rough and Ready."

Scott captured Veracruz in March 1847, and moving in a northwesterly direction from there (much as Spanish conquistador Hernán Cortés had done in 1519), he slowly closed in on the capital. Every step of the way was a hard-fought victory, however, and Mexican soldiers and civilians both fought bravely to save their land from the American invaders. Mexico City's defenders, including young military cadets, fought to the end. According to legend, cadet Juan Escutia's last act was to save the Mexican flag, and he leapt from the city's walls with it wrapped around his body. On September 14, 1847, Scott entered Mexico City's central plaza; the city had fallen. While Polk and other expansionists called for "all Mexico," the Mexican government and the United States negotiated for peace in 1848, resulting in the Treaty of Guadalupe Hidalgo.

The Treaty of Guadalupe Hidalgo, signed in February 1848, was a triumph for American expansionism under which Mexico ceded nearly half its land to the United States. The **Mexican Cession**, as the conquest of land west of the Rio Grande was called, included the current states of California, New Mexico, Arizona, Nevada, Utah, and portions of Colorado and Wyoming. Mexico also recognized the Rio Grande as the border with the United States. Mexican citizens in the ceded territory were promised U.S. citizenship in the future when the territories they were living in became states. In exchange, the United States agreed to assume $3.35 million worth of Mexican debts owed to U.S. citizens, paid Mexico $15 million for the loss of its land, and promised to guard the residents of the Mexican Cession from Indian raids.

In General Scott's Entrance into Mexico (1851), Carl Nebel depicts General Winfield Scott on a white horse entering Mexico City's Plaza de la Constitución as anxious residents of the city watch. One woman peers furtively from behind the curtain of an upstairs window. On the left, a man bends down to pick up a paving stone to throw at the invaders.

As extensive as the Mexican Cession was, some argued the United States should not be satisfied until it had taken all of Mexico. Many who were opposed to this idea were southerners who, while desiring the annexation of more slave territory, did not want to make Mexico's large mestizo (people of mixed Indian and European ancestry) population part of the United States. Others did not want to absorb a large group of Roman Catholics. These expansionists could not accept the idea of new U.S. territory filled with mixed-race, Catholic populations.

> Explore the U.S.-Mexican War at **PBS** to read about life in the Mexican and U.S. armies during the war and to learn more about the various battles.

CALIFORNIA AND THE GOLD RUSH

The United States had no way of knowing that part of the land about to be ceded by Mexico had just become far more valuable than anyone could have imagined. On January 24, 1848, James Marshall discovered gold in the millrace of the sawmill he had built with his partner John Sutter on the south fork of California's **American River**. Word quickly spread, and within a few weeks all of Sutter's employees had left to search for gold. When the news reached San Francisco, most of its inhabitants abandoned the town and headed for the American River. By the end of the year, thousands of California's residents had gone north to the gold fields with visions of wealth dancing in their heads, and in 1849 thousands of people from around the world followed them. The Gold Rush had begun.

The fantasy of instant wealth induced a mass exodus to California. Settlers in Oregon and Utah rushed to the American River. Easterners sailed around the southern tip of South America or to Panama's Atlantic coast, where they crossed the Isthmus of Panama to the Pacific and booked ship's passage for San Francisco. As California-bound vessels stopped in South American ports to take on

Word about the discovery of gold in California in 1848 quickly spread and thousands soon made their way to the West Coast in search of quick riches.

food and fresh water, hundreds of Peruvians and Chileans streamed aboard. Easterners who could not afford to sail to California crossed the continent on foot, on horseback, or in wagons. Others journeyed from as far away as Hawaii and Europe. Chinese people came as well, adding to the polyglot population in the California boomtowns.

This Currier & Ives lithograph from 1849 imagines the extreme lengths that people might go to in order to be part of the California Gold Rush. In addition to the men with picks and shovels trying to reach the ship from the dock, airships and rocket are shown flying overhead. (credit: Library of Congress)

Once in California, gathered in camps with names like Drunkard's Bar, Angel's Camp, Gouge Eye, and Whiskeytown, the "**forty-niners**" did not find wealth so easy to come by as they had first imagined. Although some were able to find gold by panning for it or shoveling soil from river bottoms into sieve-like contraptions called rockers, most did not. The placer gold, the gold that had been washed down the mountains into streams and rivers, was quickly exhausted, and what remained was deep below ground. Independent miners were supplanted by companies that could afford not only to purchase hydraulic mining technology but also to hire laborers to work the hills. The frustration of many a miner was expressed in the words of Sullivan Osborne. In 1857, Osborne wrote that he had arrived in California "full of high hopes and bright anticipations of the future" only to find his dreams "have long since perished." Although $550 million worth of gold was found in California between 1849 and 1850, very little of it went to individuals.

Observers in the gold fields also reported abuse of Indians by miners. Some miners forced Indians to work their claims for them; others drove Indians off their lands, stole from them, and even murdered them. Foreigners were generally disliked, especially those from South America. The most despised, however, were the thousands of Chinese migrants. Eager to earn money to send to their families in Hong Kong and southern China, they quickly earned a reputation as frugal men and hard workers who routinely took over diggings others had abandoned as worthless and worked them until every scrap of gold had been found. Many American miners, often spendthrifts, resented their presence and discriminated against them, believing the Chinese, who represented about 8 percent of the nearly 300,000 who arrived, were depriving them of the opportunity to make a living.

> Visit The Chinese in California to learn more about the experience of Chinese migrants who came to California in the Gold Rush era.

In 1850, California imposed a tax on foreign miners, and in 1858 it prohibited all immigration from China. Those Chinese who remained in the face of the growing hostility were often beaten and killed, and some Westerners made a sport of cutting off Chinese men's queues, the long braids of hair worn down their backs. In 1882, Congress took up the power to restrict immigration by banning the further immigration of Chinese.

This daguerreotype shows the bustling port of San Francisco in January 1851, just a few months after San Francisco became part of the new U.S. state of California. (credit: Library of Congress)

As people flocked to California in 1849, the population of the new territory swelled from a few thousand to about 100,000. The new arrivals quickly organized themselves into communities, and the trappings of "civilized" life—stores, saloons, libraries, stage lines, and fraternal lodges—began to appear. Newspapers were established, and musicians, singers, and acting companies arrived to entertain the gold seekers. The epitome of these Gold Rush boomtowns was San Francisco, which counted only a few hundred residents in 1846 but by 1850 had reached a population of thirty-four thousand ([link]). So quickly did the territory grow that by 1850 California was ready to enter the Union as a state. When it sought admission, however, the issue of slavery expansion and sectional tensions emerged once again.

"Pacific Chivalry: Encouragement to Chinese Immigration," which appeared in Harper's Weekly in 1869, depicts a white man attacking a Chinese man with a whip as he holds him by the queue. Americans sometimes forcefully cut off the queues of Chinese immigrants. This could have serious consequences for the victim. Until 1911, all Chinese men were required by their nation's law to wear the queue as a sign of loyalty. Miners returning to China without it could be put to death. (credit: Library of Congress)

Section Summary

President James K. Polk's administration was a period of intensive expansion for the United States. After overseeing the final details regarding the annexation of Texas from Mexico, Polk negotiated a peaceful settlement with Great Britain regarding ownership of the Oregon Country, which brought the United States what are now the states of Washington and Oregon. The acquisition of additional lands from Mexico, a country many in the United States perceived as weak and inferior, was not so bloodless. The Mexican Cession added nearly half of Mexico's territory to the United States, including New Mexico and California, and established the U.S.-Mexico border at the Rio Grande. The California Gold Rush rapidly expanded the population of the new territory, but also prompted concerns over immigration, especially from China.

https://www.openassessments.org/assessments/980

Review Question

1. Why did whites in California dislike the Chinese so much?

Answer to Review Question

1. The Chinese were seemingly more disciplined than the majority of the white miners, gaining a reputation for being extremely hard-working and frugal. White miners resented the mining successes that the Chinese earned. They believed the Chinese were unfairly depriving them of the means to earn a living.

Glossary

Californios Mexican residents of California

forty-niners the nickname for those who traveled to California in 1849 in hopes of finding gold

Mexican Cession the lands west of the Rio Grande ceded to the United States by Mexico in 1848, including California, Arizona, New Mexico, Nevada, Utah, and parts of Wyoming and Colorado

Attributions

CC licensed content, Shared previously

- US History. **Authored by**: P. Scott Corbett, Volker Janssen, John M. Lund, Todd Pfannestiel, Paul Vickery, and Sylvie Waskiewicz. **Provided by**: OpenStax College. **Located at**: http://openstaxcollege.org/textbooks/us-history. **License**: CC BY: Attribution. **License Terms**: Download for free at http://cnx.org/content/col11740/latest/

Free Soil or Slave? The Dilemma of the West

Learning Objectives

By the end of this section, you will be able to:

- Describe the terms of the Wilmot Proviso
- Discuss why the Free-Soil Party objected to the westward expansion of slavery
- Explain why sectional and political divisions in the United States grew
- Describe the terms of the Compromise of 1850

The 1848 treaty with Mexico did not bring the United States domestic peace. Instead, the acquisition of new territory revived and intensified the debate over the future of slavery in the western territories, widening the growing division between North and South and leading to the creation of new single-issue parties. Increasingly, the South came to regard itself as under attack by radical northern abolitionists, and many northerners began to speak ominously of a southern drive to dominate American politics for the purpose of protecting slaveholders' human property. As tensions mounted and both sides hurled accusations, national unity frayed. Compromise became nearly impossible and antagonistic sectional rivalries replaced the idea of a unified, democratic republic.

THE LIBERTY PARTY, THE WILMOT PROVISO, AND THE ANTISLAVERY MOVEMENT

Committed to protecting white workers by keeping slavery out of the lands taken from Mexico, Pennsylvania congressman David Wilmot attached to an 1846 revenue bill an amendment that would prohibit slavery in the new territory. The **Wilmot Proviso** was not entirely new. Other congressmen had drafted similar legislation, and Wilmot's language was largely copied from the 1787 Northwest Ordinance that had banned slavery in that territory. His ideas were very controversial in the 1840s, however, because his proposals would prevent American slaveholders from bringing what they viewed as their lawful property, their slaves, into the western lands. The measure passed the House but was defeated in the Senate. When Polk tried again to raise revenue the following year (to pay for lands taken from Mexico), the Wilmot Proviso was reintroduced, this time calling for the prohibition of slavery not only in the Mexican Cession but in all U.S. territories. The revenue bill passed, but without the proviso.

That Wilmot, a loyal Democrat, should attempt to counter the actions of a Democratic president hinted at the party divisions that were to come. The 1840s were a particularly active time in the creation and reorganization of political parties and constituencies, mainly because of discontent with the positions of the mainstream Whig and Democratic Parties in regard to slavery and its extension into the territories. The first new party, the small and politically weak **Liberty Party** founded in 1840, was a single-issue party, as were many of those that followed it. Its members were abolitionists who fervently believed slavery was evil and should be ended, and that this was best accomplished by political means.

The Wilmot Proviso captured the "antislavery" sentiments during and after the Mexican War. Antislavery advocates differed from the abolitionists. While abolitionists called for the end of slavery everywhere, antislavery advocates, for various reasons, did not challenge the presence of slavery in the states where it already existed. Those who supported antislavery fervently opposed its expansion westward because, they argued, slavery would degrade white labor and reduce its value, cast a stigma upon hard-working whites, and deprive them of a chance to advance economically. The western lands, they argued, should be open to white men only—small farmers and urban workers for whom the West held the promise of economic advancement. Where slavery was entrenched, according to antislavery advocates, there was little land left for small farmers to purchase, and such men could not compete fairly with slaveholders who held large farms and gangs of slaves. Ordinary laborers suffered also; no one would pay a white man a decent wage when a slave worked for nothing. When labor was associated with loss of freedom, antislavery supporters argued, all white workers carried a stigma that marked them as little better than slaves.

Wilmot opposed the extension of slavery into the Mexican Cession not because of his concern for African Americans, but because of his belief that slavery hurt white workers, and that lands acquired by the government should be used to better the position of white small farmers and laborers. Work was not simply something that people did; it gave them dignity, but in a slave society, labor had no dignity. In response to these arguments, southerners maintained that laborers in northern factories were treated worse than slaves. Their work was tedious and low paid. Their meager income was spent on inadequate food, clothing, and shelter. There was no dignity in such a life. In contrast, they argued, southern slaves were provided with a home, the necessities of life, and the protection of their masters. Factory owners did not care for or protect their employees in the same way.

THE FREE-SOIL PARTY AND THE ELECTION OF 1848

The Wilmot Proviso was an issue of great importance to the Democrats. Would they pledge to support it? At the party's New York State convention in Buffalo, Martin Van Buren's antislavery supporters—called **Barnburners** because they were likened to farmers who were willing to burn down their own barn to get rid of a rat infestation—spoke in favor of the proviso. Their opponents, known as Hunkers, refused to support it. Angered, the Barnburners organized their own convention, where they chose antislavery, pro–Wilmot Proviso delegates to send to the Democrats' national convention in Baltimore. In this way, the controversy over the expansion of slavery divided the Democratic Party.

At the national convention, both sets of delegates were seated—the pro-proviso ones chosen by the Barnburners and the anti-proviso ones chosen by the Hunkers. When it came time to vote for the party's presidential nominee, the majority of votes were for Lewis Cass, an advocate of popular sovereignty. Popular sovereignty was the belief that citizens should be able to decide issues based on the principle of majority rule; in this case, residents of a territory should have the right to decide whether slavery would be allowed in it. Theoretically, this doctrine would allow slavery to become established in any U.S. territory, including those from which it had been banned by earlier laws.

Disgusted by the result, the Barnburners united with antislavery Whigs and former members of the Liberty Party to form a new political party—the **Free-Soil Party**, which took as its slogan "Free Soil, Free Speech, Free Labor, and Free Men." The party had one real goal—to oppose the extension of slavery into the territories. In the minds of its members and many other northerners of the time, southern slaveholders had marshaled their wealth and power to control national politics for the purpose of protecting the institution of slavery and extending it into the territories. Many in the Free-Soil Party believed in this far-reaching conspiracy of the slaveholding elite to control both foreign affairs and domestic policies for their own ends, a cabal that came to be known as the **Slave Power**.

This political cartoon depicts Martin Van Buren and his son John, both Barnburners, forcing the slavery issue within the Democratic Party by "smoking out" fellow Democrat Lewis Cass on the roof. Their support of the Wilmot Proviso and the new Free-Soil Party is demonstrated by John's declaration, "That's you Dad! more 'Free-Soil.' We'll rat 'em out yet. Long life to Davy Wilmot." (credit: Library of Congress)

In the wake of the Mexican War, antislavery sentiment entered mainstream American politics when the new Free-Soil party promptly selected Martin Van Buren as its presidential candidate. For the first time, a national political party committed itself to the goal of stopping the expansion of slavery. The Democrats chose Lewis Cass, and the Whigs nominated General Zachary Taylor, as Polk had assumed they would. On Election Day, Democrats split their votes between Van Buren and Cass. With the strength of the Democratic vote diluted, Taylor won. His popularity with the American people served him well, and his status as a slaveholder helped him win the South.

> Visit the archives of the Gilder Lehrman Institute to read an August 1848 letter from Gerrit Smith, a staunch abolitionist, regarding the Free-Soil candidate, Martin Van Buren. Smith played a major role in the Liberty Party and was their presidential candidate in 1848.

THE COMPROMISE OF 1850

The election of 1848 did nothing to quell the controversy over whether slavery would advance into the Mexican Cession. Some slaveholders, like President Taylor, considered the question a moot point because the lands acquired from Mexico were far too dry for growing cotton and therefore, they thought, no slaveholder would want to move there. Other southerners, however, argued that the question was not whether slaveholders *would* want to move to the lands of the Mexican Cession, but whether they *could* and still retain control of their slave property. Denying them the right to freely relocate with their lawful property was, they maintained, unfair and unconstitutional. Northerners argued, just as fervidly, that because Mexico had abolished slavery, no slaves currently lived in the Mexican Cession, and to introduce slavery there would extend it to a new territory, thus furthering the institution and giving the Slave Power more control over the United States. The strong current of antislavery sentiment—that is, the desire to protect white labor—only increased the opposition to the expansion of slavery into the West.

Most northerners, except members of the Free-Soil Party, favored popular sovereignty for California and the New Mexico territory. Many southerners opposed this position, however, for they feared residents of these regions might choose to outlaw slavery. Some southern politicians spoke ominously of secession from the United States. Free-Soilers rejected popular sovereignty and demanded that slavery be permanently excluded from the territories.

Beginning in January 1850, Congress worked for eight months on a compromise that might quiet the growing sectional conflict. Led by the aged Henry Clay, members finally agreed to the following:

> 1. California, which was ready to enter the Union, was admitted as a free state in accordance with its state constitution.
> 2. Popular sovereignty was to determine the status of slavery in New Mexico and Utah, even though Utah and part of New Mexico were north of the Missouri Compromise line.
> 3. The slave trade was banned in the nation's capital. Slavery, however, was allowed to remain.
> 4. Under a new fugitive slave law, those who helped runaway slaves or refused to assist in their return would be fined and possibly imprisoned.
> 5. The border between Texas and New Mexico was established.

The **Compromise of 1850** brought temporary relief. It resolved the issue of slavery in the territories for the moment and prevented secession. The peace would not last, however. Instead of relieving tensions between North and South, it had actually made them worse.

Section Summary

The acquisition of lands from Mexico in 1848 reawakened debates regarding slavery. The suggestion that slavery be barred from the Mexican Cession caused rancorous debate between North and South and split the Democratic Party when many northern members left to create the Free-Soil Party. Although the Compromise of 1850 resolved the question of whether slavery would be allowed in the new territories, the solution pleased no one. The peace brought by the compromise was short-lived, and the debate over slavery continued.

https://www.openassessments.org/assessments/981

Review Question

1. Describe the events leading up to the formation of the Free-Soil Party.

Answer to Review Question

1. At the party's national convention in 1848, the majority of Democrats voted for a candidate who supported popular sovereignty. A faction of the party was dismayed by this outcome; they opposed popular sovereignty and wanted to restrict the expansion of slavery in order to protect the value of white workers' labor. They united with antislavery Whigs and former members of the Liberty Party to form a new political party—the Free-Soil Party—which had one goal, to oppose the extension of slavery into the territories.

Critical Thinking Questions

1. Consider the role of filibusters in American expansion. What are some arguments in favor of filibustering? What are some arguments against it?
2. What are the economic and political issues raised by having an imbalance between free and slave states? Why did the balance of free and slave states matter?
3. How did Anglo-American settlers in Texas see themselves? Did they adopt a Mexican identity because they were living in Mexican territory? Why or why not?
4. Consider the annexation of Texas and the Mexican-American War from a Mexican perspective. What would you find objectionable about American actions, foreign policy, and attitudes in the 1840s?
5. Describe the place of Texas in the history of American westward expansion by comparing Texas's early history to the Missouri Crisis in 1819–1820. What are the similarities and what are the differences?
6. Consider the arguments over the expansion of slavery made by both northerners and southerners in the aftermath of the U.S. victory over Mexico. Who had the more compelling case? Or did each side make equally significant arguments?

Glossary

Barnburners northern Democrats loyal to Martin Van Buren who opposed the extension of slavery into the territories and broke away from the main party when it nominated a pro-popular sovereignty candidate

Compromise of 1850 five separate laws passed by Congress in September 1850 to resolve issues stemming from the Mexican Cession and the sectional crisis

Free-Soil Party a political party that sought to exclude slavery from the western territories, leaving these areas open for settlement by white farmers and ensuring that white laborers would not have to compete with slaves

Liberty Party a political party formed in 1840 by those who believed political measures were the best means by which abolition could be accomplished

Slave Power a term northerners used to describe the disproportionate influence that they felt elite southern slaveholders wielded in both domestic and international affairs

Wilmot Proviso an amendment to a revenue bill that would have barred slavery from all the territory acquired from Mexico

Attributions

CC licensed content, Shared previously

- US History. **Authored by**: P. Scott Corbett, Volker Janssen, John M. Lund, Todd Pfannestiel, Paul Vickery, and Sylvie Waskiewicz. **Provided by**: OpenStax College. **Located at**: http://openstaxcollege.org/textbooks/us-history. **License**: *CC BY: Attribution*. **License Terms**: Download for free at http://cnx.org/content/col11740/latest/

Primary Source Reading: The Great Nation of Futurity

The Great Nation of Futurity

John L. O'Sullivan

The American people having derived their origin from many other nations, and the Declaration of National Independence being entirely based on the great principle of human equality, these facts demonstrate at once our disconnected position as regards any other nation; that we have, in reality, but little connection with the past history of any of them, and still less with all antiquity, its glories, or its crimes. On the contrary, our national birth was the beginning of a new history, the formation and progress of an untried political system, which separates us from the past and connects us with the future only; and so far as regards the entire development of the natural rights of man, in moral, political, and national life, we may confidently assume that our country is destined to be *the great nation* of futurity.

It is so destined, because the principle upon which a nation is organized fixes its destiny, and that of equality is perfect, is universal. It presides in all the operations of the physical world, and it is also the conscious law of the soul—the self-evident dictate of morality, which accurately defines the duty of man to man, and consequently man's rights as man. Besides, the truthful annals of any nation furnish abundant evidence, that its happiness, its greatness, its duration, were always proportionate to the democratic equality in its system of government.

How many nations have had their decline and fall, because the equal rights of the minority were trampled on by the despotism of the majority; or the interests of the many sacrificed to the aristocracy of the few; or the rights and interests of all given up to the monarchy of one? These three kinds of government have figured so frequently and so largely in the ages that have passed away, that their history, through all time to come, can only furnish a resemblance. Like causes produce like effects, and the true philosopher of history will easily discern the principle of equality, or of privilege, working out its inevitable result. The first is regenerative, because it is natural and right; the latter is destructive to society, because it is unnatural and wrong.

What friend of human liberty, civilization, and refinement, can cast his view over the past history of the monarchies and aristocracies of antiquity, and not deplore that they ever existed? What philanthropist can contemplate the oppressions, the cruelties, and injustice inflicted by them on the masses of mankind, and not turn with moral horror from the retrospect?

America is destined for better deeds. It is our unparalleled glory that we have no reminiscences of battle fields, but in defence of humanity, of the oppressed of all nations, of the rights of conscience, the rights of personal enfranchisement. Our annals describe no scenes of horrid carnage, where men were led on by hundreds of thousands to slay one another, dupes and victims to emperors, kings, nobles, demons in the human form called heroes. We have had patriots to defend our homes, our liberties, but no aspirants to crowns or thrones; nor have the American people ever suffered themselves to be led on by wicked ambition to depopulate the land, to spread desolation far and wide, that a human being might be placed on a seat of supremacy.

We have no interest in the scenes of antiquity, only as lessons of avoidance of nearly all their examples. The expansive future is our arena, and for our history. We are entering on its untrodden space, with the truths of God in our minds, beneficent objects in our hearts, and with a clear conscience unsullied by the past. We are the nation of human progress, and who will, what can, set limits to our onward march? Providence is with us, and no earthly power can. We point to the everlasting truth on the first page of our national declaration, and we proclaim to the millions of other lands, that "the gates of hell—"the powers of aristocracy and monarchy—"shall not prevail against it."

The far-reaching, the boundless future will be the era of American greatness. In its magnificent domain of space and time, the nation of many nations is destined to manifest to mankind the excellence of divine principles; to establish on earth the noblest temple ever dedicated to the worship of the Most High—the Sacred and the True. Its floor shall be a hemisphere—its roof the firmament of the star-studded heavens, and its congregation an Union of many Republics, comprising hundreds of happy millions, calling, owning no man master, but governed by God's natural and moral law of equality, the law of brotherhood—of "peace and good will amongst men."

But although the mighty constituent truth upon which our social and political system is founded will assuredly work out the glorious destiny herein shadowed forth, yet there are many untoward circumstances to retard our progress, to procrastinate the entire fruition of the greatest good to the human race. There is a tendency to imitativeness, prevailing amongst our professional and literary men, subversive of originality of thought, and wholly unfavorable to progress. Being in early life devoted to the study of the laws, institutions, and antiquities of other nations, they are far behind the mind and movement of the age in which they live: so much so, that the spirit of improvement, as well as of enfranchisement, exists chiefly in the great masses—the agricultural and mechanical population.

This propensity to imitate foreign nations is absurd and injurious. It is absurd, for we have never yet drawn on our mental resources that we have not found them ample and of unsurpassed excellence; witness our constitutions of government, where we had no foreign ones to imitate. It is injurious, for never have we followed foreign examples in legislation; witness our laws, our charters of monopoly, that we did not inflict evil on ourselves, subverting common right, in violation of common sense and common justice. The halls of legislation and the courts of law in a Republic are necessarily the public schools of the adult population. If, in these institutions, foreign precedents are legislated, and foreign decisions adjudged over again, is it to be wondered at that an imitative propensity predominates amongst professional and business men. Taught to look abroad for the highest standards of law, judicial wisdom, and literary excellence, the native sense is subjugated to a most obsequious idolatry of the tastes, sentiments, and prejudices of Europe. Hence our legislation, jurisprudence, literature, are more reflective of foreign aristocracy than of American democracy.

European governments have plunged themselves in debt, designating burthens on the people "national blessings." Our State Legislatures, humbly imitating their pernicious example, have pawned, bonded the property, labor, and credit of their constituents to the subjects of monarchy. It is by our own labor, and with our own materials, that our internal improvements are constructed, but our British-law-trained legislators have enacted that we shall be in debt for them, paying interest, but never to become owners. With various climates, soils, natural resources, and products, beyond any other country, and producing more real capital annually than any other sixteen millions of people on earth, we are, nevertheless, borrowers, paying tribute to the money powers of Europe.

Our business men have also conned the lesson of example, and devoted themselves body and mind to the promotion of foreign interests. If States can steep themselves in debt, with any propriety in times of peace, why may not merchants import merchandise on credit? If the one can bond the labor and property of generations yet unborn, why may not the other contract debts against the yearly crops and daily labor of their contemporary fellow citizens?

And our literature!—Oh, when will it breathe the spirit of our republican institutions? When will it be imbued with the God-like aspiration of intellectual freedom—the elevating principle of equality? When will it assert *its* national independence, and speak the soul—the heart of the American people? Why cannot our literati comprehend the matchless sublimity of our position amongst the nations of the world —our high destiny—and cease bending the knee to foreign idolatry, false tastes, false doctrines, false principles? When will they be inspired by the magnificent scenery of our own world, imbibe the fresh enthusiasm of a new heaven and a new earth, and soar upon the expanded wings of truth and liberty? Is not nature as original—her truths as captivating—her aspects as various, as lovely, as grand—her Promethean fire as glowing in this, our Western hemisphere, as in that of the East? And above all, is not our private life as morally beautiful and good—is not our public life as politically right, as indicative of the brightest prospects of humanity, and therefore as inspiring of the highest conceptions? Why, then, do our authors aim at no higher degree of merit, than a successful imitation of English writers of celebrity?

But with all the retrograde tendencies of our laws, our judicature, our colleges, our literature, still they are compelled to follow the mighty impulse of the age; they are carried onward by the increasing tide of progress; and though they cast many a longing look behind, they cannot stay the glorious movement of the masses, nor induce them to venerate the rubbish, the prejudices, the superstitions of other times and other lands, the theocracy of priests, the divine right of kings, the aristocracy of blood, the metaphysics of colleges, the irrational stuff of law libraries. Already the brightest hopes of philanthropy, the most enlarged speculations of true philosophy, are inspired by the indications perceptible amongst the mechanical and agricultural population. There, with predominating influence, beats the vigorous national heart of America, propelling the onward march of the multitude, propagating and extending, through the present and the future, the powerful purpose of soul, which, in the seventeenth century, sought a refuge among savages, and reared in the wilderness the sacred altars of intellectual freedom. This was the seed that produced individual equality, and political liberty, as its natural fruit; and this is our true nationality. American patriotism is not of soil; we are not aborigines, nor of ancestry, for we are of all nations; but it is essentially personal enfranchisement, for "where liberty dwells," said Franklin, the sage of the Revolution, "there is my country."

Such is our distinguishing characteristic, our popular instinct, and never yet has any public functionary stood forth for the rights of conscience against any, or all, sects desirous of predominating over such right, that he was not sustained by the people. And when a venerated patriot of the Revolution appealed to his fellow-citizens against the overshadowing power of a monarch institution, they came in their strength, and the moneyed despot was brought low. Corporate powers and privileges shrink to nothing when brought in conflict against the rights of individuals. Hence it is that our professional, literary, or commercial aristocracy, have no faith in the virtue, intelligence or capability of the people. The latter have never responded to their exotic sentiments nor promoted their views of a strong government irresponsible to the popular majority, to the will of the masses.

Yes, we are the nation of progress, of individual freedom, of universal enfranchisement. Equality of rights is the cynosure of our union of States, the grand exemplar of the correlative equality of individuals; and while truth sheds its effulgence, we cannot retrograde, without dissolving the one and subverting the other. We must onward to the fulfilment of our mission—to the entire development of the principle of our organization—freedom of conscience, freedom of person, freedom of trade and business pursuits, universality of freedom and equality. This is our high destiny, and in nature's eternal, inevitable decree of cause and effect we must accomplish it. All this will be our future history, to establish on earth the moral dignity and salvation of man—the immutable truth and beneficence of God. For this blessed mission to the nations of the world, which are shut out from the life-giving light of truth, has America been chosen; and her high example shall smite unto death the tyranny of kings, hierarchs, and oligarchs, and carry the glad tidings of peace and good will where myriads now endure an existence scarcely more enviable than that of beasts of the field. Who, then, can doubt that our country is destined to be the great nation of futurity?

(http://en.wikisource.org/wiki/The_Great_Nation_of_Futurity)

Attributions

Public domain content

- The Great Nation of Futurity. **Authored by**: John L. O'Sullivan. **Provided by**: Wikisource. **Located at**: https://en.wikisource.org/wiki/The_Great_Nation_of_Futurity. **License**: *Public Domain: No Known Copyright*

12. Cotton is King: The Antebellum South, 1800-1860

Introduction

Nine new slave states entered the Union between 1789 and 1860, rapidly expanding and transforming the South into a region of economic growth built on slave labor. In the image above, innumerable slaves load cargo onto a steamship in the Port of New Orleans, the commercial center of the antebellum South, while two well-dressed white men stand by talking. Commercial activity extends as far as the eye can see.

By the mid-nineteenth century, southern commercial centers like New Orleans had become home to the greatest concentration of wealth in the United States. While most white southerners did not own slaves, they aspired to join the ranks of elite slaveholders, who played a key role in the politics of both the South and the nation. Meanwhile, slavery shaped the culture and society of the South, which rested on a racial ideology of white supremacy and a vision of the United States as a white man's republic. Slaves endured the traumas of slavery by creating their own culture and using the Christian message of redemption to find hope for a world of freedom without violence.

Bateaux à Vapeur Géant, la Nouvelle-Orléans 1853 (Giant Steamboats at New Orleans, 1853), by Hippolyte Sebron, shows how New Orleans, at the mouth of the Mississippi River, was the primary trading hub for the cotton that fueled the growth of the southern economy.

Attributions

CC licensed content, Shared previously

- US History. **Authored by**: P. Scott Corbett, Volker Janssen, John M. Lund, Todd Pfannestiel, Paul Vickery, and Sylvie Waskiewicz. **Provided by**: OpenStax College. **Located at**: http://openstaxcollege.org/textbooks/us-history. **License**: CC BY: Attribution. **License Terms**: Download for free at http://cnx.org/content/col11740/latest/

The Economics of Cotton

Learning Objectives

By the end of this section, you will be able to:

- Explain the labor-intensive processes of cotton production
- Describe the importance of cotton to the Atlantic and American antebellum economy

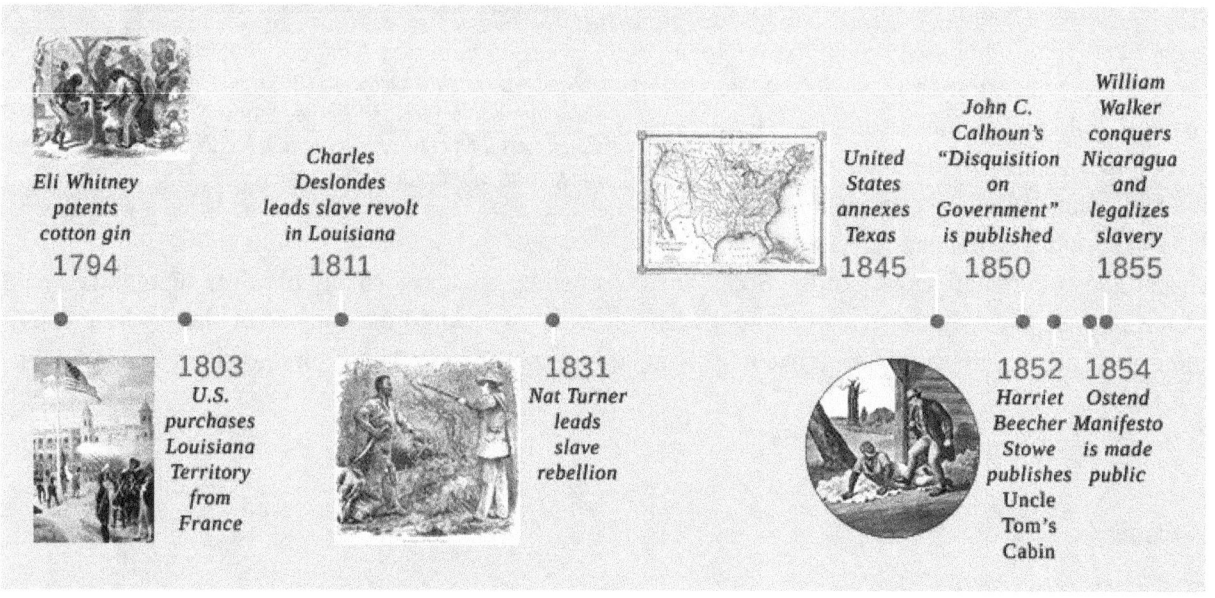

In the **antebellum** era—that is, in the years before the Civil War—American planters in the South continued to grow Chesapeake tobacco and Carolina rice as they had in the colonial era. Cotton, however, emerged as the antebellum South's major commercial crop, eclipsing tobacco, rice, and sugar in economic importance. By 1860, the region was producing two-thirds of the world's cotton. In 1793, Eli Whitney revolutionized the production of cotton when he invented the **cotton gin**, a device that separated the seeds from raw cotton. Suddenly, a process that was extraordinarily labor-intensive when done by hand could be completed quickly and easily. American plantation owners, who were searching for a successful staple crop to compete on the world market, found it in cotton.

As a commodity, cotton had the advantage of being easily stored and transported. A demand for it already existed in the industrial textile mills in Great Britain, and in time, a steady stream of slave-grown American cotton would also supply northern textile mills. Southern cotton, picked and processed by American slaves, helped fuel the nineteenth-century Industrial Revolution in both the United States and Great Britain.

KING COTTON

Almost no cotton was grown in the United States in 1787, the year the federal constitution was written. However, following the War of 1812, a huge increase in production resulted in the so-called **cotton boom**, and by midcentury, cotton became the key **cash crop** (a crop grown to sell rather than for the farmer's sole use) of the southern economy and the most important American commodity. By 1850, of the 3.2 million slaves in the country's fifteen slave states, 1.8 million were producing cotton; by 1860, slave labor was producing over two billion pounds of cotton per year. Indeed, American cotton soon made up two-thirds of the global supply, and production continued to soar. By the time of the Civil War, South Carolina politician James Hammond confidently proclaimed that the North could never threaten the South because "cotton is king."

The crop grown in the South was a hybrid: *Gossypium barbadense,* known as Petit Gulf cotton, a mix of Mexican, Georgia, and Siamese strains. Petit Gulf cotton grew extremely well in different soils and climates. It dominated cotton production in the Mississippi River Valley—home of the new slave states of Louisiana, Mississippi, Arkansas, Tennessee, Kentucky, and Missouri—as well as in other states like Texas. Whenever new slave states entered the Union, white slaveholders sent armies of slaves to clear the land in order to grow and pick the lucrative crop. The phrase "to be sold down the river," used by Harriet Beecher Stowe in her 1852 novel *Uncle Tom's Cabin,* refers to this forced migration from the upper southern states to the Deep South, lower on the Mississippi, to grow cotton.

The slaves who built this cotton kingdom with their labor started by clearing the land. Although the Jeffersonian vision of the settlement of new U.S. territories entailed white yeoman farmers single-handedly carving out small independent farms, the reality proved quite different. Entire old-growth forests and cypress swamps fell to the axe as slaves labored to strip the vegetation to make way for cotton. With the land cleared, slaves readied the earth by plowing and planting. To ambitious white planters, the extent of new land available for cotton production seemed almost limitless, and many planters simply leapfrogged from one area to the next, abandoning their fields every ten to fifteen years after the soil became exhausted. Theirs was a world of mobility and restlessness, a constant search for the next area to grow the valuable crop. Slaves composed the vanguard of this American expansion to the West.

Cotton planting took place in March and April, when slaves planted seeds in rows around three to five feet apart. Over the next several months, from April to August, they carefully tended the plants. Weeding the cotton rows took significant energy and time. In August, after the cotton plants had flowered and the flowers had begun to give way to cotton bolls (the seed-bearing capsule that contains the cotton fiber), all the plantation's slaves—men, women, and children—worked together to pick the crop. On each day of cotton picking, slaves went to the fields with sacks, which they would fill as many times as they could. The effort was laborious, and a white "driver" employed the lash to make slaves work as quickly as possible.

Cotton planters projected the amount of cotton they could harvest based on the number of slaves under their control. In general, planters expected a good "hand," or slave, to work ten acres of land and pick two hundred pounds of cotton a day. An overseer or master measured each individual slave's daily yield. Great pressure existed to meet the expected daily amount, and some masters whipped slaves who picked less than expected.

Cotton picking occurred as many as seven times a season as the plant grew and continued to produce bolls through the fall and early winter. During the picking season, slaves worked from sunrise to sunset with a ten-minute break at lunch; many slaveholders tended to give them little to eat, since spending on food would cut into their profits. Other slaveholders knew that feeding slaves could increase productivity and therefore provided what they thought would help ensure a profitable crop. The slaves' day didn't end after they picked the cotton; once they had brought it to the gin house to be weighed, they then had to care for the animals and perform other chores. Indeed, slaves often maintained their own gardens and livestock, which they tended after working the cotton fields, in order to supplement their supply of food.

In the late nineteenth century, J. N. Wilson captured this image of harvest time at a southern plantation. While the workers in this photograph are not slave laborers, the process of cotton harvesting shown here had changed little from antebellum times.

Sometimes the cotton was dried before it was ginned (put through the process of separating the seeds from the cotton fiber). The cotton gin allowed a slave to remove the seeds from fifty pounds of cotton a day, compared to one pound if done by hand. After the seeds had been removed, the cotton was pressed into bales. These bales, weighing about four hundred to five hundred pounds, were wrapped in burlap cloth and sent down the Mississippi River.

> Visit the Internet Archive to watch a 1937 WPA film showing cotton bales being loaded onto a steamboat.

As the cotton industry boomed in the South, the Mississippi River quickly became the essential water highway in the United States. Steamboats, a crucial part of the transportation revolution thanks to their enormous freight-carrying capacity and ability to navigate shallow waterways, became a defining component of the cotton kingdom. Steamboats also illustrated the class and social distinctions of the antebellum age. While the decks carried precious cargo, ornate rooms graced the interior. In these spaces, whites socialized in the ship's saloons and dining halls while black slaves served them.

Investors poured huge sums into steamships. In 1817, only seventeen plied the waters of western rivers, but by 1837, there were over seven hundred steamships in operation. Major new ports developed at St. Louis, Missouri; Memphis, Tennessee; and other locations. By 1860, some thirty-five hundred vessels were steaming in and out of New Orleans, carrying an annual cargo made up primarily of cotton that amounted to $220 million worth of goods (approximately $6.5 billion in 2014 dollars).

As in this depiction of the saloon of the Mississippi River steamboat Princess, elegant and luxurious rooms often occupied the interiors of antebellum steamships, whose decks were filled with cargo.

New Orleans had been part of the French empire before the United States purchased it, along with the rest of the Louisiana Territory, in 1803. In the first half of the nineteenth century, it rose in prominence and importance largely because of the cotton boom, steam-powered river traffic, and its strategic position near the mouth of the Mississippi River. Steamboats moved down the river transporting cotton grown on plantations along the river and throughout the South to the port at New Orleans. From there, the bulk of American cotton went to Liverpool, England, where it was sold to British manufacturers who ran the cotton mills in Manchester and elsewhere. This lucrative international trade brought new wealth and new residents to the city. By 1840, New Orleans alone had 12 percent of the nation's total banking capital, and visitors often commented on the great cultural diversity of the city. In 1835, Joseph Holt Ingraham wrote: "Truly does New-Orleans represent every other city and nation upon earth. I know of none where is congregated so great a variety of the human species." Slaves, cotton, and the steamship transformed the city from a relatively isolated corner of North America in the eighteenth century to a thriving metropolis that rivaled New York in importance.

THE DOMESTIC SLAVE TRADE

The South's dependence on cotton was matched by its dependence on slaves to harvest the cotton. Despite the rhetoric of the Revolution that "all men are created equal," slavery not only endured in the American republic but formed the very foundation of the country's economic success. Cotton and slavery occupied a central—and intertwined—place in the nineteenth-century economy.

This print of The Levee – New Orleans (1884) shows the bustling port of New Orleans with bales of cotton waiting to be shipped. The sheer volume of cotton indicates its economic importance throughout the century.

In 1807, the U.S. Congress abolished the foreign slave trade, a ban that went into effect on January 1, 1808. After this date, importing slaves from Africa became illegal in the United States. While smuggling continued to occur, the end of the international slave trade meant that domestic slaves were in very high demand. Fortunately for Americans whose wealth depended upon the exploitation of slave labor, a fall in the price of tobacco had caused landowners in the Upper South to reduce their production of this crop and use more of their land to grow wheat, which was far more profitable. While tobacco was a labor-intensive crop that required many people to cultivate it, wheat was not. Former tobacco farmers in the older states of Virginia and Maryland found themselves with "surplus" slaves whom they were obligated to feed, clothe, and shelter. Some slaveholders responded to this situation by freeing slaves; far more decided to sell their excess bondsmen. Virginia and Maryland therefore took the lead in the **domestic slave trade**, the trading of slaves within the borders of the United States.

The domestic slave trade offered many economic opportunities for white men. Those who sold their slaves could realize great profits, as could the slave brokers who served as middlemen between sellers and buyers. Other white men could benefit from the trade as owners of warehouses and pens in which slaves were held, or as suppliers of clothing and food for slaves on the move. Between 1790 and 1859, slaveholders in Virginia sold more than half a million slaves. In the early part of this period, many of these slaves were sold to people living in Kentucky, Tennessee, and North and South Carolina. By the 1820s, however, people in Kentucky and the Carolinas had begun to sell many of their slaves as well. Maryland slave dealers sold at least 185,000 slaves. Kentucky slaveholders sold some seventy-one thousand individuals. Most of the slave traders carried these slaves further south to Alabama, Louisiana, and Mississippi. New Orleans, the hub of commerce, boasted the largest slave market in the United States and grew to become the nation's fourth-largest city as a result. Natchez, Mississippi, had the second-largest market. In Virginia, Maryland, the Carolinas, and elsewhere in the South, slave auctions happened every day.

All told, the movement of slaves in the South made up one of the largest forced internal migrations in the United States. In each of the decades between 1820 and 1860, about 200,000 people were sold and relocated. The 1800 census recorded over one million African Americans, of which nearly 900,000 were slaves. By 1860, the total number of African Americans increased to 4.4 million, and of that number, 3.95 million were held in bondage. For many slaves, the domestic slave trade incited the terror of being sold away from family and friends.

Solomon Northup Remembers the New Orleans Slave Market

Solomon Northup was a free black man living in Saratoga, New York, when he was kidnapped and sold into slavery in 1841. He later escaped and wrote a book about his experiences: *Twelve Years a Slave. Narrative of Solomon Northup, a Citizen of New-York, Kidnapped in Washington City in 1841 and Rescued in 1853* (the basis of a 2013 Academy Award–winning film). This excerpt derives from Northup's description of being sold in New Orleans, along with fellow slave Eliza and her children Randall and Emily.

> One old gentleman, who said he wanted a coachman, appeared to take a fancy to me. . . .
>
> The same man also purchased Randall. The little fellow was made to jump, and run across the floor, and perform many other feats, exhibiting his activity and condition. All the time the trade was going on, Eliza was crying aloud, and wringing her hands. She besought the man not to buy him, unless he also bought her self and Emily. . . . Freeman turned round to her, savagely, with his whip in his uplifted hand, ordering her to stop her noise, or he would flog her. He would not have such work—such snivelling; and unless she ceased that minute, he would take her to the yard and give her

a hundred lashes. . . . Eliza shrunk before him, and tried to wipe away her tears, but it was all in vain. She wanted to be with her children, she said, the little time she had to live. All the frowns and threats of Freeman, could not wholly silence the afflicted mother.

What does Northup's narrative tell you about the experience of being a slave? How does he characterize Freeman, the slave trader? How does he characterize Eliza?

THE SOUTH IN THE AMERICAN AND WORLD MARKETS

The first half of the nineteenth century saw a market revolution in the United States, one in which industrialization brought changes to both the production and the consumption of goods. Some southerners of the time believed that their region's reliance on a single cash crop and its use of slaves to produce it gave the South economic independence and made it immune from the effects of these changes, but this was far from the truth. Indeed, the production of cotton brought the South more firmly into the larger American and Atlantic markets. Northern mills depended on the South for supplies of raw cotton that was then converted into textiles. But this domestic cotton market paled in comparison to the Atlantic market. About 75 percent of the cotton produced in the United States was eventually exported abroad. Exporting at such high volumes made the United States the undisputed world leader in cotton production. Between the years 1820 and 1860, approximately 80 percent of the global cotton supply was produced in the United States. Nearly all the exported cotton was shipped to Great Britain, fueling its burgeoning textile industry and making the powerful British Empire increasingly dependent on American cotton and southern slavery.

The power of cotton on the world market may have brought wealth to the South, but it also increased its economic dependence on other countries and other parts of the United States. Much of the corn and pork that slaves consumed came from farms in the West. Some of the inexpensive clothing, called "slops," and shoes worn by slaves were manufactured in the North. The North also supplied the furnishings found in the homes of both wealthy planters and members of the middle class. Many of the trappings of domestic life, such as carpets, lamps, dinnerware, upholstered furniture, books, and musical instruments—all the accoutrements of comfortable living for southern whites—were made in either the North or Europe. Southern planters also borrowed money from banks in northern cities, and in the southern summers, took advantage of the developments in transportation to travel to resorts at Saratoga, New York; Litchfield, Connecticut; and Newport, Rhode Island.

Section Summary

In the years before the Civil War, the South produced the bulk of the world's supply of cotton. The Mississippi River Valley slave states became the epicenter of cotton production, an area of frantic economic activity where the landscape changed dramatically as land was transformed from pinewoods and swamps into cotton fields. Cotton's profitability relied on the institution of slavery, which generated the product that fueled cotton mill profits in the North. When the international slave trade was outlawed in 1808, the domestic slave trade exploded, providing economic opportunities for whites involved in many aspects of the trade and increasing the possibility of slaves' dislocation and separation from kin and friends. Although the larger American and Atlantic markets relied on southern cotton in this era, the South depended on these other markets for food, manufactured goods, and loans. Thus, the market revolution transformed the South just as it had other regions.

https://www.openassessments.org/assessments/982

Review Question

1. Why did some southerners believe their region was immune to the effects of the market revolution? Why was this thinking misguided?

Answer to Review Question

1. Some southerners believed that their region's monopoly over the lucrative cotton crop—on which both the larger American and Atlantic markets depended—and their possession of a slave labor force allowed the South to remain independent from the market revolution. However, the very cotton that provided the South with such economic potency also increased its reliance on the larger U.S. and world markets, which supplied—among other things—the food and clothes slaves needed, the furniture and other manufactured goods that defined the southern standard of comfortable living, and the banks from which southerners borrowed needed funds.

Glossary

antebellum a term meaning "before the war" and used to describe the decades before the American Civil War began in 1861

cash crop a crop grown to be sold for profit instead of consumption by the farmer's family

cotton boom the upswing in American cotton production during the nineteenth century

cotton gin a device, patented by Eli Whitney in 1794, that separated the seeds from raw cotton quickly and easily

domestic slave trade the trading of slaves within the borders of the United States

Attributions

CC licensed content, Shared previously

- US History. **Authored by**: P. Scott Corbett, Volker Janssen, John M. Lund, Todd Pfannestiel, Paul Vickery, and Sylvie Waskiewicz. **Provided by**: OpenStax College. **Located at**: http://openstaxcollege.org/textbooks/us-history. **License**: *CC BY: Attribution*. **License Terms**: Download for free at http://cnx.org/content/col11740/latest/

African Americans in the Antebellum United States

> *Learning Objectives*
>
> By the end of this section, you will be able to:
> - Discuss the similarities and differences in the lives of slaves and free blacks
> - Describe the independent culture and customs that slaves developed

In addition to cotton, the great commodity of the antebellum South was human chattel. Slavery was the cornerstone of the southern economy. By 1850, about 3.2 million slaves labored in the United States, 1.8 million of whom worked in the cotton fields. Slaves faced arbitrary power abuses from whites; they coped by creating family and community networks. Storytelling, song, and Christianity also provided solace and allowed slaves to develop their own interpretations of their condition.

LIFE AS A SLAVE

Southern whites frequently relied upon the idea of **paternalism**—the premise that white slaveholders acted in the best interests of slaves, taking responsibility for their care, feeding, discipline, and even their Christian morality—to justify the existence of slavery. This grossly misrepresented the reality of slavery, which was, by any measure, a dehumanizing, traumatizing, and horrifying human disaster and crime against humanity. Nevertheless, slaves were hardly passive victims of their conditions; they sought and found myriad ways to resist their shackles and develop their own communities and cultures.

Slaves often used the notion of paternalism to their advantage, finding opportunities within this system to engage in acts of resistance and win a degree of freedom and autonomy. For example, some slaves played into their masters' racism by hiding their intelligence and feigning childishness and ignorance. The slaves could then slow down the workday and sabotage the system in small ways by "accidentally" breaking tools, for example; the master, seeing his slaves as unsophisticated and childlike, would believe these incidents were accidents rather than rebellions. Some slaves engaged in more dramatic forms of resistance, such as poisoning their masters slowly. Other slaves reported rebellious slaves to their masters, hoping to gain preferential treatment. Slaves who informed their masters about planned slave rebellions could often expect the slaveholder's gratitude and, perhaps, more lenient treatment. Such expectations were always tempered by the individual personality and caprice of the master.

Slaveholders used both psychological coercion and physical violence to prevent slaves from disobeying their wishes. Often, the most efficient way to discipline slaves was to threaten to sell them. The lash, while the most common form of punishment, was effective but not efficient; whippings sometimes left slaves incapacitated or even dead. Slave masters also used punishment gear like neck braces, balls and chains, leg irons, and paddles with holes to produce blood blisters. Slaves lived in constant terror of both physical violence and separation from family and friends.

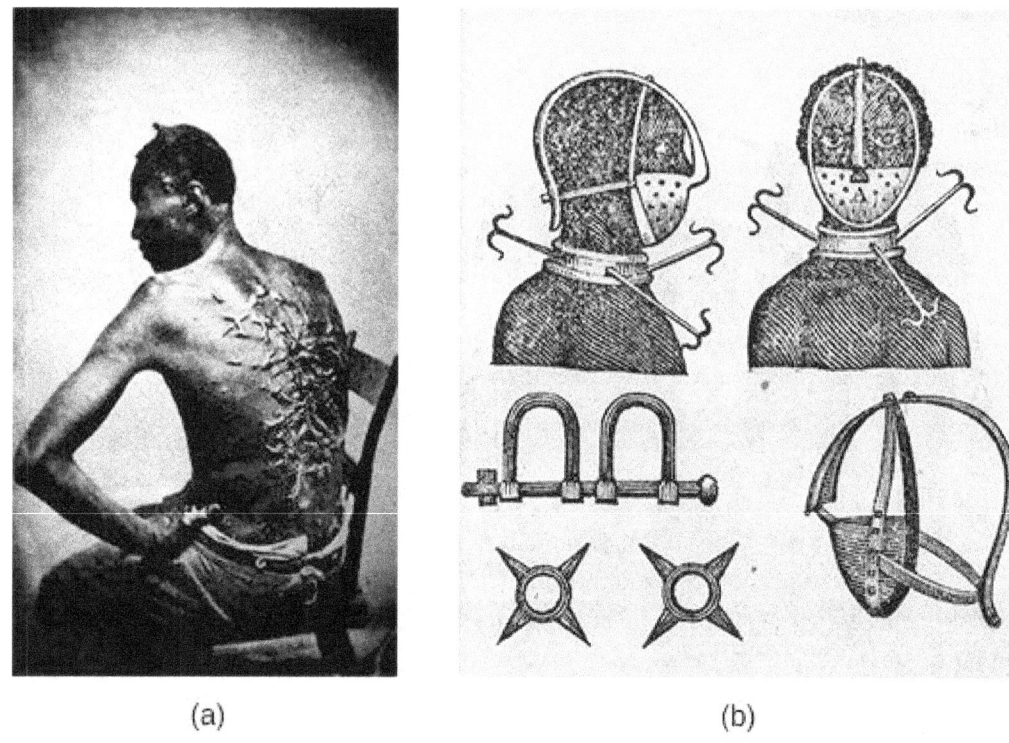

The original caption of this photograph of a slave's scarred back (a), taken in Baton Rouge, Louisiana, in 1863, reads as follows: "Overseer Artayou Carrier whipped me. I was two months in bed sore from the whipping. My master come after I was whipped; he discharged the overseer. The very words of poor Peter, taken as he sat for his picture." Images like this one helped bolster the northern abolitionist message of the inhumanity of slavery. The drawing of an iron mask, collar, leg shackles, and spurs (b) demonstrates the various cruel and painful instruments used to restrain slaves.

Under southern law, slaves could not marry. Nonetheless, some slaveholders allowed marriages to promote the birth of children and to foster harmony on plantations. Some masters even forced certain slaves to form unions, anticipating the birth of more children (and consequently greater profits) from them. Masters sometimes allowed slaves to choose their own partners, but they could also veto a match. Slave couples always faced the prospect of being sold away from each other, and, once they had children, the horrifying reality that their children could be sold and sent away at any time.

Browse a collection of first-hand narratives of slaves and former slaves at the National Humanities

Center to learn more about the experience of slavery.

Slave parents had to show their children the best way to survive under slavery. This meant teaching them to be discreet, submissive, and guarded around whites. Parents also taught their children through the stories they told. Popular stories among slaves included tales of tricksters, sly slaves, or animals like Brer Rabbit, who outwitted their antagonists. Such stories provided comfort in humor and conveyed the slaves' sense of the wrongs of slavery. Slaves' work songs commented on the harshness of their life and often had double meanings—a literal meaning that whites would not find offensive and a deeper meaning for slaves.

African beliefs, including ideas about the spiritual world and the importance of African healers, survived in the South as well. Whites who became aware of non-Christian rituals among slaves labeled such practices as witchcraft. Among Africans, however, the rituals and use of various plants by respected slave healers created connections between the African past and the American South while also providing a sense of community and identity for slaves. Other African customs, including traditional naming patterns, the making of baskets, and the cultivation of certain native African plants that had been brought to the New World, also endured.

Brer Rabbit, depicted here in an illustration from Uncle Remus, His Songs and His Sayings: The Folk-Lore of the Old Plantation (1881) by Joel Chandler Harris, was a trickster who outwitted his opponents.

African Americans and Christian Spirituals

Many slaves embraced Christianity. Their masters emphasized a scriptural message of obedience to whites and a better day awaiting slaves in heaven, but slaves focused on the uplifting message of being freed from bondage.

The styles of worship in the Methodist and Baptist churches, which emphasized emotional responses to scripture, attracted slaves to those traditions and inspired some to become preachers. Spiritual songs that referenced the Exodus (the biblical account of the Hebrews' escape from slavery in Egypt), such as "Roll, Jordan, Roll," allowed slaves to freely express messages of hope, struggle, and overcoming adversity.

This version of "Roll, Jordan, Roll" was included in Slave Songs of the United States, *the first published collection of African American music, which appeared in 1867.*

What imagery might the Jordan River suggest to slaves working in the Deep South? What lyrics in this song suggest redemption and a better world ahead?

> Listen to a rendition of "Roll, Jordan, Roll" from the movie based on Solomon Northup's memoir and life.https://youtu.be/7oFcFzJT7Tw

THE FREE BLACK POPULATION

Complicating the picture of the antebellum South was the existence of a large free black population. In fact, more free blacks lived in the South than in the North; roughly 261,000 lived in slave states, while 226,000 lived in northern states without slavery. Most free blacks did not live in the Lower, or Deep South: the states of Alabama, Arkansas, Florida, Georgia, Louisiana, Mississippi, South Carolina, and Texas. Instead, the largest number lived in the upper southern states of Delaware, Maryland, Virginia, North Carolina, and later Kentucky, Missouri, Tennessee, and the District of Columbia.

Part of the reason for the large number of free blacks living in slave states were the many instances of manumission—the formal granting of freedom to slaves—that occurred as a result of the Revolution, when many slaveholders put into action the ideal that "all men are created equal" and freed their slaves. The transition in the Upper South to the staple crop of wheat, which did not require large numbers of slaves to produce, also spurred manumissions. Another large group of free blacks in the South had been free residents of Louisiana before the 1803 Louisiana Purchase, while still other free blacks came from Cuba and Haiti.

Most free blacks in the South lived in cities, and a majority of free blacks were lighter-skinned women, a reflection of the interracial unions that formed between white men and black women. Everywhere in the United States blackness had come to be associated with slavery, the station at the bottom of the social ladder. Both whites and those with African ancestry tended to delineate varying degrees of lightness in skin color in a social hierarchy. In the slaveholding South, different names described one's distance from blackness or whiteness: mulattos (those with one black and one white parent), quadroons (those with one black grandparent), and octoroons (those with one black great-grandparent). Lighter-skinned blacks often looked down on their darker counterparts, an indication of the ways in which both whites and blacks internalized the racism of the age.

Some free blacks in the South owned slaves of their own. Andrew Durnford, for example, was born in New Orleans in 1800, three years before the Louisiana Purchase. His father was white, and his mother was a free black. Durnford became an American citizen after the Louisiana Purchase, rising to prominence as a Louisiana sugar planter and slaveholder. William Ellison, another free black who amassed great wealth and power in the South, was born a slave in 1790 in South Carolina. After buying his freedom and that of his wife and daughter, he proceeded to purchase his own slaves, whom he then put to work manufacturing cotton gins. By the eve of the Civil War, Ellison had become one of the richest and largest slaveholders in the entire state.

In this late eighteenth-century painting, a free woman of color stands with her quadroon daughter in New Orleans. Families with members that had widely varying ethnic characteristics were not uncommon at the time, especially in the larger cities.

The phenomenon of free blacks amassing large fortunes within a slave society predicated on racial difference, however, was exceedingly rare. Most free blacks in the South lived under the specter of slavery and faced many obstacles. Beginning in the early nineteenth century, southern states increasingly made manumission of slaves illegal. They also devised laws that divested free blacks of their rights, such as the right to testify against whites in court or the right to seek employment where they pleased. Interestingly, it was in the upper southern states that such laws were the harshest. In Virginia, for example, legislators made efforts to require free blacks to leave the state. In parts of the Deep South, free blacks were able to maintain their rights more easily. The difference in treatment between free blacks in the Deep South and those in the Upper South, historians have surmised, came down to economics. In the Deep South, slavery as an institution was strong and profitable. In the Upper South, the opposite was true. The anxiety of this economic uncertainty manifested in the form of harsh laws that targeted free blacks.

SLAVE REVOLTS

Slaves resisted their enslavement in small ways every day, but this resistance did not usually translate into mass uprisings. Slaves understood that the chances of ending slavery through rebellion were slim and would likely result in massive retaliation; many also feared the risk that participating in such actions would pose to themselves and their families. White slaveholders, however, constantly feared uprisings and took drastic steps, including torture and mutilation, whenever they believed that rebellions might be simmering. Gripped by the fear of insurrection, whites often imagined revolts to be in the works even when no uprising actually happened.

At least two major slave uprisings did occur in the antebellum South. In 1811, a major rebellion broke out in the sugar parishes of the booming territory of Louisiana. Inspired by the successful overthrow of the white planter class in Haiti, Louisiana slaves took up arms against planters. Perhaps as many five hundred slaves joined the rebellion, led by Charles Deslondes, a mixed-race slave driver on a sugar plantation owned by Manuel Andry.

The revolt began in January 1811 on Andry's plantation. Deslondes and other slaves attacked the Andry household, where they killed the slave master's son (although Andry himself escaped). The rebels then began traveling toward New Orleans, armed with weapons gathered at Andry's plantation. Whites mobilized to stop the rebellion, but not before Deslondes and the other rebelling slaves set fire to three plantations and killed numerous whites. A small white force led by Andry ultimately captured Deslondes, whose body was mutilated and burned following his execution. Other slave rebels were beheaded, and their heads placed on pikes along the Mississippi River.

The second rebellion, led by the slave Nat Turner, occurred in 1831 in Southampton County, Virginia. Turner had suffered not only from personal enslavement, but also from the additional trauma of having his wife sold away from him. Bolstered by Christianity, Turner became convinced that like Christ, he should lay down his life to end slavery. Mustering his relatives and friends, he began the rebellion August 22, killing scores of whites in the county. Whites mobilized quickly and within forty-eight hours had brought the rebellion to an end. Shocked by Nat Turner's Rebellion, Virginia's state legislature considered ending slavery in the state in order to provide greater security. In the end, legislators decided slavery would remain and that their state would continue to play a key role in the domestic slave trade.

SLAVE MARKETS

As discussed above, after centuries of slave trade with West Africa, Congress banned the further importation of slaves beginning in 1808. The domestic slave trade then expanded rapidly. As the cotton trade grew in size and importance, so did the domestic slave trade; the cultivation of cotton gave new life and importance to slavery, increasing the value of slaves. To meet the South's fierce demand for labor, American smugglers illegally transferred slaves through Florida and later through Texas. Many more slaves arrived illegally from Cuba; indeed, Cubans relied on the smuggling of slaves to prop up their finances. The largest number of slaves after 1808, however, came from the massive, legal internal slave market in which slave states in the Upper South sold enslaved men, women, and children to states in the Lower South. For slaves, the domestic trade presented the full horrors of slavery as children were ripped from their mothers and fathers and families destroyed, creating heartbreak and alienation.

Some slaveholders sought to increase the number of slave children by placing male slaves with fertile female slaves, and slave masters routinely raped their female slaves. The resulting births played an important role in slavery's expansion in the first half of the nineteenth century, as many slave children were born as a result of rape. One account written by a slave named William J. Anderson captures the horror of sexual exploitation in the antebellum South. Anderson wrote about how a Mississippi slaveholder

> divested a poor female slave of all wearing apparel, tied her down to stakes, and whipped her with a handsaw until he broke it over her naked body. In process of time he ravished [raped] her person, and became the father of a child by her. Besides, he always kept a colored Miss in the house with him. This is another curse of Slavery—concubinage and illegitimate connections—which is carried on to an alarming extent in the far South. A poor slave man who lives close by his wife, is permitted to visit

her but very seldom, and other men, both white and colored, cohabit with her. It is undoubtedly the worst place of incest and bigamy in the world. A white man thinks nothing of putting a colored man out to carry the fore row [front row in field work], and carry on the same sport with the colored man's wife at the same time.

Anderson, a devout Christian, recognized and explains in his narrative that one of the evils of slavery is the way it undermines the family. Anderson was not the only critic of slavery to emphasize this point. Frederick Douglass, a Maryland slave who escaped to the North in 1838, elaborated on this dimension of slavery in his 1845 narrative. He recounted how slave masters had to sell their own children whom they had with slave women to appease the white wives who despised their offspring.

The selling of slaves was a major business enterprise in the antebellum South, representing a key part of the economy. White men invested substantial sums in slaves, carefully calculating the annual returns they could expect from a slave as well as the possibility of greater profits through natural increase. The domestic slave trade was highly visible, and like the infamous Middle Passage that brought captive Africans to the Americas, it constituted an equally disruptive and horrifying journey now called the **second middle passage**. Between 1820 and 1860, white American traders sold a million or more slaves in the domestic slave market. Groups of slaves were transported by ship from places like Virginia, a state that specialized in raising slaves for sale, to New Orleans, where they were sold to planters in the Mississippi Valley. Other slaves made the overland trek from older states like North Carolina to new and booming Deep South states like Alabama.

New Orleans had the largest slave market in the United States. Slaveholders brought their slaves there from the East (Virginia, Maryland, and the Carolinas) and the West (Tennessee and Kentucky) to be sold for work in the Mississippi Valley. The slave trade benefited whites in the Chesapeake and Carolinas, providing them with extra income: A healthy young male slave in the 1850s could be sold for $1,000 (approximately $30,000 in 2014 dollars), and a planter who could sell ten such slaves collected a windfall.

In Sale of Estates, Pictures and Slaves in the Rotunda, New Orleans (1853) by J. M. Starling, it is clear that slaves are considered property to be auctioned off, just like pictures or other items.

In fact, by the 1850s, the demand for slaves reached an all-time high, and prices therefore doubled. A slave who would have sold for $400 in the 1820s could command a price of $800 in the 1850s. The high price of slaves in the 1850s and the inability of natural increase to satisfy demands led some southerners to demand the reopening of the international slave trade, a movement that caused a rift between the Upper South and the Lower South. Whites in the Upper South who sold slaves to their counterparts in the Lower South worried that reopening the trade would lower prices and therefore hurt their profits.

John Brown on Slave Life in Georgia

A slave named John Brown lived in Virginia, North Carolina, and Georgia before he escaped and moved to England. While there, he dictated his autobiography to someone at the British and Foreign Anti-Slavery Society, who published it in 1855.

> I really thought my mother would have died of grief at being obliged to leave her two children, her mother, and her relations behind. But it was of no use lamenting, the few things we had were put together that night, and we completed our preparations for being parted for life by kissing one another over and over again, and saying good bye till some of us little ones fell asleep. . . . And here I may as well tell what kind of man our new master was. He was of small stature, and thin, but very strong. He had sandy hair, a very red face, and chewed tobacco. His countenance had a very cruel expression, and his disposition was a match for it. He was, indeed, a very bad man, and used to flog us dreadfully. He would make his slaves work on one meal a day, until quite night, and after supper, set them to burn brush or spin cotton. We worked from four in the morning till twelve before we broke our fast, and from that time till eleven or twelve at night . . . we labored eighteen hours a day.
>
> —John Brown, *Slave Life in Georgia: A Narrative of the Life, Sufferings, and Escape of John Brown, A Fugitive Slave, Now in England*, 1855

What features of the domestic slave trade does Brown's narrative illuminate? Why do you think he brought his story to an antislavery society? How do you think people responded to this narrative?

> Read through several narratives at "Born in Slavery," part of the American Memory collection at the Library of Congress. Do these narratives have anything in common? What differences can you find between them?

Section Summary

Slave labor in the antebellum South generated great wealth for plantation owners. Slaves, in contrast, endured daily traumas as the human property of masters. Slaves resisted their condition in a variety of ways, and many found some solace in Christianity and the communities they created in the slave quarters. While some free blacks achieved economic prosperity and even became slaveholders themselves, the vast majority found themselves restricted by the same white-supremacist assumptions upon which the institution of slavery was based.

https://www.openassessments.org/assessments/983

Review Question

1. How did both slaveholders and slaves use the concept of paternalism to their advantage?

> ### Answer to Review Question
>
> 1. Southern whites often used paternalism to justify the institution of slavery, arguing that slaves, like children, needed the care, feeding, discipline, and moral and religious education that they could provide. Slaves often used this misguided notion to their advantage: By feigning ignorance and playing into slaveholders' paternalistic perceptions of them, slaves found opportunities to resist their condition and gain a degree of freedom and autonomy.

> ### Glossary
>
> **paternalism** the premise that southern white slaveholders acted in the best interests of their slaves
>
> **second middle passage** the internal forced migration of slaves to the South and West in the United States

Attributions

CC licensed content, Shared previously

- US History. **Authored by**: P. Scott Corbett, Volker Janssen, John M. Lund, Todd Pfannestiel, Paul Vickery, and Sylvie Waskiewicz. **Provided by**: OpenStax College. **Located at**: http://openstaxcollege.org/textbooks/us-history. **License**: *CC BY: Attribution*. **License Terms**: Download for free at http://cnx.org/content/col11740/latest/

Primary Source Reading: Twelve Years a Slave

Solomon Northup, Twelve Years a Slave (Selections)

Solomon Northup (July 1808–1863?) was an American abolitionist and the primary author of the memoir Twelve Years a Slave. *A free-born African American from New York, he was the son of a freed slave and free woman of color. A farmer and violinist, Northup owned land in Hebron, New York. In 1841, he was offered a traveling musician's job and went to Washington, D.C. (where slavery was legal), where he was kidnapped, and sold as a slave. He was shipped to New Orleans, purchased by a planter, and held as a slave for 12 years in the Red River region of Louisiana, mostly in Avoyelles Parish. He remained in slavery until he met a Canadian working on his plantation who helped get word to New York, where state law provided for aid to free New York citizens kidnapped into slavery. Family and friends enlisted the aid of the Governor of New York, Washington Hunt, and Northup regained his freedom on January 3, 1853.*

The slave trader in Washington, D.C., James H. Birch, was arrested and tried, but acquitted because District of Columbia law prohibited Northup as a black man from testifying against white people. Later, in New York State, his northern kidnappers were located and charged, but the case was tied up in court for two years due to jurisdictional challenges and finally dropped when Washington, D.C., was found to have jurisdiction. The D.C. government did not pursue the case. Those who had kidnapped and enslaved Northup received no punishment.

In his first year of freedom, Northup wrote and published a memoir, Twelve Years a Slave *(1853). He lectured on behalf of the abolitionist movement, giving more than two dozen speeches throughout the Northeast about his experiences, to build momentum against slavery. He largely disappears from the historical record in 1857 (although a letter later reported him alive in early 1863); some commentators thought he had been kidnapped again, but historians believe it unlikely, as he would have been considered too old to bring a good price. The details of his death have never been documented.*

EDWIN EPPS, of whom much will be said during the remainder of this history, is a large, portly, heavy-bodied man with light hair, high cheek bones, and a Roman nose of extraordinary dimensions. He has blue eyes, a fair complexion, and is, as I should say, full six feet high. He has the sharp, inquisitive expression of a jockey. His manners are repulsive and coarse, and his language gives speedy and unequivocal evidence that he has never enjoyed the advantages of an education. He has the faculty of saying most provoking things, in that respect even excelling old Peter Tanner. At the time I came into his possession, Edwin Epps was fond of the bottle, his "sprees" sometimes extending over the space of two whole weeks. Latterly, however, he had reformed his habits, and when I left him, was as strict a specimen of temperance as could be found on Bayou Boeuf When "in his Cups," Master Epps was a roystering, blustering, noisy fellow, whose chief delight was in dancing with his "niggers," or lashing them about the yard with his long whip, just for the pleasure of hearing them screech and scream, as the great welts were planted on their backs. When sober, he was silent, reserved and cunning, not beating us indiscriminately, as in his drunken moments, but sending the end of his rawhide to some tender spot of a lagging slave, with a sly dexterity peculiar to himself.

He had been a driver and overseer in his younger years, but at this time was in possession of a plantation on Bayou Huff Power, two and a half miles from Holmesville, eighteen from Marksville, and twelve from Cheneyville. It belonged to Joseph B. Roberts, his wife's uncle, and was leased by Epps. His principal business was raising cotton, and inasmuch as some may read this book who have never seen a cotton field, a description of the manner of its culture may not be out of place.

The ground is prepared by throwing up beds or ridges, with the plough—back-furrowing, it is called. Oxen and mules, the latter almost exclusively, are used in ploughing. The women as frequently as the men perform this labor, feeding, currying, and taking care of their teams, and in all respects doing the field and stable work, precisely as do the ploughboys of the North.

The beds, or ridges, are six feet wide, that is, from water furrow to water furrow. A plough drawn by one mule is then run along the top of the ridge or center of the bed, making the drill, into which a girl usually drops the seed, which she carries in a bag hung round her neck. Behind her comes a mule and harrow, covering up the seed, so that two mules three slaves, a plough and harrow, are employed in planting a row of cotton. This is done in the months of March and April. Corn is planted in February. When there are no cold rains, the cotton usually makes its appearance in a week. In the course of eight or ten days afterwards the first hoeing is commenced. This is performed in part, also, by the aid of the plough and mule. The plough passes as near as possible to the cotton on both sides, throwing the furrow from it. Slaves follow with their hoes, cutting up the grass and cotton, leaving hills two feet and a half apart. This is called scraping cotton. In two weeks more commences the second hoeing. This time the furrow is thrown towards the cotton. Only one stalk, the largest, is now left standing in each hill. In another fortnight it is hoed the third time, throwing the furrow towards the cotton in the same manner as before, and killing all the grass between the rows. About the first of July, when it is a foot high or thereabouts, it is hoed the fourth and last time. Now the whole space between the rows is ploughed, leaving a deep water furrow in the center. During all these hoeings the overseer or driver follows the slaves on horseback with a whip, such as has been described. The fastest hoer takes the lead row. He is usually about a rod in advance of his companions. If one of them passes him, he is whipped. If one falls behind or is a moment idle, he is whipped. In fact, the lash is flying from morning until night, the whole day long. The hoeing season thus continues from April until July, a field having no sooner been finished once, than it is commenced again.

In the latter part of August begins the cotton picking season. At this time each slave is presented with a sack. A strap is fastened to it, which goes over the neck, holding the mouth of the sack breast high, while the bottom reaches nearly to the ground. Each one is also presented with a large basket that will hold about two barrels. This is to put the cotton in when the sack is filled. The baskets are carried to the field and placed at the beginning of the rows.

When a new hand, one unaccustomed to the business, is sent for the first time into the field, he is whipped up smartly, and made for that day to pick as fast as he can possibly. At night it is weighed, so that his capability in cotton picking is known. He must bring in the same weight each night following. If it falls short, it is considered evidence that he has been laggard, and a greater or less number of lashes is the penalty.

An ordinary day's work is two hundred pounds. A slave who is accustomed to picking, is punished, if he or she brings in a less quantity than that. There is a great difference among them as regards this kind of labor. Some of them seem to have a natural knack, or quickness, which enables them to pick with great celerity, and with both hands, while others, with whatever practice or industry, are utterly unable to come up to the ordinary standard. Such hands are taken from the cotton field and employed in other business. Patsey, of whom I shall have more to say, was known as the most remarkable cotton picker on Bayou Boeuf. She picked with both hands and with such surprising rapidity, that five hundred pounds a day was not unusual for her.

Each one is tasked, therefore, according to his picking abilities, none, however, to come short of two hundred weight. I, being unskillful always in that business, would have satisfied my master by bringing in the latter quantity, while on the other hand, Patsey would surely have been beaten if she failed to produce twice as much.

The cotton grows from five to seven feet high, each stalk having a great many branches, shooting out in all directions, and lapping each other above the water furrow.

There are few sights more pleasant to the eye, than a wide cotton field when it is in the bloom. It presents an appearance of purity, like an immaculate expanse of light, new-fallen snow.

Sometimes the slave picks down one side of a row, and back upon the other, but more usually, there is one on either side, gathering all that has blossomed, leaving the unopened boils for a succeeding picking. When the sack is filled, it is emptied into the basket and trodden down. It is necessary to be extremely careful the first time going through the field, in order not to break the branches off the stalks. The cotton will not bloom upon a broken branch. Epps never failed to inflict the severest chastisement on the unlucky servant who, either carelessly or unavoidably, was guilty in the least degree in this respect.

The hands are required to be in the cotton field as soon as it is light in the morning, and, with the exception of ten or fifteen minutes, which is given them at noon to swallow their allowance of cold bacon, they are not permitted to be a moment idle until it is too dark to see, and when the moon is full, they often times labor till the middle of the night. They do not dare to stop even at dinner time, nor return to the quarters, however late it be, until the order to halt is given by the driver.

The day's work over in the field, the baskets are "toted," or in other words, carried to the gin-house, where the cotton is weighed. No matter how fatigued and weary he may be—no matter how much he longs for sleep and rest—a slave never approaches the gin-house with his basket of cotton but with fear. If it falls short in weight—if he has not performed the full task appointed him, he knows that he must suffer. And if he has exceeded it by ten or twenty pounds, in all probability his master will measure the next day's task accordingly. So, whether he has too little or too much, his approach to the gin-house is always with fear and trembling. Most frequently they have too little, and therefore it is they are not anxious to leave the field. After weighing, follow the whippings; and then the baskets are carried to the cotton house, and their contents stored away like hay, all hands being sent in to tramp it down. If the cotton is not dry, instead of taking it to the gin-house at once, it is laid upon platforms, two feet high, and some three times as wide, covered with boards or plank, with narrow walks running between them.

This done, the labor of the day is not yet ended, by any means. Each one must then attend to his respective chores. One feeds the mules, another the swine—another cuts the wood, and so forth; besides, the packing is all done by candle light. Finally, at a late hour, they reach the quarters, sleepy and overcome with the long day's toil. Then a fire must be kindled in the cabin, the corn ground in the small hand-mill, and supper, and dinner for the next day in the field, prepared. All that is allowed them is corn and bacon, which is given out at the corncrib and smoke-house every Sunday morning. Each one receives, as his weekly allowance, three and a half pounds of bacon, and corn enough to make a peck of meal. That is all—no tea, coffee, sugar, and with the exception of a very scanty sprinkling now and then, no salt. I can say, from a ten years' residence with Master Epps, that no slave of his is ever likely to suffer from the gout, superinduced by excessive high living. Master Epps' hogs were fed on shelled corn—it was thrown out to his "niggers" in the ear. The former, he thought, would fatten faster by shelling, and soaking it in the water—the latter, perhaps, if treated in the same manner, might grow too fat to labor. Master Epps was a shrewd calculator, and knew how to manage his own animals, drunk or sober.

The corn mill stands in the yard beneath a shelter. It is like a common coffee mill, the hopper holding about six quarts. There was one privilege which Master Epps granted freely to every slave he had. They might grind their corn nightly, in such small quantities as their daily wants required, or they might grind the whole week's allowance at one time, on Sundays, just as they preferred. A very generous man was Master Epps!

I kept my corn in a small wooden box, the meal in a gourd; and, by the way, the gourd is one of the most convenient and necessary utensils on a plantation. Besides supplying the place of all kinds of crockery in a slave cabin, it is used for carrying water to the fields. Another, also, contains the dinner. It dispenses with the necessity of pails, dippers, basins, and such tin and wooden superfluities altogether.

When the corn is ground, and fire is made, the bacon is taken down from the nail on which it hangs a slice cut off and thrown upon the coals to broil. The majority of slaves have no knife, much less a fork. They cut their bacon with the axe at the woodpile. The corn meal is mixed with a little water, placed in the fire, and baked. When it is "done brown," the ashes are scraped off; and being placed upon a chip, which answers for a table, the tenant of the slave hut is ready to sit down upon the ground to supper. By this time it is usually midnight. The same fear of punishment with which they approach the gin-house, possesses them again on lying down to get a snatch of rest. It is the fear of oversleeping in the morning. Such an offence would certainly be attended with not less than twenty lashes. With a prayer that he may be on his feet and wide awake at the first sound of the horn, he sinks to his slumbers nightly.

The softest couches in the world are not to be found in the log mansion of the slave. The one whereon I reclined year after year, was a plank twelve inches wide and ten feet long. My pillow was a stick of wood. The bedding was a coarse blanket, and not a rag or shred beside. Moss might be used, were it not that it directly breeds a swarm of fleas.

The cabin is constructed of logs, without floor or window. The latter is altogether unnecessary, the crevices between the logs admitting sufficient light. In stormy weather the rain drives through them, rendering it comfortless and extremely disagreeable. The rude door hangs on great wooden hinges. In one end is constructed an awkward fire-place.

An hour before day light the horn is blown. Then the slaves arouse, prepare their breakfast, fill a gourd with water, in another deposit their dinner of cold bacon and corn cake, and hurry to the field again. It is an offence invariably followed by a flogging, to be found at the quarters after daybreak. Then the fears and labors of another day begin; and until its close there is no such thing as rest. He fears he will be caught lagging through the day; he fears to approach the gin-house with his basket-load of cotton at night; he fears, when he lies down, that he will oversleep himself in the morning. Such is a true, faithful, unexaggerated picture and description of the slave's daily life, during the time of cotton-picking, on the shores of Bayou Boeuf.

In the month of January, generally, the fourth and last picking is completed. Then commences the harvesting, of corn. This is considered a secondary crop, and receives far less attention than the cotton. It is planted, as already mentioned, in February. Corn is grown in that region for the purpose of fattening hogs and feeding slaves; very little, if any, being sent to market. It is the white variety, the ear of great size, and the stalk growing to the height of eight, and often times ten feet. In August the leaves are stripped off, dried in the sun, bound in small bundles, and stored away as provender for the mules and oxen. After this the slaves go through the field, turning down the ear, for the purpose of keeping the rains from penetrating to the grain. It is left in this condition until after cotton-picking is over, whether earlier or later. Then the ears are separated from the stalks, and deposited in the corncrib with the husks on; otherwise, stripped of the husks, the weevil would destroy it. The stalks are left standing in the field.

The Carolina, or sweet potato, is also grown in that region to some extent. They are not fed, however, to hogs or cattle, and are considered but of small importance. They are preserved by placing them upon the surface of the ground, with a slight covering of earth or cornstalks. There is not a cellar on Bayou Boeuf. The ground is so low it would fill with water. Potatoes are worth from two to three "bits," or shillings a barrel; corn, except when there is an unusual scarcity, can be purchased at the same rate.

As soon as the cotton and corn crops are secured, the stalks are pulled up, thrown into piles and burned. The ploughs are started at the same time, throwing up the beds again, preparatory to another planting. The soil, in the parishes of Rapides and Avoyelles, and throughout the whole country, so far as my observation extended, is of exceeding richness and fertility. It is a kind of marl, of a brown or reddish color. It does not require those invigorating composts necessary to more barren lands, and on the same field the same crop is grown for many successive years.

Ploughing, planting, picking cotton, gathering the corn, and pulling and burning stalks, occupies the whole of the four seasons of the year. Drawing and cutting wood, pressing cotton, fattening and killing hog's, are but incidental labors.

In the month of September or October, the hogs are run out of the swamps by dogs, and confined in pens. On a cold morning, generally about New Year's day, they are slaughtered. Each carcass is cut into six parts, and piled one above the other in salt, upon large tables in the smoke-house. In this condition it remains a fortnight, when it is hung up, and a fire built, and continued more than half the time during the remainder of the year. This thorough smoking is necessary to prevent the bacon from becoming infested with worms. In so warm a climate it is difficult to preserve it, and very many times myself and my companions have received our weekly allowance of three pounds and a half, when it was full of these disgusting vermin.

Although the swamps are overrun with cattle, they are never made the source of profit, to any considerable extent. The planter cuts his mark upon the ear, or brands his initials upon the side, and turns them into the swamps, to roam unrestricted within their almost limitless confines. They are the Spanish breed, small and spike-horned. I have known of droves being taken from Bayou Boeuf, but it is of very rare occurrence. The value of the best cows is about five dollars each. Two quarts at one milking, would be considered an unusual large quantity. They furnish little tallow, and that of a soft, inferior quality. Notwithstanding the great number of cows that throng the swamps, the planters are indebted to the North for their cheese and butter, which is purchased in the New-Orleans market. Salted beef is not an article of food either in the great house, or in the cabin.

Master Epps was accustomed to attend shooting matches for the purpose of obtaining what fresh beef he required. These sports occurred weekly at the neighboring village of Holmesville. Fat beeves are driven thither and shot at, a stipulated price being demanded for the privilege. The lucky marksman divides the flesh among his fellows, and in this manner the attending planters are supplied.

The great number of tame and untamed cattle which swarm the woods and swamps of Bayou Boeuf, most probably suggested that appellation to the French, inasmuch as the term, translated, signifies the creek or river of the wild ox.

Garden products, such as cabbages, turnips and the like, are cultivated for the use of the master and his family. They have greens and vegetables at all times and seasons of the year. "The grass withereth and the flower fadeth" before the desolating winds of autumn in the chill northern latitudes, but perpetual verdure overspreads the hot lowlands, and flowers bloom in the heart of winter, in the region of Bayou Boeuf.

There are no meadows appropriated to the cultivation of the grasses. The leaves of the corn supply a sufficiency of food for the laboring cattle, while the rest provide for themselves all the year in the evergrowing pasture.

There are many other peculiarities of climate, habit, custom, and of the manner of living and laboring at the South, but the foregoing, it is supposed, will give the reader an insight and general idea of life on a cotton plantation in Louisiana. The mode of cultivating cane, and the process of sugar manufacturing, will be mentioned in another place.

Twelve Years a Slave:

Narrative of Solomon Northup, a Citizen of New-York,

Kidnapped in Washington City in 1841, and Rescued in 1853:

Electronic Edition.

Solomon Northup (b. 1808)

Text scanned (OCR) by Christopher Gwyn

Text encoded by Natalia Smith.

This work is the property of the University of North Carolina at Chapel Hill. It may be used freely by individuals for research, teaching and personal use as long as this statement of availability is included in the text.

Attributions

CC licensed content, Shared previously

- Introduction to Solomon Northrup. **Provided by**: Wikipedia. **Located at**: http://en.wikipedia.org/wiki/Solomon_Northup. **License**: *CC BY: Attribution*

Public domain content

- Twelve Years a Slave: Narrative of Solomon Northup, a Citizen of New-York, Kidnapped in Washington City in 1841, and Rescued in 1853:. **Authored by**: Solomon Northup. **Located at**: http://docsouth.unc.edu/fpn/northup/northup.html. **Project**: Documenting The American South. **License**: *Public Domain: No Known Copyright*

Primary Source Reading: John Calhoun on Slavery

John C. Calhoun, Slavery a Positive Good (1837)

Introduction

John Caldwell Calhoun (March 18, 1782 – March 31, 1850) was a leading American politician and political theorist during the first half of the 19th century. Hailing from South Carolina, Calhoun began his political career as a nationalist, modernizer, and proponent of a strong national government and protective tariffs. After 1830, his views evolved and he became a greater proponent of states' rights, limited government, nullification and free trade; as he saw these means as the only way to preserve the Union. He is best known for his intense and original defense of slavery as something positive, his distrust of majoritarianism, and for pointing the South toward secession from the Union. …

Calhoun died eleven years before the start of the American Civil War, but he was an inspiration to the secessionists of 1860–61. Nicknamed the "cast-iron man" for his ideological rigidity [2][3] as well as for his determination to defend the causes he believed in,[4] Calhoun supported states' rights and nullification, under which states could declare null and void federal laws which they viewed as unconstitutional. He was an outspoken proponent of the institution of slavery, which he defended as a "positive good" rather than as a "necessary evil".[5] His rhetorical defense of slavery was partially responsible for escalating Southern threats of secession in the face of mounting abolitionist sentiment in the North. (http://en.wikipedia.org/wiki/John_C._Calhoun)

Speech

Delivered February 6, 1837

I do not belong, said Mr. C., to the school which holds that aggression is to be met by concession. Mine is the opposite creed, which teaches that encroachments must be met at the beginning, and that those who act on the opposite principle are prepared to become slaves. In this case, in particular I hold concession or compromise to be fatal. If we concede an inch, concession would follow concession—compromise would follow compromise, until our ranks would be so broken that effectual resistance would be impossible. We must meet the enemy on the frontier, with a fixed determination of maintaining our position at every hazard. Consent to receive these insulting petitions, and the next demand will be that they be referred to a committee in order that they may be deliberated and acted upon. At the last session we were modestly asked to receive them, simply to lay them on the table, without any view to ulterior action. . . . I then said, that the next step would be to refer the petition to a committee, and I already see indications that such is now the intention. If we yield, that will be followed by another, and we will thus proceed, step by step, to the final consummation of the object of these petitions. We are now told that the most effectual mode of arresting the progress of abolition is, to reason it down; and with this view it is urged that the petitions ought to be referred to a committee. That is the very ground which was taken at the last session in the other House, but instead of arresting its progress it has since advanced more rapidly than ever. The most unquestionable right may be rendered doubtful, if once admitted to be a subject of controversy, and that would be the case in the present instance. The subject is beyond the jurisdiction of Congress – they have no right to touch it in any shape or form, or to make it the subject of deliberation or discussion. . . .

As widely as this incendiary spirit has spread, it has not yet infected this body, or the great mass of the intelligent and business portion of the North; but unless it be speedily stopped, it will spread and work upwards till it brings the two great sections of the Union into deadly conflict. This is not a new impression with me. Several years since, in a discussion with one of the Senators from Massachusetts (Mr. Webster), before this fell spirit had showed itself, I then predicted that the doctrine of the proclamation and the Force Bill—that this Government had a right, in the last resort, to determine the extent of its own powers, and enforce its decision at the point of the bayonet, which was so warmly maintained by that Senator, would at no distant day arouse the dormant spirit of abolitionism. I told him that the doctrine was tantamount to the assumption of unlimited power on the part of the Government, and that such would be the impression on the public mind in a large portion of the Union. The consequence would be inevitable. A large portion of the Northern States believed slavery to be a sin, and would consider it as an obligation of conscience to abolish it if they should feel themselves in any degree responsible for its continuance, and that this doctrine would necessarily lead to the belief of such responsibility. I then predicted that it would commence as it has with this fanatical portion of society, and that they would begin their operations on the ignorant, the weak, the young, and the thoughtless —and gradually extend upwards till they would become strong enough to obtain political control, when he and others holding the highest stations in society, would, however reluctant, be compelled to yield to their doctrines, or be driven into obscurity. But four years have since elapsed, and all this is already in a course of regular fulfilment.

Standing at the point of time at which we have now arrived, it will not be more difficult to trace the course of future events now than it was then. They who imagine that the spirit now abroad in the North, will die away of itself without a shock or convulsion, have formed a very inadequate conception of its real character; it will continue to rise and spread, unless prompt and efficient measures to stay its progress be adopted. Already it has taken possession of the pulpit, of the schools, and, to a considerable extent, of the press; those great instruments by which the mind of the rising generation will be formed.

However sound the great body of the non—slaveholding States are at present, in the course of a few years they will be succeeded by those who will have been taught to hate the people and institutions of nearly one-half of this Union, with a hatred more deadly than one hostile nation ever entertained towards another. It is easy to see the end. By the necessary course of events, if left to themselves, we must become, finally, two people. It is impossible under the deadly hatred which must spring up between the two great nations, if the present causes are permitted to operate unchecked, that we should continue under the same political system. The conflicting elements would burst the Union asunder, powerful as are the links which hold it together. Abolition and the Union cannot coexist. As the friend of the Union I openly proclaim it—and the sooner it is known the better. The former may now be controlled, but in a short time it will be beyond the power of man to arrest the course of events. We of the South will not, cannot, surrender our institutions. To maintain the existing relations between the two races, inhabiting that section of the Union, is indispensable to the peace and happiness of both. It cannot be subverted without drenching the country or the other of the races. . . . But let me not be understood as admitting, even by implication, that the existing relations between the two races in the slaveholding States is an evil:—far otherwise; I hold it to be a good, as it has thus far proved itself to be to both, and will continue to prove so if not disturbed by the fell spirit of abolition. I appeal to facts. Never before has the black race of Central Africa, from the dawn of history to the present day, attained a condition so civilized and so improved, not only physically, but morally and intellectually.

In the meantime, the white or European race, has not degenerated. It has kept pace with its brethren in other sections of the Union where slavery does not exist. It is odious to make comparison; but I appeal to all sides whether the South is not equal in virtue, intelligence, patriotism, courage, disinterestedness, and all the high qualities which adorn our nature.

But I take higher ground. I hold that in the present state of civilization, where two races of different origin, and distinguished by color, and other physical differences, as well as intellectual, are brought together, the relation now existing in the slaveholding States between the two, is, instead of an evil, a good—a positive good. I feel myself called upon to speak freely upon the subject where the honor and interests of those I represent are involved. I hold then, that there never has yet existed a wealthy and civilized society in which one portion of the community did not, in point of fact, live on the labor of the other. Broad and general as is this assertion, it is fully borne out by history. This is not the proper occasion, but, if it were, it would not be difficult to trace the various devices by which the wealth of all civilized communities has been so unequally divided, and to show by what means so small a share has been allotted to those by whose labor it was produced, and so large a share given to the non-producing classes. The devices are almost innumerable, from the brute force and gross superstition of ancient times, to the subtle and artful fiscal contrivances of modern. I might well challenge a comparison between them and the more direct, simple, and patriarchal mode by which the labor of the African race is, among us, commanded by the European. I may say with truth, that in few countries so much is left to the share of the laborer, and so little exacted from him, or where there is more kind attention paid to him in sickness or infirmities of age. Compare his condition with the tenants of the poor houses in the more civilized portions of Europe—look at the sick, and the old and infirm slave, on one hand, in the midst of his family and friends, under the kind superintending care of his master and mistress, and compare it with the forlorn and wretched condition of the pauper in the poorhouse. But I will not dwell on this aspect of the question; I turn to the political; and here I fearlessly assert that the existing relation between the two races in the South, against which these blind fanatics are waging war, forms the most solid and durable foundation on which to rear free and stable political institutions. It is useless to disguise the fact. There is and always has been in an advanced stage of wealth and civilization, a conflict between labor and capital. The condition of society in the South exempts us from the disorders and dangers resulting from this conflict; and which explains why it is that the political condition of the slaveholding States has been so much more stable and quiet than that of the North. . . . Surrounded as the slaveholding States are with such imminent perils, I rejoice to think that our means of defense are ample, if we shall prove to have the intelligence and spirit to see and apply them before it is too late. All we want is concert, to lay aside all party differences and unite with zeal and energy in repelling approaching dangers. Let there be concert of action, and we shall find ample means of security without resorting to secession or disunion. I speak with full knowledge and a thorough examination of the subject, and for one see my way clearly. . . . I dare not hope that anything I can say will arouse the South to a due sense of danger; I fear it is beyond the power of mortal voice to awaken it in time from the fatal security into which it has fallen.

Attributions

Public domain content

- Slavery a Positive Good. **Authored by**: John C. Calhoun. **Provided by**: Wikisource. **Located at**: https://en.wikisource.org/wiki/Slavery_a_Positive_Good. **License**: *Public Domain: No Known Copyright*

Primary Source Reading: Fredrick Douglass

Fredrick Douglass, Autobiography (1845)

Introduction

Frederick Douglass (born Frederick Augustus Washington Bailey, c. February 1818 – February 20, 1895) was an African-American social reformer, orator, writer, and statesman. After escaping from slavery, he became a leader of the abolitionist movement, gaining note for his dazzling oratory and incisive antislavery writing. He stood as a living counter-example to slaveholders' arguments that slaves lacked the intellectual capacity to function as independent American citizens. Many Northerners also found it hard to believe that such a great orator had been a slave.

Douglass wrote several autobiographies. He described his experiences as a slave in his 1845 autobiography, Narrative of the Life of Frederick Douglass, an American Slave, which became a bestseller and influential in supporting abolition, as did the second, My Bondage and My Freedom (1855). After the Civil War, Douglass remained an active campaigner against slavery and wrote his last autobiography, Life and Times of Frederick Douglass. First published in 1881 and revised in 1892, three years before his death, it covered events through and after the Civil War. Douglass also actively supported women's suffrage, and held several public offices. Without his approval, Douglass became the first African American nominated for Vice President of the United States as the running mate and Vice Presidential nominee of Victoria Woodhull on the impracticable, small, but far foreseeing Equal Rights Party ticket.

A firm believer in the equality of all people, whether black, female, Native American, or recent immigrant, Douglass famously said, "I would unite with anybody to do right and with nobody to do wrong."

Selections

CHAPTER I

I was born in Tuckahoe, near Hillsborough, and about twelve miles from Easton, in Talbot county, Maryland. I have no accurate knowledge of my age, never having seen any authentic record containing it. By far the larger part of the slaves know as little of their ages as horses know of theirs, and it is the wish of most masters within my knowledge to keep their slaves thus ignorant. I do not remember to have ever met a slave who could tell of his birthday. They seldom come nearer to it than planting-time, harvesttime, cherry-time, spring-time, or fall-time. A want of information concerning my own was a source of unhappiness to me even during childhood. The white children could tell their ages. I could not tell why I ought to be deprived of the same privilege. I was not allowed to make any inquiries of my master concerning it. He deemed all such inquiries on the part of a slave improper and impertinent, and evidence of a restless spirit. The nearest estimate I can give makes me now between twenty-seven and twentyeight years of age. I come to this, from hearing my master say, some time during 1835, I was about seventeen years old.

My mother was named Harriet Bailey. She was the daughter of Isaac and Betsey Bailey, both colored, and quite dark. My mother was of a darker complexion than either my grandmother or grandfather.

My father was a white man. He was admitted to be such by all I ever heard speak of my parentage. The opinion was also whispered that my master was my father; but of the correctness of this opinion, I know nothing; the means of knowing was withheld from me. My mother and I were separated when I was but an infant–before I knew her as my mother. It is a common custom, in the part of Maryland from which I ran away, to part children from their mothers at a very early age. Frequently, before the child has reached its twelfth month, its mother is taken from it, and hired out on some farm a considerable distance off, and the child is placed under the care of an old woman, too old for field labor. For what this separation is done, I do not know, unless it be to hinder the development of the child's affection toward its mother, and to blunt and destroy the natural affection of the mother for the child. This is the inevitable result.

I never saw my mother, to know her as such, more than four or five times in my life; and each of these times was very short in duration, and at night. She was hired by a Mr. Stewart, who lived about twelve miles from my home. She made her journeys to see me in the night, travelling the whole distance on foot, after the performance of her day's work. She was a field hand, and a whipping is the penalty of not being in the field at sunrise, unless a slave has special permission from his or her master to the contrary–a permission which they seldom get, and one that gives to him that gives it the proud name of being a kind master. I do not recollect of ever seeing my mother by the light of day. She was with me in the night. She would lie down with me, and get me to sleep, but long before I waked she was gone. Very little communication ever took place between us. Death soon ended what little we could have while she lived, and with it her hardships and suffering. She died when I was about seven years old, on one of my master's farms, near Lee's Mill. I was not allowed to be present during her illness, at her death, or burial. She was gone long before I knew any thing about it. Never having enjoyed, to any considerable extent, her soothing presence, her tender and watchful care, I received the tidings of her death with much the same emotions I should have probably felt at the death of a stranger.

Called thus suddenly away, she left me without the slightest intimation of who my father was. The whisper that my master was my father, may or may not be true; and, true or false, it is of but little consequence to my purpose whilst the fact remains, in all its glaring odiousness, that slaveholders have ordained, and by law established, that the children of slave women shall in all cases follow the condition of their mothers; and this is done too obviously to administer to their own lusts, and make a gratification of their wicked desires profitable as well as pleasurable; for by this cunning arrangement, the slaveholder, in cases not a few, sustains to his slaves the double relation of master and father.

I know of such cases; and it is worthy of remark that such slaves invariably suffer greater hardships, and have more to contend with, than others. They are, in the first place, a constant offence to their mistress.

She is ever disposed to find fault with them; they can seldom do any thing to please her; she is never better pleased than when she sees them under the lash, especially when she suspects her husband of showing to his mulatto children favors which he withholds from his black slaves. The master is frequently compelled to sell this class of his slaves, out of deference to the feelings of his white wife; and, cruel as the deed may strike any one to be, for a man to sell his own children to human flesh-mongers, it is often the dictate of humanity for him to do so; for, unless he does this, he must not only whip them himself, but must stand by and see one white son tie up his brother, of but few shades darker complexion than himself, and ply the gory lash to his naked back; and if he lisp one word of disapproval, it is set down to his parental partiality, and only makes a bad matter worse, both for himself and the slave whom he would protect and defend.

Every year brings with it multitudes of this class of slaves. It was doubtless in consequence of a knowledge of this fact, that one great statesman of the south predicted the downfall of slavery by the inevitable laws of population. Whether this prophecy is ever fulfilled or not, it is nevertheless plain that a very different-looking class of people are springing up at the south, and are now held in slavery, from those originally brought to this country from Africa; and if their increase do no other good, it will do away the force of the argument, that God cursed Ham, and therefore American slavery is right. If the lineal descendants of Ham are alone to be scripturally enslaved, it is certain that slavery at the south must soon become unscriptural; for thousands are ushered into the world, annually, who, like myself, owe their existence to white fathers, and those fathers most frequently their own masters.

I have had two masters. My first master's name was Anthony. I do not remember his first name. He was generally called Captain Anthony–a title which, I presume, he acquired by sailing a craft on the Chesapeake Bay. He was not considered a rich slaveholder. He owned two or three farms, and about thirty slaves. His farms and slaves were under the care of an overseer. The overseer's name was Plummer. Mr. Plummer was a miserable drunkard, a profane swearer, and a savage monster. He always went armed with a cowskin and a heavy cudgel. I have known him to cut and slash the women's heads so horribly, that even master would be enraged at his cruelty, and would threaten to whip him if he did not mind himself. Master, however, was not a humane slaveholder. It required extraordinary barbarity on the part of an overseer to affect him. He was a cruel man, hardened by a long life of slaveholding. He would at times seem to take great pleasure in whipping a slave. I have often been awakened at the dawn of day by the most heart-rending shrieks of an own aunt of mine, whom he used to tie up to a joist, and whip upon her naked back till she was literally covered with blood. No words, no tears, no prayers, from his gory victim, seemed to move his iron heart from its bloody purpose. The louder she screamed, the harder he whipped; and where the blood ran fastest, there he whipped longest. He would whip her to make her scream, and whip her to make her hush; and not until overcome by fatigue, would he cease to swing the blood-clotted cowskin. I remember the first time I ever witnessed this horrible exhibition. I was quite a child, but I well remember it. I never shall forget it whilst I remember any thing. It was the first of a long series of such outrages, of which I was doomed to be a witness and a participant. It struck me with awful force. It was the blood-stained gate, the entrance to the hell of slavery, through which I was about to pass. It was a most terrible spectacle. I wish I could commit to paper the feelings with which I beheld it.

This occurrence took place very soon after I went to live with my old master, and under the following circumstances. Aunt Hester went out one night,-where or for what I do not know,–and happened to be absent when my master desired her presence. He had ordered her not to go out evenings, and warned her that she must never let him catch her in company with a young man, who was paying attention to her belonging to Colonel Lloyd. The young man's name was Ned Roberts, generally called Lloyd's Ned. Why master was so careful of her, may be safely left to conjecture. She was a woman of noble form, and of graceful proportions, having very few equals, and fewer superiors, in personal appearance, among the colored or white women of our neighborhood.

Aunt Hester had not only disobeyed his orders in going out, but had been found in company with Lloyd's Ned; which circumstance, I found, from what he said while whipping her, was the chief offence. Had he been a man of pure morals himself, he might have been thought interested in protecting the innocence of my aunt; but those who knew him will not suspect him of any such virtue. Before he commenced whipping Aunt Hester, he took her into the kitchen, and stripped her from neck to waist, leaving her neck, shoulders, and back, entirely naked. He then told her to cross her hands, calling her at the same time a d——d b——h. After crossing her hands, he tied them with a strong rope, and led her to a stool under a large hook in the joist, put in for the purpose. He made her get upon the stool, and tied her hands to the hook. She now stood fair for his infernal purpose. Her arms were stretched up at their full length, so that she stood upon the ends of her toes. He then said to her, "Now, you d——d b——h, I'll learn you how to disobey my orders!" and after rolling up his sleeves, he commenced to lay on the heavy cowskin, and soon the warm, red blood (amid heart-rending shrieks from her, and horrid oaths from him) came dripping to the floor. I was so terrified and horror-stricken at the sight, that I hid myself in a closet, and dared not venture out till long after the bloody transaction was over. I expected it would be my turn next. It was all new to me. I had never seen any thing like it before. I had always lived with my grandmother on the outskirts of the plantation, where she was put to raise the children of the younger women. I had therefore been, until now, out of the way of the bloody scenes that often occurred on the plantation.

CHAPTER II

My master's family consisted of two sons, Andrew and Richard; one daughter, Lucretia, and her husband, Captain Thomas Auld. They lived in one house, upon the home plantation of Colonel Edward Lloyd. My master was Colonel Lloyd's clerk and superintendent. He was what might be called the overseer of the overseers. I spent two years of childhood on this plantation in my old master's family. It was here that I witnessed the bloody transaction recorded in the first chapter; and as I received my first impressions of slavery on this plantation, I will give some description of it, and of slavery as it there existed. The plantation is about twelve miles north of Easton, in Talbot county, and is situated on the border of Miles River. The principal products raised upon it were tobacco, corn, and wheat. These were raised in great abundance; so that, with the products of this and the other farms belonging to him, he was able to keep in almost constant employment a large sloop, in carrying them to market at Baltimore. This sloop was named Sally Lloyd, in honor of one of the colonel's daughters. My master's son-in-law, Captain Auld, was master of the vessel; she was otherwise manned by the colonel's own slaves. Their names were Peter, Isaac, Rich, and Jake. These were esteemed very highly by the other slaves, and looked upon as the privileged ones of the plantation; for it was no small affair, in the eyes of the slaves, to be allowed to see Baltimore.

Colonel Lloyd kept from three to four hundred slaves on his home plantation, and owned a large number more on the neighboring farms belonging to him. The names of the farms nearest to the home plantation were Wye Town and New Design. "Wye Town" was under the overseership of a man named Noah Willis. New Design was under the overseership of a Mr. Townsend. The overseers of these, and all the rest of the farms, numbering over twenty, received advice and direction from the managers of the home plantation. This was the great business place. It was the seat of government for the whole twenty farms. All disputes among the overseers were settled here. If a slave was convicted of any high misdemeanor, became unmanageable, or evinced a determination to run away, he was brought immediately here, severely whipped, put on board the sloop, carried to Baltimore, and sold to Austin Woolfolk, or some other slave-trader, as a warning to the slaves remaining.

Here, too, the slaves of all the other farms received their monthly allowance of food, and their yearly clothing. The men and women slaves received, as their monthly allowance of food, eight pounds of pork, or its equivalent in fish, and one bushel of corn meal. Their yearly clothing consisted of two coarse linen shirts, one pair of linen trousers, like the shirts, one jacket, one pair of trousers for winter, made of coarse negro cloth, one pair of stockings, and one pair of shoes; the whole of which could not have cost more than seven dollars. The allowance of the slave children was given to their mothers, or the old women having the care of them. The children unable to work in the field had neither shoes, stockings, jackets, nor trousers, given to them; their clothing consisted of two coarse linen shirts per year. When these failed them, they went naked until the next allowance-day. Children from seven to ten years old, of both sexes, almost naked, might be seen at all seasons of the year.

There were no beds given the slaves, unless one coarse blanket be considered such, and none but the men and women had these. This, however, is not considered a very great privation. They find less difficulty from the want of beds, than from the want of time to sleep; for when their day's work in the field is done, the most of them having their washing, mending, and cooking to do, and having few or none of the ordinary facilities for doing either of these, very many of their sleeping hours are consumed in preparing for the field the coming day; and when this is done, old and young, male and female, married and single, drop down side by side, on one common bed,–the cold, damp floor,–each covering himself or herself with their miserable blankets; and here they sleep till they are summoned to the field by the driver's horn. At the sound of this, all must rise, and be off to the field. There must be no halting; every one must be at his or her post; and woe betides them who hear not this morning summons to the field; for if they are not awakened by the sense of hearing, they are by the sense of feeling: no age nor sex finds any favor. Mr. Severe, the overseer, used to stand by the door of the quarter, armed with a large hickory stick and heavy cowskin, ready to whip any one who was so unfortunate as not to hear, or, from any other cause, was prevented from being ready to start for the field at the sound of the horn.

Mr. Severe was rightly named: he was a cruel man. I have seen him whip a woman, causing the blood to run half an hour at the time; and this, too, in the midst of her crying children, pleading for their mother's release. He seemed to take pleasure in manifesting his fiendish barbarity. Added to his cruelty, he was a profane swearer. It was enough to chill the blood and stiffen the hair of an ordinary man to hear him talk. Scarce a sentence escaped him but that was commenced or concluded by some horrid oath. The field was the place to witness his cruelty and profanity. His presence made it both the field of blood and of blasphemy. From the rising till the going down of the sun, he was cursing, raving, cutting, and slashing among the slaves of the field, in the most frightful manner. His career was short. He died very soon after I went to Colonel Lloyd's; and he died as he lived, uttering, with his dying groans, bitter curses and horrid oaths. His death was regarded by the slaves as the result of a merciful providence.

Mr. Severe's place was filled by a Mr. Hopkins. He was a very different man. He was less cruel, less profane, and made less noise, than Mr. Severe. His course was characterized by no extraordinary demonstrations of cruelty. He whipped, but seemed to take no pleasure in it. He was called by the slaves a good overseer.

The home plantation of Colonel Lloyd wore the appearance of a country village. All the mechanical operations for all the farms were performed here. The shoemaking and mending, the blacksmithing, cartwrighting, coopering, weaving, and grain-grinding, were all performed by the slaves on the home plantation. The whole place wore a business-like aspect very unlike the neighboring farms. The number of houses, too, conspired to give it advantage over the neighboring farms. It was called by the slaves the ~Great House Farm.~ Few privileges were esteemed higher, by the slaves of the out-farms, than that of being selected to do errands at the Great House Farm. It was associated in their minds with greatness. A representative could not be prouder of his election to a seat in the American Congress, than a slave on one of the out-farms would be of his election to do errands at the Great House Farm. They regarded it as evidence of great confidence reposed in them by their overseers; and it was on this account, as well as a constant desire to be out of the field from under the driver's lash, that they esteemed it a high privilege, one worth careful living for. He was called the smartest and most trusty fellow, who had this honor conferred upon him the most frequently. The competitors for this office sought as diligently to please their overseers, as the office-seekers in the political parties seek to please and deceive the people. The same traits of character might be seen in Colonel Lloyd's slaves, as are seen in the slaves of the political parties.

The slaves selected to go to the Great House Farm, for the monthly allowance for themselves and their fellow-slaves, were peculiarly enthusiastic. While on their way, they would make the dense old woods, for miles around, reverberate with their wild songs, revealing at once the highest joy and the deepest sadness. They would compose and sing as they went along, consulting neither time nor tune. The thought that came up, came out–if not in the word, in the sound;–and as frequently in the one as in the other. They would sometimes sing the most pathetic sentiment in the most rapturous tone, and the most rapturous sentiment in the most pathetic tone. Into all of their songs they would manage to weave something of the Great House Farm. Especially would they do this, when leaving home. They would then sing most exultingly the following words:–

"I am going away to the Great House Farm!

O, yea! O, yea! O!" This they would sing, as a chorus, to words which to many would seem unmeaning jargon, but which, nevertheless, were full of meaning to themselves. I have sometimes thought that the mere hearing of those songs would do more to impress some minds with the horrible character of slavery, than the reading of whole volumes of philosophy on the subject could do.

I did not, when a slave, understand the deep meaning of those rude and apparently incoherent songs. I was myself within the circle; so that I neither saw nor heard as those without might see and hear. They told a tale of woe which was then altogether beyond my feeble comprehension; they were tones loud, long, and deep; they breathed the prayer and complaint of souls boiling over with the bitterest anguish. Every tone was a testimony against slavery, and a prayer to God for deliverance from chains. The hearing of those wild notes always depressed my spirit, and filled me with ineffable sadness. I have frequently found myself in tears while hearing them. The mere recurrence to those songs, even now, afflicts me; and while I am writing these lines, an expression of feeling has already found its way down my cheek. To those songs I trace my first glimmering conception of the dehumanizing character of slavery. I can never get rid of that conception. Those songs still follow me, to deepen my hatred of slavery, and quicken my sympathies for my brethren in bonds. If any one wishes to be impressed with the soul-killing effects of slavery, let him go to Colonel Lloyd's plantation, and, on allowance-day, place himself in the deep pine woods, and there let him, in silence, analyze the sounds that shall pass through the chambers of his soul,–and if he is not thus impressed, it will only be because "there is no flesh in his obdurate heart."

I have often been utterly astonished, since I came to the north, to find persons who could speak of the singing, among slaves, as evidence of their contentment and happiness. It is impossible to conceive of a greater mistake. Slaves sing most when they are most unhappy. The songs of the slave represent the sorrows of his heart; and he is relieved by them, only as an aching heart is relieved by its tears. At least, such is my experience. I have often sung to drown my sorrow, but seldom to express my happiness. Crying for joy, and singing for joy, were alike uncommon to me while in the jaws of slavery. The singing of a man cast away upon a desolate island might be as appropriately considered as evidence of contentment and happiness, as the singing of a slave; the songs of the one and of the other are prompted by the same emotion.

Attributions

CC licensed content, Shared previously

- Introduction: Frederick Douglass. **Provided by**: Wikipedia. **Located at**: https://en.wikipedia.org/wiki/Frederick_Douglass. **License**: *CC BY-SA: Attribution-ShareAlike*

Public domain content

- Autobiography. **Authored by**: Frederick Douglass. **Located at**: http://legacy.fordham.edu/Halsall/mod/DUGLAS11.asp. **Project**: Internet Modern History Sourcebook. **License**: *Public Domain: No Known Copyright*

Primary Source Reading: The Life of Plantation Field Hands

The Life of Plantation Field Hands, 1857

Introduction

James Stirling, was a British writer who visited the American South in 1857. He wrote a book – Letters from the Slave States – which contains interviews plantation owners and former slaves.

Source

In judging of the welfare of the slaves, it is necessary to distinguish the different conditions of slavery. The most important distinction, both as regards numbers and its influence on the wellbeing of the slave, is that between houseservants and farm or fieldhands. The houseservant is comparatively well off. He is frequently born and bred in the family he belongs to; and even when this is not the case, the constant association of the slave and his master, and master's family, naturally leads to such an attachment as ensures good treatment. There are not wanting instances of devoted attachment on both sides in such cases. There is even a danger that the affection on the part of the owner may degenerate into overindulgence. It is no uncommon thing to make pets of slaves, as we do of other inferior animals; and when this is the case, the real welfare of the slave is sacrificed to an indiscriminating attachment. I was struck with the appearance of the slaves in the streets of Charleston on a Sunday afternoon. A large proportion of them were well dressed and of decent bearing, and had all the appearance of enjoying a holiday. I was informed they were principally houseservants belonging to the town; and there could be no doubt the control of public opinion, natural to a large city, had exercised a favourable influence on the condition of these poor people.

The position of the fieldhands is very different; of those, especially, who labour on large plantations. Here there are none of those humanizing influences at work which temper the rigour of the system, nor is there the same check of public opinion to control abuse. The 'force' is worked en masse, as a great human mechanism; or, if you will, as a drove of human cattle. The proprietor is seldom present to direct and control. Even if he were, on large estates the numbers are too great for his personal attention to details of treatment. On all large plantations the comfort of the slave is practically at the disposal of the white overseer, and his subordinate, the negrodriver. There are many estates which the proprietor does not visit at all, or visits perhaps once a year; and where, during his absence, the slaves are left to the uncontrolled caprice of the overseer and his assistants, not another white man, perhaps, being within miles of the plantation. Who can say what passes in those voiceless solitudes7 Happen what may, there is none to tell. Whatever the slave may suffer there is none to bear witness to his wrong. It needs a large amount of charity to believe that power so despotic, so utterly uncontrolled even by opinion, will never degenerate into violence. It could only be so if overseers were saints, and drivers angels.

It is often said that the interest of the slaveowner is sufficient guarantee for the good treatment of the slave; that no man will voluntarily injure the value of his property. This reasoning assumes, first, that slaveowners will take an intelligent view of their own interests; and, secondly, that they will be guided by the passion of gain rather than by other passions. But we find the Cuba slave-owner working his slaves to death, at the rate of 3 per cent. per annum. And again, slavery is a system which evokes passions more powerful even than the love of gain. Against the action of these angry passions, the distant calculation of mere profit can avail but little with men of violent dispositions.

But even if we grant the restraint placed on the passions of the master by considerations of pecuniary interest, we cannot allow the same effect to be produced on the overseer. On the contrary, the interest of the overseer is to exhibit a large production as the result of his exertions; and the more remote consideration of being a prudent husbandman of his forces will only affect a superior mind. On this point I prefer giving the opinions of slaveowners themselves. In an article in De Bow's Review, on the management of slaves, I find some interesting remarks on this subject, in a report to a committee of slave-holders. After pointing out the interest of the owners in the good treatment of their slaves, it continues:-'There is one class of our community to whom all the motives referred to, to induce us to kindness to our slaves, do not apply. Your committee refer to our overseers. As they have no property in our slaves, of course they lack the check of selfinterest. As their only aim, in general, is to get the largest possible crop for the year, we can readily conceive the strong inducement they have to overwork our slaves, and masters are often much to blame for inadvertently encouraging this feeling in their overseers.'

It appears, then, that nothing but high principle on the part of the overseer could ensure the good treatment of the slave on large plantations. But all testimony concurs in representing the overseers as a very inferior class in point of character. A Virginian slaveowner used this language to Olmsted:-'They (the overseers) are the curse of this country, sir; the worst men in the community.' Yet these are the men on whom devolves, practically, the management of the great bulk of the agricultural slave population, in the cotton, rice, and sugar districts.

Midway between houseservants and plantationhands stand the farmservants of small proprietors. Of all slaves these are, probably, the best off. They are neither spoiled like pet domestics, nor abused like plantation cattle. They live much in the farmer's family, work with himself and his children, take an interest in his affairs, and, in return, become objects of his regard. Such is the condition of many slaves among the small farmers in the upland districts of Virginia, Kentucky, Tennessee, Georgia, and the Carolinas. The same applies also to many proprietors in Texas, and, I believe, Arkansas. In general it may be affirmed, that the welfare of the slaves is in an inverse ratio to their numbers.

Source: James Stirling, Letters From the Slave States (New York: Kraus Reprint Co., 1969), pp. 28791 .

This text is part of the Internet Modern History Sourcebook. The Sourcebook is a collection of public domain and copy-permitted texts for introductory level classes in modern European and World history.

Unless otherwise indicated the specific electronic form of the document is copyright. Permission is granted for electronic copying, distribution in print form for educational purposes and personal use. If you do reduplicate the document, indicate the source. No permission is granted for commercial use of the Sourcebook.

(c)Paul Halsall Aug 1997

Attributions

CC licensed content, Shared previously

- Letters From the Slave States. **Authored by**: James Stirling. **Located at**: http://legacy.fordham.edu/halsall/mod/1857stirling.asp. **Project**: Internet Modern History Sourcebook. **License**: *Public Domain: No Known Copyright*

13. Troubled Times: The Tumultuous 1850s

Introduction

The heated sectional controversy between the North and the South reached new levels of intensity in the 1850s. Southerners and northerners grew ever more antagonistic as they debated the expansion of slavery in the West. The notorious confrontation between Representative Preston Brooks of South Carolina and Massachusetts senator Charles Sumner depicted in the image above, illustrates the contempt between extremists on both sides. The "Caning of Sumner" in May 1856 followed upon a speech given by Sumner two days earlier in which he condemned slavery in no uncertain terms, declaring: "[Admitting Kansas as a slave state] is the rape of a virgin territory, compelling it to the hateful embrace of slavery; and it may be clearly traced to a depraved longing for a new slave state, the hideous offspring of such a crime, in the hope of adding to the power of slavery in the national government." Sumner criticized proslavery legislators, particularly attacking a fellow senator and relative of Preston Brooks. Brooks responded by beating Sumner with a cane, a thrashing that southerners celebrated as a manly defense of gentlemanly honor and their way of life. The episode highlights the violent clash between pro- and antislavery factions in the 1850s, a conflict that would eventually lead to the traumatic unraveling of American democracy and civil war.

In Southern Chivalry: Argument versus Club's (1856), by John Magee, South Carolinian Preston Brooks attacks Massachusetts senator Charles Sumner after his speech denouncing "border ruffians" pouring into Kansas from Missouri. For southerners, defending slavery meant defending southern honor.

Attributions

CC licensed content, Shared previously

- US History. **Authored by**: P. Scott Corbett, Volker Janssen, John M. Lund, Todd Pfannestiel, Paul Vickery, and Sylvie Waskiewicz. **Provided by**: OpenStax College. **Located at**: http://openstaxcollege.org/textbooks/us-history. **License**: *CC BY: Attribution*. **License Terms**: Download for free at http://cnx.org/content/col11740/latest/

The Compromise of 1850

Learning Objectives

By the end of this section, you will be able to:

- Explain the contested issues that led to the Compromise of 1850
- Describe and analyze the reactions to the 1850 Fugitive Slave Act

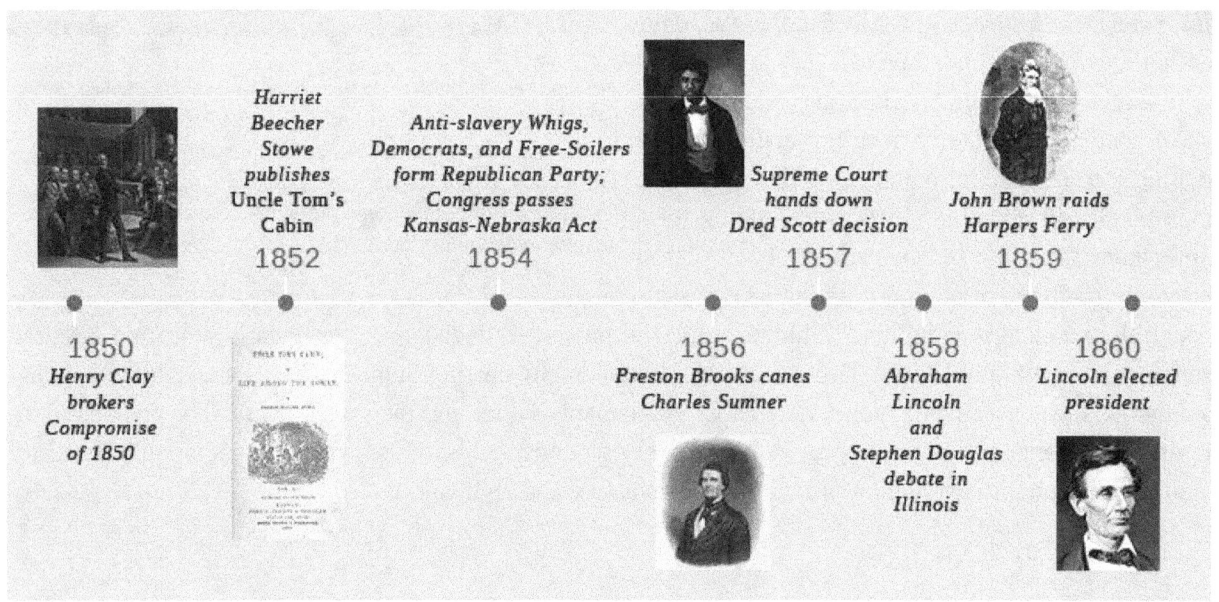

At the end of the Mexican-American War, the United States gained a large expanse of western territory known as the Mexican Cession. The disposition of this new territory was in question; would the new states be slave states or free-soil states? In the long run, the Mexican-American War achieved what abolitionism alone had failed to do: it mobilized many in the North against slavery.

Antislavery northerners clung to the idea expressed in the 1846 Wilmot Proviso: slavery would not expand into the areas taken, and later bought, from Mexico. Though the proviso remained a proposal and never became a law, it defined the sectional division. The Free-Soil Party, which formed at the conclusion of the Mexican-American War in 1848 and included many members of the failed Liberty Party, made this position the centerpiece of all its political activities, ensuring that the issue of slavery and its expansion remained at the front and center of American political debate. Supporters of the Wilmot Proviso and members of the new Free-Soil Party did not want to abolish slavery in the states where it already existed; rather, Free-Soil advocates demanded that the western territories be kept free of slavery for the benefit of white laborers who might settle there. They wanted to protect white workers from having to compete with slave labor in the West. (Abolitionists, in contrast, looked to destroy slavery everywhere in the United States.) Southern extremists, especially wealthy slaveholders, reacted with outrage at this effort to limit slavery's expansion. They argued for the right to bring their slave property west, and they vowed to leave the Union if necessary to protect their way of life—meaning the right to own slaves—and ensure that the American empire of slavery would continue to grow.

BROKERING THE COMPROMISE

The issue of what to do with the western territories added to the republic by the **Mexican Cession** consumed Congress in 1850. Other controversial matters, which had been simmering over time, complicated the problem further. Chief among these issues were the slave trade in the District of Columbia, which antislavery advocates hoped to end, and the fugitive slave laws, which southerners wanted to strengthen. The border between Texas and New Mexico remained contested because many Texans hoped to enlarge their state further, and, finally, the issue of California had not been resolved. California was the crown jewel of the Mexican Cession, and following the discovery of gold, it was flush with thousands of emigrants. By most estimates, however, it would be a free state, since the former Mexican ban on slavery still remained in force and slavery had not taken root in California. The map below shows the disposition of land before the 1850 compromise.

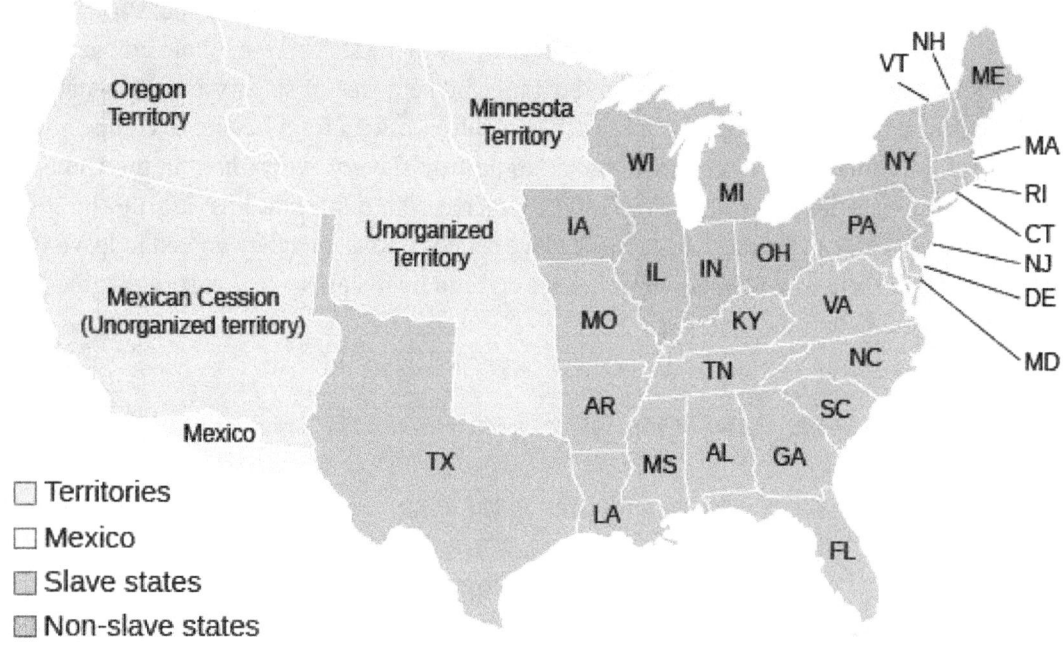

This map shows the states and territories of the United States as they were in 1849–1850. (credit "User:Golbez"/Wikimedia Commons)

The presidential election of 1848 did little to solve the problems resulting from the Mexican Cession. Both the Whigs and the Democrats attempted to avoid addressing the issue of slavery publicly as much as possible. The Democrats nominated Lewis Cass of Michigan, a supporter of the idea of popular sovereignty, or letting the people in the territories decide the issue of whether or not to permit slavery based on majority rule. The Whigs nominated General Zachary Taylor, a slaveholder from Kentucky, who had achieved national prominence as a military hero in the Mexican-American War. Taylor did not take a personal stand on any issue and remained silent throughout the campaign. The fledgling Free-Soil Party put forward former president Martin Van Buren as their candidate. The Free-Soil Party attracted northern Democrats who supported the Wilmot Proviso, northern Whigs who rejected Taylor because he was a slaveholder, former members of the Liberty Party, and other abolitionists.

Both the Whigs and the Democrats ran different campaigns in the North and South. In the North, all three parties attempted to win voters with promises of keeping the territories free of slavery, while in the South, Whigs and Democrats promised to protect slavery in the territories. For southern voters, the slaveholder Taylor appeared the natural choice. In the North, the Free-Soil Party took votes away from Whigs and Democrats and helped to ensure Taylor's election in 1848.

As president, Taylor sought to defuse the sectional controversy as much as possible, and, above all else, to preserve the Union. Although Taylor was born in Virginia before relocating to Kentucky and owned more than one hundred slaves by the late 1840s, he did not push for slavery's expansion into the Mexican Cession. However, the California Gold Rush made California's statehood into an issue demanding immediate attention. In 1849, after California residents adopted a state constitution prohibiting slavery, President Taylor called on Congress to admit California and New Mexico as free states, a move that infuriated southern defenders of slavery who argued for the right to bring their slave property wherever they chose. Taylor, who did not believe slavery could flourish in the arid lands of the Mexican Cession because the climate prohibited plantation-style farming, proposed that the Wilmot Proviso be applied to the entire area.

In Congress, Kentucky senator Henry Clay, a veteran of congressional conflicts, offered a series of resolutions addressing the list of issues related to slavery and its expansion. Clay's resolutions called for the admission of California as a free state; no restrictions on slavery in the rest of the Mexican Cession (a rejection of the Wilmot Proviso and the Free-Soil Party's position); a boundary between New Mexico and Texas that did not expand Texas (an important matter, since Texas allowed slavery and a larger Texas meant more opportunities for the expansion of slavery); payment of outstanding Texas debts from the Lone Star Republic days; and the end of the slave trade (but not of slavery) in the nation's capital, coupled with a more robust federal fugitive slave law. Clay presented these proposals as an omnibus bill, that is, one that would be voted on its totality.

Clay's proposals ignited a spirited and angry debate that lasted for eight months. The resolution calling for California to be admitted as a free state aroused the wrath of the aged and deathly ill John C. Calhoun, the elder statesman for the proslavery position. Calhoun, too sick to deliver a speech, had his friend Virginia senator James Mason present his assessment of Clay's resolutions and the current state of sectional strife.

In Calhoun's eyes, blame for the stalemate fell squarely on the North, which stood in the way of southern and American prosperity by limiting the zones where slavery could flourish. Calhoun called for a vigorous federal law to ensure that runaway slaves were returned to their masters. He also proposed a constitutional amendment specifying a dual presidency—one office that would represent the South and another for the North—a suggestion that hinted at the possibility of disunion. Calhoun's argument portrayed an embattled South faced with continued northern aggression—a line of reasoning that only furthered the sectional divide.

Several days after Mason delivered Calhoun's speech, Massachusetts senator Daniel Webster countered Calhoun in his "Seventh of March" speech. Webster called for national unity, famously declaring that he spoke "not as a Massachusetts man, not as a Northern man, but as an American." Webster asked southerners to end threats of disunion and requested that the North stop antagonizing the South by harping on the Wilmot Proviso. Like Calhoun, Webster also called for a new federal law to ensure the return of runaway slaves.

Webster's efforts to compromise led many abolitionist sympathizers to roundly denounce him as a traitor. Whig senator William H. Seward, who aspired to be president, declared that slavery—which he characterized as incompatible with the assertion in the Declaration of Independence that "all men are created equal"—would one day be extinguished in the United States. Seward's speech, in which he invoked the idea of a higher moral law than the Constitution, secured his reputation in the Senate as an advocate of abolition.

The speeches made in Congress were published in the nation's newspapers, and the American public followed the debates with great interest, anxious to learn how the issues of the day, especially the potential advance of slavery, would be resolved. Colorful reports of wrangling in Congress further piqued public interest. Indeed, it was not uncommon for arguments to devolve into fistfights or worse. One of the most astonishing episodes of the debate occurred in April 1850, when a quarrel erupted between Missouri Democratic senator Thomas Hart Benton, who by the time of the debate had become a critic of slavery (despite owning slaves), and Mississippi Democratic senator Henry S. Foote. When the burly Benton appeared ready to assault Foote, the Mississippi senator drew his pistol.

This 1850 print, Scene in Uncle Sam's Senate, depicts Mississippi senator Henry S. Foote taking aim at Missouri senator Thomas Hart Benton. In the print, Benton declares: "Get out of the way, and let the assassin fire! let the scoundrel use his weapon! I have no arm's! I did not come here to assassinate!" Foote responds, "I only meant to defend myself!" (credit: Library of Congress)

President Taylor and Henry Clay, whose resolutions had begun the verbal fireworks in the Senate, had no patience for each other. Clay had long harbored ambitions for the White House, and, for his part, Taylor resented Clay and disapproved of his resolutions. With neither side willing to budge, the government stalled on how to resolve the disposition of the Mexican Cession and the other issues of slavery. The drama only increased when on July 4, 1850, President Taylor became gravely ill, reportedly after eating an excessive amount of fruit washed down with milk. He died five days later, and Vice President Millard Fillmore became president. Unlike his predecessor, who many believed would be opposed to a compromise, Fillmore worked with Congress to achieve a solution to the crisis of 1850.

In the end, Clay stepped down as leader of the compromise effort in frustration, and Illinois senator Stephen Douglas pushed five separate bills through Congress, collectively composing the Compromise of 1850. First, as advocated by the South, Congress passed the Fugitive Slave Act, a law that provided federal money—or "bounties"—to slave-catchers. Second, to balance this concession to the South, Congress admitted California as a free state, a move that cheered antislavery advocates and abolitionists in the North. Third, Congress settled the contested boundary between New Mexico and Texas by favoring New Mexico and not allowing for an enlarged Texas, another outcome pleasing to the North. Fourth, antislavery advocates welcomed Congress's ban on the slave trade in Washington, DC, although slavery continued to thrive in the nation's capital. Finally, on the thorny issue of whether slavery would expand into the territories, Congress avoided making a direct decision and instead relied on the principle of popular sovereignty. This put the onus on residents of the territories to decide for themselves whether to allow slavery. Popular sovereignty followed the logic of American democracy; majorities in each territory would decide the territory's laws. The compromise, however, further exposed the sectional divide as votes on the bills divided along strict regional lines.

Most Americans breathed a sigh of relief over the deal brokered in 1850, choosing to believe it had saved the Union. Rather than resolving divisions between the North and the South, however, the compromise stood as a truce in an otherwise white-hot sectional conflict. Tensions in the nation remained extremely high; indeed, southerners held several conventions after the compromise to discuss ways to protect the South. At these meetings, extremists who called for secession found themselves in the minority, since most southerners committed themselves to staying in the Union—but only if slavery remained in the states where it already existed, and if no effort was made to block its expansion into areas where citizens wanted it, thereby applying the idea of popular sovereignty.

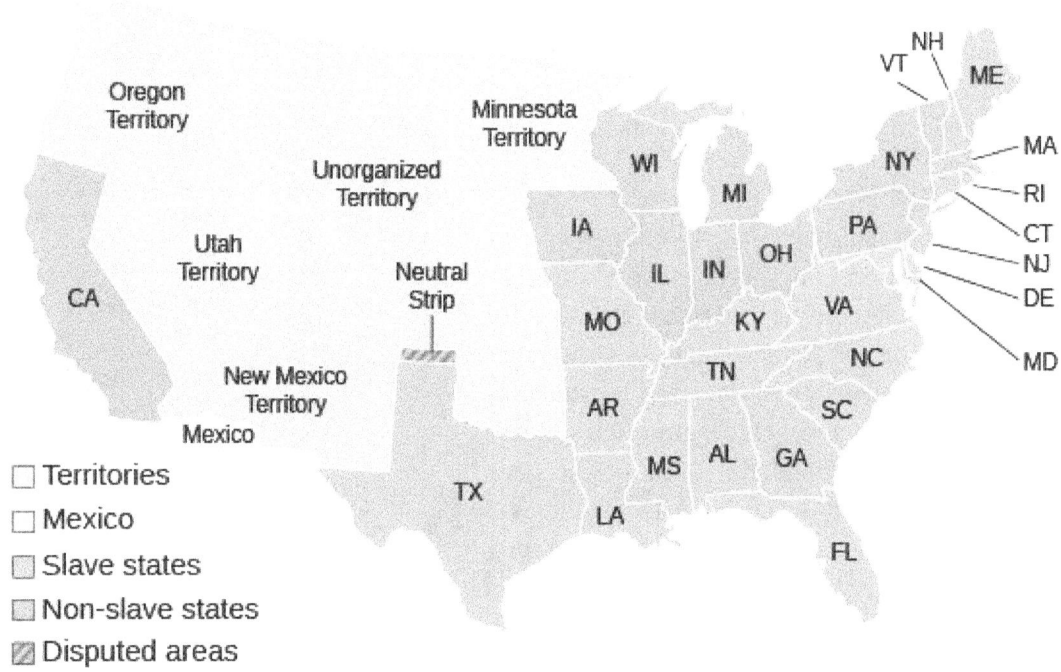

This map shows the states and territories of the United States as they were from 1850 to March 1853. (credit "User:Golbez"/Wikimedia Commons)

THE FUGITIVE SLAVE ACT AND ITS CONSEQUENCES

The hope that the Compromise of 1850 would resolve the sectional crisis proved short-lived when the Fugitive Slave Act turned into a major source of conflict. The federal law imposed heavy fines and prison sentences on northerners and midwesterners who aided runaway slaves or refused to join posses to catch fugitives. Many northerners felt the law forced them to act as slave-catchers against their will.

The law also established a new group of federal commissioners who would decide the fate of fugitives brought before them. In some instances, slave-catchers even brought in free northern blacks, prompting abolitionist societies to step up their efforts to prevent kidnappings. The commissioners had a financial incentive to send fugitives and free blacks to the slaveholding South, since they received ten dollars for every African American sent to the South and only five if they decided the person who came before them was actually free. The commissioners used no juries, and the alleged runaways could not testify in their own defense.

The operation of the law further alarmed northerners and confirmed for many the existence of a **"Slave Power"**—that is, a minority of elite slaveholders who wielded a disproportionate amount of power over the federal government, shaping domestic and foreign policies to suit their interests. Despite southerners' repeated insistence on states' rights, the Fugitive Slave Act showed that slaveholders were willing to use the power of the federal government to bend people in other states to their will. While rejecting the use of federal power to restrict the expansion of slavery, proslavery southerners turned to the federal government to protect and promote the institution of slavery.

The actual number of runaway slaves who were not captured within a year of escaping remained very low, perhaps no more than one thousand per year in the early 1850s. Most stayed in the South, hiding in plain sight among free blacks in urban areas. Nonetheless, southerners feared the influence of a vast **Underground Railroad**: the network of northern whites and free blacks who sympathized with runaway slaves and provided safe houses and safe passage from the South. Quakers, who had long been troubled by slavery, were especially active in this network. It is unclear how many slaves escaped through the Underground Railroad, but historians believe that between 50,000 and 100,000 slaves used the network in their bids for freedom. Meanwhile, the 1850 Fugitive Slave Act greatly increased the perils of being captured. For many thousands of fugitives, escaping the United States completely by going to southern Ontario, Canada, where slavery had been abolished, offered the best chance of a better life beyond the reach of slaveholders.

This 1851 poster, written by Boston abolitionist Theodore Parker, warned that any black person, free or slave, risked kidnapping by slave-catchers.

Harriet Tubman, one of the thousands of slaves who made their escape through the Underground Railroad, distinguished herself for her efforts in helping other enslaved men and women escape. Born a slave in Maryland around 1822, Tubman, who suffered greatly under slavery but found solace in Christianity, made her escape in the late 1840s. She returned to the South more than a dozen times to lead other slaves, including her family and friends, along the Underground Railroad to freedom.

Harriet Tubman: An American Moses?

Harriet Tubman was a legendary figure in her own time and beyond. An escaped slave herself, she returned to the South thirteen times to help over three hundred slaves through the Underground Railroad to liberty in the North. In 1869, printer William J. Moses published Sarah H. Bradford's *Scenes in the Life of Harriet*

Tubman. Bradford was a writer and biographer who had known Tubman's family for years. The excerpt below is from the beginning of her book, which she updated in 1886 under the title *Harriet, the Moses of Her People*.

This full-length portrait of Harriet Tubman hangs in the National Portrait Gallery of the Smithsonian.

It is proposed in this little book to give a plain and unvarnished account of some scenes and adventures in the life of a woman who, though one of earth's lowly ones, and of dark-hued skin, has shown an amount of heroism in her character rarely possessed by those of any station in life. Her name (we say it advisedly and without exaggeration) deserves to be handed down to posterity side by side with the names of Joan of Arc, Grace Darling, and Florence Nightingale; for not one of these women has shown more courage and power of endurance in facing danger and death to relieve human suffering, than has this woman in her heroic and successful endeavors to reach and save all whom she might of her oppressed and suffering race, and to pilot them from the land of Bondage to the promised land of Liberty. Well has she been called "Moses," for she has been a leader and deliverer unto hundreds of her people.

—Sarah H. Bradford, *Scenes in the Life of Harriet Tubman*

How does Bradford characterize Tubman? What language does Bradford use to tie religion into the fight for freedom?

The Fugitive Slave Act provoked widespread reactions in the North. Some abolitionists, such as Frederick Douglass, believed that standing up against the law necessitated violence. In Boston and elsewhere, abolitionists tried to protect fugitives from federal authorities. One case involved Anthony Burns, who had escaped slavery in Virginia in 1853 and made his way to Boston. When federal officials arrested Burns in 1854, abolitionists staged a series of mass demonstrations and a confrontation at the courthouse. Despite their best efforts, however, Burns was returned to Virginia when President Franklin Pierce supported the Fugitive Slave Act with federal troops. Boston abolitionists eventually bought Burns's freedom. For many northerners, however, the Burns incident, combined with Pierce's response, only amplified their sense of a conspiracy of southern power.

The most consequential reaction against the Fugitive Slave Act came in the form of a novel, *Uncle Tom's Cabin*. In it, author Harriet Beecher Stowe, born in Connecticut, made use of slaves' stories she had heard firsthand after marrying and moving to Ohio, then on the country's western frontier. Her novel first appeared as a series of stories in a Free-Soil newspaper, the *National Era*, in 1851 and was published as a book the following year. Stowe told the tale of slaves who were sold by their Kentucky master. While Uncle Tom is indeed sold down the river, young Eliza escapes with her baby. The story highlighted the idea that slavery was a sin because it destroyed families, ripping children from their parents and husbands and wives from one another. Stowe also emphasized the ways in which slavery corrupted white citizens. The cruelty of some of the novel's white slaveholders (who genuinely believe that slaves don't feel things the way that white people do) and the brutality of the slave dealer Simon Legree, who beats slaves and sexually exploits a slave woman, demonstrate the dehumanizing effect of the institution even on those who benefit from it.

Anthony Burns, drawn ca. 1855 by an artist identified only as "Barry," shows a portrait of the fugitive slave surrounded by scenes from his life, including his escape from Virginia, his arrest in Boston, and his address to the court.

This drawing from Uncle Tom's Cabin, captioned "Eliza comes to tell Uncle Tom that he is sold, and that she is running away to save her child," illustrates the ways in which Harriet Beecher Stowe's antislavery novel bolstered abolitionists' arguments against slavery.

This photograph shows Harriet Beecher Stowe, the author of Uncle Tom's Cabin, in 1852. Stowe's work was an inspiration not only to abolitionists, but also to those who believed that women could play a significant role in upholding the nation's morality and shaping public opinion.

Stowe's novel proved a runaway bestseller and was the most-read novel of the nineteenth century, inspiring multiple theatrical productions and musical compositions. It was translated into sixty languages and remains in print to this day. Its message about the evils of slavery helped convince many northerners of the righteousness of the cause of abolition. The novel also demonstrated the power of women to shape public opinion. Stowe and other American women believed they had a moral obligation to mold the conscience of the United States, even though they could not vote.

> Visit the Documenting the American South collection on the University of North Carolina at Chapel Hill website to read the memoirs of Levi Coffin, a prominent Quaker abolitionist who was known as the "president" of the Underground Railroad for his active role in helping slaves to freedom. The memoirs include the story of Eliza Harris, which inspired Harriet Beecher Stowe's famous character.

The backlash against the Fugitive Slave Act, fueled by *Uncle Tom's Cabin* and well-publicized cases like that of Anthony Burns, also found expression in personal liberty laws passed by eight northern state legislatures. These laws emphasized that the state would provide legal protection to anyone arrested as a fugitive slave, including the right to trial by jury. The personal liberty laws stood as a clear-cut example of the North's use of states' rights in opposition to federal power while providing further evidence to southerners that northerners had no respect for the Fugitive Slave Act or slaveholders' property rights.

> Go to an archived page from the Michigan Department of Natural Resources site to read the original text of Michigan's 1855 personal liberty laws. How do these laws refute the provisions of the federal Fugitive Slave Act of 1850?

Section Summary

The difficult process of reaching a compromise on slavery in 1850 exposed the sectional fault lines in the United States. After several months of rancorous debate, Congress passed five laws—known collectively as the Compromise of 1850—that people on both sides of the divide hoped had solved the nation's problems. However, many northerners feared the impact of the Fugitive Slave Act, which made it a crime not only to help slaves escape, but also to fail to help capture them. Many Americans, both black and white, flouted the Fugitive Slave Act by participating in the Underground Railroad, providing safe houses for slaves on the run from the South. Eight northern states passed personal liberty laws to counteract the effects of the Fugitive Slave Act.

https://www.openassessments.org/assessments/991

Review Question

1. Why did many in the North resist the Fugitive Slave Act?

Answer to Review Question

1. This federal law appeared to northerners to be further proof of a "Slave Power" conspiracy and elite slaveholders' disproportionate influence over U.S. domestic policy. Northerners also resented being compelled to serve as de facto slave-catchers, as the law punished people not only for helping fugitive slaves, but also for failing to aid in efforts to return them. Finally, the law rankled many northerners for the hypocrisy that it exposed, given southerners' arguments in favor of states' rights and against the federal government's meddling in their affairs.

Glossary

Compromise of 1850 five laws passed by Congress to resolve issues stemming from the Mexican Cession and the sectional crisis

Free-Soil Party a political party committed to ensuring that white laborers would not have to compete with unpaid slaves in newly acquired territories

popular sovereignty the principle of letting the people residing in a territory decide whether or not to permit slavery in that area based on majority rule

Underground Railroad a network of free blacks and northern whites who helped slaves escape bondage through a series of designated routes and safe houses

Attributions

CC licensed content, Shared previously

- US History. **Authored by**: P. Scott Corbett, Volker Janssen, John M. Lund, Todd Pfannestiel, Paul Vickery, and Sylvie Waskiewicz. **Provided by**: OpenStax College. **Located at**: http://openstaxcollege.org/textbooks/us-history. **License**: CC BY: Attribution. **License Terms**: Download for free at http://cnx.org/content/col11740/latest/

The Kansas-Nebraska Act and the Republican Party

Learning Objectives

By the end of this section, you will be able to:

- Explain the political ramifications of the Kansas-Nebraska Act
- Describe the founding of the Republican Party

In the early 1850s, the United States' sectional crisis had abated somewhat, cooled by the Compromise of 1850 and the nation's general prosperity. In 1852, voters went to the polls in a presidential contest between Whig candidate Winfield Scott and Democratic candidate Franklin Pierce. Both men endorsed the Compromise of 1850. Though it was considered unseemly to hit the campaign trail, Scott did so—much to the benefit of Pierce, as Scott's speeches focused on forty-year-old battles during the War of 1812 and the weather. In New York, Scott, known as "Old Fuss and Feathers," talked about a thunderstorm that did not occur and greatly confused the crowd. In Ohio, a cannon firing to herald Scott's arrival killed a spectator.

Pierce was a supporter of the "Young America" movement of the Democratic Party, which enthusiastically anticipated extending democracy around the world and annexing additional territory for the United States. Pierce did not take a stance on the slavery issue. Helped by Scott's blunders and the fact that he had played no role in the bruising political battles of the past five years, Pierce won the election. The brief period of tranquility between the North and South did not last long, however; it came to an end in 1854 with the passage of the Kansas-Nebraska Act. This act led to the formation of a new political party, the Republican Party, that committed itself to ending the further expansion of slavery.

THE KANSAS-NEBRASKA ACT

The relative calm over the sectional issue was broken in 1854 over the issue of slavery in the territory of Kansas. Pressure had been building among northerners to organize the territory west of Missouri and Iowa, which had been admitted to the Union as a free state in 1846. This pressure came primarily from northern farmers, who wanted the federal government to survey the land and put it up for sale. Promoters of a transcontinental railroad were also pushing for this westward expansion.

Southerners, however, had long opposed the Wilmot Proviso's stipulation that slavery should not expand into the West. By the 1850s, many in the South were also growing resentful of the Missouri Compromise of 1820, which established the 36° 30′ parallel as the geographical boundary of slavery on the north-south axis. Proslavery southerners now contended that popular sovereignty should apply to all territories, not just Utah and New Mexico. They argued for the right to bring their slave property wherever they chose.

Attitudes toward slavery in the 1850s were represented by a variety of regional factions. Throughout the South, slaveholders entrenched themselves in defense of their "way of life," which depended on the ownership of slaves. Since the 1830s, abolitionists, led by journalist and reformer William Lloyd Garrison, had cast slavery as a national sin and called for its immediate end. For three decades, the abolitionists remained a minority, but they had a significant effect on American society by bringing the evils of slavery into the public consciousness. By the 1850s, some abolitionists advocated the use of violence against those who owned slaves. In 1840, the Liberty Party, whose members came from the ranks of ministers, was founded; this group sought to work within the existing political system, a strategy Garrison and others rejected. Meanwhile, the Free-Soil Party committed itself to ensuring that white laborers would find work in newly acquired territories and not have to compete with unpaid slaves.

It is important to note that, even among those who opposed the expansion of slavery in the West, very different attitudes toward slavery existed. Some antislavery northerners wanted the West to be the best country for poor whites to go and seek opportunity. They did not want white workers to have to compete with slave labor, a contest that they believed demeaned white labor. Radical abolitionists, in contrast, envisioned the end of all slavery, and a society of equality between blacks and whites. Others opposed slavery in principle, but believed that the best approach was colonization; that is, settling freed slaves in a colony in Africa.

The growing political movement to address the issue of slavery stiffened the resolve of southern slaveholders to defend themselves and their society at all costs. Prohibiting slavery's expansion, they argued, ran counter to basic American property rights. As abolitionists fanned the flames of antislavery sentiment, southerners solidified their defense of their enormous investment in human chattel. Across the country, people of all political stripes worried that the nation's arguments would cause irreparable rifts in the country.

THE HURLY-BURLY POT.

In this 1850 political cartoon, the artist takes aim at abolitionists, the Free-Soil Party, Southern states' rights activists, and others he believes risk the health of the Union.

As these different factions were agitating for the settlement of Kansas and Nebraska, leaders of the Democratic Party in 1853 and 1854 sought to bind their party together in the aftermath of intraparty fights over the distribution of patronage jobs. Illinois Democratic senator Stephen Douglas believed he had found a solution—the **Kansas-Nebraska bill**—that would promote party unity and also satisfy his colleagues from the South, who detested the Missouri Compromise line. In January 1854, Douglas introduced the bill. The act created two territories: Kansas, directly west of Missouri; and Nebraska, west of Iowa. The act also applied the principle of popular sovereignty, dictating that the people of these territories would decide for themselves whether to adopt slavery. In a concession crucial to many southerners, the proposed bill would also repeal the 36° 30′ line from the Missouri Compromise. Douglas hoped his bill would increase his political capital and provide a step forward on his quest for the presidency. Douglas also wanted the territory organized in hopes of placing the eastern terminus of a transcontinental railroad in Chicago, rather than St. Louis or New Orleans.

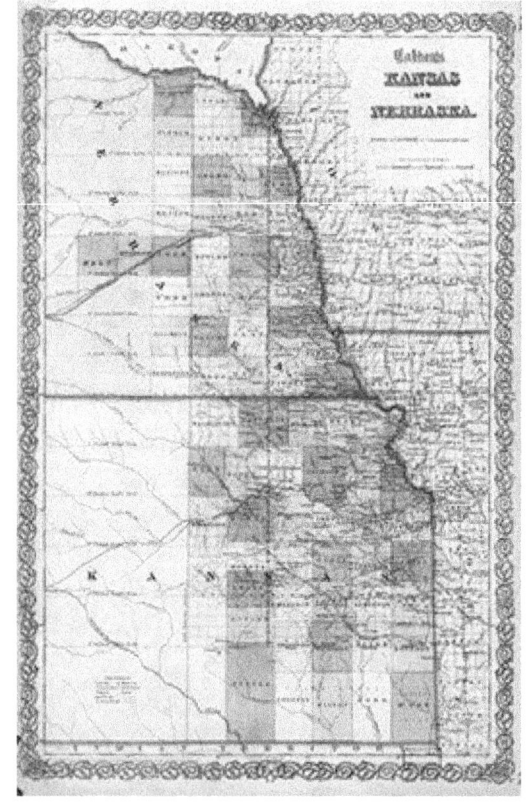

This 1855 map shows the new territories of Kansas and Nebraska, complete with proposed routes of the transcontinental railroad.

After heated debates, Congress narrowly passed the Kansas-Nebraska Act. (In the House of Representatives, the bill passed by a mere three votes: 113 to 110.) This move had major political consequences. The Democrats divided along sectional lines as a result of the bill, and the Whig party, in decline in the early 1850s, found its political power slipping further. Most important, the Kansas-Nebraska Act gave rise to the **Republican Party**, a new political party that attracted northern Whigs, Democrats who shunned the Kansas-Nebraska Act, members of the Free-Soil Party, and assorted abolitionists. Indeed, with the formation of the Republican Party, the Free-Soil Party ceased to exist.

The new Republican Party pledged itself to preventing the spread of slavery into the territories and railed against the Slave Power, infuriating the South. As a result, the party became a solidly northern political organization. As never before, the U.S. political system was polarized along sectional fault lines.

BLEEDING KANSAS

In 1855 and 1856, pro- and antislavery activists flooded Kansas with the intention of influencing the popular-sovereignty rule of the territories. Proslavery Missourians who crossed the border to vote in Kansas became known as **border ruffians**; these gained the advantage by winning the territorial elections, most likely through voter fraud and illegal vote counting. (By some estimates, up to 60 percent of the votes cast in Kansas were fraudulent.) Once in power, they wrote a proslavery constitution, known as the Lecompton Constitution because President Pierce approved it at Lecompton, Kansas.

The Lecompton Constitution

Kansas was home to no fewer than four state constitutions in its early years. Its first constitution, the Topeka Constitution, would have made Kansas a free-soil state. A proslavery legislature, however, created the 1857 Lecompton Constitution to enshrine the institution of slavery in the new Kansas-Nebraska territories. In January 1858, Kansas voters defeated the proposed Lecompton Constitution, excerpted below, with an overwhelming margin of 10,226 to 138.

> ARTICLE VII.—SLAVERY
>
> SECTION 1. The right of property is before and higher than any constitutional sanction, and the right of the owner of a slave to such slave and its increase is the same and as inviolable as the right of the owner of any property whatever.
>
> SEC. 2. The Legislature shall have no power to pass laws for the emancipation of slaves without the consent of the owners, or without paying the owners previous to their emancipation a full equivalent in money for the slaves so emancipated. They shall have no power to prevent immigrants to the State from bringing with them such persons as are deemed slaves by the laws of any one of the United States or Territories, so long as any person of the same age or description shall be continued in slavery by the laws of this State: Provided, That such person or slave be the bona fide property of such immigrants.

How are slaves defined in the 1857 Kansas constitution? How does this constitution safeguard the rights of slaveholders?

The majority in Kansas, however, were Free-Soilers who seethed at the border ruffians' co-opting of the democratic process. Many had come from New England to ensure a numerical advantage over the border ruffians. The New England Emigrant Aid Society, a northern antislavery group, helped fund these efforts to halt the expansion of slavery into Kansas and beyond.

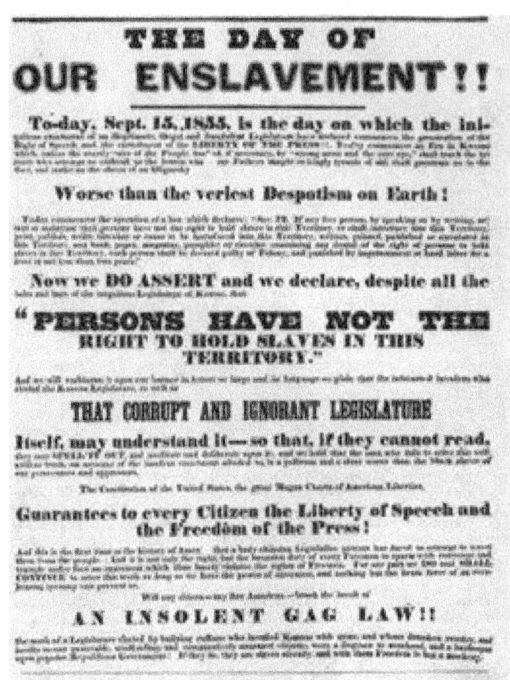

This full-page editorial ran in the Free-Soiler Kansas Tribune on September 15, 1855, the day Kansas' Act to Punish Offences against Slave Property of 1855 went into effect. This law made it punishable by death to aid or abet a fugitive slave, and it called for punishment of no less than two years for anyone who might: "print, publish, write, circulate, or cause to be introduced into this Territory . . . [any materials] . . . containing any denial of the right of persons to hold slaves in this Territory."

> Go to the Kansas Historical Society's Kansapedia to read the four different state constitutions that Kansas had during its early years as a United States Territory. What can you deduce about the authors of each constitution?

In 1856, clashes between antislavery Free-Soilers and border ruffians came to a head in Lawrence, Kansas. The town had been founded by the New England Emigrant Aid Society, which funded antislavery settlement in the territory and were determined that Kansas should be a free-soil state. Proslavery emigrants from Missouri were equally determined that no "abolitionist tyrants" or "negro thieves" would control the territory. In the spring of 1856, several of Lawrence's leading antislavery citizens were indicted for treason, and federal marshal Israel Donaldson called for a posse to help make arrests. He did not have trouble finding volunteers from Missouri. When the posse, which included Douglas County sheriff Samuel Jones, arrived outside Lawrence, the antislavery town's "committee of safety" agreed on a policy of nonresistance. Most of those who were indicted fled. Donaldson arrested two men without incident and dismissed the posse.

However, Jones, who had been shot during an earlier confrontation in the town, did not leave. On May 21, falsely claiming that he had a court order to do so, Jones took command of the posse and rode into town armed with rifles, revolvers, cutlasses and bowie knives. At the head of the procession, two flags flew: an American flag and a flag with a crouching tiger. Other banners followed, bearing the words "Southern rights" and "The Superiority of the White Race." In the rear were five artillery pieces, which were dragged to the center of town. The posse smashed the presses of the two newspapers, *Herald of Freedom* and the *Kansas Free State*, and burned down the deserted Free State Hotel. When the posse finally left, Lawrence residents found themselves unharmed but terrified.

The next morning, a man named John Brown and his sons, who were on their way to provide Lawrence with reinforcements, heard the news of the attack. Brown, a strict, God-fearing Calvinist and staunch abolitionist, once remarked that "God had raised him up on purpose to break the jaws of the wicked." Disappointed that the citizens of Lawrence did not resist the "slave hounds" of Missouri, Brown opted not to go to Lawrence, but to the homes of proslavery settlers near Pottawatomie Creek in Kansas. The group of seven, including Brown's four sons, arrived on May 24, 1856, and announced they were the "Northern Army" that had come to serve justice. They burst into the cabin of proslavery Tennessean James Doyle and marched him and two of his sons off, sparing the youngest at the desperate request of Doyle's wife, Mahala. One hundred yards down the road, Owen and Salmon Brown hacked their captives to death with broadswords and John Brown shot a bullet into Doyle's forehead. Before the night was done, the Browns visited two more cabins and brutally executed two other proslavery settlers. None of those executed owned any slaves or had had anything to do with the raid on Lawrence.

This undated image shows the aftermath of the sacking of Lawrence, Kansas, by border ruffians. Shown are the ruins of the Free State Hotel.

Brown's actions precipitated a new wave of violence. All told, the guerilla warfare between proslavery "border ruffians" and antislavery forces, which would continue and even escalate during the Civil War, resulted in over 150 deaths and significant property loss. The events in Kansas served as an extreme reply to Douglas's proposition of popular sovereignty. As the violent clashes increased, Kansas became known as "**Bleeding Kansas**." Antislavery advocates' use of force carved out a new direction for some who opposed slavery. Distancing themselves from William Lloyd Garrison and other pacifists, Brown and fellow abolitionists believed the time had come to fight slavery with violence.

The violent hostilities associated with Bleeding Kansas were not limited to Kansas itself. It was the controversy over Kansas that prompted the caning of Charles Sumner, introduced at the beginning of this chapter with the political cartoon *Southern Chivalry: Argument versus Club's*. Note the title of the cartoon; it lampoons the southern ideal of chivalry, the code of behavior that Preston Brooks believed he was following in his attack on Sumner. In Sumner's "Crime against Kansas" speech he went much further than politics, filling his verbal attack with allusions to sexuality by singling out fellow senator Andrew Butler from South Carolina, a zealous supporter of slavery and Brooks's uncle. Sumner insulted Butler by comparing slavery to prostitution, declaring, "Of course he [Butler] has chosen a mistress to whom he has made his vows, and who, though ugly to others, is always lovely to him; though polluted in the sight of the world, is chaste in his sight. I mean the harlot Slavery." Because Butler was aged, it was his nephew, Brooks, who sought satisfaction for Sumner's attack on his family and southern honor. Brooks did not challenge Sumner to a duel; by choosing to beat him with a cane instead, he made it clear that he did not consider Sumner a gentleman. Many in the South rejoiced over Brooks's defense of slavery, southern society, and family honor, sending him hundreds of canes to replace the one he had broken assaulting Sumner. The attack by Brooks left Sumner incapacitated physically and mentally for a long period of time. Despite his injuries, the people of Massachusetts reelected him.

THE PRESIDENTIAL ELECTION OF 1856

The electoral contest in 1856 took place in a transformed political landscape. A third political party appeared: the anti-immigrant **American Party**, a formerly secretive organization with the nickname "the Know-Nothing Party" because its members denied knowing anything about it. By 1856, the American or Know-Nothing Party had evolved into a national force committed to halting further immigration. Its members were especially opposed to the immigration of Irish Catholics, whose loyalty to the Pope, they believed, precluded their loyalty to the United States. On the West Coast, they opposed the entry of immigrant laborers from China, who were thought to be too foreign to ever assimilate into a white America.

The election also featured the new Republican Party, which offered John C. Fremont as its candidate. Republicans accused the Democrats of trying to nationalize slavery through the use of popular sovereignty in the West, a view captured in the 1856 political cartoon *Forcing Slavery Down the Throat of a Free Soiler*. The cartoon features the image of a Free-Soiler settler tied to the Democratic Party platform while Senator Douglas (author of the Kansas-Nebraska Act) and President Pierce force a slave down his throat. Note that the slave cries out "Murder!!! Help—neighbors help, O my poor Wife and Children," a reference to the abolitionists' argument that slavery destroyed families.

This 1856 political cartoon, Forcing Slavery Down the Throat of a Free Soiler, by John Magee, shows Republican resentment of the Democratic platform—here represented as an actual platform—of expanding slavery into new western territories.

The Democrats offered James Buchanan as their candidate. Buchanan did not take a stand on either side of the issue of slavery; rather, he attempted to please both sides. His qualification, in the minds of many, was that he was out of the country when the Kansas-Nebraska Act was passed. In the above political cartoon, Buchanan, along with Democratic senator Lewis Cass, holds down the Free-Soil advocate. Buchanan won the election, but Fremont garnered more than 33 percent of the popular vote, an impressive return for a new party. The Whigs had ceased to exist and had been replaced by the Republican Party. Know-Nothings also transferred their allegiance to the Republicans because the new party also took an anti-immigrant stance, a move that further boosted the new party's standing. (The Democrats courted the Catholic immigrant vote.) The Republican Party was a thoroughly northern party; no southern delegate voted for Fremont.

Section Summary

The application of popular sovereignty to the organization of the Kansas and Nebraska territories ended the sectional truce that had prevailed since the Compromise of 1850. Senator Douglas's Kansas-Nebraska Act opened the door to chaos in Kansas as proslavery and Free-Soil forces waged war against each other, and radical abolitionists, notably John Brown, committed themselves to violence to end slavery. The act also upended the second party system of Whigs and Democrats by inspiring the formation of the new Republican Party, committed to arresting the further spread of slavery. Many voters approved its platform in the 1856 presidential election, though the Democrats won the race because they remained a national, rather than a sectional, political force.

https://www.openassessments.org/assessments/992

Review Question

1. How did the "Bleeding Kansas" incident change the face of antislavery advocacy?

Answer to Review Question

1. In response to proslavery forces' destruction of the antislavery press and Free State Hotel, radical abolitionists, including John Brown, murdered proslavery settlers at Pottawatomie. This was a turning point for Brown and many other radical abolitionists, who—unlike their largely pacifist counterparts, such as William Lloyd Garrison—came to believe that slavery must be extinguished by any means necessary, including open violence.

Glossary

American Party also called the Know-Nothing Party, a political party that emerged in 1856 with an anti-immigration platform

Bleeding Kansas a reference to the violent clashes in Kansas between Free-Soilers and slavery supporters

border ruffians proslavery Missourians who crossed the border into Kansas to influence the legislature

Republican Party an antislavery political party formed in 1854 in response to Stephen Douglas's Kansas-Nebraska Act

Attributions

CC licensed content, Shared previously

- US History. **Authored by**: P. Scott Corbett, Volker Janssen, John M. Lund, Todd Pfannestiel, Paul Vickery, and Sylvie Waskiewicz. **Provided by**: OpenStax College. **Located at**: http://openstaxcollege.org/textbooks/us-history. **License**: *CC BY: Attribution*. **License Terms**: Download for free at http://cnx.org/content/col11740/latest/

John Brown and the Election of 1860

> **Learning Objectives**
>
> By the end of this section, you will be able to:
>
> - Describe John Brown's raid on Harpers Ferry and its results
> - Analyze the results of the election of 1860

Events in the late 1850s did nothing to quell the country's sectional unrest, and compromise on the issue of slavery appeared impossible. Lincoln's 1858 speeches during his debates with Douglas made the Republican Party's position well known; Republicans opposed the extension of slavery and believed a Slave Power conspiracy sought to nationalize the institution. They quickly gained political momentum and took control of the House of Representatives in 1858. Southern leaders were divided on how to respond to Republican success. Southern extremists, known as "**Fire-Eaters**," openly called for secession. Others, like Mississippi senator Jefferson Davis, put forward a more moderate approach by demanding constitutional protection of slavery.

JOHN BROWN

In October 1859, the radical abolitionist John Brown and eighteen armed men, both blacks and whites, attacked the federal arsenal in **Harpers Ferry**, Virginia. They hoped to capture the weapons there and distribute them among slaves to begin a massive uprising that would bring an end to slavery. Brown had already demonstrated during the 1856 Pottawatomie attack in Kansas that he had no patience for the nonviolent approach preached by pacifist abolitionists like William Lloyd Garrison. Born in Connecticut in 1800, Brown spent much of his life in the North, moving from Ohio to Pennsylvania and then upstate New York as his various business ventures failed. To him, slavery appeared an unacceptable evil that must be purged from the land, and like his Puritan forebears, he believed in using the sword to defeat the ungodly.

John Brown, shown here in a photograph from 1859, was a radical abolitionist who advocated the violent overthrow of slavery.

Brown had gone to Kansas in the 1850s in an effort to stop slavery, and there, he had perpetrated the killings at Pottawatomie. He told other abolitionists of his plan to take Harpers Ferry Armory and initiate a massive slave uprising. Some abolitionists provided financial support, while others, including Frederick Douglass, found the plot suicidal and refused to join. On October 16, 1859, Brown's force easily took control of the federal armory, which was unguarded. However, his vision of a mass uprising failed completely. Very few slaves lived in the area to rally to Brown's side, and the group found themselves holed up in the armory's engine house with townspeople taking shots at them. Federal troops, commanded by Colonel Robert E. Lee, soon captured Brown and his followers. On December 2, Brown was hanged by the state of Virginia for treason.

John Brown's raid on Harpers Ferry represented the radical abolitionist's attempt to start a revolt that would ultimately end slavery. This 1859 illustration, captioned "Harper's Ferry insurrection—Interior of the Engine-House, just before the gate is broken down by the storming party—Col. Washington and his associates as captives, held by Brown as hostages," is from Frank Leslie's Illustrated Magazine. Do you think this image represents a southern or northern version of the raid? How are the characters in the scene depicted?

Visit the Avalon Project on Yale Law School's website to read the impassioned speech that Henry David Thoreau delivered on October 30, 1859, arguing against the execution of John Brown. How does Thoreau characterize Brown? What does he ask of his fellow citizens?

John Brown's raid on Harpers Ferry generated intense reactions in both the South and the North. Southerners grew especially apprehensive of the possibility of other violent plots. They viewed Brown as a terrorist bent on destroying their civilization, and support for secession grew. Their anxiety led several southern states to pass laws designed to prevent slave rebellions. It seemed that the worst fears of the South had come true: A hostile majority would stop at nothing to destroy slavery. Was it possible, one resident of Maryland asked, to "live under a government, a majority of whose subjects or citizens regard John Brown as a martyr and Christian hero?" Many antislavery northerners did in fact consider Brown a martyr to the cause, and those who viewed slavery as a sin saw easy comparisons between him and Jesus Christ.

THE ELECTION OF 1860

The election of 1860 triggered the collapse of American democracy when the elevation of Abraham Lincoln to the presidency inspired secessionists in the South to withdraw their states from the Union.

Lincoln's election owed much to the disarray in the Democratic Party. The Dred Scott decision and the Freeport Doctrine had opened up huge sectional divisions among Democrats. Though Brown did not intend it, his raid had furthered the split between northern and southern Democrats. Fire-Eaters vowed to prevent a northern Democrat, especially Illinois's Stephen Douglas, from becoming their presidential candidate. These proslavery zealots insisted on a southern Democrat.

The Democratic nominating convention met in April 1860 in Charleston, South Carolina. However, it broke up after northern Democrats, who made up a majority of delegates, rejected Jefferson Davis's efforts to protect slavery in the territories. These northern Democratic delegates knew that supporting Davis on this issue would be very unpopular among the people in their states. A second conference, held in Baltimore, further illustrated the divide within the Democratic Party. Northern Democrats nominated Stephen Douglas, while southern Democrats, who met separately, put forward Vice President John Breckinridge from Kentucky. The Democratic Party had fractured into two competing sectional factions.

By offering two candidates for president, the Democrats gave the Republicans an enormous advantage. Also hoping to prevent a Republican victory, pro-Unionists from the border states organized the Constitutional Union Party and put up a fourth candidate, John Bell, for president, who pledged to end slavery agitation and preserve the Union but never fully explained how he'd accomplish this objective. In a pro-Lincoln political cartoon of the time, the presidential election is presented as a baseball game. Lincoln stands on home plate. A skunk raises its tail at the other candidates. Holding his nose, southern Democrat John Breckinridge holds a bat labeled "Slavery Extension" and declares "I guess I'd better leave for Kentucky, for I smell something strong around here, and begin to think, that we are completely skunk'd."

The national game. Three "outs" and one "run" (1860), by Currier and Ives, shows the two Democratic candidates and one Constitutional Union candidate who lost the 1860 election to Republican Lincoln, shown at right.

The Republicans nominated Lincoln, and in the November election, he garnered a mere 40 percent of the popular vote, though he won every northern state except New Jersey. (Lincoln's name was blocked from even appearing on many southern states' ballots by southern Democrats.) More importantly, Lincoln did gain a majority in the Electoral College. The Fire-Eaters, however, refused to accept the results. With South Carolina leading the way, Fire-Eaters in southern states began to withdraw formally from the United States in 1860. South Carolinian Mary Boykin Chesnut wrote in her diary about the reaction to the Lincoln's election. "Now that the black radical Republicans have the power," she wrote, "I suppose they will Brown us all." Her statement revealed many southerners' fear that with Lincoln as President, the South could expect more mayhem like the John Brown raid.

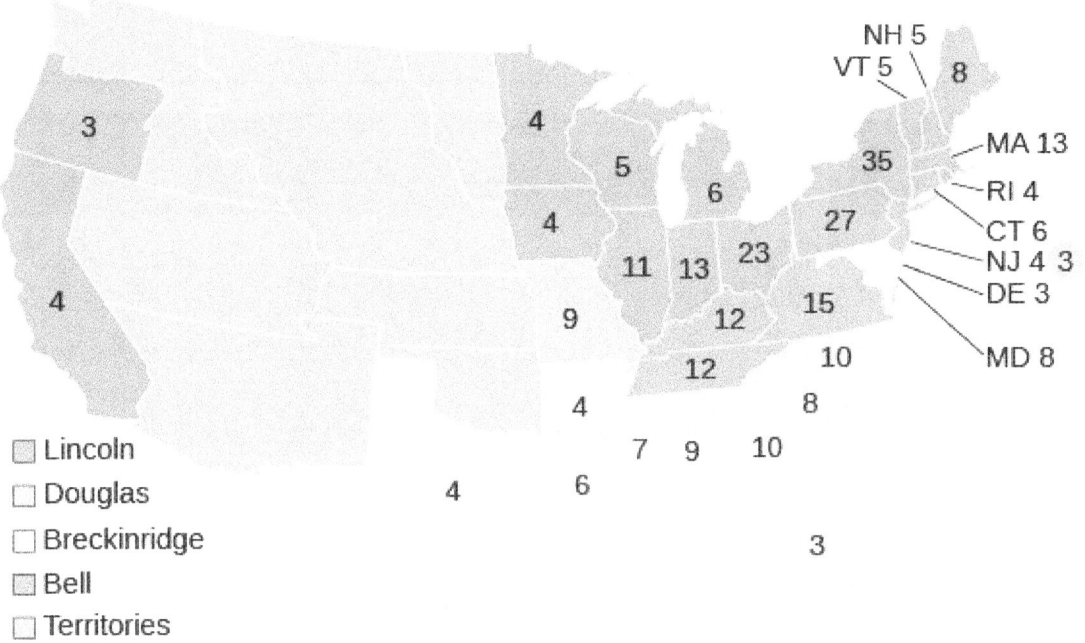

This map shows the disposition of electoral votes for the election of 1860. The votes were divided along almost perfect sectional lines.

Section Summary

A new level of animosity and distrust emerged in 1859 in the aftermath of John Brown's raid. The South exploded in rage at the northern celebration of Brown as a heroic freedom fighter. Fire-Eaters called openly for disunion. Poisoned relations split the Democrats into northern and southern factions, a boon to the Republican candidate Lincoln. His election triggered the downfall of the American experiment with democracy as southern states began to leave the Union.

https://www.openassessments.org/assessments/993

Review Question

1. What were southerners' and northerners' views of John Brown?

Answer to Review Question

1. Antislavery northerners tended to view Brown as a martyr for the antislavery cause; some saw in him a Christ-like figure who died for his beliefs. Southerners, for their part, consid-

ered Brown a terrorist. They felt threatened by northerners' deification of Brown and worried about the potential for other, similar armed insurrections.

Critical Thinking Questions

1. Why would Americans view the Compromise of 1850 as a final solution to the sectional controversy that began with the Wilmot Proviso in 1846?
2. If you were a proslavery advocate, how would you feel about the platform of the newly formed Republican Party?
3. Based on the text of the Lincoln–Douglas debates, what was the position of the Republican Party in 1858? Was the Republican Party an abolitionist party? Why or why not?
4. John Brown is often described as a terrorist. Do you agree with this description? Why or why not? What attributes might make him fit this profile?
5. Was it possible to save American democracy in 1860? What steps might have been taken to maintain unity? Why do you think these steps were not taken?

Glossary

Harpers Ferry the site of a federal arsenal in Virginia, where radical abolitionist John Brown staged an ill-fated effort to end slavery by instigating a mass uprising among slaves

Fire-Eaters radical southern secessionists

Attributions

CC licensed content, Shared previously

- US History. **Authored by**: P. Scott Corbett, Volker Janssen, John M. Lund, Todd Pfannestiel, Paul Vickery, and Sylvie Waskiewicz. **Provided by**: OpenStax College. **Located at**: http://openstaxcollege.org/textbooks/us-history. **License**: *CC BY: Attribution*. **License Terms**: Download for free at http://cnx.org/content/col11740/latest/

The Dred Scott Decision and Sectional Strife

> ### Learning Objectives
>
> By the end of this section, you will be able to:
> - Explain the importance of the Supreme Court's Dred Scott ruling
> - Discuss the principles of the Republican Party as expressed by Abraham Lincoln in 1858

As president, Buchanan confronted a difficult and volatile situation. The nation needed a strong personality to lead it, and Buchanan did not possess this trait. The violence in Kansas demonstrated that applying popular sovereignty—the democratic principle of majority rule—to the territory offered no solution to the national battle over slavery. A decision by the Supreme Court in 1857, which concerned the slave Dred Scott, only deepened the crisis.

DRED SCOTT

In 1857, several months after President Buchanan took the oath of office, the Supreme Court ruled in *Dred Scott v. Sandford*. Dred Scott, born a slave in Virginia in 1795, had been one of the thousands forced to relocate as a result of the massive internal slave trade and taken to Missouri, where slavery had been adopted as part of the Missouri Compromise. In 1820, Scott's owner took him first to Illinois and then to the Wisconsin territory. However, both of those regions were part of the Northwest Territory, where the 1787 Northwest Ordinance had prohibited slavery. When Scott returned to Missouri, he attempted to buy his freedom. After his owner refused, he sought relief in the state courts, arguing that by virtue of having lived in areas where slavery was banned, he should be free.

This 1888 portrait by Louis Schultze shows Dred Scott, who fought for his freedom through the American court system.

In a complicated set of legal decisions, a jury found that Scott, along with his wife and two children, were free. However, on appeal from Scott's owner, the state Superior Court reversed the decision, and the Scotts remained slaves. Scott then became the property of John Sanford (his name was misspelled as "Sandford" in later court documents), who lived in New York. He continued his legal battle, and because the issue involved Missouri and New York, the case fell under the jurisdiction of the federal court. In 1854, Scott lost in federal court and appealed to the United States Supreme Court.

In 1857, the Supreme Court—led by Chief Justice Roger Taney, a former slaveholder who had freed his slaves—handed down its decision. On the question of whether Scott was free, the Supreme Court decided he remained a slave. The court then went beyond the specific issue of Scott's freedom to make a sweeping and momentous judgment about the status of blacks, both free and slave. Per the court, blacks could never be citizens of the United States. Further, the court ruled that Congress had no authority to stop or limit the spread of slavery into American territories. This proslavery ruling explicitly made the Missouri Compromise unconstitutional; implicitly, it made Douglas's popular sovereignty unconstitutional.

Roger Taney on *Dred Scott v. Sandford*

In 1857, the United States Supreme Court ended years of legal battles when it ruled that Dred Scott, a slave who had resided in several free states, should remain a slave. The decision, written by Chief Justice Roger Taney, also stated that blacks could not be citizens and that Congress had no power to limit the spread of slavery. The excerpt below is from Taney's decision.

> A free negro of the African race, whose ancestors were brought to this country and sold as slaves, is not a "citizen" within the meaning of the Constitution of the United States. . . .

> The only two clauses in the Constitution which point to this race treat them as persons whom it was morally lawfully to deal in as articles of property and to hold as slaves. . . .
>
> Every citizen has a right to take with him into the Territory any article of property which the Constitution of the United States recognises as property. . . .
>
> The Constitution of the United States recognises slaves as property, and pledges the Federal Government to protect it. And Congress cannot exercise any more authority over property of that description than it may constitutionally exercise over property of any other kind. . . .
>
> Prohibiting a citizen of the United States from taking with him his slaves when he removes to the Territory . . . is an exercise of authority over private property which is not warranted by the Constitution, and the removal of the plaintiff [Dred Scott] by his owner to that Territory gave him no title to freedom.

How did the Supreme Court define Dred Scott? How did the court interpret the Constitution on this score?

The Dred Scott decision infuriated Republicans by rendering their goal—to prevent slavery's spread into the territories—unconstitutional. To Republicans, the decision offered further proof of the reach of the South's Slave Power, which now apparently extended even to the Supreme Court. The decision also complicated life for northern Democrats, especially Stephen Douglas, who could no longer sell popular sovereignty as a symbolic concession to southerners from northern voters. Few northerners favored slavery's expansion westward.

THE LINCOLN-DOUGLAS DEBATES

The turmoil in Kansas, combined with the furor over the Dred Scott decision, provided the background for the 1858 senatorial contest in Illinois between Democratic senator Stephen Douglas and Republican hopeful Abraham Lincoln. Lincoln and Douglas engaged in seven debates before huge crowds that met to hear the two men argue the central issue of slavery and its expansion. Newspapers throughout the United States published their speeches. Whereas Douglas already enjoyed national recognition, Lincoln remained largely unknown before the debates. These appearances provided an opportunity for him to raise his profile with both northerners and southerners.

Douglas portrayed the Republican Party as an abolitionist effort—one that aimed to bring about **miscegenation**, or race-mixing through sexual relations or marriage. The "black Republicans," Douglas declared, posed a dangerous threat to the Constitution. Indeed, because Lincoln declared the nation could not survive if the slave state–free state division continued, Douglas claimed the Republicans aimed to destroy what the founders had created.

For his part, Lincoln said: "A house divided against itself cannot stand. I believe this government cannot endure permanently half Slave and half Free. I do not expect the Union to be dissolved—I do not expect the house to fall—but I do expect it will cease to be divided. It will become all one thing, or all the other. Either the opponents of slavery will arrest the further spread of it, and place it where the public mind shall rest in the belief that it is in the course of ultimate extinction: or its advocates will push it forward till it shall became alike lawful in all the States—old as well as new, North as well as South." Lincoln interpreted the Dred Scott decision and the Kansas-Nebraska Act as efforts to nationalize slavery: that is, to make it legal everywhere from New England to the Midwest and beyond.

(a)   (b)

In 1858, Abraham Lincoln (a) debated Stephen Douglas (b) seven times in the Illinois race for the U.S. Senate. Although Douglas won the seat, the debates propelled Lincoln into the national political spotlight.

The Lincoln-Douglas Debates

On August 21, 1858, Abraham Lincoln and Stephen Douglas met in Ottawa, Illinois, for the first of seven debates. People streamed into Ottawa from neighboring counties and from as far away as Chicago. Reporting on the event was strictly partisan, with each of the candidates' supporters claiming victory for their candidate. In this excerpt, Lincoln addresses the issues of equality between blacks and whites.

> [A]nything that argues me into his idea of perfect social and political equality with the negro, is but a specious and fantastic arrangement of words, . . . I have no purpose, directly or indirectly, to interfere with the institution of slavery in the States where it exists. I believe I have no lawful right to do so, and I have no inclination to do so. I have no purpose to introduce political and social equality between the white and the black races. There is a physical difference between the two, which, in my judgment, will probably forever forbid their living together upon the footing of perfect equality, . . . I, as well as Judge Douglas, am in favor of the race to which I belong having the superior position. . . . [N]otwithstanding all this, there is no reason in the world why the negro is not entitled to all the natural rights enumerated in the Declaration of Independence, the right to life, liberty, and the pursuit of happiness. I hold that he is as much entitled to these as the white man. . . . [I]n the right to eat the bread, without the leave of anybody else, which his own hand earns, he is my equal and the equal of Judge Douglas, and the equal of every living man.
>
> —Lincoln's speech on August 21, 1858, in Ottawa, Illinois

How would you characterize Lincoln's position on equality between blacks and whites? What types of equality exist, according to Lincoln?

Go to the Lincoln Home National Historic Site on the National Park Service's website to read excerpts from and full texts of the debates. Then, visit The Lincoln/Douglas Debates of 1858 on the Northern Illinois University website to read different newspaper accounts of the debates. Do you see any major differences in the way the newspapers reported the debates? How does the commentary vary, and why?

During the debates, Lincoln demanded that Douglas explain whether or not he believed that the 1857 Supreme Court decision in the Dred Scott case trumped the right of a majority to prevent the expansion of slavery under the principle of popular sovereignty. Douglas responded to Lincoln during the second debate at Freeport, Illinois. In what became known as the **Freeport Doctrine**, Douglas adamantly upheld popular sovereignty, declaring: "It matters not what way the Supreme Court may hereafter decide as to the abstract question whether slavery may or may not go into a territory under the Constitution, the people have the lawful means to introduce it or exclude it as they please." The Freeport Doctrine antagonized southerners and caused a major rift in the Democratic Party. The doctrine did help Douglas in Illinois, however, where most voters opposed the further expansion of slavery. The Illinois legislature selected Douglas over Lincoln for the senate, but the debates had the effect of launching Lincoln into the national spotlight. Lincoln had argued that slavery was morally wrong, even as he accepted the racism inherent in slavery. He warned that Douglas and the Democrats would nationalize slavery through the policy of popular sovereignty. Though Douglas had survived the election challenge from Lincoln, his Freeport Doctrine undermined the Democratic Party as a national force.

Section Summary

The Dred Scott decision of 1857 went well beyond the question of whether or not Dred Scott gained his freedom. Instead, the Supreme Court delivered a far-reaching pronouncement about African Americans in the United States, finding they could never be citizens and that Congress could not interfere with the expansion of slavery into the territories. Republicans erupted in anger at this decision, which rendered their party's central platform unconstitutional. Abraham Lincoln fully articulated the Republican position on the issue of slavery in his 1858 debates with Senator Stephen Douglas. By the end of that year, Lincoln had become a nationally known Republican icon. For the Democrats' part, unity within their party frayed over both the Dred Scott case and the Freeport Doctrine, undermining the Democrats' future ability to retain control of the presidency.

https://www.openassessments.org/assessments/994

Review Question

1. What are the main points of the Dred Scott decision?

Answer to Review Question

1. The Supreme Court decided that Dred Scott had not earned freedom by virtue of having lived in a free state; thus, Scott and his family would remain enslaved. More broadly, the Court ruled that blacks could never be citizens of the United States and that Congress had no authority to stop or limit the spread of slavery into American territories.

Glossary

Dred Scott v. Sandford an 1857 case in which the Supreme Court ruled that blacks could not be citizens and Congress had no jurisdiction to impede the expansion of slavery

Freeport Doctrine a doctrine that emerged during the Lincoln-Douglas debates in which Douglas reaffirmed his commitment to popular sovereignty, including the right to halt the spread of slavery, despite the 1857 Dred Scott decision affirming slaveholders' right to bring their property wherever they wished

miscegenation race-mixing through sexual relations or marriage

term meaning of the term

Attributions

CC licensed content, Shared previously

- US History. **Authored by**: P. Scott Corbett, Volker Janssen, John M. Lund, Todd Pfannestiel, Paul Vickery, and Sylvie Waskiewicz. **Provided by**: OpenStax College. **Located at**: http://openstaxcollege.org/textbooks/us-history. **License**: *CC BY: Attribution*. **License Terms**: Download for free at http://cnx.org/content/col11740/latest/

14. The Civil War, 1860-1865

Introduction

This photograph by John Reekie, entitled, "A burial party on the battle-field of Cold Harbor," drives home the brutality and devastation wrought by the Civil War. Here, in April 1865, African Americans collect the bones of soldiers killed in Virginia during General Ulysses S. Grant's Wilderness Campaign of May–June 1864.

In May 1864, General Ulysses S. Grant ordered the Union's Army of the Potomac to cross the Rapidan River in Virginia. Grant knew that Confederate general Robert E. Lee would defend the Confederate capital at Richmond at all costs, committing troops that might otherwise be sent to the Shenandoah or the Deep South to stop Union general William Tecumseh Sherman from capturing Atlanta, a key Confederate city. For two days, the Army of the Potomac fought Lee's troops in the Wilderness, a wooded area along the Rapidan River. Nearly ten thousand Confederate soldiers were killed or wounded, as were more than seventeen thousand Union troops. A few weeks later, the armies would meet again at the Battle of Cold Harbor, where another fifteen thousand men would be wounded or killed. As in many battles, the bodies of those who died were left on the field where they fell. A year later, African Americans, who were often called upon to perform menial labor for the Union army, collected the skeletal remains of the dead for a proper burial. The state of the graves of many Civil War soldiers partly inspired the creation of Memorial Day, a day set aside for visiting and decorating the graves of the dead.

Attributions

CC licensed content, Shared previously

- US History. **Authored by**: P. Scott Corbett, Volker Janssen, John M. Lund, Todd Pfannestiel, Paul Vickery, and Sylvie Waskiewicz. **Provided by**: OpenStax College. **Located at**: http://openstaxcollege.org/textbooks/us-history. **License**: *CC BY: Attribution*. **License Terms**: Download for free at http://cnx.org/content/col11740/latest/

The Origins and Outbreak of the Civil War

Learning Objectives

By the end of this section, you will be able to:

- Explain the major events that occurred during the Secession Crisis
- Describe the creation and founding principles of the Confederate States of America

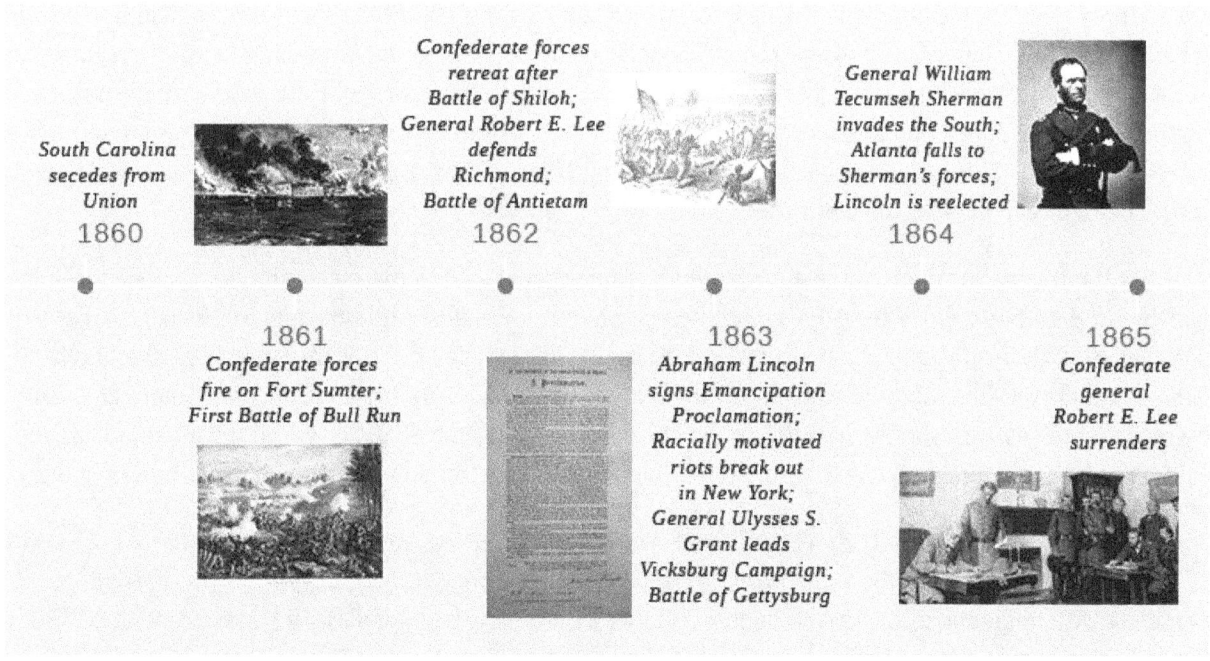

(credit "1865": modification of work by "Alaskan Dude"/Wikimedia Commons)

The 1860 election of Abraham Lincoln was a turning point for the United States. Throughout the tumultuous 1850s, the Fire-Eaters of the southern states had been threatening to leave the Union. With Lincoln's election, they prepared to make good on their threats. Indeed, the Republican president-elect appeared to be their worst nightmare. The Republican Party committed itself to keeping slavery out of the territories as the country expanded westward, a position that shocked southern sensibilities. Meanwhile, southern leaders suspected that Republican abolitionists would employ the violent tactics of John Brown to deprive southerners of their slave property. The threat posed by the Republican victory in the election of 1860 spurred eleven southern states to leave the Union to form the Confederate States of America, a new republic dedicated to maintaining and expanding slavery. The Union, led by President Lincoln, was unwilling to accept the departure of these states and committed itself to restoring the country. Beginning in 1861 and continuing until 1865, the United States engaged in a brutal Civil War that claimed the lives of over 600,000 soldiers. By 1863, the conflict had become not only a war to save the Union, but also a war to end slavery in the United States. Only after four years of fighting did the North prevail. The Union was preserved, and the institution of slavery had been destroyed in the nation.

THE CAUSES OF THE CIVIL WAR

Lincoln's election sparked the southern secession fever into flame, but it did not cause the Civil War. For decades before Lincoln took office, the sectional divisions in the country had been widening. Both the Northern and southern states engaged in inflammatory rhetoric and agitation, and violent emotions ran strong on both sides. Several factors played into the ultimate split between the North and the South.

One key irritant was the question of slavery's expansion westward. The debate over whether new states would be slave or free reached back to the controversy over statehood for Missouri beginning in 1819 and Texas in the 1830s and early 1840s. This question arose again after the Mexican-American War (1846–1848), when the government debated whether slavery would be permitted in the territories taken from Mexico. Efforts in Congress to reach a compromise in 1850 fell back on the principle of popular sovereignty—letting the people in the new territories south of the 1820 Missouri Compromise line decide whether to allow slavery. This same principle came to be applied to the Kansas-Nebraska territories in 1854, a move that added fuel to the fire of sectional conflict by destroying the Missouri Compromise boundary and leading to the birth of the Republican Party. In the end, popular sovereignty proved to be no solution at all. This was especially true in "Bleeding Kansas" in the mid-1850s, as pro- and antislavery forces battled each another in an effort to gain the upper hand.

The small but very vocal abolitionist movement further contributed to the escalating tensions between the North and the South. Since the 1830s, abolitionists, led by journalist and reformer William Lloyd Garrison, had cast slavery as a national sin and called for its immediate end. For three decades, the abolitionists—a minority even within the antislavery movement—had had a significant effect on American society by bringing the evils of slavery into the public consciousness. By the 1850s, some of the most radical abolitionists, such as John Brown, had resorted to violence in their efforts to destroy the institution of slavery.

The formation of the Liberty Party (1840), the Free-Soil Party (1848), and the Republican Party (1854), all of which strongly opposed the spread of slavery to the West, brought the question solidly into the political arena. Although not all those who opposed the westward expansion of slavery had a strong abolitionist bent, the attempt to limit slaveholders' control of their human property stiffened the resolve of southern leaders to defend their society at all costs. Prohibiting slavery's expansion, they argued, ran counter to fundamental American property rights. Across the country, people of all political stripes worried that the nation's arguments would cause irreparable rifts in the country.

Despite the ruptures and tensions, by the 1860s, some hope of healing the nation still existed. Before Lincoln took office, John Crittenden, a senator from Kentucky who had helped form the Constitutional Union Party during the 1860 presidential election, attempted to diffuse the explosive situation by offering six constitutional amendments and a series of resolutions, known as the **Crittenden Compromise**. Crittenden's goal was to keep the South from seceding, and his strategy was to transform the Constitution to explicitly protect slavery forever. Specifically, Crittenden proposed an amendment that would restore the 36°30′ line from the Missouri Compromise and extend it all the way to the Pacific Ocean, protecting and ensuring slavery south of the line while prohibiting it north of the line. He further proposed an amendment that would prohibit Congress from abolishing slavery anywhere it already existed or from interfering with the interstate slave trade.

Crittenden's Compromise would protect slavery in all states where it already existed. More importantly, however, it proposed to allow the western expansion of slavery into states below the Missouri Compromise line.

Republicans, including President-elect Lincoln, rejected Crittenden's proposals because they ran counter to the party's goal of keeping slavery out of the territories. The southern states also rejected Crittenden's attempts at compromise, because it would prevent slaveholders from taking their human chattel north of the 36°30′ line. On December 20, 1860, only a few days after Crittenden's proposal was introduced in Congress, South Carolina began the march towards war when it seceded from the United States. Three more states of the Deep South—Mississippi, Florida, and Alabama—seceded before the U.S. Senate rejected Crittenden's proposal on January 16, 1861. Georgia, Louisiana, and Texas joined them in rapid succession on January 19, January 26, and February 1, respectively. In many cases, these secessions occurred after extremely divided conventions and popular votes. A lack of unanimity prevailed in much of the South.

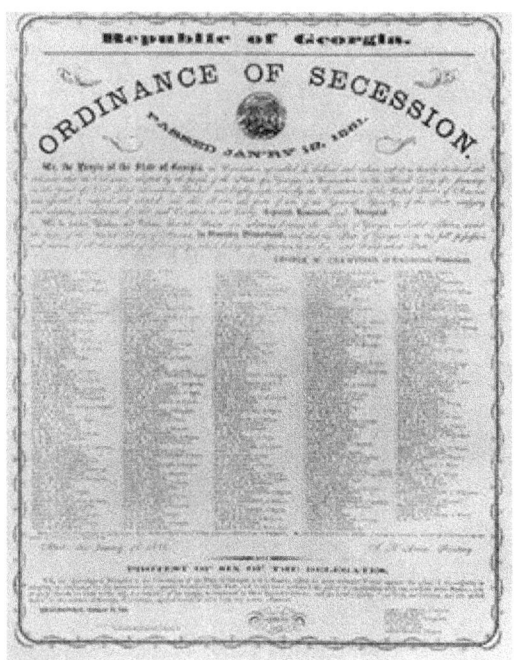

Georgia's Ordinance of Secession and those of the other Deep South states were all based on that of South Carolina, which was drafted just a month after Abraham Lincoln was elected.

Explore the causes, battles, and aftermath of the Civil War at the interactive website offered by the National Parks Service.

THE CREATION OF THE CONFEDERATE STATES OF AMERICA

The seven Deep South states that seceded quickly formed a new government. In the opinion of many Southern politicians, the federal Constitution that united the states as one nation was a contract by which individual states had agreed to be bound. However, they maintained, the states had not sacrificed their autonomy and could withdraw their consent to be controlled by the federal government. In their eyes, their actions were in keeping with the nature of the Constitution and the social contract theory of government that had influenced the founders of the American Republic.

The new nation formed by these men would not be a federal union, but a confederation. In a confederation, individual member states agree to unite under a central government for some purposes, such as defense, but to retain autonomy in other areas of government. In this way, states could protect themselves, and slavery, from interference by what they perceived to be an overbearing central government. The constitution of the Confederate States of America (CSA), or the **Confederacy**, drafted at a convention in Montgomery, Alabama, in February 1861, closely followed the 1787 Constitution. The only real difference between the two documents centered on slavery. The Confederate Constitution declared that the new nation existed to defend and perpetuate racial slavery, and the leadership of the slaveholding class. Specifically, the constitution protected the interstate slave trade, guaranteed that slavery would exist in any new territory gained by the Confederacy, and, perhaps most importantly, in Article One, Section Nine, declared that "No . . . law impairing or denying the right of property in negro slaves shall be passed." Beyond its focus on slavery, the Confederate Constitution resembled the 1787 U.S. Constitution. It allowed for a Congress composed of two chambers, a judicial branch, and an executive branch with a president to serve for six years.

The convention delegates chose Jefferson Davis of Mississippi to lead the new provisional government as president and Alexander Stephens of Georgia to serve as vice president until elections could be held in the spring and fall of 1861. By that time, four new states—Virginia, Arkansas, Tennessee, and North Carolina—had joined the CSA. As 1861 progressed, the Confederacy claimed Missouri and Kentucky, even though no ordinance of secession had been approved in those states. Southern nationalism ran high, and the Confederacy, buoyed by its sense of purpose, hoped that their new nation would achieve eminence in the world.

By the time Lincoln reached Washington, DC, in February 1861, the CSA had already been established. The new president confronted an unprecedented crisis. A conference held that month with delegates from the Southern states failed to secure a promise of peace or to restore the Union. On inauguration day, March 4, 1861, the new president repeated his views on slavery: "I have no purpose, directly or indirectly, to interfere with the institution of slavery in the States where it exists. I believe I have no lawful right to do so, and I have no inclination to do so." His recognition of slavery in the South did nothing to mollify slaveholders, however, because Lincoln also pledged to keep slavery from expanding into the new western territories. Furthermore, in his inaugural address, Lincoln made clear his commitment to maintaining federal power against the secessionists working to destroy it. Lincoln declared that the Union could not be dissolved by individual state actions, and, therefore, secession was unconstitutional.

> Read Lincoln's entire inaugural address at the Yale Avalon project's website. How would Lincoln's audience have responded to this speech?

FORT SUMTER

President Lincoln made it clear to Southern secessionists that he would fight to maintain federal property and to keep the Union intact. Other politicians, however, still hoped to avoid the use of force to resolve the crisis. In February 1861, in an effort to entice the rebellious states to return to the Union without resorting to force, Thomas Corwin, a representative from Ohio, introduced a proposal to amend the Constitution in the House of Representatives. His was but one of several measures proposed in January and February 1861, to head off the impending conflict and save the United States. The proposed amendment would have made it impossible for Congress to pass any law abolishing slavery. The proposal passed the House on February 28, 1861, and the Senate passed the proposal on March 2, 1861. It was then sent to the states to be ratified. Once ratified by three-quarters of state legislatures, it would become law. In his inaugural address, Lincoln stated that he had no objection to the amendment, and his predecessor James Buchanan had supported it. By the time of Lincoln's inauguration, however, seven states had already left the Union. Of the remaining states, Ohio ratified the amendment in 1861, and Maryland and Illinois did so in 1862. Despite this effort at reconciliation, the Confederate states did not return to the Union.

Indeed, by the time of the Corwin amendment's passage through Congress, Confederate forces in the Deep South had already begun to take over federal forts. The loss of **Fort Sumter**, in the harbor of Charleston, South Carolina, proved to be the flashpoint in the contest between the new Confederacy and the federal government. A small Union garrison of fewer than one hundred soldiers and officers held the fort, making it a vulnerable target for the Confederacy. Fire-Eaters pressured Jefferson Davis to take Fort Sumter and thereby demonstrate the Confederate government's resolve. Some also hoped that the Confederacy would gain foreign recognition, especially from Great Britain, by taking the fort in the South's most important Atlantic port. The situation grew dire as local merchants refused to sell food to the fort's Union soldiers, and by mid-April, the garrison's supplies began to run out. President Lincoln let it be known to Confederate leaders that he planned to resupply the Union forces. His strategy was clear: The decision to start the war would rest squarely on the Confederates, not on the Union. On April 12, 1861, Confederate forces in Charleston began a bombardment of Fort Sumter. Two days later, the Union soldiers there surrendered.

The Confederacy's attack on Fort Sumter, depicted here in an 1861 lithograph by Currier and Ives, stoked pro-war sentiment on both sides of the conflict.

The attack on Fort Sumter meant war had come, and on April 15, 1861, Lincoln called upon loyal states to supply armed forces to defeat the rebellion and regain Fort Sumter. Faced with the need to choose between the Confederacy and the Union, border states and those of the Upper South, which earlier had been reluctant to dissolve their ties with the United States, were inspired to take action. They quickly voted for secession. A convention in Virginia that had been assembled earlier to consider the question of secession voted to join the Confederacy on April 17, two days after Lincoln called for troops. Arkansas left the Union on May 6 along with Tennessee one day later. North Carolina followed on May 20.

Not all residents of the border states and the Upper South wished to join the Confederacy, however. Pro-Union feelings remained strong in Tennessee, especially in the eastern part of the state where slaves were few and consisted largely of house servants owned by the wealthy. The state of Virginia—home of revolutionary leaders and presidents such as George Washington, Thomas Jefferson, James Madison, and James Monroe—literally was split on the issue of secession. Residents in the north and west of the state, where few slaveholders resided, rejected secession. These counties subsequently united to form "West Virginia," which entered the Union as a free state in 1863. The rest of Virginia, including the historic lands along the Chesapeake Bay that were home to such early American settlements as Jamestown and Williamsburg, joined the Confederacy. The addition of this area gave the Confederacy even greater hope and brought General Robert E. Lee, arguably the best military commander of the day, to their side. In addition, the secession of Virginia brought Washington, DC, perilously close to the Confederacy, and fears that the border state of Maryland would also join the CSA, thus trapping the U.S. capital within Confederate territories, plagued Lincoln.

The Confederacy also gained the backing of the Five Civilized Tribes, as they were called, in the Indian Territory. The Five Civilized Tribes comprised the Choctaws, Chickasaws, Creeks, Seminoles, and Cherokees. The tribes supported slavery and many members owned slaves. These Indian slaveholders, who had been forced from their lands in Georgia and elsewhere in the Deep South during the presidency of Andrew Jackson, now found unprecedented common cause with white slaveholders. The CSA even allowed them to send delegates to the Confederate Congress.

While most slaveholding states joined the Confederacy, four crucial slave states remained in the Union. Delaware, which was technically a slave state despite its tiny slave population, never voted to secede. Maryland, despite deep divisions, remained in the Union as well. Missouri became the site of vicious fighting and the home of pro-Confederate guerillas but never joined the Confederacy. Kentucky declared itself neutral, although that did little to stop the fighting that occurred within the state. In all, these four states deprived the Confederacy of key resources and soldiers.

This map illustrates the southern states that seceded from the Union and formed the Confederacy in 1861, at the outset of the Civil War.

Section Summary

The election of Abraham Lincoln to the presidency in 1860 proved to be a watershed event. While it did not cause the Civil War, it was the culmination of increasing tensions between the proslavery South and the antislavery North. Before Lincoln had even taken office, seven Deep South states had seceded from the Union to form the CSA, dedicated to maintaining racial slavery and white supremacy. Last-minute efforts to reach a compromise, such as the proposal by Senator Crittenden and the Corwin amendment, went nowhere. The time for compromise had come to an end. With the Confederate attack on Fort Sumter, the Civil War began.

https://www.openassessments.org/assessments/995

> ### Review Question
>
> 1. Why did the states of the Deep South secede from the Union sooner than the states of the Upper South and the border states?

> ### Answer to Review Question
>
> 1. Slavery was more deeply entrenched in the Deep South than it was in the Upper South or the border states. The Deep South was home to larger numbers of both slaveholders and slaves. Pro-Union sentiment remained strong in parts of the Upper South and border states, particularly those areas with smaller populations of slaveholders.

> ### Glossary
>
> **Confederacy** the new nation formed by the seceding southern states, also known as the Confederate States of America (CSA)
>
> **Crittenden Compromise** a compromise, suggested by Kentucky senator John Crittenden, that would restore the 36°30′ line from the Missouri Compromise and extend it to the Pacific Ocean, allowing slavery to expand into the southwestern territories
>
> **Fort Sumter** a fort in the harbor of Charleston, South Carolina, where the Union garrison came under siege by Confederate forces in an attack on April 12, 1861, beginning the Civil War

Attributions

CC licensed content, Shared previously

- US History. **Authored by**: P. Scott Corbett, Volker Janssen, John M. Lund, Todd Pfannestiel, Paul Vickery, and Sylvie Waskiewicz. **Provided by**: OpenStax College. **Located at**: http://openstaxcollege.org/textbooks/us-history. **License**: *CC BY: Attribution*. **License Terms**: Download for free at http://cnx.org/content/col11740/latest/

Early Mobilization and War

> ### Learning Objectives
>
> By the end of this section, you will be able to:
>
> - Assess the strengths and weaknesses of the Confederacy and the Union
> - Explain the strategic importance of the Battle of Bull Run and the Battle of Shiloh

In 1861, enthusiasm for war ran high on both sides. The North fought to restore the Union, which Lincoln declared could never be broken. The Confederacy, which by the summer of 1861 consisted of eleven states, fought for its independence from the United States. The continuation of slavery was a central issue in the war, of course, although abolitionism and western expansion also played roles, and Northerners and Southerners alike flocked eagerly to the conflict. Both sides thought it would be over quickly. Militarily, however, the North and South were more equally matched than Lincoln had realized, and it soon became clear that the war effort would be neither brief nor painless. In 1861, Americans in both the North and South romanticized war as noble and positive. Soon the carnage and slaughter would awaken them to the horrors of war.

THE FIRST BATTLE OF BULL RUN

After the fall of Fort Sumter on April 15, 1861, Lincoln called for seventy-five thousand volunteers from state militias to join federal forces. His goal was a ninety-day campaign to put down the Southern rebellion. The response from state militias was overwhelming, and the number of Northern troops exceeded the requisition. Also in April, Lincoln put in place a naval blockade of the South, a move that gave tacit recognition of the Confederacy while providing a legal excuse for the British and the French to trade with Southerners. The Confederacy responded to the blockade by declaring that a state of war existed with the United States. This official pronouncement confirmed the beginning of the Civil War. Men rushed to enlist, and the Confederacy turned away tens of thousands who hoped to defend the new nation.

Many believed that a single, heroic battle would decide the contest. Some questioned how committed Southerners really were to their cause. Northerners hoped that most Southerners would not actually fire on the American flag. Meanwhile, Lincoln and military leaders in the North hoped a quick blow to the South, especially if they could capture the Confederacy's new capital of Richmond, Virginia, would end the rebellion before it went any further. On July 21, 1861, the two armies met near Manassas, Virginia, along **Bull Run Creek**, only thirty miles from Washington, DC. So great was the belief that this would be a climactic Union victory that many Washington socialites and politicians brought picnic lunches to a nearby area, hoping to witness history unfolding before them. At the First Battle of Bull Run, also known as First Manassas, some sixty thousand troops assembled, most of whom had never seen combat, and each side sent eighteen thousand into the fray. The Union forces attacked first, only to be pushed back. The Confederate forces then carried the day, sending the Union soldiers and Washington, DC, onlookers scrambling back from Virginia and destroying Union hopes of a quick, decisive victory. Instead, the war would drag on for four long, deadly years.

The First Battle of Bull Run, which many Northerners thought would put a quick and decisive end to the South's rebellion, ended with a Confederate victory.

BALANCE SHEET: THE UNION AND THE CONFEDERACY

As it became clearer that the Union would not be dealing with an easily quashed rebellion, the two sides assessed their strengths and weaknesses. At the onset on the war, in 1861 and 1862, they stood as relatively equal combatants.

The Confederates had the advantage of being able to wage a defensive war, rather than an offensive one. They had to protect and preserve their new boundaries, but they did not have to be the aggressors against the Union. The war would be fought primarily in the South, which gave the Confederates the advantages of the knowledge of the terrain and the support of the civilian population. Further, the vast coastline from Texas to Virginia offered ample opportunities to evade the Union blockade. And with the addition of the Upper South states, especially Virginia, North Carolina, Tennessee, and Arkansas, the Confederacy gained a much larger share of natural resources and industrial might than the Deep South states could muster.

Still, the Confederacy had disadvantages. The South's economy depended heavily on the export of cotton, but with the naval blockade, the flow of cotton to England, the region's primary importer, came to an end. The blockade also made it difficult to import manufactured goods. Although the secession of the Upper

South added some industrial assets to the Confederacy, overall, the South lacked substantive industry or an extensive railroad infrastructure to move men and supplies. To deal with the lack of commerce and the resulting lack of funds, the Confederate government began printing paper money, leading to runaway inflation. The advantage that came from fighting on home territory quickly turned to a disadvantage when Confederate armies were defeated and Union forces destroyed Southern farms and towns, and forced Southern civilians to take to the road as refugees. Finally, the population of the South stood at fewer than nine million people, of whom nearly four million were black slaves, compared to over twenty million residents in the North. These limited numbers became a major factor as the war dragged on and the death toll rose.

The Confederacy started printing paper money at an accelerated rate, causing runaway inflation and an economy in which formerly well-off people were unable to purchase food.

The Union side held many advantages as well. Its larger population, bolstered by continued immigration from Europe throughout the 1860s, gave it greater manpower reserves to draw upon. The North's greater industrial capabilities and extensive railroad grid made it far better able to mobilize men and supplies for the war effort. The Industrial Revolution and the transportation revolution, beginning in the 1820s and continuing over the next several decades, had transformed the North. Throughout the war, the North was able to produce more war materials and move goods more quickly than the South. Furthermore, the farms of New England, the Mid-Atlantic, the Old Northwest, and the prairie states supplied Northern civilians and Union troops with abundant food throughout the war. Food shortages and hungry civilians were common in the South, where the best land was devoted to raising cotton, but not in the North.

Unlike the South, however, which could hunker down to defend itself and needed to maintain relatively short supply lines, the North had to go forth and conquer. Union armies had to establish long supply lines, and Union soldiers had to fight on unfamiliar ground and contend with a hostile civilian population off the battlefield. Furthermore, to restore the Union—Lincoln's overriding goal, in 1861—the United States, after defeating the Southern forces, would then need to pacify a conquered Confederacy, an area of over half a million square miles with nearly nine million residents. In short, although it had better resources and a larger population, the Union faced a daunting task against the well-positioned Confederacy.

MILITARY STALEMATE

The military forces of the Confederacy and the Union battled in 1861 and early 1862 without either side gaining the upper hand. The majority of military leaders on both sides had received the same military education and often knew one another personally, either from their time as students at West Point or as commanding officers in the Mexican-American War. This familiarity allowed them to anticipate each other's strategies. Both sides believed in the use of concentrated armies charged with taking the capital city of the enemy. For the Union, this meant the capture of the Confederate capital in Richmond, Virginia, whereas Washington, DC, stood as the prize for Confederate forces. After hopes of a quick victory faded at Bull Run, the months dragged on without any major movement on either side.

As this cartoon indicates, the fighting strategy at the beginning of the war included watchful waiting by the leaders of the North and South.

General George B. McClellan, the **general in chief** of the army, responsible for overall control of Union land forces, proved especially reluctant to engage in battle with the Confederates. In direct command of the **Army of the Potomac**, the Union fighting force operating outside Washington, DC, McClellan believed, incorrectly, that Confederate forces were too strong to defeat and was reluctant to risk his troops in battle. His cautious nature made him popular with his men but not with the president or Congress. By 1862, however, both President Lincoln and the new Secretary of War Edwin Stanton had tired of waiting. The Union put forward a new effort to bolster troop strength, enlisting one million men to serve for three-year stints in the Army of the Potomac. In January 1862, Lincoln and Stanton ordered McClellan to invade the Confederacy with the goal of capturing Richmond.

To that end, General McClellan slowly moved 100,000 soldiers of the Army of the Potomac toward Richmond but stopped a few miles outside the city. As he did so, a Confederate force led by Thomas "Stonewall" Jackson moved north to take Washington, DC. To fend off Jackson's attack, somewhere between one-quarter and one-third of McClellan's soldiers, led by Major General Irvin McDowell, returned to defend the nation's capital, a move that Jackson hoped would leave the remaining troops near Richmond more vulnerable. Having succeeding in drawing off a sizable portion of the Union force, he joined General Lee to launch an attack on McClellan's remaining soldiers near Richmond. From June 25 to July 1, 1862, the two sides engaged in the brutal Seven Days Battles that killed or wounded almost twenty thousand Confederate and ten thousand Union soldiers. McClellan's army finally returned north, having failed to take Richmond.

General Lee, flush from his success at keeping McClellan out of Richmond, tried to capitalize on the Union's failure by taking the fighting northward. He moved his forces into northern Virginia, where, at the Second Battle of Bull Run, the Confederates again defeated the Union forces. Lee then pressed into Maryland, where his troops met the much larger Union forces near Sharpsburg, at Antietam Creek. The ensuing one-day battle on September 17, 1862, led to a tremendous loss of life. Although there are varying opinions about the total number of deaths, eight thousand soldiers were killed or wounded, more than on any other single day of combat. Once again, McClellan, mistakenly believing that the Confederate troops outnumbered his own, held back a significant portion of his forces. Lee withdrew from the field first, but McClellan, fearing he was outnumbered, refused to pursue him.

The Union army's inability to destroy Lee's army at **Antietam** made it clear to Lincoln that McClellan would never win the war, and the president was forced to seek a replacement. Lincoln wanted someone who could deliver a decisive Union victory. He also personally disliked McClellan, who referred to the president as a "baboon" and a "gorilla," and constantly criticized his decisions. Lincoln chose General Ambrose E. Burnside to replace McClellan as commander of the Army of the Potomac, but Burnside's efforts to push into Virginia failed in December 1862, as Confederates held their position at Fredericksburg and devastated Burnside's forces with heavy artillery fire. The Union's defeat at Fredericksburg harmed morale in the North but bolstered Confederate spirits. By the end of 1862, the Confederates were still holding their ground in Virginia. Burnside's failure led Lincoln to make another change in leadership, and Joseph "Fighting Joe" Hooker took over command of the Army of the Potomac in January 1863.

General Ulysses S. Grant's **Army of the West**, operating in Kentucky, Tennessee, and the Mississippi River Valley, had been more successful. In the western campaign, the goal of both the Union and the Confederacy was to gain control of the major rivers in the west, especially the Mississippi. If the Union could control the Mississippi, the Confederacy would be split in two. The fighting in this campaign initially centered in Tennessee, where Union forces commanded by Grant pushed Confederate troops back and gained control of the state. The major battle in the western theater took place at Pittsburgh Landing, Tennessee, on April 6 and 7, 1862. Grant's army was camped on the west side of the Tennessee River near a small log church called Shiloh, which gave the battle its name. On Sunday morning, April 6, Confederate forces under General Albert Sidney Johnston attacked Grant's encampment with the goal of separating them from their supply line on the Tennessee River and driving them into the swamps on the river's western side, where they could be destroyed. Union general William Tecumseh Sherman tried to rally the Union forces as Grant, who had been convalescing from an injured leg when the attack began and was unable to walk without crutches, called for reinforcements and tried to mount a defense. Many of Union troops fled in terror.

Unfortunately for the Confederates, Johnston was killed on the afternoon of the first day. Leadership of the Southern forces fell to General P. G. T. Beauregard, who ordered an assault at the end of that day. This assault was so desperate that one of the two attacking columns did not even have ammunition. Heavily reinforced Union forces counterattacked the next day, and the Confederate forces were routed. Grant had maintained the Union foothold in the western part of the Confederacy. The North could now concentrate on its efforts to gain control of the Mississippi River, splitting the Confederacy in two and depriving it of its most important water route.

> Read a first-hand account from a Confederate soldier at the Battle at Shiloh, followed by the perspective of a Union soldier at the same battle.

In the spring and summer of 1862, the Union was successful in gaining control of part of the Mississippi River. In April 1862, the Union navy under Admiral David Farragut fought its way past the forts that guarded New Orleans and fired naval guns upon the below-sea-level city. When it became obvious that New Orleans could no longer be defended, Confederate major general Marshall Lovell sent his artillery upriver to Vicksburg, Mississippi. Armed civilians in New Orleans fought the Union forces that entered the city. They also destroyed ships and military supplies that might be used by the Union. Upriver, Union naval forces also bombarded Fort Pillow, forty miles from Memphis, Tennessee, a Southern industrial center and one of the largest cities in the Confederacy. On June 4, 1862, the Confederate defenders abandoned the fort. On June 6, Memphis fell to the Union after the ships defending it were destroyed.

Section Summary

Many in both the North and the South believed that a short, decisive confrontation in 1861 would settle the question of the Confederacy. These expectations did not match reality, however, and the war dragged on into a second year. Both sides mobilized, with advantages and disadvantages on each side that led to a rough equilibrium. The losses of battles at Manassas and Fredericksburg, Virginia, kept the North from achieving the speedy victory its generals had hoped for, but the Union did make gains and continued to press forward. While they could not capture the Southern capital of Richmond, they were victorious in the Battle of Shiloh and captured New Orleans and Memphis. Thus, the Confederates lost major ground on the western front.

https://www.openassessments.org/assessments/996

Review Question

1. What military successes and defeats did the Union experience in 1862?

Answer to Review Question

1. In the eastern part of the Confederacy, the Army of the Potomac met with mixed success. The Union army failed to capture Richmond and won at Antietam only because the Confederates withdrew from the field first. In the western part of the Confederacy, the Army of the West won the Battle of Shiloh, and the Union navy captured New Orleans and Memphis.

Glossary

Army of the Potomac the Union fighting force operating outside Washington, DC

Army of the West the Union fighting force operating in Kentucky, Tennessee, and the Mississippi River Valley

general in chief the commander of army land forces

Attributions

CC licensed content, Shared previously

- US History. **Authored by**: P. Scott Corbett, Volker Janssen, John M. Lund, Todd Pfannestiel, Paul Vickery, and Sylvie Waskiewicz. **Provided by**: OpenStax College. **Located at**: http://openstaxcollege.org/textbooks/us-history. **License**: *CC BY: Attribution*. **License Terms**: Download for free at http://cnx.org/content/col11740/latest/

1863: The Changing Nature of the War

> **Learning Objectives**
>
> By the end of this section, you will be able to:
>
> - Explain what is meant by the term "total war" and provide examples
> - Describe mobilization efforts in the North and the South
> - Explain why 1863 was a pivotal year in the war

Wars have their own logic; they last far longer than anyone anticipates at the beginning of hostilities. As they drag on, the energy and zeal that marked the entry into warfare often wane, as losses increase and people on both sides suffer the tolls of war. The American Civil War is a case study of this characteristic of modern war.

Although Northerners and Southerners both anticipated that the battle between the Confederacy and the Union would be settled quickly, it soon became clear to all that there was no resolution in sight. The longer the war continued, the more it began to affect life in both the North and the South. Increased need for manpower, the issue of slavery, and the ongoing challenges of keeping the war effort going changed the way life on both sides as the conflict progressed.

MASS MOBILIZATION

By late 1862, the course of the war had changed to take on the characteristics of **total war**, in which armies attempt to demoralize the enemy by both striking military targets and disrupting their opponent's ability to wage war through destruction of their resources. In this type of war, armies often make no distinction between civilian and military targets. Both the Union and Confederate forces moved toward total war, although neither side ever entirely abolished the distinction between military and civilian. Total war also requires governments to mobilize all resources, extending their reach into their citizens' lives as never before. Another reality of war that became apparent in 1862 and beyond was the influence of combat on the size and scope of government. Both the Confederacy and the Union governments had to continue to grow in order to manage the logistics of recruiting men and maintaining, feeding, and equipping an army.

Confederate Mobilization

The Confederate government in Richmond, Virginia, exercised sweeping powers to ensure victory, in stark contradiction to the states' rights sentiments held by many Southern leaders. The initial emotional outburst of enthusiasm for war in the Confederacy waned, and the Confederate government instituted a military draft in April 1862. Under the terms of the draft, all men between the ages of eighteen and thirty-five would serve three years. The draft had a different effect on men of different socioeconomic classes. One loophole permitted men to hire substitutes instead of serving in the Confederate army. This provision favored the wealthy over the poor, and led to much resentment and resistance. Exercising its power over the states, the Confederate Congress denied state efforts to circumvent the draft.

In order to fund the war, the Confederate government also took over the South's economy. The government ran Southern industry and built substantial transportation and industrial infrastructure to make the weapons of war. Over the objections of slaveholders, it impressed slaves, seizing these workers from their owners and forcing them to work on fortifications and rail lines. Concerned about the resistance to and unhappiness with the government measures, in 1862, the Confederate Congress gave President Davis the power to suspend the writ of **habeas corpus**, the right of those arrested to be brought before a judge or court to determine whether there is cause to hold the prisoner. With a stated goal of bolstering national security in the fledgling republic, this change meant that the Confederacy could arrest and detain indefinitely any suspected enemy without giving a reason. This growth of the Confederate central government stood as a glaring contradiction to the earlier states' rights argument of pro-Confederate advocates.

The war efforts were costing the new nation dearly. Nevertheless, the Confederate Congress heeded the pleas of wealthy plantation owners and refused to place a tax on slaves or cotton, despite the Confederacy's desperate need for the revenue that such a tax would have raised. Instead, the Confederacy drafted a taxation plan that kept the Southern elite happy but in no way met the needs of the war. The government also resorted to printing immense amounts of paper money, which quickly led to runaway inflation. Food prices soared, and poor, white Southerners faced starvation. In April 1863, thousands of hungry people rioted in Richmond, Virginia. Many of the rioters were mothers who could not feed their children. The riot ended when President Davis threatened to have Confederate forces open fire on the crowds.

One of the reasons that the Confederacy was so economically devastated was its ill-advised gamble that cotton sales would continue during the war. The government had high hopes that Great Britain and France, which both used cotton as the raw material in their textile mills, would ensure the South's economic strength—and therefore victory in the war—by continuing to buy. Furthermore, the Confederate government hoped that Great Britain and France would make loans to their new nation in order to ensure the continued flow of raw materials. These hopes were never realized. Great Britain in particular did not wish to risk war with the United States, which would have meant the invasion of Canada. The United States was also a major source of grain for Britain and an important purchaser of British goods. Furthermore, the blockade made Southern trade with Europe difficult. Instead, Great Britain, the major consumer of American cotton, found alternate sources in India and Egypt, leaving the South without the income or alliance it had anticipated.

Rampant inflation in the 1860s made food too expensive for many Southerners, leading to widespread starvation.

Dissent within the Confederacy also affected the South's ability to fight the war. Confederate politicians disagreed over the amount of power that the central government should be allowed to exercise. Many states' rights advocates, who favored a weak central government and supported the sovereignty of individual states, resented President Davis's efforts to conscript troops, impose taxation to pay for the war, and requisition necessary resources. Governors in the Confederate states often proved reluctant to provide supplies or troops for the use of the Confederate government. Even Jefferson Davis's vice president Alexander Stephens opposed conscription, the seizure of slave property to work for the Confederacy, and suspension of habeas corpus. Class divisions also divided Confederates. Poor whites resented the ability of wealthy slaveholders to excuse themselves from military service. Racial tensions plagued the South as well. On those occasions when free blacks volunteered to serve in the Confederate army, they were turned away, and enslaved African Americans were regarded with fear and suspicion, as whites whispered among themselves about the possibility of slave insurrections.

Union Mobilization

Mobilization for war proved to be easier in the North than it was in the South. During the war, the federal government in Washington, DC, like its Southern counterpart, undertook a wide range of efforts to ensure its victory over the Confederacy. To fund the war effort and finance the expansion of Union infrastructure, Republicans in Congress drastically expanded government activism, impacting citizens' everyday lives through measures such as new types of taxation. The government also contracted with major suppliers of food, weapons, and other needed materials. Virtually every sector of the Northern economy became linked to the war effort.

In keeping with their longstanding objective of keeping slavery out of the newly settled western territories, the Republicans in Congress (the dominant party) passed several measures in 1862. First, the Homestead

Act provided generous inducements for Northerners to relocate and farm in the West. Settlers could lay claim to 160 acres of federal land by residing on the property for five years and improving it. The act not only motivated free-labor farmers to move west, but it also aimed to increase agricultural output for the war effort. The federal government also turned its attention to creating a transcontinental railroad to facilitate the movement of people and goods across the country. Congress chartered two companies, the Union Pacific and the Central Pacific, and provided generous funds for these two businesses to connect the country by rail.

The Republican emphasis on free labor, rather than slave labor, also influenced the 1862 Land Grant College Act, commonly known as the **Morrill Act** after its author, Vermont Republican senator Justin Smith Morrill. The measure provided for the creation of agricultural colleges, funded through federal grants, to teach the latest agricultural techniques. Each state in the Union would be granted thirty thousand acres of federal land for the use of these institutions of higher education.

Congress paid for the war using several strategies. They levied a tax on the income of the wealthy, as well as a tax on all inheritances. They also put high tariffs in place. Finally, they passed two National Bank Acts, one in 1863 and one in 1864, calling on the U.S. Treasury to issue war bonds and on Union banks to buy the bonds. A Union campaign to convince individuals to buy the bonds helped increase sales. The Republicans also passed the Legal Tender Act of 1862, calling for paper money—known as **greenbacks**—to be printed. Some $150 million worth of greenbacks became legal tender, and the Northern economy boomed, although high inflation also resulted.

The Union began printing these paper "greenbacks" to use as legal tender as one of its strategies for funding the war effort.

Like the Confederacy, the Union turned to conscription to provide the troops needed for the war. In March 1863, Congress passed the Enrollment Act, requiring all unmarried men between the ages of twenty and twenty-five, and all married men between the ages of thirty-five and forty-five—including immigrants who had filed for citizenship—to register with the Union to fight in the Civil War. All who registered were subject to military service, and draftees were selected by a lottery system. As in the South, a loophole in the law allowed individuals to hire substitutes if they could afford it. Others could avoid enlistment by paying $300 to the federal government. In keeping with the Supreme Court decision in *Dred Scott v. Sandford*, African Americans were not citizens and were therefore exempt from the draft.

The Union tried to provide additional incentives for soldiers, in the form of bounties, to enlist without waiting for the draft, as shown in recruitment posters (a) and (b).

Like the Confederacy, the Union also took the step of suspending habeas corpus rights, so those suspected of pro-Confederate sympathies could be arrested and held without being given the reason. Lincoln had selectively suspended the writ of habeas corpus in the slave state of Maryland, home to many Confederate sympathizers, in 1861 and 1862, in an effort to ensure that the Union capital would be safe. In March 1863, he signed into law the Habeas Corpus Suspension Act, giving him the power to detain suspected Confederate operatives throughout the Union. The Lincoln administration also closed down three hundred newspapers as a national security measure during the war.

In both the North and the South, the Civil War dramatically increased the power of the belligerent governments. Breaking all past precedents in American history, both the Confederacy and the Union employed the power of their central governments to mobilize resources and citizens.

Women's Mobilization

As men on both sides mobilized for the war, so did women. In both the North and the South, women were forced to take over farms and businesses abandoned by their husbands as they left for war. Women organized themselves into ladies' aid societies to sew uniforms, knit socks, and raise money to purchase necessities for the troops. In the South, women took wounded soldiers into their homes to nurse. In the North, women volunteered for the United States Sanitary Commission, which formed in June 1861. They inspected military camps with the goal of improving cleanliness and reducing the number of soldiers who died from disease, the most common cause of death in the war. They also raised money to buy medical supplies and helped with the injured. Other women found jobs in the Union army as cooks and laundresses. Thousands volunteered to care for the sick and wounded in response to a call by reformer Dorothea Dix, who was placed in charge of the Union army's nurses. According to rumor, Dix sought respectable women over the age of thirty who were "plain almost to repulsion in dress" and thus could be trusted not to form romantic liaisons with soldiers. Women on both sides also acted as spies and, disguised as men, engaged in combat.

EMANCIPATION

Early in the war, President Lincoln approached the issue of slavery cautiously. While he disapproved of slavery personally, he did not believe that he had the authority to abolish it. Furthermore, he feared that making the abolition of slavery an objective of the war would cause the border slave states to join the Confederacy. His one objective in 1861 and 1862 was to restore the Union.

Lincoln's Evolving Thoughts on Slavery

President Lincoln wrote the following letter to newspaper editor Horace Greeley on August 22, 1862. In it, Lincoln states his position on slavery, which is notable for being a middle-of-the-road stance. Lincoln's later public speeches on the issue take the more strident antislavery tone for which he is remembered.

> I would save the Union. I would save it the shortest way under the Constitution. The sooner the national authority can be restored the nearer the Union will be "the Union as it was." If there be those who would not save the Union unless they could at the same time save Slavery, I do not agree with them. If there be those who would not save the Union unless they could at the same time destroy Slavery, I do not agree with them. My paramount object in this struggle is to save the Union, and is not either to save or destroy Slavery. If I could save the Union without freeing any slave, I would do it, and if I could save it by freeing all the slaves, I would do it, and if I could save it by freeing some and leaving others alone, I would also do that. What I do about Slavery and the colored race, I do because I believe it helps to save this Union, and what I forbear, I forbear because I do not believe it would help to save the Union. I shall do less whenever I shall believe what I am doing hurts the cause, and I shall do more whenever I shall believe doing more will help the cause. I shall try to correct errors when shown to be errors; and I shall adopt new views so fast as they shall appear to be true views. I have here stated my purpose according to my view of official duty, and I intend no modification of my oft-expressed personal wish that all men, everywhere, could be free. Yours, A. LINCOLN.

How would you characterize Lincoln's public position in August 1862? What was he prepared to do for slaves, and under what conditions?

Since the beginning of the war, thousands of slaves had fled to the safety of Union lines. In May 1861, Union general Benjamin Butler and others labeled these refugees from slavery **contrabands**. Butler reasoned that since Southern states had left the United States, he was not obliged to follow federal fugitive slave laws. Slaves who made it through the Union lines were shielded by the U.S. military and not returned to slavery. The intent was not only to assist slaves but also to deprive the South of a valuable source of manpower.

Congress began to define the status of these ex-slaves in 1861 and 1862. In August 1861, legislators approved the Confiscation Act of 1861, empowering the Union to seize property, including slaves, used by the Confederacy. The Republican-dominated Congress took additional steps, abolishing slavery in Washington, DC, in April 1862. Congress passed a second Confiscation Act in July 1862, which extended freedom to runaway slaves and those captured by Union armies. In that month, Congress also addressed the issue of slavery in the West, banning the practice in the territories. This federal law made the 1846 Wilmot Proviso and the dreams of the Free-Soil Party a reality. However, even as the Union government took steps to aid individual slaves and to limit the practice of slavery, it passed no measure to address the institution of slavery as a whole.

Lincoln moved slowly and cautiously on the issue of abolition. His primary concern was the cohesion of the Union and the bringing of the Southern states back into the fold. However, as the war dragged on and many thousands of contrabands made their way north, Republicans in Congress continued to call for the end of slavery. Throughout his political career, Lincoln's plans for former slaves had been to send them to Liberia. As late as August 1862, he had hoped to interest African Americans in building a colony for former slaves in Central America, an idea that found favor neither with black leaders nor with abolitionists, and thus was abandoned by Lincoln. Responding to Congressional demands for an end to slavery, Lincoln presented an ultimatum to the Confederates on September 22, 1862, shortly after the Confederate retreat at Antietam. He gave the Confederate states until January 1, 1863, to rejoin the Union. If they did, slavery would continue in the slave states. If they refused to rejoin, however, the war would continue and all slaves would be freed at its conclusion. The Confederacy took no action. It had committed itself to maintaining its independence and had no interest in the president's ultimatum.

On January 1, 1863, Lincoln made good on his promise and signed the **Emancipation Proclamation**. It stated "That on the first day of January, in the year of our Lord one thousand eight hundred and sixty-three, all persons held as slaves within any State or designated part of a State, the people whereof shall then be in rebellion against the United States, shall be then, thenceforward, and forever free." The proclamation did not immediately free the slaves in the Confederate states. Although they were in rebellion against the United States, the lack of the Union army's presence in such areas meant that the president's directive could not be enforced. The proclamation also did not free slaves in the border states, because these states were not, by definition, in rebellion. Lincoln relied on his powers as commander-in-chief in issuing the Emancipation Proclamation. He knew the proclamation could be easily challenged in court, but by excluding the territories still outside his control, slaveholders and slave governments could not sue him. Moreover, slave states in the Union, such as Kentucky, could not sue because the proclamation did not apply to them. Slaveholders in Kentucky knew full well that if the institution were abolished throughout the South, it would not survive in a handful of border territories. Despite the limits of the proclamation, Lincoln dramatically shifted the objective of the war increasingly toward ending slavery. The Emancipation Proclamation became a monumental step forward on the road to changing the character of the United States.

> Read through the full text of the Emancipation Proclamation at the National Archives website.

The proclamation generated quick and dramatic reactions. The news created euphoria among slaves, as it signaled the eventual end of their bondage. Predictably, Confederate leaders raged against the proclamation, reinforcing their commitment to fight to maintain slavery, the foundation of the Confederacy. In the North, opinions split widely on the issue. Abolitionists praised Lincoln's actions, which they saw as the fulfillment of their long campaign to strike down an immoral institution. But other Northerners, especially Irish, working-class, urban dwellers loyal to the Democratic Party and others with racist beliefs, hated the new goal of emancipation and found the idea of freed slaves repugnant. At its core, much of this racism had an economic foundation: Many Northerners feared competing with emancipated slaves for scarce jobs.

In New York City, the Emancipation Proclamation, combined with unhappiness over the Union draft, which began in March 1863, fanned the flames of white racism. Many New Yorkers supported the Confederacy for business reasons, and, in 1861, the city's mayor actually suggested that New York City leave the Union. On July 13, 1863, two days after the first draft lottery took place, this racial hatred erupted into violence. A volunteer fire company whose commander had been drafted initiated a riot, and the violence spread quickly across the city. The rioters chose targets associated either with the Union army or with

African Americans. An armory was destroyed, as was a Brooks Brothers' store, which supplied uniforms to the army. White mobs attacked and killed black New Yorkers and destroyed an African American orphanage. On the fourth day of the riots, federal troops dispatched by Lincoln arrived in the city and ended the violence. Millions of dollars in property had been destroyed. More than one hundred people died, approximately one thousand were left injured, and about one-fifth of the city's African American population fled New York in fear.

The race riots in New York showed just how divided the North was on the issue of equality, even as the North went to war with the South over the issue of slavery.

UNION ADVANCES

The war in the west continued in favor of the North in 1863. At the start of the year, Union forces controlled much of the Mississippi River. In the spring and summer of 1862, they had captured New Orleans—the most important port in the Confederacy, through which cotton harvested from all the Southern states was exported—and Memphis. Grant had then attempted to capture Vicksburg, Mississippi, a commercial center on the bluffs above the Mississippi River. Once Vicksburg fell, the Union would have won complete control over the river. A military bombardment that summer failed to force a Confederate surrender. An assault by land forces also failed in December 1862.

In April 1863, the Union began a final attempt to capture Vicksburg. On July 3, after more than a month of a Union siege, during which Vicksburg's residents hid in caves to protect themselves from the bombardment and ate their pets to stay alive, Grant finally achieved his objective. The trapped Confederate forces surrendered. The Union had succeeded in capturing Vicksburg and splitting the Confederacy. This victory inflicted a serious blow to the Southern war effort.

As Grant and his forces pounded Vicksburg, Confederate strategists, at the urging of General Lee, who had defeated a larger Union army at Chancellorsville, Virginia, in May 1863, decided on a bold plan to invade the North. Leaders hoped this invasion would force the Union to send troops engaged in the Vicksburg campaign east, thus weakening their power over the Mississippi. Further, they hoped the aggressive action of pushing north would weaken the Union's resolve to fight. Lee also hoped that a significant Confederate victory in the North would convince Great Britain and France to extend support to Jefferson Davis's government and encourage the North to negotiate peace.

In this illustration, Union gun boats fire on Vicksburg in the campaign that helped the Union take control of the Mississippi River.

Beginning in June 1863, General Lee began to move the Army of Northern Virginia north through Maryland. The Union army—the Army of the Potomac—traveled east to end up alongside the Confederate forces. The two armies met at Gettysburg, Pennsylvania, where Confederate forces had gone to secure supplies. The resulting battle lasted three days, July 1–3 and remains the biggest and costliest battle ever fought in North America. The climax of the Battle of Gettysburg occurred on the third day. In the morning, after a fight lasting several hours, Union forces fought back a Confederate attack on Culp's Hill, one of the Union's defensive positions. To regain a perceived advantage and secure victory, Lee ordered a frontal assault, known as Pickett's Charge (for Confederate general George Pickett), against the center of the Union lines on Cemetery Ridge. Approximately fifteen thousand Confederate soldiers took part, and more than half lost their lives, as they advanced nearly a mile across an open field to attack the entrenched Union forces. In all, more than a third of the Army of Northern Virginia had been lost, and on the evening of July 4, Lee and his men slipped away in the rain. General George Meade did not pursue them. Both sides suffered staggering losses. Total casualties numbered around twenty-three thousand for the Union and some twenty-eight thousand among the Confederates. With its defeats at Gettysburg and Vicksburg, both on the same day, the Confederacy lost its momentum. The tide had turned in favor of the Union in both the east and the west.

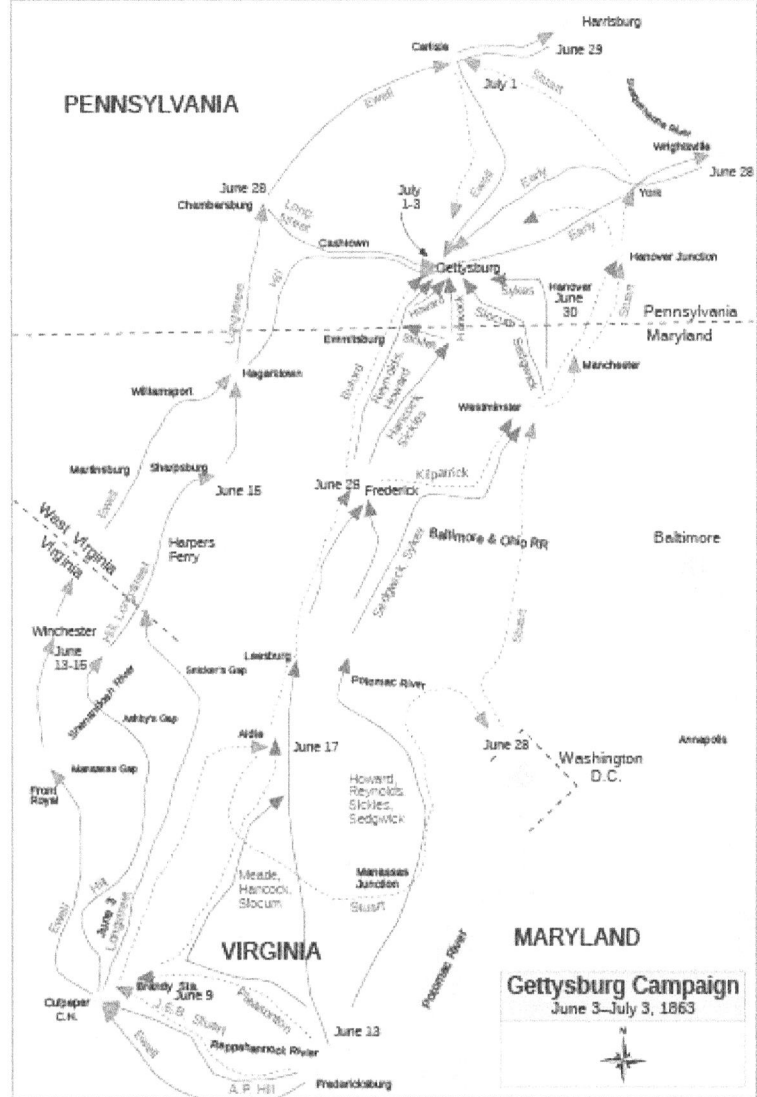

As this map indicates, the battlefield at Gettysburg was the farthest north that the Confederate army advanced. (credit: Hal Jesperson)

Following the Battle of Gettysburg, the bodies of those who had fallen were hastily buried. Attorney David Wills, a resident of Gettysburg, campaigned for the creation of a national cemetery on the site of the battlefield, and the governor of Pennsylvania tasked him with creating it. President Lincoln was invited to attend the cemetery's dedication. After the featured orator had delivered a two-hour speech, Lincoln addressed the crowd for several minutes. In his speech, known as the **Gettysburg Address**, which he had finished writing while a guest in David Wills' home the day before the dedication, Lincoln invoked the Founding Fathers and the spirit of the American Revolution. The Union soldiers who had died at Gettysburg, he proclaimed, had died not only to preserve the Union, but also to guarantee freedom and equality for all.

Lincoln's Gettysburg Address

Several months after the battle at Gettysburg, Lincoln traveled to Pennsylvania and, speaking to an audience at the dedication of the new Soldiers' National Ceremony near the site of the battle, he delivered his now-famous Gettysburg Address to commemorate the turning point of the war and the soldiers whose sacrifices had made it possible. The two-minute speech was politely received at the time, although press reactions split along party lines. Upon receiving a letter of congratulations from Massachusetts politician and orator William Everett, whose speech at the ceremony had lasted for two hours, Lincoln said he was glad to know that his brief address, now virtually immortal, was not "a total failure."

> Four score and seven years ago our fathers brought forth on this continent, a new nation, conceived in Liberty, and dedicated to the proposition that all men are created equal.
>
> Now we are engaged in a great civil war, testing whether that nation, or any nation so conceived and so dedicated, can long endure. We are met on a great battle-field of that war. We have come to dedicate a portion of that field, as a final resting place for those who here gave their lives that that nation might live. It is altogether fitting and proper that we should do this.
>
> It is for us the living . . . to be here dedicated to the great task remaining before us—that from these honored dead we take increased devotion to that cause for which they gave the last full measure of devotion—that we here highly resolve that these dead shall not have died in vain—that this nation, under God, shall have a new birth of freedom—and that government of the people, by the people, for the people, shall not perish from the earth.
>
> —Abraham Lincoln, Gettysburg Address, November 19, 1863

What did Lincoln mean by "a new birth of freedom"? What did he mean when he said "a government of the people, by the people, for the people, shall not perish from the earth"?

Acclaimed filmmaker Ken Burns has created a documentary about a small boys' school in Vermont where students memorize the Gettysburg Address. It explores the value the address has in these boys' lives, and why the words still matter.

Section Summary

The year 1863 proved decisive in the Civil War for two major reasons. First, the Union transformed the purpose of the struggle from restoring the Union to ending slavery. While Lincoln's Emancipation Proclamation actually succeeded in freeing few slaves, it made freedom for African Americans a cause of the Union. Second, the tide increasingly turned against the Confederacy. The success of the Vicksburg Campaign had given the Union control of the Mississippi River, and Lee's defeat at Gettysburg had ended the attempted Confederate invasion of the North.

https://www.openassessments.org/assessments/997

Review Question

1. Why is 1863 considered a turning point in the Civil War?

Answer to Review Question

1. At the beginning of 1863, Abraham Lincoln issued the Emancipation Proclamation, which freed all slaves in areas under rebellion. This changed the war from one in which the North fought to preserve the Union to one in which it fought to free enslaved African Americans. On the battlefield, Union forces led by Grant captured Vicksburg, Mississippi, splitting the Confederacy in two and depriving it of a major avenue of transportation. In the east, General Meade stopped a Confederate invasion of the North at Gettysburg, Pennsylvania.

Glossary

Emancipation Proclamation signed on January 1, 1863, the document with which President Lincoln transformed the Civil War into a struggle to end slavery

Gettysburg Address a speech by Abraham Lincoln dedicating the military cemetery at Gettysburg on November 19, 1863

greenbacks paper money the United States began to issue during the Civil War

habeas corpus the right of those arrested to be brought before a judge or court to determine whether there is cause to hold the prisoner

total war a state of war in which the government makes no distinction between military and civilian targets, and mobilizes all resources, extending its reach into all areas of citizens' lives

contrabands slaves who escaped to the Union army's lines

Attributions

CC licensed content, Shared previously

- US History. **Authored by**: P. Scott Corbett, Volker Janssen, John M. Lund, Todd Pfannestiel, Paul Vickery, and Sylvie Waskiewicz. **Provided by**: OpenStax College. **Located at**: http://openstaxcollege.org/textbooks/us-history. **License**: *CC BY: Attribution*. **License Terms**: Download for free at http://cnx.org/content/col11740/latest/

The Union Triumphant

Learning Objectives

By the end of this section, you will be able to:

- Describe the reasons why many Americans doubted that Abraham Lincoln would be reelected
- Explain how the Union forces overpowered the Confederacy

By the outset of 1864, after three years of war, the Union had mobilized its resources for the ongoing struggle on a massive scale. The government had overseen the construction of new railroad lines and for the first time used standardized rail tracks that allowed the North to move men and materials with greater ease. The North's economy had shifted to a wartime model. The Confederacy also mobilized, perhaps to a greater degree than the Union, its efforts to secure independence and maintain slavery. Yet the Confederacy experienced ever-greater hardships after years of war. Without the population of the North, it faced a shortage of manpower. The lack of industry, compared to the North, undercut the ability to sustain and wage war. Rampant inflation as well as food shortages in the South lowered morale.

THE RELATIONSHIP WITH EUROPE

From the beginning of the war, the Confederacy placed great hope in being recognized and supported by Great Britain and France. European intervention in the conflict remained a strong possibility, but when it did occur, it was not in a way anticipated by either the Confederacy or the Union.

Napoleon III of France believed the Civil War presented an opportunity for him to restore a French empire in the Americas. With the United States preoccupied, the time seemed ripe for action. Napoleon's target was Mexico, and in 1861, a large French fleet took Veracruz. The French then moved to capture Mexico City, but the advance came to an end when Mexican forces defeated the French in 1862. Despite this setback, France eventually did conquer Mexico, establishing a regime that lasted until 1867. Rather than coming to the aid of the Confederacy, France used the Civil War to provide a pretext for efforts to reestablish its former eighteenth-century colonial holdings.

Still, the Confederacy had great confidence that it would find an ally in Great Britain despite the antislavery sentiment there. Southerners hoped Britain's dependence on cotton for its textile mills would keep the country on their side. The fact that the British proved willing to build and sell ironclad ships intended to smash through the Union naval blockade further raised Southern hopes. The Confederacy purchased two of these armored blockade runners, the CSS *Florida* and the CSS *Alabama*. Both were destroyed during the war.

The Confederacy's staunch commitment to slavery eventually worked against British recognition and support, since Great Britain had abolished slavery in 1833. The 1863 Emancipation Proclamation ended any doubts the British had about the goals of the Union cause. In the aftermath of the proclamation, many in Great Britain cheered for a Union victory. Ultimately, Great Britain, like France, disappointed the Confederacy's hope of an alliance, leaving the outnumbered and out-resourced states that had left the Union to fend for themselves.

AFRICAN AMERICAN SOLDIERS

At the beginning of the war, in 1861 and 1862, Union forces had used contrabands, or escaped slaves, for manual labor. The Emancipation Proclamation, however, led to the enrollment of African American men as Union soldiers. Huge numbers, former slaves as well as free blacks from the North, enlisted, and by the end of the war in 1865, their numbers had swelled to over 190,000. Racism among whites in the Union army ran deep, however, fueling the belief that black soldiers could never be effective or trustworthy. The Union also feared for the fate of captured black soldiers. Although many black soldiers saw combat duty, these factors affected the types of tasks assigned to them. Many black regiments were limited to hauling supplies, serving as cooks, digging trenches, and doing other types of labor, rather than serving on the battlefield.

This 1865 daguerreotype illustrates three of the Union's distinct advantages: African American soldiers, a stream of cannons and supplies, and an extensive railroad grid. (credit: Library of Congress)

African American soldiers also received lower wages than their white counterparts: ten dollars per month, with three dollars deducted for clothing. White soldiers, in contrast, received thirteen dollars monthly, with no deductions. Abolitionists and their Republican supporters in Congress worked to correct this discriminatory practice, and in 1864, black soldiers began to receive the same pay as white soldiers plus retroactive pay to 1863.

For their part, African American soldiers welcomed the opportunity to prove themselves. Some 85 percent were former slaves who were fighting for the liberation of all slaves and the end of slavery. When given the opportunity to serve, many black regiments did so heroically. One such regiment, the Fifty-Fourth Regiment of Massachusetts Volunteers, distinguished itself at Fort Wagner in South Carolina by fighting valiantly against an entrenched Confederate position. They willingly gave their lives for the cause.

The Confederacy, not surprisingly, showed no mercy to African American troops. In April 1864, Southern forces attempted to take Fort Pillow in Tennessee from the Union forces that had captured it in 1862. Confederate troops under Major General Nathan Bedford Forrest, the future founder of the Ku Klux Klan, quickly overran the fort, and the Union defenders surrendered. Instead of taking the African American soldiers prisoner, as they did the white soldiers, the Confederates executed them. The massacre outraged the North, and the Union refused to engage in any future exchanges of prisoners with the Confederacy.

African American and white soldiers of the Union army pose together in this photograph, although in reality, black soldiers were often kept separate and given only menial jobs.

THE CAMPAIGNS OF 1864 AND 1865

In the final years of the war, the Union continued its efforts on both the eastern and western fronts while bringing the war into the Deep South. Union forces increasingly engaged in total war, not distinguishing between military and civilian targets. They destroyed everything that lay in their path, committed to breaking the will of the Confederacy and forcing an end to the war. General Grant, mastermind of the Vicksburg campaign, took charge of the war effort. He understood the advantage of having large numbers of soldiers at his disposal and recognized that Union soldiers could be replaced, whereas the Confederates, whose smaller population was feeling the strain of the years of war, could not. Grant thus pushed forward relentlessly, despite huge losses of men. In 1864, Grant committed his forces to destroying Lee's army in Virginia.

In the Virginia campaign, Grant hoped to use his larger army to his advantage. But at the Battle of the Wilderness, fought from May 5 to May 7, Confederate forces stopped Grant's advance. Rather than retreating, he pushed forward. At the Battle of Spotsylvania on May 8 through 12, Grant again faced determined Confederate resistance, and again his advance was halted. As before, he renewed the Union campaign. At the Battle of Cold Harbor in early June, Grant had between 100,000 and 110,000 soldiers, whereas the Confederates had slightly more than half that number. Again, the Union advance was halted, if only momentarily, as Grant awaited reinforcements. An attack on the Confederate position on June 3 resulted in heavy casualties for the Union, and nine days later, Grant led his army away from Cold Harbor to Petersburg, Virginia, a rail center that supplied Richmond. The immense losses that Grant's forces suffered severely hurt Union morale. The war seemed unending, and with the tremendous loss of life, many in the North began to question the war and desire peace. Undaunted by the changing opinion in the North and hoping to destroy the Confederate rail network in the Upper South, however, Grant laid siege to Petersburg for nine months. As the months wore on, both sides dug in, creating miles of trenches and gun emplacements.

The other major Union campaigns of 1864 were more successful and gave President Lincoln the advantage that he needed to win reelection in November. In August 1864, the Union navy captured Mobile Bay. General Sherman invaded the Deep South, advancing slowly from Tennessee into Georgia, confronted at every turn by the Confederates, who were commanded by Johnston. When President Davis replaced Johnston with General John B. Hood, the Confederates made a daring but ultimately costly direct attack on the Union army that failed to drive out the invaders. Atlanta fell to Union forces on September 2, 1864. The fall of Atlanta held tremendous significance for the war-weary Union and helped to reverse the North's sinking morale. In keeping with the logic of total war, Sherman's forces cut a swath of destruction to Savannah. On **Sherman's March to the Sea**, the Union army, seeking to demoralize the South, destroyed everything in its path, despite strict instructions regarding the preservation of civilian property. Although towns were left standing, houses and barns were burned. Homes were looted, food was stolen, crops were destroyed, orchards were burned, and livestock was killed or confiscated. Savannah fell on December 21, 1864—a Christmas gift for Lincoln, Sherman proclaimed. In 1865, Sherman's forces invaded South Carolina, capturing Charleston and Columbia. In Columbia, the state capital, the Union army burned slaveholders' homes and destroyed much of the city. From South Carolina, Sherman's force moved north in an effort to join Grant and destroy Lee's army.

Dolly Sumner Lunt on Sherman's March to the Sea

The following account is by Dolly Sumner Lunt, a widow who ran her Georgia cotton plantation after the death of her husband. She describes General Sherman's march to Savannah, where he enacted the policy of total war by burning and plundering the landscape to inhibit the Confederates' ability to keep fighting.

> Alas! little did I think while trying to save my house from plunder and fire that they were forcing my boys [slaves] from home at the point of the bayonet. One, Newton, jumped into bed in his cabin, and declared himself sick. Another crawled under the floor,—a lame boy he was,—but they pulled him out, placed him on a horse, and drove him off. Mid, poor Mid! The last I saw of him, a man had him going around the garden, looking, as I thought, for my sheep, as he was my shepherd. Jack came crying to me, the big tears coursing down his cheeks, saying they were making him go. I said: 'Stay in my room.'
>
> But a man followed in, cursing him and threatening to shoot him if he did not go; so poor Jack had to yield. . . .
>
> Sherman himself and a greater portion of his army passed my house that day. All day, as the sad moments rolled on, were they passing not only in front of my house, but from behind; they tore down my garden palings, made a road through my back-yard and lot field, driving their stock and riding through, tearing down my fences and desolating my home—wantonly doing it when there was no necessity for it. . . .
>
> About ten o'clock they had all passed save one, who came in and wanted coffee made, which was done, and he, too, went on. A few minutes elapsed, and two couriers riding rapidly passed back. Then, presently, more soldiers came by, and this ended the passing of Sherman's army by my place, leaving me poorer by thirty thousand dollars than I was yesterday morning. And a much stronger Rebel!

According to this account, what was the reaction of slaves to the arrival of the Union forces? What did the Union forces do with the slaves? For Lunt, did the strategy of total war work as planned?

THE ELECTION OF 1864

Despite the military successes for the Union army in 1863, in 1864, Lincoln's status among many Northern voters plummeted. Citing the suspension of the writ of habeas corpus, many saw him as a dictator, bent on grabbing power while senselessly and uncaringly drafting more young men into combat. Arguably, his greatest liability, however, was the Emancipation Proclamation and the enlistment of African American soldiers. Many whites in the North found this deeply offensive, since they still believed in racial inequality. The 1863 **New York City Draft Riots** illustrated the depth of white anger.

Northern Democrats railed against Lincoln and the war. Republicans labeled these vocal opponents of the President **Copperheads**, a term that many antiwar Democrats accepted. As the anti-Lincoln poster below illustrates, his enemies tried to paint him as an untrustworthy and suspect leader. It seemed to most in the North that the Democratic candidate, General George B. McClellan, who did not support abolition and was replaced with another commander by Lincoln, would win the election.

The Republican Party also split over the issue of reelecting Lincoln. Those who found him timid and indecisive, and favored extending full rights to African Americans, as well as completely refashioning the South after its defeat, earned the name Radicals. A moderate faction of Republicans opposed the Radicals. For his part, Lincoln did not align himself with either group.

The tide of the election campaign turned in favor of Lincoln, however, in the fall of 1864. Above all else, Union victories, including the fall of Atlanta in September and General Philip Sheridan's successes in the Shenandoah Valley of Virginia, bolstered Lincoln's popularity and his reelection bid. In November 1864, despite earlier forecasts to the contrary, Lincoln was reelected. Lincoln won all but three states—New Jersey and the border states of Delaware and Kentucky. To the chagrin of his opponent, McClellan, even Union army troops voted overwhelmingly for the incumbent President.

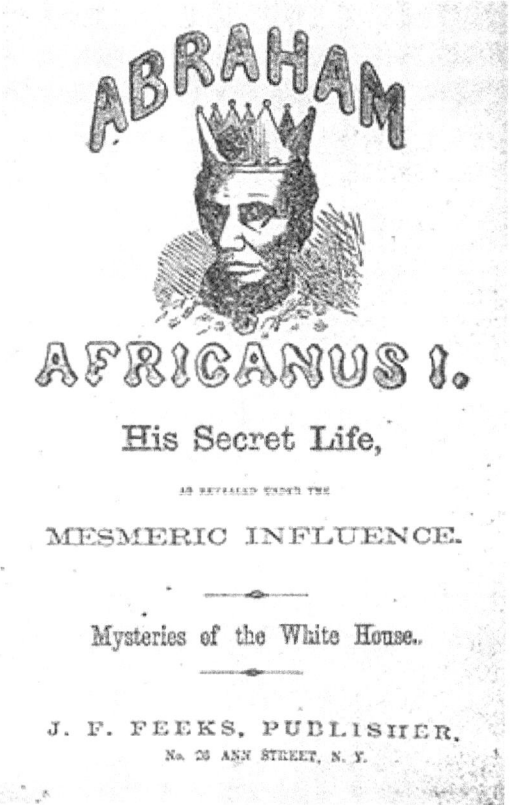

Anti-Lincoln sentiment in the North ran high in 1864, and many believed he would not be reelected president that year.

THE WAR ENDS

By the spring of 1865, it had become clear to both sides that the Confederacy could not last much longer. Most of its major cities, ports, and industrial centers—Atlanta, Savannah, Charleston, Columbia, Mobile, New Orleans, and Memphis—had been captured. In April 1865, Lee had abandoned both Petersburg and

Richmond. His goal in doing so was to unite his depleted army with Confederate forces commanded by General Johnston. Grant effectively cut him off. On April 9, 1865, Lee surrendered to Grant at Appomattox Court House in Virginia. By that time, he had fewer than 35,000 soldiers, while Grant had some 100,000. Meanwhile, Sherman's army proceeded to North Carolina, where General Johnston surrendered on April 19, 1865. The Civil War had come to an end. The war had cost the lives of more than 600,000 soldiers. Many more had been wounded. Thousands of women were left widowed. Children were left without fathers, and many parents were deprived of a source of support in their old age. In some areas, where local volunteer units had marched off to battle, never to return, an entire generation of young women was left without marriage partners. Millions of dollars' worth of property had been destroyed, and towns and cities were laid to waste. With the conflict finally over, the very difficult work of reconciling North and South and reestablishing the United States lay ahead.

Vastly outnumbered by the Union army, the Confederate general Robert E. Lee (seated at the left) surrendered to Ulysses S. Grant at Appomattox Courthouse. (credit: "Alaskan Dude"/Wikimedia Commons)

Section Summary

Having failed to win the support it expected from either Great Britain or France, the Confederacy faced a long war with limited resources and no allies. Lincoln won reelection in 1864, and continued to pursue the Union campaign, not only in the east and west, but also with a drive into the South under the leadership of General Sherman, whose March to the Sea through Georgia destroyed everything in its path. Cut off and outnumbered, Confederate general Lee surrendered to Union general Grant on April 9 at Appomattox Court House in Virginia. Within days of Lee's surrender, Confederate troops had lay down their arms, and the devastating war came to a close.

https://www.openassessments.org/assessments/998

Critical Thinking Questions

1. Could the differences between the North and South have been worked out in late 1860 and 1861? Could war have been avoided? Provide evidence to support your answer.

2. Why did the North prevail in the Civil War? What might have turned the tide of the war *against* the North?

3. If you were in charge of the Confederate war effort, what strategy or strategies would you have pursued? Conversely, if you had to devise the Union strategy, what would you propose? How does your answer depend on your knowledge of how the war actually played out?

4. What do you believe to be the enduring qualities of the Gettysburg Address? Why has this two-minute speech so endured?

5. What role did women and African Americans play in the war?

Glossary

Copperheads Democrats who opposed Lincoln in the 1864 election

Sherman's March to the Sea the scorched-earth campaign employed in Georgia by Union general William Tecumseh Sherman

Attributions

CC licensed content, Shared previously

- US History. **Authored by**: P. Scott Corbett, Volker Janssen, John M. Lund, Todd Pfannestiel, Paul Vickery, and Sylvie Waskiewicz. **Provided by**: OpenStax College. **Located at**: http://openstaxcollege.org/textbooks/us-history. **License**: *CC BY: Attribution*. **License Terms**: Download for free at http://cnx.org/content/col11740/latest/

Primary Source Reading: The Emancipation Proclamation

Introduction

The Emancipation Proclamation was a presidential proclamation and executive order issued by President Abraham Lincoln on January 1, 1863, as a war measure during the American Civil War, directed to all of the areas in rebellion and all segments of the executive branch (including the Army and Navy) of the United States. It proclaimed the freedom of slaves in the ten states that were still in rebellion. Because it was issued under the President's war powers, it necessarily excluded areas not in rebellion – it applied to more than 3 million of the 4 million slaves in the U.S. at the time. The Proclamation was based on the president's constitutional authority as commander in chief of the armed forces; it was not a law passed by Congress. The Proclamation also ordered that suitable persons among those freed could be enrolled into the paid service of United States' forces, and ordered the Union Army (and all segments of the Executive branch) to "recognize and maintain the freedom of" the ex-slaves. The Proclamation did not compensate the owners, did not outlaw slavery, and did not grant citizenship to the ex-slaves (called freedmen). It made the eradication of slavery an explicit war goal, in addition to the goal of reuniting the Union.

https://en.wikipedia.org/wiki/Emancipation_Proclamation

The Proclamation

The Emancipation Proclamation is the popular name given to two complementary Presidential Proclamations issued 100 days apart from each other by United States President Abraham Lincoln during the American Civil War. These are officially known as Proclamation 93 and Proclamation 95.

Proclamation 93, the preliminary Emancipation Proclamation, was issued on September 22, 1862. It declared the freedom of all slaves in any state of the Confederate States of America as did not return to Union control by January 1, 1863. Proclamation 95, the final Emancipation Proclamation was issued on January 1, 1863. This enumerated the specific states where it applied.

Proclamation 95

By the President of the United States of America:

A PROCLAMATION.

Whereas, on the twenty-second day of September, in the year of our Lord one thousand eight hundred and sixty-two, a proclamation was issued by the President of the United States, containing, among other things, the following, to wit:

"That on the first day of January, in the year of our Lord one thousand eight hundred and sixty-three, all persons held as slaves within any State or designated part of a State, the people whereof shall then be in rebellion against the United States, shall be then, thenceforward, and forever free; and the Executive Government of the United States, including the military and naval authority thereof, will recognize and maintain the freedom of such persons, and will do no act or acts to repress such persons, or any of them, in any efforts they may make for their actual freedom.

"That the Executive will, on the first day of January aforesaid, by proclamation, designate the States and parts of States, if any, in which the people thereof, respectively, shall then be in rebellion against the United States; and the fact that any State, or the people thereof, shall on that day be, in good faith, represented in the Congress of the United States by members chosen thereto at elections wherein a majority of the qualified voters of such State shall have participated, shall, in the absence of strong countervailing testimony, be deemed conclusive evidence that such State, and the people thereof, are not then in rebellion against the United States."

Now, Therefore, I, Abraham Lincoln, President of the United States, by virtue of the power in me vested as Commander-in-Chief, of the Army and Navy of the United States in time of actual armed rebellion against the authority and government of the United States, and as a fit and necessary war measure for suppressing said rebellion, do, on this first day of January, in the year of our Lord one thousand eight hundred and sixty-three, and in accordance with my purpose so to do publicly proclaimed for the full period of one hundred days, from the day first above mentioned, order and designate as the States and parts of States wherein the people thereof respectively, are this day in rebellion against the United States, the following, to wit:

Arkansas, Texas, Louisiana (except the parishes of St. Bernard, Plaquemines, Jefferson, St. John, St. Charles, St. James, Ascension, Assumption, Terrebone, Lafourche, St. Mary, St. Martin, and Orleans, including the city of New Orleans), Mississippi, Alabama, Florida, Georgia, South Carolina, North Carolina, and Virginia (except the forty-eight counties designated as West Virginia, and also the counties of Berkeley, Accomac, Northhampton, Elizabeth City, York, Princess Anne, and Norfolk, including the cities of Norfolk and Portsmouth), and which excepted parts, are for the present, left precisely as if this proclamation were not issued.

And by virtue of the power, and for the purpose aforesaid, I do order and declare that all persons held as slaves within said designated States, and parts of States, are, and henceforward shall be free; and that the Executive government of the United States, including the military and naval authorities thereof, will recognize and maintain the freedom of said persons.

And I hereby enjoin upon the people so declared to be free to abstain from all violence, unless in necessary self-defence; and I recommend to them that, in all cases when allowed, they labor faithfully for reasonable wages.

And I further declare and make known, that such persons of suitable condition, will be received into the armed service of the United States to garrison forts, positions, stations, and other places, and to man vessels of all sorts in said service.

And upon this act, sincerely believed to be an act of justice, warranted by the Constitution, upon military necessity, I invoke the considerate judgment of mankind, and the gracious favor of Almighty God.

In Witness Whereof, I have hereunto set my hand and caused the seal of the United States to be affixed.

Done US Great Seal 1877 drawing.png at the City of Washington, this first day of January, in the year of our Lord one thousand eight hundred and sixty three, and of the Independence of the United States of America the eighty-seventh.

[Abraham Lincoln]

By the President:
William H. Seward,
Secretary of State.
Attributions

CC licensed content, Shared previously

- Introduction to the Emancipation Proclamation. **Provided by**: Wikipedia. **Located at**: https://en.wikipedia.org/wiki/Emancipation_Proclamation. **License**: *CC BY-SA: Attribution-ShareAlike*

Public domain content

- The Emancipation Proclamation. **Provided by**: Wikisource. **Located at**: https://en.wikisource.org/wiki/The_Emancipation_Proclamation. **License**: *Public Domain: No Known Copyright*

Primary Source Reading: Lincoln's 2nd Inaugural Address

Lincoln, 2nd Inaugural Address (1865)

Introduction

Abraham Lincoln delivered his second inaugural address on March 4, 1865, during his second inauguration as President of the United States. At a time when victory over the secessionists in the American Civil War was within days and slavery was near an end, Lincoln did not speak of happiness, but of sadness. Some see this speech as a defense of his pragmatic approach to Reconstruction, in which he sought to avoid harsh treatment of the defeated South by reminding his listeners of how wrong both sides had been in imagining what lay before them when the war began four years earlier. Lincoln balanced that rejection of triumphalism, however, with recognition of the unmistakable evil of slavery, which he described in the most concrete terms possible. John Wilkes Booth, David Herold, George Atzerodt, Lewis Paine, John Surratt and Edmund Spangler, some of the conspirators involved with Lincoln's assassination, were present in the crowd at the inauguration. The address is inscribed, along with the Gettysburg Address, in the Lincoln Memorial.

Source

Fellow Countrymen:

At this second appearing to take the oath of the presidential office, there is less occasion for an extended address than there was at the first. Then a statement, somewhat in detail, of a course to be pursued, seemed fitting and proper. Now, at the expiration of four years, during which public declarations have been constantly called forth on every point and phase of the great contest which still absorbs the attention, and engrosses the energies [sic] of the nation, little that is new could be presented. The progress of our arms, upon which all else chiefly depends, is as well known to the public as to myself; and it is, I trust, reasonably satisfactory and encouraging to all. With high hope for the future, no prediction in regard to it so ventured.

On the occasion corresponding to this four years ago, all thoughts were anxiously directed to an impending civil-war. All dreaded it–all sought to avert it. While the inaugural address was being delivered from this place, devoted altogether to saving the Union without war, insurgent agents were in the city seeking to destroy it without war–seeking to dissolve the Union, and divide effects, by negotiation. Both parties deprecated war; but one of them would make war rather than let the nation survive; and others would accept war rather than let it perish. And the war came.

One eighth of the whole population were colored slaves, not distributed generally over the Union, but localized in the Southern part of it. These slaves constituted a peculiar and powerful interest. All knew that this interest was somehow, the cause of the war. To strengthen, perpetuate, and extend this interest was the object for which the insurgents would rend the Union, even by war; while the government claimed no right to do more than to restrict the territorial enlargement of it. Neither party expected for the war, the magnitude, or the duration, which it has already attained. Neither anticipated that the cause of the conflict might cease with, or even before, the conflict itself should cease. Each looked for an easier triumph, and a result less fundamental and astounding. Both read the same Bible, and pray to the same God; and each invokes His aid against the other. It may seem strange that any men should dare ask a just God s assistance in wringing their bread from the sweat of other men's faces; but let us judge not that we will be not judged. The prayers of both could not be answered; that of neither has been answered fully. The Almighty has His own purposes. Woe unto the world because of offenses! for it must needs be that offenses come; but woe to that man by whom the offense cometh! (2) If we shall suppose that American Slavery is one of those offenses which, in the providence of God, must needs come, but which, having continued through His appointed time, He now wills to remove, and that He gives to both North and South, this terrible war, as the woe due to those by whom the offense came, shall we discern therein any departure from those divine attributes which the believers in a Living God always ascribe to Him? Fondly do we hope–fervently do we pray–that this mighty scourge of war may speedily pass away. Yet, if God wills that it continue, until all the wealth piled by the bond-man s two hundred and fifty years of unrequited toil shall be sunk, and until every drop of blood drawn with the lash, shall be paid by another drawn with the sword, as was said three thousand years ago, so still it must be said the judgments of the Lord, are true and righteous altogether.

With malice toward none; with charity for all; with firmness in the right, as God gives us to see the right, let us strive on to finish the work we are in, to bind up the nation s wounds; to care for him who shall have borne the battle, and for his widow, and his orphan–to do all which may achieve and cherish a just, and a lasting piece, among ourselves, and with all nations.

Notes

(1) Matthew 7:1.

(2) Matthew 18:7.

(3) Psalms 19:9

Attributions

Public domain content

- Abraham Lincoln: Second Inaugural Address, March 4, 1865. **Authored by**: Abraham Lincoln. **Located at**: http://legacy.fordham.edu/Halsall/mod/1865lincoln-aug2.asp. **Project**: Internet Modern History Sourcebook. **License**: *Public Domain: No Known Copyright*

Primary Source Reading: Stephens' Cornerstone Address

Alexander H. Stephens (1812-1883): Cornerstone Address, March 21, 1861

Introduction

The Cornerstone Speech, also known as the Cornerstone Address, was an oration delivered by Confederate Vice President Alexander Stephens at the Athenaeum in Savannah, Georgia on March 21, 1861.

Delivered extemporaneously a few weeks before the Confederacy would start the American Civil War by firing on the U.S. Army at Fort Sumter, Stephens' speech explained what the fundamental differences were between the constitutions of the Confederacy and that of the United States, contrasts between U.S. and Confederate ideologies and beliefs, laid out the Confederacy's causes for starting the American Civil War, and defended slavery.

Source

Alexander H. Stephens (1812-1883), although originally opposed to secession, was elected vice-president of the Confederacy. After the war he returned to political service in Georgia and in the House of Representatives. He was elected governor of Georgia in 1882 and died in office.

We are in the midst of one of the greatest epochs in our history. The last ninety days will mark one of the most memorable eras in the history of modern civilization.

... we are passing through one of the greatest revolutions in the annals of the world-seven States have, within the last three months, thrown off an old Government and formed a new. This revolution has been signally marked, up to this time, by the fact of its having been accomplished without the loss of a single drop of blood. [Applause.] This new Constitution, or form of government, constitutes the subject to which your attention will be partly invited.

In reference to it, I make this first general remark: It amply secures all our ancient rights, franchises, and privileges. All the great principles of Magna Chartal are retained in it. No citizen is deprived of life, liberty, or property, but by the judgment of his peers, under the laws of the land. The great principle of religious liberty, which was the honor and pride of the old Constitution, is still maintained and secured. All the essentials of the old Constitution, which have endeared it to the hearts of the American people, have been preserved and perpetuated.... So, taking the whole new Constitution, I have no hesitancy in giving it as my judgment, that it is decidedly better than the old. [Applause.] Allow me briefly to allude to some of these improvements. The question of building up class interests, or fostering one branch of industry to the prejudice of another, under the exercise of the revenue power, which gave us so much trouble under the old Constitution, is put at rest forever under the new. We allow the imposition of no duty with a view of giving advantage to one class of persons, in any trade or business, over those of another. All, under our system, stand upon the same broad principles of perfect equality. Honest labor and enterprise are left free and unrestricted in whatever pursuit they may be engaged in ....

But not to be tedious in enumerating the numerous changes for the better, allow me to allude to one other-though last, not least: the new Constitution has put at rest forever all the agitating questions relating to our peculiar institutions-African slavery as it exists among us-the proper status of the negro in our form of civilization. This was the immediate cause of the late rupture and present revolution. Jefferson, in his forecast, had anticipated this, as the "rock upon which the old Union would split." He was right. What was conjecture with him, is now a realized fact. But whether he fully comprehended the great truth upon which that rock stood and stands, may be doubted. The prevailing ideas entertained by him and most of the leading statesmen at the time of the formation of the old Constitution were, that the enslavement of the African was in violation of the laws of nature; that it was wrong in principle, socially, morally and politically. It was an evil they knew not well how to deal with; but the general opinion of the men of that day was, that, somehow or other, in the order of Providence, the institution would be evanescent and pass away. This idea, though not incorporated in the Constitution, was the prevailing idea at the time. The Constitution, it is true, secured every essential guarantee to the institution while it should last, and hence no argument can be justly used against the constitutional guarantees thus secured, because of the common sentiment of the day. Those ideas, however, were fundamentally wrong. They rested upon the assumption of the equality of races. This was an error. It was a sandy foundation, and the idea of a Government built upon it-when the "storm came and the wind blew, it fell."

Our new Government is founded upon exactly the opposite ideas; its foundations are laid, its cornerstone rests, upon the great truth that the negro is not equal to the white man; that slavery, subordination to the superior race, is his natural and moral condition. [Applause.] This, our new Government, is the first, in the history of the world, based upon this great physical, philosophical, and moral truth. This truth has been slow in the process of its development, like all other truths in the various departments of science. It is so even amongst us. Many who hear me, perhaps, can recollect well that this truth was not generally admitted, even within their day. The errors of the past generation still clung to many as late as twenty years ago. Those at the North who still cling to these errors with a zeal above knowledge, we justly denominate fanatics. All fanaticism springs from an aberration of the mind; from a defect in reasoning. It is a species of insanity. One of the most striking characteristics of insanity, in many instances, is, forming correct conclusions from fancied or erroneous premises; so with the anti-slavery fanatics: their conclusions are right if their premises are. They assume that the negro is equal, and hence conclude that he is entitled to equal privileges and rights, with the white man.... I recollect once of having heard a gentleman from one of the Northern States, of great power and ability, announce in the House of Representatives, with imposing effect, that we of the South would be compelled, ultimately, to yield upon this subject of slavery; that it was as impossible to war successfully against a principle in politics, as it was in physics or mechanics. That the principle would ultimately prevail. That we, in maintaining slavery as it exists with us, were warring against a principle-a principle founded in nature, the principle of the equality of man. The reply I made to him was, that upon his own grounds we should succeed, and that he and his associates in their crusade against our institutions would ultimately fail. The truth announced, that it was as impossible to war successfully against a principle in politics as well as in physics and mechanics, I admitted, but told him it was he and those acting with him who were warring against a principle. They were attempting to make things equal which the Creator had made unequal.

In the conflict thus far, success has been on our side, complete throughout the length and breadth of the Confederate States. It is upon this, as I have stated, our social fabric is firmly planted; and I cannot permit myself to doubt the ultimate success of a full recognition of this principle throughout the civilized and enlightened world.

As I have stated, the truth of this principle may be slow in development, as all truths are, and ever have been, in the various branches of science. It was so with the principles announced by Galileo-it was so with Adam Smith and his principles of political economy. It was so with Harvey, and his theory of the circulation of the blood. It is stated that not a single one of the medical profession, living at the time of the announcement of the truths made by him, admitted them. Now, they are universally acknowledged. May we not therefore look with confidence to the ultimate universal acknowledgment of the truths upon which our system rests? It is the first Government ever instituted upon principles in strict conformity to nature, and the ordination of Providence, in furnishing the materials of human society. Many Governments have been founded upon the principles of certain classes; but the classes thus enslaved, were of the same race, and in violation of the laws of nature. Our system commits no such violation of nature's laws. The negro by nature, or by the curse against Canaan, [note: A reference to Genesis, 9:20-27, which was used as a justification for slavery] is fitted for that condition which he occupies in our system. The architect, in the construction of buildings, lays the foundation with the proper material-the granite-then comes the brick or the marble. The substratum of our society is made of the material fitted by nature for it, and by experience we know that it is the best, not only for the superior but for the inferior race, that it should be so. It is, indeed, in conformity with the Creator. It is not for us to inquire into the wisdom of His ordinances or to question them. For His own purposes He has made one race to differ from another, as He has made "one star to differ from another in glory."

The great objects of humanity are best attained, when conformed to his laws and degrees [sic], in the formation of Governments as well as in all things else. Our Confederacy is founded upon principles in strict conformity with these laws. This stone which was rejected by the first builders "is become the chief stone of the corner" in our new edifice.

Source: Alexander H. Stephens, "Cornerstone Address, March 21, 1861 " in The Rebellion Record: A Diary of American Events with Documents, Narratives, Illustrative Incidents, Poetry, etc., vol. 1, ed. Frank Moore (New York: O.P. Putnam, 1862), pp. 44-46.

This text is part of the Internet Modern History Sourcebook. The Sourcebook is a collection of public domain and copy-permitted texts for introductory level classes in modern European and World history.

Unless otherwise indicated the specific electronic form of the document is copyright. Permission is granted for electronic copying, distribution in print form for educational purposes and personal use. If you do reduplicate the document, indicate the source. No permission is granted for commercial use of the Sourcebook. © Paul Halsall, July 1998

Attributions

CC licensed content, Shared previously

- Introduction to the Cornerstone Speech. **Provided by**: Wikipedia. **Located at**: https://en.wikipedia.org/wiki/Cornerstone_Speech. **License**: *CC BY-SA: Attribution-ShareAlike*

Public domain content

- Alexander H. Stephens (1812-1883): Cornerstone Address, March 21, 1861. **Located at**: http://www.southalabama.edu/history/faculty/faust/Alexander%20Stephens%20Cornerstone%20Address,%201861.html. **Project**: Internet Modern History Sourcebook. **License**: *Public Domain: No Known Copyright*

Appendices

The Declaration of Independence

When in the Course of human events, it becomes necessary for one people to dissolve the political bands which have connected them with another, and to assume among the powers of the earth, the separate and equal station to which the Laws of Nature and of Nature's God entitle them, a decent respect to the opinions of mankind requires that they should declare the causes which impel them to the separation.

We hold these truths to be self-evident, that all men are created equal, that they are endowed by their Creator with certain unalienable Rights, that among these are Life, Liberty and the pursuit of Happiness. —That to secure these rights, Governments are instituted among Men, deriving their just powers from the consent of the governed, —That whenever any Form of Government becomes destructive of these ends, it is the Right of the People to alter or to abolish it, and to institute new Government, laying its foundation on such principles and organizing its powers in such form, as to them shall seem most likely to effect their Safety and Happiness. Prudence, indeed, will dictate that Governments long established should not be changed for light and transient causes; and accordingly all experience hath shewn, that mankind are more disposed to suffer, while evils are sufferable, than to right themselves by abolishing the forms to which they are accustomed. But when a long train of abuses and usurpations, pursuing invariably the same Object evinces a design to reduce them under absolute Despotism, it is their right, it is their duty, to throw off such Government, and to provide new Guards for their future security. —Such has been the patient sufferance of these Colonies; and such is now the necessity which constrains them to alter their former Systems of Government. The history of the present King of Great Britain is a history of repeated injuries and usurpations, all having in direct object the establishment of an absolute Tyranny over these States. To prove this, let Facts be submitted to a candid world.

He has refused his Assent to Laws, the most wholesome and necessary for the public good.

He has forbidden his Governors to pass Laws of immediate and pressing importance, unless suspended in their operation till his Assent should be obtained; and when so suspended, he has utterly neglected to attend to them.

He has refused to pass other Laws for the accommodation of large districts of people, unless those people would relinquish the right of Representation in the Legislature, a right inestimable to them and formidable to tyrants only.

He has called together legislative bodies at places unusual, uncomfortable, and distant from the depository of their public Records, for the sole purpose of fatiguing them into compliance with his measures.

He has dissolved Representative Houses repeatedly, for opposing with manly firmness his invasions on the rights of the people.

He has refused for a long time, after such dissolutions, to cause others to be elected; whereby the Legislative powers, incapable of Annihilation, have returned to the People at large for their exercise; the State remaining in the mean time exposed to all the dangers of invasion from without, and convulsions within.

He has endeavoured to prevent the population of these States; for that purpose obstructing the Laws for Naturalization of Foreigners; refusing to pass others to encourage their migrations hither, and raising the conditions of new Appropriations of Lands.

He has obstructed the Administration of Justice, by refusing his Assent to Laws for establishing Judiciary powers.

He has made Judges dependent on his Will alone, for the tenure of their offices, and the amount and payment of their salaries.

He has erected a multitude of New Offices, and sent hither swarms of Officers to harrass our people, and eat out their substance.

He has kept among us, in times of peace, Standing Armies without the Consent of our legislatures.

He has affected to render the Military independent of and superior to the Civil power.

He has combined with others to subject us to a jurisdiction foreign to our constitution, and unacknowledged by our laws; giving his Assent to their Acts of pretended Legislation:

For Quartering large bodies of armed troops among us:

For protecting them, by a mock Trial, from punishment for any Murders which they should commit on the Inhabitants of these States:

For cutting off our Trade with all parts of the world:

For imposing Taxes on us without our Consent:

For depriving us in many cases, of the benefits of Trial by Jury:

For transporting us beyond Seas to be tried for pretended offences:

For abolishing the free System of English Laws in a neighbouring Province, establishing therein an Arbitrary government, and enlarging its Boundaries so as to render it at once an example and fit instrument for introducing the same absolute rule into these Colonies:

For taking away our Charters, abolishing our most valuable Laws, and altering fundamentally the Forms of our Governments:

For suspending our own Legislatures, and declaring themselves invested with power to legislate for us in all cases whatsoever.

He has abdicated Government here, by declaring us out of his Protection and waging War against us.

He has plundered our seas, ravaged our Coasts, burnt our towns, and destroyed the lives of our people.

He is at this time transporting large Armies of foreign Mercenaries to compleat the works of death, desolation and tyranny, already begun with circumstances of Cruelty & perfidy scarcely paralleled in the most barbarous ages, and totally unworthy the Head of a civilized nation.

He has constrained our fellow Citizens taken Captive on the high Seas to bear Arms against their Country, to become the executioners of their friends and Brethren, or to fall themselves by their Hands.

He has excited domestic insurrections amongst us, and has endeavoured to bring on the inhabitants of our frontiers, the merciless Indian Savages, whose known rule of warfare, is an undistinguished destruction of all ages, sexes and conditions.

In every stage of these Oppressions We have Petitioned for Redress in the most humble terms: Our repeated Petitions have been answered only by repeated injury. A Prince whose character is thus marked by every act which may define a Tyrant, is unfit to be the ruler of a free people.

Nor have We been wanting in attentions to our Brittish brethren. We have warned them from time to time of attempts by their legislature to extend an unwarrantable jurisdiction over us. We have reminded them of the circumstances of our emigration and settlement here. We have appealed to their native justice and magnanimity, and we have conjured them by the ties of our common kindred to disavow these usurpations, which, would inevitably interrupt our connections and correspondence. They too have been deaf to the voice of justice and of consanguinity. We must, therefore, acquiesce in the necessity, which denounces our Separation, and hold them, as we hold the rest of mankind, Enemies in War, in Peace Friends.

We, therefore, the Representatives of the united States of America, in General Congress, Assembled, appealing to the Supreme Judge of the world for the rectitude of our intentions, do, in the Name, and by Authority of the good People of these Colonies, solemnly publish and declare, That these United Colonies are, and of Right ought to be Free and Independent States; that they are Absolved from all Allegiance to the British Crown, and that all political connection between them and the State of Great Britain, is and ought to be totally dissolved; and that as Free and Independent States, they have full Power to levy War, conclude Peace, contract Alliances, establish Commerce, and to do all other Acts and Things which Independent States may of right do. And for the support of this Declaration, with a firm reliance on the protection of divine Providence, we mutually pledge to each other our Lives, our Fortunes and our sacred Honor.

The 56 signatures on the Declaration appear in the positions indicated:

Column 1
Georgia:
Button Gwinnett
Lyman Hall
George Walton
Column 2
North Carolina:

William Hooper
Joseph Hewes
John Penn
South Carolina:
Edward Rutledge
Thomas Heyward, Jr.
Thomas Lynch, Jr.
Arthur Middleton
Column 3
Massachusetts:
John Hancock
Maryland:
Samuel Chase
William Paca
Thomas Stone
Charles Carroll of Carrollton
Virginia:
George Wythe
Richard Henry Lee
Thomas Jefferson
Benjamin Harrison
Thomas Nelson, Jr.
Francis Lightfoot Lee
Carter Braxton
Column 4
Pennsylvania:
Robert Morris
Benjamin Rush
Benjamin Franklin
John Morton
George Clymer
James Smith
George Taylor
James Wilson
George Ross
Delaware:
Caesar Rodney
George Read
Thomas McKean
Column 5
New York:
William Floyd
Philip Livingston
Francis Lewis
Lewis Morris
New Jersey:

Richard Stockton
John Witherspoon
Francis Hopkinson
John Hart
Abraham Clark
Column 6
New Hampshire:
Josiah Bartlett
William Whipple
Massachusetts:
Samuel Adams
John Adams
Robert Treat Paine
Elbridge Gerry
Rhode Island:
Stephen Hopkins
William Ellery
Connecticut:
Roger Sherman
Samuel Huntington
William Williams
Oliver Wolcott
New Hampshire:
Matthew Thornton

Attributions

CC licensed content, Shared previously

- US History. **Authored by**: P. Scott Corbett, Volker Janssen, John M. Lund, Todd Pfannestiel, Paul Vickery, and Sylvie Waskiewicz. **Provided by**: OpenStax College. **Located at**: http://openstaxcollege.org/textbooks/us-history. **License**: *CC BY: Attribution*. **License Terms**: Download for free at http://cnx.org/content/col11740/latest/

The Constitution of the United States

We the People of the United States, in Order to form a more perfect Union, establish Justice, insure domestic Tranquility, provide for the common defence, promote the general Welfare, and secure the Blessings of Liberty to ourselves and our Posterity, do ordain and establish this Constitution for the United States of America.

Article. I.

Section. 1.

All legislative Powers herein granted shall be vested in a Congress of the United States, which shall consist of a Senate and House of Representatives.

Section. 2.

The House of Representatives shall be composed of Members chosen every second Year by the People of the several States, and the Electors in each State shall have the Qualifications requisite for Electors of the most numerous Branch of the State Legislature.

No Person shall be a Representative who shall not have attained to the Age of twenty five Years, and been seven Years a Citizen of the United States, and who shall not, when elected, be an Inhabitant of that State in which he shall be chosen.

Representatives and direct Taxes shall be apportioned among the several States which may be included within this Union, according to their respective Numbers, which shall be determined by adding to the whole Number of free Persons, including those bound to Service for a Term of Years, and excluding Indians not taxed, three fifths of all other Persons. The actual Enumeration shall be made within three Years after the first Meeting of the Congress of the United States, and within every subsequent Term of ten Years, in such Manner as they shall by Law direct. The Number of Representatives shall not exceed one for every thirty Thousand, but each State shall have at Least one Representative; and until such enumeration shall be made, the State of New Hampshire shall be entitled to chuse three, Massachusetts eight, Rhode-Island and Providence Plantations one, Connecticut five, New-York six, New Jersey four, Pennsylvania eight, Delaware one, Maryland six, Virginia ten, North Carolina five, South Carolina five, and Georgia three.

When vacancies happen in the Representation from any State, the Executive Authority thereof shall issue Writs of Election to fill such Vacancies.

The House of Representatives shall chuse their Speaker and other Officers; and shall have the sole Power of Impeachment.

Section. 3.

The Senate of the United States shall be composed of two Senators from each State, chosen by the Legislature thereof, for six Years; and each Senator shall have one Vote.

Immediately after they shall be assembled in Consequence of the first Election, they shall be divided as equally as may be into three Classes. The Seats of the Senators of the first Class shall be vacated at the Expiration of the second Year, of the second Class at the Expiration of the fourth Year, and of the third Class at the Expiration of the sixth Year, so that one third may be chosen every second Year; and if Vacancies happen by Resignation, or otherwise, during the Recess of the Legislature of any State, the Executive thereof may make temporary Appointments until the next Meeting of the Legislature, which shall then fill such Vacancies.

No Person shall be a Senator who shall not have attained to the Age of thirty Years, and been nine Years a Citizen of the United States, and who shall not, when elected, be an Inhabitant of that State for which he shall be chosen.

The Vice President of the United States shall be President of the Senate, but shall have no Vote, unless they be equally divided.

The Senate shall chuse their other Officers, and also a President pro tempore, in the Absence of the Vice President, or when he shall exercise the Office of President of the United States.

The Senate shall have the sole Power to try all Impeachments. When sitting for that Purpose, they shall be on Oath or Affirmation. When the President of the United States is tried, the Chief Justice shall preside: And no Person shall be convicted without the Concurrence of two thirds of the Members present.

Judgment in Cases of Impeachment shall not extend further than to removal from Office, and disqualification to hold and enjoy any Office of honor, Trust or Profit under the United States: but the Party convicted shall nevertheless be liable and subject to Indictment, Trial, Judgment and Punishment, according to Law.

Section. 4.

The Times, Places and Manner of holding Elections for Senators and Representatives, shall be prescribed in each State by the Legislature thereof; but the Congress may at any time by Law make or alter such Regulations, except as to the Places of chusing Senators.

The Congress shall assemble at least once in every Year, and such Meeting shall be on the first Monday in December, unless they shall by Law appoint a different Day.

Section. 5.

Each House shall be the Judge of the Elections, Returns and Qualifications of its own Members, and a Majority of each shall constitute a Quorum to do Business; but a smaller Number may adjourn from day to day, and may be authorized to compel the Attendance of absent Members, in such Manner, and under such Penalties as each House may provide.

Each House may determine the Rules of its Proceedings, punish its Members for disorderly Behaviour, and, with the Concurrence of two thirds, expel a Member.

Each House shall keep a Journal of its Proceedings, and from time to time publish the same, excepting such Parts as may in their Judgment require Secrecy; and the Yeas and Nays of the Members of either House on any question shall, at the Desire of one fifth of those Present, be entered on the Journal.

Neither House, during the Session of Congress, shall, without the Consent of the other, adjourn for more than three days, nor to any other Place than that in which the two Houses shall be sitting.

Section. 6.

The Senators and Representatives shall receive a Compensation for their Services, to be ascertained by Law, and paid out of the Treasury of the United States. They shall in all Cases, except Treason, Felony and Breach of the Peace, be privileged from Arrest during their Attendance at the Session of their respective Houses, and in going to and returning from the same; and for any Speech or Debate in either House, they shall not be questioned in any other Place.

No Senator or Representative shall, during the Time for which he was elected, be appointed to any civil Office under the Authority of the United States, which shall have been created, or the Emoluments whereof shall have been encreased during such time; and no Person holding any Office under the United States, shall be a Member of either House during his Continuance in Office.

Section. 7.

All Bills for raising Revenue shall originate in the House of Representatives; but the Senate may propose or concur with Amendments as on other Bills.

Every Bill which shall have passed the House of Representatives and the Senate, shall, before it become a Law, be presented to the President of the United States; If he approve he shall sign it, but if not he shall return it, with his Objections to that House in which it shall have originated, who shall enter the Objections at large on their Journal, and proceed to reconsider it. If after such Reconsideration two thirds of that House shall agree to pass the Bill, it shall be sent, together with the Objections, to the other House, by which it shall likewise be reconsidered, and if approved by two thirds of that House, it shall become a Law. But in all such Cases the Votes of both Houses shall be determined by yeas and Nays, and the Names of the Persons voting for and against the Bill shall be entered on the Journal of each House respectively. If any Bill shall not be returned by the President within ten Days (Sundays excepted) after it shall have been presented to him, the Same shall be a Law, in like Manner as if he had signed it, unless the Congress by their Adjournment prevent its Return, in which Case it shall not be a Law.

Every Order, Resolution, or Vote to which the Concurrence of the Senate and House of Representatives may be necessary (except on a question of Adjournment) shall be presented to the President of the United

States; and before the Same shall take Effect, shall be approved by him, or being disapproved by him, shall be repassed by two thirds of the Senate and House of Representatives, according to the Rules and Limitations prescribed in the Case of a Bill.

Section. 8.

The Congress shall have Power To lay and collect Taxes, Duties, Imposts and Excises, to pay the Debts and provide for the common Defence and general Welfare of the United States; but all Duties, Imposts and Excises shall be uniform throughout the United States;

To borrow Money on the credit of the United States;

To regulate Commerce with foreign Nations, and among the several States, and with the Indian Tribes;

To establish an uniform Rule of Naturalization, and uniform Laws on the subject of Bankruptcies throughout the United States;

To coin Money, regulate the Value thereof, and of foreign Coin, and fix the Standard of Weights and Measures;

To provide for the Punishment of counterfeiting the Securities and current Coin of the United States;

To establish Post Offices and post Roads;

To promote the Progress of Science and useful Arts, by securing for limited Times to Authors and Inventors the exclusive Right to their respective Writings and Discoveries;

To constitute Tribunals inferior to the supreme Court;

To define and punish Piracies and Felonies committed on the high Seas, and Offences against the Law of Nations;

To declare War, grant Letters of Marque and Reprisal, and make Rules concerning Captures on Land and Water;

To raise and support Armies, but no Appropriation of Money to that Use shall be for a longer Term than two Years;

To provide and maintain a Navy;

To make Rules for the Government and Regulation of the land and naval Forces;

To provide for calling forth the Militia to execute the Laws of the Union, suppress Insurrections and repel Invasions;

To provide for organizing, arming, and disciplining, the Militia, and for governing such Part of them as may be employed in the Service of the United States, reserving to the States respectively, the Appointment of the Officers, and the Authority of training the Militia according to the discipline prescribed by Congress;

To exercise exclusive Legislation in all Cases whatsoever, over such District (not exceeding ten Miles square) as may, by Cession of particular States, and the Acceptance of Congress, become the Seat of the

Government of the United States, and to exercise like Authority over all Places purchased by the Consent of the Legislature of the State in which the Same shall be, for the Erection of Forts, Magazines, Arsenals, dock-Yards, and other needful Buildings;—And

To make all Laws which shall be necessary and proper for carrying into Execution the foregoing Powers, and all other Powers vested by this Constitution in the Government of the United States, or in any Department or Officer thereof.

Section. 9.

The Migration or Importation of such Persons as any of the States now existing shall think proper to admit, shall not be prohibited by the Congress prior to the Year one thousand eight hundred and eight, but a Tax or duty may be imposed on such Importation, not exceeding ten dollars for each Person.

The Privilege of the Writ of Habeas Corpus shall not be suspended, unless when in Cases of Rebellion or Invasion the public Safety may require it.

No Bill of Attainder or ex post facto Law shall be passed.

No Capitation, or other direct, Tax shall be laid, unless in Proportion to the Census or enumeration herein before directed to be taken.

No Tax or Duty shall be laid on Articles exported from any State.

No Preference shall be given by any Regulation of Commerce or Revenue to the Ports of one State over those of another: nor shall Vessels bound to, or from, one State, be obliged to enter, clear, or pay Duties in another.

No Money shall be drawn from the Treasury, but in Consequence of Appropriations made by Law; and a regular Statement and Account of the Receipts and Expenditures of all public Money shall be published from time to time.

No Title of Nobility shall be granted by the United States: And no Person holding any Office of Profit or Trust under them, shall, without the Consent of the Congress, accept of any present, Emolument, Office, or Title, of any kind whatever, from any King, Prince, or foreign State.

Section. 10.

No State shall enter into any Treaty, Alliance, or Confederation; grant Letters of Marque and Reprisal; coin Money; emit Bills of Credit; make any Thing but gold and silver Coin a Tender in Payment of Debts; pass any Bill of Attainder, ex post facto Law, or Law impairing the Obligation of Contracts, or grant any Title of Nobility.

No State shall, without the Consent of the Congress, lay any Imposts or Duties on Imports or Exports, except what may be absolutely necessary for executing it's inspection Laws: and the net Produce of all Duties and Imposts, laid by any State on Imports or Exports, shall be for the Use of the Treasury of the United States; and all such Laws shall be subject to the Revision and Controul of the Congress.

No State shall, without the Consent of Congress, lay any Duty of Tonnage, keep Troops, or Ships of War in time of Peace, enter into any Agreement or Compact with another State, or with a foreign Power, or engage in War, unless actually invaded, or in such imminent Danger as will not admit of delay.

Article. II.

Section. 1.

The executive Power shall be vested in a President of the United States of America. He shall hold his Office during the Term of four Years, and, together with the Vice President, chosen for the same Term, be elected, as follows

Each State shall appoint, in such Manner as the Legislature thereof may direct, a Number of Electors, equal to the whole Number of Senators and Representatives to which the State may be entitled in the Congress: but no Senator or Representative, or Person holding an Office of Trust or Profit under the United States, shall be appointed an Elector.

The Electors shall meet in their respective States, and vote by Ballot for two Persons, of whom one at least shall not be an Inhabitant of the same State with themselves. And they shall make a List of all the Persons voted for, and of the Number of Votes for each; which List they shall sign and certify, and transmit sealed to the Seat of the Government of the United States, directed to the President of the Senate. The President of the Senate shall, in the Presence of the Senate and House of Representatives, open all the Certificates, and the Votes shall then be counted. The Person having the greatest Number of Votes shall be the President, if such Number be a Majority of the whole Number of Electors appointed; and if there be more than one who have such Majority, and have an equal Number of Votes, then the House of Representatives shall immediately chuse by Ballot one of them for President; and if no Person have a Majority, then from the five highest on the List the said House shall in like Manner chuse the President. But in chusing the President, the Votes shall be taken by States, the Representation from each State having one Vote; A quorum for this Purpose shall consist of a Member or Members from two thirds of the States, and a Majority of all the States shall be necessary to a Choice. In every Case, after the Choice of the President, the Person having the greatest Number of Votes of the Electors shall be the Vice President. But if there should remain two or more who have equal Votes, the Senate shall chuse from them by Ballot the Vice President.

The Congress may determine the Time of chusing the Electors, and the Day on which they shall give their Votes; which Day shall be the same throughout the United States.

No Person except a natural born Citizen, or a Citizen of the United States, at the time of the Adoption of this Constitution, shall be eligible to the Office of President; neither shall any Person be eligible to that Office who shall not have attained to the Age of thirty five Years, and been fourteen Years a Resident within the United States.

In Case of the Removal of the President from Office, or of his Death, Resignation, or Inability to discharge the Powers and Duties of the said Office, the Same shall devolve on the Vice President, and the Congress may by Law provide for the Case of Removal, Death, Resignation or Inability, both of the President and Vice President, declaring what Officer shall then act as President, and such Officer shall act accordingly, until the Disability be removed, or a President shall be elected.

The President shall, at stated Times, receive for his Services, a Compensation, which shall neither be encreased nor diminished during the Period for which he shall have been elected, and he shall not receive within that Period any other Emolument from the United States, or any of them.

Before he enter on the Execution of his Office, he shall take the following Oath or Affirmation:—"I do solemnly swear (or affirm) that I will faithfully execute the Office of President of the United States, and will to the best of my Ability, preserve, protect and defend the Constitution of the United States."

Section. 2.

The President shall be Commander in Chief of the Army and Navy of the United States, and of the Militia of the several States, when called into the actual Service of the United States; he may require the Opinion, in writing, of the principal Officer in each of the executive Departments, upon any Subject relating to the Duties of their respective Offices, and he shall have Power to grant Reprieves and Pardons for Offences against the United States, except in Cases of Impeachment.

He shall have Power, by and with the Advice and Consent of the Senate, to make Treaties, provided two thirds of the Senators present concur; and he shall nominate, and by and with the Advice and Consent of the Senate, shall appoint Ambassadors, other public Ministers and Consuls, Judges of the supreme Court, and all other Officers of the United States, whose Appointments are not herein otherwise provided for, and which shall be established by Law: but the Congress may by Law vest the Appointment of such inferior Officers, as they think proper, in the President alone, in the Courts of Law, or in the Heads of Departments.

The President shall have Power to fill up all Vacancies that may happen during the Recess of the Senate, by granting Commissions which shall expire at the End of their next Session.

Section. 3.

He shall from time to time give to the Congress Information of the State of the Union, and recommend to their Consideration such Measures as he shall judge necessary and expedient; he may, on extraordinary Occasions, convene both Houses, or either of them, and in Case of Disagreement between them, with Respect to the Time of Adjournment, he may adjourn them to such Time as he shall think proper; he shall receive Ambassadors and other public Ministers; he shall take Care that the Laws be faithfully executed, and shall Commission all the Officers of the United States.

Section. 4.

The President, Vice President and all civil Officers of the United States, shall be removed from Office on Impeachment for, and Conviction of, Treason, Bribery, or other high Crimes and Misdemeanors.

Article III.

Section. 1.

The judicial Power of the United States, shall be vested in one supreme Court, and in such inferior Courts as the Congress may from time to time ordain and establish. The Judges, both of the supreme and inferior Courts, shall hold their Offices during good Behaviour, and shall, at stated Times, receive for their Services, a Compensation, which shall not be diminished during their Continuance in Office.

Section. 2.

The judicial Power shall extend to all Cases, in Law and Equity, arising under this Constitution, the Laws of the United States, and Treaties made, or which shall be made, under their Authority;—to all Cases affecting Ambassadors, other public Ministers and Consuls;—to all Cases of admiralty and maritime Jurisdiction;—to Controversies to which the United States shall be a Party;—to Controversies between two or more States;— between a State and Citizens of another State,—between Citizens of different States,—between Citizens of the same State claiming Lands under Grants of different States, and between a State, or the Citizens thereof, and foreign States, Citizens or Subjects.

In all Cases affecting Ambassadors, other public Ministers and Consuls, and those in which a State shall be Party, the supreme Court shall have original Jurisdiction. In all the other Cases before mentioned, the supreme Court shall have appellate Jurisdiction, both as to Law and Fact, with such Exceptions, and under such Regulations as the Congress shall make.

The Trial of all Crimes, except in Cases of Impeachment, shall be by Jury; and such Trial shall be held in the State where the said Crimes shall have been committed; but when not committed within any State, the Trial shall be at such Place or Places as the Congress may by Law have directed.

Section. 3.

Treason against the United States, shall consist only in levying War against them, or in adhering to their Enemies, giving them Aid and Comfort. No Person shall be convicted of Treason unless on the Testimony of two Witnesses to the same overt Act, or on Confession in open Court.

The Congress shall have Power to declare the Punishment of Treason, but no Attainder of Treason shall work Corruption of Blood, or Forfeiture except during the Life of the Person attainted.

Article. IV.

Section. 1.

Full Faith and Credit shall be given in each State to the public Acts, Records, and judicial Proceedings of every other State. And the Congress may by general Laws prescribe the Manner in which such Acts, Records and Proceedings shall be proved, and the Effect thereof.

Section. 2.

The Citizens of each State shall be entitled to all Privileges and Immunities of Citizens in the several States.

A Person charged in any State with Treason, Felony, or other Crime, who shall flee from Justice, and be found in another State, shall on Demand of the executive Authority of the State from which he fled, be delivered up, to be removed to the State having Jurisdiction of the Crime.

No Person held to Service or Labour in one State, under the Laws thereof, escaping into another, shall, in Consequence of any Law or Regulation therein, be discharged from such Service or Labour, but shall be delivered up on Claim of the Party to whom such Service or Labour may be due.

Section. 3.

New States may be admitted by the Congress into this Union; but no new State shall be formed or erected within the Jurisdiction of any other State; nor any State be formed by the Junction of two or more States, or Parts of States, without the Consent of the Legislatures of the States concerned as well as of the Congress.

The Congress shall have Power to dispose of and make all needful Rules and Regulations respecting the Territory or other Property belonging to the United States; and nothing in this Constitution shall be so construed as to Prejudice any Claims of the United States, or of any particular State.

Section. 4.

The United States shall guarantee to every State in this Union a Republican Form of Government, and shall protect each of them against Invasion; and on Application of the Legislature, or of the Executive (when the Legislature cannot be convened), against domestic Violence.

Article. V.

The Congress, whenever two thirds of both Houses shall deem it necessary, shall propose Amendments to this Constitution, or, on the Application of the Legislatures of two thirds of the several States, shall call a Convention for proposing Amendments, which, in either Case, shall be valid to all Intents and Purposes, as Part of this Constitution, when ratified by the Legislatures of three fourths of the several States, or by Conventions in three fourths thereof, as the one or the other Mode of Ratification may be proposed by the Congress; Provided that no Amendment which may be made prior to the Year One thousand eight hundred and eight shall in any Manner affect the first and fourth Clauses in the Ninth Section of the first Article; and that no State, without its Consent, shall be deprived of its equal Suffrage in the Senate.

Article. VI.

All Debts contracted and Engagements entered into, before the Adoption of this Constitution, shall be as valid against the United States under this Constitution, as under the Confederation.

This Constitution, and the Laws of the United States which shall be made in Pursuance thereof; and all Treaties made, or which shall be made, under the Authority of the United States, shall be the supreme Law of the Land; and the Judges in every State shall be bound thereby, any Thing in the Constitution or Laws of any State to the Contrary notwithstanding.

The Senators and Representatives before mentioned, and the Members of the several State Legislatures, and all executive and judicial Officers, both of the United States and of the several States, shall be bound by Oath or Affirmation, to support this Constitution; but no religious Test shall ever be required as a Qualification to any Office or public Trust under the United States.

Article. VII.

The Ratification of the Conventions of nine States, shall be sufficient for the Establishment of this Constitution between the States so ratifying the Same.

Done in Convention by the Unanimous Consent of the States present the Seventeenth Day of September in the Year of our Lord one thousand seven hundred and Eighty seven and of the Independance of the United States of America the Twelfth In witness whereof We have hereunto subscribed our Names,

G. Washington

Presidt and deputy from Virginia

Delaware
Geo: Read
Gunning Bedford jun
John Dickinson
Richard Bassett
Jaco: Broom
Maryland
James McHenry
Dan of St Thos. Jenifer
Danl. Carroll
Virginia
John Blair
James Madison Jr.
North Carolina
Wm. Blount
Richd. Dobbs Spaight
Hu Williamson
South Carolina
J. Rutledge
Charles Cotesworth Pinckney
Charles Pinckney
Pierce Butler
Georgia
William Few
Abr Baldwin
New Hampshire
John Langdon
Nicholas Gilman
Massachusetts
Nathaniel Gorham
Rufus King
Connecticut
Wm. Saml. Johnson
Roger Sherman
New York
Alexander Hamilton
New Jersey
Wil: Livingston
David Brearley
Wm. Paterson
Jona: Dayton
Pensylvania
B Franklin
Thomas Mifflin

Robt. Morris
Geo. Clymer
Thos. FitzSimons
Jared Ingersoll
James Wilson
Gouv Morris

Constitutional Amendments

The U.S. Bill of Rights (Amendments 1–10)

The Preamble to The Bill of Rights

Congress of the United States begun and held at the City of New-York, on Wednesday the fourth of March, one thousand seven hundred and eighty nine.

The Conventions of a number of the States, having at the time of their adopting the Constitution, expressed a desire, in order to prevent misconstruction or abuse of its powers, that further declaratory and restrictive clauses should be added: And as extending the ground of public confidence in the Government, will best ensure the beneficent ends of its institution.

Resolved by the Senate and House of Representatives of the United States of America, in Congress assembled, two thirds of both Houses concurring, that the following Articles be proposed to the Legislatures of the several States, as amendments to the Constitution of the United States, all, or any of which Articles, when ratified by three fourths of the said Legislatures, to be valid to all intents and purposes, as part of the said Constitution; viz.

Articles in addition to, and Amendment of the Constitution of the United States of America, proposed by Congress, and ratified by the Legislatures of the several States, pursuant to the fifth Article of the original Constitution.

Note: The following text is a transcription of the first ten amendments to the Constitution in their original form. These amendments were ratified December 15, 1791, and form what is known as the "Bill of Rights."

Amendment I

Congress shall make no law respecting an establishment of religion, or prohibiting the free exercise thereof; or abridging the freedom of speech, or of the press; or the right of the people peaceably to assemble, and to petition the Government for a redress of grievances.

Amendment II

A well regulated Militia, being necessary to the security of a free State, the right of the people to keep and bear Arms, shall not be infringed.

Amendment III

No Soldier shall, in time of peace be quartered in any house, without the consent of the Owner, nor in time of war, but in a manner to be prescribed by law.

Amendment IV

The right of the people to be secure in their persons, houses, papers, and effects, against unreasonable searches and seizures, shall not be violated, and no Warrants shall issue, but upon probable cause, supported by Oath or affirmation, and particularly describing the place to be searched, and the persons or things to be seized.

Amendment V

No person shall be held to answer for a capital, or otherwise infamous crime, unless on a presentment or indictment of a Grand Jury, except in cases arising in the land or naval forces, or in the Militia, when in actual service in time of War or public danger; nor shall any person be subject for the same offence to be twice put in jeopardy of life or limb; nor shall be compelled in any criminal case to be a witness against himself, nor be deprived of life, liberty, or property, without due process of law; nor shall private property be taken for public use, without just compensation.

Amendment VI

In all criminal prosecutions, the accused shall enjoy the right to a speedy and public trial, by an impartial jury of the State and district wherein the crime shall have been committed, which district shall have been previously ascertained by law, and to be informed of the nature and cause of the accusation; to be confronted with the witnesses against him; to have compulsory process for obtaining witnesses in his favor, and to have the Assistance of Counsel for his defence.

Amendment VII

In Suits at common law, where the value in controversy shall exceed twenty dollars, the right of trial by jury shall be preserved, and no fact tried by a jury, shall be otherwise re-examined in any Court of the United States, than according to the rules of the common law.

Amendment VIII

Excessive bail shall not be required, nor excessive fines imposed, nor cruel and unusual punishments inflicted.

Amendment IX

The enumeration in the Constitution, of certain rights, shall not be construed to deny or disparage others retained by the people.

Amendment X

The powers not delegated to the United States by the Constitution, nor prohibited by it to the States, are reserved to the States respectively, or to the people.

Amendment XI

The Judicial power of the United States shall not be construed to extend to any suit in law or equity, commenced or prosecuted against one of the United States by Citizens of another State, or by Citizens or Subjects of any Foreign State.

Amendment XII

The Electors shall meet in their respective states and vote by ballot for President and Vice-President, one of whom, at least, shall not be an inhabitant of the same state with themselves; they shall name in their ballots the person voted for as President, and in distinct ballots the person voted for as Vice-President, and they shall make distinct lists of all persons voted for as President, and of all persons voted for as Vice-President, and of the number of votes for each, which lists they shall sign and certify, and transmit sealed to the seat of the government of the United States, directed to the President of the Senate; — the President of the Senate shall, in the presence of the Senate and House of Representatives, open all the certificates and the votes shall then be counted; — The person having the greatest number of votes for President, shall be the President, if such number be a majority of the whole number of Electors appointed; and if no person have such majority, then from the persons having the highest numbers not exceeding three on the list of those voted for as President, the House of Representatives shall choose immediately, by ballot, the President. But in choosing the President, the votes shall be taken by states, the representation from each state having one vote; a quorum for this purpose shall consist of a member or members from two-thirds of the states, and a majority of all the states shall be necessary to a choice. [And if the House of Representatives shall not choose a President whenever the right of choice shall devolve upon them, before the fourth day of March next following, then the Vice-President shall act as President, as in case of the death or other constitutional disability of the President. —]* The person having the greatest number of votes as Vice-President, shall be the Vice-President, if such number be a majority of the whole number of Electors appointed, and if no person have a majority, then from the two highest numbers on the list, the Senate shall choose the Vice-President; a quorum for the purpose shall consist of two-thirds of the whole number of Senators, and a majority of the whole number shall be necessary to a choice. But no person constitutionally ineligible to the office of President shall be eligible to that of Vice-President of the United States.

Superseded by Section 3 of the 20th amendment.

Amendment XIII

Section 1.

Neither slavery nor involuntary servitude, except as a punishment for crime whereof the party shall have been duly convicted, shall exist within the United States, or any place subject to their jurisdiction.

Section 2.

Congress shall have power to enforce this article by appropriate legislation.

Amendment XIV

Section 1.

All persons born or naturalized in the United States, and subject to the jurisdiction thereof, are citizens of the United States and of the State wherein they reside. No State shall make or enforce any law which shall abridge the privileges or immunities of citizens of the United States; nor shall any State deprive any person of life, liberty, or property, without due process of law; nor deny to any person within its jurisdiction the equal protection of the laws.

Section 2.

Representatives shall be apportioned among the several States according to their respective numbers, counting the whole number of persons in each State, excluding Indians not taxed. But when the right to vote at any election for the choice of electors for President and Vice-President of the United States, Representatives in Congress, the Executive and Judicial officers of a State, or the members of the Legislature thereof, is denied to any of the male inhabitants of such State, being twenty-one years of age,* and citizens of the United States, or in any way abridged, except for participation in rebellion, or other crime, the basis of representation therein shall be reduced in the proportion which the number of such male citizens shall bear to the whole number of male citizens twenty-one years of age in such State.

Section 3.

No person shall be a Senator or Representative in Congress, or elector of President and Vice-President, or hold any office, civil or military, under the United States, or under any State, who, having previously taken an oath, as a member of Congress, or as an officer of the United States, or as a member of any State legislature, or as an executive or judicial officer of any State, to support the Constitution of the United States, shall have engaged in insurrection or rebellion against the same, or given aid or comfort to the enemies thereof. But Congress may by a vote of two-thirds of each House, remove such disability.

Section 4.

The validity of the public debt of the United States, authorized by law, including debts incurred for payment of pensions and bounties for services in suppressing insurrection or rebellion, shall not be questioned. But neither the United States nor any State shall assume or pay any debt or obligation incurred in aid of insurrection or rebellion against the United States, or any claim for the loss or emancipation of any slave; but all such debts, obligations and claims shall be held illegal and void.

Section 5.

The Congress shall have the power to enforce, by appropriate legislation, the provisions of this article.

Changed by Section 1 of the 26th amendment.

Amendment XV

Section 1.

The right of citizens of the United States to vote shall not be denied or abridged by the United States or by any State on account of race, color, or previous condition of servitude—

Section 2.

The Congress shall have the power to enforce this article by appropriate legislation.

Amendment XVI

The Congress shall have power to lay and collect taxes on incomes, from whatever source derived, without apportionment among the several States, and without regard to any census or enumeration.

Amendment XVII

The Senate of the United States shall be composed of two Senators from each State, elected by the people thereof, for six years; and each Senator shall have one vote. The electors in each State shall have the qualifications requisite for electors of the most numerous branch of the State legislatures.

When vacancies happen in the representation of any State in the Senate, the executive authority of such State shall issue writs of election to fill such vacancies: *Provided,* That the legislature of any State may empower the executive thereof to make temporary appointments until the people fill the vacancies by election as the legislature may direct.

This amendment shall not be so construed as to affect the election or term of any Senator chosen before it becomes valid as part of the Constitution.

Amendment XVIII

Section 1.

After one year from the ratification of this article the manufacture, sale, or transportation of intoxicating liquors within, the importation thereof into, or the exportation thereof from the United States and all territory subject to the jurisdiction thereof for beverage purposes is hereby prohibited.

Section 2.

The Congress and the several States shall have concurrent power to enforce this article by appropriate legislation.

Section 3.

This article shall be inoperative unless it shall have been ratified as an amendment to the Constitution by the legislatures of the several States, as provided in the Constitution, within seven years from the date of the submission hereof to the States by the Congress.

Amendment XIX

The right of citizens of the United States to vote shall not be denied or abridged by the United States or by any State on account of sex.

Congress shall have power to enforce this article by appropriate legislation.

Amendment XX

Section 1.

The terms of the President and the Vice President shall end at noon on the 20th day of January, and the terms of Senators and Representatives at noon on the 3d day of January, of the years in which such terms would have ended if this article had not been ratified; and the terms of their successors shall then begin.

Section 2.

The Congress shall assemble at least once in every year, and such meeting shall begin at noon on the 3d day of January, unless they shall by law appoint a different day.

Section 3.

If, at the time fixed for the beginning of the term of the President, the President elect shall have died, the Vice President elect shall become President. If a President shall not have been chosen before the time fixed for the beginning of his term, or if the President elect shall have failed to qualify, then the Vice President elect shall act as President until a President shall have qualified; and the Congress may by law provide for the case wherein neither a President elect nor a Vice President elect shall have qualified, declaring who shall then act as President, or the manner in which one who is to act shall be selected, and such person shall act accordingly until a President or Vice President shall have qualified.

Section 4.

The Congress may by law provide for the case of the death of any of the persons from whom the House of Representatives may choose a President whenever the right of choice shall have devolved upon them, and for the case of the death of any of the persons from whom the Senate may choose a Vice President whenever the right of choice shall have devolved upon them.

Section 5.

Sections 1 and 2 shall take effect on the 15th day of October following the ratification of this article.

Section 6.

This article shall be inoperative unless it shall have been ratified as an amendment to the Constitution by the legislatures of three-fourths of the several States within seven years from the date of its submission.

Amendment XXI

Section 1.

The eighteenth article of amendment to the Constitution of the United States is hereby repealed.

Section 2.

The transportation or importation into any State, Territory, or possession of the United States for delivery or use therein of intoxicating liquors, in violation of the laws thereof, is hereby prohibited.

Section 3.

This article shall be inoperative unless it shall have been ratified as an amendment to the Constitution by conventions in the several States, as provided in the Constitution, within seven years from the date of the submission hereof to the States by the Congress.

Amendment XXII

Section 1.

No person shall be elected to the office of the President more than twice, and no person who has held the office of President, or acted as President, for more than two years of a term to which some other person was elected President shall be elected to the office of the President more than once. But this Article shall not apply to any person holding the office of President when this Article was proposed by the Congress, and shall not prevent any person who may be holding the office of President, or acting as President, during the term within which this Article becomes operative from holding the office of President or acting as President during the remainder of such term.

Section 2.

This article shall be inoperative unless it shall have been ratified as an amendment to the Constitution by the legislatures of three-fourths of the several States within seven years from the date of its submission to the States by the Congress.

Amendment XXIII

Section 1.

The District constituting the seat of Government of the United States shall appoint in such manner as the Congress may direct:

A number of electors of President and Vice President equal to the whole number of Senators and Representatives in Congress to which the District would be entitled if it were a State, but in no event more than the least populous State; they shall be in addition to those appointed by the States, but they shall be considered, for the purposes of the election of President and Vice President, to be electors appointed by a State; and they shall meet in the District and perform such duties as provided by the twelfth article of amendment.

Section 2.

The Congress shall have power to enforce this article by appropriate legislation.

Amendment XXIV

Section 1.

The right of citizens of the United States to vote in any primary or other election for President or Vice President, for electors for President or Vice President, or for Senator or Representative in Congress, shall not be denied or abridged by the United States or any State by reason of failure to pay any poll tax or other tax.

Section 2.

The Congress shall have power to enforce this article by appropriate legislation.

Amendment XXV

Section 1.

In case of the removal of the President from office or of his death or resignation, the Vice President shall become President.

Section 2.

Whenever there is a vacancy in the office of the Vice President, the President shall nominate a Vice President who shall take office upon confirmation by a majority vote of both Houses of Congress.

Section 3.

Whenever the President transmits to the President pro tempore of the Senate and the Speaker of the House of Representatives his written declaration that he is unable to discharge the powers and duties of his office, and until he transmits to them a written declaration to the contrary, such powers and duties shall be discharged by the Vice President as Acting President.

Section 4.

Whenever the Vice President and a majority of either the principal officers of the executive departments or of such other body as Congress may by law provide, transmit to the President pro tempore of the Senate and the Speaker of the House of Representatives their written declaration that the President is unable to discharge the powers and duties of his office, the Vice President shall immediately assume the powers and duties of the office as Acting President.

Thereafter, when the President transmits to the President pro tempore of the Senate and the Speaker of the House of Representatives his written declaration that no inability exists, he shall resume the powers and duties of his office unless the Vice President and a majority of either the principal officers of the executive department or of such other body as Congress may by law provide, transmit within four days to the President pro tempore of the Senate and the Speaker of the House of Representatives their written declaration that the President is unable to discharge the powers and duties of his office. Thereupon Congress shall decide the issue, assembling within forty-eight hours for that purpose if not in session. If the Congress, within twenty-one days after receipt of the latter written declaration, or, if Congress is not in session, within twenty-one days after Congress is required to assemble, determines by two-thirds vote of both Houses that the President is unable to discharge the powers and duties of his office, the Vice President shall continue to discharge the same as Acting President; otherwise, the President shall resume the powers and duties of his office.

Amendment XXVI

Section 1.

The right of citizens of the United States, who are eighteen years of age or older, to vote shall not be denied or abridged by the United States or by any State on account of age.

Section 2.

The Congress shall have power to enforce this article by appropriate legislation.

Amendment XXVII

No law, varying the compensation for the services of the Senators and Representatives, shall take effect, until an election of Representatives shall have intervened.

Attributions

CC licensed content, Shared previously

- US History. **Authored by**: P. Scott Corbett, Volker Janssen, John M. Lund, Todd Pfannestiel, Paul Vickery, and Sylvie Waskiewicz. **Provided by**: OpenStax College. **Located at**: http://openstaxcollege.org/textbooks/us-history. **License**: *CC BY: Attribution*. **License Terms**: Download for free at http://cnx.org/content/col11740/latest/

Presidents of the United States of America

Presidents of the United States of America

Order	Election Year	President
1	1788–1789	George Washington
1	1792	George Washington
2	1796	John Adams
3	1800	Thomas Jefferson
3	1804	Thomas Jefferson
4	1808	James Madison
4	1812	James Madison
5	1816	James Monroe
5	1820	James Monroe
6	1824	John Quincy Adams
7	1828	Andrew Jackson
7	1832	Andrew Jackson
8	1836	Martin Van Buren
9	1840	William Henry Harrison
10	1840	John Tyler
11	1844	James K. Polk
12	1848	Zachary Taylor
13	1848	Mallard Fillmore
14	1852	Franklin Pierce
15	1856	James Buchanan
16	1860	Abraham Lincoln
16	1864	Abraham Lincoln
17	1864	Andrew Johnson
18	1868	Ulysses S. Grant
18	1872	Ulysses S. Grant

Order	Election Year	President
19	1876	Rutherford B. Hayes
20	1880	James A. Garfield
21	1880	Chester A. Arthur
22	1884	Grover Cleveland
23	1888	Benjamin Harrison
24	1892	Grover Cleveland
25	1896	William McKinley
25	1900	William McKinley
26	1904	Theodore Roosevelt
27	1908	William Howard Taft
28	1912	Woodrow Wilson
28	1916	Woodrow Wilson
29	1920	Warren G. Harding
30	1924	Calvin Coolidge
31	1928	Herbert Hoover
32	1932	Franklin D. Roosevelt
32	1936	Franklin D. Roosevelt
32	1940	Franklin D. Roosevelt
32	1944	Franklin D. Roosevelt
33	1948	Harry S. Truman
34	1952	Dwight D. Eisenhower
34	1956	Dwight D. Eisenhower
35	1960	John F. Kennedy
36	1964	Lyndon B. Johnson
37	1968	Richard Nixon
37	1972	Richard Nixon
38	1972	Gerald Ford
39	1976	Jimmy Carter
40	1980	Ronald Reagan
40	1984	Ronald Reagan
41	1988	George H. W. Bush
42	1992	Bill Clinton
42	1996	Bill Clinton
43	2000	George W. Bush
43	2004	George W. Bush
44	2008	Barack Obama
44	2012	Barack Obama

Attributions

CC licensed content, Shared previously

- US History. **Authored by**: P. Scott Corbett, Volker Janssen, John M. Lund, Todd Pfannestiel, Paul Vickery, and Sylvie Waskiewicz. **Provided by**: OpenStax College. **Located at**: http://openstaxcollege.org/textbooks/us-history. **License**: *CC BY: Attribution*.

License Terms: Download for free at http://cnx.org/content/col11740/latest/

U.S. Political Map

(credit: U.S. Department of the Interior, U.S. Geological Survey, The National Atlas of the United States of America/nationalatlas.gov)

Attributions

CC licensed content, Shared previously

- US History. **Authored by**: P. Scott Corbett, Volker Janssen, John M. Lund, Todd Pfannestiel, Paul Vickery, and Sylvie Waskiewicz. **Provided by**: OpenStax College. **Located at**: http://openstaxcollege.org/textbooks/us-history. **License**: *CC BY: Attribution*. **License Terms**: Download for free at http://cnx.org/content/col11740/latest/

U.S. Topographical Map

Attributions

CC licensed content, Shared previously

- US History. **Authored by**: P. Scott Corbett, Volker Janssen, John M. Lund, Todd Pfannestiel, Paul Vickery, and Sylvie Waskiewicz. **Provided by**: OpenStax College. **Located at**: http://openstaxcollege.org/textbooks/us-history. **License**: CC BY: Attribution. **License Terms**: Download for free at http://cnx.org/content/col11740/latest/

United States Population Chart

United States Population Chart[1]

Census Year	Population	Census Year	Population
1610	350	1820	9,638,453
1620	2,302	1830	12,866,020
1630	4,646	1840	17,069,453
1640	26,634	1850	23,191,876
1650	50,368	1860	31,443,321
1660	75,058	1870	38,558,371
1670	111,935	1880	50,189,209
1680	151,507	1890	62,979,766
1690	210,372	1900	76,212,168
1700	250,888	1910	92,228,496
1710	331,711	1920	106,021,537
1720	466,185	1930	123,202,624
1730	629,445	1940	132,164,569
1740	905,563	1950	151,325,798
1750	1,170,760	1960	179,323,175
1760	1,593,625	1970	203,211,926
1770	2,148,076	1980	226,656,805
1780	2,780,369	1990	248,709,873
1790	3,929,214	2000	281,421,906
1800	5,308,483	2010	308,745,538
1810	7,239,881		

Footnotes

1. Population figures for the decades before the first U.S. census in 1790 are estimates.

Attributions

CC licensed content, Shared previously

- US History. **Authored by**: P. Scott Corbett, Volker Janssen, John M. Lund, Todd Pfannestiel, Paul Vickery, and Sylvie Waskiewicz. **Provided by**: OpenStax College. **Located at**: http://openstaxcollege.org/textbooks/us-history. **License**: *CC BY: Attribution*. **License Terms**: Download for free at http://cnx.org/content/col11740/latest/

Further Reading

THE PRE-COLUMBIAN WORLD AND EARLY GLOBALIZATION

Alchon, Suzanne Austin. 2003. *A Pest in the Land: New World Epidemics in a Global Perspective*. Albuquerque: University of New Mexico Press.

Brown, Kathleen M. 1996. *Good Wives, Nasty Wenches, and Anxious Patriarchs: Gender, Race, and Power in Colonial Virginia*. Chapel Hill: University of North Carolina Press.

Clendinnen, Inga. 1991. *Aztecs: An Interpretation*. Cambridge: Cambridge University Press.

Cook, Harold John. 2007. *Matters of Exchange: Commerce, Medicine, and Science in the Dutch Golden Age*. New Haven: Yale University Press.

Curtin, Philip D. 1990. *The Rise and Fall of the Plantation Complex: Essays in Atlantic History*. Cambridge: Cambridge University Press.

Leon, Portilla Miguel. (1992) 2006. *The Broken Spears: The Aztec Account of the Conquest of Mexico*. Boston: Beacon Press.

Mann, Charles C. 2005. *1491: New Revelations of the Americas Before Columbus*. New York: Knopf.

—. 2011. *1493: Uncovering the New World Columbus Created*. New York: Knopf.

Meltzer, David J. 2009. *First Peoples in a New World: Colonizing Ice Age America*. Berkeley: University of California Press.

Niane, Djibril Tamsir. 1965. *Sundiata: An Epic of Old Mali*. Translated by G. D. Pickett. London: Longmans.

Northrup, David. 2013. *Africa's Discovery of Europe*. Oxford: Oxford University Press.

Pagden, Anthony. 1995. *Lords of all the World: Ideologies of Empire in Spain, Britain and France c.1500–c.1800*. New Haven: Yale University Press.

Prescott, William Hickling. 1936. *History of the Conquest of Mexico, and History of the Conquest of Peru*. New York: Modern Library.

Seed, Patricia. 1995. *Ceremonies of Possession in Europe's Conquest of the New World, 1492–1640*. Cambridge: Cambridge University Press.

Taylor, Alan. 2002. *American Colonies*. New York: Penguin Books.

Thornton, John K. 1992. *Africa and Africans in the Making of the Atlantic World, 1400–1680*. Cambridge: Cambridge University Press.

Wey Gómez, Nicolás. 2008. *The Tropics of Empire: Why Columbus Sailed South to the Indies*. Cambridge, MA: MIT Press.

THE COLONIAL AMERICAS

Bailyn, Bernard. 2012. *The Barbarous Years: The Peopling of British North America: The Conflict of Civilizations, 1600–1675*. New York: Vintage Books.

Berlin, Ira. 1998. *Many Thousands Gone: The First Two Centuries of Slavery in North America*. Cambridge, MA: Belknap Press.

Calloway, Colin G. 2011. *First Peoples: A Documentary Survey of American Indian History*. Fourth edition, Boston: Bedford/St. Martin's Press.

Elliott, J. H. 2006. *Empires of the Atlantic World: Britain and Spain in America, 1492–1830*. New Haven: Yale University Press.

Fischer, David H. 1989. *Albion's Seed: Four British Folkways in America*. New York: Oxford University Press.

Gaustad, Edwin S. 1982. *A Documentary History of Religion in America*. Grand Rapids, MI: Eerdmans.

Gibson, Charles. 1964. *The Aztecs Under Spanish Rule: A History of the Indians of the Valley of Mexico, 1519–1810*. Stanford, CA: Stanford University Press.

Hatfield, April Lee. 2004. *Atlantic Virginia: Intercolonial Relations in the Seventeenth Century*. Philadelphia: University of Pennsylvania Press.

Liss, Peggy K. 1975. *Mexico Under Spain, 1521–1556: Society and the Origins of Nationality*. Chicago: University of Chicago Press.

Morgan, Edmund S. 1958. *The Puritan Dilemma: The Story of John Winthrop*. Boston: Little, Brown.

Rediker, Marcus. 2007. *The Slave Ship: A Human History*. New York: Viking Books.

Richter, Daniel K. 2001. *Facing East from Indian Country: A Native History of Early America*. Cambridge, MA: Harvard University Press.

Roberts, David. 2004. *The Pueblo Revolt: The Secret Rebellion that Drove the Spaniards Out of the Southwest*. New York: Simon & Schuster.

Spicer, Edward Holland. 1962. *Cycles of Conquest: The Impact of Spain, Mexico, and the United States on the Indians of the Southwest, 1533–1960*. Tucson: University of Arizona Press.

Twinam, Ann. 1982. *Miners, Merchants, and Farmers in Colonial Colombia*. Austin: University of Texas Press.

Weber, David J. 1992. *The Spanish Frontier in North America*. New Haven: Yale University Press.

REFORM, PROTEST, AND REVOLUTION

Anderson, Fred. 2005. *The War That Made America: A Short History of the French and Indian War*. New York: Viking Books.

Bailyn, Bernard. 1986. *The Peopling of British North America: An Introduction*. New York: Knopf Doubleday.

Breen, Timothy H. 2004. *The Marketplace of Revolution: How Consumer Politics Shaped American Independence*. Oxford: Oxford University Press.

Butler, Jon. 2000. *Becoming America: The Revolution before 1776*. Cambridge, MA: Harvard University Press.

Calloway, Colin G. 1995. *The American Revolution in Indian Country: Crisis and Diversity in Native American Communities*. Cambridge: Cambridge University Press.

Cook, Don. 1995. *The Long Fuse: How England Lost the American Colonies, 1760–1785*. New York: Atlantic Monthly Press.

Egerton, Douglas R. 2009. *Death or Liberty: African Americans and Revolutionary America*. Oxford: Oxford University Press.

Ellis, Joseph J. 2003. *Founding Brothers: The Revolutionary Generation*. New York: Random House.

Fischer, David Hackett. 2004. *Washington's Crossing*. Oxford: Oxford University Press.

Fleming, Thomas J. 1997. *Liberty! The American Revolution*. New York: Viking Books.

Holton, Woody. 1999. *Forced Founders: Indians, Debtors, Slaves, and the Making of the American Revolution in Virginia*. Chapel Hill: University of North Carolina Press.

—. 2007. *Unruly Americans and the Origins of the Constitution*. New York: Hill and Wang.

Isaac, Rhys. 1982. *The Transformation of Virginia, 1740-1790*. Chapel Hill: University of North Carolina Press.

Lovejoy, David S. 1972. *The Glorious Revolution in America*. New York: Harper & Row.

McCullough, David. 2005. *1776*. New York: Simon & Schuster.

Middlekauff, Robert. 1982. *The Glorious Cause: The American Revolution, 1763–1789.* New York: Oxford University Press.

Noll, Mark A. 2003. *The Rise of Evangelicalism: The Age of Edwards, Whitefield, and the Wesleys.* Downers Grove, IL: InterVarsity Press.

Norton, Mary Beth. 1980. *Liberty's Daughters: The Revolutionary Experience of American Women, 1750–1800.* Boston: Little, Brown.

Olwell, Robert. 1998. *Masters, Slaves & Subjects: The Culture of Power in the South Carolina Low Country, 1740–1790.* Ithaca, NY: Cornell University Press.

Rakove, Jack N. 2010. *Revolutionaries: A New History of the Invention of America.* Boston: Houghton Mifflin Harcourt.

Raphael, Ray. 2001. *A People's History of the American Revolution: How Common People Shaped the Fight for Independence.* New York: New Press.

Stout, Harry S. 1991. *The Divine Dramatist: George Whitefield and the Rise of Modern Evangelicalism.* Grand Rapids, MI: Eerdmans.

Webb, Stephen Saunders. 1995. *Lord Churchill's Coup: The Anglo-American Empire and the Glorious Revolution Reconsidered.* New York: Knopf.

Wood, Gordon S. 1992. *The Radicalism of the American Revolution.* New York: Knopf.

Young, Alfred Fabian. 1999. *The Shoemaker and the Tea Party: Memory and the American Revolution.* Boston: Beacon Press.

THE EARLY REPUBLIC

Appleby, Joyce Oldham. 2000. *Inheriting the Revolution: The First Generation of Americans.* Cambridge, MA: Belknap Press.

Dubois, Laurent. 2004. *Avengers of the New World: The Story of the Haitian Revolution.* Cambridge, MA: Belknap Press.

Ellis, Joseph J. 1997. *American Sphinx: The Character of Thomas Jefferson.* New York: Knopf.

Ferling, John. 2004. *Adams vs. Jefferson: The Tumultuous Election of 1800.* New York: Oxford University Press.

Hickey, Donald R. 1989. *The War of 1812: A Forgotten Conflict.* Urbana: University of Illinois Press.

Kamensky, Jane. 2008. *The Exchange Artist: A Tale of High-Flying Speculation and America's First Banking Collapse.* New York: Viking Books.

Langguth, A. J. 2006. *Union 1812: The Americans Who Fought the Second War of Independence.* New York: Simon & Schuster.

Litwack, Leon F. 1961. *North of Slavery: The Negro in the Free States, 1790–1860*. Chicago: University of Chicago Press.

Maier, Pauline. 1997. *American Scripture: Making the Declaration of Independence*. New York: Knopf.

Smith, Jean Edward. 1996. *John Marshall: Definer of a Nation*. New York: Holt.

Taylor, Alan. 2010. *The Civil War of 1812: American Citizens, British Subjects, Irish Rebels, & Indian Allies*. New York: Vintage Books.

INDUSTRIALIZATION AND TRANSFORMATION

Blackmar, Elizabeth. 1989. *Manhattan for Rent, 1785–1850*. Ithaca, NY: Cornell University Press.

Howe, Daniel Walker. 2007. *What Hath God Wrought: The Transformation of America, 1815–1848*. New York: Oxford University Press.

Igler, David. 2013. *The Great Ocean: Pacific Worlds from Captain Cook to the Gold Rush*. Oxford: Oxford University Press.

Johnson, Paul E. 1978. *A Shopkeeper's Millennium: Society and Revivals in Rochester, New York, 1815–1837*. New York: Hill and Wang.

Johnson, Walter. 1999. *Soul by Soul: Life Inside the Antebellum Slave Market*. Cambridge, MA: Harvard University Press.

Marx, Leo. 1964. *The Machine in the Garden: Technology and the Pastoral Ideal in America*. New York: Oxford University Press.

Rees, Jonathan. 2013. *Industrialization and the Transformation of American Life: A Brief Introduction*. Armonk, NY: M.E. Sharpe.

Sandage, Scott A. 2005. *Born Losers: A History of Failure in America*. Cambridge, MA: Harvard University Press.

JACKSONIAN DEMOCRACY

Allgor, Catherine. 2000. *Parlor Politics: In Which the Ladies of Washington Help Build a City and a Government*. Charlottesville: University of Virginia Press.

Deloria, Philip Joseph. 1998. *Playing Indian*. New Haven: Yale University Press.

Deyle, Steven. 2005. *Carry Me Back: The Domestic Slave Trade in American Life*. New York: Oxford University Press.

Dippie, Brian W. 1982. *The Vanishing American: White Attitudes and U.S. Indian Policy*. Middletown, CT: Wesleyan University Press.

Feller, Daniel. 1995. *The Jacksonian Promise: America, 1815–1840*. Baltimore: Johns Hopkins University Press.

Marszalek, John F. 1997. *The Petticoat Affair: Manners, Mutiny, and Sex in Andrew Jackson's White House*. New York: Free Press.

Meacham, Jon. 2008. *American Lion: Andrew Jackson in the White House*. New York: Random House.

Mihm, Stephen. 2007. *A Nation of Counterfeiters: Capitalists, Con Men, and the Making of the United States*. Cambridge, MA: Harvard University Press.

Saxton, Alexander. 1990. *The Rise and Fall of the White Republic: Class Politics and Mass Culture in Nineteenth-Century America*. London: Verso.

Sellers, Charles. 1991. *The Market Revolution: Jacksonian America, 1815–1846*. New York: Oxford University Press.

Steinberg, Theodore. 1991. *Nature Incorporated: Industrialization and the Waters of New England*. Cambridge: Cambridge University Press.

Watson, Harry L. 1990. *Liberty and Power: The Politics of Jacksonian America*. New York: Hill and Wang.

—. 1998. *Andrew Jackson vs. Henry Clay: Democracy and Development in Antebellum America*. Boston: Bedford/St. Martin's Press.

Wilentz, Sean. 2005. *The Rise of American Democracy: Jefferson to Lincoln*. New York: Norton.

THE ANTEBELLUM SOUTH

Berlin, Ira. 2003. *Generations of Captivity: A History of African-American Slaves*. Cambridge, MA: Belknap Press.

Clark, Emily. 2013. *The Strange History of the American Quadroon: Free Women of Color in the Revolutionary Atlantic World*. Chapel Hill: University of North Carolina Press.

Delfino, Susanna, and Michele Gillespie. 2002. *Neither Lady nor Slave: Working Women of the Old South*. Chapel Hill: University of North Carolina Press.

Fox-Genovese, Elizabeth. 1988. *Within the Plantation Household: Black and White Women of the Old South*. Chapel Hill: University of North Carolina Press.

Genovese, Eugene D. 1974. *Roll, Jordan, Roll: The World the Slaves Made*. New York: Pantheon Books.

Hall, Gwendolyn Midlo. 1992. *Africans in Colonial Louisiana: The Development of Afro-Creole Culture in the Eighteenth Century*. Baton Rouge: Louisiana State University Press.

Johnson, Walter. 1999. *Soul by Soul: Life Inside the Antebellum Slave Market*. Cambridge, MA: Harvard University Press.

McCurry, Stephanie. 1995. *Masters of Small Worlds: Yeoman Households, Gender Relations, and the Political Culture of the Antebellum South Carolina Low Country*. New York: Oxford University Press.

Potter, David Morris, and Don E. Fehrenbacher. 1976. *The Impending Crisis, 1848–1861*. New York: Harper & Row.

Rasmussen, Daniel. 2011. *American Uprising: The Untold Story of America's Largest Slave Revolt*. New York: HarperCollins.

Wyatt-Brown, Bertram. 1982. *Southern Honor: Ethics and Behavior in the Old South*. New York: Oxford University Press.

REFORM AND ABOLITION

DuBois, Ellen Carol. 1978. *Feminism and Suffrage: The Emergence of an Independent Women's Movement in America, 1848-1869*. Ithaca, NY: Cornell University Press.

DuBois, Ellen Carol, and Lynn Dumenil. 2005. *Through Women's Eyes: An American History with Documents*. Boston: Bedford/St. Martin's Press.

Heyrman, Christine Leigh. 1997. *Southern Cross: The Beginnings of the Bible Belt*. New York: Knopf.

Mayer, Henry. 1998. *All On Fire: William Lloyd Garrison and the Abolition of Slavery*. New York: Bedford/St. Martin's Press.

Mintz, Steven. 1995. *Moralists and Modernizers: America's Pre-Civil War Reformers*. Baltimore: Johns Hopkins University Press.

Rorabaugh, W. J. 1979. *The Alcoholic Republic, an American Tradition*. New York: Oxford University Press.

Stewart, James Brewer. 1976. *Holy Warriors: The Abolitionists and American Slavery*. New York: Hill and Wang.

CIVIL WAR AND RECONSTRUCTION

Alcott, Louisa May, and Bessie Zahan Jones. 1960. *Hospital Sketches*. Cambridge, MA: Harvard University Press.

Berlin, Ira, Joseph P. Reidy, and Leslie S. Rowland. 1998. *Freedom's Soldiers: The Black Military Experience in the Civil War*. Cambridge: Cambridge University Press.

Blight, David W. 2001. *Race and Reunion: The Civil War in American Memory*. Cambridge, MA: Belknap Press.

Catton, Bruce. 1962. *Mr. Lincoln's Army*. Garden City, NY: Doubleday.

Donald, David Herbert. 1960. *Charles Sumner and the Coming of the Civil War*. New York: Knopf.

Earle, Jonathan Halperin. 2008. *John Brown's Raid on Harpers Ferry: A Brief History with Documents*. Boston: Bedford/St. Martin's Press.

Egerton, Douglas R. 2014. *The Wars of Reconstruction: The Brief, Violent History of America's Most Progressive Era*. London: Bloomsbury Press.

Emberton, Carole. 2013. *Beyond Redemption: Race, Violence, and the American South After the Civil War*. Chicago: University of Chicago Press.

Faust, Drew Gilpin. 2008. *This Republic of Suffering: Death and the American Civil War*. New York: Knopf.

Fehrenbacher, Don E. 1978. *The Dred Scott Case, Its Significance in American Law and Politics*. New York: Oxford University Press.

Foner, Eric. 1970. *Free Soil, Free Labor, Free Men: The Ideology of the Republican Party Before the Civil War*. New York: Oxford University Press.

—. 2006. *Forever Free: The Story of Emancipation and Reconstruction*. New York: Vintage Books.

Gallagher, Gary W. 2011. *The Union War*. Cambridge, MA: Harvard University Press.

—. 2013. *Becoming Confederates: Paths to a New National Loyalty*. Atlanta: University of Georgia Press.

Gienapp, William E. 2002. *Abraham Lincoln and Civil War America: A Biography*. New York: Oxford University Press.

Goodwin, Doris Kearns. 2006. *Team of Rivals: The Political Genius of Abraham Lincoln*. New York: Simon & Schuster.

Guelzo, Allen C. 2013. *Gettysburg: The Last Invasion*. New York: Knopf

Hahn, Steven. 2003. *A Nation Under Our Feet: Black Political Struggles in the Rural South, from Slavery to the Great Migration*. Cambridge, MA: Belknap Press.

Holt, Michael F. 1978. *The Political Crisis of the 1850s*. New York: Wiley.

LaFantasie, Glenn W. 2007. *Twilight at Little Round Top: July 2, 1863—The Tide Turns at Gettysburg*. New York: Vintage Books.

Lemann, Nicholas. 2006. *Redemption: The Last Battle of the Civil War*. New York: Farrar, Straus & Giroux.

Levine, Bruce C., and Eric Foner. 1992. *Half Slave and Half Free: The Roots of Civil War*. New York: Hill and Wang.

Manning, Chanda. 2008. *What this Cruel War Was Over: Soldiers, Slavery, and the Civil War*. New York: Vintage Books.

McPherson, James M. 1994. *What They Fought For 1861–1865*. Baton Rouge: Louisiana State University Press.

Oates, Stephen B. 1970. *To Purge This Land with Blood: A Biography of John Brown*. New York: Harper & Row.

Richardson, Heather Cox. 2001. *The Death of Reconstruction: Race, Labor, and Politics in the Post-Civil War North, 1865–1901*. Cambridge, MA: Harvard University Press.

Stampp, Kenneth M. 1990. *America in 1857: A Nation on the Brink*. New York: Oxford University Press.

Thomas, Emory M. 1991. *The Confederacy as a Revolutionary Experience*. Columbia: University of South Carolina Press.

Vorenberg, Michael. 2001. *Final Freedom: The Civil War, the Abolition of Slavery, and the Thirteenth Amendment*. Cambridge: Cambridge University Press.

Williams, Heather Andrea. 2005. *Self-Taught: African American Education in Slavery and Freedom*. Chapel Hill: University of North Carolina Press.

WESTWARD EXPANSION

Brown, Dee. 1970. *Bury My Heart at Wounded Knee: An Indian History of the American West*. New York: Holt Rinehart Winston.

Dando-Collins, Stephen. 2008. *Tycoon's War: How Cornelius Vanderbilt Invaded a Country to Overthrow America's Most Famous Military Adventurer*. Philadelphia: Da Capo Press.

Greenberg, Amy S. 2012. *A Wicked War: Polk, Clay, Lincoln, and the 1846 U.S. Invasion of Mexico*. New York: Knopf.

Madley, Benjamin. 2012. "The Genocide of California's Yana Indians." In *Centuries of Genocide: Essays and Eyewitness Accounts*, edited by Samuel Totten and Williams S. Parsons, 16–53. New York: Routledge.

Mahon, John K. 1967. *History of the Second Seminole War, 1835–1842*. Gainesville: University of Florida Press.

Neihardt, John G. 1975. *Black Elk Speaks: Being the Life Story of a Holy Man of the Oglala Sioux*. New York: Pocket Books.

Richardson, Heather Cox. 2008. *West from Appomattox: The Reconstruction of America After the Civil War*. New Haven: Yale University Press.

Soluri, John. 2005. *Banana Cultures: Agriculture, Consumption, and Environmental Change in Honduras and the United States*. Austin: University of Texas Press.

Stephanson, Anders. 1995. *Manifest Destiny: American Expansionism and the Empire of Right*. New York: Hill and Wang.

White, Richard. 2011. *Railroaded: The Transcontinentals and the Making of Modern America*. New York: Norton.

FROM THE GILDED AGE TO THE PROGRESSIVE ERA

Addams, Jane, and Norah Hamilton. 1910. *Twenty Years at Hull-House: With Autobiographical Notes.* New York: Macmillan.

Bederman, Gail. 1995. *Manliness & Civilization: A Cultural History of Gender and Race in the United States, 1880–1917.* Chicago: University of Chicago Press.

Berg, A. Scott. 2013. *Wilson.* New York: Simon & Schuster.

Boyer, Paul S. 1978. *Urban Masses and Moral Order in America, 1820–1920.* Cambridge, MA: Harvard University Press.

Chauncey, George. 1994. *Gay New York: Gender, Urban Culture, and the Makings of the Gay Male World, 1890-1940.* New York: Basic Books.

Cronon, William. 1991. *Nature's Metropolis: Chicago and the Great West.* New York: Norton.

Dalton, Kathleen. 2002. *Theodore Roosevelt: A Strenuous Life.* New York: Knopf.

Dewey, John. 1915. *The School and Society.* Chicago: The University of Chicago Press.

Du Bois, W. E. B., David W. Blight, and Robert Gooding-Williams. 1997. *The Souls of Black Folk.* Boston: Bedford Books.

Fitzpatrick, Ellen F., Lincoln Steffens, Ida M. Tarbell, and Ray Stannard Baker. 1994. *Muckraking: Three Landmark Articles.* Boston: Bedford/St. Martin's Press.

Gilmore, Glenda E. 1996. *Gender and Jim Crow: Women and the Politics of White Supremacy in North Carolina.* Chapel Hill: University of North Carolina Press.

Goodwin, Doris Kearns. 2013. *The Bully Pulpit: Theodore Roosevelt, William Howard Taft, and the Golden Age of Journalism.* New York: Simon & Schuster.

Goodwyn, Lawrence. 1976. *Democratic Promise: The Populist Moment in America.* New York: Oxford University Press.

Hershkowitz, Leo. 1977. *Tweed's New York: Another Look.* Garden City, NY: Anchor Press.

James, William. 1975. *Pragmatism.* Cambridge, MA: Harvard University Press.

Kraditor, Aileen S. 1981. *The Ideas of the Woman Suffrage Movement 1890–1920.* New York: Norton.

Lears, T. J. Jackson. 2009. *Rebirth of a Nation: The Making of Modern America, 1877–1920.* New York: HarperCollins.

Lunardini, Christine A. 1986. *From Equal Suffrage to Equal Rights: Alice Paul and the National Woman's Party, 1910–1928.* New York: New York University Press.

Matthews, Jean V. 2003. *The Rise of the New Woman: The Women's Movement in America, 1875–1930.* Chicago: Dee.

Osofsky, Gilbert. 1971. *Harlem: The Making of a Ghetto. Negro New York, 1890–1930*. New York: Harper & Row.

Pegram, Thomas R. 1998. *Battling Demon Rum: The Struggle for a Dry America, 1800–1933*. Chicago: Dee.

Peiss, Kathy Lee. 1986. *Cheap Amusements: Working Women and Leisure in Turn-of-the-Century New York*. Philadelphia: Temple University Press.

Quammen, David. 2008. *Charles Darwin On the Origin of Species: The Illustrated Edition*. New York: Sterling.

Riis, Jacob A. 1971. *How the Other Half Lives: Studies Among the Tenements of New York*. New York: Dover.

Sinclair, Upton. 1971. *The Jungle*. Cambridge, MA: Bentley.

Von Drehle, David. 2003. *Triangle: The Fire That Changed America*. New York: Atlantic Monthly Press.

Washington, Booker T. 1963. *Up from Slavery, An Autobiography*. Garden City, NY: Doubleday.

Wiebe, Robert H. *The Search for Order, 1877–1920*. New York: Hill and Wang.

Woodward, C. Vann. 1957. *The Strange Career of Jim Crow*. New York: Oxford University Press.

IMPERIAL EXPANSION AND THE FIRST WORLD WAR

Barry, John M. 2004. *The Great Influenza: The Epic Story of the Deadliest Plague in History*. New York: Viking Books.

Eisenhower, John S. D. 2001. *Yanks: The Epic Story of the American Army in World War I*. New York: Simon & Schuster.

Fromkin, David. 2004. *Europe's Last Summer: Who Started the Great War in 1914?* New York: Knopf.

Hart, Peter. 2007. *Aces Falling: War Above the Trenches, 1918*. London: Weidenfeld & Nicolson.

Hoganson, Kristin L. 1998. *Fighting for American Manhood: How Gender Politics Provoked the Spanish-American and Philippine-American Wars*. New Haven: Yale University Press.

Kaplan, Amy. 2002. *The Anarchy of Empire in the Making of U.S. Culture*. Cambridge, MA: Harvard University Press.

Kennedy, David M. 1980. *Over Here: The First World War and American Society*. New York: Oxford University Press.

Lengel, Edward G. 2008. *To Conquer Hell: The Meuse-Argonne, 1918*. New York: Holt.

Maier, Charles S. 2006. *Among Empires: American Ascendancy and Its Predecessors*. Cambridge, MA: Harvard University Press.

McCullough, David G. 1977. *The Path between the Seas: The Creation of the Panama Canal, 1870–1914*. New York: Simon & Schuster.

Thomas, Evan. 2010. *The War Lovers: Roosevelt, Lodge, Hearst, and the Rush to Empire, 1898*. New York: Little, Brown.

Tooze, J. Adam. 2014. *The Deluge: The Great War and the Remaking of Global Order 1916–1931*. New York: Viking Books.

Twain, Mark. 2009. *Following the Equator A Journey Around the World*. Waiheke Island: Floating Press.

THE ROARING TWENTIES

Allen, Frederick Lewis. 1931. *Only Yesterday: An Informal History of the Nineteen-Twenties*. New York: Harper & Bros.

Bryson, Bill. 2013. *One Summer: America, 1927*. New York: Anchor Books.

Davison M. Douglas. 2005. *Jim Crow Moves North: The Battle over Northern School Desegregation, 1865–1954*. New York: Cambridge University Press.

Moore, Lucy. 2010. *Anything Goes: A Biography of the Roaring Twenties*. New York: Overlook Press.

Robinson, Thomas A., and Lanette R. Ruff. 2011. *Out of the Mouths of Babes: Girl Evangelists in the Flapper Era*. New York: Oxford University Press.

Russell, Francis. 1968. *The Shadow of Blooming Grove: Warren G. Harding in His Times*. New York: McGraw-Hill.

Shlaes, Amity. 2013. *Coolidge*. New York: Harper.

Watts, Steven. 2005. *The People's Tycoon: Henry Ford and the American Century*. New York: Knopf.

THE GREAT DEPRESSION AND THE NEW DEAL

Browder, Laura. 1998. *Rousing the Nation Radical Culture in Depression America*. Amherst: University of Massachusetts Press.

Cohen, Lizabeth. 1990. *Making a New Deal: Industrial Workers in Chicago, 1919–1939*. Cambridge: Cambridge University Press.

Domhoff, G. William, and Michael J. Webber. 2011. *Class and Power in the New Deal: Corporate Moderates, Southern Democrats, and the Liberal-Labor Coalition*. Stanford, CA: Stanford University Press.

Hamby, Alonzo L. 2004. *For the Survival of Democracy: Franklin Roosevelt and the World Crisis of the 1930s*. New York: Free Press.

Hofstadter, Richard. 1955. *The Age of Reform: From Bryan to F.D.R.* New York: Knopf.

Hurt, R. Douglas. 1984. *The Dust Bowl: An Agricultural and Social History*. Chicago: Nelson-Hall.

Katznelson, Ira. 2013. *Fear Itself: The New Deal and the Origins of Our Time*. New York: Norton.

Kennedy, David M. 1999. *Freedom from Fear: The American People in Depression and War, 1929–1945*. New York: Oxford University Press.

Lumley, Darwyn H. 2009. *Breaking the Banks in Motor City: The Auto Industry, the 1933 Detroit Banking Crisis and the Start of the New Deal*. Jefferson, NC: McFarland.

Poppendieck, Janet, and Marion Nestle. 2014. *Breadlines Knee-Deep in Wheat: Food Assistance in the Great Depression*. Berkeley: University of California Press.

Shindo, Charles J. 1997. *Dust Bowl Migrants in the American Imagination*. Lawrence: University of Kansas Press.

Shlaes, Amity. 2007. *The Forgotten Man: A New History of the Great Depression*. New York: HarperCollins.

Smith, Fred C. 2014. *Trouble in Goshen: Plain Folk, Roosevelt, Jesus, and Marx in the Great Depression South*. Jackson: University Press of Mississippi.

Solomon, William. 2002. *Literature, Amusement, and Technology in the Great Depression*. Cambridge: Cambridge University Press.

Terkel, Studs. 1970. *Hard Times: An Oral History of the Great Depression*. New York: Pantheon Books.

WORLD WAR, COLD WAR, AND AMERICAN PROSPERITY

Dobrynin, Anatoly. 1995. *In Confidence: Moscow's Ambassador to America's Six Cold War Presidents*. New York: Crown.

Doenecke, Justus D., and Mark A. Stoler. 2005. *Debating Franklin D. Roosevelt's Foreign Policies, 1933–1945*. Lanham, MD: Rowman & Littlefield.

Fischer, Conan. 2003. *The Ruhr Crisis, 1923–1924*. Oxford: Oxford University Press.

Homan, Lynn M., and Thomas Reilly. 2001. *Black Knights: The Story of the Tuskegee Airmen*. Gretna, LA: Pelican.

Kessler-Harris, Alice. 1982. *Out to Work: A History of Wage-Earning Women in the United States*. New York: Oxford University Press.

Mitchell, Greg. 1998. *Tricky Dick and the Pink Lady: Richard Nixon vs. Helen Gahagan Douglas—Sexual Politics and the Red Scare, 1950*. New York: Random House.

O'Sullivan, John. 2006. *The President, the Pope, and the Prime Minister: Three Who Changed the World*. New York: Regnery.

Overy, R. J. 1995. *Why the Allies Won*. New York: Norton.

Robinson, Jo Ann Gibson, and David J. Garrow. 1987. *The Montgomery Bus Boycott and the Women Who Started It: The Memoir of Jo Ann Gibson Robinson*. Knoxville: University of Tennessee Press.

Schweizer, Peter. 2002. *Reagan's War: The Epic Story of His Forty-Year Struggle and Final Triumph over Communism*. New York: Doubleday.

Sone, Monica Itoi. 1979. *Nisei Daughter*. Seattle: University of Washington Press.

Weinberg, Gerhard L. 1994. *A World at Arms: A Global History of World War II*. Cambridge: Cambridge University Press.

Wyman, David S. 1998. *The Abandonment of the Jews: America and the Holocaust 1941–1945*. New York: New Press.

FROM CAMELOT TO CULTURE WARS

Appy, Christian G. 2003. *Patriots: The Vietnam War Remembered from All Sides*. New York: Viking Books.

Branch, Taylor. 1988. *Parting the Waters: America in the King Years, 1954–63*. New York: Simon & Schuster.

Clendinen, Dudley, and Adam Nagourney. 1999. *Out for Good: The Struggle to Build a Gay Rights Movement in America*. New York: Simon & Schuster.

Clinton, Bill. 2004. *My Life*. New York: Knopf.

Cowie, Jefferson. 2010. *Stayin' Alive: The 1970s and the Last Days of the Working Class*. New York: New Press.

Delpla, Isabelle, Xavier Bougarel, and Jean-Louis Fournel, eds. 2012. *Investigating Srebrenica: Institutions, Facts, Responsibilities*. New York: Berghahn Books.

Dudziak, Mary L. 2000. *Cold War Civil Rights: Race and the Image of American Democracy*. Princeton, NJ: Princeton University Press.

Farber, David R. 1994. *The Age of Great Dreams: America in the 1960s*. New York: Hill and Wang.

Frank, Thomas. 2004. *What's the Matter with Kansas? How Conservatives Won the Heart of America*. New York: Metropolitan Books.

Friedan, Betty. 1963. *The Feminine Mystique*. New York: Norton.

Gitlin, Todd. 1993. *The Sixties: Years of Hope, Days of Rage*. New York: Bantam Books.

Goodwin, Doris Kearns. 1976. *Lyndon Johnson and the American Dream*. New York: Harper & Row.

Karnow, Stanley. 1983. *Vietnam, a History*. New York: Viking Press.

King, Martin Luther. 1986. *A Testament of Hope: The Essential Writings of Martin Luther King, Jr*. Edited by James Melvin Washington. San Francisco: Harper & Row.

Levy, Ariel. 2006. *Female Chauvinist Pigs: Women and the Rise of Raunch Culture*. New York: Free Press.

McCain, John, and Mark Salter. 1999. *Faith of My Fathers*. New York: Random House.

Meriwether, James. 2008. "'Worth a Lot of Negro Votes:' Black Voters, Africa, and the 1960 Presidential Campaign." *Journal of American History* 95(3): 737–63.

Murch, Donna Jean. 2010. *Living for the City: Migration, Education, and the Rise of the Black Panther Party in Oakland, California*. Chapel Hill: University of North Carolina Press.

Schlesinger, Arthur M. 1965. A *Thousand Days: John F. Kennedy in the White House*. Boston: Houghton Mifflin.

Selvin, Joel. 1994. *Summer of Love: The Inside Story of LSD, Rock & Roll, Free Love, and High Times in the Wild West*. New York: Dutton.

Stein, Judith. 2010. *Pivotal Decade: How the United States Traded Factories for Finance in the Seventies*. New Haven: Yale University Press.

Warren Commission. 1964. *Report of the Warren Commission on the Assassination of President Kennedy*. New York: McGraw-Hill.

X, Malcolm. 1992. *The Autobiography of Malcolm X*. Edited by Alex Haley. New York: One World/Ballantine Books.

TWENTY-FIRST-CENTURY PROBLEMS

Bravin, Jess. 2013. *The Terror Courts: Rough Justice at Guantanamo Bay*. New Haven: Yale University Press.

Cowen, Tyler. 2001. *The Great Stagnation: How America Ate All the Low-Hanging Fruit of Modern History, Got Sick, and Will (Eventually) Feel Better*. New York: Dutton.

Ehrenreich, Barbara. 2001. *Nickel and Dimed: On (Not) Getting by in America*. New York: Metropolitan Books.

Gerges, Fawaz A. 2011. *The Rise and Fall of Al-Qaeda*. Oxford: Oxford University Press.

Gordon, Joy. 2010. *Invisible War: The United States and the Iraq Sanctions*. Cambridge, MA: Harvard University Press.

John Cannan, 2013. "A Legislative History of the Affordable Care Act: How Legislative Procedure Shapes Legislative History." *Law Library Journal* 105(2): 132–73.

Keen, D. 2012. *Useful Enemies: When Waging Wars Is More Important than Winning Them*. New Haven: Yale University Press.

Lance, Peter. 2004. *1000 Years for Revenge: International Terrorism and the FBI*. New York: Regan Books.

Lewis, Michael. 2010. *The Big Short: Inside the Doomsday Machine*. New York: Norton.

Little, Douglas. 2002. *American Orientalism: The United States and the Middle East since 1945*. Chapel Hill: University of North Carolina Press.

Oreskes, Naomi, and Erik M. Conway. 2010. *Merchants of Doubt: How a Handful of Scientists Obscured the Truth on Issues from Tobacco Smoke to Global Warming*. New York: Bloomsbury Press.

Rivoli, Pietra. 2005. *The Travels of a T-Shirt in the Global Economy: An Economist Examines the Markets, Power and Politics of World Trade*. Hoboken, NJ: Wiley.

Simon, Bryant. 2009. *Everything but the Coffee: Learning About America from Starbucks*. Berkeley: University of California Press.

Wright, Lawrence. 2006. *The Looming Tower: Al-Qaeda and the Road to 9/11*. New York: Knopf.

Attributions

CC licensed content, Shared previously

- US History. **Authored by**: P. Scott Corbett, Volker Janssen, John M. Lund, Todd Pfannestiel, Paul Vickery, and Sylvie Waskiewicz. **Provided by**: OpenStax College. **Located at**: http://openstaxcollege.org/textbooks/us-history. **License**: *CC BY: Attribution*. **License Terms**: Download for free at http://cnx.org/content/col11740/latest/

www.ingramcontent.com/pod-product-compliance
Lightning Source LLC
Chambersburg PA
CBHW080537230426
43663CB00015B/2620